PARLIAMENTARY OVERSIGHT OF THE EXECUTIVES

The oversight of the executive is a key function of parliament, and is central to the relationship between branches of government. Recently, however, the influence of parliament on policymaking has been diluted. This book plots trends in parliaments across Europe to illustrate points of convergence and divergence. It compares the tools and methods developed by parliaments to bolster their crucial oversight role, and it demonstrates that oversight of the executive itself – more than lawmaking – is the pivotal dimension of parliaments in Europe for regaining their spheres of influence and democratic control over decision-making.

Volume 4 in the series Parliamentary Democracy in Europe

Parliamentary Democracy in Europe

The European Union is founded on the idea of 'representative democracy'. Its citizens are directly represented in the European Parliament, but Union democracy is equally based on indirect forms of representation especially through the European Council and the Council – two Union institutions whose members will be democratically accountable to their national parliaments. The good functioning of the Union democracy assumes, therefore, the good functioning of the democratic institutions of each Member State.

What is the role and relationship between the European and the national parliaments in the democratic functioning of the Union? Do they exercise distinct or complementary functions? Has the European Parliament adopted a structure similar to national parliaments; and how do national parliaments assume their 'European' functions? These questions have gained particular relevance in recent years. Not only has the Lisbon Treaty conferred new functions upon national parliaments, especially concerning the scrutiny on the compliance with the subsidiarity principle (the so called 'Early Warning System'), the coordination of fiscal and economic policies at the European level has led to significant restrictions of national parliamentary powers.

The new Hart Series on 'Parliamentary Democracy in Europe', encompassing both monographs and edited collections, aims to answer some of these questions. The series offers new insights into rules and conventions shaping parliaments and parliamentary democracy in Europe. Its aim is to provide a better understanding of the role parliaments are playing in European constitutional law and its idea of 'representative democracy'.

Series Editors

Nicola Lupo
Robert Schütze

Interparliamentary Cooperation in the Composite European Constitution
Edited by Nicola Lupo and Cristina Fasone

The Italian Parliament in the European Union
Edited by Nicola Lupo and Giovanni Piccirilli

The Principle of Subsidiarity and its Enforcement in the EU Legal Order:
The Role of National Parliaments in the Early Warning System
Katarzyna Granat

Parliamentary Oversight of the Executives: Tools and Procedure in Europe
Elena Griglio

Parliamentary Oversight of the Executives

Tools and Procedures in Europe

Elena Griglio

·HART·

OXFORD · LONDON · NEW YORK · NEW DELHI · SYDNEY

HART PUBLISHING

Bloomsbury Publishing Plc

Kemp House, Chawley Park, Cumnor Hill, Oxford, OX2 9PH, UK

1385 Broadway, New York, NY 10018, USA

HART PUBLISHING, the Hart/Stag logo, BLOOMSBURY and the Diana logo are
trademarks of Bloomsbury Publishing Plc

First published in Great Britain 2020

A catalogue record for this book is available from the British Library.

Library of Congress Cataloging-in-Publication data

Names: Griglio, Elena, 1978- author.

Title: Parliamentary oversight of the executives : tools and procedures in Europe / Elena Griglio.

Description: Oxford, UK ; New York, NY : Hart Publishing, 2020. | Series: Parliamentary
democracy in Europe ; volume 4 | Includes bibliographical references and index.

Identifiers: LCCN 2020016742 (print) | LCCN 2020016743 (ebook) |
ISBN 9781509925681 (hardcover) | ISBN 9781509925698 (Epub)

Subjects: LCSH: Legislative oversight—Europe.

Classification: LCC KJC5315 .G75 2020 (print) | LCC KJC5315 (ebook) | DDC 328.4/07456—dc23

LC record available at https://lccn.loc.gov/2020016742

LC ebook record available at https://lccn.loc.gov/2020016743

ISBN: HB: 978-1-50992-568-1
ePDF: 978-1-50992-570-4
ePub: 978-1-50992-569-8

Typeset by Compuscript Ltd, Shannon

To find out more about our authors and books visit www.hartpublishing.co.uk.
Here you will find extracts, author information, details of forthcoming events
and the option to sign up for our newsletters.

Ideoque providimus, anno quolibet, in festo felicet omnium Sanctorum, in Siciliae partibus generalem Curiam celebrari (a); in qua nobis adesse statuimus, Comites, Barones, e universitatum quarumlibet syndicos idoneos, e sufficientes, instructos, e alios ad hoc opportunos, e utiles ad providendum nobiscum, procurandum, e exaltandum nostrae Majestatis, ipsius Insulae, e omnium, specialiter Siculorum, flatum salutiferum, e felicem; ad examinandum etiam, e puniendum j(g)ustitiariorum, judicum, notarium, e officialum quorumlibet defectus, negligentias, e excessus; ac praesatus sindycos, pro referendis, e denunciandis officialium ipsorum erratis, apparere praecipimus plenius informatos; ubi officiales eosdem de cunctis eorum peccatis mandabimus, quos expedierit, e sicut expedierit, syndicari; e que etiam in praedicta Curia.

De generali curia semel in anno facienda, 1296, in H M Brancifortii et al, *Capitula Regni Siciliae quae ad hodiernum diem lata sunt, edita cura ejusdem regni deputatorum,* I (Panormi, excudebat A. Felicella, 1741) 48

To Maria Rita and Valerio who brought me up to the values of democracy and control

TABLE OF CONTENTS

PART I

Constitutional Features of Parliamentary Oversight in Europe

1

Introduction: Oversight of the Executives. A European Approach

I. What Parliamentary Oversight Serves: In Search of a Definition

Oversight of the executives has always been a major function of parliaments.[1] One of the fundamental tasks of representative assemblies according to liberal thought,[2] parliamentary oversight has turned out to be one essential mechanism for limiting[3] and, at the same time, sharing executive power. It is part of the wider sphere of constitutional controls whose aim is to keep government within its limits, prevent abuse of power and protect fundamental liberties.[4] The settlement of parliamentary oversight offers an answer to the fundamental question, 'Is power concentrated in the hands of a single power holder or state organ, or is it mutually shared and reciprocally controlled by several power holders or state organs?'.[5] Oversight is closely intertwined with the principle of responsibility of governing bodies, but at the same time it is something more than a formal mechanism for implementing this doctrine.[6] It is both the possibility to determine political decisions with the intimation or application of a serious penalty,[7] and the positive act of participating in government action

---

[1] P Ihalainen, C Ilie and K Palonen, 'Parliament as a Conceptual Nexus' in P Ihalainen, C Ilie and K Palonen (eds), *Parliament and Parliamentarism: A Comparative History of a European Concept* (New York, Berghahan, 2016) 8.

[2] JS Mill, 'Considerations on Representative Government' (1861) in JS Mill, *The Collected Works of John Stuart Mill, XIX – Essays on Politics and Society*, 3rd edn (London, Longman-Green, 1865) 430 ff; W Wilson, *Congressional Government. A Study in American Politics* (Boston, MA, Houghton Mifflin Company, 1885) 297.

[3] F von Hayek, *Law, Legislation and Liberty. A New Statement of the Liberal Principles of Justice and Political Economy*, III (London, Routledge, 1979) 20 ff. S McCune Lindsay, 'Constitutional Limitations on Government Powers' (1915) 5 *Proceedings of the Academy of Political Science in the City of New York* 93.

[4] CH McIlwain, *Constitutionalism Ancient and Modern* (Ithaca, NY, Cornell University Press, 1940) 24; CJ Friedrich, *Constitutional Government and Democracy: Theory and Practice in Europe and America*, 4th edn (Waltham, MA, Blaisdell, 1968); S Gordon, *Controlling the State: Constitutionalism from Ancient Athens to Today* (Cambridge, MA, Harvard University Press, 1999) 5; A Sajó, *Limiting Government: An Introduction to Constitutionalism* (Budapest, Central European Press, 1999) x.

[5] K Loewenstein, *Political Power and the Governmental Process* (Chicago, IL, University of Chicago Press, 1957) 29. See also MJC Vile, *Constitutionalism and the Separation of Powers* (Oxford, Oxford University Press, 1967) 13; and C Möllers, *The Three Branches: A Comparative Model of Separation of Powers* (Oxford, Oxford University Press, 2013) 10.

[6] L Sánchez Agesta, 'Gobierno y responsabilidad' (1960) 113–14 *Revista de estudios políticos* 35, 39 f.

[7] HD Lasswell and A Kaplan, *Power and Society. A Framework for Political Inquiry* (New Haven, CT, Routledge, 1950) 75.

by influencing – persuading or dissuading – decision-making.[8] It is therefore co-essential to the very notion of constitution.[9]

Placed at the heart of the relationship between the executive and the legislative powers, parliamentary oversight may come in many forms. There is no universal principle to iden-tify the nature, scope, functioning and constitutional implications of the oversight function. This is an ever-changing prerogative, whose transformation is continuously being fostered by constitutional and political factors at both national and supranational level. At the begin-ning of the twenty-first century, the oversight function is considered to be a marker of parliaments' relevance.[10] Its potentialities are not always fully appreciated by MPs and yet oversight is deemed to have the potential of being an extremely powerful function. This trend is fostered by two parallel processes.

On the one hand, whereas law-making has long been perceived as the pivotal function of representative assemblies, legislation is increasingly being controlled by governments and the legislative room for manoeuvre left to parliaments is being reduced more and more.[11] This situation fosters the idea that parliaments have become law-influencing legislatures[12] rather than law-makers: at times, they seem to succeed better in influencing the decisions made by other authorities than in acting as fully-fledged legislators. On the other hand, in recent decades, the social claim for effective political oversight has grown stronger. Civil society is increasingly sceptical of the effectiveness of political oversight. However, both the parliament and the government often find little incentive to take the oversight demand seriously. As citizens are pushing for increased control on the conduct of politics and on its outcomes, this pressure leads parliaments to take counter-actions.[13]

In fact, ahead of these rather general trends, 'personne ne sait très bien ce qu'est le contrôle' ('Nobody really knows what oversight is').[14] We not only lack a universal vision of the scope, purpose, nature and organisation of the oversight function. More radically, we also lack linguistic consistency in defining this prerogative. A large number of linguistic formulae, ranging from oversight to scrutiny, from control to supervision, from evalua-tion to monitoring, from surveillance to assessment, are currently used in the institutional and academic debate to define the privileged right of critique[15] exercised by representative

---

[8] FE Oppenheim, 'An Analysis of Political Control: Actual and Potential' (1958) 3 *Journal of Politics* 515.

[9] M Aragón Reyes, 'El control como elemento inseparable del concepto del Constitución' (1987) 19 *Revista Española de Derecho Constitucional* 15, 52. On the oversight theory as an inseparable part of the theory of the Constitution, see the Decision of the Spanish Tribunal Constitucional, STC 124/2018, of 14 November.

[10] Inter-Parliamentary Union (IPU) and United Nations Development Programme (UNDP), *Global Parliamen-tary Report 2017. Parliament's power to hold government to account: Realities and perspectives on oversight* (France, Courand et Associés, 2017) 11.

[11] U Karpen, 'Comparative Law: Perspectives of Legislation' (2003) 17 *Anuario Iberoamericano de Justicia Constitucional* 141, 145. On the concern over the so-called 'rubber-stamp legislation', see J Blondel, *Comparative Legislatures* (Englewood Cliffs, NJ, Prentice-Hall, 1973) 11 ff; D Olson and P Norton, 'Legislatures in Democratic Transition' (1996) 2 *The Journal of Legislative Studies* 1, 7; SM Saiegh, 'Lawmaking' in S Martin, T Saalfeld and KW Strøm (eds), *The Oxford Handbook of Legislative Studies* (Oxford, Oxford University Press, 2014).

[12] P Norton, 'Parliaments: A Framework for Analysis' (1990) 13 *West European Politics* 1, 5 ff.

[13] N Grandguillaume, 'Le demande de contrôle' (2000) 318 *La Revue Administrative* 641, 643.

[14] N Grandguillaume, *Théorie générale du contrôle* (Paris, Economica, 1994) 1.

[15] I Jennings, *Cabinet Government*, 2nd edn (Cambridge, Cambridge University Press, 1951) 439; P Lauvaux, 'Le contrôle, source du régime parlementaire, priorité du régime présidentiel' (2010) 3 *Pouvoirs* 23, 26; GU Rescigno, *La responsabilità politica* (Milano, Giuffrè, 1967) 90 ff.

assemblies with regard to government bodies. Different stylistic options are similarly used in legal acts, including constitutions.[16] These terms are often used as synonyms, although from a constitutional perspective they are not perfectly equivalent.

The two most recurring terms in the English language are the notions of *oversight* and *scrutiny*, which have been used to cover two rather distinct constitutional approaches, often referred to as presidential and parliamentary regimes respectively (see below chapter two, section II).[17] The other terms can be considered either as generic variations (this is the case, inter alia, for the notions of *supervision*,[18] *surveillance, monitoring*)[19] or as sectorial implementations (this is the case for *audit*, applied to the budgetary sector, *evaluation*,[20] referred to the evaluation of public policies and legislation, and *assessment*, developed in terms of 'impact assessment').

The reference to the notion of *control*[21] is instead more equivocal; it is recurring in literature, but can be considered as an 'imported' notion. Its spreading is apparently explained by two parallel factors. On the one hand, this notion is semantically corresponding to the terms most diffused in other European languages: *contrôle* in France, *kontrolle* in Germany, *controllo* in Italy and *control* in Spain. On the other hand, it enables the oversight dimension to gain back a certain legalistic conception of the relationship between the controller and the controlled that is typical in the French *contrôle*.[22] The etymological origins of the word *contrôle* derive from the contraction of two words, 'contre' and 'rôle', which, in its original meaning, referred to a double-entry bookkeeping where one entry is used to check the reliability of the other. It gives the idea of a check aimed at assessing the compliance to a model,[23] thus including two opposite dimensions: verification and censure.[24] This meaning has exercised a major influence on the Napoleonic tradition of administrative law, where the notion has been interpreted as a manifestation of power and authority (on this point,

---

[16] 'Scrutiny and oversight of the executive action' is the formula used in section 42(3) of the Constitution of South Africa. The terms *kontrollrechte, contrôle* and the verb *controlan* are respectively used by art 52 of the Austrian Constitution, art 24 of the French Constitution and art 66 (2) of the Spanish Constitution.

[17] D Olson, 'Legislatures and Administration in Oversight and Budgets: Constraints, Means, and Executives' in R Stapenhurst, R Pelizzo, D Olson and L von Trapp (eds), *Legislative Oversight and Budgeting: A World Perspective* (Washington DC, World Bank, 2008).

[18] M Weber, 'Parliament and Government in a Reconstructed Germany' (1918) in M Weber, *Economy and Society. An Outline of Interpretive Sociology* (New York, Bedminster, 1968) 1421.

[19] See Blondel (n 11) 68 for the use of the terms 'scrutiny', 'control' and 'supervision' as synonyms, referred to the US committees' 'continuous control (or at least supervision) of administrative activities'.

[20] A Schick, 'Congress and the "details" of administration' (1976) 36 *Public Administration Review* 516, 521 (oversight 'is clearly a legislative responsibility', by contrast, evaluation 'does not operate with a differentiation of legislative and executive roles', because both branches can evaluate).

[21] This is defined as 'the legislature's ability to constrain executive behaviour' by P Pennings, 'Beyond dichotomous explanations: Explaining constitutional control of the executive with fuzzy sets' (2003) 42 *European Journal of Political Research* 541. The term 'control' is the one most frequently used in the collective volume by H Döering (ed), *Parliaments and Majority Rule in Western Europe* (New York, St Martin's Press, 1995).

[22] O Rozenberg, 'Comparer les parlements' in JM de Waele and Y Déloye (eds), *Politique comparé* (Bruxelles, Bruylant, 2018) 348 (on the difference between the English notion of *scrutiny* – a multiprocedural and multipurpose function that aims at influencing and reorienting government action – and the French *contrôle* – a dimension associated with the enforcement of government responsibility).

[23] G Cornu (ed), *Vocabulaire juridique*, 12th edn (Paris, PUF, 2018) 345 ff.

[24] P Avril, 'L'introuvable contrôle parlementaire (après la révision constitutionnelle française de 2008' (2009) 3 *Jus Politicum* 1, 2.

see below chapter two, sections I and V.A)[25] and associated with Parliament's capacity to enforce government responsibility.[26] The multilinguistic approach enriches the multifaceted dimensions of parliamentary oversight, showing manifold ways of expressing this function. This is the case, inter alia, of the *sindacato ispettivo* (parliamentary inspection)[27] or the *control-fiscalización* (supervision),[28] respectively used in the Italian and Spanish parliamentary traditions to highlight the investigative/supervisory capacity of the legislative branch corresponding to the duty of the executive to reply, provide information, produce a document, and appear before Parliament.[29]

On the whole, this linguistic pluralism witnesses the proliferation of rather antithetic theoretical approaches to parliamentary oversight. This is often considered as a comprehensive power, the 'quintessential' parliamentary function,[30] inclusive of the legislative interaction between the parliament and the government.[31] Alternatively, it is seen as a residual domain, comprising all the non-legislative activities of Parliament – the so-called 'other powers' – like the censure of the executive or the budget-related powers.[32] Oversight may be framed in the general legislative–executive relationship as to also include the processes of government formation and dismissal; or it can be specifically referred to the outcome of government activity, hence the formula of 'legislative oversight'[33] or 'administrative oversight',[34] whose meaning and definition are often overlapping. The formula 'legislative

[25] The English word 'control' has a stronger meaning compared with the French 'contrôle', because it means not only surveillance, but also dominance and ownership. Avril (n 24) 4. *Contra*, Rozenberg, 'Comparer les parlements' (n 22) fn 14.

[26] A Delcamp, 'La perception du contrôle parlementaire. Comment le rendre plus attractif?' (2010) 134 *Pouvoirs* 109, 110.

[27] G Amato, *L'ispezione parlamentare* (Milano, Giuffrè, 1968); M Morichetti Franchi, 'Efficacia e limiti del sindacato ispettivo parlamentare' (1989) 19 *Nuovi studi politici* 105.

[28] E Alvarez Conde, *Curso de Derecho Constitucional*, II (Madrid, Tecnos, 1993) 166. A Arévalo Gutiérrez, 'Las comisiones de investigación de las Cortes generales y de las Asambleas legislativas de las Comunidades Autónomas' (1995) 43 *Revista Española de Derecho Constitucional* 113, 128.

[29] On other linguistic formulae used to identify different dimensions of parliamentary oversight, see S Galeotti, *Introduzione alla teoria dei controlli costituzionali* (Milano, Giuffrè, 1963) 34 ff; and I Fernández Sarasola, 'El control parlamentario y su regulación en el ordenamiento español' (2000) 60 *Revista Española de Derecho Constitucional* 89 ff.

[30] ST Siefken, *Parlamentarische Kontrolle im Wandel: Theorie und Praxis des Deutschen Bundestages* (Baden-Baden, Nomos, 2018) 27 ff.

[31] E Thiers, 'Le contrôle parlementaire et ses limites juridiques: un pouvoir presque sans entraves' (2010) 134 *Pouvoirs* 71, 72. This interpretation is also supported by the Spanish Tribunal Constitucional in the STC 124/2018, para 7 (see below ch 2, section III).

[32] The expression 'other powers' confirms the traditional view of the 'legislature' as a body basically entitled to initiate legislation and to adopt it; see the Joint Dissenting Opinion of Judge Sir John Freeland and Judge Jungwiert in the European Court of Human Rights, *Case of Matthews v the United Kingdom* (App no 24833/94), 18 February 1999, para 5.

[33] G Sartori, *Comparative Constitutional Engineering. An Inquiry into Structures, Incentives and Outcomes*, 2nd edn (New York, NYU Press, 1997) 161 f (*legislative* oversight refers to parliaments' capacity to submit, amend, defer and veto legislative proposals; *political* oversight is their capacity to follow up the implementation of legislative decisions).

[34] The formula, introduced by SP Huntington, 'Congressional Responses to the Twentieth Century' in DB Truman (ed), *The Congress and America's Future* (Englewood Cliffs, NJ, Prentice Hall, 1965) 30; and RA Packenham, 'Legislatures and Political Development' in A Kornberg and LD Musolf (eds), *Legislatures in Developmental Perspective* (Durham, NC, Duke University Press, 1970), is analysed in its procedural consequences by P Norton, *Parliament in British Politics*, 2nd edn (New York, Palgrave, 2013) 111.

oversight' is used by some scholars mostly referring to presidential systems and having regard to the review of law execution by the administration.[35]

The variety of linguistic and theoretical approaches confirms that there are many different ways of implementing this function, depending on a number of contextual factors. As a core function of the legislative–executive interaction, parliamentary oversight is a normative conception shared by all theories of democratic constitutionalism. However, there is not one universal constitutional standard for accomplishing this task.[36]

Presidential and parliamentary systems are specifically acknowledging two rather antithetic ways of fulfilling the same requirement of how to involve representative assemblies in the democratic control of executive business (see below chapter two, section II). The scope and extension of parliamentary oversight is one of the main criteria for distinguishing between the two regimes.[37] Parliamentarism finds its constitutive feature in the executive authority's 'permanent' dependence[38] on the confidence scheme, so that the government emerges from and is responsible before the legislative authority.[39] Under a parliamentary government, oversight of the executive discloses some apparent paradoxes. Whereas the confidence relationship calls the government to be as close as possible to Parliament, the oversight prerogative assumes that some distance is established between the controller and the controlled.[40] The paradox is maximal in the case of constitutional arrangements of a Westminster type leading to the fusion of the executive and legislative branches in Parliament and to a one-party majority government supported by strong party discipline.[41] Moreover, oversight can be both about monitoring and about overthrowing the executive.[42] In this vein, the underlying question is what type of 'oversight' could possibly be exercised by the Parliament in regard to a body that, due to the confidence relationship, is by definition an expression of its own majority.[43] It is this question, strictly referred to parliamentary democracies, that the monograph addresses.

To answer this question, it is necessary to investigate the distinctive nature of the oversight dynamics as a relational mechanism of a political nature. This task clearly exceeds

---

[35] Schick (n 20) 519 ff; BA Rockman, 'Legislative-executive relations and legislative oversight' (1984) 9 *Legislative Studies Quarterly* 387; R Stapenhurst, R Pelizzo, D Olson and L von Trapp (eds), *Legislative Oversight and Government Accountability: A World Perspective* (Washington DC, World Bank Publications, 2008); R Pelizzo and F Stapenhurst, *Parliamentary Oversight Tools. A Comparative Analysis* (New York, Routledge, 2011) 14 ff.

[36] F Meinel, 'Confidence and Control in Parliamentary Government: Parliamentary Questioning, Executive Knowledge, and the Transformation of Democratic Accountability' (2018) 66 *The American Journal of Comparative Law* 317, 318 ff.

[37] Lauvaux (n 15) 23. D Verney, 'Parliamentary Government and Presidential Government' in A Lijphart (ed), *Parliamentary Versus Presidential Government* (Oxford, Oxford University Press, 1992).

[38] On government in parliamentary experiences as a permanent emanation of the legislative branch, see L Elia, 'Governo (forme di)' in *Enciclopedia del diritto*, XIX (Milano, Giuffrè, 1970) 642.

[39] B Mirkine-Guetzévitch, *Les nouvelles tendances du droit constitutionnel* (Paris, Marcel Giard, 1931) 7 ff; Y Gouet, 'Qu'est-ce que le Régime Parlementaire' (1932) *Revue de Droit Public* 179; LD Epstein, 'Parliamentary Government' in *International Encyclopedia of the Social Sciences*, II (New York, Macmillan, 1968) 419 ff.

[40] Meinel (n 36) 340.

[41] M Shepard, 'Administrative Review and Oversight: The Experience of Westminster' in R Pelizzo, R Stapenhurst and D Olson (eds), *Trends in Parliamentary Oversight* (Washington DC, World Bank Institute, 2004).

[42] F Hamon and M Troper, *Droit constitutionnel*, 26th edn (Paris, LGDJ, 1999) 613. *Contra*, Thiers (n 31) 74 questions the idea that overthrowing the government is part of the oversight function *stricto sensu*.

[43] A Le Divellec, 'Des effets du contrôle parlementaire' (2010) 134 *Pouvoirs* 123. The question of parliamentary oversight's dependence on the confidence relationship is addressed by the Spanish Tribunal Constitucional in the STC 124/2018, see below ch 2, section III.

the pure constitutional legal analysis. The constitutional law of parliamentary oversight is rather poor and vague[44] insofar as legal norms regulating the tools and procedures available to Parliament for holding the government to account find rather limited space at constitutional level.[45] The right to oversee the executive is in fact better found in the inherent powers of parliamentary regimes rather than in specific provisions.[46]

Beyond this constitutional base, the domain of parliamentary oversight lies in the Rules of Procedure and Standing Orders that set the internal organisation and functioning of every representative assembly. The preference for a rather flexible legal basis[47] does not contradict the constitutional relevance of this function; rather, this is the only solution compatible with the inherently relational and political nature of parliamentary oversight. Not by chance, the notion of 'control' falls within the family of words called 'influence terms': these are defined as a casual relation among one actor's preferences and another actor's actions.[48]

Under the relational perspective, oversight can hence be defined as the activity performed by the Parliament to control the action of another political body, enforce its statutory or general accountability, and adopt any necessary measures to restore infringed public interests.[49] This perspective unfolds through three fundamental stages: assessment, enforcement of government accountability, and restoration of infringed public interests. Implementation of these stages involves: identifying which areas of government action are subject to parliamentary oversight; gathering and analysing evidence to enable Parliament to assess the government's ability to discharge its mandate and ascertain the executive achievements; expressing a judgement on the effectiveness and efficiency of government action; defining expected follow-up initiatives; and urging the government, either directly or indirectly, to acknowledge requested adjustments.

II. Placing the Oversight Function in the European Constitutional Legal Order

Parliamentarism is at the core of the European constitutional tradition[50] and its regime 'can legitimately be seen as characteristically European'.[51] This is true both retrospectively

---

[44] Meinel (n 36) 325.

[45] See above (n 16). Examples of constitutional clauses are to be found in art 66.2 of the Spanish Constitution ('[The *Cortes Generales*] control the action of the Government'); arts 24, 47, 48 and 51 of the French Constitution, as amended in 2008; art 4 ('The Riksdag shall examine the government and administration of the Realm'); and 6 ('[The Government] is accountable to the Riksdag') of the Swedish Instrument of Government.

[46] On this point, see Conseil constitutionnel, Décision no 64-27 DC of 18 December 1964; and L Hamon, '[Note sous décision n° 64-27 DC]' (1966) *Recueil Dalloz* 17, 19.

[47] Thiers (n 31) 79.

[48] R Dahl, *Modern Political Analysis*, 5th edn (Englewood Cliffs, NJ, Prentice-Hall, 1991) 32.

[49] A Manzella, *Il Parlamento* (Bologna, Il Mulino, 2003) 441; and, similarly, Loewenstein (n 5) 48 ff. Delcamp (n 26) 111 (for a definition of the oversight function centred on the legal and non-legal tools available to Parliament to hold the government accountable). Olson, 'Legislatures and Administration' (n 17) 324 ff (on the defining aspects of parliamentary oversight).

[50] AW Bradley and C Pinelli, 'Parliamentarism' in M Rosenfeld and A Sajó (eds), *The Oxford Handbook of Comparative Constitutional Law* (Oxford, Oxford University Press, 2012).

[51] Ihalainen, Ilie and Palonen (n 1) 11.

as well as contemporaneously. At the national level, the structure of the system of government is defined by the confidence relationship between the executive and the legislative branch.[52] At the European Union (EU) level, the confidence scheme shows rather distinctive features, not fully comparable to national standards.[53] In fact, for the purposes of this book, it is not so much relevant to solve the atavistic dispute on the parliamentary or presidential structure of the EU system of government,[54] which 'instead of a constitutionally established balance of powers, exhibits a dynamic confusion of powers'.[55] Rather, the EU dimension serves to understand how the oversight relationship is enforced in the daily experience of European parliamentary democracies.[56] Participation in the EU has deeply affected the rationale, subjects, scope, purposes and implementing mechanisms of parliamentary oversight. Therefore, it is no more possible to isolate the domestic from the supranational perspective.

It is sometimes argued that the EU is a 'weak' constitutionalism,[57] grounded on a 'parasitic legitimacy' derived from the more robust constitutionalism of the Member States.[58] In fact, the EU constitutional legal order comprises the constitutional law of EU treaties and the constitutional law of the Member States, which are seen as deeply integrated[59] and not merely juxtaposed.[60] Different explicative models have been advanced in literature to account for the complex set of interactions between the European, national and sub-national legal orders.[61] The formula of *multilevel constitutionalism*[62]

---

[52] With the exception of Cyprus, single case for presidentialism, all EU Member States have either a parliamentary or a semi-presidential form of government (P Kubicek, *European Politics*, 2nd edn (New York, Routledge, 2017) 176 ff), unfolding through the confidence relationship. See DJ Samuels and MS Shugart, *Presidents, Parties, and Prime Ministers. How the Separation of Powers Affects Party Organization and Behavior* (New York, Cambridge University Press, 2010) 15; M Laver and KA Shepsle (eds), *Cabinet Ministers and Parliamentary Government* (Cambridge, Cambridge University Press, 1994) 290.

[53] D Praino, 'The Structure of the EU System of Government' (2015) 5 ARENA Working Papers 1, 15. See also below ch 7, section II.A.

[54] On the apparent 'parliamentarisation' of the EU form of government, B Rittberger, '"No integration without representation!" European integration, parliamentary democracy, and two forgotten Communities' (2006) 13 *Journal of European Public Policy* 1211; B Rittberger and T Winzen, 'The EU's Multilevel Parliamentary System' in J Richardson and S Mazey (eds), *European Union: Power and Policy-Making*, 4th edn (London, Routledge, 2015) 109 ff. *Contra*, S Fabbrini, 'The European Union and the puzzle of parliamentary government' (2015) 37 *Journal of European Integration* 571.

[55] V Schmidt, 'European "Federalism" and its Encroachments on National Institutions' (1999) 29 *Publius: The Journal of Federalism* 19f. F Fabbrini, EH Ballin and F Somsen, 'Introduction: A New Look at the Form of Government of the European Union and the Eurozone' in F Fabbrini, EH Ballin and F Somsen (eds), *What Form of Government for the European Union and the Eurozone?* (Oxford, Hart Publishing, 2015) 2.

[56] Meinel (n 36) 344.

[57] P Lindseth '"Weak" Constitutionalism? Reflections on Comitology and Transnational Governance in the European Union' (2001) 21 *Oxford Journal of Legal Studies* 145.

[58] K Tuori, *European Constitutionalism* (Cambridge, Cambridge University Press, 2015) 4 and 36.

[59] L Besselink, *A Composite European Constitution* (Groningen, Europa Law Publishing, 2007); A Manzella and N Lupo (eds), *Il sistema parlamentare euro-nazionale. Lezioni* (Torino, Giappichelli, 2014).

[60] I Pernice, 'Multilevel Constitutionalism in the European Union' (2002) 5 *European Law Review* 511. *Contra*, on 'administrative' interpretations of EU law, G Majone, 'The European Community: An "Independent Fourth Branch of Government?"' in G Brüggemeier (ed), *Verfassungen für ein ziviles Europa* (Baden-Baden, Nomos, 1994) 25 ff; A Somek 'Administration Without Sovereignty' in P Dobner and M Loughlin (eds), *The Twilight of Constitutionalism* (Oxford, Oxford University Press, 2010).

[61] S Fabbrini, 'Intergovernmentalism and its Limits: Assessing the European Union's Answer to the Euro Crisis' (2013) 46 *Comparative Political Studies* 1003, 1005 ff.

[62] Pernice (n 60).

or *multilevel parliamentary field*[63] respectively suggest the idea of the separateness and hierarchy between the orders or assume that the 'field' acts with no fixed hierarchies and with often overlapping constituencies. By contrast, the vision embraced in this volume conceives the EU as a composite constitutional dimension,[64] supported by a euro-national parliamentary system.[65] Relying on a '*dual* government, *dual* sovereignty and also *dual* citizenship',[66] the constitutional order of the EU results from the integration and mutual transformation of European and domestic rules, actors and procedures.

This legal arrangement has changed irreversibly the relationship between the legislative and the executive branches at the national level.[67] The 'domestic' interaction between the branches has become a constitutive component of the 'polycentric' paradigm of parliamentary oversight in the EU constitutional architecture.[68] This integration has deeply affected the traditional oversight scheme rooted in the tradition of national parliamentarism.

On the one hand, the EU is a laboratory where hybrid instances of parliamentary oversight, derived from the blending of different political and regulatory patterns, are experienced.[69] Political patterns are inherited from national traditions of parliamentary government and they are based on the confidence scheme. Regulatory patterns have specifically grown out of the EU 'model',[70] with visible influences from presidential regimes. They conceive democratic oversight as a function grounded on instances of direct democracy (such as petitions, the ombudsman, transparency rules and consultations on the web) and evaluation of public policies[71] that are not based on the exclusive relationship between the executive and the legislative branches. These two patterns of democratic oversight, originally conceived as radically opposed, are now seen as functionally integrated and complementary.[72] Their blending has produced a new 'style' of parliamentary politics, composed of elements derived from national constitutional traditions and other instances that are typical of EU governance, combining both representative and direct democracy tools.

---

[63] B Crum and JE Fossum, 'The Multilevel Parliamentary Field: a framework for theorizing representative democracy in the EU' (2009) 1 *European Political Science Review* 249.

[64] Besselink, *A Composite European Constitution* (n 59). In fact, the use of the term 'composite' referred to the EU constitutional legal order can be first referred to the French version of I Pernice and FC Mayer, 'De la Constitution composée de l'Europe' (2000) 36 *Revue trimestrielle de droit européen* 623.

[65] Manzella and Lupo (eds) (n 59). N Lupo, 'Parlamento europeo e Parlamenti nazionali nella Costituzione "composita" dell'Unione europea: le diverse letture possibili' in A Ciancio (ed), *Nuove strategie per lo sviluppo democratico e l'integrazione politica in Europa* (Roma, Aracne, 2014).

[66] R Schütze, *From Dual to Cooperative Federalism. The Changing Structure of EU Law* (Oxford, Oxford University Press, 2009) 29.

[67] D Fromage and A Hérranz-Surallés (eds), *Executive–Legislative (Im)balance in the European Union* (Oxford, Hart Publishing, forthcoming).

[68] L Besselink, 'National Parliaments in the EU's Composite Constitution: a Plea for a Shift in Paradigm' in P Kiiver (ed), *National and Regional Parliaments in the European Constitutional Order* (Groningen, Europa Law Publishing, 2006).

[69] See also below ch 7, section I.

[70] A Héritier, 'Elements of democratic legitimation in Europe: an alternative perspective' (1999) 6 *Journal of European Public Policy* 269. G Majone, 'Regulatory Legitimacy' in G Majone (ed), *Regulating Europe* (New York, Routledge, 1996).

[71] On the difference between oversight and evaluation, Avril, 'L'introuvable contrôle' (n 24) 4. On the blending of the two dimensions, G Filippetta, 'Il controllo parlamentare e le trasformazioni della rappresentanza politica' (2014) *Rivista AIC* 1. See also below ch 3, section III.A.

[72] P Magnette, 'Appointing and censuring the European Commission: the adaptation of parliamentary institutions to the Community context' (2001) 7 *European Law Journal* 292, 293 ff.

On the other hand, the nature of EU constitutionalism has deeply affected the identity and role of the two main subjects of the oversight relationship: the Parliament (controller) and the government (controlled). In the EU legal and political framework, parliaments are clearly no more comparable to the sovereign institutions described by the constitutionalism of the nineteenth and the first half of the twentieth century. The identity and nature of the European Parliament are still highly controversial,[73] but this body is experiencing a process of irreversible empowerment.[74] National parliaments seem to have lost shares of sovereign power and they have experienced a significant limitation in their law-making function;[75] nonetheless, they have seen their informative and participatory rights in EU decision-making strengthened.[76] Regardless of what functions they serve, both the European and national channels of parliamentary representation grounded on Article 10 of the Treaty on European Union (TEU) have been recognised as fundamental components of representative democracy in the EU.[77] Besides their individual prerogatives, national parliaments and the European Parliament have gradually been involved as 'collective' actors in a network of representative assemblies with the aim of fostering new patterns of 'joint' oversight.[78] Moreover, in Member States with federal or regional governance, representation is further enriched by sub-national assemblies, especially when endowed with full legislative powers. In a broad perspective, the EU dimension allocates the role of 'controller' among several parliamentary bodies, with different features and capacities, thus paving the way to a wide range of oversight relations, sometimes closer to a separation of powers system.[79]

---

[73] R Dehousse, 'European institutional architecture after Amsterdam: parliamentary system or regulatory structure?' (1998) 35 *Common Market Law Review* 595, 598; O Costa, *Le Parlement européen, assemblée deliberante* (Bruxelles, Editions de l'Université de Bruxelles, 2001); R Corbett, F Jacobs and M Shackleton, 'The European Parliament at Fifty: A View from the Inside' (2003) 41 *Journal of Common Market Studies* 353, 366 ff; A Kreppel, 'Understanding the European Parliament from a Federalist Perspective: The Legislatures of the United States and the European Union Compared' in A Menon and MA Schain (eds), *Comparative Federalism. The European Union and the United States in Comparative Perspective* (Oxford, Oxford University Press, 2006); M Kohler, 'European Governance and the European Parliament: From Talking Shop to Legislative Powerhouse' (2014) 52 *Journal of Common Market Studies* 600, 602; M Shackleton, 'Transforming representative democracy in the EU? The role of the European Parliament' (2017) 39 *Journal of European Integration* 191.

[74] B Rittberger, 'Institutionalizing Representative Democracy in the European Union: The Case of the European Parliament' (2012) 50 *Journal of Common Market Studies* 18. See also B de Witte et al, 'Legislating after Lisbon. New Opportunities for the European Parliament' (2010) 1 *EUDO Report* 1.

[75] W Wessels, 'National Parliaments and the EP in Multi-tier Governance: In Search for an Optimal Multi-level Parliamentary Architecture. Analysis, Assessment, Advice' in I Pernice et al (eds), *Challenges of Multi-tier Governance in the European Union* (Brussels, European Parliament – Directorate General for Internal Policies, 2013) 104; K Auel and O Höing, 'Parliaments in the Euro Crisis: can the losers of integration still fight back?' (2014) 52 *Journal of Common Market Studies* 1184, 1192; C Neuhold and J Smith, 'Conclusion' in C Hefftler, C Neuhold, O Rozenberg and J Smith (eds), *The Palgrave Handbook of National Parliaments and the European Union* (London, Palgrave, 2015); O Rozenberg, *The Role of National Parliaments in the EU After Lisbon: Potentialities and Challenges* (Brussels, European Parliament – Directorate General for Internal Policies, 2017).

[76] See below ch 7, section III.

[77] A von Bogdandy, 'The European Lesson for International Democracy: The Significance of Articles 9–12 EU Treaty for International Organizations' (2012) 23 *European Journal of International Law* 315.

[78] See below ch 7, section IV.

[79] As argued by T Tiilikainen, 'The concepts of parliamentarism in the EU's political system. Approaching the choice between two models' (2019) 108 *FIIA Working Papers* 7, among the different understandings of parliamentarism that shaped the formation of the EU's political system, the key role taken by the directly elected bodies, both the European Parliament and national parliaments, comes closer to an understanding of parliamentary powers in a presidential, or separation of powers system.

Also, on the side of the executive branch, the EU constitutional order has brought about some epochal changes. Broadly speaking, it could be argued that the 'executive', using the singular, does not exist and that the executive dimension can only be referred to in the plural. In the history of constitutionalism, the terms 'executive' and 'government' have been approached in multiple ways. Since Rousseau's contribution to the theory and language of constitutional law,[80] it has been debated whether the two terms might be considered as synonyms[81] or whether the term 'government' should comprise only the political bodies responsible for setting the directions of public policies. The point is that these terms cannot any more be understood without including participation in the EU executive dimension. That's why the formula of the 'fragmented EU government(s)' has been advanced[82] to explain the coexistence of supranational bodies (the European Commission), intergovernmental institutions (such as the Council and the European Council), independent authorities (including the European Central Bank and the European agencies) and other less formalised intergovernmental bodies (among which are the Euro-group and the Euro-Summits). Many of these institutions are more or less directly participated in by national executives, which implies that executive responsibilities in the EU are shared by bodies with a legitimacy grounded both nationally and supranationally.[83] It is this fragmented and multicentric executive domain that the title of the monograph tries to capture by referring to the 'executives', in the plural.

This conceptualisation explains in what sense it is assumed that participation in the EU has changed the arrangement and implementation of parliamentary oversight at the domestic level.[84] In the EU democratic system, national parliaments have more subjects to oversee, because the executive has fragmented into a plurality of bodies acting at both national and EU level. The oversight scheme has therefore become increasingly complex and diffuse.[85] It has been argued that 'the intentionally diffuse and fragmented character of authority … makes the identification of lines of political oversight vastly more challenging in the European case'.[86] It is the complex and ever-evolving dynamics of political oversight, structurally grounded in the integration between the European and the national levels, that the volume tackles.

III. A Selective Approach to Parliamentary Oversight

The monograph addresses the current challenges of parliamentary oversight from a constitutional comparative perspective that aims to identify, assess and classify the relationship

---

[80] JJ Rousseau, *Du contrat social*, III (Paris, Bordas, 1762) ch I, 125 ff.

[81] On the ambiguity of the expression 'executive power', G Vedel, *Manuel élémentaire de droit constitutionnel* (Paris, Recueil Sirey, 1949) 160.

[82] D Curtin, 'Challenging Executive Dominance in European Democracy' (2014) 77 *Modern Law Review* 12, 29 ff.

[83] P Lindseth, AC Aman and AC Raul, *Oversight* (Chicago, American Bar Association, 2008) 5.

[84] G Rivosecchi, 'La funzione di controllo parlamentare tra Parlamento europeo e Parlamenti nazionali' in A Lucarelli and A Patroni Griffi (eds), *Studi sulla Costituzione europea: percorsi e ipotesi* (Napoli, ESI, 2003).

[85] D Curtin, *Executive Power of the European Union. Law, Practices, and the Living Constitution* (Oxford, Oxford University Press, 2009); Curtin, 'Challenging Executive Dominance in European Democracy' (n 82).

[86] Lindseth, Aman and Raul (n 83) 3.

linking the legislative and the executive branches in the oversight domain. This approach looks for the constitutive elements featuring the oversight function as a relational dimension mirroring the position of the parliament vis-a-vis the government(s) in the remit of non-legislative activity.[87] Some authors (mainly in political science)[88] include formal law-making powers within the tools that parliaments can use in the oversight function. In fact, parliaments oversee the executive in their capacity as legislative bodies, but at the same time from the constitutional viewpoint this eschews the legislative process.[89] In practice, oversight tools do not draw on the law in the expected output. Therefore, 'legislative' oversight, as an instance of oversight performed through Parliament's participation in the legislative function,[90] is beyond the remit of this work.

The constitutive differences between the conception of the oversight function in presidential and parliamentary forms of government justify the focus on systems featuring a relationship of confidence between the legislative and the executive. Following a minimal definition of parliamentary government,[91] some benchmark cases (Denmark, France, Germany, Italy, Spain, Sweden and the UK) have been selected to allow the comparison of the oversight function in parliamentary regimes that differ according to many variables, including the role of the Parliament in government formation and resignation and the type of democracy.[92]

These regimes range from the Westminster model to the hybrid semi-presidential system of France, from the German chancellor democracy to the ill-rationalised parliamentary regime of Italy. They include examples of positive (Germany, Italy and Spain) and negative (Denmark, France and Sweden) parliamentarism. They cover different models of the executive–parties dimension and federal-unitary arrangement (for example: majoritarian democracy in Britain; minority parliamentarism in the experience of Denmark and Sweden; grand coalitions as special forms of consensual government in Germany; party system de-institutionalisation in Italy; coalition governments open to regional parties in Spain). The benchmark is expected to represent both unicameral parliaments (Denmark

---

[87] The distinction between legislative and non-legislative functions is emphasised by R Blackburn and A Kennon et al, *Griffith and Ryle on Parliament: Functions, Practice and Procedures* (London, Sweet & Maxwell, 2003); C Leston Bandeira and L Thompson, *Exploring Parliament* (Oxford, Oxford University Press, 2018); P Blachèr, *Le Parlement en France* (Paris, LGDJ, 2012); R Dickmann and S Staiano (eds), *Funzioni parlamentari non legislative e forma di governo. L'esperienza dell'Italia* (Milano, Giuffrè, 2008); and R Dickmann and S Staiano (eds), *Le funzioni parlamentari non legislative. Studi di diritto comparato* (Milano, Giuffrè, 2009).

[88] P Furlong, 'Institutional fragmentation in parliamentary control: the Italian case' (2004) 10 *The Journal of Legislative Studies* 174 (on the importance of law-making in the Italian Parliament as a form of parliamentary control). Similarly, D Arter, 'From "Parliamentary Control" to "Accountable Government"? The role of public committee hearings in the Swedish Riksdag' (2008) 61 *Parliamentary Affairs* 122 with regard to the Swedish Riksdag.

[89] G Sartori, *Elementi di scienza politica* (Bologna, Il Mulino, 1987) (highlights the distinction between the legislative and the political oversight).

[90] B Chantebout (ed), *Le contrôle parlementaire* (Paris, La Documentation Française, 1998) 11 (conceptualising law-making as a form of parliamentary oversight of government legislative Bills). Similarly, A Kimmel, *L'Assemblée nationale sous la Cinquième République* (Paris, Presses de Sciences Po, 1991).

[91] K Strøm, 'Delegation and accountability in parliamentary democracies' (2000) 37 *European Journal of Political Research* 261, 265 defines parliamentary government as 'a system of government in which the prime minister and his or her cabinet are accountable to any majority of the members of parliament and can voted out of office by the latter'.

[92] A Lijphart, *Patterns of Democracy. Government Forms and Performance in Thirty-Six Countries*, 2nd edn (New Haven, CT, Yale University Press, 2012) 12.

and Sweden) and bicameral systems, either symmetric (Italy) or asymmetric, the latter of which featured in the presence of Upper Houses differing in the type of representation, relationship with the government, composition, organisation and functions performed (France, Germany, Spain and the UK). Benchmark cases are intended to compare executive–legislative oversight traditions in northern and southern European countries. Moreover, they are specifically selected to represent different legal orders from the Germanic area (Germany and the related Spanish body of law), Roman law (Italy and France), common law (the UK) and Nordic countries (Sweden and Denmark).[93]

Practices of parliamentary oversight in the EU institutional system are also included in the benchmark. From a methodological point of view, this choice does not correspond to any *prise de position* on the presidential or parliamentary nature of the EU system of government. Rather, the EU case is included in the comparative overview because it has irreversibly changed the national parliamentary dimension, its interaction with the executive and the exercise of the oversight function. Based on the idea that 'comparative Law in the light of European Legal Space is today's business',[94] the monograph addresses parliamentary oversight matching the *ius commune* with the European experience in order to fulfil a dual purpose: understanding how domestic traditions of parliamentary oversight, combined with the European common dimension, have come to shape the relationship between the legislative and executive branch at the EU level; and assessing how requirements of democratic oversight experimented in the EU architecture have influenced the way parliamentary oversight is performed and arranged at national level.[95]

From a methodological point of view, parliamentary oversight is analysed from a comparative perspective focusing on the oversight tools and procedures included in the legal framework of benchmark parliaments and on related implementing practices. The purpose of this analysis is to assess not only the formal outcomes on the executive–legislative relationship, but also the influence capacity of parliaments (see below, section IV). All legislatures have some level of oversight capacity, which can be evaluated by comparing their internal oversight tools and procedures. In fact, comparative studies[96] have demonstrated that, in a political perspective, the oversight effectiveness is influenced by a variety of institutional and extra-institutional factors (such as the socio-economic conditions and the level of democracy) and cannot be reduced to the number of oversight tools available. Issues of oversight effectiveness are only occasionally addressed in the monograph.

Parliamentary oversight does not exhaust all the existing forms of democratic oversight in contemporary parliamentary systems. It is no longer self-evident that democratic control is entirely satisfied by elective representatives, as was once believed.[97] Other instances of 'popular' oversight, directly performed by citizens or based on a close interaction with civil society, are gaining increasing relevance. Old and new tools of 'direct' or 'participatory'

---

[93] Karpen (n 11) 142 f.

[94] A von Bogdandy, P Cruz Villalón and PM Huber (eds), *Handbuch Ius Publicum Europaeum*, I (Heidelberg, Müller, 2007).

[95] L Verhey, P Kiiver and S Loeffen (eds), *Political Accountability and European Integration* (Groningen, Europa Law Publishing, 2009).

[96] R Pelizzo and F Stapenhurst, *Government Accountability and Legislative Oversight* (New York, Routledge, 2014) 43 f.

[97] S Scher, 'Conditions for Legislative Control' (1963) 25 *Journal of Politics* 526.

democracy are currently used to satisfy these requirements, from popular consultations to the ombudsman, from petitions to e-democracy tools.[98] They find their main doctrine in the principle of transparency which 'fosters accountability, but not specifically in the parliamentary sense': the more executive action is made transparent, the more parliamentary oversight is bypassed by other forms of popular or interest-based control of the executive power.[99] At the same time, oversight experiences the boost in independent evaluation bodies that sideline the traditional structures providing reinforced technical expertise and critical capacity.[100] These instances are gaining increased relevance at the EU level, where they satisfy the requirements of the 'regulatory' democracy[101] that has played a major role in explaining the original dynamics of the European supranational dimension.

The reasons behind the success of this model are complex and manifold. One main explanation lies in the assumed insufficiency of parliamentary institutions to satisfy the social claim for enhanced political oversight advanced by citizens. It is often assumed that parliamentary institutions are not able to offer a serious answer to these pushes. A sort of 'bureaucratisation' of the oversight function is detected: in response to social demand, we face instances of parliamentary oversight that are performed only in the form of 'des contrôle alibis, imaginaires, pour satisfaire l'opinion, improvisés, ou des contrôles formels, ou encore des contrôles parcellaires, inadaptés' ('control-alibis, fictional, aimed at satisfying public opinion, improvised, or of ceremonial controls or even of incomplete, unsuited controls').[102] These trends are taken into account when examining the parliamentary oversight dimension and yet they do not represent the core subject of this work.

Similarly, the monograph focuses on parliamentary oversight at the national and European levels, with only limited references to the sub-national dimension. In fact, the federal or regional arrangement of the form of state is not neutral on the exercise of parliamentary oversight. On the one hand, in highly decentralised systems, sub-national entities are usually represented at national parliamentary level and participate in the oversight of the national executive.[103] On the other hand, sub-national interests can penetrate the legislative–executive interaction, intruding into the political cleavages between the government, the parliamentary majority and the opposition an 'external' perspective that may enrich the standard dynamics of parliamentary oversight.[104]

---

[98] M Luciani, 'Democrazia rappresentativa e democrazia partecipativa' in Vv Aa, *La sovranità popolare nel penisero di Esposito, Crisafulli, Paladin* (Padova, Cedam, 2004) 181. T Schiller, 'Direct Democracy and Theories of Participatory Democracy: some observations' in ZT Pállinger, B Kaufmann, W Marxer, T Schiller (eds), *Direct Democracy in Europe. Developments and Prospects* (Wiesbaden, Springer, 2007) 52; JP Gaudin, *La démocratie participative* (Paris, Armand Collin, 2007); H Ottman and P Barisic (eds), *Deliberative Demokratie* (Baden-Baden, Nomos, 2015).

[99] Meinel (n 36) 332.

[100] R Bustos Gisbert, *La responsabilidad política del Gobierno: Realidad o ficción?* (Madrid, Colex, 2001) 21 ff.

[101] Héritier (n 70) 269 ff. Majone, 'Regulatory Legitimacy' (n 70).

[102] Grandguillaume, 'Le demande' (n 13) 644.

[103] M Russell, 'The Territorial Role of Second Chambers' in N Baldwin and D Shell (eds), *Second Chambers* (London, Frank Cass, 2001). W Swenden, *Federalism and Second Chambers. Regional Representation in Parliamentary Federations: The Australian Senate and German Bundesrat Compared* (Brussels, Peter Lang, 2004). See also below ch 5.

[104] M Burgess and GA Tarr, 'Introduction: Sub-national Constitutionalism and Constitutional Development' in M Burgess and GA Tarr (eds), *Constitutional Dynamics in Federal Systems: Sub-national Perspectives* (Montreal, McGill-Queen's University Press, 2012).

IV. The Fortune of the Oversight Function in Scholarship

Literature on parliamentary oversight is extremely vast and heterogeneous; however the concept is still deemed to be under-theorised.[105]

Over the decades, parliamentary oversight has been approached by a multitude of constitutional and political science studies concerned with either the executive–legislative relationship or with the functioning of parliaments. Constitutional law and political science approaches differ in terms of theoretical framework, conceptualisation of the function, categorisation of its mechanisms and research methodologies. Both general theoretical perspectives and empirical analysis have been used to address the function. Nonetheless, systematic studies on the oversight function per se are not so common.

At a first approximation, in many continental European countries (namely Germany, Italy and Spain), the 'golden age' of theoretical constitutional studies on parliamentary oversight was in the 1970s and 1980s. In previous decades, with some exceptions,[106] parliamentary oversight was mostly approached within general theoretical studies on the role of Parliament and its relationship with the executive.[107] By contrast, in the 1970s and 1980s, some constitutional studies published in Germany, Italy and Spain addressed parliamentary oversight as their main theoretical field of interest.[108] One main question addressed by these contributions is whether parliamentary oversight can be considered as a form of legal

---

[105] Pelizzo and Stapenhurst, *Parliamentary Oversight Tools* (n 35) 14. On this point, see also A Le Divellec, 'Le Gouvernement, portion dirigeante du Parlement. Quelques aspects de la réception juridique hésitante du modèle de Westminster dans les Etats européens' (2009) 1 *Jus Politicum* 185, 188.

[106] See the studies published in the 1960s by Galeotti (n 29); M Ameller, *Les questions, instrument du contrôle parlementaire* (Paris, LGDJ, 1964); R Baümlin, *Die Kontrolle des Parlaments über Regierung und Verwaltung* (Basel, Helbing & Lichtenhahn, 1966).

[107] See, eg, L Duguit, *Traité de droit constitutionnel*, II, 3rd edn (Paris, E de Boccard, 1928) 806 ff; B Mirkine-Guetzévitch, 'Le régime parlementaire dans les récentes Constitutions européennes' (1950) 2–4 *Revue internationale de droit comparé* 605, 610 ff; Jennings (n 15) 439 ff; E Friesenhahn et al (eds), *Parlement und Regierung in modernen Staat. Die Organisationsgewalt* (Berlin, Walter de Gruyter, 1966); E Cheli, *Atto politico e funzione di indirizzo politico* (Milano, Giuffrè, 1968); N Gehrig, *Parlament – Regierung – Opposition. Dualismus als Voraussetzung für eine parlamentarische Kontrolle der Regierung* (München, Beck, 1969); Elia (n 38).

[108] See, in Germany: U Thaysen, 'Zur Praxis eines grundlegenden parlamentarischen Kontrollrechts: die herbeirufung von regierungsmitgliedern durch das Parlament' (1974) 5 *Zeitschrift für Parlamentsfragen* 459; DG Bodenheim, *Kollision parlamentarischer Kontrollrechte Zum verfassungsrechtlichen Verhältnis von parlamentarischem Frage – und Untersuchungsrecht* (Hamburg, Joachim Heitmann, 1979); N Achterberg, 'Parlamentarische Kontrollrechte' (1977) 30 *Die öffentliche verwaltung* 548; KU Meyn, *Kontrolle als Verfassungsprinzip* (Baden-Baden, Nomos, 1982); E Busch, *Parlamentarische Kontrolle. Ausgestaltung und Wirkung* (Heidelberg, Decker und Müller, 1983); W Krebs, *Kontrolle in staatlichen Entscheidungsprozessen. Ein Beitrag zur rechtlichen Analyse von gerichtlichen, parlamentarischen und Rechnungshof-Kontrollen* (Heildelberg, Muller, 1984); P Stadler, *Die parlamentarische Kontrolle der Bundesregierung* (Berlin, Springer, 1984); W Steffani, 'Formen, Verfahren und Wirkungen der parlamentarischen Kontrolle' in HP Schneider and W Zeh (eds), *Parlamentsrecht und Parlamentspraxis* (Berlin, De Gruyter, 1989). In Italy: Amato (n 27); A Manzella, *I controlli parlamentari* (Milano, Giuffrè, 1970); C Chimenti, *Il controllo parlamentare nell'ordinamento italiano* (Milano, Giuffrè, 1974); A Baldassarre, 'I poteri di indirizzo-controllo del parlamento' in Vv Aa, *Il parlamento: analisi e proposte di riforma* (Roma, Editori Riuniti, 1978); S Sicardi, 'Controllo e indirizzo parlamentare' in *Digesto delle discipline pubblicistiche*, IV (Torino, Utet, 1989). In Spain: F Santaolalla López, *El Parlamento y sus instrumentos de información (preguntas, interpelaciones y Comisiones de investigación)* (Madrid, EDERSA, 1982); JR Montero Gibert, *El control parlamentario* (Madrid, Tecnos, 1984); J García Morillo and JR Montero, *El control parlamentario* (Madrid, Tecnos, 1984); J García Morillo, *El control parlamentario del Gobierno en el ordenamiento español* (Madrid, Congreso de los Diputados, 1985); M Aragón Reyes, 'El control parlamentario como control político' (1986) 23 *Revista de Derecho Político* 9.

control (exercised on the basis of a given parameter and supported by the use of sanctions) or a form of political control. The preference for a flexible conception of parliamentary oversight as a multifaceted function, associated with different implications in the executive–legislative interaction,[109] laid the foundations for successive works on the multi-procedural nature of this power.[110]

In the following years, for a certain period, the oversight function ceased to be a topical issue in constitutional studies.[111] From the 1990s, the number of monographs devoted to a theoretical approach on parliamentary oversight sharply decreased.[112] However, parliamentary oversight continued to be studied from more specific perspectives of analysis: the interaction with the right to information and citizens' participation;[113] the potential of Parliament and of the government to act as a unitary subject in triggering or answering to oversight action;[114] the evaluation of public policies;[115] and the position of the different political aggregations (majority, opposition and parliamentary groups) in the exercise of the oversight function.[116]

After this apparent fade-out, in the last decade a plurality of factors renewed the interest in parliamentary oversight both among scholars and in the institutional debate.

---

[109] Manzella, *I controlli parlamentari* (n 108); Busch (n 108); and Aragón Reyes, 'El control parlamentario' (n 108); J García Morillo, 'Control parlamentario' in JJ González Encinar (ed), *Diccionario del sistema político español* (Madrid, Akal, 1984); J García Morillo, 'Aproximación a un concepto del control parlamentario' (1986) 10 *Revista de la Facultad de Derecho de la Universidad Complutense* 31; and F Rubio Llorente, 'El control parlamentario' (1985) 1 *Revista Parlamentaria de Habla Hispana* 83, now in F Rubio Llorente, *La forma del poder (Estudios sobre la Constitución)* (Madrid, CEC, 1993).

[110] HP Schneider, *Entscheidungsdefizite der Parlamente: über die Notwendigkeit einer Wiederbelebung der Parlamentsreform* (Tübingen, Mohr Siebeck, 1980); A Embid Irujo, 'El control parlamentario y el principio de la mayoria parlamentaria' (1992) 25 *Revista de las Cortes Generales* 7, 8 ff.

[111] For an exhaustive bibliographical analysis of the Italian and Spanish literature on parliamentary oversight, see Rivosecchi (n 84); and FJ García Roca and R Ibrido, 'El control parlamentario en Italia. Un estudio comparado sobre el concepto y algunas de sus mejores prácticas: el Comité para la legislación y la Comisión de presupuestos' in F Pau i Vall (ed), *El control del Gobierno en democracia* (Madrid, Tecnos, 2013).

[112] Some exceptions are represented by M Carducci, *Controllo parlamentare e teorie costituzionali* (Padova, Cedam, 1996); Bustos Gisbert (n 100); S Emmerling, *Kontrolle im parlamentarischen Regierungssystem der Bundesrepublik Deutschland* (Kiel, Grin, 2004); J Schmidt, *Die demokratische Legitimationsfunktion der parlamentarischen Kontrolle* (Berlin, Duncker & Humblot, 2007); Siefken (n 30). In France, the academic debate on parliamentary oversight gained relevance after the 2008 constitutional amendment (see below (n 117)).

[113] A Janssen, *Über die Grenzen des legislativen Zugriffsrechts* (Tübingen, Mohr, 1990); E Cobreros Mendazona, 'El status parlamentario como derecho fundamental' in Vv Aa, *Estudios sobre la Constitución española. Homenaje al profesor E Garcia de Enterrìa*, III (Madrid, Ed Civitas, 1991) 2168 ff.

[114] FJ García Roca, 'El control del Gobierno desde la perspectiva individual del parlamentario (y a la luz del art. 23.2 de la Constitución)' (1995) 42 *Revista Vasca de Administración Publica* 161; J García Fernández, 'El control parlamentario desde la perspectiva del Gobierno' (1997) 2 *Cuadernos de Derecho Público* 195.

[115] Chantebout (n 90); A Delcamp, JL Bergel and A Dupas, *Contrôle parlementaire et évaluation* (Paris, La Documentation française, 1995); JP Duprat, 'Le parlement évaluateur' (1998) 2 *Revue Internationale de Droit Comparé* 551; A Pariente, 'Evaluation parlementaire et responsabilité politique du Gouvernement' (2000) 14 *Les Petites Affiches* 9.

[116] Embid Irujo (n 110) 8 ff; L López Guerra, 'El control parlamentario como instrumento de las minorías' (1996) 8 *Anuario de derecho constitucional y parlamentario* 81; S Sicardi, 'Il problematico rapporto tra controllo parlamentare e ruolo dell'opposizione nell'esperienza repubblicana' (2002) 44 *Rassegna parlamentare* 961; E Schuett-Wetschky, 'Gouvernementale Parlamentskontrolle? Politische Führung, Regierungsmehrheiten und das Verhältnis von Parlament und Regierung' in W Patzelt and E Holtmann (eds), *Parlamentarische Regierungskontrolle – Gouvernementale Parlamentskontrolle. Theorie und Fallbeispiele* (Lesk, Opladen, 2004); L Ciaurro, 'Maggioranza e opposizioni nelle procedure di controllo parlamentare: l'esperienza del Senato' in E Rossi (ed), *Maggioranza e opposizioni nelle procedure parlamentari* (Padova, Cedam, 2004); P Mattei, 'Party system change and parliamentary scrutiny of the executive in Italy' (2005) 11 *Journal of Legislative Studies* 16.

First, changes affecting the constitutional relevance of the oversight function have recently occurred at national level, fostered by formal paths of constitutional revision (as in the case of the 2008 amendment to the French Constitution),[117] spontaneous processes of constitutional adaptation (as in the German debate on parliamentary oversight of EU affairs started by the Lissabon Urteil)[118] or by major reforms of the EU legal order (including the European economic governance launched in response to the 2008 Euro crisis).[119]

Second, parliamentary oversight has been significantly affected by ongoing transformations experienced by parliamentary democracy in the EU, in a dual direction. On the one hand, oversight procedures are a typical case of institutional transplant forged in the context of national parliamentary systems and then integrated into the architecture of the EU.[120] EU policy-making relies on various forms of oversight from national parliaments as a due component of the democratic legitimacy circuit.[121] On the other hand, the transplant has affected the way national oversight mechanisms are implemented at domestic level, attracting ever-increasing interest in the 'Europeanisation' of the oversight function as a whole.[122]

---

[117] *Ex multis*, P Türk, *Le contrôle parlementaire en France* (Paris, LGDJ, 2011) and the Special Issue 'Le contrôle parlementaire' (2010) 134 *Pouvoirs* 5. The 'evaluation' task of Parliament has represented a privileged perspective; see P Avril, 'Le contrôle. Exemple du Comité d'évaluation et de contrôle des politiques publiques' (2008) 6 *Jus Politicum* 1; L Baghestani, 'A propos de la loi tendant à renforcer les moyens du Parlement en matière de contrôle de l'action du Gouvernement et d'évaluation des politiques publiques' (2011) 78 *Les Petites affiches* 3 f.

[118] E Röper, 'Europapolitische Bundesratsbeschlüsse ohne demokratisch-parlamentarische Kontrolle' (2009) 40 *Zeitschrift für Parlamentsfragen* 3; R Hönle, 'Bundesrat und Europapolitik – kein kontrollfreier Raum. Eine Replik auf Erich Röper' (2009) 40 *Zeitschrift für Parlamentsfragen* 683; F Schorkopf, 'The European Union as an Association of Sovereign States: Karlsruhe's Ruling on the Treaty of Lisbon' (2009) 10 *German Law Journal* 1219; PC Müller-Graff, 'Das Karlsruher Lissabon-Urteil: Bedingungen, Grenzen, Orakel und integrative Optionen' (2009) 32 *Integration* 331; A Benz and J Broschek, *Nationale Parlamente in der europäischen Politik: Funktionen, Probleme und Lösungen* (Berlin, Friedrich-Ebert-Stiftung: Internationale Politikanalyse, 2010).

[119] E Griglio and N Lupo, 'Parliamentary democracy and the Eurozone crisis' (2012) 1 *Law and Economics Yearly Review* II, 313, 345 ff; F Allemand and F Martucci, 'La légitimité démocratique de la gouvernance économique européenne: la mutation de la fonction parlementaire' (2014) 134 *Revue de l'OFCE* 115; K Auel and O Höing, 'National Parliaments and the Eurozone Crisis: Taking Ownership in Difficult Times?' (2015) 38 *West European Politics* 375; V Kreilinger, *National Parliaments, Surveillance Mechanisms and Ownership in the EuroArea* (Berlin, Jacques Delors Institute Studies and Report, 2016); D Jančić, *National Parliaments after the Lisbon Treaty and the Euro Crisis: Resilience or Resignation?* (Oxford, Oxford University Press, 2017).

[120] P Lindseth, *Power and Legitimacy. Reconciling Europe and the Nation-State* (Oxford, Oxford University Press, 2010).

[121] Besselink, 'National Parliaments in the EU' (n 68); Crum and Fossum (n 63); T Raunio, 'The gatekeepers of European integration? The functions of national parliaments in the EU political system' (2011) 33 *Journal of European Integration* 303, 315 ff; G Martinico, 'Dating Cinderella: On Subsidiarity as a Political Safeguard of Federalism in the European Union' (2011) 4 *European Public Law* 649; W Wessels and O Rozenberg (eds), *Democratic Control in the Member States of the European Council and the Euro Zone Summits* (Brussels, EU Parliament – Directorate General for Internal Policies, 2013); K Boronska-Hryniewiecka, 'Legitimacy through Subsidiarity? The Parliamentary Control of EU Policy-making' (2013) 1 *Polish Political Science Review* 84; D Fromage, *Les Parlements dans l'Union Européenne après le Traité de Lisbonne – La Participation des Parlements allemands, britanniques, espagnols, français et italiens* (Paris, Harmattan, 2015).

[122] *Ex multis*, E Damgaard and H Jensen, 'Europeanisation of Executive–Legislative Relations: Nordic Perspectives' (2005) 11 *The Journal of Legislative Studies* 394; K Auel, 'Democratic Accountability and National Parliaments: Redefining the Impact of Parliamentary Scrutiny in EU Affairs' (2007) 13 *European Law Journal* 487; C Sprungk, 'Ever more or ever better scrutiny? Analysing the conditions of effective national parliamentary involvement in EU affairs' (2010) 14 *European Integration Online Papers* 1; C Neuhold and R de Ruiter, 'Out of reach? Parliamentary control of EU affairs in the Netherlands and the UK' (2010) 16 *The Journal of Legislative Studies* 57; J Karlas, 'National Parliamentary Control of EU Affairs: Institutional Design after Enlargement' (2012) 35 *West European Politics* 1095; T Winzen, 'National Parliamentary Control of European Union Affairs: A Cross-national

In the European framework, due also to the blending together of national approaches, parliamentary oversight is often viewed as a counterpart of accountability discourse;[123] it is increasingly approached as a potential opportunity for rethinking the role of the legislature in the eyes of the executive and public opinion. This trend confirms that literature on parliamentary oversight in the EU has recently experienced a sort of hybridisation between classic constitutional law and political science approaches to the issue. Studies on EU democratic accountability seem to have implicitly (and often unconsciously) derived from mainstream political science approaches the two main insights that, over the decades, have fostered comparative politics research on parliamentary oversight.

The first insight relates to parliamentary oversight as the masterpiece of the agency theory framing representation as delegation, embodied by the principal–agent relationship.[124] This is the approach shared by a large part of political science literature dealing with issues of accountability and oversight.[125] According to the agency theory, parliamentary oversight aims to limit the fundamental risk inherent in the chain of representation through delegation: that is, the possibility that the agent (ie, the executive) might act in violation of the principal's (ie, Parliament's) interests. Through the oversight function, parliaments address

---

and Longitudinal Comparison' (2012) 35 *West European Politics* 657; C Neuhold and A Streklov, 'New opportunity structures for the "unusual suspects"? Implications of the Early Warning System for the role of national parliaments within the EU system of governance' (2012) 4 *OPAL online Paper Series* 1; K Auel, O Rozenberg and A Tacea, 'To Scrutinise or Not to Scrutinise? Explaining Variation in EU-Related Activities in National Parliaments' (2015) 38 *West European Politics* 282.

[123] T Bergman and E Damgaard (eds), *Delegation and Accountability in European Integration: The Nordic Parliamentary Democracies and the European Union* (London, Frank Cass, 2000); O Costa, N Jabko, C Lequesne and P Magnette, 'La diffusion des mécanismes de contrôle dans l'Union européenne: vers une nouvelle forme de démocratie?' (2001) 51 *Revue française de science politique* 859; C Harlow, *Accountability in the European Union* (Oxford, Oxford University Press, 2002); C Harlow and R Rawlings, 'Promoting Accountability in Multi-Level Governance: A Network Approach' (2007) 13 *European Law Journal* 542; D Curtin and A Wille (eds), *Meaning and Practice of Accountability in the EU Multi-Level Context* (Mannheim, Connex Report Series No 07, 2008); S Gustavsson, C Karlsson and T Persson (eds), *The Illusion of Accountability in the European Union* (New York, Routledge, 2009); M Bovens, D Curtin and P 't Hart, *The Real World of EU Accountability. What Deficit?* (Oxford, Oxford University Press, 2010); D Curtin, P Mair and I Papadopoulos (eds), *Accountability and European Governance* (London, Routledge, 2012); A Cygan, *Accountability, Parliamentarism and Transparency in the EU* (Cheltenham, Edward Elgar, 2013); C Geslot, PY Monjal and J Rossetto (eds), *La responsabilité politique des exécutifs des États membres du fait de leur action européenne* (Brussels, Bruylant, 2016); M Costa, *The Accountability Gap in EU Law: Mind the Gap* (New York, Routledge, 2016); B Crum, 'Parliamentary accountability in multilevel governance: what role for parliaments in post-crisis EU economic governance?' (2017) 25 *Journal of European Public Policy* 268.

[124] BM Mitnick, 'Agency Theory' in RE Freeman and OH Werhane (eds), *The Blackwell Encyclopedic Dictionary of Business Ethics* (Malden, Blackwell, 1998) 12; RW Waterman and KJ Meier, 'Principal-agent models: an expansion?' (1998) 8 *Journal of Public Administration Research and Theory* 173; G Majone, 'Two logics of delegation: agency and fiduciary relations in EU governance' (2001) 2 *European Union Politics* 103.

[125] See MD McCubbins and T Schwartz, 'Congressional oversight overlooked: police patrol versus fire alarms' (1984) 28 *American Journal of Political Science* 165; DR Kiewiet and MD McCubbins, *The Logic of Delegation* (Chicago, IL, University of Chicago Press, 1991); J Ferejohn, 'Accountability and Authority: Toward a Theory of Political Accountability' in A Przeworski, SC Stokes and B Manin (eds), *Democracy, Accountability, and Representation* (Cambridge, Cambridge University Press, 1999); Strøm, 'Delegation and accountability' (n 91) 271 ff; R Maffio, '*Qui custodiet ipsos custodes? Il controllo parlamentare dell'attività di governo in prospettiva comparata*' (2002) 9 *Quaderni di scienza politica* 333; K Strøm, 'Parliamentary Democracy and Delegation' in K Strøm, W Müller and T Bergman (eds), *Delegation and Accountability in Parliamentary Democracies* (Oxford, Oxford University Press, 2003) 67 ff; A Lupia, 'Delegation and its Perils' in K Strøm, W Müller and T Bergman (eds), *Delegation and Accountability in Parliamentary Democracies* (Oxford, Oxford University Press, 2003) 44 ff; Pelizzo and Stapenhurst, *Government Accountability* (n 96).

problems of adverse selection, related to the asymmetry of information between the principal and the agent, and moral hazard, raised by an agent that does not act consistently with the principal's directions and expectations. To face the former, parliaments implement ex ante oversight mechanisms that take place in the first stage of the delegation chain linking citizens to representatives, before the 'contract' is made, during the appointing or electing of the executive.[126] Risks of moral hazard are instead addressed through ex post oversight mechanisms, operating in the subsequent stage of the delegation chain, when the contract has been made and the agents have been entrusted with their mandate.[127]

The second insight is instead derived from political science studies concerned with the notion of parliamentary 'influence' as opposed to formal powers vested in parliaments, based on constitutional or statutory arrangements. A long-standing approach to this notion argued that the Parliament should spend less time on 'ritualistic forms of debates and divisions on legislation which is going to be passed anyway' and more on the scrutiny of administration, to be exercised in terms of influence rather than direct power, advice rather than command, criticism instead of obstruction, scrutiny instead of initiation.[128] The term *influence* is used in assorted meanings in contemporary comparative politics,[129] but it usually describes 'what power parliament exercises in practice within or despite its formal constraints'.[130] It may refer to the factual *control* exercised by Parliament not just in the legislative process (usually labelled as 'legislative influence',[131] following Meyer's conceptualisation)[132] but also in non-legislative procedures, including oversight.[133] This non-technical use of the noun *control* can be misleading if confronted with the notion of formal oversight. Moreover, a distinction should be made between the notion of *influence capacity*, focusing on the tools and procedures available to parliaments for exercising their influence,[134] and *influence effectiveness*, as a means to assess what amount of influence is effectively achieved in the decision-making process.[135] Consideration for the effectiveness of executive oversight

---

[126] T Bergman, 'Formation rules and minority governments' (1993) 23 *European Journal of Political Research* 55; L De Winter, 'The Role of Parliament in Government Formation and Resignation' in H Döering (ed), *Parliaments and Majority Rule in Western Europe* (New York, St Martin's Press, 1995).

[127] T Saalfeld, 'Members of parliament and governments in Western Europe: agency relations and problems of oversight' (2000) 37 *European Journal of Political Research* 353; and Strøm, 'Parliamentary Democracy and Delegation' (n 125) 67 ff.

[128] B Crick, *The Reform of Parliament* (London, Weidenfeld and Nicolson, 1964) 193.

[129] For instance, U Sieberer, 'The institutional power of Western European Parliaments: a multidimensional analysis' (2011) 34 *West European Politics* 731 develops parliamentary power as a multidimension concept comprising direct influence on policy-making, ex ante selection of external officeholders, and ex post control of the Cabinet.

[130] M Russell and M Benton, 'Assessing the policy impact of Parliament: methodological challenges and possible future approaches' (2009) Paper for PSA Legislative Studies Specialist Group Conference. For an overview of literature, see O Rozenberg, 'Comparer les parlements' (n 22) 323 ff.

[131] A Maurer, 'The legislative powers and impact of the European Parliament' (2003) 41 *Journal of Common Market Studies* 227; A Kreppel, 'Moving beyond procedure. An empirical analysis of European Parliament legislative influence' (2002) 35 *Comparative Political Studies* 784.

[132] K Meyer, 'Legislative influence: toward theory development through casual analysis' (1980) 5 *Legislative Studies Quarterly* 563.

[133] M Russell, 'Assessing the policy impact of Parliament: methodological challenges and possible future approaches' (2009) Paper for PSA Legislative Studies Specialist Group Conference, 24 June 2009.

[134] MS Ogul, 'Congressional Oversight: Structure and Incentives' in L Dodd and B Oppenheimer (eds), *Congress Reconsidered* (New York, Praeger, 1977).

[135] D Arter, 'Conclusion. Questioning the "Mezey Question": an interrogatory framework for the comparative study of legislatures' (2006) 12 *The Journal of Legislative Studies* 462; Pelizzo and Stapenhurst, *Government Accountability* (n 96).

in Parliament has led to the recognition of the influence of behaviour on institutions: individual MPs' motivational and attitudinal changes, alongside formal institutional reforms, are therefore detected as fundamental determinants of the oversight function.[136]

As for the evaluation of the amount of 'influence' that a Parliament can exercise, different classifications and approaches have been advanced, comparing formal powers, contextual factors[137] and parliaments' performances in the policy-making process. For our purposes, it is appropriate to recall the distinction by Philip Norton between *policy-influencing* and *policy-making* parliaments,[138] which is based on the traditional Mezey classification of parliaments according to their formal powers and level of support by the public or the elites.[139] Another relevant distinction is the one advanced by Polsby in 1975,[140] based on previous studies,[141] between *working parliaments* and *talking parliaments*, which however some political scientists have considered not fully suited to describe parliaments in continental Europe.[142] Assemblies focused on executive oversight and public debate have instead been labelled as *arena type legislatures* so as to distinguish them from the *transformative legislatures* that rather aim at exercising a direct influence on policy-making.[143]

Finally, several non-academic comparative studies on parliamentary oversight have been published on behalf of or under the label of parliamentary bodies and organisations (at both national and international level).[144] They may either result from interparliamentary conferences or arise from systematic comparative studies developed by means of questionnaires and surveys. Comparative evidence is usually provided in an extensive manner, combining results from extremely heterogeneous institutional and political systems.

The review of literature confirms that there is no single conceptualisation of the oversight function when one moves from consideration of the formal delegation-accountability

---

[136] P Norton, *Parliament in the 1980s* (Oxford, Basil Blackwell, 1985).

[137] Saalfeld (n 127).

[138] Norton, 'Parliaments: A Framework for Analysis' (n 12) 5 ff; GW Copeland and SC Patterson (eds), *Parliaments in the Modern World* (Ann Arbor, MI, Michigan University Press, 1997). See also P Norton (ed), *Parliaments in Western Europe* (London, Frank Cass, 1990).

[139] M Mezey, *Comparative Legislatures* (Durham, NC, Duke University Press, 1979). See also D Arter, 'Introduction: comparing the legislative performance of legislatures' (2006) 12 *Journal of Legislative Studies* 245.

[140] NW Polsby, 'Legislatures' in FI Greenstein and NW Polsby (eds), *Handbook of Political Science*, V (Reading, Addison-Wesley, 1975).

[141] M Weber, 'Parliament and Government in Germany under a New Political Order' (1917) in P Lassman and R Speirs (eds), *Weber: Political Writings* (Cambridge, Cambridge University Press, 1994) 176 ff.

[142] A Panebianco, 'Parlamento-arena e partiti' (1987) 17 *Rivista italiana di scienza politica* 203; G Pasquino and R Pelizzo, *Parlamenti democratici* (Bologna, Il Mulino, 2006).

[143] Rozenberg, 'Comparer les parlements' (n 22) 325.

[144] H Yamamoto, *Tools for Parliamentary Oversight: A Comparative Study of 88 National Parliaments* (Geneva, Inter-Parliamentary Union, 2007). IPU and UNDP, *Global Parliamentary Report 2017* (n 10). In the OECD context, see the OECD Background documents of OECD Parliamentary Budget Officials and Independent Fiscal Institutions and the essays published in the *OECD Journal on Budgeting*. Many comparative publications on parliamentary oversight of budget are edited by the World Bank Institute and the International Monetary Fund; see I Lienert, 'Who Controls the Budget: The Legislature or the Executive?' (2005) 5/115 IMF Working Paper 1; R Pelizzo, R Stapenhurst and D Olson, *The Role of Parliaments in the Budget Process* (Washington, World Bank Institute, 2005); Stapenhurst, Pelizzo, Olson and von Trapp (eds), *Legislative Oversight* (n 35). In the last few years, the Directorate General for internal policies of the European Parliament has also published comparative publications on parliamentary oversight addressing different fields of action. See AM Kanis (ed), *Parliamentary Control of Budget Implementation* (Brussels, European Parliament, 2012); A Wills and M Vermeulen (eds), *Parliamentary*

argument to the evaluation of its actual implementation in the institutional decision-making process. Nonetheless, these studies have offered a privileged point of view for analysing the way in which oversight is concretely operationalised by representative assemblies, beyond formal arrangements; and for assessing its effects on policy-making. Therefore, they will be considered in the monograph when analysing the constitutional factors that shape the oversight function.

oversight of security and intelligence agencies in the European Union (EU Parliament – Directorate General for Internal Policies, 2011); Wessels and Rozenberg (eds) (n 121). Extensive research on the role of parliaments in the oversight of the security sector has been conducted on behalf of the Geneva Centre for the Democratic Control of Armed Forces (DCAF); see H Born, PH Fluri and S Lunn (eds), *Oversight and guidance: the relevance of parliamentary oversight for the security sector and its reform. A collection of articles on foundational aspects of parliamentary oversight of the security sector* (Brussels, DCAF and NATO Parliamentary Assembly, 2003).

2

Oversight as a Relational Function Linking Parliaments to Executives

Chapter two presents the macro factors influencing parliamentary oversight: those relating to the legal constitutional design (comprising the constitutional tradition, the form of government and the legal framework), and those relating to the political and pre-legal factors (including the executive–parties dimension and party system).

I. At the Origins of Parliamentarism in Europe

The origins of parliamentary oversight date back to the rise of Western democracies. According to liberal thought, the 'control' of executive business identified one of the fundamental tasks of elected assemblies. The basic idea was that

> an effective representative body, gifted with the power to rule, ought ... not only to speak the will of the nation ... but also to lead it to its conclusions, to utter the voice of its opinions, and to serve as its eyes in superintending all matters of government.[1]

Surprisingly, the assumption was advanced by Woodrow Wilson while deploring the nature of the US Congress as a merely legislative body rather than a 'parliament'.[2] In his vision, the Congress was overdoing the business of legislation, whereas it should learn to be 'the eyes and the voice' of the constituents by looking diligently into every affair of government. The undertaking of this role by political representatives was perceived as a guarantee for the government against the risk of irresponsive and half-informed criticism. The oversight capacity vested on parliaments in Europe served as a reference model.

In Europe, the debate on parliamentary oversight dates back to the settlement of the constitutional theory of the state in the nineteenth century. The origins of this power should be traced back to the peculiar arrangement of the doctrine of separation of powers found in different parliamentary regimes. Regardless of national variations, what enabled the 'surveillance' of the parliament on the 'government' was the softening of the separation doctrine by means of agreement and cooperation between the legislative and the executive powers.[3]

---

[1] W Wilson, *Congressional Government. A Study in American Politics* (Boston, MA, Houghton Mifflin Company, 1885) 297.

[2] ibid, 300. See also DK Price, 'The Parliamentary and Presidential Systems' (1943) 3 *Public Administration Review* 317.

[3] 'Si dans un État libre, la puissance législative ne doit pas avoir le droit d'arrêter la puissance exécutrice, elle a droit, et doit avoir la faculté d'examiner de quelle manière les lois qu'elle a faites ont été exécutées' is the the logical consequence brought in by C de Secondat de Montesquieu, *De l'esprit des lois*, XI, ch VI (Paris, Nourse, 1772) 198 f.

The doctrine of representative (or responsible) government grown in the Westminster parliamentary system[4] is one that best represents this arrangement. The formula provides that the executive power is held by the Cabinet, a committee that is appointed and removable by the House of Commons. The Cabinet is responsible to the Commons, and the Commons responsible to the people. The meaning of this formula is that 'the whole people, or some numerous portion of them, exercise through deputies periodically elected by themselves the ultimate controlling power'.[5] In the British liberal tradition, the 'scrutiny', 'control' or 'review' function of Parliament in regard to the executive was therefore clearly implicated by the broader theory of 'checks and balances' as a singular approximation to the separation of the legislative and executive authorities.[6] The function was instrumental to pursue the *balance* between the branches of government.

John Stuart Mill is probably the author who best developed this suggestion. He laid the theoretical foundation of parliamentary oversight in the British system of government based on two main premises: controlling the business of government and actually doing it should be vested on two different bodies; the task that a representative assembly can possibly fulfil is not that of doing the business, but rather 'causing it to be done, determining to whom it should be confided and assessing it when performed':[7]

> Instead of the function of governing, for which it is radically unfit, the proper office of a representative assembly is to watch and control the government; to throw the light of publicity on its acts; to compel a full exposition and justification of all of them which any one considers questionable; to censure them if found condemnable and, if the men who compose the government abuse their trust, or fulfil it in a manner which conflicts with the deliberate sense of the nation, to expel them from office, and either expressly or virtually appoint their successors.[8]

Combined with the formula of Cabinet government, the British doctrine of representative government contributed to anchoring the control of business in Parliament on behalf of the Crown in the executive–legislative interaction.[9] This vision spread throughout Europe[10] however remained quite unique to the British system: rather different approaches prevailed at that time on the Continent.[11]

The British experience exercised a major influence on the process of 'parliamentarisation' of Nordic countries. Sweden had a long-standing constitutional and parliamentary tradition, directly inspired by England.[12] Transition to parliamentarism was completed quite late, in the political conjuncture of 1915 to 1917 when the introduction of an 'extraordinary' oversight power enabled the Parliament to overthrow the executive. However,

---

[4] W Bagehot, *The English Constitution*, 2nd edn (London, HS King, 1872) *passim*.

[5] JS Mill, 'Considerations on Representative Government' (1861) in JS Mill, *The Collected Works of John Stuart Mill, XIX – Essays on Politics and Society*, 3rd edn (London, Longman-Green, 1865) 430.

[6] Bagehot (n 4) 43 and 49.

[7] Mill (n 5) 430.

[8] ibid, 432.

[9] A Todd, *On Parliamentary Government in England. Its Origin, Development and Practical Operation*, II, 2nd edn (London, Longmans, Green and Co, 1889) 390 ff.

[10] L Sánchez Agesta, 'Gobierno y responsabilidad' (1960) 113–14 *Revista de estudios políticos* 35, 52 ff.

[11] P Lindseth, 'The Paradox of Parliamentary Supremacy: Delegation, Democracy and Dictatorship in Germany and France, 1920s–1950s' (2004) 49 *University of Connecticut School of Law Articles and Working Papers* 1341, 1343.

[12] F Sterzel, *Riksdagen Kontrollmakt* (Stockholm, PA Norstedt, 1969).

the 1809 Instrument of Government and the 1810 Riksdag Act had already introduced at parliamentary level their own mechanisms for scrutinising the Cabinet.[13] Compared with the British parliamentary tradition, Sweden developed a distinctive 'model' of executive accountability.[14] This was based not so much on ministerial responsibility, because ministers were not MPs and their relations with the Riksdag[15] differed from the accountability patterns typical to the Westminster model; rather, it focused on 'representativeness' as the dominant principle.[16] Prior to the adoption of the 1974 Instrument of Government, the 1809 'Constitution' prevented ministers from attending Riksdag committee meetings. As a matter of fact, the Swedish model of parliamentary oversight was based on the sharp separation of the two channels of the administrative and political responsibility of the executive. This was implemented through the contribution of two ad hoc control instruments: the parliamentary ombudsman and the Constitution Committee. The former is a monocratic body that – in the name of the people – was given the task of supervising the observance of the laws and statutes as applied by the courts, by public officials and employees.[17] The role of the ombudsman was introduced by the 1809 Instrument of Government and this figure is still a fundamental component of parliamentary oversight today. The other control instrument was the Constitution Committee which, dating back to the 1809 Instrument of Government, represents the oldest parliamentary committee still in use in the Nordic countries. This committee conducts a permanent supervision of the handling of government business and the exercise of ministers' duties.[18]

In the rest of Europe, the historical origins of parliamentary oversight showed rather different developments. In Spain, from 1834 until the dictatorship of Primo de Rivera there was no real experience of parliamentary oversight. The Spanish Constitutions of 1869 and 1931 formally recognised the power to censure and question the government as a prerogative respectively of each Chamber and each MP. However, in the constitutional practice, until the entry into force of the Constitution of 1978 the Cortes had no real power over the formation, mandate and dismissal of the executive.[19]

In France, after the Revolution of 1789, the legislature, in its capacity as representative of the *volonté generale*, was perceived as a real, almost unlimited, law-making authority. Government was charged to give execution to the general will.[20] Parliament's surveillance

---

[13] O Petersson, 'Constitutional History' in J Pierre (ed), *The Oxford Handbook of Swedish Politics* (Oxford, Oxford University Press, 2016) 94 f. MF Metcalf, *The Riksdag: A History of the Swedish Parliament* (Stockholm, Bank of Sweden Tercentenary Foundation, 1987). B Thorarensen, 'Mechanisms for Parliamentary Control of the Executive' in H Krunke and B Thorarensen (eds), *The Nordic Constitutions: A Comparative and Contextual Study* (Oxford, Hart Publishing, 2018) 69 ff.

[14] D Arter, 'From "Parliamentary Control" to "Accountable Government"? The role of public committee hearings in the Swedish Riksdag' (2008) 61 *Parliamentary Affairs* 122.

[15] ibid, 138 f.

[16] L Lewin, 'Majoritarian and Consensus Democracy: the Swedish Experience' (1998) 21 *Scandinavian Political Studies* 195, 203.

[17] B Wieslander, *The Parliamentary Ombudsman in Sweden* (Stockholm, Bank of Sweden Tercentenary Foundation, 1994).

[18] O Petersson, 'The Swedish Constitution of 1809' in E Özdalga and S Persson (eds), *Contested Sovereignties: Government and Democracy in Middle Eastern and European Perspectives* (Istanbul, Swedish Research Institute in Istanbul, 2009).

[19] See J Varela Suárez, 'El control parlamentario del gobierno en la Historia constitucional española' in Vv Aa, *El Parlamento a debate* (Madrid, Trotta, 1997) 66 ff.

[20] JJ Rousseau, *Du contrat social*, III (Paris, Bordas, 1762) 122 ff.

represented the natural implication of the subordination of the executive power,[21] which 'reste sous le contrôle du parlement quant à l'ensemble et au detail de ses actes' ('is kept under parliamentary scrutiny for its acts either as a whole or singularly').[22] In the post-French Revolution framework, the traditional British conception of parliamentary scrutiny as instrumental to the balance of powers was therefore substituted by the idea of 'oversight-subjection' centred on parliamentary monism.[23]

The notion of ministerial responsibility itself differed from the conceptualisation grown in British constitutionalism, focusing on the penal, rather than on the political aspects of responsibility.[24] Ministerial responsibility was mentioned in the *Cahiers des doléances* drafted by the *Etats Généraux* in 1789 without specifying what kind of responsibility should be involved. Acting as a guarantee against any risks of power abuse, the penal dimension played a dominant role.[25] For a long time, the political and penal dimensions were combined to define the ministerial responsibility around the formula advanced by Benjamin Constant of the 'mauvais usage d'un pouvoir légal' ('misuse of a lawful power').[26] The formula defined the abuse of legal power by a minister, done in an official capacity, which harms the state or its citizens without any justification on the grounds of public interest.

On the whole, what we would define today as 'political' control on the management of daily affairs was not a crucial competence in the nineteenth century French Parliament. In a system that placed all the power in the hands of the *volunté générale* (general will), interpreted by the majority,[27] there was not even space for any control from minority groups. Nonetheless, quite surprisingly, the first exhaustive overview of parliamentary tools and procedures dates back to this period. Between the end of the nineteenth century and the beginning of the twentieth century, some authors provided a list of the tools available to Parliament for controlling and reviewing the government.[28] These include the right to enquiry on any political or administrative matter and the right to submit questions and interpellations. Both tools showed continuous overlapping between the penal and the political dimension of ministerial responsibility: questions and inquiries were seen as a preliminary examination in order to assess whether an accusation could be formulated and resignation demanded.[29]

---

[21] Montesquieu (n 3). On the subordination of the executive power as a means for 'preserving' the Constitution, JJ Rousseau, 'Considerations sur le gouvernement de la Pologne et sur sa réformation projetée (1771–1772)' in *Collection complète des oeuvres de JJ Rousseau*, I (Genève, Société typographique de Genève, 1780–89) 450; and M Bluntschi, *Théorie générale de l'Etat*, fr trad (Paris, Librairie Guillaumin, 1877) 446.

[22] E Fuzier-Herman, *La séparation des pouvoirs d'après l'histoire et le droit constitutionnel* (Paris, Librairie de A Marescq Aîné, 1880) 296.

[23] I Fernández Sarasola, 'El control parlamentario' y su regulación en el ordenamiento español' (2000) 60 *Revista Española de Derecho Constitucional* 89, 92.

[24] A Esmein, *Eléments de droit constitutionnel*, 1st edn (Paris, Larose et Forcel, 1896) 6 ff.

[25] L Michon, *Le Gouvernement perlementaire sous la Restauration* (Paris, Librairie générale de droit et de jurisprudence, 1905).

[26] B Constant, *De la responsabilité des ministres* (Paris, H Nicolle, 1815) *passim*. See also A de Broglie, *Vues sur le Gouvernement de la France* (Paris, Michel Levy Frères, 1870) 324 f.

[27] Rousseau, *Du contrat social* (n 20) 98.

[28] There is no perfect correspondence in the list of tools that satisfy the requirements of parliamentary oversight: Fuzier-Herman (n 22) 343 f also includes some 'preventive' tools, such as the authorisation to declare war and the authorisation to ratify international treaties. By contrast, J Barthélémy, *L'introduction du régime parlementaire en France sous Louis XVIII et Charles X* (Paris, Giard & Brière, 1904) 219 ff also refers to the messages from the Chambers to the king and to petitions.

[29] Barthélémy (n 28) 220 and 246 ff.

A rather different approach to the oversight role of Parliament marked the German constitutional tradition. In the constellation of the German Empire, the Prussian constitutional system hindered any quest for parliamentary government, blamed to be a sort of 'majority despotism'.[30] In sharp contrast to the British, Belgian or Italian monarchies and to the French and American republics, the Prussian government pertained to the strong monarchy that identified in the king the source of law and political authority.[31] In this system, the 'oversight' notion grew out of the antagonism between the monarchical and the parliamentary power known as *Zweischlächtigkeit*.[32] This was introduced to legitimise the parliament acting as a 'counter-power' to the almost absolute monarchy.[33] It was conceived of as a status (well described by the German term '*Macht*', expressive of the parliamentary power as influence and sanction on the king) rather than as a function.[34]

In daily practice, the executive–legislative interaction remained a 'dualistic arrangement of mutual veto powers: parliaments could block laws and executive expenditure, but governments could not be ousted by parliamentary censure'.[35] The dimension of political parliamentary oversight instrumental to making the government accountable to Parliament (and hence to citizens) was therefore outside the remit of the two Prussian representative Chambers, the Reichstag (popular Chamber) and the Bundesrat (the federal Chamber). Ministers were not politically responsible to the Reichstag; they were subject to instances of legal oversight as to ensure the superiority of law-making over the stage of the execution.[36] It was argued that the Reichstag 'in a measure controls. But only in a measure',[37] having regard to the fact that its assent was necessary to the validity of all legislation.[38] As a matter of fact, the Reichstag's power to 'control' executive action was overlapping with the exercise of the legislative function. Even the *Interpellationsrecht*, the right to interpellate the executive, was considered not an oversight prerogative of Parliament[39] but rather a tool that, regulating the relationship between different bodies, served the purposes of state sovereignty.[40] In fact, the

---

[30] G Roethe in D Schäfer, G Roethe and A Wagner (eds), *Preussen. Deutschlands Vergangenheit und Deutschland Zukunft* (Berlin, von Reimar Hobbing, 1913) 112. WW Willoughby, 'The Prussian Theory of Government' (1918) 12 *The American Journal of International Law* 266, 267 f.

[31] P Laband, *Des Staatsrecht des Deutschen Reiches*, I (Tubingen, Laupp, 1876) 27.

[32] FE Oppenheimer, *System der soziologie*, I (Jena, Fischer, 1992) 893.

[33] P Laband, *Das Budgetrech nach den Bestimmungen der Preussichen Verfassungsurkunde* (Berlin, Guttentag, 1871) 68 ff (linking the origin of parliamentary oversight to the *Budgetrecht*, the power to approve the budget vested on the Reichstag).

[34] O Hintze, 'Preussens Entwicklung zum Rechtstaat' (1920) in O Hintze, *Geist und Epochen der preussichen Geschichte*, III (Leipzig, Koehler & Amelang, 1943) 184. This conception of parliamentary oversight was criticised by the Marxist theory; see H Draper, 'Marx on Democratic Forms of Government' (1974) *Social Register* 101, 113 ff.

[35] H Spenkuch, 'Prussian Governance' in M Jefferies (ed), *The Ashgate Research Companion to Imperial Germany* (London, Routledge, 2015) 35.

[36] H Kelsen, *General Theory of Law and State* (Cambridge, MA, Harvard University Press, 1945) 283 ff.

[37] W Wilson, *The State: Elements of Historical and Practical Politics* (Boston, MA, DC Heath & Co, 1911) 265.

[38] ibid, 267.

[39] DG Bodenheim, *Kollision parlamentarischer Kontrollrechte. Zum verfassungsrechtlichen Verhältnis von parlamentarischem Frage – und Untersuchungsrecht* (Hamburg, Joachim Heitmann, 1979) 12 ff (on the transformation of the *Interpellationsrecht* into the dimension of *Fragerecht*, sovereign power of observation).

[40] HL Rosegger, *Das parlamentarische Interpellationsrecht. Rechts-vergl eichende und politische Studie* (Leipzig, von Duncker & Humblot, 1907) 15 ff; J Hatschek, *Das Interpellationsrecht im Rahmen der modern Ministerverantwortlichkeit* (Leipzig, GJ Göschen, 1909) 111; T Nipperdey, *Deutsche Geschichte 1866-1918*, II (München, Beck, 1992) 104.

'limited' nature of the Prussian monarchy that did not allow the enforcement of (political) ministerial responsibility created the premise for placing the heart of parliamentary oversight in the Reichstag committees. Executive oversight was strongly focused on the role of standing committees that matched this prerogative with the scrutiny of legislative Bills. The Bundestag is the inheritor of this tradition.[41]

As for the Bundesrat, not legislation but superintendence of administration was deemed to be the main prerogative of the federal Chamber.[42] Having regard to the 'executive function' of the Bundesrat, it was therefore assumed that

> the administrative function of the federal chamber may be summed up in the word oversight. It considers all defects or needs which discover themselves in the administrative arrangement of the Empire in the course of the execution of the laws, and may, in all cases where that duty has not been otherwise bestowed, formulate the necessary regulation to cure such defects and meet such needs.[43]

In this sphere, there was no space for real political control, as the Bundesrat's 'superintendence' was interpreted and implemented as a strictly administrative form of surveillance. It can therefore be concluded that the origins of parliamentary oversight in Germany are deeply embedded in the lack of a parliamentary tradition and in the influence of the federal structure on the role of the two Chambers.

Elements of the French and of the German tradition contributed to the consolidation of the oversight power in the Italian regime of the *Statuto albertino* that entered into force in 1848. On the one hand, similar to the French experience, parliamentary oversight was approached in Italy as an implication of the traditional dogma of parliamentary sovereignty, originally based on the supremacy of the law and hence on the independence of the legislative power. The dogma evolved over decades, when new modules for the implementation of state functions emerged. The gradual empowerment of the government in the adoption of legislative acts and regulations resulted in a complete rebalancing of the two powers.[44] Their relationship ceased to be legislative centred. New acts – such as the interpellations, votes of confidence, resolutions, motions and recommendations – came to dominate the executive-legislative interaction. At this stage, the connection of parliamentary oversight with the confidence relationship (that was 'presumed')[45] became clearly evident.[46] This new conceptualisation was the result of the parliamentarisation of the Italian form of government,[47] which explains why similar results could not be obtained in Germany.

On the other hand, similar to Germany, the origins of parliamentary oversight in Italy were based on an atechnical conception: the oversight power was not opposed to the other

---

[41] P Lauvaux, 'Le contrôle, source du régime parlementaire, priorité du régime présidentiel' (2010) 3 *Pouvoirs* 23, 35.

[42] Laband, *Des Staatsrecht* (n 31) 34.

[43] Wilson, *The State* (n 37) 261.

[44] G Arcoleo, *Il gabinetto nei governi parlamentari* (Napoli, Jovene, 1881) 124 ff. VE Orlando, 'La decadenza del sistema parlamentare' (1884) 2 *Rassegna di scienze sociali e politiche* 589.

[45] Arcoleo, *Il gabinetto* (n 44) 215.

[46] T Perassi, *Le attuali istituzioni e la bancarotta del parlamentarismo* (Pavia, Officina d'arti grafiche, 1907). A Bragaglia, *Il sindacato parlamentare, principi, norme, forme: studio giuridico e politico* (Torino, Casa Editrice Nazionale, 1903).

[47] S Sonnino, *Del governo rappresentativo in Italia* (Roma, Botta, 1872).

parliamentary powers, including law-making. One of the means for assessing government will was supporting a generalised ex post judgement, with no real power to scrutinise single decisions or acts.[48] This led to an overlap between the power to set the political directions (the so-called '*indirizzo politico*', well known to Italian scholars)[49] and the power to control how these directions were implemented.[50] Two main features qualified the oversight function: the postponement of government action and the ancillary nature.[51] Moreover, in the nineteenth century, there was no clear concept of the scope of parliamentary oversight, whether it was only covering the political activity of government or whether it could also affect 'administrative' acts.[52] The latter interpretation was the one that prevailed in practice. Many factors contributed to this outcome. However, the procedural implementation of the oversight function remained stuck in a rather 'individualistic' approach: most often, MPs resorted to oversight tools urged by personal interests, addressing the responsibility of individual ministers or pressing them for action.[53]

Giving regard to the whole picture, a different 'balanced union'[54] of executive and legislative powers featured the coming out of parliamentary oversight in national constitutional traditions. Contrary to the British formula of 'cabinet government',[55] in Continental Europe the nineteenth-century dominant approach to parliamentary oversight was based on a dualistic vision of the legislative and the executive branches, conceived as opposed to one another. In France and Italy, the oversight power was the natural implication of parliamentary sovereignty, and hence of the parliamentary dominion over the executive. In Germany, this function was rather enacted as a defensive measure to promote Parliament's empowerment over the executive dominance. A clear conception of parliamentary oversight's procedural implications was lacking at that time. Whereas in the British tradition it was approached as a strictly non-legislative function, in Continental Europe it was commonly regarded as equivalent to the standard legislative and political power vested in representative assemblies.[56]

This conception of parliamentary oversight experienced a radical transformation in the twentieth century. The recognition of popular sovereignty as the sole legitimation for the exercise of political power led to a reconsideration of parliamentary oversight as the unilateral prerogative of the legislative power. The function was hence reframed in the 'peer-to-peer' political relationship based on the confidence between the government and the parliament.[57] An extensive conception of the 'control of business in Parliament'

---

[48] F Racioppi and I Brunelli, *Commento allo Statuto*, III (Torino, Unione tipografico editrice, 1909) 386 f.

[49] V Crisafulli, 'Per una teoria giuridica dell'indirizzo politico' (1939) 1–2 *Studi urbinati* 53, now in V Crisafulli, *Prima e dopo la Costituzione* (Napoli, Editoriale Scientifica, 2015); and C Mortati, *L'ordinamento del governo nel nuovo diritto pubblico italiano* (Roma, Anonima Romana Editoriale, 1931). See below ch 3, section II.B.

[50] G Arangio-Ruiz, *Delle guarentigie costituzionali* (Napoli, Pierro, 1886) 230 ff.

[51] M Carducci, *Controllo parlamentare e teorie costituzionali* (Padova, Cedam, 1996) 118 ff.

[52] L Palma, *Corso di diritto costituzionale*, II (Firenze, Pellas, 1884) 450. I Santangelo Spoto, *La giustizia nell'amministrazione: la burocrazia ed il Governo parlamentare* (Torino, Unione tipografico-editrice, 1902) 190 ff.

[53] M Carducci, 'Controllo parlamentare e "autonomia" politica del governo' (1993) 41 *Studi Parmensi* 53, 94 ff.

[54] Bagehot (n 4).

[55] Todd (n 9) 179.

[56] See R Gneist, *L'amministrazione e il diritto amministrativo inglese*, III (Torino, Unione Tipografico-editrice, 1896) 429 ff.

[57] N Achterberg, 'Parlamentarische Kontrollrechte' (1977) 30 *Die öffentliche verwaltung* 548; and N Achterberg, *Parlamentsrecht* (Tübingen, Mohr, 1984) 28 (referring to the critiques of the traditional liberal doctrine boosted at the beginning of the twentieth century).

started spreading: this was not only covering the scope of evaluation and assessment but also enabling an 'influence' over the sphere of the controlled. Such an extensive conception, introduced by Todd in the British tradition at the end of the nineteenth century,[58] was hence rediscovered and deepened in the twentieth century both in Germany[59] and in Italy.[60]

II. Oversight or Scrutiny? A Comparison with Presidential Experiences

The capacity to look diligently into every affair of government was identified by Woodrow Wilson as one differential between the US Congress and European 'parliaments'. Beyond engaging in the business of law-making, the former 'superintends administration by the exercise of semi-judicial powers of investigation, whose limitations and insufficiency are manifest'.[61] The latter, by contrast, 'command administration and verify their name of "parliaments" by talking official acts into notoriety'.[62] These words give an idea of the diverging conception that the oversight of the executive meets in parliamentary and presidential regimes.[63] The requirement of providing democratic control of government action is designed in a radically different manner depending on two factors: where the executive finds its legitimacy, whether it is from direct popular election or confidence in Parliament; and what role is vested in elective assemblies – whether they play the role of a pure law-making authority (what is considered a pure 'legislature') or whether they are also deemed to appoint and control the executive (thus acting as a real 'parliament').[64]

Due to the combination of these two factors, presidential or parliamentary assemblies do not just differ in the scope and enforcement associated with executive oversight.[65]

---

[58] Todd (n 9) 390 ff.

[59] G Anschütz, *Die Verfassung des Deutschen Reiches vom 11. 8. 1919*, 14th edn (Berlin, Georg Stilke, 1933) 213 ff.

[60] P Virga, 'Dibattito sulle inchieste parlamentari' (1959) 4 *Giurisprudenza costituzionale* 596.

[61] Wilson, *Congressional Government* (n 1) 297. The idea that Congress' oversight is under-developed exercised a major influence on subsequent literature, see SP Huntington, 'Congressional Responses to the Twentieth Century' in DB Truman (ed), *The Congress and America's Future* (Englewood Cliffs, NJ, Prentice Hall, 1965) 30; WJ Oleszek, 'Towards a Stronger Legislative Branch' (1975) 3 *The Bureaucrat* 456, 457 ff; MS Ogul, *Congress Oversees the Bureaucracy: Studies in Legislative Supervision* (Pittsburgh, University of Pittsburgh Press, 1976) 5 ff.

[62] Wilson, *Congressional Government* (n 1) 297.

[63] R Pelizzo and F Stapenhurst, *Government Accountability and Legislative Oversight* (New York, Routledge, 2014) 13 f.

[64] The difference between 'legislature' and 'Parliament' is stressed by M Laver, 'Overview: Legislatures and Parliaments in Comparative Context' in B Weingast and D Wittman (eds), *Oxford Handbook of Political Economy* (Oxford, Oxford University Press, 2008); and A Kreppel, 'Understanding the European Parliament from a Federalist Perspective: The Legislatures of the United States and the European Union Compared' in A Menon and MA Schain (eds), *Comparative Federalism. The European Union and the United States in Comparative Perspective* (Oxford, Oxford University Press, 2006). In fact, due to the variety of institutional denominations adopted, a certain degree of confusion surrounds the terms 'parliaments', 'legislatures' and 'legislative bodies'; see C Fasone, 'What is a legislature in the twenty-first century? Classification and evolution of a contested notion' (2019) 15 *Federalismi.it* 1, 4.

[65] W McKay and CW Johnson, *Parliament and Congress: Representation and Scrutiny in the Twenty-first Century* (Oxford, Oxford University Press, 2010) 307 ff.

The asymmetries affect the guiding principles and hence the nature of the function.[66] They are so manifest that different linguistic formulae have been used to explain the variation. In this vein, according to some authors,[67] the term *oversight*, stemming from the American separation-of-power system, would specifically refer to 'the review of policy implementation'.[68] This activity is instrumental both to executive surveillance and to the prevention of future violations.[69] By contrast, the term *scrutiny*, typical of Westminster systems, would rather support a broad meaning, inclusive of all executive–legislative relations. *Oversight* and *scrutiny* would therefore differ in the ex ante and ex post time frame, respectively referred to the stage that preludes the formal adoption of a government decision and to the implementing stage. *Oversight* would act as a form of ex post review in presidential systems,[70] *scrutiny* as a residual and cross-cutting function in parliamentary regimes, able to also cover the ex ante stage.[71]

This argument, however, only explains part of the picture. The linguistic dualism between *oversight* and *scrutiny* can only be justified by referring to the structural causes that, based on the form of government, shape the executive-legislative interaction. Five factors should specifically be taken into consideration.

First, a different assortment of extraordinary and ordinary oversight instances features presidential and parliamentary regimes.[72] In presidential systems, the aprioristic refusal for any form of extraordinary political oversight has led to the promotion of a capillary system of ordinary oversight mechanisms.[73] Under this regime, the need to preserve the independence of the executive excludes 'radical' instances of political oversight that enforce government responsibility up to the point of its dismissal. What remains is a rather weakened form of extraordinary oversight (the so-called impeachment), limited to the most serious charges and similar to the bringing of an accusation in criminal law.[74] These limits are compensated by the introduction of rather intrusive and effective ordinary oversight settings,[75] comprising not just select committee investigations or hearings but also informal

---

[66] F Meinel, 'Confidence and Control in Parliamentary Government: Parliamentary Questioning, Executive Knowledge, and the Transformation of Democratic Accountability' (2018) 66 *The American Journal of Comparative Law* 317, 339. *Contra*, FJ García Roca, 'Control parlamentario y convergencia entre presidencialismo y parlamentarismo' (2016) 38 *Teoría y Realidad Constitucional* 61, 75 f (stressing the analogies in large part of the oversight tools available to presidential and parliamentary systems). Lauvaux, 'Le contrôle' (n 41).

[67] D Olson, 'Legislatures and Administration in Oversight and Budgets: Constraints, Means, and Executives' in R Stapenhurst, R Pelizzo, D Olson and L von Trapp (eds), *Legislative Oversight and Budgeting: A World Perspective* (Washington DC, World Bank, 2008) 324 stresses the difference between the notions of *oversight* and *scrutiny*. *Contra*, J Blondel, *Comparative Legislatures* (Englewood Cliffs, NJ, Prentice-Hall, 1973) 68 refers the term *scrutiny* both to presidential and to parliamentary systems.

[68] Olson (n 67) 324.

[69] This is the 'police-patrol oversight' discussed in MD McCubbins and T Schwartz, 'Congressional oversight overlooked: police patrol versus fire alarms' (1984) 28 *The American Journal of Political Science* 165.

[70] R Maffio, '*Qui custodiet ipsos custodes?* Il controllo parlamentare dell'attività di governo in prospettiva comparata' (2002) 9 *Quaderni di scienza politica* 333.

[71] K Strøm, 'Delegation and accountability in parliamentary democracies' (2000) 37 *European Journal of Political Research* 261, 273.

[72] Lauvaux, 'Le contrôle' (n 41) 25 (instances of oversight can be defined as 'extraordinary' insofar as they allow the application of radical political sanctions to enforce government responsibility).

[73] JD Aberbach, *Keeping a Watchful Eye: The Politics of Congressional Oversight* (Washington DC, Brookings Institution, 1990).

[74] FM Kaiser, WJ Oleszek and TB Tatelman, *Congressional Oversight Manual* (Washington, Congressional Oversight Service, 2011) 22 f.

[75] García Roca, 'Control parlamentario' (n 66) 75.

meetings between legislators and executive officials and the use of inspecting offices outside Congress.[76] An opposite arrangement features parliamentary regimes.

Second, a rather different pattern of interaction supports the parliamentary control of executive business in presidential and parliamentary regimes.[77] The former ground the function on the competitive relationship between Parliament and government, fostered by the sharp separation of power and by the mutual independence of the two branches.[78] In performing the oversight function, Parliament tends to behave as a single institutional agent involved in the checks and balances dynamics,[79] thereby bypassing the cleavage between parties.[80] A far more complex and multifaceted pattern of interaction features the dynamics of parliamentary scrutiny in systems that support a confidence relationship between the two branches of government. In such regimes, the scrutiny function is deeply embedded in the interdependence and interaction of government, parliamentary majority and opposition.[81] It is nourished by either cooperative patterns (fostered by the majority) or antagonistic approaches (boosted by the opposition) where great prominence is given to political parties,[82] although bipartisan modules are often allowed.[83]

Third, in presidential systems oversight is strictly interpreted as an ex post assessment of government conduct,[84] it is always perceived as binding in nature[85] and in most cases it is interpreted and implemented as a real veto power.[86] In parliamentary regimes, the prerogatives of the legislature with regard to the executive power cover the entire policy-making process;[87] however, Parliament may lack a real 'political' independence from the government. The confidence relationship brings along Parliament's capacity to scrutinise the government in the ex ante stage of the preparation and direction of executive action:[88]

---

[76] FM Kaiser, 'Congressional Oversight of the Presidency' (1988) 499 *The Annals of the American Academy of Political and Social Science* 75; and Aberbach (n 73).

[77] J Krause, 'Der Bedeutungswandel parlamentarischer Kontrolle: Deutscher Bundestag und US-Kongreß im Vergleich' (1999) 30 *Zeitschrift für Parlamentsfragen* 534.

[78] A Stepan and C Skach, 'Constitutional frameworks and democratic consolidation: Parliamentarism and presidentialism' (1993) 46 *World Politics* 1.

[79] A McCanse Wright, 'Constitutional Conflict and Congressional Oversight' (2014) 98 *Marquette Law Review* 881.

[80] Strøm, 'Delegation and accountability' (n 71) 272 f; P Norton, 'La nature du contrôle parlementaire' (2010) 134 *Le Seuil* 5, 13 f.

[81] O Rozenberg, 'Comparer les parlements' in JM de Waele and Y Déloye (eds), *Politique comparé* (Bruxelles, Bruylant, 2018) 307.

[82] Strøm, 'Delegation and accountability' (n 71) 274.

[83] HP Schneider, *Entscheidungsdefizite der Parlamente: über die Notwendigkeit einer Wiederbelebung der Parlamentsreform* (Tübingen, Mohr Siebeck, 1980) *passim*; E Busch, *Parlamentarische Kontrolle. Ausgestaltung und Wirkung* (Heidelberg, Decker und Müller, 1983) *passim*; M Aragón Reyes, 'El control parlamentario como control político' (1986) 23 *Revista de Derecho Político* 9; A Embid Irujo, 'El control parlamentario del gobierno en la jurisprudencia del Tribunal constitucional' (1991) 31 *Revista Vasca de Administración Pública* 179.

[84] JP Harris, *Congressional Control of Administration* (Washington DC, Brookings Institution, 1964) 9; Ogul (n 61) 11; WJ Oleszek, 'Integration and Fragmentation: Key Themes of Congressional Change' (1983) 466 *The Annals of the American Academy of Political and Social Science* 193, 200 f.

[85] P Pennings, 'Beyond dichotomous explanations: Explaining constitutional control of the executive with fuzzy sets' (2003) 42 *European Journal of Political Research* 541.

[86] T Lowi and B Ginsberg, *American Government: Freedom and Power* (London, WW Norton, 1996) 104. A Schick, 'Congress and the "details" of administration' (1976) 36 *Public Administration Review* 516, 522 (if congressional oversight always follows administrative action, the congressional veto of proposed executive action is activated in the course of the administrative process).

[87] P Norton, *Does Parliament Matter?* (Hemel Hempstead, Harvester Wheatsheaf, 1993).

[88] Rozenberg, 'Comparer les parlements' (n 81) fn 14.

Parliament uses its power to indirectly influence executive future action rather than to assess government past conduct.

Fourth, congressional oversight has a high degree of legal formalisation. Oversight tools, procedures and powers have a solid legal basis, either at constitutional or at sub-constitutional level. The oversight relationship is legal in nature and the executive has the legal duty to comply with formal requests (for example, to provide information, to appear in Parliament, to produce documents) submitted by the legislature, regardless of any specific investigative procedure.[89] A radically different political conception of the oversight function features parliamentary forms of government: parliamentary oversight is inherent in the confidence relationship and comes out of the government's political interaction with every single component of Parliament. The government has the political responsibility, but not the legal duty (with the only exception of inquiry procedures) to follow up oversight requests advanced by any MP.

Fifth, presidential models acknowledge multiple and complex lines of accountability that allow both ministers/secretaries of state and civil servants to be directly accountable not just to the president, but also to the legislative chambers.[90] The scope of parliamentary oversight is hence directly covering the political and the administrative components of the executive branch.[91] By contrast, the line of accountability and delegation in parliamentary democracies follows the singularity principle, taking the form of a long and singular chain that finds its bottleneck in the Prime Minister. It is up to the Prime Minister to connect the elected representatives of the people and the administrators of the state[92] that are not directly responsible before Parliament, as the case of *Crichel Down* discussed in 1937 in the UK clearly showed.[93] Only the Cabinet is directly subject to parliamentary oversight both for its 'political' action and for the conduct of administrative affairs.[94] Due to this arrangement, in parliamentary systems 'it would be impossible to strengthen parliamentary control of administration without appreciably weakening the Government'.[95]

Notwithstanding these structural differences, over the decades parliamentary and presidential regimes have developed similar methodologies to face the problem of complexity,[96] consisting of the creation of specialised bodies, the development of auxiliary structures and the use of modern information technologies and scientific competences.[97] As a matter of fact, Parliament's control of executive business is not exactly the same function in presidentialism and parliamentarism, but this finding does not seem to support a strict terminological

---

[89] Meinel (n 66) 343.

[90] Strøm, 'Delegation and accountability' (n 71) 269. Against this theory, SG Calabresi and CS Yoom, *The Unitary Executive. Presidential Power from Washington to Bush* (New Haven, CT, Yale University Press, 2008) 30 f (the President holds ultimate responsibility before the Congress of all the actions made by public administrations, including agencies).

[91] A Le Divellec, 'La problématique du contrôle parlementaire de l'administration' in B Seiller (ed), *Le contrôle parlementaire de l'administration* (Paris, Dalloz, 2010) 9 f.

[92] A comparison on parliamentary means for overseeing administrative action in Europe and in the US is offered in B Seiller (ed), *Le contrôle parlementaire de l'administration* (Paris, Dalloz, 2010).

[93] A critique to this approach is offered by H Finer, 'The Individual Responsibility of Ministers' (1956) *Public Administration* 377, 378 ff.

[94] Todd (n 9) 216 f.

[95] I Jennings, *Cabinet Government* 2nd edn (Cambridge, Cambridge University Press, 1951) 451.

[96] R Pelizzo and R Stapenhurst, 'Legislature and Oversight: a note' (2004) 9 *Quaderni di scienza politica* 175 (discussing the difference between parliamentary and presidential systems in terms of oversight capacity).

[97] Krause, 'Der Bedeutungswandel' (n 77); and García Roca, 'Control parlamentario' (n 66) 80 ff.

Figure 1 Structural differences in the arrangement of parliamentary oversight in presidential and parliamentary systems

Variables	Presidential system	Parliamentary system
Time frame When does parliamentary oversight meet executive action?	*Ex post* (review of policy implementation)	Both *ex ante* and *ex post* (inclusive of all the executive–legislative relations)
Enabling circumstances Which instances of parliamentary oversight are prevailing (with regard to exceptional/current political circumstances)?	Prevalence of ordinary over extraordinary instances of parliamentary oversight	Both extraordinary and ordinary instances of oversight
Pattern of interaction What type of legislative–executive interaction does it produce?	Competitive	Cooperative
Expected outcome How does oversight impact on executive action?	Veto power	Influence
Executive duties What types of duties are incumbent upon the government?	Legal duties (eg, to provide information, to appear in Parliament, to produce documents)	Political responsibility to follow up oversight requests submitted by any MP
Scope Which spheres of executive action does oversight directly cover?	Both the political and the administrative sphere of executive action	Only the political component, that is responsible to Parliament also for the administrative action

distinction between *oversight* as a presidential prerogative and *scrutiny* as parliamentary in nature. This is why the monograph, although focusing only on parliamentary systems, relies on the *oversight* notion, making use of the term *scrutiny* when appropriate, based on the customary parliamentary use and on comparative research.[98]

III. Oversight in Contemporary European Forms of Government

Within parliamentary democracies, Westminster and European Continental systems offer distinct approaches to the oversight of the executive. Two factors structure this difference:

[98] H Yamamoto, *Tools for Parliamentary Oversight: A Comparative Study of 88 National Parliaments* (Geneva, Inter-Parliamentary Union, 2007). Pelizzo and Stapenhurst, *Government Accountability* (n 63). Inter-Parliamentary Union (IPU) and United Nations Development Programme (UNDP), *Global Parliamentary Report 2017. Parliament's power to hold government to account: Realities and perspectives on oversight* (France, Courand et Associés, 2017).

the electoral rules for the formation of parliament and the respective position of the legislative and the executive branches according to the formula of 'Cabinet' government.

On the one hand, different implications derive from the option for a majority or a proportional electoral system. In Westminster democracies shaped according to majority rules, the electoral system favours the supremacy of one single party in both the executive and the legislative branches and the accent is put on the presence of a strong government.[99] Executive dominance, based on the doctrine of the 'party mandate',[100] is expected to limit Parliament's capacity to fulfil its oversight prerogative[101] and parliamentary oversight is biased by the natural inclination of parliamentary majority towards protecting the government.[102] Nonetheless, the sharp division between majority and opposition may create favourable conditions for scrutinising the conduct of government affairs. By contrast, in Continental Europe, where proportional electoral systems prevail, there is no absolute guarantee that one single party gains a majority in Parliament. Negotiations among parties for executive formation and policy-making limit the capacity of government to control Parliament. Therefore, continental-type parliamentary systems may be perceived as best suited to oversee the executive, at least compared with Westminster systems.[103] However, due to the absence of a clear-cut cleavage between parliamentary majority and minorities, political conditions for implementing effective oversight tend to vary significantly (see also below, section IV).

On the other hand, the different fortune met in Continental Europe by the traditional Westminster formula of 'Cabinet government' has enhanced the divergencies in the approach to parliamentary oversight. Due to the lack of a written constitution, to the doctrine of parliamentary sovereignty and the fusion between the two branches of government,[104] the Cabinet formula has found in the principle of ministerial responsibility its cornerstone against the risk of excesses of the executive. The idea of ministerial responsibility was introduced to define the role of ministers in accounting to Parliament for the actions of their departments. Therefore, the core issue is clearly the position of the government vis-a-vis the parliament, rather than the action that the latter can force on the former. The role of Parliament in scrutinising a government's action is not addressed in a 'hierarchical' perspective as one of the prerogatives and formal powers of the legislature. Rather, it is appreciated for its instrumental contribution to the political relationship between the executive and the legislative branches.[105]

By contrast, in Continental Europe, the possibility to also select ministers outside Parliament has loosened the fusion between the executive and the legislative branches.[106]

---

[99] Jennings (n 95) 440.

[100] I Budge, 'Great Britain and Ireland: Variations on Dominant Party Government' in JM Colomer (ed), *Political Institutions in Europe*, 3rd edn (London, Routledge, 2008) 18 ff.

[101] Norton, 'La nature du contrôle' (n 80) 15.

[102] García Roca, 'Control parlamentario' (n 66) 82.

[103] ibid.

[104] Bagehot (n 4) 65.

[105] AH Birch, *Representative and Responsible Government. An Essay on the British Constitution* (Toronto, University of Toronto Press, 1969); G Marshall, *Constitutional Conventions: The Rules and Forms of Political Accountability* (Oxford, Oxford University Press, 1987) 54; and G Marshall (ed), *Ministerial Responsibility* (Oxford, Oxford University Press, 1989); C Turpin, 'Responsibility in Government' (1996) 11 *Public Policy and Administration* 35.

[106] P Badura, 'Die Parlamentarische Verantwortlichkeit Der Minister' (1980) 11 *Zeitschrift Für Parlamentsfragen* 573.

This trend has reached its apex in Sweden, where the incompatibility between being a member of government and of Parliament has led to the development of a rather different pattern of accountability relations.[107] At the same time, the introduction of legal mechanisms for ensuring government stability has hardened the confidence relationship,[108] leading to what is defined as *parliamentarisme rationalisé* (rationalised parliamentarism).[109]

A different mix of these factors creates in each national form of government peculiar constitutional conditions for the exercise of parliamentary oversight. Where the fusion between the executive and legislative branches is greater, oversight participates both in the cooperation between government and parliamentary majority and in the competition of the opposition towards the executive. Where elements of separation between the branches are introduced and the rationalisation of the government formula is higher, the oversight function meets instances of the competitive approach of Parliament, as a whole, in regard to the executive, in line with congressional trends.

As a matter of fact, the intrusion of 'external' factors into the traditional Cabinet formula, jointly with the presence of written constitutions and the influence of administrative law on the theory of (constitutional) controls, has deeply affected the approach to the legislative–executive relationship. It has specifically led to a shift in the focus from ministerial responsibility to parliamentary oversight as a due prerogative vested in representative assemblies to counterbalance executive powers and prevent the risk that the government may act independently from Parliament. Oversight has thus become for Parliament, in its capacity as direct representative of the popular will, a means for enforcing authority over the executive bodies. This perspective derives from the 'oversight-subjection' conception developed in the post-French Revolution framework (see above, section I).

In fact, the transformation of the French form of government and the adoption of a semi-presidential system – featured by the coexistence of the confidence relationship with the direct election of the head of state[110] and by the presence of a 'dual' executive[111] – has

---

[107] See above, section I (n 15).

[108] Mechanisms of this sort are typical in the German and Spanish Constitutions; see T Oppermann et al, *Das parlamentarische Regierungssystem des Grundgesetzes. Organisierte Einwirkungen auf die Verwaltung* (Berlin, Walter de Gruyter, 1975) 8 ff; R Dolzer et al, *Das parlamentarische Regierungssystem und der Bundesrat – Entwicklungsstand und Reformbedarf. Rechtliche Optimierungsgebote oder Rahmensetzungen für das Verwaltungshandeln?* (Berlin, Walter de Gruyter, 1999) 8 ff; M Sánchez de Dios, *La moción de censura* (Madrid, Congreso de los Diputados, 1992) 268 f; CF Juberías, 'Spain: Delegation and Accountability in a Newly Established Democracy' in K Strøm, W Müller and T Bergman (eds), *Delegation and Accountability in Parliamentary Democracies* (Oxford, Oxford University Press, 2003).

[109] B Mirkine-Guetzévitch, *Les nouvelles tendances du droit constitutionnel* (Paris, Marcel Giard, 1931); and B Mirkine-Guetzévitch, 'Le régime parlementaire dans les récentes Constitutions européennes' (1950) 2–4 *Revue internationale de droit comparé* 605.

[110] H Beuve-Méry, 'De la dictature temporaire au régime semi-présidentiel' *Le Monde* (8 January 1959), now in D Colas and C Émeri (eds), *Droit, institutions et systèmes politiques: mélanges en hommage à Maurice Duverger* (Paris, PUF, 1988); M Duverger, *Institutions politiques et droit constitutionnel*, 11th edn (Paris, PUF, 1970) 277; and M Duverger, 'A new political system model: semi-presidential government' (1980) 8 *European Journal of Political Research* 165; P Türk, *Les institutions de la Ve République*, 12th edn (Paris, LGDJ, 2019/2020).

[111] R Capitant, 'L'aménagement du pouvoir exécutif et la question du chef de l'État' in *Encyclopédie française. Tome X: L'État* (Paris, Société nouvelle de l'Encyclopédie française, 1964) 153; P Avril, 'La nature de la Ve République' (2001) 300 *Cahiers français* 3, 4 f; G Carcassonne, 'La primauté de l'élection présidentielle: rapports entre les consultations populaires. La leçon des résultats' in N Wahl and JL Quermonne (eds), *La France présidentielle: l'influence du suffrage universel sur la vie politique* (Paris, Presses de Sciences Po, 1995) 32 f.

introduced another variation in the legislative–executive relationship of Continental Europe. The semi-presidential arrangement deeply influences the approach to parliamentary oversight both in legal and political terms. From a constitutional point of view, the scope of parliamentary oversight is limited, because it does not formally cover the head of the executive branch, whose political responsibility is not before Parliament, but directly before the electorate.[112] Pursuant to article 23.2 of the French Constitution, the function of members of government is incompatible with the exercise of the parliamentary mandate.[113] From the point of view of the political relations, parliamentary majority is deemed to have limited autonomy in holding the government to account and parliamentary opposition is seen as sufficiently 'associated' with decision-making.[114] In this framework, featured by the priority of legislation, the uncertainty of majority and the incapability of the opposition, Parliament's oversight activity is very limited.[115]

In 2007, the 'atony' of parliamentary oversight in France was deplored in the Balladur Report.[116] To counterbalance this situation and gain back spheres of oversight in favour of the Parliament, a constitutional amendment was required in 2008, providing an extensive legal basis to the oversight function. Four constitutional clauses were introduced, enabling the Parliament to control the action of the government and assess public policies (article 24), allowing each House to set up inquiry committees in order to gather information (article 51.2), urging the Cour des comptes to support the Parliament in the control of the government and in the evaluation of public policies (article 47.2), allotting adequate time in the parliamentary agenda to the control and evaluation functions (article 48.4). The constitutional amendment led to the approval of Loi no 2011-140,[117] aiming at reinforcing the means of the Parliament in monitoring the government's action and in evaluating public policies, and to the 2009 reform of the Houses' Rules of Procedures. Broadly speaking, the 2008 French constitutional amendment pursued a durable convergence of presidential and parliamentary features, based on the idea that the only possible way to revitalise the oversight function was to disconnect it from the issue of political responsibility and develop oversight tools in favour of the opposition.[118] As a matter of fact, this formal change brought the French semi-presidential system closer to the competitive approach of presidential forms of government rather than to the informal cooperation among the branches of government featuring parliamentary systems.[119]

Regardless of national specificities, the common feature shown by the oversight function in all parliamentary systems is its intimate connection with the confidence relationship.

---

[112] *Ex multis*, A Chandernagor, *Un parlement pour quoi faire?* (Paris, Gallimard, 1967); P Birnbaun, F Hamon and M Troper, *Reinventer le parlement* (Paris, Flammarion, 1978); JM Belorgey, *Le Parlement à refaire* (Paris, Gallimard, 1991).

[113] C Vintzel, 'Renforcer le Parlement français: Les leçons du droit comparé' (2017) 17 *Jus Politicum*.

[114] A Delcamp, 'La perception du contrôle' parlementaire. Comment le rendre plus attractif?' (2010) 134 *Pouvoirs* 109, 110; and R Dosière, 'Le contrôle ordinaire' (2010) 134 *Pouvoirs* 37.

[115] P Avril, 'Quel équilibre entre exécutif et législatif?' (2002) 1–2 *Revue du droit public* 268, 277.

[116] E Balladur, *Une Ve République plus démocratique – Comité de réflexion et de proposition sur la modernisation et le rééquilibrage des institutions de la Ve République* (Paris, La Documentation Française, 2007) 103.

[117] L Baghestani, 'A propos de la loi tendant à renforcer les moyens du Parlement en matière de contrôle de l'action du Gouvernement et d'évaluation des politiques publiques' (2011) 78 *Les Petites affiches* 3 f.

[118] B Nabli, 'L'opposition parlementaire: un contre-pouvoir politique saisi par le droit' (2010) 133 *Pouvoirs* 125, 133 ff.

[119] Lauvaux, 'Le contrôle' (n 41) 36.

Confidence is the vehicle through which oversight mechanisms can produce their effects on the executive. It is also the main limit against an antagonistic interaction between the controller and the controlled. The point is whether confidence is also the premise for the exercise of oversight powers. This question was addressed by the Spanish Tribunal Constitucional in Decision STC 124/2018 of 14 November 2018, a unique judgment that, in response to the first conflict of power raised by Parliament against the government in Spanish constitutional history, offered a comprehensive theory of oversight as a constitutional safeguard. The Decision was called to solve an unprecedented situation:[120] the presence of a government that for almost a year, from December 2015 until October 2016, lacked the confidence of the newly elected Congreso and acted in an *interim* situation; and the government's refusal to submit to parliamentary oversight, by attending a committee hearing, because it was not supported by confidence in Parliament.

Upholding the arguments raised by the two Houses, the Tribunal Constitucional challenged the idea of the full identification of the oversight function with the confidence relationship, but admitted that the two dimensions are closely related one another. It is necessary to distinguish between the oversight powers and the requirements of political responsibility: whereas the latter are exclusively vested in the Lower House, the Congreso, the former are attributed to both Houses, thus confirming that the Senate is engaged in the oversight function without having a confidence relationship with the executive.[121] Moreover, not all the oversight tools find their final purpose in the breaking of the confidence relationship. Insofar as the caretaker government continues to perform its duties, executive action cannot evade the domain of parliamentary oversight.[122] It is therefore established that the confidence relationship is not strictly required for the exercise of the oversight function, whose legitimacy relies on the representative nature of Parliament and on the parliamentary form of government, because any limitation of this function would undermine the constitutional balance of power.

IV. The Influence of the Executive-Parties Dimension

In parliamentary systems, oversight insists on what Philip Norton defines as a 'paradox':[123] whereas Parliament is in theory a powerful institution, due to pressure from political parties, it is the executive that plays a dominant role in the relationship. Beyond constitutional features, the political arrangement resulting from party interaction is of vital importance to understand the different modes of relation between the executive and legislative branches,

---

[120] FJ García Roca, 'Puede rechazar el control parlamentario un Gobierno en funciones?' in E Aranda Álvarez (ed), *Lecciones constitucionales de 314 días con el Gobierno en funciones* (Barcelona, Tirant lo Blanch, 2017).

[121] STC 124/2018, para 7.

[122] JM Herreros López, 'El control parlamentario del Gobierno en funciones. Comentario de la STC 124/2018, de 14 de noviembre' (2019) 6 *Actualidad administrativa* 1. M Férnandez-Fontecha Torres, 'Un Gobierno en funciones: su responsabilidad. Comentario a la Sentencia del Tribunal Constitucional 124/2018 de 14 de noviembre, en el conflicto entre órganos constitucionales 3102-2016 (B.O.E. núm.301, de 14 de diciembre 2018)' (2019) 106 *Revista de las Cortes Generales* 595.

[123] Norton, 'La nature du contrôle' (n 80) 14.

including the enforcement of the oversight relation.[124] The 'political' factor conditions the set of oversight incentives met by Parliament, the mode of interaction with the controlled and the types of mechanisms implemented.[125]

From a broad perspective, under a parliamentary government, due to the intertwining of oversight and confidence, the party dimension draws a cleavage between two opposing modes of serving the function of holding the government to account. Oversight is structured to be performed both by the parliamentary majority and by the opposition, in a different manner. On the one hand, the parliamentary majority exercises what can be defined as an 'internal' oversight, associated with 'co-decision' and 'co-management'.[126] The constitutional relevance of the internal oversight exercised by members of the parliamentary majority in regard to the government was clearly recognised by the German Federal Constitutional Court.[127] Under this pattern, oversight is addressed to other members of the same party in their acting capacity as members of the government. The aim of this function is to provide legitimacy to those who have been appointed to run public affairs;[128] and to grant protection to fundamental values, acting as a mechanism for preserving constitutional stability.[129] Moreover, oversight from the majority enables the orientation of *a priori* government action, thus serving as an anticipated and directional power.[130] Oversight mechanisms that unfold through a vote (especially in the plenary) and ex ante oversight tools are clear examples of this dimension.

On the other hand, the opposition may be considered as the more authentic oversight actor: its main role is to watch with a keen eye the conduct of the government it opposes.[131] Not being politically aligned to the government, it is in a position to better serve the purposes of independent parliamentary oversight.[132] Since this function may unfold also through non-deliberative mechanisms that merely aim to foster public debate, there is much space for the intervention of the opposition.[133] Not by chance, the 2008 amendment of the French Constitution, while strengthening the oversight prerogatives of Parliament, modified

---

[124] D Sternberger, 'Gewaltenteilung und parlamentarische Regierung in der Bundesrepublik Deutschland' in T Stammen (ed), *Strukturwandel der modernen Regierung* (Darmstadt, Wissenschaftliche Buchgesellschaft, 1967); N Gehrig, *Parlament – Regierung – Opposition. Dualismus als Voraussetzung für eine parlamentarische Kontrolle der Regierung* (München, Beck, 1969) 228; G Leibholz, 'Die Kontrollfunktion des Parlaments' in *Macht und Ohnmacht der Parlamente* (Stuttgart, Friedrich-Naumann-Stiftung, 1965) 61; M Duverger, *La monarchie républicaine* (Paris, Robert Laffont, 1974) 199 f; JC Colliard, *Les régimes parlementaires contemporains* (Paris, Presses de la Fondation nationale des sciences politiques, 1978) 277.

[125] M Cotta, 'Il sotto-sistema governo-parlamento' (1987) 2 *Rivista italiana di Scienza Politica* 254.

[126] A Le Divellec, *Le gouvernement parlementaire en Allemagne. Contribution à une théorie générale* (Paris, LGDJ, 2004) 309 f.

[127] BverfG, Urt V 03.05.2016, 2 BvE 4/14 (the opposition plays a fundamental role in overseeing the executive, § 90, but all MPs are potentially able to fulfil the role of critique and oversight regarding the government. The reserve of oversight prerogatives to the opposition would place MPs who support the government in an unfavourable position, § 103).

[128] A Le Divellec, 'Des effets du contrôle parlementaire' (2010) 134 *Pouvoirs* 123, 129.

[129] This is the dimension of the *control-garantía*, defined by Fernández Sarasola (n 23) 94, following the theory of constitutional controls by S Galeotti, *Introduzione alla teoria dei controlli costituzionali* (Milano, Giuffrè, 1963) 111 ff.

[130] K Eichenberger, 'Die Problematik der parlamentarischen Kontrolle im Verwaltungsstaat' (1965) 18 *Schweizerische Juristen-Zeitung* 269.

[131] Todd (n 9) 413.

[132] McKay and Johnson (n 65) 307 ff.

[133] Fernández Sarasola (n 23) 90.

article 51.1 by allowing each parliamentary assembly to set the rights of opposition and minority groups.[134] As a matter of fact, recent political studies seem to demonstrate that the amount of opposition prerogatives is a criterium for assessing the capacity of Parliament, as a whole, to exercise influence on the government.[135] It is therefore commonly believed that the oversight function is suited more to the opposition than to the majority.[136] Historically, this perspective has found its fortune in the evolution of British parliamentarism that, with the formula of the 'Shadow Cabinet', came to recognise the constitutional role of the opposition in providing an alternative to the governing party.[137] In fact, in 'real' politics the relationship between government, parliamentary majority and opposition is never so sharp.

What should be considered of utmost importance for its impact on the oversight arrangement is the difference between majoritarian and consensus democracies: the former featuring a model of a majority Cabinet, two-party system, disproportional electoral system, unitary and centralised government; the latter supporting a power-sharing model based on a broad coalition Cabinet, a proportional electoral system, a multiparty system, and a decentralised government.[138] With regard to these two types of democracy, combining the constitutional features and electoral outcomes, attention should therefore be focused on the 'horizontal' executive-parties dimension, comprising the degree of electoral disproportionality, the effective number and size of the parties, the frequency of single-party government, and the average length of Cabinet.[139] At the same time, some features of the 'vertical' federal-unitary dimension, including bicameralism, federalism and judicial review, might be taken into consideration.[140]

With regard to the former, the advantage of including the party dimension in the analysis of executive–legislative relations was clearly demonstrated by Anthony King:

> [I]f we wish to examine the influences brought to bear on the Government by Parliament, we ought if possible to avoid using the term 'Parliament' since what we are interested in is not the whole of Parliament, but Parliament … minus the Government of the day. The presence of party groupings in the chamber further suggests that we should use as our units of analysis not Parliament as a whole or even Parliament minus the Government but rather these party groupings and/or combinations of them.[141]

When analysing the enforcement of parliamentary oversight, it is therefore not to 'Parliament' as a whole that we should refer, but rather to its internal party components, in

---

[134] On this point, see Vintzel (n 113).

[135] JL Garritzmann, 'How much power do opposition have? Comparing the opportunity structures of parliamentary oppositions in 21 democracies' (2017) 23 *The Journal of Legislative Studies* 1.

[136] Delcamp (n 114) 116.

[137] G De Vergottini, *Lo 'Shadow Cabinet'. Saggio comparativo sul rilievo costituzionale dell'opposizione nel regime parlamentare britannico* (Milano, Giuffrè, 1973) 49 ff.

[138] A Lijphart, *Democracies. Patterns of Majoritarian and Consensus Government in Twenty-One Countries* (New Haven, CT, Yale University Press, 1984). LW Martin and G Vanberg, *Parliaments and Coalitions: The Role of Legislative Institutions in Multiparty Governance* (Oxford, Oxford University Press, 2011).

[139] Olson (n 67) 325 ff.

[140] ibid.

[141] A King, 'Modes of Executive–Legislative Relations: Great Britain, France, and West Germany' (1976) 1 *Legislative Studies Quarterly* 13 f. G Pasquino, 'Executive–legislative relations in Southern Europe' in R Gunther, P Nikiforos Diamandourous and HJ Puhle (eds), *The Politics of Democratic Consolidation. Southern Europe in Comparative Perspective* (Baltimore, MD, John Hopkins University Press, 1995) 261.

their interaction with the government. Three modes of executive–legislative relations should be considered.[142] The *intra-party* mode, internal to parliamentary majority, is fostered by the intra-party relationship between the government and the MPs that vote on confidence motions; it intertwines with the inter-party mode in consensual democracies. The *opposition* mode is defined by conflict between those who support and oppose the government. The *non-party* mode unfolds through decisions that 'are made deliberately (not to say self-consciously) on non-party basis';[143] it finds a variation in the cross-party mode[144] that finds specific implementation in the representation of regional or sectoral interests that do not coincide with a specific party position.[145]

Of these modes, it is the non-party mode that, instinctively, everyone would associate with Parliament's capacity to oversee the executive.[146] The effectiveness of parliamentary investigation is indeed considered by literature as subordinate either to cross-party or non-party patterns. Paradoxically, in terms of political effectiveness, this mode often turns out to be the least important.[147] Nevertheless, the non-party mode is gaining new relevance in the scrutiny of EU affairs: the involvement both of the majority and of opposition members is one fundamental prerequisite for national parliaments' proactive scrutiny of EU decisions.[148] European affairs do not usually follow the major political cleavage between majority and opposition,[149] as many studies on the functioning of the Early Warning System clearly demonstrate.[150] When this condition is satisfied, parliamentary assemblies prove themselves capable of developing the role of 'unitary scrutiniser' advocated by some scholars in the transition to a new form of parliamentary democracy in the EU.[151]

Whereas each mode has a distinctive set of incentives and range of mechanisms for enforcing parliamentary oversight, selected case studies offer a rather comprehensive picture of these alternative patterns. Great Britain is an example of a majoritarian democracy where the fusion between the legislative and executive branches and strong party discipline[152] make parliamentary oversight of the Cabinet a real challenge. In practice, the *continuum*

---

[142] King (n 141) 14 ff. Pennings (n 85) offers a distinct categorisation, distinguishing between *partisan control*, voiced by opposition, *non-partisan control* and *control with a penalty*.

[143] TK Jensen, 'Party Cohesion' in P Esaiasson and K Heidar (eds), *Beyond Westminster and Congress. The Nordic Experience* (Columbus, OH, Ohio State University Press, 2000).

[144] Rozenberg, 'Comparer les parlements' (n 81) 338 considers the *cross-party* interaction as an autonomous mode in executive–legislative relations.

[145] RB Andeweg, 'Role Specialisation or Role Switching? Dutch MPs between Electorate and Executive' (1997) 3 *The Journal of Legislative Studies* 110, 116.

[146] RB Andeweg and L Nijzink, 'Beyond the Two-Body Image: Relations between Ministers and MPs' in H Döering (ed), *Parliaments and Majority Rule in Western Europe* (New York, St Martin's Press, 1995) 176.

[147] Referring to the British system, King (n 141) 20.

[148] C Sprungk, 'Ever more or ever better scrutiny?' Analysing the conditions of effective national parliamentary involvement in EU affairs' (2010) 14 *European Integration Online Papers* 1.

[149] D Finke and A Herbel, 'Coalition Politics and Parliamentary Oversight in the European Union' (2018) 53 *Government and Opposition* 388.

[150] K Gattermann and C Hefftler, 'Political motivation and institutional capacity: assessing national parliaments' incentives to participate in the early warning mechanism' (2013) 15 *OPAL Online Paper Series* 1; C Neuhold and A Strelkov, 'New opportunity structures for the "unusual suspects"? Implications of the Early Warning System for the role of national parliaments within the EU system of governance' (2012) 4 *OPAL Online Paper Series* 13.

[151] C Sprungk, 'A New Type of Representative Democracy? Reconsidering the Role of National Parliaments in the European Union' (2013) 35 *Journal of European Integration* 547.

[152] CJ Kam, *Party Discipline and Parliamentary Politics* (Cambridge, Cambridge University Press, 2009).

between government and its parliamentary majority is weakened by the emergence of coalition governments, providing case studies for the intra-coalition dynamics.[153] The intra-party mode is ordinarily fostered by the rather unique interaction between government and backbenchers, fed by mutual needs and reciprocal bargaining resources.[154] This intra-party bargaining reaches its maximum in cases of a coalition government. Moreover, parliamentary oversight is fostered by the opposition mode as the larger dimension of party politics in Britain,[155] with Parliament acting as one of the arenas for party battle. This is confirmed by the highly oppositional style of debates on the floor of the House of Commons. The non-party mode is present and alive, as witnessed by the practice of select committees concerned with investigating the conduct of government affairs or protecting citizens' rights (see below chapter four, section VI.B); however, it is deemed to be not politically influential.[156]

The arrangement of executive–party modes featuring France's semi-presidentialism creates a rather different environment for parliamentary oversight. The opportunity of an internal oversight based on the intra-party mode is weakened by two factors: the intrusion of inter-party mode, fostered by the multiparty composition of government;[157] and the formal restriction related to the direct election of the President that limits MPs' opportunities to put pressure on the government.[158] Oversight based on the opposition mode is also undermined by the fact there is more than one minority group, which hinders the possibility of a unitary policy action. In this framework, the non-party mode has represented the privileged pattern for fulfilling parliamentary oversight as a constitutional duty; most of the procedural innovations brought about by the constitutional reform of 2008 rely on this pattern. This scenario significantly changed in the cases – recurring in France between 1986 and 2002 – labelled as 'co-habitation',[159] when the head of state and parliamentary majority had different party affiliations. Under such conditions, which the constitutional reforms of 2000 and 2008 tried to limit,[160] there is no place for the intra-party mode and the oversight of the executive rather tends to follow the modes of 'pure' parliamentary regimes.

Germany offers a relevant example of executive–legislative modes based on coalitions:[161] since the formation of the Federal Republic, German executives have always been coalitions of at least two parties. Coalition governments show two main features: the separate

---

[153] R Hazell and B Young, *The Politics of Coalition: How the Conservative–Liberal Democrat Government Works* (London, Bloomsbury Publishing, 2012).

[154] M Russell and P Cowley, 'The Policy Power of the Westminster Parliament: The Parliamentary State and the Empirical Evidence' (2017) 29 *Governance* 121.

[155] King (n 141) 17.

[156] ibid, 20.

[157] Y Mény, 'France: The Institutionalization of Leadership' in JM Colomer (ed), *Political Institutions in Europe*, 3rd edn (London, Routledge, 2008).

[158] King (n 141) 23.

[159] B Daugeron, 'La cohabitation et ses faux-semblants: réflexions sur le présidentialisme minoritaire' (2004) 1 *Revue du droit public* 67, 72; and J Massot, 'La cohabitation, quelles conséquences pour les institutions?' (2001) 300 *Cahiers français* 28.

[160] P Lauvaux, *Destins du présidentialisme* (Paris, PUF, 2002) 15 ff. R Ghevontian, 'La révision de la Constitution et le Président de la République: l'hyperprésidentialisation n'a pas eu lieu' (2009) 70 *Revue française de droit constitutionnel* 119.

[161] MG Schmidt, 'Germany: The Grand Coalition State' in JM Colomer (ed), *Political Institutions in Europe*, 3rd edn (London, Routledge, 2008).

identities of parties in the coalition and their parliamentary followings; and the complete separation between the organisation of Cabinet and parliamentary party leadership, so that the Chancellor and the leader of the parliamentary majority group are not the same person.[162] This situation has had a major influence on the practice of parliamentary oversight. In Germany, intra-party mode is pervaded by different patterns of inter-party relations: intense inter-party bargaining, often taking place outside Parliament,[163] influences the formation and dismissal of government, thus strongly affecting the 'extraordinary' oversight instances. The opposition mode is strongly rooted in committee work, where opposition parties are allowed to play a strong role. Non-party mode, too, is diffused: it enables standing committees of the Bundestag to function in a genuinely 'legislative' style, with intense specialisation, recurring cross-voting, and chairmen not necessarily belonging to the majority party.[164] These two modes account for the solid German tradition of parliamentary oversight in committee. Finally, the cross-party mode is fostered by the federal arrangement, with oversight permeated by the representation of *Länder* interests mostly within the Bundesrat.

In Italy, the solid tradition of coalition governments, jointly with intense party fragmentation[165] and with the ongoing swing between proportional and hybrid electoral systems,[166] creates a rather unique framework for parliamentary oversight, deeply influenced by the overlapping of the executive–party modes. The frequent repositioning of political parties creates lines of division between the government and its parliamentary majority.[167] This sets the conditions for an adversarial style of parliamentary oversight even within the intra-party and inter-party mode, with the opposition being offered a welcome opportunity to assert its clout by means of active participation in floor and committee votes.[168] The de-institutionalisation of the party system has not enabled the consolidation of a solid parliamentary framework for the opposition mode.[169] Limited instances of non-party mode are possible within certain oversight mechanisms, including inquiry committees.

Denmark and Sweden offer two privileged examples of consensual democracies where party cohesion and discipline are a fundamental component of the executive accountability before Parliament and lead to the consolidation of solid inter-party modes.[170] This political arrangement 'has meant that the effective lines of accountability of the political executive to

---

[162] K Loewenstein, *Political Power and the Governmental Process* (Chicago, IL, University of Chicago Press, 1957) 217. R Katz, 'Party Government: A Rationalistic Conception' in F Castles and R Wildenmann (eds), *The Future of Party Government. Vol I: Visions and Realities of Party Government* (Berlin, De Gruyter, 1987).

[163] WJ Patzelt, 'Ein latenter Verfassungskonflikt? Die Deutschen und ihr parlamentarisches Regierungssystem' (1998) 39 *Politische Vierteljahresschrift* 725.

[164] King (n 141) 31.

[165] A Pappalardo, 'Dal pluralismo polarizzato al pluralismo moderato. Il modello di Sartori e la transizione italiana' (1996) 26 *Rivista Italiana di Scienza Politica* 103.

[166] G Pasquino, 'Tricks and Threats: The 2005 Italian Electoral Law and Its Consequences' (2007) 12 *South European Society & Politics* 79.

[167] V Crisafulli, 'Aspetti problematici del sistema parlamentare vigente in Italia' (1958) 2 *Jus* 151.

[168] G Pasquino, 'Italy: The Never-ending Transition of a Democratic Regime' in JM Colomer (ed), *Political Institutions in Europe*, 3rd edn (London, Routledge, 2008) 150.

[169] G Rizzoni, *Opposizione parlamentare e democrazia deliberativa. Ordinamenti europei a confronto* (Bologna, Il Mulino, 2012) 298 f. V Casamassima, *L'opposizione parlamentare: le esperienze britannica ed italiana a confronto* (Pisa, Il Campano, 2008).

[170] K von Beyme, 'Does the Constitution Need Reforming?' in O Petersson et al (eds), *Democracy the Swedish Way* (Stockholm, SNS Forlag, 1999) 23.

the legislature do not run through the plenary account debates or committee questioning, but through the party groups on the governing side'.[171] Moreover, the frequency of minority governments in both countries[172] has made the executive dependent on legislative coalitions, often created ad hoc, with one or more parties in opposition. The flexibility of this arrangement, emphasised by the presence of a fluid multipartism, has boosted the consolidation of the intra-party, non-party and opposition modes. This is mirrored, in Denmark, by the capacity demonstrated over the decades by some parties to exercise a strong influence on government policies, regardless of their position as members of the majority or of the opposition. A significant example is offered by the influence exercised in the 1980s by the Radical Party which, as part of the opposition or member of the government coalition, has been able to keep in the Folketing a solid majority oriented against the use of nuclear weapons.[173] The long life of many Swedish minority governments confirms that the combination of these modes does not necessarily result in executive instability.[174] In Sweden, since 2004, the intensified bipolar 'bloc of politics', grown out of the strengthened cooperation between four non-socialist opposition parties, has led to more adversarial legislative–executive relations.[175]

In Continental Europe, with its tradition of single-party governments supported by minority voting, Spain is the country that shows patterns of executive–legislative relations more similar to the Westminster model. The debate on parliamentary oversight started in the mid-1980s, when the executive hegemony supported by the absolute majority of the socialist party (PSOE) fostered the idea that control from elected representatives was required to balance the different branches of government.[176] Since 1978, the Spanish party system has evolved from moderate multipartism to high polarisation between the two larger nationwide Spanish parties, which is supplemented only by a number of regional parties.[177] The rules on executive appointment and control concede only a limited role to the Parliament: the intra-party mode is solidly under the control of the party leadership and provides government stability,[178] thanks also to strong party discipline.[179] A form of 'external' oversight is exercised by regional parties that, either in the inter-party mode (if they support the majority) or through the opposition mode try to give voice to their territorial

---

[171] D Arter, 'Parliamentary Democracy in Scandinavia' (2004) 57 *Parliamentary Affairs* 581, 592.

[172] E Damgaard and P Svensson, 'Who Governs? Parties and Policies in Denmark' (1989) 17 *European Journal of Political Research* 731. A Sannerstedt and M Sjölin, 'Sweden: Changing Party Relations in a More Active Parliament' in E Damgaard (ed), *Parliamentary Change in the Nordic Countries* (Oslo, Scandinavian University Press, 1992).

[173] Le Divellec, 'Des effets du contrôle parlementaire' (n 128) 135.

[174] Arter, 'Parliamentary Democracy in Scandinavia' (n 171) 586.

[175] Arter, 'From "Parliamentary Control"' (n 14) 136.

[176] García Roca, 'Control parlamentario' (n 66) 68.

[177] JL Cascajo, 'El Congreso de los Diputados y la forma de gobierno en Espana' in A Martinez (ed), *El Congreso de los Diputados* (Madrid, Tecnos, 2000).

[178] JM Colomer, 'Spain and Portugal: Rule by Party Leadership' in JM Colomer (ed), *Political Institutions in Europe*, 3rd edn (London, Routledge, 2008) 187 ff; A Mujica and I Sanchez-Cuenca, 'Consensus and Parliamentary Opposition: the Case of Spain' (2006) 41 *Government and Opposition* 86.

[179] M Herrero, 'El Estado de partidos y la vida parlamentaria' in M Ramirez (ed), *El Parlamento en debate* (Madrid, Trotta, 1997) 45; E Sáenz Royo, 'El papel del parlamento español en la democracia de partidos' (2007) 73 *Revista de Derecho Político* 149.

interests. The latter are therefore channelled in the standard party dynamics rather than through non-party modes of relations.

Comparing these executive–party arrangements demonstrates that the intensity and quality of parliamentary oversight changes according to the political framework.[180] The capacity of majority groups to oversee the executive is more limited in Westminster system countries (where the government has a solid power to set the political directions) and in France (due to the semi-presidential regime), but it tends to expand in countries ruled by a coalition (such as Italy, Spain, Denmark and Sweden) or where the majority is fully conscious of its strength (as in the case of Germany).

V. Oversight Serving the Requirements of Executive Accountability

In defining parliamentary government, it is often argued that 'the decisive property is ex post accountability, and not ex ante selection'.[181] Government accountability before Parliament may therefore be considered as the cornerstone of parliamentary democracy. Whereas its origins date back to democracy in ancient Athens,[182] literature has long debated the relevance of accountability as a fundamental component of representative government. The notion of *accountability* is actually 'an amorphous concept' that does not find corresponding translations in most other European languages.[183] This concept, derived from literature on public management,[184] has grown out of the contraction experienced by the notion of ministerial *responsibility* in Westminster system countries.[185] The difference between the two nouns is still somewhat blurred.[186] However, core accountability seems to go beyond the traditional branches of the collective responsibility convention, as set in British constitutionalism.[187]

The *accountability* notion covers both a procedural and a substantial dimension. From a procedural point of view, the accountability relationship involves two distinct stages.[188] The first is the traditional 'constitutional' doctrine of government responsibility in terms of *answerability* before Parliament.[189] This stage makes members of government answerable

---

[180] Le Divellec, 'Des effets du contrôle parlementaire' (n 128) 135.

[181] Strøm, 'Delegation and accountability' (n 71) 266.

[182] In ancient Athens, office holders were subject to confirmation hearings and accountability examinations at the end of their mandate; see S Gordon, *Controlling the State: Constitutionalism from Ancient Athens to Today* (Cambridge, MA, Harvard University Press, 1999) 74 f.

[183] Pelizzo and Stapenhurst, *Government Accountability* (n 63) 2.

[184] BS Romzek and MJ Dubnick, 'Accountability in the public sector: lessons from the challenger tragedy' (1987) 47 *Public Administration Review* 227. B Stone, 'Administrative accountability in "Westminster" democracies: towards a new conceptual framework' (1995) 8 *Governance* 505. On accountability as a polymorphic concept, see N Balmforth and P Leyland, 'Introduction: Accountability in the Contemporary Constitution' in N Balmforth and P Leyland (eds), *Accountability in the Contemporary Constitution* (Oxford, Oxford University Press, 2013).

[185] M Flinders, *The Politics of Accountability in the Modern State* (Aldershot, Ashgate Publishing, 2001).

[186] D Woodhouse, *Ministers and Parliament: Accountability in Theory and Practice* (Oxford, Oxford University Press, 1994) *passim*.

[187] Marshall, *Constitutional Conventions* (n 105) 54 ff.

[188] Pelizzo and Stapenhurst, *Government Accountability* (n 63) 3.

[189] Finer (n 93) 378 f.

to Parliament and censurable *for* their mistakes before Parliament.[190] These two dimensions are clearly distinguished in the history of British parliamentarism: the Scott Report[191] demonstrated the difference between ministers' generalised duty to account to Parliament for the conduct of their departments and the duty to resign when they are personally involved in an action or decision. *Answerability* implies the government's obligation to answer questions affecting the conduct of its mandate, transmitting information and providing explanations/justifications. *Enforcement* is the second stage of the accountability process. It involves the capacity of the controller to sanction the accountee in case of contravening behaviour and to provide remedies.

From the substantial point of view, accountability encompasses two other implications of the noun *responsibility*; namely, the expectation vested on the executive branch to satisfy the fundamental needs of citizens and to account for the conduct of public policies, and the moral attitude of a government that strives in selecting the best policies to satisfy societal needs.[192] In this vein, it is specifically applied to cover issues affecting the relationship between citizens, elected politicians and bureaucrats (that is: how voters can make elected representatives accountable to their policies; and how legislators can scrutinise the actions of public servants and make them responsible for their mistakes).[193]

A. The Connection with Political Accountability

Once the conceptual implications of political accountability on responsible government have been clarified, it remains to be explained how parliamentary oversight may serve the requirements of executive accountability, what is the intimate nature of these two dimensions, and what is the connection between them. To answer these questions, one potentially suggestive gateway is offered by the *agency theory*[194] featuring the chain of delegation as mirrored by a corresponding chain of accountability that runs in the reverse direction. In this view, 'an agent is accountable to his principal if (1) he is obliged to act on the latter's behalf, and (2) the latter is empowered to reward or punish him for his performance in this capacity'.[195] Referring to the legislative–executive relationship, this theory offers an interpretation of parliamentary oversight as a means for ensuring that executive authorities are held accountable for the powers delegated to them.[196]

However, the theory is best suited to serve presidential regimes based on a dualistic division of power.[197] The fusion between the executive and legislative branches serving

---

[190] R Bustos Gisbert, *La responsabilidad política del Gobierno: Realidad o ficción?* (Madrid, Colex, 2001) 16.
[191] *Return to an Address of the Honourable House of Commons dated 15 February 1996 for the Report the Inquiry into the Export of Defence Equipment and Dual-use Goods to Iraq and related prosecutions* (1995–96 HC 115).
[192] Birch (n 105) 4 ff.
[193] R Mulgan, 'Accountability: An Ever-Expanding Concept? (2000) 78 *Public Administration* 555.
[194] See above ch 1 (nn 124–27).
[195] Strøm, 'Delegation and accountability' (n 71) 267; and JD Fearon, 'Electoral Accountability and the Control of Politicians: Selecting Food Types Versus Sanctioning Poor Performance' in A Przeworski, SC Stokes and B Manin (eds), *Democracy, Accountability, and Representation* (Cambridge, Cambridge University Press, 1999).
[196] K Strøm, 'Parliamentary Government and Legislative Organisation' in H Döering (ed), *Parliaments and Majority Rule in Western Europe* (New York, St Martin's Press, 1995) 61.
[197] GJ Miller, 'The Political Evolution of Principal-Agent Models' (2005) 8 *Annual Review of Political Science* 203.

parliamentary democracies makes the agency theory a potentially misleading conceptual framework for understanding the oversight–accountability relation. In parliamentary democracies much more than in presidential systems, Parliament does not act as a unitary subject when executive accountability is at stake, creating different modes of interaction that the principal–agent relationship is not able to explain.[198]

A different way of approaching the above-mentioned questions, based on a focused constitutional perspective, is by reflecting on the political relationship as the *fil rouge* linking parliamentary oversight to executive accountability. To investigate this dimension, it is necessary to recall the distinctive nature of political oversight vis-a-vis other forms of legal control that are a constitutive part of democratic constitutionalism. These two dimensions, in fact, have often been improperly overlapped. Instances of legal control are those performed by the judicial branch and by public administration. The former strictly rely on legal parameters and involve the so-called 'legality check'; their aim is to assess the enforcement of law obligations and to activate sanctions in case of any infringements. By contrast, the latter can rely on legal or pre- and extra-legal parameters.

Administrative controls may unfold through the 'legality' or 'regularity' checks whose purpose is to assess the respect of legal rules that are deemed to be compulsory for all the subordinate parts.[199] Their main concern is that the individuals may find due protection of their fundamental rights against public administration, which was at the very origins of the development of administrative law in the nineteenth century.[200] Administrative law also experiences other instances of 'opportunity' checks that are not based on pre-defined rules: their aim is to assess the discretionary exercise of power by public administration, evaluating the effectiveness and efficiency of public management. Although they lack a legal parameter, these checks are legal in nature as they are always enforceable through a system of sanctions. This second category of administrative checks has often been blurred with the notion of political oversight because its theoretical justification lies in the principle of democratic legitimacy that also plays a major role in the field of executive accountability and parliamentary oversight. Legitimacy arguments require that the administration, as a body that is independent and separate from political authorities, should be subject to political control.[201] These traditional categories of administrative checks, jointly with their theoretical justifications, are becoming increasingly overlapped and blurred in contemporary democracies.[202] The notion of 'administrative' control in itself is losing consistency,

---

[198] Rozenberg, 'Comparer les parlements' (n 81) 341.

[199] See G Marcou, 'Les inspections générales et le contrôle de l'administration' in G Marcou (ed), *Le contrôle de l'administration par elle-même* (Paris, Editions du CNRS, 1983) 10 ff; P Milloz, *Les inspections générales ministérielles dans l'administration française* (Paris, Economica, 1983).

[200] O Mayer, *Deutsches Verwaltungsrecht*, 1st edn (Leipzig, Duncker & Humblot, 1895); and A Merkl, *Allgemeines Vewaltungsrech* (Berlin, Springer, 1927); M Hauriou, *Précis de droit administratif: contenant le droit public et le droit administratif* (Paris, Larose, 1892); and E Laferrière, *Traité de la jurisdiction administrative et des recours contentieux* (Paris, Berge-Levrault, 1896); VE Orlando (ed), *Primo trattato completo di diritto amministrativo italiano* (Milano, Società Editrice Libraria, 1900).

[201] This idea was probably best explained by Max Weber, 'Parliament and Government' in a Reconstructed Germany' (1918) in M Weber, *Economy and Society. An Outline of Interpretive Sociology* (New York, Bedminster, 1968) 1421, but the theoretical basis of legitimacy requirements dates back to the classical liberal theories on parliamentary democracy by Bagehot, Mill and Rousseau (see above, section I).

[202] G Marcou, 'Le Contrôle de l'Administration Aujourd'hui' (2011) 45 *Zbornik Radova* 797, 799.

torn between the multiplication of the legal parameters and the fulfilment of ever more complex purposes, including the evaluation of public policies.[203]

Notwithstanding these ongoing transformations, the category of legal (administrative) controls, in its original design,[204] has exercised a major impact on the conceptualisation of political oversight. This is particularly true in Continental Europe where, due to the spread of the Napoleonic tradition, administrative law has deeply affected both the theory of (constitutional) controls[205] and the discourse on political responsibility. The influence of administrative law has fostered the idea that political responsibility is associated with the imposition of sanctions, thus opening, beyond the positive dimension of the 'accounting for', to the negative dimension of the civil law responsibility enforced by means of sanctions and denial of confidence.[206] In this vein, government responsibility has been associated with the idea of subordination: since the controlling authority may issue sanctions, its action virtually implies injunction and subpoena.[207]

The contamination of the legal and political perspective in defining the scope and nature of political responsibility and parliamentary oversight seems to have lost momentum in literature. The polymorphic meaning of the noun 'responsibility' supports the identification of political responsibility as a third attribute, additional to civil and penal responsibility.[208] This is increasingly perceived as a purely political dimension, only marginally dependent on legal factors.[209] Such a vision has been deeply influenced by the spread of the responsibility/accountability discourse also outside Westminster system countries.[210]

This historical and theoretical background explains that what links the dimensions of executive responsibility/accountability/oversight is the machinery of the political relationship based on confidence. On the one hand, parliamentary oversight is instrumental to

---

[203] JL Pissaloux, 'Les inspections générales au sein de l'administration française: structures, fonctions et évolution' (2015) 155 *Revue française de l'administration publique* 601.

[204] R Chapus, *Droit administratif général*, I, 13th edn (Paris, Montchrestien, 1999) 388.

[205] S Galeotti, 'Controlli costituzionali' in *Enciclopedia del Diritto*, X (Milano, Giuffrè, 1962); MS Giannini, 'Controllo: nozioni e problemi' (1974) 4 *Rivista trimestrale di diritto pubblico* 1263. F Rubio Llorente, *La forma del poder (Estudios sobre la Constitución)* (Madrid, CEC, 1993).

[206] D Baranger, *Parlementarisme des origines. Essai sur les conditions de formation d'un exécutif responsable en Angleterre* (Paris, PUF, 1999) 25 f; and O Beaud and JM Blanquer, 'Comment réintroduire une responsabilité des gouvernants sous la Vᵛ République' in O Beaud and JM Blanquer (eds), *La responsabilité des gouvernants* (Paris, Descartes & Cie, 1999) 12.

[207] P Avril, 'Responsabilité et *accountability*' in O Beaud and JM Blanquer (eds), *La responsabilité des gouvernants* (Paris, Descartes & Cie, 1999) 85. In Italy and Spain, for a long time the notion of political responsibility was framed within Rescigno's theory (GU Rescigno, *La responsabilità politica* (Milano, Giuffrè, 1967)) of the stable and continuous relation linking the government to the Parliament that makes the former subject to the latter's will.

[208] G Pitruzzella, 'Responsabilità politica' in *Digesto delle discipline pubblicistiche*, XIII (Torino, Utet, 1997) 290 ff; F Donati, *La responsabilità politica dei ministri nella forma di governo italiana* (Torino, Giappichelli, 1997); B Manin, *Los principios del Gobierno representativo* (Madrid, Alianza Editorial, 1998); E Millard, 'La signification juridique de la responsabilité politique' in P Ségur (ed), *Gouvernants, quelle responsabilité?*, 1st edn (Paris, PUF, 1998) 81 ff; P Ségur, *La responsabilité politique* (Paris, PUF, 1998); M Volpi, 'La responsabilité politique en Italie' in Vv Aa, *La responsabilité en droit public: aspects contemporains: colloque de Beyrouth, 3–4 novembre 2004* (Bruxelles, Bruylant, 2005).

[209] S Stammati, 'Qualche riflessione ulteriore su democrazia, rappresentanza e responsabilità: dalla rappresentanza democratica alla rappresentanza "sbagliata"' in Vv Aa, *Scritti in onore di Lorenza Carlassare: il diritto costituzionale come regola e limite al potere*, V (Napoli, Jovene, 2009); V Angiolini, 'La difficile convivenza tra responsabilità politica e responsabilità giuridica' in N Zanon and F Biondi (eds), *Percorsi e vicende attuali della rappresentanza e della responsabilità politica: atti del convegno* (Milano, Giuffrè, 2001).

[210] See the Special Issue published on the review (2010) *Pouvoirs* 134, and above ch 1, section IV.

serve political, not legal, accountability. Parliament's capacity to hold the government to account relies on the political authority of the parliamentary institution as a whole and of its components more than on legal rules.[211] To enforce executive accountability, Parliament theoretically does not need to resort to judicial reasoning or legal argument. On the other hand, there is no strict legal duty incumbent upon the government to answer parliamentary questions or to provide explanations, information and documents. Executive members react to the oversight requests submitted by MPs to comply with the requirements of ministerial responsibility and with the unwritten rules of the confidence relationship.

As a matter of fact, parliamentary oversight and executive accountability are two faces of a relation that is strictly political in nature. Oversight is the hinge between responsibility and representation: it is the means through which the solidarity between these two notions empirically manifests itself.[212] By selecting and combining oversight approaches and procedures, parliaments react to the challenges of executive accountability in complex societies.[213]

The oversight dimension in Upper Houses only apparently challenges this perspective. These assemblies are actually exercising oversight powers that contribute to executive accountability, but outside a dimension of fully-fledged political responsibility.[214] Their involvement in the oversight-accountability mechanism is based on their representative nature[215] which, although potentially disconnected from the political majoritarian mechanisms supporting Lower Houses, provides alternative channels of democratic legitimacy.[216] Oversight by Upper Houses may therefore act as a dimension instrumental to the fulfilment of 'other' instances of executive responsibility, either related to the territorial sphere and to the relationship with sub-national entities or connected to the protection of supreme constitutional values uncoupled from majoritarian politics.

B. Parliamentary Oversight of Public Administration

In parliamentary regimes, executive accountability should also be examined from the perspective of the internal relation between the political and the administrative responsibility.

---

[211] Meinel (n 66) 341.

[212] P Avril, 'L'introuvable contrôle' parlementaire (après la révision constitutionelle française de 2008' (2009) 3 *Jus Politicum* 1, 6. The close connection between the accountability and oversight notions is also true in a negative sense; as a matter of fact, 'Weak systems of accountability within government are compounded by weak parliamentary scrutiny', B Guerin, J McCrae and M Shepheard, 'Accountability in modern government: what are the issues? A discussion paper' (London, Institute for Government, 2018) 4.

[213] D Oliver, 'Executive Accountability: A Key Concept' in L Verhey, P Kiiver and S Loeffen (eds), *Political Accountability and European Integration* (Groningen, Europa Law Publishing, 2009).

[214] This thesis is argued in the STC 124/2018, para 7 (see above, section III). In this vein, M Luciani, 'Funzione di controllo e riforma del Senato' (2016) 1 *Rivista AIC* 1, 2, distinguishes the *institutional* responsibility, which implies a confidence relationship, from the *diffused* responsibility which, according to GU Rescigno, 'Responsabilità (diritto costituzionale)' in *Enciclopedia del diritto*, XXXIX (Milano, Giuffrè, 1988) 1347, relates political bodies, per se, to an indefinite and variable number of actors.

[215] On the difference between 'political' and 'social' representativeness referred to Upper Houses, see P Dorey and M Purvis, 'Representation in the Lords' in C Leston Bandeira and L Thompson (eds), *Exploring Parliament* (Oxford, Oxford University Press, 2018) 251 ff.

[216] On the prerogative vested on Upper Houses to oversee the executive especially when their political majority and powers diverge from those of the Lower Houses, see Norton, 'La nature du contrôle' (n 80) 16.

From a broad perspective, the notion of responsibility can be referred not just to political representatives, but also to public servants. When applied to public administration, the dimension of responsibility assumes three different meanings:[217] it relates to the capacity and authority of public servants to perform the duties and tasks set by laws and regulations; it acts as the commitment of being accountable before superior authorities, providing information and explanation for the execution of administrative duties; and it consists of legal liability for the acts falling under the field of authority of the ultimate responsible official, which implies the obligation to dismiss staff or to undergo disciplinary sanctions in case of misbehaviours and administrative failures. These dimensions correspond to a regime composed of three types of control: bureaucratic, political and legal. Bureaucratic control verifies the respect of the 'three Es' of public auditing (economy, efficiency and effectiveness), political control tests the fulfilment of policy objectives and outcomes, and legal control checks the compliance to the law.[218]

Of the three dimensions, the second, linking responsibility to accountability, is the pivotal perspective for highlighting the connection with parliamentary oversight. Under a parliamentary regime, this dimension falls under the scope of ministerial responsibility:[219] the latter also covers the conduct of public administration that may be called to provide evidence but not to give explanations of its actions before Parliament. Therefore, senior officials of departmental administrations are responsible before their minister but not before Parliament.[220] This assumption apparently seems to prove that the surveillance over public administration is excluded from the scope of parliamentary oversight; oversight of public administration in parliamentary regimes turns out to be an 'illusion',[221] if compared with presidential systems, where a variety of oversight tools, unfolding through direct contacts between senior officials and congressional bodies, enable the exercise of an extensive oversight of public administration.[222]

In fact, the picture is far more complex and multifaceted: even in parliamentary regimes, legislatures always have the possibility to evaluate how public administration is working in practice and to make a political judgement on its performance.[223] However, the pursuit of the political and administrative responsibility in Parliament changes according to a number of variables. Depending on the nature of the public administration involved and the type of activity performed, two situations can be identified.

---

[217] GE Caiden, 'The Problem of Ensuring the Public Accountability of Public Officials' in JG Jabbra and OP Dwivedi (eds), *Public Service Accountability: A Comparative Perspective* (West Hartford, CT Kumarian, 1989); and M Bovens, *The Quest for Responsibility: Accountability and Citizenship in Complex Organisations* (Cambridge, Cambridge University Press, 1998).

[218] P Cane, *Controlling Administrative Power: An Historical Comparison* (Cambridge, Cambridge University Press, 2016) 146 ff.

[219] BW Hogwood, 'Autonomía burocrática y responsabilidad' (1999) 15 *Gestion y Análisis de Políticas Públicas* 19.

[220] On existing gaps in this circuit of parliamentary oversight, J Schmidt, *Die demokratische Legitimationsfunktion der parlamentarischen Kontrolle* (Berlin, Duncker & Humblot, 2007) *passim*.

[221] Le Divellec, *Le gouvernement parlementaire* (n 126).

[222] See above, section II. A Bar Cendón, 'Accountability and Public Administration: Concepts, Dimensions, Developments' in M Kelly (ed), *Openness and Transparency in Governance: Challenges and Opportunities* (Bratislava, NISPAcee Press, 2000) 27.

[223] ST Siefken, *Parlamentarische Kontrolle im Wandel: Theorie und Praxis des Deutschen Bundestages* (Baden-Baden, Nomos, 2018) 27 ff. JM Gil-Robles y Gil-Delgado and F Marín Riaño, 'Naturaleza jurídica del control sobre el Gobierno y la Administración' in Vv Aa, *Gobierno y Administración en la Constitución*, I (Madrid, Instituto de Estudios Fiscales, 1988) 731 ff.

On the one hand, traditional administrative structures in the shape of a department perform executive activity that is directly instrumental to the fulfilment of the general directives of government policy. These activities are subject to parliamentary oversight in an indirect and mild form,[224] unfolding through the evaluation of the ministerial conduct of departmental policy. Under such circumstances, Parliament can oversee the executive action evaluating both the appropriateness and the discretionary use of administrative power.[225] In contemporary democracies, the capacity of the minister to account for the whole of the departmental administrative activity is seriously challenged by the complexity of the internal organisation[226] and the increasing technical specialisation of structures.[227] Moreover, the shortcomings and deficiencies associated with the traditional formula of ministerial responsibility before Parliament have fostered the evolution of alternative forms of accountability, including managerial and judicial accountability.[228] Nonetheless, the formal arrangement of the ministerial responsibility is still there to cover all these administrative spheres of activity. This implies that if an administrative failure is detected, the only solutions available to Parliament are either pursuing a minister's responsibility (at least in severe cases) or pushing the minister to remove or sanction the responsible officials.

On the other hand, autonomous administrative units and bodies that are not directly responsible to a minister are constantly growing in number. A varied range of agencies and independent authorities whose governance cannot be directly referred to traditional departmental structures are now controlling large spheres of public action.[229] Agencies and independent authorities have spread throughout Europe following the example of European agencies: these are assumed to operate free of political influence which allows credible and longer-term commitments.[230] The principle of non-interference by politicians in their activity 'renders traditional forms of upward accountability toward political principals (ministers and parliaments) problematic, as autonomy and accountability have an uneasy relationship'.[231] Nonetheless, from the perspective of the chain of accountability, the autonomisation of large sectors of public administration does not automatically determine the ousting of the ministerial responsibility. The relevant minister still holds a relationship of accountability with Parliament regarding political programming and the implementation of

---

[224] Le Divellec, 'La problématique du contrôle' (n 91) 16. Stone (n 184).

[225] Le Divellec, 'La problématique du contrôle' (n 91) 11. Bar Cendón (n 222) 31.

[226] AW Bradley and KD Ewing, *Constitutional and Administrative Law*, 15th edn (London, Longman, 2011) 277 (in the UK, since the 1990s, with the creation of a wide range of non-departmental bodies, a distinction was introduced between a minister's accountability before Parliament for departmental activity and his/her irresponsibility for the faults and omissions of civil servants).

[227] Siefken (n 223) 45 ff. O Beaud, 'Le transfert de la responsabilité politique du ministre verse ses proches subordonnés' in O Beaud and JM Blanquer (eds), *La responsabilité des gouvernants* (Paris, Descartes & Cie, 1999) 203 f.

[228] Flinders (n 185).

[229] C Gusy, 'Privatisierung und parlamentarische Kontrolle' (1998) 31 *Zeitschrift für Rechtspolitik* 265.

[230] B Crum and D Curtin, 'The Challenge of Making European Union Executive Power Accountable' in S Piattoni (ed), *The European Union: Democratic Principles and Institutional Architectures in Times of Crisis* (Oxford, Oxford University Press, 2015) 74.

[231] K Verhoest, A Molenveld and T Willems, 'Explaining Self-Perceived Accountability of Regulatory Agencies in Comparative Perspective: How Do Formal Independence and De Facto Managerial Autonomy Interact' in AC Bianculli, X Fernández-i-Marín and J Jordana (eds), *Accountability and Regulatory Governance. Audiences, Controls and Responsibilities in the Politics of Regulation* (London, Palgrave, 2015) 51. Accountability concerns raised by standards of discretion allowed to administrative agencies are also at issue in presidential systems; see C Coglianese, 'Administrative Law: The US and Beyond' (2016) 1656 *Faculty Scholarship Paper* 1, 3 ff.

the designed policies falling under the scope of independent authorities or agencies.[232] The latter, at the same time, may be asked to give account directly to Parliament of the results achieved in the fulfilment of their mandate. In parliamentary systems, the accountability obligations are far more limited than in presidential regimes, because they do not include the power to dismiss the directors of autonomous agencies and independent authorities. However, it is not unusual that representatives of these bodies are requested in Parliament for public hearings or for evidence sessions where the performance of the agency or authority is put under scrutiny.[233]

National parliaments in the EU have started engaging in such forms of 'mild' surveillance and vigilance in regard to autonomous administrations, involving in their field of intervention both the national and European agencies.[234] Also, the vigilance exercised by national parliaments in regard to banking supervision of the European Central Bank can be included in this experience.[235] National legislatures have undoubtedly benefited from the positive trend started by the European Parliament leading to an increased accountability arrangement for European agencies. The original model for this type of accountability arrangement is offered by the US Congress' control in regard to bureaucracy, well explained by the group of scholars defined as the 'theorists of congressional dominance'.[236]

The European Parliament has engaged in a sort of 'accountability game' with EU-level agencies, fostered by the overcoming of the Meroni doctrine, according to which discretionary 'executive-type' powers could only be delegated to treaty-based institutions.[237] At first, the European Parliament was rather indifferent to the performance of these bodies: the annual reports on the activity accomplished were not debated in committee or in plenary sessions and there was no practice of questioning the directors for assessing the outcomes achieved. The establishment of the latest agencies marked a shift of approach.[238] The constitutive statutes now mandate the European Parliament to invite the executive director to report on the conduct of the agency's duties and tasks. Based on these provisions, the European Parliament has started promoting annual meetings with the directors of different agencies, questioning sessions have been activated and the agencies' budgets have been placed under the budgetary powers of the European Parliament (insofar as they

---

[232] Bar Cendón (n 222) 51.

[233] A Katsaitis and A Eriksen, 'Accountability through Mutual Attunement: Parliamentary Hearings & Agency Oversight in the European Union' (2019) Paper prepared for EUSA, Denver, 9–11 May 2019.

[234] M Chamon, *EU Agencies: Legal and Political Limits to the Transformation of the EU Administration* (Oxford, Oxford University Press, 2016) 316 ff; and M Simoncini, *Administrative Regulation Beyond the Non-Delegation Doctrine. A Study on EU Agencies* (Oxford, Hart Publishing, 2018).

[235] The reference is to the 'banking dialogues' based on art 21 of Regulation no 2014/2013/UE; see D Fromage and R Ibrido, 'Democratic Accountability and Parliamentary Oversight over the ECB. The Banking Union Experience' (2016) 49 SOG Working Papers 1, 10 ff; and R Ibrido, *L'Unione bancaria europea. Profili costituzionali* (Torino, Giappichelli, 2017) 259 ff. For further details, see below ch 7.

[236] See M Guidi, 'Modelling the Relationship Between Independence and Accountability of Regulatory Agencies' in AC Bianculli, X Fernández-i-Marín and J Jordana (eds), *Accountability and Regulatory Governance. Audiences, Controls and Responsibilities in the Politics of Regulation* (London, Palgrave, 2015).

[237] M Busuioc, *European Agencies. Law and Practices of Accountability* (Oxford, Oxford University Press, 2013); and M Egeberg and J Trondal, 'Researching European Union Agencies: What Have We Learnt (and Where Do We Go from Here)?' (2017) 55 *Journal of Common Market Studies* 657.

[238] N Font, 'Designing Accountability Regimes at the European Union Level' in AC Bianculli, X Fernández-i-Marín and J Jordana (eds), *Accountability and Regulatory Governance. Audiences, Controls and Responsibilities in the Politics of Regulation* (London, Palgrave, 2015).

form part of the non-compulsory expenditures of the EU budget).[239] It is argued that 'the accountability system of agencies has developed in a "muddling through" manner, more as an afterthought rather than a thought-through process of institutional design'.[240] As a matter of fact, improvements on the grounds of transparency, sharing of information, accessibility and debate have not led to a clear definition of the overall political responsibility structure of European agencies.

Searching for a legitimacy framework, instances of political accountability for autonomous administrations should therefore be confronted with the patterns derived from the regulatory oversight model that has exercised a major influence on the design of EU integration.[241] The regulatory approach has boosted an alternative form of legitimacy, based not on the democratic inputs and processes, but on the standards achieved in the implementation of laws, rules or principles prescribed by EU authorities to control or govern public conduct. Following the EU model, in the last few decades principles of regulatory oversight have gained relevance at national level also. This has enhanced the horizontal dimension of administrative accountability of autonomous agencies both before citizens[242] and before external bodies of supervision, such as the ombudsmen.[243] In both cases, parliaments can exercise a key role in the accountability chain. On the one hand, their interaction with autonomous administrations may serve the purposes of the democratic accountability before public society.[244] On the other hand, they may collect the results of the surveillance exercised by external controllers to instruct a process of political accountability involving both the conduct of autonomous administrations and the management of related public policies.

VI. The Problem of Enforcement: Comparing Hard and Soft Oversight

Instances of political oversight differ from legal controls in two dimensions. On the one hand, the premises for enforcing political oversight are entirely left at the remit of political actors and there is no binding rule that can condition or limit this field of discretion.[245] On the other hand, the consequences related to political responsibility are not predetermined and rather depend on the overall political context.[246] Accordingly, enforcement of political oversight shows a peculiar relationship with the use of sanctions.

---

[239] Crum and Curtin (n 230) 75 f.

[240] Busuioc (n 237) 281 f.

[241] See above ch 1, section II (n 70). G Majone, 'Europe's "Democratic Deficit": The Question of Standards' (1998) 4 *European Law Journal* 5.

[242] This corresponds to the elaboration of downward accountability mechanisms towards stakeholders, peers and target groups; see Verhoest, Molenveld and Willems (n 231) 51 ff.

[243] Bar Cendón (n 222) 37.

[244] B Rosen, *Holding Government Bureaucracies Accountable* (New York, Praeger, 1982) 72 ff; D Osborne and T Gaebler, *Reinventing Government: How the Entrepreneurial Spirit is Transforming the Public Sector* (Reading, Addison-Wesley, 1992) 49 ff.

[245] GU Rescigno, 'Responsabilità politica e responsabilità giuridica' (2012) 3 *Rivista italiana per le scienze giuridiche* 333, 337.

[246] ibid.

It has been argued that the accountability-oversight circuit involves two stages: answerability and enforcement. Both stages should be considered as a due component of the accountability relation, because 'answerability without enforcement and sanctions without enforcement significantly diminish accountability'.[247] It is common opinion that parliamentary regimes lack a real system of sanctions applicable to the executive. In fact, it should rather be noted that the notion of 'sanction' cannot be considered in a strict legal perspective.

Parliamentary oversight is not just about enforcing government responsibility.[248] First, political responsibility pursued in Parliament is the apex of the oversight relation,[249] but government duty to account for elected representatives follows a gradual *iter* that finds in the resignation or censure of a minister or prime minister its very final and unlikely event.[250] The relationship with formal sanctions is strongly dependent on the form of government. This explains why the possibility to connect political oversight to the use of sanctions has been deeply challenged in France, following the jurisprudence of the Conseil constitutionnel. Since Decision no 59-2 of 24 July 1959, the Conseil constitutionnel has clarified that the mechanisms enforcing parliamentary oversight should not overpass the constitutional rules (article 49 of the Constitution) that regulate government responsibility. In other words, the power to oversee should not be turned into the power to sanction.[251]

A different approach to the notion of 'sanction' should therefore be embraced. In this vein, sanction is not just the application of the penalty embodied in a legal act but it may also represent the exposition to a 'soft' enforcement mechanism, such as public exposure or negative publicity.[252] In parliamentary regimes, government responsibility works alongside the chain of confidence between the executive and legislative branches, which permeates all parliamentary functions. It therefore manifests itself as informative, explicative and channelling responsibility, which respectively imply the duty to share data and information, provide justifications and channel the relationship of public administration with Parliament.

Second, parliamentary oversight interacts with the logic of 'diffused' responsibility, which is urged by public opinion and worked through media exposure.[253] This is defined as an institutional and free instance of political responsibility: it is institutional, because it complements and potentially substitutes the traditional instance of political responsibility; it is free, because it is exclusively based on the freedom of expression.[254] In this vein, parliamentary oversight comprises instances of evidence-gathering, disclosure of information and public debate which are instrumental to government accountability but do not directly require the application of sanctions. In most cases, as the analysis of oversight tools clearly demonstrates, this part of the oversight circuit works better if it is supported by patterns of cooperation between the executive and the legislative branches.

---

[247] Pelizzo and Stapenhurst, *Government Accountability* (n 63) 2. Avril, 'L'introuvable contrôle' (n 24) 2.

[248] Fernández Sarasola (n 23) 95 f.

[249] A Esmein, *Éléments de Droit Français et comparé*, I (Paris, Recueil Sirey, 1927) 484; V Hermán and F Mendel (eds), *Parliaments of the World* (London, Macmillan, 1976) 825.

[250] Bustos Gisbert (n 190) 67 f.

[251] E Thiers, 'Le contrôle' parlementaire et ses limites juridiques: un pouvoir presque sans entraves' (2010) 134 *Pouvoirs* 71, 74.

[252] ibid. A Manzella, *Il Parlamento* (Bologna, Il Mulino, 2003) 355 f.

[253] Rescigno, *La responsabilità politica* (n 207) 115 ff.

[254] Rescigno, 'Responsabilità politica' (n 245) 352 f.

Following this argument, from the point of view of the enforcing mechanisms, two different conceptions of the oversight function can be identified. On the one hand, it is the conception of the 'hard' oversight available to parliaments in view of holding the government to account in a binding manner. The hard conception frames oversight as a vertical means to enforce executive accountability in Parliament.[255] On the other hand, the conception of the 'soft' oversight is instrumental to strengthening the informative prerogatives of legislatures and supporting their representative and communicative functions.[256] Under this conception, parliamentary oversight is interpreted as a horizontal dimension serving Parliament's attempt to exercise influence over the executive.

Emphasis has traditionally been placed on 'hard' instances of parliamentary oversight that may lead to the overthrow of a government. In fact, parliamentary practice shows a large variety of unsanctioned oversight tools, from parliamentary questioning to government reporting duties, from debates to hearings. The importance of non-sanctioning accountability has recently been recognised as a means of reinforcing the 'constructive' part of the oversight process, instrumental to identifying problems and promoting better management, in connection with the civil society.[257]

It might be questioned whether the use made by parliamentary assemblies of the hard and soft instances of parliamentary oversight is justiciable, and hence may be subject to an external evaluation from the judiciary. The answer is no, even in those countries, including France, that admit constitutional review of the parliamentary Rules of Procedure:[258] the Conseil constitutionnel has the right to review the Rules of Procedure of the assemblies, but it is not allowed to assess oversight activities *in concreto*. As a matter of fact, the enforcement of parliamentary oversight is created on a case-by-case basis and it is completely left to the discretionary evaluation of elected assemblies, which are exclusively answerable to their electors.[259]

---

[255] N Grandguillaume, *Théorie générale du contrôle* (Paris, Economica, 1994).
[256] Meinel (n 66) 318 ff.
[257] A Schedler, L Diamond and M Plattner, *The Self-Restraining State: Power and Accountability in New Democracies* (Boulder, CO, Lynne Rienner Publishers, 1999).
[258] See Thiers (n 251) 79.
[259] ibid.

3

Instances of Parliamentary Oversight: In Dialogue with Other Parliamentary Functions

The oversight function is hard to define and frame due to its multifaceted nature. For a long time, parliamentary oversight was marked out in negative terms, based on a residual definition that covered all the spheres of activity apart from budget and law-making.[1] In fact, contemporary approaches rather describe oversight of the executive as a polymorphic function that appears in different guises, forms and varieties.[2] This vision is consistent with the description of parliamentary procedures as versatile, interchangeable and multifunctional.[3] The polymorphism is particularly true in parliamentary systems, where the oversight function covers all the stages of government formation, tenure and dismissal and all the phases of policy-making.

Different categories of parliamentary oversight have been proposed by constitutional scholars in order to isolate alternative dimensions of this function. The terminological solutions vary from country to country, but it is probably in Italy and Spain where these categorisations have gained major success. This is the case, among others, for the formula

---

[1] FJ García Roca, 'Control parlamentario y convergencia entre presidencialismo y parlamentarismo' (2016) 38 *Teoría y Realidad Constitucional* 61, 63. G Ferrara, 'Bicameralismo e riforme del Parlamento' (1981) 21 *Democrazia e diritto* 11, 24 ff; and L Paladin, 'Bicameralismo' in *Enciclopedia giuridica*, V (Roma, Treccani, 1988) 1 ff (on parliamentary oversight as an auxiliary function, which serves all the other major functions of Parliament).

[2] BA Rockman, 'Legislative-executive relations and legislative oversight' (1984) 9 *Legislative Studies Quarterly* 387, specifically referring to congressional oversight. With regard to parliamentary systems, *ex multis*, HP Schneider, *Entscheidungsdefizite der Parlamente: über die Notwendigkeit einer Wiederbelebung der Parlamentsreform* (Tübingen, Mohr Siebeck, 1980); E Busch, *Parlamentarische Kontrolle Ausgestaltung und Wirkung* (Heidelberg, Decker und Müller, 1983); M Aragón Reyes, 'El control parlamentario como control político' (1986) 23 *Revista de Derecho Político* 9; M Embid Irujo, 'El control parlamentario del gobierno en la jurisprudencia del Tribunal constitucional' (1991) 31 *Revista Vasca de Administración Pública* 179; F Rubio Llorente, *La forma del poder (Estudios sobre la Constitución)* (Madrid, CEC, 1993) 256; N Grandguillaume, *Théorie générale du contrôle* (Paris, Economica, 1994); FJ García Roca, 'El control del Gobierno desde la perspectiva individual del parlamentario (y a la luz del art. 23.2 de la Constitución)' (1995) 42 *Revista Vasca de Administración Publica* 161; P Avril, 'L'introuvable contrôle parlementaire (après la révision constitutionelle française de 2008' (2009) 3 *Jus Politicum* 1, 6; N Lupo, 'Funkcja kontrolna parlamentu we Włoszech (La funzione di controllo parlamentare nell'ordinamento italiano)' in Z Witkowski, GC De Martin and KM Witkowska-Chrzczonowicz (eds), *Gwarancje konstytucyjne i srodki kontroli w panstwie demokratycznym z perspektywy dorobku konstytucyjnego Włoch i Polski* (Torun, Tnoik, 2008) 108; A Manzella, 'La funzione di controllo' in Vv Aa, *Associazione italiana dei costituzionalisti, Annuario 2000. Il Parlamento* (Padova, Cedam, 2001) 213 f.

[3] A Manzella, *Il Parlamento* (Bologna, Il Mulino, 2003) *passim*. I Molas and I Pitarch, *Las Cortes Generales en el sistema parlamentario de Gobierno* (Madrid, Tecnos, 1987). I Fernández Sarasola, 'El control parlamentario y su regulación en el ordenamiento español' (2000) 60 *Revista Española de Derecho Constitucional* 89.

of the *control-fiscalización* and *control-responsabilidad política* in Spain,[4] *controllo-direzione*, *controllo-verifica* and *controllo-ispezione* in Italy.[5]

The following sections will account for these parallel dimensions by highlighting how parliamentary oversight interacts with other fully-fledged parliamentary functions, namely the formation of government, the setting of political directions, the scrutiny of legislative enactment and impact assessment and the informative function.[6] Oversight of the executive is also intertwined with the audit of budget, but the interconnection between these two functions will be examined below (see below chapter eight).

I. Parliamentary Appraisal of Executive Appointments in Government Formation: Oversight or Elective Function?

It is argued that 'government formation is at the very heart of representative politics'.[7] In parliamentary systems, the process of appointing the executive always requires the consent (either explicit or implicit) of one or more Houses of Parliament. In unicameral and bicameral systems that provide an asymmetric role to the two Houses, it is only the Lower House that participates in the formation of government. The case of Italy is rather unique in this perspective, because both Houses are required to support the executive with a vote of confidence.[8]

Constitutional law textbooks usually refer to this dimension as a manifestation of the 'elective function'[9] vested in representative assemblies – 'la face anticipée et positive de la responsabilité politique' ('the early and positive stage of the political responsibility') – whose origin lies in the formula of Cabinet government.[10] Government formation is indeed 'an intensely political as well as a legal process'; therefore, 'its nature and outcome can depend as much on political circumstances as on the written (or even unwritten) constitutional rules'.[11] In contrast, in political science the power to decide on the formation and composition of the executive is considered as 'the most important ex ante form of control'.[12] The appointment of the government gives parties, depending on their role of majority and opposition, a rather unique opportunity to control government offices and policies.[13] It is at this stage that, especially when no party gains an overall majority in

---

[4] García Roca, 'Control parlamentario' (n 1) 64.

[5] V Di Ciolo and L Ciaurro, *Il diritto parlamentare nella teoria e nella pratica* (Milano, Giuffrè, 2013) 718.

[6] A Manzella, 'Il Parlamento come organo costituzionale di controllo' (2017) 1 *Nomos* 1, 2 (on existing difficulties to trace the interconnection with the other parliamentary functions).

[7] M Laver and KA Shepsle, *Making and Breaking Governments: Cabinets and Legislatures in Parliamentary Democracies* (Cambridge, Cambridge University Press, 1996) 4.

[8] L Trivelli, *Le Bicamérisme. Institutions Comaparées. Étude historique, statistique et critique des rapports entre le conseil national et le conseil des états* (Lausanne, Diffusion Payot, 1975); G Tsebelis and J Money, *Bicameralism* (Cambridge, Cambridge University Press, 1997); J Uhr, 'Bicameralism' in RAW Rhodes, SA Binder and B Rockman (eds), *The Oxford Handbook of Political Institutions* (Oxford, Oxford University Press, 2006).

[9] The elective (that is Parliament's influence over selecting the executive) is deemed to be the most important function of the House of Commons by Bagehot, W Bagehot, *The English Constitution*, 2nd edn (London, HS King, 1872) 118.

[10] A Le Divellec, 'Des effets du contrôle parlementaire' (2010) 134 *Pouvoirs* 123, 129.

[11] E Bulmer, *Government Formation and Removal Mechanisms* (Stockholm, International IDEA, 2017) 9.

[12] I Budge and H Keman, *Parties and Democracy. Coalition Formation and Government Functioning in Twenty States* (Oxford, Oxford University Press, 1990).

[13] K Strøm, *Minority Government and Majority Rule* (Cambridge, Cambridge University Press, 1990). M Laver and N Schofield, *Multiparty Government. The Politics of Coalitions in Europe* (Oxford, Oxford University Press, 1990).

Parliament, political bargaining and negotiations may lead to unexpected outcomes in the final composition of government.[14]

For the purposes of this monograph, it is assumed that parliamentary appraisal of executive appointments in government formation may represent a manifestation of either the elective or the oversight function, depending on the mechanisms that rule this process and on the related prerogatives vested in parliaments.[15] Assessing this assumption is not an easy task, from a comparative perspective. In most European countries, government formation constitutes a quite complex decision-making process that involves a wide variety of actors, unfolds through informal practices beyond formal rules, and produces unpredictable outcomes that strongly depend on the political framework of the hour.[16]

Broadly speaking, one key variable in this analysis is the level of formal parliamentary control over the government formation process,[17] based on the difference between positive and negative parliamentarism.[18] Constitutions may either require a vote of investiture or provide that there is no requirement for a formal parliamentary vote to select or approve a prime minister. If the government cannot be formed unless an explicit investiture is voted in Parliament, the model of positive parliamentarism is applied. By contrast, in the case of negative parliamentarism, government formation does not strictly require a formal endorsement by Parliament.[19]

The difference between positive and negative parliamentarism can be considered a relevant parameter for describing the formal power that Parliament can exercise during government formation. Models of positive parliamentarism may take various forms. Parliament may be involved in the initial phase of the process or, more commonly, in the final phase. In some cases, MPs are asked to vote in an uncontested election for or against the candidate appointed to the office of Prime Minister; in others, they participate in a contested election in which two or more candidates are presented to Parliament. Some constitutions provide that the Parliament participates through a vote of confidence in the investiture of the government as a whole after it is formally appointed by the head of state; others refer the nomination of the Prime Minister by Parliament, usually through a resolution.[20]

---

[14] T Saalfeld, 'Institutions, Chance and Choices. The Dynamics of Cabinet Survival in the Parliamentary Democracies of Western Europe' in K Strøm, WC Müller and T Bergman (eds), *Cabinets and Coalition Bargaining: The Democratic Life Cycle in Western Europe* (Oxford, Oxford University Press, 2008).

[15] O Rozenberg, 'Comparer les parlements' in JM de Waele and Y Déloye (eds), *Politique comparé* (Bruxelles, Bruylant, 2018) 333 (on the substitutability between investiture and censure: parliaments that are powerful in the process of government formation are less influential when the government is in charge).

[16] L De Winter, 'The Role of Parliament in Government Formation and Resignation' in H Döring (ed), *Parliaments and Majority Rule in Western Europe* (New York, St Martin's Press, 1995) 116.

[17] A detailed comparative overview is available in M Brunclik, 'Patterns of Government Formation in Europe: The Role of the Head of State' (2015) 1 *Czech Journal of Political Science* 26, 32 f.

[18] T Bergman, 'Formation rules and minority governments' (1993) 23 *European Journal of Political Research* 55. B Seyd, *Coalition Government in Britain: Lessons from Overseas* (London, The Constitution Unit, 2002) 38 ff. Bulmer (n 11) 15 f (on the existence of a third category, labelled 'minimal' parliamentarism, when the process of government formation is not regulated in detail by the constitution and mostly relies on unwritten conventions and sub-constitutional rules).

[19] BE Rasch, S Martin and JA Cheibub (eds), *Parliaments and Government Formation: Unpacking Investiture Rules* (Oxford, Oxford University Press, 2015). V Bogdanor, 'The Government Formation Process in the Constitutional Monarchies of North-West Europe' in D Kavanagh and G Peele (eds), *Comparative Government and Politics: Essays in Honour of SE Finer* (London, Heinemann, 1984).

[20] Bulmer (n 11) 20.

Regardless of these procedural variations, cases of positive parliamentarism allow that the investiture of government is filtered by a public debate. The latter offers MPs the chance to express a judgment on government proposals and to formulate their views, expectations and desires on the conduct of executive affairs. The opportunities of interaction are apparently more limited in a framework of negative parliamentarism. It would therefore be possible to argue that Parliament is given a real chance to exercise an *ex ante* oversight during government formation only in those systems, such as Germany, Italy, Spain and Sweden, that belong to positive parliamentarism. In fact, the picture turns out to be more complex than expected. Even in those countries, such as Denmark, France and the United Kingdom, that represent an example of negative parliamentarism, the process of government formation experiences some instances of parliamentary *ex ante* oversight (although most often limited to members of the parliamentary majority and exercised on informal grounds).

A more exhaustive picture of what space Parliament is given for overseeing the stage of government formation should consequently consider other contextual elements. The role reserved to Parliament in the investiture procedure is deeply influenced by the scope and nature of the task entrusted on the formateur, whether it is the monarch, the head of state[21] or the speaker (as in the rather unique case of Sweden).[22] This aspect, in its turn, depends on different sets of factors.

One is the recognition of rules, ie, the constitutional principles that identify who is to assume the role of the *formateur*, that is asked to form the government, what type of powers are entrusted on this actor[23] and in which order different subjects might be invited to assume this task.[24] In some cases, the *formateur* has large margins of discretion in identifying and appointing a prime minister who is likely to gain the confidence of Parliament on the basis of the results of parliamentary elections.[25] In these hypotheses, Parliament formally intervenes ex post, after the *formateur* has formalised the candidature and completed the appointment; however, different MPs – depending on their party position and role in Parliament – may be informally consulted *ex ante* by the *formateur* to get a detailed view of the overall party orientations. Italy offers a paradigmatic example of informal consultations with the Speakers of both Houses and the representatives of parliamentary groups and political parties by the *formateur* (the head of state). This is not formally provided for in the Constitution, but it is followed as a constitutional convention.[26]

In other cases, the role of the *formateur* is a ceremonial one. This happens especially when the recognition rules provide the legal requirement of a parliamentary vote not just to confirm the confidence to the newly appointed executive, but beforehand to also nominate formally the incoming Prime Minister.[27] Versions of this type of procedure are

---

[21] Brunclik (n 17).

[22] T Larsson, 'Sweden: The New Constitution' in J Blondel and F Müller-Rommel (eds), *Cabinets in Western Europe* (London, Macmillan, 1988). T Bergman, 'Constitution rules and party goals in coalition formation: an analysis of winning minority governments in Sweden' (Umeå, Umeå universitet, 1995) 40 ff.

[23] De Winter (n 16) 123.

[24] P Schleiter, V Belu and R Hazell, 'Hung Parliaments and the Need for Clearer Rules of Government Formation' (2017) 88 *The Political Quarterly* 404.

[25] Bulmer (n 11) 8.

[26] L Paladin, 'Presidente della Repubblica' in *Enciclopedia del diritto* XXXV (Milano, Giuffrè, 1986) 24.

[27] Schleiter, Belu and Hazell (n 24) 411; W Müller and K Strøm, 'Conclusion: Coalition Governance in Western Europe' in W Müller and K Strøm (eds), *Coalition Governments in Western Europe* (Oxford, Oxford University Press, 2000) 567.

applied in different parliamentary systems. In Germany, the President of the Republic selects a candidate for the office of chancellor, but the nominee must be approved by the Bundestag either by an absolute majority (in which case the head of state is obliged to formalise the appointment) or by simple majority (in this hypothesis, it is up to the President of the Republic to decide between a minority government or the dissolution of the Bundestag).[28] In Spain, the Congreso is asked to intervene before the formal appointment of the Prime Minister, in two subsequent stages: the candidature can be formalised by the king through the Speaker of the Congreso after having consulted the political groups represented in Parliament; the nominee is then submitted to the Congreso for being formally approved by an absolute majority or, after 48 hours, in case of failure, by simple majority.[29] These arrangements offer Parliament the possible largest formal role in the formation of government.

The second set of factors, investigated in political studies,[30] turns around the electoral system, whether it offers parliamentary groups or even individual MPs the opportunity to exercise a formal or informal role in the formation of government. The process is usually a fairly complex one in systems that are not able to produce single party majorities: long-lasting negotiations during government formation may give single components in Parliament the opportunity to exercise an informal influence. By contrast, the formation of government is a relatively simple and mechanical process in majority systems, where the party leader and the government programme are pre-known and the main unknown variable lies in the selection of ministers.[31] In fact, even majority systems have raised the risk that general elections produce 'hung parliaments in which no single party commanded an overall majority';[32] in these circumstances, rules applicable to government formation are not clear from the beginning. If the outcome is the formation of minority governments, formal or informal contacts might be activated with opposition parliamentary groups or members.[33]

Finally, in the rather distinctive case of Italy, the involvement of both Houses in the formation of government makes the bicameral factor a fundamental issue for understanding

---

[28] Art 63 Basic Law. See S Ganghof and C Stecker, 'Investiture Rules in Germany: Stacking the Deck against Minority Government' in B Rasch, S Martin and JA Cheibub (eds), *Parliaments and Government Formation Unpacking Investiture Rules* (Oxford, Oxford University Press, 2015); SO Proksch and JB Slapin, 'Institutions and Coalition Formation: The German Election of 2005' (2006) 29 *West European Politics* 540.

[29] Art 99 Constitution. See M Revenga Sánchez, *La formación del gobierno en la Constitución española de 1978* (Madrid, Centro de Estudios Constitucionales, 1988); L Aguiar de Luque, 'La estructura del proceso de formación de gobierno: el caso español en el marco del Derecho comparado' (1980) 6 *Revista de derecho político* 61.

[30] D Diermeier and P van Roozendaal, 'The duration of cabinet formation processes in western multi-party democracies' (1998) 28 *British Journal of Political Science* 609; K von Beyme, *Parliamentary Democracy* (Basingstoke, Macmillan, 2000); LW Martin and RT Stevenson, 'Government Formation in Parliamentary Democracies' (2001) 45 *Journal of Political Science* 33; M Laver, S de Marchi and H Mutlu, 'Negotiation in Legislatures over Government Formation' (2011) 147 *Public Choice* 285; M Golder, S Golder and DA Siegel, 'Modeling the Institutional Foundations of Parliamentary Government Formation' (2012) 74 *Journal of Politics* 427.

[31] De Winter (n 16) 117.

[32] Schleiter, Belu and Hazell (n 24) 404, referring to the consequences of the general elections in 2010 and 2017 in the UK. On the notion of 'hung parliaments' as well as on pre-existing experiences, D Butler, *Governing without a majority. Dilemmas for Hung Parliaments in Britain* (Basingstoke, Macmillan, 1987) 10; D Butler, 'Hung Parliaments: Context and Background' in A Brazier and S Kalitowski (eds), *No Overall Control: The Impact of a 'Hung Parliament' on British Politics* (London, Hansard Society, 2008). G Pasquino, 'Governments in European Politics' in JM Magone (ed), *Routledge Handbook of European Politics* (London, Routledge, 2015) 296.

[33] T Bergman, 'When Minority Cabinets are the Rule and Majority Coalitions the Exception' in W Müller and K Strøm (eds), *Coalition Governments* (Oxford, Oxford University Press, 2000).

the role of Parliament. In fact, the need to gain a vote of confidence both in the Chamber of Deputies and in the Senate does not seem to represent an added value that enriches the Italian Parliament's capacity to oversee the investiture of government. Rather, over the decades, it has represented an 'aggravated' factor[34] that, in cases of uncertain electoral outcomes and inconsistencies in the majorities of the two Houses, has required a gradual increase in the discretionary power reserved for the President of the Republic to overcome risks of stalemate in the investiture procedure.[35] In this vein, Italy also offers a distinctive case for the large variety of recognition rules that, over the years, have been applied to the process of government formation.[36]

The combination of these factors creates a rather heterogeneous picture[37] that does not allow conclusions to be drawn on the effective opportunities offered to Parliament to oversee the process. Nonetheless, evidence gathered from the comparison of different parliamentary models seems to offer two main insights. On the one hand, where no clear recognition rules exist, it is on the informal ground rather than through formal procedures that Parliament is offered the opportunity to have a say on the fundamental decisions that affect the formation of government, from the selection of the Prime Minister to the definition of the governmental programme, up to the appointment of ministers.[38] This assumption is also true for cases of positive parliamentarism, where official debates and votes on the appointment of government usually turn out to be mere attempts to make formal decisions already agreed in the informal negotiations. On the other hand, the involvement of Parliament in the process of government formation draws a clear cleavage between majority and opposition that does not allow the consideration of the role of the institution as a whole. Rather, spaces for ex ante oversight should be distinctively evaluated for single parliamentary groups and even for single MPs, depending on their position in regard to the government.

II. Ex Ante Parliamentary Oversight: Setting the Political Direction

In parliamentary systems, the legislature engages in the oversight of the executive from the very beginning, before the 'contract' is made, during the appointing or electing stage. Nonetheless, it is in the exercise of government's full mandate that the oversight function gains major momentum. During this stage, two distinct dimensions can be identified: ex ante and ex post oversight. The terms *ex ante* and *ex post* find their parameter in the time

---

[34] Pasquino (n 32) 299.

[35] See E Cheli, 'Articolo 89' in G Branca (ed), *Commentario alla Costituzione. Articoli 88–91: Il Presidente della Repubblica. Tomo II* (Bologna, Zanichelli, 1983) 129 ff; M Luciani, 'Un giroscopio costituzionale. Il Presidente della Repubblica dal mito alla realtà (passando per il testo della costituzione)' (2017) 2 *Rivista AIC* 1.

[36] M Valbruzzi, 'When populists meet technocrats. The Italian innovation in government formation' (2018) 23 *Journal of Modern Italian Studies* 460.

[37] BE Rasch, S Martin and JA Cheibub, 'Investiture Rules Unpacked' in BE Rasch, S Martin and JA Cheibub (eds), *Parliaments and Government Formation: Unpacking Investiture Rules* (Oxford, Oxford University Press, 2015) 352.

[38] Seyd (n 18) 34.

frame of government action.[39] The former refers to the stage that preludes to the formal adoption of government decision or action,[40] the latter to the implementing stage.

A. The Purpose of Ex Ante Oversight

Executive action can be decided and formalised in multiple ways. Legislation remains at the core of policy-making and certain political goals require a legislative act to be accomplished.[41] However, policy-making goes beyond the scope of legislation, encompassing the adoption of other types of acts and decisions of an administrative nature, including elements of 'soft law'.[42] The formal vest of the decisions under control does not substantially alter the nature of the oversight function performed by Parliament. Rather, it is the time frame of Parliament intervention, related to the time frame of government decision, that changes the mechanisms enforceable.

The traditional conception of parliamentary oversight defines this function as an ex post activity, whose purpose is to check the action of the government and place a remedy against inefficiencies or misbehaviours.[43] This dimension of the oversight function is partial and limited. Parliaments cannot restrain their role to a *posteriori* surveillance, since this form of verification turns out to be either ineffective or excessive. On the one hand, Parliament is often incapable of compelling the government to revise its decisions. On the other, available binding ex post tools may prove too much, as they produce irreversible consequences on the government mandate.[44] In both cases, once the policy is implemented, it may be difficult to provide concrete remedies able to fix inefficiencies or misbehaviours.

More than in the ex post, it is therefore in the ex ante stage that legislatures can play a strategic role. Engaging in what is defined as 'preventative control' or 'foresight'[45] offers two main advantages: it contributes to the improvement of the quality of government policies and programmes; and it strengthens the democratic legitimacy of these decisions.[46] Since the sphere of ex ante oversight is rather blurred, some clarity is required on the associated dimensions.

---

[39] This use of the notions of *ex ante* and *ex post* oversight is advanced among others by R Maffio, '*Qui custodiet ipsos custodes? Il controllo parlamentare dell'attività di governo in prospettiva comparata*' (2002) 9 *Quaderni di scienza politica* 333, 333 f.

[40] K Eichenberger, 'Die Problematik der parlamentarischen Kontrolle im Verwaltungsstaat' (1965) 18 *Schweizerische Juristen-Zeitung* 269.

[41] VCRAC Crabbe, 'The ethics of legislative drafting' (2010) 36 *Commonwealth Law Bulletin* 11.

[42] DM Trubek, P Cottrell and M Nance, '"Soft Law", "Hard Law", and EU Integration' in G de Búrca and J Scott (eds), *New Governance, Law and Constitutionalism* (Oxford, Hart Publishing, 2006).

[43] A Le Divellec, 'La problématique du contrôle parlementaire de l'administration' in B Seiller (ed), *Le contrôle parlementaire de l'administration* (Paris, Dalloz, 2010) (n 235) 15 recalls the traditional definition of the term 'contrôle' as 'opposed to the action' provided by E Littré, *Dictionnaire de la langue française*, 1st edn (Paris, Hachette, 1973).

[44] K Strøm, 'Delegation and accountability in parliamentary democracies' (2000) 37 *European Journal of Political Research* 261, 273 ('It is the very existence of ex post cabinet accountability to the parliamentary majority that defines parliamentary government. But the no confidence threat is a blunt and unwieldy instrument').

[45] R Pelizzo and F Stapenhurst, *Government accountability and Legislative Oversight* (New York, Routledge, 2014) 17.

[46] ibid. Manzella, 'La funzione di controllo' (n 2) 213 f; Lupo, 'Funkcja kontrolna' (n 2).

For instance, the formula of 'pre-legislative scrutiny', developed in literature to define Parliament's intervention before a Bill is drafted and formally submitted in the legislative process, is not part of the ex ante dimension of parliamentary oversight. As a form of pre-drafting instrumental to the quality of legislation,[47] pre-legislative scrutiny is a complex process, open to the participation of multiple actors,[48] that may involve parliaments in their capacity as legislators,[49] not as controllers of the executive.[50] Pre-legislative scrutiny is in fact serving the legislative more than the oversight function, because it does not drain Parliament's amending power once the Bill is formally submitted.

Rather, it is in the setting of political directions – which is co-determined between Parliament and government – where ex ante oversight finds more fertile ground. Parliament's participation in the exercise of the direction of power, consisting of the ability to identify the fundamental political goals of executive action, is at the very core of the parliamentary regime. In these systems, political directions are jointly set by the legislative and the executive branches. Yet, on theoretical grounds, this function is not equally acknowledged in all European constitutional traditions.

The 'political direction' function can be traced back to the Liberal State when, especially in France and Germany, the notion started being debated in literature to legitimise the transfer of powers from Parliament to government.[51] The original situation of a parliament that exceeded its powers, with the government unable to even start the legislative process, urged a counterbalance to protect executive interests.[52] It is in this period that scholars started distinguishing government from executive power to justify the conferral on the former of further powers, additional to the implementation of legislation.[53] Government was identified as an autonomous function that is primarily, but not exclusively, in the hands of the executive branch,[54] since the political direction of the state is jointly exercised with Parliament.[55]

In the following century, the notion acknowledged a rather different contextualisation. The development of the welfare state required new forms of ex ante coordination of the multiple spheres of public regulation and intervention. The breakdown of the pillars of the Liberal State – the principle of separation of powers and the primacy of law – urged

---

[47] GC Thornton, *Legislative Drafting*, 4th edn (London, Butterworths, 1996) 128.

[48] Z Ntaba, 'Pre-legislative scrutiny' in C Stefanou and H Xanthaki (eds), *Drafting Legislation: A Modern Approach* (London, Routledge, 2008) 119.

[49] Hansard Society Commission on the Legislative Process, *Making the Law* (London, Hansard Society, 1992); and J Garrett, *Westminster: Does Parliament Work?* (London, Gollancz, 1992).

[50] In fact, the interference between the legislative and the oversight function is at the basis of some studies on pre-legislative scrutiny of Bills; see J Smookler, 'Making a difference? The effectiveness of pre-legislative scrutiny' (2006) 59 *Parliamentary Affairs* 522.

[51] I Fernández Sarasola, 'Dirección política y función del gobierno en la Historia constitucional' (2003) 4 *Revista Electrónica de Historia Constitucional* para 62. E Cheli, *Atto politico e funzione di indirizzo politico* (Milano, Giuffrè, 1968) 43 ff.

[52] P Colombo, 'La question du pouvoir exécutif dans l'évolution institutionelle et le débat politique révolutionnaire' (2000) 319 *Annales historiques de la Révolution française* 1.

[53] R Smend, *Die politische Gewalt im Verfassungsstaat und das Problem der Staatsform* (Tübingen, Mohr, 1923) 11 ff. Sieyès' contribution to this debate is highlighted by P Pasquino, 'Sieyès, Constant e il "governo dei moderni". Contributo alla storia del concetto di rappresentanza politica' (1987) 1 *Filosofia politica* 77.

[54] This acknowledgement was enabled by the formal recognition of the notion of 'political act', fostered for the first time in France by the Conseil d'Etat, Ord 1 mai 1822, Laffitte, requête numéro 5363, Rec 1821–1825, 202.

[55] R Carré de Malberg, *Contribution à la Théorie Genérale de l'Etat*, II (Paris, Recueil Sirey, 1929) 108. M Hariou, *Précis de Droit Constitutionnel*, 2nd edn (Paris, Recueil Sirey, 1929) 383 ff.

the arrival of new mechanisms of preventative determination of the fundamental political goals that a plurality of public bodies was now expected to fulfil. The relationship between the executive and the legislative branches was overturned.[56] However, what remained is the idea that the political direction of state intervention is not an exclusive function of the government but should be exercised jointly with Parliament.[57] The challenge is determining what type of contribution is actually required from the legislative branch in the fulfilment of this function, whether it is the co-sharing of government power, the exercise of a form of 'influence' or the oversight of government action.

B. The Sphere of the *Indirizzo Politico*

To solve this dilemma, it can be useful to recall the doctrine of the political direction function developed by the Italian constitutional scholars through the notion of the *indirizzo politico*, indicating the setting of the fundamental goals that the state as a public entity is expected to fulfil.[58] This expression has found its fortune in Spain, where the formula *dirección política* (or *impulso politico*) has been coined,[59] but it does not seem to find corresponding transla- tions[60] in the Westminster tradition or in Nordic countries.

The doctrine of the *indirizzo politico* offers its original contribution by highlighting that the setting of political directions enables the legislative body to limit the excesses of the executive power derived from the *parliamentarisme rationalisé*.[61] As an activity that is instrumental to the fulfilment of the Constitution,[62] the *indirizzo politico* is shared

---

[56] J Barthélémy, *Le rôle du pouvoir exécutif dans le Républiques modernes* (Paris, Giard et Brière, 1906).

[57] E Friesenhahn, 'Die politischen Grundlagen des Bonner Grundgesetzes' in H Wandersleb (ed), *Recht, Staat, Wirtschaft*, II (Dusseldorf, Schwann, 1950) 164 f; G Burdüau, *Traité de Science Politique* (Paris, Librairie Genérale de Droit et de Jurisprudence, 1976) 393 ff; K Stern, *Staatsrecht*, I (Munich, Beck, 1977) 757.

[58] C Mortati, *L'ordinamento del governo nel nuovo diritto pubblico italiano* (Roma, Anonima Romana Editoriale, 1931); V Crisafulli, 'Per una teoria giuridica dell'indirizzo politico' (1939) 1–2 *Studi urbinati* 53; A Tesauro, 'Le funzioni fondamentali dello Stato' (1957) 12 *Rassegna di diritto pubblico* 533; T Martines, 'Indirizzo politico' in *Enciclopedia del diritto*, XXI (Milano, Giuffrè, 1971) 134; M Galizia, *Studi sui rapporti fra Parlamento e Governo*, I (Milano, Giuffrè, 1972); A Mannino, *Indirizzo politico e fiducia nei rapporti fra governo e parlamento* (Milano, Giuffrè, 1973); A Predieri, 'Mediazione e indirizzo nel parlamento italiano' (1975) 5 *Rivista italiana di scienze politiche* 407; M Dogliani, *Indirizzo politico. Riflessioni su regole e regolarità nel diritto costituzionale* (Napoli, Jovene, 1985); and M Dogliani, 'Indirizzo politico' in *Digesto delle discipline pubblicistiche*, VIII (Torino, Utet, 1993).

[59] Fernández Sarasola, 'Dirección política' (n 51). A Sáiz Arnáiz, 'El Gobierno y la dirección de la política' (1992) 34 *Revista Vasca de Administración Pública* 189; IM Giménez Sánchez, 'Indirizzo politico, dirección política, impulso político: el papel del Parlamento' (2008) 18 *Revista Jurídica de la Universidad de Madrid* 83. Critiques of this transplant were expressed by FJ García Roca, 'Del principio de la división de poderes' (2000) 108 *Revista de Estudios Políticos* 61.

[60] U Liebert, 'The Centrality of Parliament in the Consolidation of Democracy: A Theoretical Exploration' (1989) 7 Political Science Institute Heidelberg – Working Paper 12; L Gianniti, 'The 2016 Attempted Reform of the Italian Senate in a European Perspective' in N Lupo and G Piccirilli (eds), *The Italian Parliament in the European Union* (Oxford, Hart Publishing, 2017).

[61] C Chimenti, *Il controllo parlamentare nell'ordinamento italiano* (Milano, Giuffrè, 1974) 84; and C Chimenti, 'Centralità e funzionalità del Parlamento' (1978) 4 *Democrazia e diritto* 627. A Manzella, 'Le origini dei regolamenti parlamentari a quarant'anni dal 1971' in A Manzella (ed), *I regolamenti parlamentari a quarant'anni dal 1971* (Bologna, Il Mulino, 2012).

[62] Crisafulli (n 58) 74 ff (against the idea of the *indirizzo politico* as a 'fourth' function of the state). S Cassese and R Perez, *Istituzioni di Diritto Pubblico* (Roma, La Nuova Italia Scientifica, 1989) 58.

between government and Parliament: the vote of confidence, based on the general government programme,[63] reconciles the requirement of coordination in the definition of state political directions with the respect of the independence and autonomy of either branch of government.[64] Parliament participates in the setting of the *indirizzo politico* by issuing political instructions in regard to the executive.[65] In practice, the procedural decline of the *indirizzo politico* formula is so broad and undefined[66] that its connection with other parliamentary functions, including the oversight of the executive, is still questioned.

On the one hand, it has been argued that the *indirizzo politico* is external to the dimension of the oversight of the executive. Two sets of reasons support this argument. First, whereas the oversight function is permeated by manifold patterns of interaction between the government and the political components represented in Parliament, the *indirizzo politico* is strongly rooted in the *continuum* between government and its parliamentary majority.[67] Second, political directions may be addressed to the executive branch in the stages of government formation and policy-making,[68] but they usually do not involve the stage of policy implementation and follow-up that are among the domain of parliamentary oversight.

On the other hand, the identification of different dimensions of parliamentary oversight – referable to the *controllo-direzione* (*control-dirección*), beside the *controllo-verifica* (*control-fiscalización*)[69] – has implicitly contributed to highlight the intimate connection of the oversight and the political direction functions. Whereas the latter (*controllo verifica*) corresponds to the ex post dimension of parliamentary oversight as a mechanism for evaluating the results achieved by the executive branch in the fulfilment and implementation of a certain policy,[70] the former (*controllo-direzione*) specifically attains the ex ante stage of policy-making. It indicates the dimension of the oversight function that is aiming to fulfil government's duty to conform the conduct of executive affairs to the directions imparted by the Parliament. This dimension of the oversight power is (in its original conception) the domain of parliamentary majority[71] that, through

---

[63] P Furlong, 'Institutional fragmentation in parliamentary control: the Italian case' (2004) 10 *The Journal of Legislative Studies* 174, 187.

[64] Galizia (n 58) 186 ff.

[65] Manzella, *Il Parlamento* (n 3) 303 (on the difference between the *indirizzo politico* 'of the government' – which is defined exclusively by the executive branch – and the 'governmental' *indirizzo politico* – which must be defined jointly by the government and the Parliament). A Manzella, 'Le funzioni del Parlamento in Italia' (1974) 24 *Rivista Trimestrale di Diritto Pubblico* 375.

[66] ML Mazzoni Honorati, *Lezioni di diritto parlamentare*, 3rd edn (Torino, Giappichelli, 1999) 316.

[67] A Rinella, 'L'opposizione parlamentare. Profili di diritto costituzionale' in G Dalla Torre (ed), *Studi in onore di Giovanni Giacobbe*, II (Milano, Giuffrè, 2010) 201 f (only the parliamentary majority participates in the setting of political directions, jointly with the government; by contrast, the opposition has the task of overseeing the *indirizzo politico* of the government). *Contra*, A Mannino, *Rapporti tra maggioranza e opposizioni. Note introduttive* (Milano, Giuffrè, 1999) 199.

[68] A Manzella, *I controlli parlamentari* (Milano, Giuffrè, 1970) 8.

[69] S Sicardi, 'Controllo e indirizzo parlamentare' in *Digesto delle discipline pubblicistiche*, IV (Torino, Utet, 1989) 102; Baldassarre, 'Il Parlamento come soggetto di indirizzo e di controllo politico' in Vv Aa, *Attualità e attuazione della Costituzione* (Roma, Bari, 1979).

[70] V Casamassima, *L'opposizione in parlamentare: le esperienze britannica ed italiana a confronto* (Pisa, Il Campano, 2008) 431.

[71] L Ciaurro, 'Maggioranza e opposizioni nelle procedure di controllo parlamentare: l'esperienza del Senato' in E Rossi (ed), *Maggioranza e opposizioni nelle procedure parlamentari* (Padova, Cedam, 2004) 103.

the approval of acts in the plenary (such as motions and resolutions), serves its role as a 'transmission belt' between Parliament and government.

The latter perspective captures the most dynamic side of the oversight function. It is the fulfilment of a cyclical conception of the executive–legislative relationship that, through the definition of clear political directions in the ex ante stage, sets the premises of the ex post evaluation. In this cycle of action, the traditional cleavage between the *indirizzo politico* as a majority-centred domain and the oversight as the dominion of the opposition is reconfigured. Oversight also instrumental to the setting of political directions addresses a plurality of technical policy issues that cannot be defined by the majority alone, as they require a larger political consensus.[72] An example of how effectively the ex ante oversight can be used by Parliament to orient and sideline executive decisions is offered by the German Bundestag, where the notions of *Begleitende Kontrolle* (accompanying oversight) and *Richtungskontrolle* (directional oversight) respectively define the majority's action in the guidance and direction of ministerial and even administrative decisions.[73] This instance of ex ante oversight may occur at different stages and manifest itself in different forms, unfolding through the participation in plenary or committee debates, the drafting of reports, the submission of questions and resolutions, thus potentially involving all the available oversight tools.[74]

This vision, that stresses the interference of the direction of political power with the oversight prerogatives of Parliament, has gained increased relevance in the ever-expanding field of the scrutiny of EU affairs.[75] After the entry into force of the Lisbon Treaty, many parliaments were deprived of the oversight machinery of the 'mandates' available to legislatures in Denmark, Sweden, Austria, Estonia, Finland, Latvia, Poland and Slovakia.[76] The only possible way to overcome this limitation was by activating the standard mechanisms of the *indirizzo politico*. As a matter of fact, in the hybrid architecture of the EU, parliamentary oversight at all levels (European, national and sub-national) is often permeated by the purpose of issuing instructions addressed to the government and evaluating ex ante its conduct of EU affairs.[77]

These trends make it irrelevant to solve the original dilemma on the nature of the *indirizzo politico* in the parliamentary practice, whether it sets an autonomous function of

---

[72] A Manzella, 'Controllo parlamentare e forme di governo' (1995) 15 *Quaderni costituzionali* 311, 313.

[73] M Schwarzmeier, *Parlamentarische Mitsteuerung* (Wiesbaden, Westdeutscher, 2001); and J Krause, 'Der Bedeutungswandel parlamentarischer Kontrolle: Deutscher Bundestag und US-Kongreß im Vergleich' (1999) 30 *Zeitschrift für Parlamentsfragen* 534, 535. A Le Divellec, *Le gouvernement parlementaire en Allemagne. Contribution à une théorie générale* (Paris, LGDJ, 2004) 307 ff; and A Le Divellec, 'La problématique du contrôle parlementaire de l'administration' in B Seiller (ed), *Le contrôle parlementaire de l'administration* (Paris, Dalloz, 2010).

[74] ST Siefken, *Parlamentarische Kontrolle im Wandel: Theorie und Praxis des Deutschen Bundestages* (Baden-Baden, Nomos, 2018) 105 ff.

[75] Manzella, 'Il Parlamento come organo' (n 6) 2.

[76] See D Finke and M Melzer, *Parliamentary Scrutiny of EU Law Proposals in Denmark: Why do Governments Request a Negotiation Mandate?* (Vienna, Institute for Advanced Studies, 2012); K Auel, O Rozenberg and A Thomas, 'Lost in Transaction? Parliamentary Reserves in EU Bargains' (2012) 10 *OPAL Online Paper Series*. See below ch 4, section II.B (nn 78–83).

[77] National parliaments' participation in the EWS is often conveyed by the approval of resolutions, preventative opinions, authorisations (see below ch 4, section IV.C (nn 259–70). N Lupo, 'The Scrutiny of the Principle of Subsidiarity in the Procedures and Reasoned Opinions of the Italian Chamber and Senate' in A Jonsson Cornell and M Goldoni (eds), *National and Regional Parliaments in the EU-Legislative Procedure Post-Lisbon The Impact of the Early Warning Mechanism* (Oxford, Hart Publishing, 2017).

the legislative body[78] or, rather, it is part of a macro-function labelled 'indirizzo, surveillance and oversight' through which Parliament tries to extend and strengthen its prerogatives in regard to the executive.[79] The latter perspective is actually gaining increased relevance in all those policy areas where parliaments are unable to exercise an effective decision-making power by means of their legislative function.

III. The Ex Post Dimension of Parliamentary Oversight: Post-Legislative Scrutiny and the Evaluation of Public Policies

The ex post dimension of parliamentary oversight can be referred to as the implementation and enforcement stage, which presides over law enactment and policy execution.[80] Since by common rule government action finds its legal basis in a legislative act, this sphere of intervention is labelled 'post-legislative scrutiny'.[81] The ex post stage of law-making was traditionally conceived as instrumental to the evaluation of the formal implementation of legislative acts, serving as a purely legal dimension to assess law enactment (*narrow dimension*). However, in the framework of what has been described as the 'end-to-end' nature of an effective legislative process,[82] the substantial dimension of ex post impact assessment, whose purpose is to evaluate the effectiveness and efficiency of public policies,[83] has gained increased momentum (*broad dimension*).[84]

In contemporary democracies, the scope of the ex post stage of law-making is related both to the monitoring of how laws are implemented and to the evaluation of what impact they produce.[85] As a consequence, by 'post-legislative scrutiny' we consider all the activities carried out by parliaments in the ex post stage of legislation; the label 'evaluation of public policies' is instead covering the impact assessment carried out to check the effects produced by a specific policy or piece of legislation. Although different institutions are involved in this stage, keeping legal implementation under control is primarily considered a task for the Parliament.[86]

---

[78] V Longhi, *Elementi di diritto e procedura parlamentare* (Milano, Giuffrè, 1982) 167.

[79] Giménez Sánchez (n 59) 97. On the *indirizzo político* as part of the oversight function, ML Díez-Picazo Giménez, 'Actos de los procedimientos de control, impulso e información' in F Sáinz Moreno (ed), *Los actos del Parlamento (Instituciones de Derecho Parlamentario II)* (Vitoria, Parlamento Vasco, 1999) 144.

[80] U Karpen, 'Introduction' in U Karpen and H Xanthaki (eds), *Legislation in Europe. A Comprehensive Guide for Scholars and Practitioners* (Oxford, Hart Publishing, 2017) 9 f.

[81] A Brazier, 'Post-Legislative Scrutiny' (2017) 8 *Global Partners Governance, Guide to Parliaments* 1.

[82] ibid. U Karpen, 'Good Governance through Transparent Application of the Rule of Law' (2009) 11 *European Journal of Law Reform* 213, 219.

[83] F De Vrieze, *Principles of Post-Legislative Scrutiny by Parliaments* (London, Westminster Foundation for Democracy, 2018) 4. S Naundorf and C Radaelli, 'Regulatory Evaluation *Ex Ante* and *Ex Post*: Best Practice, Guidance and Methods' in U Karpen and H Xanthaki (eds), *Legislation in Europe* (eds), *A Comprehensive Guide for Scholars and Practitioners* (Oxford, Hart Publishing, 2017).

[84] U Karpen, 'On the State of Legislation Studies in Europe' (2005) 7 *European Journal of Law Reform* 59, 62 ff (the narrow dimension relates to legal analytics, legal methodology and legal technique; the broader dimension is supported by the research of effectiveness).

[85] A Meuwese and P Popelier, 'The Legal Implications of Better Regulation: An Introduction' (2011) 17 *European Public Law* 455.

[86] U Karpen, 'Comparative Law: Perspectives of Legislation' (2003) 17 *Anuario Iberoamericano de Justicia Constitucional* 141, 168.

It is at this stage that parliamentary oversight enters the domain of the evaluation of public policies; the boundaries between these two spheres of activities are extremely blurred, up to the point that it is extremely difficult to establish whether they represent two distinct functions or whether, by contrast, the evaluation of public policies constitutes a specific implementation of the traditional oversight function.[87]

A. Oversight, Post-Legislative Scrutiny and Evaluation

There are several ways to classify parliamentary functions, depending on the constitutional tradition, on the legal framework and also on the selected approach (legal or political).[88] However, neither post-legislative scrutiny, nor the evaluation of public policies are among the traditional functions.

Some national constitutions acknowledge the evaluation of public policies as a formal task of Parliament, thus setting the premises for its proceduralisation and recognition as a 'real' function. Mentions in the constitution are still extremely rare. Switzerland was the first country in the world to introduce an evaluation clause at the constitutional level.[89] Also, France[90] and Sweden[91] have their constitutional clauses. However, these are still isolated cases, often resulting from recent reforms. In the large majority of countries, post-legislative scrutiny and ex post evaluation have a weak legal basis and are rather part of the 'unseen' and informal work that is carried out in parliaments.[92] From a theoretical standpoint, these are not fully-fledged parliamentary functions and can hardly be considered functions at all, for three sets of reasons.

First, post-legislative scrutiny is not at all physiologically a 'parliamentary' activity: a wide range of institutions and agencies are involved in the post-legislative stage. Government or independent authorities are, in most cases, preferred bodies for performing regulatory

---

[87] A Delcamp, 'La perception du contrôle parlementaire. Comment le rendre plus attractif?' (2010) 134 *Pouvoirs* 109, 114 (it is doubtful whether evaluation is part of the oversight function or whether these are two distinct and complementary activities).

[88] Bagehot, *The English Constitution* (n 9) *passim* (distinguishing among the elective, expressive, teaching and informing, legislative functions). JS Mill, *Considerations* on Representative Government' (1861) in JS Mill, *The Collected Works of John Stuart Mill, XIX – Essays on Politics and Society*, 3rd edn (London, Longman-Green, 1865) 430 (highlighting the importance of the function of 'controlling the business of government'). R Blackburn and A Kennon et al, *Griffith and Ryle on Parliament: Functions, Practice and Procedures* (London, Sweet & Maxwell, 2003); C Leston Bandeira and L Thompson, *Exploring Parliament* (Oxford, Oxford University Press, 2018); P Blachèr, *Le Parlement en France* (Paris, LGDJ, 2012) (on the distinction between legislative and non-legislative functions).

[89] See art 170 of the Swiss Confederal Constitution of 18 April 1999 (calling the Federal Assembly to ensure that federal measures are evaluated with regard to their effectiveness), further implemented by arts 27 and 40 of the Swiss Parliament Act.

[90] Art 24 of the French Constitution, amended in 2008, and further implemented by *Loi no 96-517*, 14 June 1996, by the *Loi organique no 2001-692*, 1 August 2001, on the *lois de finances* (so-called *LOLF*), and by the two Houses' Rules of Procedure.

[91] Chapter 4, art 8 of the Instrument of Government that entered into force on 1 January 2011, which is further regulated by the Riksdag Act and by the Riksdag guidelines adopted in 2001 and 2006 (Riksdag, *Forskning och framtid, uppföljning och utvärdering. Arbetsgruppen för genomförande av Riksdagskommitténs förslag*, Stockholm, Riksdagstryckeriet, 2006).

[92] W Bagehot, 'The Non-Legislative Functions of Parliament' (1860) in N St John-Stevas (ed), *The Collected Works of Walter Bagehot*, VI (London, The Economist, 1986) 41; and W Bagehot, 'The Unseen Work of Parliament' (1861) in N St John-Stevas (ed), *The Collected Works of Walter Bagehot*, VI (London, The Economist, 1986) 47 f.

impact assessment.[93] In multilayer systems such as the EU, post-legislative scrutiny strongly relies on inter-institutional dynamics.[94] Many reasons seem to stand against the structural involvement of parliaments in this activity, among which are political, resource, organisation and time constraint.[95]

Second, post-legislative scrutiny and ex post evaluation rarely have the structure of a proper function.[96] There is no one single definition of what constitutes a function in public law and in political science. However, the administrative Napoleonic tradition defines the 'function' as an action associated to the fulfilment of a well-defined goal, supported by the appropriate means. In the field of parliamentary law, no explicit constitutional basis is strictly required to identify the functions entrusted in representative assemblies; the latter can be derived from constitutional or other equivalent provisions on parliamentary prerogatives and powers. Yet, conventionally parliamentary functions are expected to draw on a political decision or activity that results in a formal vote in committee or in the plenary or in any case produces a procedural outcome.[97] Since post-legislative scrutiny is most often developed on an informal basis and kept at the 'administrative' level with no procedural outcome, the conditions for structuring a formal function are not always met.

Third, comparative data on the experience of different European parliaments seem to confirm that under the label 'post-legislative scrutiny' legislatures comprise a vast range of activities. Parliaments' involvement in this sphere might be supported either by 'administrative' strategies, such as the strengthening of the documentation and evaluation capacity, or by 'political' strategies focused on the reinforcement of parliaments' influence on government in the ex post stage. Three models have subsequently been identified to describe the main attitudes of parliaments with regard to these mechanisms: passive, informal and formal scrutinisers (see below, section B).[98] On the whole, practices are quite inconsistent, which makes it challenging to trace a common line of development in different countries.

Combining all these reasons, a more radical question can be raised: why should representative assemblies be concerned about policy evaluation and impact assessment? These tools are either implemented in presidential systems to control how delegated agencies exercise the regulatory powers;[99] or they are promoted in the EU context to enhance the

---

[93] P Popelier, 'Management of Legislation' in U Karpen and H Xanthaki (eds), *Legislation in Europe. A Comprehensive Guide for Scholars and Practitioners* (Oxford, Hart Publishing, 2017) 55 f.

[94] See the Interinstitutional Agreement on Better Law-Making, 13 April 2016, OJ L 123/1, 1–14, which replaces a former agreement dating back to 16 December 2003, OJ C 321, 12–18; CM Meuwese, *Impact Assessment in EU Lawmaking* (The Netherlands, Kluwer Law International, 2008) 51 ff.

[95] A Renda, *Impact Assessment in the EU. The State of the Art and the Art of the State* (Brussels, Centre for European Policy Studies, 2006) 43 ff; Karpen, 'On the State of Legislation Studies in Europe' (n 84) 68 ff (the control of standards cannot harness the political nature of parliaments' engagement in law-making). Some counter-arguments are offered in E Griglio, 'Better Law-Making and the Integration of Impact Assessment in the Decision-Making Process: The Role of National Parliaments' in A De Feo and B Laffan (eds), *Scrutiny of EU Policies* (Fiesole, European University Institute, 2017).

[96] L Boulet, 'La notion de fonction administrative' (1966) 113 *La Revue administrative* 474, 478 ff.

[97] E Fuzier-Herman, *La séparation des pouvoirs d'après l'histoire et le droit constitutionnel* (Paris, Librairie de A Marescq Ainé, 1880) 342 ff; and J Barthélémy, *L'introduction du régime parlementaire en France sous Louis XVIII et Charles X* (Paris, Giard & Brière, 1904) 219 ff.

[98] E Griglio, 'Post-Legislative Scrutiny as a Form of Executive Oversight. Tools and Practices in Europe' (2019) 2 *European Journal of Law Reform* 118.

[99] CM Radaelli and F De Francesco, 'Regulatory impact assessment' in R Baldwin, M Cave and M Lodge (eds), *The Oxford Handbook of Regulation* (Oxford, Oxford University Press, 2010).

position of the European Commission in the law-making and foster stronger democratic legitimacy.[100] Similar conditions are not met in national parliamentary systems, where the legislative assembly is endowed with a direct legitimation and a firm position in the legislative process. In the national context, therefore, post-legislative scrutiny is used to complement and support the 'traditional' parliamentary functions (law-making and oversight of the executive, primarily),[101] providing extra accountability to the circuit of representation and decision-making.

The thesis assumed in the monograph is that parliaments' engagement in post-legislative scrutiny can be included in the exercise of parliamentary oversight, since it is in this stage that government might be asked to account for its conduct of executive affairs. On the one hand, the cyclical conception of the law-making process[102] – whereby the entry into force of the statutory Act continues in the law enforcement stage where premises for the inception of future legislative initiatives are also set[103] – would clearly identify post-legislative scrutiny as an extension of the legislative function.[104] The cyclical conception of law-making is instrumental to the better regulation discourse and has become a permanent programme of the Organisation for Economic Co-operation and Development (OECD) and a pivotal target in the institutional agenda of the EU. To fulfil this task, parliaments often resort to specific legislative techniques, such as the introduction of sunset or review clauses.[105] In this vein, post-legislative scrutiny serves as a learning process for legislatures willing to ascertain the impact of legislation and check that the needs of relevant stakeholders are met.[106]

On the other hand, it is the connection with the oversight function that best serves the purposes of post-legislative scrutiny and gives this dimension procedural practicability. Legislative bodies can play a concrete role in the ex post stage of law-making not on account of their decision-making power, but through the oversight relationship with the executive. Parliaments cannot bypass executive action in the post-legislative stage, since they must rely on government bodies for information and data on legislative implementation. At the same time, governments are also the actual addressees of parliamentary engagement in post-legislative scrutiny. Therefore, parliaments can try to orient, mould, monitor and evaluate executive action by holding the government accountable for the conduct of public policies.

To fulfil this task, the post-legislative dimension relies on both technical and political mechanisms.[107] Expertise, access to information and technical analytical capacity are a prerequisite for effective post-legislative scrutiny. However, the final outcome should be

---

[100] P Popelier, 'Governance and Better Regulation: Dealing with the Legitimacy Paradox' (2011) 17 *European Public Law* 555, 558 ff; and P Popelier, 'A legal perspective on Regulatory Impact Assessment' (2017) Paper for the International Symposium on Regulatory Impact Analysis, Luxembourg – 23, 24 November 2017.

[101] Griglio, 'Post-Legislative Scrutiny' (n 98).

[102] S Weatherhill, *Better Regulation* (Oxford, Hart Publishing, 2007).

[103] L Mader, 'Evaluating the Effects: A Contribution to the Quality of Legislation' (2001) 22 *Statute Law Review* 119. Theoretically, this vision turns out to be consistent with the procedural rationality advocated by N Luhmann, *Legitimation durch Verfahren*, 6th edn (Frankfurt am Main, Suhrkamp, 2006).

[104] P Noll, *Gesetzgebungslehre* (Hamburg, Reinbeck, 1973) (on 'legisprudence' or 'legistics' as a theoretical and practical science aiming at improving the quality of norms through a focus on the whole regulation cycle).

[105] A Kouroutakis, *The Constitutional Value of Sunset Clauses: An Historical and Normative Analysis* (New York, Routledge, 2017).

[106] F De Vrieze, 'Introduction to Post-Legislative Study' (2019) 21 *European Journal of Law Reform* 84, 84 f.

[107] M De Benedetto, M Martelli and N Rangone, *La qualità delle regole* (Bologna, Il Mulino, 2011) 126.

referred to the political relationship between the executive and legislative branches. As a matter of fact, two types of parliamentary tools serve post-legislative scrutiny: the fact-finding tools, aimed at seeking information, explanation and policy positions from the government; and the oversight tools directed at holding the government to account for the outcomes achieved. The two dimensions are equally relevant to give parliaments effective means of judgement and influence.

B. Comparing Parliaments' Approaches to Post-Legislative Scrutiny

Post-legislative scrutiny can be analysed from a comparative perspective based on a combination of structural and marginal factors assumed as explanatory variables. Structural factors are the exogenous conditions – constitutional and political – which contribute towards shaping the 'oversight-accountability' relationship. Marginal factors consist of endogenous features or strategic choices met or set by Parliament when facing post-legislative scrutiny. Combining these factors, three main approaches to post-legislative scrutiny emerge.[108]

The first approach – 'passive scrutinisers' – identifies the basic instance of post-legislative scrutiny. Parliaments limit their role to the assessment of the scrutiny conducted by governmental bodies or external agencies. Under this 'passive' attitude, parliaments do not directly engage in monitoring legislative implementation and impact assessment, relying on 'external' reports and evaluations. Since most OECD countries lack a strong parliamentary tradition in respect of impact assessment,[109] this approach may sound particularly attractive when post-legislative scrutiny covers the broad dimension. The German Bundestag is deemed to fall under the category of passive scrutinisers. An ex post review of law enactment is conducted by the Bundestag resorting to the standard scrutiny/oversight mechanisms and by the Bundesrat through its constitutionally settled powers on the federal oversight of law execution (Articles 80, 83, 84 and 85 of the Constitution). As for the broad dimension of post-legislative scrutiny, the Bundestag indirectly scrutinises the ex-post assessment carried out either by the government or by two independent bodies, the Federal Statistical Office and the National Regulatory Reform Council, established by federal law in 2006.[110]

The second approach – 'informal scrutinisers' – also comprises the goals and tasks of the first approach. Parliaments may decide to engage in a proactive approach that goes beyond the outsourcing of post-legislative scrutiny to the government or to external agencies. The first step requires establishing ad hoc administrative parliamentary structures, such as research and evaluation units providing ex post analysis of legislative implementation and impact assessment.[111] Whereas these tasks may ordinarily be fulfilled by 'traditional'

---

[108] Griglio, 'Post-Legislative Scrutiny' (n 98). Developing on this categorisation, a fourth approach, labelled 'independent scrutinisers', is detected by F De Vrieze, *Post-Legislative Scrutiny in Europe. How the oversight on the implementation of legislation by Parliaments in Europe is getting stronger* (London, Westminster Foundation for Democracy, 2019) and associated to practices in the UK, see below (nn 122–23).

[109] OECD, *Better Regulation in Europe: Germany 2010* (Geneve, OECD, 2010). On the increasing use of impact assessment and evaluation across European parliaments, see however I Anglmayer, *Better Regulation practices in national parliaments* (Brussels, European Parliamentary Research Service Study, 2020).

[110] N Johnson, *State & Government in the Federal Republic of Germany: Executive at Work*, 2nd edn (Oxford, Pergamon Press, 2016) 101 ff; and U Karpen, 'Regulatory Impact Assessment: Current Situation and Prospects in the German Parliament' (2015) 101 *Amicus Curiae* 17.

[111] EM Poptcheva, 'Policy and legislative evaluation in the EU' (European Parliament, Library of the European Parliament Briefing, 3 April 2013).

administrative structures – such as research and documentation units[112] – the creation of ad hoc units not only confirms a strong commitment towards ex post scrutiny[113] but also enables the channelling of technical expertise beyond the traditional legal-economic background of parliamentary officials.

Parliaments falling within this category are considered 'informal' scrutinisers insofar as the connection with formal parliamentary procedures is a-systematic. There is no provision of ad hoc formal proceedings and tools able to provide a follow up on the ex post internal (administrative) analytical capacity and to address the government.[114] Parliamentary bodies can nonetheless resort to these analytical resources in their standard scrutiny/oversight of the executive. Moreover, independently of their procedural outcome, large publicity is usually provided to the analytical results achieved. The case of Italy is regarded as falling within this category.[115]

The third approach – 'formal scrutinisers' – is the most inclusive, as it is also deemed to cover the purposes and activities of the first two categories. In the most 'advanced' instance, parliaments address post-legislative scrutiny in a formal and highly institutionalised manner. The function is legally grounded, vested on parliamentary (political) bodies, supported by ad hoc procedures and inclusive of both the legal and the impact assessment. The cases of Sweden, France and, with some differences, also the UK are considered to fall within this category. The Parliament enjoys formal competence, which in the experience of Sweden and France is established in constitutional clauses resulting from recent amendments.[116] Both the formal and the substantial verification of law implementation and its outcomes are part of the scrutiny.[117] The role of committees is strategic. Follow-up and evaluation have become natural tasks for standing or select committees that can rely on multiple sources of information and documentation,[118] including the connection with the ex post budgetary control.[119]

---

[112] IPU and IFLA, 'Guidelines for Parliamentary Research Services' (2015) 20. R Miller, R Pelizzo and R Stapenhurst, *Parliamentary Libraries, Institutes and Offices: The Sources of Parliamentary Information* (Washington, World Bank, 2004) 2 ff. F Fitsilis and A Koutsogiannis, 'Strengthening the Capacity of Parliaments through Development of Parliamentary Research Services' (2017) Paper presented at the 13th Workshop of Parliamentary Scholars and Parliamentarians, Wroxton.

[113] S Gailmard and JW Patty, 'Slackers and Zealots: Civil Service, Policy Discretion, and Bureaucratic Expertise' (2007) 51 *The American Journal of Political Science* 873. C Neuhold and S Vahoonacker, 'Introduction' in C Neuhold et al (eds), *Civil Servants and Politics* (Basingstoke, Palgrave, 2013).

[114] AL Högenauer, C Neuhold and T Christiansen (eds), *Parliamentary Administrations in the European Union* (Basingstoke, Palgrave, 2016) 21.

[115] G Piccirilli and P Zuddas, 'Assisting Italian MPs in Pre-Legislative Scrutiny: The Role Played by Chambers' Counsellors and Legislative Advisors in Enhancing the Knowledge and Skills Development of Italian MPs: The Assistance Offered to an Autonomous Collection of Information' (2012) 65 *Parliamentary Affairs* 672. G Regonini, 'Parlamenti analitici' (2012) 1 *Rivista Italiana di Politiche Pubbliche* 45.

[116] P Türk, *Le contrôle parlementaire en France* (Paris, LGDJ, 2011) 176 ff. JF Calmette, 'L'évaluation des politiques publiques: un moyen de control de l'action du gouvernement' in X Magnon et al (eds), *Pouvoir exécutif et Parlement: de nouveaux équilibres?* (Aix-en-Provence, PUAM, 2012).

[117] Sénat, 'Rapport d'information fai tau nom de la délégation du Sénat pour la planification sur l'évaluation des politiques publiques en France' (2004) 391 *Annexe au procés verbale de la Séance du 30 Juin 2004* Ch 1.

[118] Art 47 of the French Constitution and art 58.2 LOLF, allowing finance committees to assign investigative tasks to the Cour des comptes.

[119] C Aström, 'Evaluation et qualité de la législation: Quel rôle pour les parlements?' (2013) 1 *Sénat, Actes de colloque*. P Amselek, 'Le budget de l'État et le parlement sous la V République' (1998) 5–6 *Revue du droit public* 1444, 1449; I Bouhadana, *Les commissions des finances des assemblées parlementaires en France: origines, évolutions et enjeux* (Paris, LDGJ, 2007) 273 ff; A Baudu, *Contribution à l'étude des pouvoirs budgétaires du Parlement en France: éclairage historique et perspectives d'évolution* (Paris, Dalloz, 2010).

Notwithstanding these common inputs, the procedural outcomes of post-legislative scrutiny cannot be taken for granted. In the Riksdag, procedimentalisation of post-legislative scrutiny triggers formal discussion of the outcomes of the evaluation process.[120] By contrast, in France ex post evaluation has led primarily to the reinforcement of fact-finding and inquiry tools, with no major procedural follow-up and only occasional unofficial interaction with the government on required implementing measures.[121] Another variation comes from the experience of the UK, where a rather proactive approach to post-legislative scrutiny has been promoted in Parliament in the last decade.[122] Post-legislative work is not only legally grounded and referred to both legal and impact assessment; it is also resulting in the drafting of parliamentary reports, accessible to the public, that require a follow-up on behalf of the government, forcing the relevant minister to provide a response.[123]

The three proposed categories are not intended to be strict. Parliaments often change their approach and combine features belonging to different formulas. The European Parliament is a relevant example of a hybrid model sharing elements of all the three categories: on the one hand, it is expected to scrutinise the ex post evaluations of the European Commission – so-called fitness checks – which are carried out to assess the regulatory framework of a policy area;[124] on the other hand, it has its own ex post IA mechanisms, centred on the work of the impact assessment service established in 2013 within the Directorate General for Parliamentary Research Service.[125] Notwithstanding its strong evaluation capacity, the procedural outcomes achieved are only occasionally able to exercise an influence on the policy cycle. The engagement of the European Parliament in the ex post stage is mainly supported by an inter-institutional vision of better law-making, involving all the bodies participating in the legislative cycle.[126] Due to the institutional architecture of the EU,[127] that makes the position of the European Parliament vis-a-vis the 'executive power' not comparable to the legislative–executive arrangement featuring domestic democracies, the oversight/accountability purposes are much weaker.

---

[120] Chapter 7 of the Riksdag Act. See A Forsberg, 'Contribution to the General Debate on "The work of parliamentary committees"' (2008) Paper presented at the Meeting of the Association of Secretary Generals of Parliament, Cape Town, April 2008.

[121] Assemblée Nationale, 'Fiche de synthèse n 52: Le contrôle de l'application des lois et l'évaluation de la législation et des politiques publiques' (6 Juin 2017). P Preuvot, 'Réflexion sur les remèdes aux difficultés d'application des lois' (2011) VIII Congrès Français de Droit constitutionnel, Nancy, 18 June 2011 16 ff.

[122] R Kelly and M Everett, 'Post-Legislative Scrutiny' (2013) SN/PC/05232 *UK House of Commons Library Standard Note* 1.

[123] For these peculiar reasons, the UK Parliament has been associated with an autonomous approach to post-legislative scrutiny, namely of independent scrutinisers; see De Vrieze, *Post-Legislative Scrutiny in Europe* (n 108) 22 f.

[124] See the Regulatory Fitness and Performance Programme (REFIT), COM (2012) 746 fin.

[125] See below ch 4, section III.B (nn 171–72). A Renda, 'European Union and Better Law-Making: Best Practices and Gaps' in The Best Practices in Legislative and Regulatory Processes in a Constitutional Perspective (workshop), Study for the AFCO Committee (Brussels, European Parliament, 2015) 5 ff. On the growing institutionalisation of ex post evaluation in the European Parliament, see I Anglmayer and A Scherrer, 'Ex-post evaluation in the European Parliament: an increasing influence on the policy cycle' (2020) *Journal of legislative studies*.

[126] The same vision is supported in OECD 'Recommendation of the Council on Regulatory Policy and Governance' (22 March 2012).

[127] P Magnette, 'Appointing and censuring the European Commission: the adaptation of parliamentary institutions to the Community context' (2001) 7 *European Law Journal* 292, 307; V Schmidt, 'Federalism and State Governance in the European Union and the United States: An Institutional perspective' in K Nicolaïdis and R Howse (eds), *The Federal Vision: Legitimacy and Levels of Governance in the United States and the European Union* (Oxford, Oxford University Press, 2001) 339; M Goldoni, 'Politicising EU Lawmaking? The Spitzenkandidaten Experiment as a Cautionary Tale' (2016) 22 *European Law Journal* 279, 285.

This comparative overview shows how post-legislative scrutiny can be implemented resorting to standard scrutiny/oversight tools or activating ad hoc procedures and bodies. A different mix of parliamentary tools instrumental to post-legislative scrutiny might lead either to 'administrative' strategies, which strengthen the research and evaluation capacity of Parliament, or to 'political' strategies, whose purpose is to enhance Parliament's influence on the government.

In all these cases, post-legislative scrutiny has the potential for executive oversight. The first approach is the weakest: since information is outsourced and the scrutiny is mediated by external bodies, independent evaluation of the work of the government is rarely allowed.[128] In the second case, the parliamentary ability to develop ex post evaluation skills is higher, but this does not automatically trigger an equivalent capacity to hold the government to account. Finally, the third attitude might result in instances of 'hard' oversight,[129] given the formal involvement of political bodies both in the conduct of preliminary fact-finding and evaluation and in the channelling of scrutiny outcomes.

In fact, beyond any categorisation, parliaments' attitudes towards post-legislative scrutiny must necessarily be framed in a broader picture, inclusive of the overall parliament–government interaction. From this perspective, it is easily understood why, under a parliamentary form of government, assemblies tend to use the outcomes of post-legislative scrutiny flexibly, leaving the follow-up of scrutiny outcomes open to the dialogue with the government.

IV. Oversight Through Parliamentary Information: Publicity and Communication

The relationship with the informative function is a structural component of parliamentary oversight. On the one hand, information is the first stage of the accountability process.[130] During this stage, fact-finding is of primary concern and Parliament needs to gather data from different sources beyond government in order to reconstruct the executive purposes and achievements *in concreto*.[131] Improving the transparency of government operations is deemed to be a fundamental step for enhancing public trust in the government, which is considered a condition of effective policy delivery.[132] On the other hand, parliamentary oversight closely interacts with what Walter Bagehot defined as the 'expressive' and the 'informing' function: Parliament's office is 'to express the mind of the … people on all matters which come before it' and 'to inform the Sovereign what was wrong', laying the grievances and the complaints before the Nation.[133] The connection with information

---

[128] G Loewenberg and SC Patterson, *Comparing Legislatures* (Boston, Little, Brown and Company, 1979) 164.
[129] See below ch 4, section VI.B (n. 392).
[130] R Mulgan, 'Accountability: An Ever-Expanding Concept?' (2000) 78 *Public Administration* 555.
[131] AJ Meijer, 'Transparent Government: Parliamentary and legal accountability in an information age' (2003) 8 *Information Polity* 69.
[132] H Yamamoto, *Tools for Parliamentary Oversight: A Comparative Study of 88 National Parliaments* (Geneva, Inter-Parliamentary Union, 2007) 10.
[133] Bagehot, *The English Constitution* (n 9) 119.

provides a means for linking the institutional dimension of the executive–legislative inter-action to the social dimension of the control by the wider public.[134] If parliaments are the *locus* where oversight departs, public society is the *locus* where oversight is directed, because it is at this stage that this function may exercise its effects.[135]

In this vein, a rather successful distinction was made in political science, based on the experience of the US Congress, between two types of oversight mechanism:[136] *police patrol* as a centralised, active and direct form of oversight, whose aim is to detect and remedy any violations of legislative goals; and *fire alarms* as a system of rules, procedures and informal practices enabling individual citizens and organised interest groups to exercise a surveillance over administrative bodies.[137] Due to its multipurpose nature, the informative function serves parliamentary oversight in two distinct ways: it acts as a tool instrumental both to the enforceability of the oversight function and to the effectiveness of its outcomes. It serves at the same time as an input and output of Parliament's engagement in the scru-tiny of government.[138] Therefore, the connection between parliamentary oversight and the informative function raises two main requirements.

First, it is the requirement of Parliament's access to relevant information concerning executive action. In this vein, parliamentary oversight has been defined as a 'right to compre-hensive information relating to all executive actions'.[139] This need is gaining increased relevance in the current institutional framework where executive dominance is reflected in the concentration of relevant information and control of the political power and financial resources in the hands of a few government members and officials.[140]

Different explanations are offered in political science and constitutional law to legitimise this right. In political science, the need to grant Parliament comprehensive information arises from the manifest asymmetries affecting the position of the legislative and execu-tive branches in the access to information on policy-making.[141] The agency relationship is strongly challenged by situations of hidden information and action between Parliament and government that limit MPs' margin for manoeuvre.[142] Problems of moral hazard, relating

---

[134] P Lauvaux 'Le contrôle, source du régime parlementaire, priorité du régime présidentiel' (2010) 134 *Pouvoirs* 23.

[135] M Aragón Reyes (n 2) 27.

[136] MD McCubbins and T Schwartz, 'Congressional oversight overlooked: police patrol versus fire alarms' (1984) 28 *The American Journal of Political Science* 165.

[137] LC Dodd and RL Schott, *Congress and the Administrative State* (New York, Wiley & Sons, 1979); and MS Ogul, 'Congressional Oversight: Structure and Incentives' in L Dodd and B Oppenheimer (eds), *Congress Reconsidered* (New York, Praeger, 1977) (on the differences between *formal* and *informal* oversight).

[138] As argued by the Spanish Tribunal Constitucional in the SSTC 203/2001, para 3 and 32/2017, para 5, informa-tion as a means for parliamentary oversight can comply its effects in the act of procurement or can be instrumental to further judgement or evaluation.

[139] C Möllers, *The Three Branches: A Comparative Model of Separation of Powers* (Oxford, Oxford University Press, 2013) 121. F Meinel, 'Confidence and Control in Parliamentary Government: Parliamentary Questioning, Executive Knowledge, and the Transformation of Democratic Accountability' (2018) 66 *The American Journal of Comparative Law* 317, 348.

[140] JK Johnson, 'The Role of Parliament in Government' (2005) WBI Working Papers 1.

[141] D Curtin, 'Challenging Executive Dominance in European Democracy' (2014) 77 *Modern Law Review* 12, 31. F Fabbrini, EH Ballin and F Somsen, 'Introduction: A New Look at the Form of Government of the European Union and the Eurozone' in F Fabbrini, EH Ballin and F Somsen (eds), *What Form of Government for the European Union and the Eurozone?* (Oxford, Hart Publishing, 2015) 2.

[142] A Lupia, 'Delegation and its Perils in K Strøm, W Müller and T Bergman (eds), *Delegation and Accountability in Parliamentary Democracies* (Oxford, Oxford University Press, 2003) 35 ff.

to ministers that find incentives to take unobservable action contrary to the Parliament's interest, may similarly arise.[143]

From a constitutional law perspective, it is correctly argued that 'an explicit power of Parliament to demand or access executive information and knowledge is not part of the textual tradition of Western constitutionalism'.[144] However, the fact that legislative assemblies need information to fulfil their constitutional functions is 'an old and common insight of constitutional theory'.[145] The constitutional framework of information basically relies on the acknowledgement of the executive's general duty to report to Parliament on the conduct of public policies. This acknowledgement is supported by two opposing arguments.

The first argument frames the executive reporting duty among the requirements implied in the confidence relationship. In any systems, there needs to be a certain degree of cooperation between the branches of government, because each side must be willing to bargain and compromise in order to get some policy benefits.[146] This statement is particularly true in parliamentary systems where members of government, irrespective of their formal status of parliamentarians or unelected ministers, have specific rights and duties to participate in the business of Parliament and to contribute to it in terms of information provided, opinions cast and debates.[147] Government reporting duty finds its limit in the protection of confidential information related to 'official' secrets set in specific fields of state activity, such as the defence and intelligence services.[148] Parliaments' access to confidential information needs to be regulated, and therefore limited. A wide scope of discretion in official secrets on the side of executive institutions is clearly incompatible with the commitment to principles of openness and democratic oversight.[149]

The opposing argument claims that reporting duties are not proper to parliamentary government since they undermine the idea of the fusion between the executive and the legislative branches, starting a dualism between the two powers.[150] The introduction of executive duties to report to Parliament can only be conceived of as compensation for the loss of substantive powers suffered by the legislature on other grounds.[151] This compensation theory is particularly convincing in explaining ongoing trends in national parliaments' access to information affecting the conduct of European affairs. Broadly speaking, in the

---

[143] K Strøm, 'Parliamentary Democracy and Delegation' in K Strøm, W Müller and T Bergman (eds), *Delegation and Accountability in Parliamentary Democracies* (Oxford, Oxford University Press, 2003) 86.

[144] Meinel (n 139) 325. T Mendel, *Parliament and Access to Information: Working for Transparent Governance*, WBI Working Paper Series (Washington, World Bank Institute, 2005) 1 (on the existence of international standards protecting MPs' right of access to information and Parliament's role as an information provider).

[145] C Harlow, 'Freedom of Information and Transparency as Administrative and Constitutional Rights' (1999) 2 *Cambridge Yearbook of European Legal Studies* 285. R Peled and Y Rabin, 'The constitutional right to information' (2011) 42 *Columbia Human Rights Law Review* 357, 358 ff.

[146] National Democratic Institute for International Affairs, 'Strengthening Legislative Capacity in Legislative-Executive Relations' (2000) 6 *NDI Legislative Research Series* 4.

[147] Yamamoto (n 132) 11.

[148] S Eskens, O van Daalen and N van Eijk, *Ten standards for oversight and transparency of national intelligence services* (Amsterdam, Institute for Information Law, 2015).

[149] V Abazi, *Official Secrets and Oversight in the EU: Law and Practices of Classified Information* (Oxford, Oxford University Press, 2019) 97 ff. C Moser, *How open is 'open as possible'? Three different approaches to transparency and openness in regulating access to EU documents* (Vienna, Institute for Advanced Studies, 2001) 5.

[150] Meinel (n 139) 354 f.

[151] ibid 348 f.

EU framework, where a confidence architecture is still lacking,[152] secrecy about the activity of certain intergovernmental bodies, such as the Council, the European Council and other less formalised organisms (Eurosummit and Eurogroup), is deemed to be the source of many 'democratic deficits': it 'weakens the position of the European Parliament ... and even worse, it curtails the controlling powers of the national parliaments'.[153] However, the above-mentioned compensation theory demonstrates why, beginning in the 1990s, alongside incremental reforms in support of European integration, in several Member States constitutional amendments were passed to promote Parliament's involvement in EU affairs.[154]

Second, the connection between the oversight and the informative function flows through the transparency of parliamentary action: this prerequisite gives civil society the right of access to a wide range of relevant information deemed necessary to participate in policy-making.[155] Under this dimension, parliaments as transparency providers[156] become a fundamental component of the transmission belt that engages citizens in the public governance and enables them to hold the final decision-makers accountable.[157] Controlling the government by publicising executive decisions and structuring a public debate is among the fundamental purposes of modern constitutionalism.[158] It is regarded as essential to the democratic process because 'without an adequate flow of information even *ex post de facto* accountability of the governors to the people is meaningless'.[159] The oversight dimension instrumental to information and transparency is a *trait d'union* between presidential and parliamentary systems.[160] It is strategic in presidential forms of government where the need to counterbalance the role of the presidency requires a corresponding growth in the transparency standards through the intervention of Parliament.[161] At the same time, it has demonstrated its potential fully in the context of the EU.[162]

---

[152] See below ch 7.

[153] A Verhoeven, 'The Right to Information: a Fundamental Right? in Vv Aa, *An Efficient, Transparent Government and the Right of Citizens to Information, Conference Proceedings* (Maastricht, EIPA, 2000) 1, 4, referring to the secrecy of the Council.

[154] Meinel (n 139) 349, referring to the German constitutional trends affecting the role of the Bundestag and the Bundesrat in the scrutiny of EU affairs.

[155] Mendel (n 144) 8 and 32 (parliaments are key stakeholders in promoting open governance).

[156] T Larsson, 'How Open Can a Government Be? The Swedish Experience' in V Deckmyn and I Thomson (eds), *Openness and Transparency in the European Union* (Maastricht, European Institute of Public Administration, 1998) 41.

[157] Moser (n 149) 4.

[158] Verhoeven (n 153) 5 (transparency of government action includes a wide range of participatory mechanisms involving citizens).

[159] D Curtin, 'Democracy, Transparency and Political Participation: Some Progress Post-Amsterdam' in V Deckmyn and I Thomson (eds), *Openness and Transparency in the European Union* (Maastricht, European Institute of Public Administration, 1998).

[160] García Roca, 'Control parlamentario' (n 1) 92.

[161] C Mora-Donatto, 'Instrumentos constitucionales para el control parlamentario' (2001) *Cuestiones constitucionales* 85.

[162] D Curtin, 'Betwixt and Between: Democracy and Transparency in the Governance of the European Union' in J Winter, D Curtin, A Kellerman and B de Witte (eds), *Reforming the Treaty on the European Union – The Legal Debate* (Maastricht, Kluwer Law International, 1996); and M Westlake, 'Maastricht, Edinburgh, Amsterdam: the "End of the Beginning"' in V Deckmyn and I Thomson (eds), *Openness and Transparency in the European Union* (Maastricht, European Institute of Public Administration, 1998) 126 f.

In fact, in contemporary democracies Parliament is no longer the only subject able to provide transparency and knowledge to civil society. Non-parliamentary actors, such as interest groups, may find a channel for accessing information and knowledge about policy-making. Freedom of information legislation contributes to the disclosure of large sectors of executive information. Private actors often satisfy their informative requirements outside the procedural and institutional framework of Parliament.[163] In this vein, from the perspective of transparency and information, it is argued that the strengthening of direct control by private stakeholders weakens the usefulness and effectiveness of political control by the legislature, thus apparently accounting for the 'disjoining of the institution and the function, ie, of parliament and control'.[164]

This assumption can be challenged from various perspectives. First, the type of control performed by private stakeholders can be defined as 'interest based, economically biased, and issue specific'.[165] On the contrary, parliamentary oversight is the outcome of a political judgement, expressing the pluralism of ideas, perceptions and visions represented in legislative assemblies, addressing either a specific or a broad area of government responsibility. Second, stakeholders' control is structurally unable to produce any follow-up on the government sphere of action. Private control is not at all neutral in regard to the executive. By mobilising the media and addressing public opinion directly through social media, it can produce rather disruptive effects on the reputation of the government in charge. However, there is no possibility to structure a formal interaction between private actors and the government, thus confirming that these control mechanisms are able to work exclusively in one direction, without supporting any form of advanced interaction between the controller and the controlled. On the contrary, the distinctive feature of parliamentary oversight lies in the instrumental connection with government accountability which can be enforced both through binding procedures, eventually associated with the application of sanctions, and through soft mechanisms resulting in the co-definition of political directions.

These trends must be confronted with the new information technologies that, fostering what has been defined as the 'mediatic democracy',[166] deeply affect both aspects of parliamentary oversight's connection with the informative function. On the one hand, information technologies are valid tools for granting parliaments timely and extensive access to a wide range of executive information, leading 'to more informational and analytical transparency of government organisations for parliamentary and legal accountability'.[167] In fact, an over-abundance of information and documents on the side of the government may paradoxically prevent parliaments from making use of this knowledge and engaging in effective scrutiny, thus resulting in a parliamentary habit of passiveness.[168] On the other hand, advanced

---

[163] Griglio, 'Better law-making' (n 95) 64 ff (an example is offered by the practice of consultations in EU better law-making that directly involves civil society but does not provide any dedicated channel of participation for national parliaments).

[164] Meinel (n 139) 347. These trends are gaining increased relevance in the EU; see D Curtin, 'Transparency and political participation in EU governance: A role for civil society?' (1999) 3 *Cultural Values* 445.

[165] Meinel (n 139) 346.

[166] Le Divellec, 'Des effets du contrôle parlementaire' (n 10) 126.

[167] Meijer (n 131) 75.

[168] AJ Meijer and M Bovens, 'Public accountability in the information age' in M Palmirani, T van Engers and MA Wimmer (eds), *Workshop in conjunction with JURIX 2003* (Laxenburg, International Federation for Information Processing, 2003) 23.

information technology is a facilitator of civil society's access to relevant information as well as of their participation in public decision-making.[169] The side effect shows the increased difficulty in filtering and interpreting a large amount of information and data that seriously limit the opportunity for an individual critical analysis.[170]

From a broader viewpoint, the two examined perspectives on the relationship between the oversight and the informative function advocate some caution. With regard to the first perspective, maximising the transparency and openness of government action does not automatically result in the enhancement of government's accountability before Parliament. Transparency is increasingly concerned with the outcomes of government action rather than with the process of holding the government to account; the emphasis is therefore on results rather than process, but in the long run 'results do not compensate for lack of process accountability'.[171] Since transparency is expected to deliver efficiency beyond democracy, the principle of democratic accountability increasingly overlaps with that of economic performance, thus mixing input and output legitimacy requirements.

On the second perspective, transparency of parliamentary action is a due premise for wider democratic control of government action, but the connection between the two stages is not always automatic. Parliamentary oversight serving the purposes of information might not necessarily result in the enforcement of 'hard' mechanisms forcing the government either to provide an answer or to follow a specific line of action. In most cases, oversight as a means of granting transparency finds its final outcome in the release of the information, in the decision to debate publicly certain issues or to disclose specific facts that were previously excluded from the domain of public opinion. This form of 'soft' oversight raises a direct 'media' accountability of the government before civil society that does not trigger any political sanctions but can nonetheless result in severe judgements on behalf of citizens.[172]

---

[169] Curtin, 'Transparency and political participation' (n 164) 460 ff; see D Lathrop and L Ruma, *Open Government: Collaboration, Transparency and Participation in Practice* (Beijing, O'Reilly, 2010) ('openness' is a value which incorporates both the right of access to documents and the right to participate in the decision-making). D Curtin and J Mendes, 'Transparence et Participation: des Principes Démocratiques Pour l'Administration de L'Union Européenne' (2011) 137–38 *Revue Française d'Administration Publique* 101 ff (open government has two components, namely 'vision' and 'voice': citizens need information to *see* what is going on within government and participation to *voice* their opinions about this).

[170] AJ Meijer, D Curtin and M Hillebrandt, 'Open Government: connecting vision and voice' (2012) 78 *International Review of Administrative Science* 15.

[171] T Erkkilä, *Government Transparency. Impacts and Unintended Consequences* (New York, Palgrave, 2012) 23.

[172] P Riddell, 'Impact of Transparency on Accountability' in N Bowles, JT Hamilton and DA Levy (eds), *Transparency in Politics and the Media. Accountability and Open Government* (New York, Palgrave, 2014).

4

Classifying Oversight Tools According
to Parliamentary Practice

The polymorphic vision of parliamentary oversight discussed in chapter three deeply influences its enforcing mechanisms. Oversight of the executive unfolds through a large variety of settings. Oversight can be manifest or latent, it can occur in official or unofficial settings, it can be direct or indirect, it may consist of planned and active or reactive and passive efforts, it can be adversarial or supportive, it can be used to evaluate executive programmes and activities or to provide leverage over its specific actions or officials.[1]

Based on long-established comparative convention,[2] literature[3] and jurisprudence[4] place within the oversight function a variety of tools to be used either in the plenary or in committee. The list of parliamentary oversight tools is not fixed and unalterable. Due to the multi-procedural nature of this function, any parliamentary tool can potentially contribute to the oversight of the executive. However, in line with the original definition of parliamentary oversight as a non-legislative sphere of activity, only non-legislative tools are included within the scope of this function. Consideration of the oversight tools available may not be an exhaustive determinant of the oversight capacity and effectiveness of a Parliament;[5] yet, the analysis of implementing mechanisms is a relevant point for comparing alternative approaches and enforcing solutions.

Oversight tools and procedures may find their legal base in the Constitution. But it's in the Rules of Procedure that they meet a more extensive regulation. At this level, the cross-fertilisation of oversight mechanisms and practices across countries is quite intense. The circulation of models and rules from the British parliamentarism to the traditional Jefferson's Textbook on Parliamentary Practices has favoured the setting of common regulatory principles and oversight procedures.[6] Nonetheless, comparative parliamentary law shows a large variety of implementing mechanisms, up to the point that the same typology

---

[1] FM Kaiser, 'Congressional Oversight of the Presidency' (1988) 499 *The Annals of the American Academy of Political and Social Science* 75, 81 f, referring to the congressional experience.

[2] See above ch 2, section I (n 28).

[3] FJ García Roca, 'Control parlamentario y convergencia entre presidencialismo y parlamentarismo' (2016) 38 *Teoría y Realidad Constitucional* 61, 79 and 88.

[4] See in particular the Decision of the Spanish Tribunal Constitucional STC 124/2018 (above ch 2, section III) that offers a (non-exhaustive) list of tools and procedures related to the oversight function.

[5] R Maffio, '*Qui custodiet? ipsos custodes?* Il controllo parlamentare dell'attività di governo in prospettiva comparata' (2002) 9 *Quaderni di scienza politica* 333 (on the correlation between oversight tools/potential/capacity). R Pelizzo and F Stapenhurst, *Government Accountability and Legislative Oversight* (New York, Routledge, 2014) 32 ff (on the other factors that influence the oversight effectiveness of a Parliament).

[6] Pelizzo and Stapenhurst, *Government Accountability* (n 5) 26–27.

Figure 1 Oversight parliamentary tools: An overview

Instances of parliamentary oversight	Informative tools instrumental to oversight[7]	(Ex ante) oversight tools	Hybrid oversight tools	(Ex post) oversight tools
PURPOSE	Collecting evidence in order to enable an informed judgement Fostering a confrontation with government members	Checking government's plans and programmes with regard to future policy actions Influencing the course of government's future policy action	Collecting information Checking government's purpose with regard to future policy actions Assessing government's past conduct of public affairs	Assessing governmental performances
TOOLS	Political tools: • Government reporting duties to Parliament • Committee informative tools (hearings; fact-finding investigations; informative missions) Technical tools: • Reports from external bodies (independent authorities and agencies, supreme audit institutions, advisory bodies, etc) • Documentation from parliamentary administration	Tools that do not involve a vote in the plenary or in committee: • Debates • Communications or statements of the government Tools that invoke the responsibility of the government: • Motions of investiture/confidence • Motions of no confidence/censure • Questions of confidence Tools that do not invoke the responsibility of the government: • Motions • Resolutions • Parliamentary mandates/reserves in the field of EU affairs • Votes on other types of 'proposal'	Questioning: • Written questions • Oral questions (in committee and in the plenary) • Premier Question Time • Interpellations	Committees of inquiry Select committees
INTERACTION WITH OTHER FUNCTIONS	Informative function	Political direction	Informative function Political direction Legislative function	Legislative function
POLICY-INFLUENCING CAPACITY	None	Strong	Weak	Weak

[7] Having regard to the two dimensions of the oversight-informative function highlighted in ch 3, section IV, only the tools supporting the first purpose (Parliament's right to information) are considered in section III; the tools supporting the second purpose (transparency as a means for connecting the oversight outcomes to the wider public) are instead mentioned in section I. Parliamentary tools serving the purposes of budgetary oversight will be examined in ch 8.

of act can correspond to substantially differing oversight standards and procedures, thus making it difficult to trace common lines of development. Due to the multifunctional nature of parliamentary procedures, oversight tools may fulfil at the same time more tasks, addressing executive accountability from different perspectives. Figure 1 offers a picture of the prevailing purposes attached to the most relevant oversight tools.[8]

After a general overview of the main classification criteria (sections I and II), the chapter analyses the parliamentary tools reported in the Table, following their prevailing purpose.

I. Pairing Oversight Tools and Procedures According to Parliamentary Practice

The tools and procedures fulfilling the oversight function can be classified in several ways, depending on their purpose, on the allocation of the power to initiate the procedure, on the participation allowed to majority and opposition groups, on the type of interaction required from the government, and on the mechanisms supporting the enforcement of parliamentary will. Another relevant criterion of classification focuses on the implementation stage in committee or in the plenary. The analysis of these criteria highlights the potential of the tools associated with each category in terms of 'capacity' and not of 'effectiveness'.[9]

Figure 2 Alternative criteria for classifying the main parliamentary oversight tools

Purpose	
Fact-finding tools	Hearings, government reports, government communications and statements, missions, fact-finding investigations, questions, interpellations
Deliberative tools	Motions, resolutions, select committees, inquiry committees
Power to initiate the procedure	
Individual tools	Written and oral questions, interpellations (in some parliaments), inquiry committees (from the viewpoint of the power to initiate the procedure), motions and resolutions (in some parliaments)
Collective tools	Interpellations (in some parliaments), motions of investiture/of no confidence, select committees, inquiry committees (with regard to the power to set the committee), missions, motions and resolutions (in some parliaments), government communications and statements

(continued)

---

[8] M Sánchez de Dios, 'Parliamentary Accountability in Europe: How do parliaments of France, Italy and Spain fight information asymmetries?' (2008) Paper prepared for the Workshop 'Comparing legislatures worldwide: roles, functions and performance in old and new democracies, ECPR Joint Sessions, Rennes, 11–16 April 2008 5 f (structures the 'menu of oversight mechanisms' distinguishing between the type of resource – oversight by MPs, general control in plenary sessions and specialised control in committee – and the task – general oversight, policy supervision, critical control, *indirizzo* or policy orientation, sanction, negotiation).

[9] Parliamentary indicators and benchmarks available in a comparative perspective to evaluate the effectiveness of tools affecting executive accountability are examined in M O'Brien, R Stapenhurst and L von Trapp, *Benchmarking and Self-Assessment for Parliaments* (Washington, World Bank Group, 2016).

Figure 2 *(Continued)*

Majority/opposition preferences in the selection of oversight tools	
Majority preferred tools	Tools resulting in a vote in plenary session
Opposition preferred tools	Committee oversight tools
	Tools that do not require a vote in Parliament (such as questions and interpellations)
Type of interaction engaged with the government	
Unilateral oversight tools	Motions, resolutions, inquiry and select committees
Participatory tools	Questions, interpellations, debates in the plenary or in committee, hearings
Enforcing mechanism	
Binding tools	Motions of investiture/of no confidence
	Inquiry committees (with regard to government's legal duty to provide evidence and to be heard in committee)
	Negotiating mandates (Denmark and Sweden)
	Appraisal of government appointments (in selected cases in Italy and France)
Non-binding tools	All the remaining tools
Implementing stage	
Committee tools	Questions, resolutions, hearings, debates, fact-finding investigations, missions, inquiries, government reports, government communications and statements
Plenary tools	Questions, interpellations, resolutions, motions, debates, government reports, government communications and statements

With regard to purpose, oversight tools approximate two main goals: opposing the search for information (fact-finding tools) and deliberation (deliberative tools). Some procedures are mostly aimed at collecting information and data from the government or from other relevant institutions in order to enable the setting up of a parliamentary evaluation framework. This is the case of hearings, government reports, missions, fact-finding commissions, questions and interpellations. On the contrary, other procedures unfold through a vote in the plenary or in committee and this deliberation fixes the will of Parliament in a certain field, formulating an evaluation of government action. Motions, resolutions, select committees, and inquiry committees are all examples of parliamentary tools that may result in the adoption of a final document, suited to be voted.

From the perspective of the power to initiate the procedure, only a few types of oversight tools are available to MPs on an individual basis. The first historic cases of oversight procedures came out of the initiative of individual parliamentarians;[10] this choice was only

---

[10] See the first question, tabled by Earl Cowper, mentioned in section V (n 279).

possible in a period that still had not experienced the development of modern political parties and groups.[11] Contemporary legislatures have inherited and confirmed the 'individual' oversight procedures rooted in the history of parliamentarism, such as questions and short debates.[12] This legacy is deemed to bring about inefficiency, because it risks overburdening the workload of parliamentary assemblies, without offering any guarantee of a real political follow-up. In fact, the chance offered to individual MPs to raise specific oversight instances, either connected to a constituency concern or to a focused policy interest,[13] can be seen as an opportunity to satisfy the requirement of pluralistic representation in the oversight function. Moreover, some of the individual procedures, such as written questions, offer the advantage of being unconstrained from the agenda setting, which is usually strictly controlled by the government.[14] Finally, information gathered through individual initiatives is shared with other MPs, thus offering a collective added value.[15] Apart from these cases, the vast majority of oversight mechanisms are vested in 'political' groups, thus becoming 'collective' tools for parliamentary oversight.[16] Some tools can be initiated only by a minimum number of MPs or by a parliamentary group. This requirement is fully compatible with the political nature of the oversight function whose dynamics in a parliamentary regime are strongly party-dependent. Cases of collective oversight tools are offered by interpellations, such as the German *Große Anfrage* (major interpellation),[17] inquiry or select committees, motions and resolutions.

Majority and opposition preferences in the selection of oversight tools set another relevant criterion of classification. The opposition tends to rely on the activation of tools and procedures that do not result in a deliberation and a vote.[18] The opposite can be said for the majority. The position of the initiator(s) also makes a difference in the implementation of the oversight procedures. By common understanding, oversight tools are suited more to the opposition than to the majority. Some tools – such as questions, interpellations, motions and resolutions – may have more opportunity to be scheduled and debated, depending on whether or not the initiator(s) belong(s) to the opposition. Parliaments have adopted different solutions to reinforce the right of the opposition to have their oversight tools and proposals placed on the agenda. The allocation of oversight lots to minority groups is among

[11] H Yamamoto, *Tools for Parliamentary Oversight: A Comparative Study of 88 National Parliaments* (Geneva, Inter-Parliamentary Union, 2007) 11.

[12] F Russo and M Wiberg, 'Parliamentary Questioning in 17 European Parliaments: Some Steps towards Comparison' (2010) 16 *The Journal of Legislative Studies* 215, 216 ff.

[13] T Saalfeld, 'Parliamentary Questions as Instruments of Substantive Representation: Visible Minorities in the UK House of Commons, 2005–10' (2011) 17 *The Journal of Legislative Studies* 271; and S Bailer, 'People's Voice or Information Pool? The Role and Reasons for Parliamentary Questions in the Swiss Parliament' (2011) 17 *The Journal of Legislative Studies* 302.

[14] H Döering, 'Time as a Scarce Resource: Government Control of the Agenda' in H Döering (ed), *Parliaments and Majority Rule in Western Europe* (New York, St Martin's Press, 1995).

[15] Yamamoto (n 11) 11.

[16] García Roca (n 3) 67.

[17] See below, section V.B.

[18] A Rinella, 'L'opposizione parlamentare Profili di diritto costituzionale' in G Dalla Torre (ed), *Studi in onore di Giovanni Giacobbe*, II (Milano, Giuffrè, 2010) 207; and AJ Sánchez Navarro, *La oposición parlamentaria* (Madrid, Congreso de los Diputados, 1997) 112 ff.

the standard guarantees associated to the 'status' of the opposition.[19] Different solutions are adopted, including the 'Opposition Days' of the House of Commons,[20] the reserve of one fifth of time available to proposals tabled by the opposition in the Italian Chamber,[21] the right allowed to each president of opposition or minority group of the French National Assembly to obtain the inscription of a debate without a vote or a questioning session in the week reserved to parliamentary oversight.[22] The allotment of committee chairs to members of the opposition is another means to channel independence and effective pluralism in the oversight action.[23] Nonetheless, parliamentary rules and practices demonstrate that oversight of the executive can be effectively exercised through cooperation between majority and opposition members.[24] This is a distinctive feature of the oversight function that can only rarely be found in law-making.

Since oversight is a relational dimension, its tools and procedures are based on a dual scheme that combines parliamentary action with government reaction. The executive is never allowed to be passive and yet the degree of government involvement changes from one procedure to another. Broadly speaking, it is possible to distinguish unilateral from participatory oversight tools. The former allow the Parliament to adopt a unilateral position in regard to the executive without asking the government to provide an answer in the Chamber, since the follow-up to the oversight initiative is postponed and externalised. In these procedures, the government is not a pivotal actor: it may be required to provide information or to state its position on a certain policy direction, but the oversight scheme does not require its intervention to be completed. Tools such as motions, resolutions, inquiry and select committees fall into this category. The opposite happens in the case of participatory oversight tools: these mechanisms start a dialogue between Parliament and government members and they are completed only once the oversight initiative from one or more MPs is followed up by the executive either providing an answer or appearing in Parliament. In such cases, receipt of the government reply is necessary to have a formal conclusion to the oversight procedure. Debates in the plenary or in committee, hearings, questions, interpellations, are examples of participatory tools.

Finally, oversight tools and procedures differ in the outcome produced. Oversight outcomes are always relational in nature, which means that they are produced to be shared directly with the government, and indirectly with the citizens. Two main types of outcome should be distinguished. Formal procedural outcomes encompass the publication of

---

[19] S Giulj, *Le Statut de l'Opposition en Europe* (Paris, La Documentation française, 1980); and S Giulj, 'Confrontation or Conciliation: the Status of the Opposition in Europe' (1981) 16 *Government and Opposition* 476, 493 f; P Norton, 'Making Sense of Opposition' (2008) 14 *The Journal of Legislative Studies* 236; P Avril, 'Le statut de l'opposition: un feuilleton inachevé? (Les articles 4 et 51-1 de la Constitution)' (2008) 254 *Petites Affiches* 9 (on the status of the opposition as a form of 'positive discrimination').

[20] Rule 14 (2–3) House of Commons Standing Orders.

[21] Art 24(3) Rules of Procedure.

[22] Resolution no 437 of 28 November 2014.

[23] See below section II.B and section VI.

[24] A Delcamp, 'La perception du contrôle parlementaire. Comment le rendre plus attractif?' (2010) 134 *Pouvoirs* 109, 116.

a report, the adoption of an act addressing the government, the inception of a dialogue between MPs and members of government or simply the scheduling in the agenda of an issue, for public debate. There is not always a predefined correspondence between oversight tools and outcomes, since each tool can produce more than one procedural exit[25] and can potentially lead to further, unforeseen, forms of executive–legislative interaction.[26] The unwritten rule of parliamentary regimes on the cooperative modes of interaction between government and Parliament actually demands for a follow-up on the side of the executive even when this is not formally required. For instance, committee reports usually make recommendations for government action which do not formally require a follow-up, but 'it is a vital part of the oversight process that government should be required to consider and respond to them formally and in a timely manner'.[27]

Beyond the formal procedural exits, the importance of informal outcomes should not be underestimated. Representative assemblies have learned that connecting with the media can be a valuable means for disseminating their oversight action. Different informal tools can support this requirement, including the graduation of the publicity regime in committee, depending on the contextual framework[28] and on the confidential nature of the issues at stake,[29] and the creation of a web portal providing full access to documents and debates.[30]

II. Oversight: A Realm for the Plenary or for Parliamentary Committees?

A relevant criterion for classifying oversight tools focuses on the implementing stage that can involve either parliamentary committees or the plenary. Parliamentary committees are deemed to exercise a pivotal role in the fulfilment of the oversight function.[31] This represents a universal feature in all legislatures:[32] the committee stage is in fact best suited to serve the basic requirements of parliamentary oversight, for example, the organisation of hearings and the collection of data, the preparation of reports and the formulation of

[25] A Le Divellec, 'La problématique du contrôle' parlementaire de l'administration' in B Seiller (ed), *Le contrôle parlementaire de l'administration* (Paris, Dalloz, 2010) 16 (the formal conclusion of the oversight procedure through a 'decision' can represent a sort of implicit threat, which encourages the executive to take the procedure seriously).

[26] Delcamp, 'La perception du contrôle' (n 24) 117.

[27] IPU and UNDP, Inter-Parliamentary Union (IPU) and United Nations Development Programme (UNDP), *Global Parliamentary Report 2017. Parliament's power to hold government to account: Realities and perspectives on oversight* (France, Courand et Associés, 2017) 54.

[28] See the graduated solutions provided by art 8.9 of the Folketing Standing Orders.

[29] According to F Meinel, 'Confidence and Control in Parliamentary Government: Parliamentary Questioning, Executive Knowledge, and the Transformation of Democratic Accountability' (2018) 66 *The American Journal of Comparative Law* 317, 324, 'the more the instruments of control are made powerful and efficient in covering classified information, the less they can be public and contestable, and hence lose their parliamentary character'.

[30] Delcamp, 'La perception du contrôle' (n 24) 117.

[31] P Norton, *Parliament in British Politics*, 2nd edn (New York, Palgrave, 2013) (a weak committee system limits the capacity of the Chamber to oversee the executive). Similarly, K Strøm, *Minority Government and Majority Rule* (New York, Cambridge University Press, 1990).

[32] KC Wheare, *Government by Committee* (Oxford, Clarendon Press, 1955) (on the ubiquity of parliamentary committees).

recommendations.[33] In this vein, following the 2008 amendment of the Constitution, French scholars remarked that enhancing the oversight function of Parliament essentially means questioning the adequacy of the committee apparatus.[34]

The composition of parliamentary committees, featured by a mostly stable membership,[35] reduces party pressures on the handling of the oversight mechanisms.[36] Moreover, it allows focus on a specific department of government, thus supporting oversight procedimentalisation in partnership with the executive. The value of committees as a tool for overseeing government lies 'in their size and accessibility: committees allow a small group of members to examine in detail and over time a range of complex matters'.[37] Not by chance, in most parliaments committees' jurisdictions tend to replicate those of executive departments.[38]

Conducting oversight in committee rather than in the plenary may favour citizens' involvement in parliamentary business. Committees can invite experts or other relevant stakeholders to give evidence; public hearings can grant public opinion full disclosure of the issues at stake; online consultations can provide a valuable source of information and recommendations instrumental to effective oversight. Committees are therefore strategic bodies for providing the Chamber with the information that is needed to oversee the government.[39]

The fortune met by parliamentary committees in the daily practice of executive oversight does not preclude the plenary from acting as a key forum in the executive–legislative relation. A wide range of tools can be used in plenary sessions to foster a dialogue between parliamentary groups and members of government. Interpellations and questions, motions and resolutions, discussions on the whole package of government policy or on sectorial proposals engage the plenary in a public confrontation with the government on the conduct of public affairs.[40] Party groups have the opportunity to require clarifications from the government and at the same time to state their political position. Since plenary sittings are

---

[33] I Mattson and K Strøm, 'Parliamentary Committees' in H Döering (ed), *Parliaments and Majority Rule in Western Europe* (New York, St Martin's Press, 1995) 253 ff; and M Shaw, 'Parliamentary Committees: A Global Perspective' (1998) 4 *The Journal of Legislative Studies* 225, 236.

[34] C Vintzel, 'Renforcer le Parlement' français: Les leçons du droit comparé' (2017) 17 *Jus Politicum*. As a matter of fact, art 145 of the National Assembly Rules of Procedure was amended to strengthen the role of committees in evidence-gathering; see Assemblée Nationale, 'Le rôle des commissions permanentes en matière de contrôle du Gouvernement' (2016) 48 *Fiche de synthèse*.

[35] O Costa, E Kerrouche and P Magnette, 'Introduction. Le temps du parlementarisme désenchanté? Les parlements face aux nouveaux modes de gouvernance' in O Costa, E Kerrouche and P Magnette (eds), *Vers un renouveau du parlementarisme en Europe?* (Brussels, Ed de l'Université de Bruxelles, 2004) 18 (on the oversight role played by committees as a sign of the functional specialisation of MPs).

[36] D Olson, *The Legislative Process: A Comparative Approach* (New York, Harper and Row, 1980) 269; and E Damgaard, 'How Parties Control Committee Members' in H Döering (ed), *Parliaments and Majority Rule in Western Europe* (New York, St Martin's Press, 1995).

[37] IPU and UNDP, *Global Parliamentary Report 2017* (n 27) 46.

[38] An exception is represented by the Danish Folketing whose committees have narrower jurisdictions than ministries. See Mattson and Strøm (n 33) 270.

[39] F Götz, 'Das Informationsungleichgewicht zwischen Regierung, Verwaltung und Parlament' (1988) 33 *Publizistik. Vierteljahresschrift für Kommunikationsforschung* 633.

[40] Shaw (n 33) 226 (on plenary meetings as 'largely a series of meetings of informal "committees"', being attended by a small number of interested members).

usually held in open sessions,[41] oversight in the Chamber provides maximum publicity and transparency,[42] which is an added value for connecting Parliament and the public.[43]

Some tools (such as questions, debates and resolutions) can be carried out both in committee and in the plenary. Other tools are specific to the committee stage (this is the case, inter alia, for hearings, informative reports, missions, inquiries). One main limit of plenary oversight tools, such as interpellations, is that they are 'repressive' tools, as they intervene once the act is done. By contrast, oversight in committee offers the opportunity of real cooperation between MPs and the government which is the best way to perform ex ante scrutiny; this corresponds to a different way of holding the government to account, mediated by participation in executive action.[44]

The difference between the two stages of implementation should be compared with the traditional distinction (now increasingly blurred) between 'working' and 'talking' parliaments.[45] From a broad perspective, oversight in committee relates to the tradition of the 'working' parliaments: being typical more to presidential than to parliamentary systems, this tradition has had a major influence on those countries (including Germany, Sweden and Denmark) that had experienced a long non-parliamentary phase.[46] Oversight in the plenary is instead linked to the tradition of the 'talking' parliaments, based on the Westminster model, that tend to approach the oversight function from the perspective of the public critique.

Some authors have argued that parliamentary oversight has suffered from an excess of separation between the rituals of the plenary sessions and the work in committee.[47] Existing difficulties in comparing and connecting these two stages are exacerbated by the fact that oversight in parliamentary committees is surprisingly under-theorised.[48] Since committees' involvement in the oversight function unfolds in a 'soft' form, through informative, cooperative and non-binding mechanisms, it is extremely difficult to evaluate and measure *in concreto* the impact produced.[49] These difficulties are heightened by existing asymmetries in the arrangement of committee systems across parliaments of the world,[50] which can be described following the distinction between committees devoted to systemic oversight of ministerial policies and ad hoc oversight committees.

---

[41] Art 48(4) of the French Constitution, amended in 2008, provides that at least one session in four is reserved in each House to the oversight of the executive and the evaluation of public policies. P Houillon, 'Le contrôle extraordinaire du parlement' (2010) 134 *Pouvoirs* 64 (the purpose of this provision is encouraging the Parliament to invest in the oversight and evaluation function, devoting to this activity the same publicity and solemnity of the legislative function).

[42] Yamamoto (n 11) 11.

[43] IPU and UNDP, *Global Parliamentary Report 2017* (n 27) 57.

[44] M Hariou, *Précis de Droit Constitutionnel*, 2nd edn (Paris, Recueil Sirey, 1929) 527 f.

[45] A Le Divellec, *Le gouvernement parlementaire en Allemagne. Contribution à une théorie générale* (Paris, LGDJ, 2004) 274. B Wessels, 'Roles and Orientations of Members of Parliament in the EU Context: Congruence or Difference? Europeanisation or not? (2005) 11 *The Journal of Legislative Studies* 446.

[46] A Le Divellec, 'Des effets du contrôle' parlementaire' (2010) 134 *Pouvoirs* 123, 127 f. O Rozenberg, 'Comparer les parlements' in JM de Waele and Y Déloye (eds), *Politique comparé* (Bruxelles, Bruylant, 2018).

[47] Delcamp, 'La perception du contrôle' (n 24) 116.

[48] M Benton and M Russell, 'Assessing the Impact of Parliamentary Oversight Committees: The Select Committees in the British House of Commons' (2013) 66 *Parliamentary Affairs* 772, 776.

[49] D Kriner and L Schwartz, 'Divided Government and Congressional Investigations' (2008) 33 *Legislative Studies Quarterly* 295, referring to presidential systems.

[50] Yamamoto (n 11) 11.

A. Systemic Oversight of Ministerial Policies: Continental Europe and Westminster Committee Systems

Parliaments are expected to oversee on a permanent basis the conduct of ministerial activities. This is the standard dimension of the executive–legislative oversight relation and it is carried out in permanent committees whose jurisdiction replicates the structure of ministries. Permanent committees, thanks to the constancy of their policy focus, contribute to what is defined as a '*systemic* oversight framework'.[51]

From a comparative perspective, two main types of committee system contribute to this purpose.[52] The majority of European parliaments vest the task of scrutinising the government in standing committees which are involved both in law-making and oversight; their scope may cover the monitoring of government departmental programmes, including budgetary performances, and at the same time the scrutiny of legislative Bills falling within their scope. This solution, derived from the committee system of the US Congress, is the preferred option in many European continental countries. In Denmark, France, Germany, Italy, Spain and – although with a distinctive arrangement – Sweden, permanent committees combine legislative and oversight tasks. This model has also been imported in the European Parliament.

The implementation of this model and the associated outcomes in terms of oversight performances change significantly from one Parliament to another. In Italy and Spain, the presence of hybrid committees has led historically to the prominence of the legislative activity, which has exhausted the capacity to invest in the oversight of the executive.[53] By contrast, in 1972 Denmark experienced a process of revision of the committee system which led to the specialisation of committee members in certain policy areas; by enabling MPs to accumulate expertise, this process resulted in a reinforced capacity to control the government and public administration.[54] In France, to prevent the imbalances of the Fourth Republic, committees were originally structured as extremely weak bodies, mostly involved in law-making. Their oversight prerogatives were substantially limited to the conduct of hearings, because the investigative function was reserved to inquiry committees. This arrangement substantially changed after the 2008 constitutional amendment, which took the number of standing committees (article 43 of the Constitution) from six to eight and contributed to the location of a well-assorted oversight and evaluation toolbox at the committee level.[55]

---

[51] IPU and UNDP, *Global Parliamentary Report 2017* (n 27) 51.

[52] J Barthélémy, *Essai sur le travail parlementaire et le système des commissions* (Paris, Librairie Delagrave, 1934) 10 ff; J Lees and M Shaw (eds), *Committees in Legislatures: A Comparative Analysis* (Oxford, Martin Robertson, 1979); J da Silva Ochoa (ed), *Las Comisiones Parlamentarias* (Vitoria, Parlamento Vasco, 1994); I Rens, 'Les commissions parlementaires en droit comparé' (1961) 13 *Revue internationale de droit comparé* 309.

[53] C Fasone, *Sistemi di commissioni parlamentari e forme di governo* (Padova, Cedam, 2008) 438; and B Vila Ramos, *Los sistemas de comisiones parlamentarias* (Madrid, Cepc, 2004) 369. J Jiménez Campo, 'Sobre el control parlamentario en Comisión' in Vv Aa, *Política y sociedad. Homenaje al profesor Murillo Ferrol* (Madrid, CIS-CEC, 1987).

[54] L Togeby et al, *Power and Democracy in Sweden. Conclusions* (Aarhus, Magtudredningen, 2004) 22. Thorarensen, 'Mechanisms for Parliamentary Control' (n 157) 83. Mattson and Strøm (n 33) 267.

[55] JP Duprat, 'Le Parlement entre modernisation et attentisme (L'article 24 de la Constitution)' (2008) 254 *Les Petites affiches* 35. JJ Urvoas, 'La lente mais irrépressible renaissance des commissions parlementaires' (2013) 146 *Pouvoirs* 21.

In Germany, the development of a hybrid committee system originated from the initial existence of a few committees with limited powers to make recommendations to the Bundestag on matters specifically referred to them. These bodies interacted with the committees of the major parties, a parallel structure with an intense evidence-gathering activity and interaction with the executive.[56] In 1969, committees were given the authority to examine any other subject in their remit and at the same time they saw their power to obtain independent information significantly reinforced.[57] In fact, the core of the oversight activity is performed outside standing committees, in ad hoc inquiry bodies.[58] In Sweden, the committee system was reorganised in 1971, in connection with the constitutional reform leading to the adoption of the 1974 Instrument of Government. Committees were brought into line with the structure of government departments and they were set as multifunctional bodies, enlisted with legislative, deliberative and investigative tasks.[59] In fact, the investigative toolbox of Swedish committees was completed quite late, with the introduction of public hearings in 1988,[60] and still today committees lack the power to start an inquiry.

Moreover, the systemic scrutiny of department activity has always been a prerogative of the Riksdag Constitution Committee, which dates back to 1809. Among its various engagements, the Committee has the task of scrutinising the work of the government and its ministers, gaining access to the records of government decisions, examining ministers' performance and the handling of government business.[61] Its investigative hearings are the only occasion on which the Swedish Prime Minister attends a Riksdag committee.[62] The Committee releases two reports yearly: the first report, published in December, offers a general overview of the administration of government, including responses to parliamentary questions and the enforcement of executive plans; the second report, staged in May, is a political review of ministers' action.[63] The Riksdag may make a formal statement to the government in consequence thereof. Some criticism has been raised towards the composition of the Committee that, reflecting the proportion between parliamentary groups, is apparently biased and unable to engage in objective evaluation of government performances; to limit this risk, since 1991 the chair of the Committee is allotted to a member of the opposition.[64]

The alternative committee system features the UK Parliament, which locates the oversight function in non-legislative committees. This solution is typical to Westminster, where

[56] N Johnson, 'Committees in the West German Bundestag' in J Lees and M Shaw (eds), *Committees in Legislatures: A Comparative Analysis* (Oxford, Martin Robertson, 1979).

[57] W Ismayr, 'Jahre Parlamentarismus in der Bundesrepublik Deutschland' (1999) 20 *Aus Politik und Zeitgeschichte* 14.

[58] H Plagemann, 'Mehr parlamentarische Kontrolle durch Untersuchungsausschüsse. Zu den Empfehlungen der Enquete-Kommission Verfassungsreform' (1977) 8 *Zeitschrift für Parlamentsfragen* 242.

[59] D Arter, *The Scottish Parliament: A Scandinavian-Style Assembly?* (New York, Routledge, 2004) 138 ff.

[60] ibid, 172 ff. See also below (n 127).

[61] Chapter 12, arts 1 and 2 of the Instrument of Government.

[62] D Arter, 'From "Parliamentary Control" to "Accountable Government"? The role of public committee hearings in the Swedish Riksdag' (2008) 61 *Parliamentary Affairs* 122, 138.

[63] ibid, 129.

[64] B Thorarensen, 'Mechanisms for Parliamentary Control of the Executive' in H Krunke and B Thorarensen (eds), *The Nordic Constitutions: A Comparative and Contextual Study* (Oxford, Hart Publishing, 2018) 80 f.

some committees (the *select committees*)[65] oversee the executive and others (including the Committee of the Whole) participate in the legislative process.[66] Different select committees are engaged in executive oversight: pursuant to Rule 152, the House of Commons appoints departmental select committees whose task is to examine the expenditure, administration and policy of the principal government departments and associated public bodies. Other non-departmental select committees may be created, including the Environmental Audit Committee.[67]

From the viewpoint of the connection with the legislative function, this arrangement corresponds to what is considered in literature as a weak committee system:[68] Westminster is actually depicted as 'the poor cousin of many European parliamentary committee systems'.[69] In fact, from the viewpoint of the oversight function, the effectiveness of executive oversight provided by the House of Commons select committees 'may exceed that in many other parliaments, where specialist committees must spend much of their time on scrutiny of government legislation'.[70] Moreover, committees that are exclusively tasked with oversight assignments are usually best equipped to perform this role from a procedural point of view. Their toolbox may include the power to send for persons, papers and records, to report from time to time, to appoint specialist advisers or to take evidence from external bodies.

As a matter of fact, compared with law-making, the evaluation of the oversight potential of any committee system is strongly dependent on the relationship with information and evidence.[71] In this vein, the main question is whether committees merely act as information providers in regard to the Chamber or whether they are also able to influence the outcomes of the oversight activity.

B. Ad Hoc Oversight Committees

Beyond the systemic oversight of ministerial policies, selected scrutiny tasks may be entrusted on ad hoc committees whose core mission is directly connected with the accomplishment of an oversight purpose. The latter may encompass the completion of fact-finding or informative activities instrumental to government accountability, the conducting of an inquiry, investigation or scrutiny mission, the vigilance or supervision of a targeted policy issue or public body.[72]

---

[65] K Mackenzie, *The English Parliament* (Middlesex, Penguin, 1959) 79 f.

[66] On recent attempts to strengthen Westminster committees, see A Kelso, *Parliamentary Reform at Westminster* (Oxford, Oxford University Press, 2009).

[67] Rule 152A House of Commons Standing Orders. See also below, section VI.B.

[68] See P Norton, 'Nascent Institutionalisation: Committees in the British Parliament' (1998) 4 *The Journal of Legislative Studies* 143 (on the British Parliament as a 'chamber-oriented institution').

[69] S Martin and R Whitaker, 'Beyond Committees: parliamentary oversight of coalition government in Britain' (2019) 42 *West European Politics* 1465; and R Fox and M Korris, *Making Better Law. Reform of the Legislative Process from Policy to Act* (London, Hansard Society, 2010) 147 f.

[70] Benton and Russell (n 48) 794.

[71] NCN Lin, 'Informative Committees and Legislative Performance in the American States' (2015) 40 *Legislative Studies Quarterly* 391 (legislative committees are not simply information providers, but also substantively influence the legislative process).

[72] See below, section III.A and section VI.

In many cases, ad hoc oversight committees have a temporary shape and they cease to function after they have concluded their mission, usually through the publication of a report.[73] The broad spectrum of inquiry committees may be included in this type of ad hoc temporary body. Temporary committees may be created to cope with emergency issues or public scandals, satisfying civil society's call for transparency and responsiveness on behalf of elected representatives. They can also be set to provide the Chamber with focused information on specific issues. This hypothesis finds explicit regulation in the German Bundestag, where study commissions may be set, also on the initiative of the opposition,[74] and in the Spanish Congress.[75] Ad hoc oversight committees may also be created on a permanent basis, to address oversight demands that escape from the traditional ministerial structure and require unconventional solutions. Different factors may lead to the assignment of an oversight task to an ad hoc permanent committee.

First, the oversight of cross-departmental policies is not always satisfied by the standard arrangement based on permanent – either hybrid or select – committees. Some spheres of decision-making require dedicated bodies, capable of covering the broad spectrum of departmental activity. The most significant examples are represented by the public accounts committees of Westminster systems, in their capacity as bodies responsible for the budgetary oversight.[76]

Another relevant case is offered by the European affairs committees which are set by national parliaments to address EU-related issues. These committees, whose composition normally reflects party representation in the plenary, may be entrusted with legislative tasks, but the bulk of their activity is scrutinising government's conduct of European affairs.[77] The set-up and tools of these committees vary across parliamentary chambers, but they typically have strong investigative powers, including the right to schedule hearings, receive periodic reports, and consult the government ahead of relevant decisions at EU level.

Probably the two strongest EU affairs committees are those in the Folketing and in the Riksdag. The Danish Parliament was in fact the first to introduce a negotiating mandate system,[78] which requires the government to obtain a mandate from the EU Affairs Committee before any decision is adopted in the Council.[79] This scrutiny model, dependent on a collective decision which (implicitly or explicitly) must be supported by a majority of committee members, has been replicated by the Riksdag. As a matter of fact, in both the Riksdag and

---

[73] Yamamoto (n 11) 15.

[74] Rule 56 of the Bundestag Rules of Procedure enables the setting up of a study commission, on a motion of one quarter of the Bundestag members, for the preparation of decisions on wide-ranging issues, to be concluded before the end of the legislative term by submitting a report for debate to the plenary.

[75] s 51 Spanish Congress Standing Orders, on the establishment of ad hoc committees, set up for a specific task.

[76] See below ch 8, section II.A.

[77] T Bergman, W Müller, K Strøm and M Blomgren, 'Democratic Delegation and Accountability: Cross-national Patterns' in K Strøm, W Müller and T Bergman (eds), *Delegation and Accountability in Parliamentary Democracies* (Oxford, Oxford University Press, 2003) 174 (European Affairs Committees are a strategic resource for connecting national parliaments to European decision-making).

[78] See the first report of the European Affairs Committee, released on 29 March 1973.

[79] T Borring Olesen, 'Denmark in Europe 1973–2015: Processes of Europeanization and "Denmarkization"' (2015) 11 *Journal of Contemporary European Research* 321.

the Folketing, the EU Affairs Committee acts as a body for consultation, not for instruct-ing decisions of the plenary, as the other committees do. The government must consult the Committee before taking any decision in the Council of Ministers, sometimes also before defining the position to be supported during negotiations,[80] and ahead of meetings of the European Council. It is up to the government to ask for a negotiating mandate for issues that are declared to be of major significance, submitting a memorandum to the Committee no later than eight days before the Council meeting. The opinion of the Committee is usually adopted by consensus, without a formal vote, and it is recorded in a report. Following the Council meeting, the minister submits a report to the Committee, which can give rise to a questioning session or request for a plenary debate. The mandate is binding on the govern-ment politically, but it is 'in practice so authoritative that it entails a quasi-legally binding instruction'.[81] Mandates are comparatively less constraining in Sweden: if the government decides to deviate from the position of the EU Committee, it must seek renewed contact and, if the divergence persists, it is expected to provide very good reasons in the report submitted after the Council meeting. This choice exposes the government to the standard oversight procedures, including interpellations and, ultimately, the vote of no confidence of the Riksdag.[82] This procedure confirms that the EU Affairs Committee may turn out to be a pivotal oversight subject, offering real opportunities to individual members and parties for holding the government accountable in the field of EU affairs.[83]

Second, in both Westminster and European Continental parliaments the oversight of highly sensitive policy areas may be located in parliamentary permanent committees holding strategic surveillance and vigilance functions. Oversight of intelligence and secu-rity action is a paradigmatic case. Intelligence oversight is actually a distinct parliamentary practice, because this sensitive issue close to the core of sovereignty 'requires confidentiality and is unsuitable to public debate and open control'.[84] To solve this apparent paradox, in many parliaments the task of monitoring how intelligence and security agencies conduct their tasks, both from the viewpoint of administrative effectiveness and in connection with the respect of individual rights,[85] is vested on ad hoc parliamentary committees which are intended to act as a constitutional guarantee.[86]

---

[80] F Laursen, 'The role of national parliamentary committees in European scrutiny: Reflections based on the Danish case' (2005) 11 *The Journal of Legislative Studies* 412 ff.

[81] P Kiiver, *The National Parliaments in the European Union: A Critical View on EU Constitution-building* (The Hague, Kluwer Law, 2006) 48.

[82] H Hegeland and C Neuhold, 'Parliamentary participation in EU affairs in Austria, Finland and Sweden: Newcomers with different approaches' (2002) 6 *European Integration Online Papers* 6, 7 f.

[83] D Finke and M Melzer, *Parliamentary Scrutiny of EU Law Proposals in Denmark: Why do Governments Request a Negotiation Mandate?* (Vienna, Institute for Advanced Studies, 2012) 30 (on the effectiveness of the Danish nego-tiating mandate as an oversight tool for the supporting third party– in the case of a minority government – and for the opposition).

[84] H Hegemann, 'Towards "normal" politics? Security, parliaments and the politicization of intelligence oversight in the German Bundestag' (2018) 20 *The British Journal of Politics and International Relations* 175, 177; and P Mello and D Peters, 'Parliaments in security policy. Involvement, politicization, and influence' (2018) 20 *The British Journal of Politics and International Relations* 3.

[85] H Born and I Leigh, *Making Intelligence Accountable: Legal Standards and Best Practice for Oversight of Intelligence* (Oslo, Parliament of Norway, 2005) 15.

[86] A Wills and M Vermeulen (eds), *Parliamentary oversight of security and intelligence agencies in the European Union* (EU Parliament – Directorate General for Internal Policies, 2011) 87.

In Italy, the Bicameral Parliamentary Committee for the Security of the Republic was established by law in 1977 and then reformed in 2007[87] and, in practice, it has strengthened its role of constitutional guarantee, also due to the significant role allotted to oppositions in the composition of the Committee. The Committee is composed of 10 members, five from each House, following the proportionality between parliamentary groups. In fact, the proportionality rule has been applied so as to provide equal representation of the majority and the minority, and the position of chair of the Committee has conventionally been filled by a member of the opposition.[88] In Germany, the Parliamentary Oversight Panel oversees the Federation's intelligence services, as set by the Law on the Parliamentary Control of Federal Intelligence,[89] but since 2009 it has found a constitutional basis.[90] In Denmark, the Intelligence Services Committee is a special committee of the Folketing, to provide supervision of the security, intelligence and defence services. Established by law in 1988, it was strengthened in 2014 with the introduction of the government's duty to submit an annual briefing on the activities of intelligence services. It consists of five MPs, appointed by the main political parties and it can be summoned on request of any member or the government. Its recommendations are not public.[91] In the UK, the Intelligence and Security Committee was originally conceived as a statutory committee (a 'constitutional anomaly') by the Intelligence Services Act 1994, but with the Justice and Security Act 2013 was transformed into a full parliamentary committee which has produced quite sensitive reports. The Committee has 10 members, appointed by Parliament, and an expanded oversight mandate, but works almost entirely in secret.[92] In Spain, a special committee was established in 1995 by the Congress to oversee the use of state secrets, with access to confidential files; in 2001 the scope of the committee was enlarged to also cover the oversight of intelligence services. The committee is composed of one representative from each parliamentary group, elected by the Congress in the plenary. Finally, in France, the Parliamentary Delegation on Intelligence was created in 2007[93] as a bicameral body providing a 'pluralistic' representation of all political groups, tasked both with overseeing government action and evaluating public policies in the field of intelligence. The Parliamentary Delegation is composed of four members from each House: the presidents of the two Houses' standing committees in charge of internal security and defence are *de jure* members; the other members are appointed by the president of each House, providing a 'pluralistic' representation.

---

[87] Law no 801 of 24 October 1977, amended by Law no 124, 3 August 2007. See C Nardone, 'Il controllo parlamentare sui servizi di informazione e sicurezza e sul segreto di Stato' in R Dickmann and S Staiano (eds), *Funzioni parlamentari non legislative e forma di governo. L'esperienza dell'Italia* (Milano, Giuffrè, 2008).

[88] C Fasone, 'Le commissioni parlamentari come "categoria a sè stante" di comitati' in Vv Aa, *Le autonomie in cammino. Scritti dedicati a Gian Candido De Martin* (Padova, CEDAM, 2012) 341 ff.

[89] J Singer, *Praxiskommentar Zum Gesetz Über Die Parlamentarische Kontrolle Nachrichtendienstichler Tätigkeit Des Bundes* (Berlin, Springer, 2016).

[90] Art 45(d) Basic Law.

[91] Denmark, Act no 632 of 12 June 2013, amending Act no 370 of 6 July 1988 establishing a committee on the Danish Security and Intelligence Service and the Danish Defence Intelligence Service. See AM Pedersen and RF Jørgensen, *National intelligence authorities and surveillance in the EU: Fundamental rights safeguards and remedies. Denmark* (Copenhagen, Danish Institute for Human Rights, 2014) para 15 f.

[92] H Bochel and A Defty, 'Parliamentary Oversight of Intelligence Agencies: Lessons from Westminster' in AW Neal (ed), *Security in a Small Nation: Scotland, Democracy, Politics* (Cambridge, Open Book Publishers, 2017).

[93] Art 6 nonies of Ordonnance no 58-1110, introduced by Law no 2007-1443 of 9 October 2007 and finally amended by Law no 2017-1510. See JJ Urvoas and F Vadillo, *Réformer les services de renseignement français: efficacité et impératifs démocratiques* (Paris, Fondation Jean Laurès, 2011) 84.

Compared with other committee structures, these oversight committees show some peculiar features. First, they tend to act as subsidiary bodies and they are not always subject to standard committee rules, including proportional representation of parties.[94] Second, they have broader control tasks and informative prerogatives, including witnessing of officials, access to confidential files and facilities; but the focus of their oversight is surely the protection of individual rights rather than the monitoring of appropriateness of intelligence service action. Third, their regime of publicity is much weaker than other committees, because committees usually work in secret, which means that little or no publicity is provided on the oversight outcomes. The connection of all these factors has raised some criticism on the effectiveness of these instances of parliamentary oversight,[95] often resulting in routine monitoring,[96] as well as on the 'political' nature of this intervention.[97]

Apart from intelligence service, the 'model' of the special Oversight Committee has found its fortune in other sectorial fields, featured by the sensitivity and technicality of issues at stake. A relevant example is offered by the Italian tradition of bicameral committees, which may be set by law to pursue different tasks, from surveillance and oversight to political direction, and cover selected policy areas, including public bodies involved in highly sensitive economic sectors.[98]

Third, ad hoc committees may be set to address some technically demanding scrutiny tasks which cannot be accomplished through the standard administrative and political capacities available to permanent committees. An example is offered by the French Committee for Evaluation and Control (CEC).[99] This ad hoc permanent unit, responsible for the evaluation of public policies, was established after the 2008 constitutional amendment, through a significant review of the National Assembly rules.[100] The Committee is chaired by the President of the Assembly and composed of members designated by parliamentary groups, fully reflecting the political make-up of the House. The CEC acts on its own initiative or at the request of a standing committee and, according to the Constitutional Council,[101] it may simply 'inform' the Assembly on almost all issues, except financial and budgetary ones, without being able to give injunctions to the government.[102]

Finally, one type of committee which does not directly exercise oversight functions but might serve as a body instrumental to the scrutiny of government activity is the Petitions Committee. Not all the countries that recognise citizens' rights to submit petitions to Parliament have a committee which is specifically competent in receiving, examining and

---

[94] Singer (n 89) 17 ff.

[95] On the functional weaknesses of the Parliamentary Oversight Panel, see A Friedel, *Blackbox Parlamentarisches Kontrollgremium des Bundestages. Defizite und Optimierungsstrategien bei der Kontrolle der Nachrichtendienste* (Berlin, Springer, 2019).

[96] P Gill, 'Evaluating intelligence oversight committees: The UK intelligence and security committee and the "war on the terror"' (2007) 22 *Intelligence and National Security* 14.

[97] Hegemann (n 84).

[98] L Califano Placci, *Le commissioni parlamentari bicamerali nella crisi del bicameralismo italiano* (Milano, Giuffrè, 1993).

[99] Art 146-2 of the National Assembly's Rules of Procedure. See P Avril, 'Le contrôle. Exemple du Comité d'évaluation et de contrôle des politiques publiques' (2008) 6 *Jus Politicum* 1.

[100] Resolution no 212, adopted on 27 May 2012.

[101] Decision no 2009-581 of 25 June 2009.

[102] Loi n 2011-140 allowed the Committee to ask for temporary inquiry powers and to liaison with the Cour des Comptes.

following up these 'proposals'.[103] Such a committee exists in Germany,[104] Spain,[105] the UK[106] and in the European Parliament.[107] Broadly speaking, when a petitions committee is present in Parliament, it is usually allowed the power to require government or agencies to submit information, documents and allow access to their facilities. Petitions committees do not ordinarily have the right to issue instructions, but rather they address recommendations to the referent Chamber. These do not produce procedural automatisms and are not binding on the plenary, but the publicity associated with the Petitions Committee's work may contribute to foster public control of a certain policy issue.

To conclude, the comparative analysis shows different types of temporary and permanent committees primarily tasked with oversight assignments in specific policy areas. If the nature, scope and powers of these committees are extremely varied, one common feature behind their existence is to be found in the idea that tackling the oversight of executive policies often requires specialisation, expertise and also protection of confidential information. From a structural and functional point of view, ad hoc committees are the only possible answer to these requirements.

III. Informative Tools Instrumental to Oversight

Oversight of the executive is dependent on information. With no evidence on the 'state-of-the-art' of government performance and policies, Parliament is unable to cover the informative gap and to formulate an effective judgement.[108] To fill in this gap, informative tools may find recognition in the constitution, within the prerogatives of elected representatives,[109] or in the parliamentary Rules of Procedure.[110] Notwithstanding the large variety of tools available, they find a common feature in their incidental or ancillary nature: they are non-autonomous items meaning they do not usually result in a formal decision, but they tend to 'serve' a 'major' procedure.[111]

Four main categories of informative tools and procedures can be identified. The first two categories comprise tools (the government's reporting duties and committee informative mechanisms) of a 'political' nature. The other two categories are instead relying on 'technical' tools, including the reporting of external bodies and the informative support of parliamentary administrations.

---

[103] Vintzel (n 34) (one main reason behind the establishment of a petitions committee is that time available to the plenaries is extremely limited).

[104] Art 45 Basic Law.

[105] AL Sanz Pérez, 'El artículo 77 de la Constitución. Las comisiones de peticiones de las Cortes Generales y las de los Parlamentos autonómicos' (2018) 31 *Corts: Anuario de derecho parlamentario* 279 (the establishment of a petitions committee in both Houses is a direct consequence of the constitutional relevance of the right of petition – arts 29 and 77 of the Constitution).

[106] Rule 145A House of Commons Standing Orders.

[107] Rule 216 European Parliament Rules of Procedure.

[108] J Parkhurst, *The Politics of Evidence: From Evidence-based Policy to the Good Governance of Evidence* (London, Routledge, 2016). On the pressures posed by the UK government in support of evidence-based policy-making, see Cabinet Office, 'White Paper: Modernising government' (March 1999).

[109] The power to require information is deemed to be a particular aspect of the oversight function vested on the Cortes Generales by Art 66.2 of the Spanish Constitution (Tribunal Constitucional, STC 203/2001, 15 October 2001, para 3).

[110] Yamamoto (n 11) 9.

[111] The difference between autonomous and non-autonomous items, inclusive of the list of associated tools, is formally regulated by Rule 75 of the Bundestag Rules of Procedure.

A. The 'Political' Tools: The Informative Role of Government and Parliamentary Committees

The first informative channel relies on government reporting duties to Parliament. This obligation is implicit to the confidence relationship but usually finds a legal basis in the constitution, which may either regulate the informing duty[112] or limit itself to recognise that government members, if required, must attend committee or plenary sittings.[113] In Parliament, government reporting duties find different forms of regulation.

The Rules of Procedure may procedimentalise the duty of the government to report on a given matter, which is usually fulfilled in writing.[114] Oral developments may sometimes be allowed, on the request also of opposition and minority groups.[115] It is however at the level of sectorial laws were government reporting duties find more extensive regulation: government is usually required to report on the implementation of statutory legislation, as to provide legislative assemblies with periodic information on the post-legislative enactment and implementation.[116] These reporting duties may become part of the post-legislative scrutiny, especially when they are supported by a review or sunset clause as set in the legislative act, delegating the Parliament to verify that the act is correctly implemented and that expected outcomes are fulfilled.[117]

The implementation of this tool finds its most significant limit in the protection of confidential information. Substantive constitutional standards may be introduced to regulate parliamentary access to information in order to prevent potential disputes. However, at the point where a legal framework is defined, 'the political momentum will in most cases be lost'.[118]

The second channel for collecting information draws on Parliament's internal informative capacity, which strongly relies on committee work. It has been argued that 'at the heart of a committee's oversight function is its power to seek evidence from a wide range of individuals and organizations on the subject under investigation'.[119] As a matter of fact, committees have different informative tools available, including hearings, missions, fact-finding investigations and reports to Parliament.

---

[112] Art 190 Spanish Constitution.

[113] Art 43 German Basic Law; Art 110 Spanish Constitution; and art 64 Italian Constitution.

[114] Supplementary provision no 3.6.2 to the Riksdag Act provides that the government must report to the Riksdag every year, no later than 1 March, on the work of commissions appointed by government decision. Written communications of the government reporting certain activities are mentioned in Supplementary provision no 2.7.1.

[115] Pursuant to Arts 109 and 110 of the Spanish Constitution, s 203 of the Spanish Congress Standing Orders regulates the appearance of members of the government before the full House or any of its committees to report on a given matter. The opposition has the opportunity to initiate the reporting procedure, although the quorum required is quite high (two parliamentary groups or one-fifth of the members of the House or of the committee). The sitting unfolds through the presentation of the government report, questions and comments from parliamentary groups and the reply of the member of government.

[116] S Rose-Ackerman, S Egidy and J Fowkes, *Due Process of Lawmaking. The United States, South Africa, Germany and the European Union* (New York, Cambridge University Press, 2015) 201 f.

[117] A Kouroutakis, *The Constitutional Value of Sunset Clauses: An Historical and Normative Analysis* (New York, Routledge, 2017).

[118] Meinel (n 29) 330.

[119] IPU and UNDP, *Global Parliamentary Report 2017* (n 27) 52.

Public hearings are among the most renowned tool used to collect information and data;[120] they can be used as a form of consultation or as a means for obtaining evidence.[121] They can serve oversight purposes in different forms, as the distinction between *oversight, investigative* and *field* hearings demonstrates.[122] They are carried out at committee level, usually by the lead committee which is in charge of a certain item of business.[123] Sometimes, the decision to hold a hearing must be approved by a simple majority at committee level; in other cases, the hearing must be authorised by the full Chamber. Procedural guarantees are usually given to the opposition both in the power to initiate the procedure[124] and in the selection of witnesses.[125] Over the last two decades, Scandinavian parliaments, where the investigative function at committee level was traditionally underdeveloped, have made important changes in support of this activity.[126] Open committee hearings were introduced in the Swedish Riksdag in 1998, in response to pushes from the opposition that started in the late 1960s. Creeping reticence in allowing open hearings was justified by the fear that committees would transform into 'mini-plenaries' and lead to party politicisation of the proceedings.[127] In Denmark, a committee may start an open 'consultation', inviting other persons to take part in committee meetings; this is held if at least three members of the committee request it.[128]

Witnesses may include government officials, who have first-hand evidence of each administrative programme, experts, representatives of interest groups and any other persons who can provide useful information.[129] One major question affects the nature of the 'call' to appear made by the relevant committee. Broadly speaking, only the hearings launched by select committees and by certain inquiry committees (see below section VI.A) are compelling for the addressee(s). By contrast, in all the other committees, as a standard rule only the hearing of members of government may be considered as a binding request, when it is supported by the presence of constitutional guarantees on the government's informing duties in Parliament.[130] For the other categories of witnesses, committees appeal

---

[120] Shaw (n 33) 230.

[121] Yamamoto (n 11) 30.

[122] W Oleszek et al, *Congressional Procedures and the Policy Process*, 11th edn (Washington, CQ Press, 2019) 90 ff, identifies five types of committee hearing. Two of them, *legislative* and *field* hearings, respectively interact with the legislative function and with the scrutiny of executive appointments. The other three categories are instead directly instrumental to the oversight function: *oversight* hearings encompass aspects of post-legislative scrutiny; *investigative* hearings aim at collecting evidence of ministerial misconduct in the discharge of his/her official duties; *field* hearings are *in loco* missions, conducted around the country.

[123] Rule 70.3 of the Bundestag Rules of Procedure also extends the right to carry out hearings to the committees asked for an opinion.

[124] According to Rule 70.1 of the Bundestag Rules of Procedure, the lead committee is obliged to hold public hearings if a quarter of its members so demand.

[125] According to Rule 70.1 of the Bundestag Rules of Procedure, when a hearing is demanded by a minority of the committee members, the persons named by that minority must be heard.

[126] D Arter, 'Parliamentary Democracy in Scandinavia' (2004) 57 *Parliamentary Affairs* 581, 591.

[127] Arter, 'From "Parliamentary Control"' (n 62) 141.

[128] Art 8.8 Folketing Standing Orders.

[129] Arts 143.2 and 143.3 Italian Chamber of Deputies Rules of Procedure; arts 46 and 47 Italian Senate Rules of Procedure. On committees' power to hear a member of government, an official or any other relevant person as a manifestation of the oversight function, see the Spanish Tribunal Constitucional, SSTC 177/2002, 7; 208/2003, 6; 89/2005, 4; 90/2005, 4.

[130] R Dickmann, 'Atti e attività parlamentari con funzione conoscitiva' in R Dickmann and S Staiano (eds), *Funzioni parlamentari non legislative* (n. 87) 504.

to the principle of faithful cooperation when they make a call to appear. In many parliaments, including in Italy and the European Parliament, no cases of opposition or denial to be heard have been recorded.[131] The French case may be considered an exception in this regard, because committees' power to conduct hearings is regulated by the Ordonnance of 17 November 1958, article 5 bis: ad hoc and permanent committees can summon all the persons whose audition they deem to be necessary and administrative sanctions are set in the case of a no-show.

In Italy, one relevant informative tool consists of the power vested in standing committees to carry out fact-finding investigations into matters that fall within their scope of competence: these investigations unfold through a set of hearings and other informative activities with any person who is able to offer evidence.[132] They have a pure 'informative' scope that does not enable pursuit of government responsibility. Another difference between fact-finding investigations and inquiries lies in the fact that the former are carried out exclusively based on the voluntary cooperation of the invited persons.[133]

The need to overcome the procedural limits associated with formal hearings has led some parliaments to engage in informal hearings,[134] usually held behind 'closed' doors or with limited publicity. This instance has the advantage of being accessible and easy to implement, enabling at the same time a spontaneous and frank confrontation with the person heard.[135] Informal hearings have become common practice in both Houses of the Italian Parliament as a means to overcome the limitations posed by the Rules of Procedure[136] in defining the categories of persons that may be asked to take testimony in committee; through informal hearings, committees can hear representatives of civil society, professional bodies and potentially any informed person.

Informative missions are another tool available to parliamentary committees: these are set up on a temporary basis to gather information, usually following the same procedure that allows a permanent committee to launch an inquiry. This tool has found extensive implementation in the French Parliament, following the 2008 constitutional amendment and the 2009 reform of the Rules of Procedure of the National Assembly, as part of the toolbox supporting the evaluation of public policies. The *missions d'information* may be created in three cases: on the initiative of one or more committees; on the initiative of the Conference of the Presidents, following the proposal of the President of the Assembly; on the request of the president of a minority group.[137] The missions created by parliamentary committees might represent in their internal composition the party grouping proportions of the plenary or in any case grant that at least one member is selected from the opposition.[138] In certain cases, the presidency of the mission or the role of rapporteur must also be given to a member of the opposition.

---

[131] Fasone, *Sistemi di commissione* (n 53) 532.

[132] Art 144 Chamber of Deputies Rules of Procedure; and art 48 Senate Rules of Procedure.

[133] V Lippolis, 'Indagini conoscitive' in *Enciclopedia giuridica*, XVI (Roma, Treccani, 1989) 1 f; and F D'Onofrio, *Le indagini conoscitive delle commissioni parlamentari. Problemi e prospettive* (San Giorgio al Cremano, Istituto Grafico Italiano, 1971) 237 ff.

[134] Dickmann, 'Atti e attività parlamentari' (n 130) 55.

[135] U Karpen, 'Regulatory Impact Assessment: Current Situation and Prospects in the German Parliament' (2015) 101 *Amicus Curiae* 17, referring to practices in the German Bundestag.

[136] Art 143 Chamber of Deputies Rules of Procedure; and art 47 Senate Rules of Procedure.

[137] These three hypotheses are respectively regulated by arts 145.2, 4 and 5 Rules of Procedure.

[138] Art 145.3 Rules of Procedure.

The missions may be set up to prepare the examination of a Bill or to monitor the implementation and evaluate a piece of legislation recently adopted; they result in the preparation of reports that can be published and give place to a debate without vote in the plenary or to a questioning session.[139] Unlike inquiries, they have no power to compel the persons heard to submit the documents required.[140] Solid guarantees are offered to opposition and minority groups in the regulation and composition of the mission.

Some of the missions of the National Assembly have been relaunched on a permanent basis from one legislative term to another. This is the case of the Evaluation and Control Mission (MEC) and the Evaluation and Control Mission of Social Security. The former, set up by the Finance Committee in 1999, is a joint committee co-chaired by one member from the majority and one from the opposition; its main task is to conduct an inquiry into the implementation of sectorial public policies.[141] The latter, set up within the Social Affairs Committee in 2004, permanently monitors the implementation of legislation financing social services. Close to the informative missions are the 'parliamentary offices', which act as unicameral or bicameral parliamentary delegations whose task is to inform the Parliament around a particular policy.[142]

In all these hypotheses, reports are the standard tool used by committees to communicate to the plenary the outcomes of their activity. Reports are usually adopted by a simple majority in committee and, after being submitted to the plenary, they can be debated and voted on in the floor of the House. They usually include the terms of reference, a summary of the proceedings and of the conclusions, the evidence and submissions received; they can also address recommendations made to the relevant government department.[143] The possibility of having minority reports is an important vehicle for submitting independent information and alternative policy options to the floor.[144] Committee reports play a pivotal role in the evaluation of public policies.[145]

B. The 'Technical' Tools: The Role of External Bodies and Parliamentary Administrations

Two other categories of informative tools instrumental to parliamentary oversight rely on technical bodies that may provide the legislature with focused information on government policies, including highly specialised sectorial measures.

---

[139] Art 145.8 Rules of Procedure.

[140] JC Videlin, 'La Mission d'information parlementaire' (1999) 40 *Revue française de droit constitutionnel* 699.

[141] D Hochedez, 'La mission d'évaluation et de côntrole (MEC). Une volonté de retour aux sources du Parlement: la défense du citoyen-contribuable' (1999) 68 *Revue française de finances publiques* 264; and I Bouhadana, *Les commission des finances des assemblées parlementaires en France: origines, évolutions et enjeux* (Paris, LDGJ, 2007) 342 ff.

[142] D Maus, 'Le parlement et les cohabitations' (1999) 91 *Pouvoirs* 71.

[143] Yamamoto (n 11) 37 ff.

[144] Mattson and Strøm (n 33) 283 (minority reports add incentives to a committee minority to specialise and take committee oversight seriously).

[145] The Swedish Riksdag shows a relevant tradition of committee reports submitted to the plenary to be debated and decided upon in the field of the evaluation of public policies. See Chapter 7 of the Riksdag Act. Pursuant to art 19A of the French Senate Rules of Procedure, every permanent committee is required to draft a yearly report of its monitoring and evaluation activity, in order to compose the *Bilan annuel de l'application des lois*, which is presented at the Conference of the Presidents and discussed in a plenary session in the presence of the government.

Some tools are instrumental to post-legislative scrutiny: this field of activity, especially when interpreted in a broad sense inclusive of the evaluation of public policies, is in fact more technically demanding than other spheres of parliamentary oversight. This is why connecting with specialist bodies, either internal or external to Parliament, is a prerequisite for any legislature willing to evaluate whether a public policy is effective or not or whether the government has performed its duties in an efficient manner.[146] To satisfy these needs, parliaments have two main options available.

On the one hand, fact-finding and analytical requirements may be satisfied by connecting with external organs and bodies: independent authorities and agencies; supreme audit institutions and advisory bodies; monocratic bodies acting in defence of citizens' rights, such as the ombudsman; university and research centres that provide the House with reports, studies and documentation. Parliamentary Rules of Procedure may regulate the submission and assignment of these reports to the relevant parliamentary body, which is usually managed by the Speaker.[147] Supreme audit institutions tend to have a privileged relationship with Parliament;[148] in some cases, including France[149] and Sweden,[150] this relationship finds direct legitimacy in the Constitution and further procedimentalisation in statutory legislation or in the Rules of Procedures. The establishment of 'fiscal councils' in response to the Fiscal Compact has significantly reinforced national parliaments' capacity to oversee government macro-economic policy.[151]

The German Bundestag's structured network of independent bodies supporting its oversight activity in the field of ex post evaluation – including the Federal Statistical Office, the National Regulatory Reform Council (NKR),[152] the Office of Technology Assessment

---

[146] SR Khandker, GB Koolwal and AS Hussain, *Handbook on Impact Evaluation: Quantitative Methods and Practices* (Washington, World Bank, 2010); JW Creswell, *Research Design: Qualitative, Quantitative, and Mixed Methods Approaches* (Thousand Oaks, CA, SAGE, 2014); and PJ Gertler, S Martinez, P Premand, LB Rawlings and CJ Vermeersch, *Impact Evaluation in Practice*, 2nd edn (Washington, World Bank Institute, 2016).

[147] *Ex multis*, see ss 199, 200 and 201 of the Spanish Congress Standing Orders that respectively regulate the receipt of the annual report of the Auditing Court, of the reports of the Defender of the People and of all other reports which, by virtue of a constitutional or legal provision, must be submitted to the Congress.

[148] Yamamoto (n 11) 74 (two types of audit are carried out by Supreme Institutions: the financial audit shows whether public money has been spent in conformity with accounting or budgetary rules; the value-for-money audit concerns the assessment of public policies from the perspective of the 'three Es').

[149] Art 47.2 of the French Constitution. JR Alventosa, 'La Cour des comptes: une place constitutionnelle confortée (L'article 47-2 de la Constitution)' (2008) 254 *Les Petites affiches* 82; art 58.2 La loi organique relative aux lois de finances (LOLF), allowing finance committees to assign investigative tasks to the Cour des comptes. Assemblée Nationale, 'Les enquêtes demandées à la Cour des comptes (art 58-2° de la LOLF)' (2011).

[150] Chapter 12, art 7 of the Swedish Instrument of Government. The Swedish Riksdag interaction with the National Audit Office (NAO) in the field of ex-post evaluation and impact assessment is regulated by the Act on Audit of State Activities (2002) and by the Act containing Instructions for the Swedish National Audit Office (2002).

[151] See below ch 8, section III.

[152] The National Regulatory Reform Council (NKR) was established by Federal Law of 14 August 2006 (Fed Gaz I 1866), amended by the Law of 16 March 2011 (Fed Gaz I 420). Pursuant to Rule 70 of the Bundestag Rules of Procedure, the Chamber can resort to the NKR in its advisory capacity, based either on formal reporting duties provided by sunset or review clauses, or on the standard rule on public hearings. H Gröhe and S Naundorf, 'Bürokratieabbau und bessere Rechtsetzung, Eckpunkte, Erfahrungen und Perspektiven' (2009) 24 *Zeitschrift für Gesetzgebung* 367; and M Rani Sharma et al, *Expert report on the implementation of ex-post evaluations. Good practice and experience in other countries* (Berlin, NKR, 2013).

(OTA)[153] and the Parliamentary Advisory Council on Sustainable Development[154] – confirms the strategic value of this relationship in view of strengthening Parliament's involvement in the oversight of government action. For instance, the opinions and appraisals of the Parliamentary Advisory Council on Sustainable Development are discussed and appraised in writing by the lead committee, thus creating a direct bridge with the oversight procedures.

The ombudsman is another key actor for parliamentary oversight. In half of the countries acknowledging this figure, ombudsmen are appointed by Parliament.[155] The traditional ombudsman system grew out of the Swedish experience, where it originated in 1809 in response to Parliament's demands for independent control over maladministration in the public sphere.[156] Denmark was the third country after Sweden to establish, in 1955, the *Folketingets Ombudsman*.[157] In the UK, the Parliamentary Commissioner for Administration was settled with the Parliamentary Commissioner Act of 1967. It is seen as an assistant to individual MPs in their task of obtaining redress from the grievances suffered by their constituents at the hands of the government. Similarly, in Spain the Defender of the People is nominated by the Cortes generales through a joint committee.[158] In other countries, the ombudsman is not elected by Parliament, but the relationship with elected representatives is always very close. This is the case in France, where the *Défenseur des droits*, introduced by the 2008 constitutional amendment, is named by the President of the Republic.[159]

Ombudsmen handle complaints from the public regarding how public administration performs its duties, thus signalling omissions, misbehaviours, negative outcomes and failures. To perform this role, ombudsmen have reinforced informative prerogatives[160] and enjoy strong independence, although parliaments may integrate and precede their role in filtering, selecting and examining the complaints submitted by citizens.[161] This work results in the drafting of reports submitted to Parliament.[162] Sometimes, specialist committees are established to examine these materials.[163] On the whole, MPs' increasing interest in these

---

[153] OTA is an independent scientific institution serving the Bundestag and its committees in an advisory capacity on research and technology.

[154] This body, composed of 17 MPs, acts as a watchdog whose task is to monitor and assist the sustainable policy of the federal government.

[155] OECD, 'The Role of Ombudsman Institutions in Open Government' (2018) OECD Working Paper on Public Governance 29 (Paris, OECD, 2018).

[156] Nowadays, pursuant to Chapter 12 – art 6 of the Swedish Instrument of Government, one or one or more parliamentary ombudsmen can be established, tasked to 'supervise the application of laws and other regulations in public activities, under terms of reference drawn up by the Riksdag'. On the election procedure, see art 10 of the Riksdag Act.

[157] Act no 473 of 12 June 1996.

[158] Art 54 of the Constitution and Organic Law no 3/1981 of 6 April.

[159] Art 71 of the Constitution by art 7 of Organic Law no 2011-333 of 29 May 2011.

[160] See for instance Chapter 12 – art 6 of the Swedish Instrument of Government.

[161] In the UK, citizen's complaints must be processed by Parliament before being submitted to the Parliamentary Commissioner for Administration (s 5 of the Parliamentary Commissioner Act 1967); and JF Garner, 'The British Ombudsman' (1968) 18 *University of Toronto Law Journal* 158). In France, complaints may be submitted to the French Défenseur des droits also through an MP (art 7 of Organic Law no 2011-333). Parliaments may also provide inputs, for instance by transferring to the office of the *ombudsperson* the petitions received.

[162] On the reporting duties of the UK Parliamentary Commissioner for Administration, see s 10 of the Parliamentary Commissioner Act 1967. For the Spanish Defensor del Pueblo, see arts 32 and 33 of Organic Law no 3/1981.

[163] In the case of Sweden, this role is entrusted on the Committee on the Constitution (art 4 and the supplementary provision 4.6.1. of the Riksdag Act).

mechanisms has been considered as a sign of an ongoing process of 'Americanisation' of parliamentary oversight.[164]

On the other hand, parliamentary administrations may play a fundamental role in supporting executive oversight. This is part of the contribution offered by civil servants in addressing, underpinning and counselling representative assemblies,[165] which is deemed to have ever more positive effects on the outcomes of parliamentary work than in any other areas of activity. Access to autonomous expertise is actually a necessary premise to entrust legislatures with effective means of evaluation of government performance.[166]

Tracing civil servants' contribution to oversight is often uneasy, because this link flows through informal procedures and relations.[167] Some empirical research has been conducted in the last 15 years, focusing on the role of parliamentary staff in the European Parliament in influencing decision-making.[168] In fact, one indicator may be found in the establishment of ad hoc administrative units with specific competence in the oversight of government implementing duties or in the evaluation of public policies. Whereas oversight is commonly supported at the administrative level by research and documentation units,[169] the creation of internal administrative units shows a strong determination of parliaments to invest energies and resources in the field.[170] In the last few years, following the Niebler Report,[171] the European Parliament has made a significant effort to structure an autonomous administrative capacity in the field of ex post evaluation and impact assessment:[172]

[164] Costa, Kerrouche and Magnette (n 35) 18.

[165] BS Romzek and A Utter, 'Congressional legislative staffs: political professional or clerks?' (1997) 41 *American Journal of Political Science* 1251; W Blischke, 'Parliamentary Staff in the German Bundestag' (1981) 6 *Legislative Studies Quarterly* 533, 556; S Campbell and J Laporte, 'The Staff of the Parliamentary Assemblies in France' (1981) 6 *Legislative Studies Quarterly* 521, 524 ff; M Pacelli, 'Le amministrazioni delle Camere tra politica e burocrazia' in L Violante (ed), *Il Parlamento* (Torino, Einaudi, 2001) 746 ff.

[166] As argued by Sánchez de Dios (n 7) 5, 'policy supervision implies a higher degree of control than general oversight'.

[167] This contribution is stressed in the definition of legislative oversight proposed by JD Lees, 'Legislatures and Oversight: A Review Article on a Neglected Area of Research' (1977) 2 *Legislative Studies Quarterly* 193, 193 where oversight is referred to as 'the behavior by legislators and their staffs, individually or collectively, which results in an impact, intended or not, on bureaucratic behavior'.

[168] K Neunreither, 'Elected legislators and their unelected assistants in the European Parliament' (2006) 8 *The Journal of Legislative Studies* 40; T Winzen, 'Technical or political? An exploration of the work of officials in the committees of the European Parliament' (2011) 17 *The Journal of Legislative Studies* 27; M Egeberg, A Gornitzka, J Trondal and M Johannessen, 'Parliament staff: Unpacking the behaviour of officials in the European Parliament' (2012) 20 *Journal of European Public Policy* 495; M Dobbels and C Neuhold, 'The Roles bureaucrats play: The input of European Parliament (EP) administrators into the ordinary legislative procedure: A case study approach' (2012) 35 *Journal of European Integration* 375; AL Högenauer, C Neuhold and T Christiansen, *Parliamentary Administrations in the European Union* (Basingstoke, Palgrave, 2016).

[169] On the establishment of research and documentation units as a means for adapting the information needs to the functional levels of Parliament, see R Miller, R Pelizzo and R Stapenhurst, *Parliamentary Libraries, Institutes and Offices: The Sources of Parliamentary Information* (Washington, World Bank, 2004) 2 f; and also F Fitsilis and A Koutsogiannis, 'Strengthening the Capacity of Parliaments through Development of Parliamentary Research Services' (2017) Paper presented at the 13th Workshop of Parliamentary Scholars and Parliamentarians, Wroxton.

[170] E Griglio, 'Post-Legislative Scrutiny as a Form of Executive Oversight. Tools and Practices in Europe' (2019) 2 *European Journal of Law Reform* 118, 121 f.

[171] European Parliament Report on guaranteeing independent impact assessments, adopted through Resolution P7-TA-(2011) 0259 on 8 June 2011.

[172] A Renda, 'European Union and Better Law-Making: Best Practices and Gaps' in The Best Practices in Legislative and Regulatory Processes in a Constitutional Perspective (workshop), Study for the AFCO Committee (Brussels, European Parliament, 2015) 17 f; and I Anglmayer, *Evaluation and Ex-post Impact Assessment at EU Level* (Brussels, European Parliamentary Research Service, 2016) 7.

in January 2012, the European Parliament set up a dedicated impact assessment service which in November 2013 was included within the Directorate General for Parliamentary Research services. Also, the Italian parliamentary administrations of the two Houses show some positive trends in this direction. On the one hand, in the Lower House, the Chamber of Deputies, the Service for Parliamentary Oversight evaluates the implementation of laws and monitors reports requested by the government.[173] On the other hand, the Upper House, the Senate, established, in 2016, the Impact Assessment Office (IAO),[174] tasked with promoting research, studies and training programmes in the analysis and evaluation of public policies.[175]

In many parliaments, the internal administrative capacity is complemented by connections with academic institutions. Available studies have revealed that academic research finds difficulties in penetrating parliamentary work, due to the lack of accessibility and poor communication.[176] The UK Parliament has made considerable efforts to overcome this problem and convey research into the work of parliamentary bodies. This has led to the launch of the 'Evidence Information Service' initiative, aimed at facilitating research engagement with parliamentarians,[177] and to the establishment of the Parliamentary Office for Science and Technology, created to provide impartial assessment of the scientific and technological background in support of sustained parliamentary scrutiny.[178] A similar body was created in France in 1983, when the Parliamentary Office for Evaluation of Scientific and Technological Options[179] was asked 'to inform Parliament of scientific and technological options in order, specifically, to make its decisions clear'.

IV. Oversight Tools Preceding Government Action

Ex ante oversight tools encompass a wide range of mechanisms, with rather different purposes. Some procedures are aimed at fostering a debate, not followed by any decisions; others are instead unfolding through a vote on a given 'proposal'; a third type of procedures involves the Parliament in the preventive examination of a proposal or document submitted

---

[173] Art 25 of the Rules on Services and Personnel of the Chamber of Deputies, last amended in 2002 (Deliberation of the Bureau no 57 of 25 March 2002, enacted through the Decree of the President no 478, 27 March 2002).

[174] See the Bureau's Deliberation no 90/2016, establishing the Impact Assessment Office, approved on 28 June 2016 and the Decree of the President of the Senate no 12480 of 19 July 2016.

[175] IAO has a hybrid nature being both a political institution (the Steering council brings together MPs and officials of the Senate bureaucracy) as well as an administrative entity (the Secretariat is organised as a typical administrative unit, responsible for developing research, documentation and training in thematic areas related to public policy analysis and evaluation). G Coppola and FS Toniato, 'La valutazione delle politiche pubbliche' in F Bassanini and A Manzella (eds), *Due Camere, un Parlamento: per far funzionare il bicameralismo* (Bagno a Ripoli, Passigli, 2017) 160 ff.

[176] C Kenny, D Rose, A Hobbs, C Tyler and J Blackstock, *The Role of Research in the UK Parliament*, I (London, Houses of Parliament, 2017) 10.

[177] AL Walker et al, 'Supporting evidence-informed policy and scrutiny: A consultation of UK research professionals' (2019) 14 *PloS one* 1.

[178] M Norton, 'Origins and Functions of the UK Parliamentary Office of Science and Technology' in J Norman and H Paschen (eds), *Parliaments and Technology: The Development of Technology Assessment in Europe* (New York, State University of New York Press, 2000) 68 ff.

[179] Law no 83-609 of 8 July 1983.

by the national or by the European executive, with the purpose of releasing an opinion or an 'authorisation'.

The preference for either type of oversight tools changes from one country to another. In UK[180] and France,[181] debates and committee reporting were traditionally considered the preferred procedures. The 2008 French constitutional reform introduced some changes in this regard, opening new channels for expressing Parliament's will beyond the traditional resolutions on EU documents pursuant to article 88 (4) of the Constitution.[182] In contrast, in Italy and Spain, where the *indirizzo politico* activity is well developed, the voting of acts, such as motions and resolutions, plays a fundamental role.[183] The EU integration process has given much relevance to the ex ante involvement of national parliaments in the scrutiny of draft proposals.

A. Debates

Focusing on the first of the three dimensions, some ex ante procedures do not automatically trigger a vote in the plenary, but are rather meant to promote a debate on a certain statement or account given by members of government.[184] In this perspective, the very basic oversight tool is the request for convening an urgent sitting or an extraordinary session of the plenary.[185] The power to start the procedure is in many cases entrusted in MPs directly, following the general power to promote a debate on a certain matter or to convene the government during plenary or committee sittings.[186] This is a relevant guarantee for the opposition.[187] In the Bundestag, the opposition makes extensive use of the *Aktuelle Stunden* (topical questions), which enables the Chamber to engage in short one-hour debates on current issues, in a real adversarial style.[188] In the House of Commons, 'half-hour adjournment' debates, occurring at the end of each day, allow MPs – especially backbenchers – to raise an issue with the government that typically refers to a constituency concern.[189] Rule 24 of the House of Commons Standing Orders allows members, at the commencement of public business on Monday, Tuesday, Wednesday and Thursday, to propose a debate on 'a specific and important matter that should have urgent consideration'.

At the same time, the principle of executive accountability before Parliament has led to the development of procedures that vest in the government the power to submit a formal

---

[180] P Norton, *Does Parliament Matter?* (Hemel Hempstead, Harvester Wheatsheaf, 1993) 89.

[181] Sánchez de Dios (n 7) 8 ff.

[182] Houillon (n 41) 64 f.

[183] ibid. G Smurra, M Caputo and A Goracci, 'Gli atti di indirizzo e di sindacato ispettivo' in R Dickmann and S Staiano (eds), *Funzioni parlamentari non legislative e forma di governo: l'esperienza dell'Italia* (Milano, Giuffrè, 2008).

[184] Yamamoto (n 11) 62 (on parliamentary debates as 'oral exchanges of opinions that are intended to facilitate the chamber's collective decision-making on certain issues').

[185] IPU and UNDP, *Global Parliamentary Report 2017* (n 27) 58. The importance of this tool for parliamentary minorities is highlighted by Vintzel (n 34).

[186] See above, section IV.

[187] Art 39.3 German Basic Law.

[188] J Magone, *Contemporary European Politics: A Comparative Introduction* (New York, Routledge, 2010) 213.

[189] M Shepard, 'Administrative Review and Oversight: The Experience of Westminster' in R Pelizzo, R Stapenhurst and D Olson (eds), *Trends in Parliamentary Oversight* (Washington DC, World Bank Institute, 2004) 42.

communication or account before the Chamber as a means of fostering a debate on a certain issue. Speeches of the head of government (or Crown) presenting the executive's programme may be held not just at the beginning of the legislative term,[190] but also at the beginning of each session or parliamentary year.[191] The opening address is usually followed by a debate, during which political groups may formulate questions and present their position. These occasions are often considered as rather 'ritualistic'[192] and yet they offer a valuable opportunity for engaging in an open confrontation on the executive programme and planned policy actions.

These annual speeches may be complemented by additional addresses, to be held during the parliamentary session or year, affecting either the government's general policy or some specific policy fields.[193] This happens in Denmark where, in addition to the account presented at the beginning of the year, the Prime Minister is allowed to render an account to the Folketing on the general state of the Realm at any time.[194] A resolution can be tabled in connection with the debate. Also ministers can make an account on a matter of public interest which is submitted in writing, unless the minister asks for a verbal account.[195]

Beyond these hypotheses, government usually recognises the opportunity/duty to make a statement or a communication before Parliament on its own initiative[196] or on request of selected proponents, usually a parliamentary group.[197] The statement can be held in a committee or plenary[198] and it can give rise to a debate, with questions and comments from MPs.[199] The procedure may be concluded with the voting of draft resolutions, on the initiative either of individual members[200] or of collective subjects.[201] In the French Assembly, the final vote can only be requested by the government and it cannot raise the responsibility of

---

[190] In the UK, the Queen's Speech is held, usually in May/June or at any other time of the year in case of anticipated elections, in the House of Lords Chamber during the State Opening of Parliament. In Sweden, the speech from the monarch was repealed in 1974, when the adoption of the new Instrument of Government removed the Crown from any involvement in the legislative process.

[191] In Denmark, pursuant to art 38 of the Constitutional Act, the Prime Minister is called to render an account at the first sitting of the sessional year. In Spain, the traditional speech of the Prime Minister on the 'State of the Nation' at the beginning of the political year does not find any legal basis in the Standing Orders (although an exception made for the general provisions of arts 196 and 197 on the 'communications' of the government), but it has represented a common practice since 1983. F Quintero González, 'Debates del estado de la nación: control parlamentario o puesta en escena para medio de comunicación?' (2014) 19 *Historia y Comunicación Social* 793.

[192] As remarked by D Arter, 'Parliamentary Democracy in Scandinavia' (2004) 57 *Parliamentary Affairs* 581, 591 'an unconvincing performance by the Prime Minister will lead to a bad press but virtually never loss of office'.

[193] For instance, in the Swedish Parliament foreign policy debates are held once a year in February (see below ch 6, section II.C (n 73)).

[194] § 19.2 Folketing Standing Orders.

[195] § 19.4 and 19.6 Folketing Standing Orders; on the report, the Speaker, 17 MPs or a committee may decide to open a debate in the plenary.

[196] Rule 132 for statements by the Commission, the Council and the European Council in the European Parliament.

[197] Art 51.1 of the French Constitution. Eight members are required by art 105 of the Senate Rules of Procedure to stage a communication from the government in the plenary.

[198] s 196 of the Spanish Congress Standing Orders. The double channel of government communications (or urgent 'informatives') in committee or in the plenary is also a practice in the Italian Parliament (see, respectively, arts 22.3 and 30.4 Chamber of Deputies Rules of Procedure and art 46.3 Senate Rules of Procedure; art 118 Chamber of Deputies Rules of Procedure and art 105 Senate Rules of Procedure).

[199] Art 51.1 of the French Constitution; s 196 of the Spanish Congress Standing Orders.

[200] Art 118 Italian Chamber of Deputies Rules of Procedure.

[201] A committee, a parliamentary group of a minimum quorum of MEPs pursuant to Rule 132.2 European Parliament Rules of Procedure.

the executive.[202] In most parliaments, the EU integration process, and the Lisbon Treaty in particular, has led to an intensification of government statements in Parliament following the fundamental stages of EU decision-making.[203]

Broadly speaking, all these instances provide a means for reinforcing the 'talking' prerogative of parliaments and strengthening its connection with the government's policy-making.[204]

B. Motions and Resolutions

In some cases, the debate can be concluded with a vote on a certain 'proposal'. This is the second instance of ex ante tools, consisting of all the procedures, including the tabling of motions and resolutions, that end with a vote in the plenary or at committee level. These procedures offer Parliament the opportunity to influence the government's behaviour, anticipating potential misalignments between its political directions and the executive conduct of public affairs.[205] therefore, they turn out to be a rather powerful mechanism, associated with a strong political weight.[206]

The basic rule behind the tabling of these tools is that it is not possible for any Parliament to vote on a motion or resolution without prior notice. There are no spontaneous procedures enabling the legislature to bind the government on a proposal that has not been anticipated in writing. No 'surprise party' is therefore allowed in the executive–legislative relations. From a comparative perspective, identifying the tools that satisfy these purposes is not an easy task. The same name is used to qualify different mechanisms, thus resulting in the overlap of the procedures associated with the terms 'resolution' or 'motion'.[207] Nonetheless, three main instances can be distinguished, based on a comparative analysis.

The first instance includes the tabling of autonomous acts that produce binding effects on government's responsibility and the confidence relationship. Investiture or confidence motions (in cases of positive parliamentarism)[208] and motions of no confidence or censure

---

[202] Art 132 of the French Assembly Rules of Procedure, modified by the 2009 reform (Résolution no 292 of 27 May 2009). The government always has the last word in the debate. Declarations not followed by the debate (but allowing only one intervention for each group) are regulated by art 132.7 of the Rules of Procedure.

[203] For instance, in Italy Law no 234 of 24 December 2012, on participation in the EU, has given a statutory basis to the practice of the government's communications before the Houses ahead of European Council meetings. G Piccirilli, 'Il ricorso alla legge per l'esercizio dei poteri "europei" da parte del Parlamento italiano. Spunti per una lettura costituzionalmente orientata' (2013) 2 *Osservatorio sulle fonti* 1. C Fasone and G Piccirilli, 'Le procedure euro-nazionali' in F Bassanini and A Manzella, *Due Camere, un Parlamento. Per fare funzionare il bicameralismo* (Firenze, Passigli, 2017).

[204] In fact, it is argued by Shepard (n 189) 40 that 'the salience of debates in the House of Commons as a means of oversight are constrained from the outset as the government controls not only the timetable but much of the ground on which it will debate'.

[205] More radically, Yamamoto (n 11) 9 (the purpose of these tools is 'to detect and prevent abuse, arbitrary behaviour, or illegal and unconstitutional conduct on the part of the government and public agencies').

[206] Maffio (n 5).

[207] F Boudet, 'La force juridique des résolutions parlementaires' (1958) *Revue du droit publique* 271.

[208] In Spain, the investiture is celebrated in two steps (Art 99 of the Constitution and s 171 of the Spanish Congress Standing Orders), respectively requiring a vote by absolute and simple majority. In Italy, 'motivated' motions of investiture are voted by both Houses according to art 94 of the Constitution by roll call. On the other cases of positive parliamentarism, see above ch 3, section I.

are deemed to be the strongest parliamentary oversight tools. They are the only real binding procedures available to Parliament and they find their legal base directly in the Constitution, which sets the basic conditions for approving and removing the confidence in the executive.

Investiture motions are not just a means of formalising Parliament's confidence in the newly appointed government; they also offer the opportunity for a preventive control on the list of policy priorities included in the political programme of the executive. Motions of no confidence or censure may determine the denial or withdrawal of confidence, which can force the government out of power. The vote can affect the government as a whole or an individual minister, in which case the government is not automatically obliged to resign. This is a 'last resort' oversight tool that serves as an ultimate sanction more than as a means of creating a new legislative–executive balance,[209] with an exception made for the hypothesis – provided by the German and Spanish constitutions – of the 'constructive' vote of no confidence.[210]

Different types of procedural guarantee are foreseen in the Constitution and in the Rules of Procedure to prevent these tools from being abused. These usually include: the setting of a minimum quorum of members for tabling the motion and the limitation of the number of subscriptions for each member;[211] the determination of a minimum time-lapse from the introduction of the motion to its vote;[212] the requirement of a majority for the motion to be passed.[213] All these guarantees are manifestations of a *parlementarisme rationalisé* (rationalised parliamentarism)[214] and their purpose is to grant stability to the government, preventing any hypothesis of a 'surprise' vote. Due to their irreversible effect on the life of the executive, motions of censure or no confidence are unlikely to pass[215] and yet, for the purposes of oversight, the simple fact of having a public confrontation between elected representatives and members of government turns out to be beneficial for Parliament and for the public.[216]

In certain cases, the government has the power to invoke its responsibility before Parliament, subjecting the prosecution of the confidence relationship to the approval of a certain proposal. This mechanism, which finds different regulations and labels in France,[217]

---

[209] Yamamoto (n 11) 9.

[210] Art 67 German Basic Law; and Art 113 Spanish Constitution.

[211] The number of members' subscriptions is one tenth in France (art 49 Constitution – on the submission and debate of the motion, see arts 152, 153, 154 and 155 of the French Assembly Rules of Procedure); Spain (Art 113 Constitution); Italy (art 94 Constitution). In Germany, the quorum for 'constructive' motions of no confidence is of one quarter of the members of the Bundestag or a parliamentary group of equal consistence (Art 67 Basic Law).

[212] The time lapse is 48 hours in France (art 49.2 Constitution) and Germany (Art 67 Basic Law); three days in Italy (art 94 Constitution).

[213] In most countries, the standard majority is required for a motion of censure to be passed. In France, the rule is the absolute majority (art 49.2 Constitution).

[214] F Bastien, 'II. Un parlementarisme "rationalisé"' in F Bastien (ed), *Le régime politique de la Ve République* (Paris, La Découverte, 2011).

[215] See the data published in IPU and UNDP, *Global Parliamentary Report 2017* (n 27) 57 f.

[216] ibid, 58.

[217] Art 49 of the Constitution, on the power of the Prime Minister to invoke the responsibility of the government before the National Assembly on the approval of a Bill concerning finance legislation or social security funding.

Italy,[218] Spain[219] and also partially in Germany,[220] is only apparently similar to the other confidence votes: it may be aimed at 'protecting' a certain proposal, which is deemed to be pivotal for the implementation of the programme, more than at raising government responsibility before Parliament. Consequently, the connection of these tools with the oversight function is highly questionable.

A second instance corresponds to the tabling of non-legislative motions (or resolutions of a non-legislative nature)[221] whose aim is to define a policy position on a certain issue without producing any implication on the confidence relationship. The case of France is paradigmatic of the potential impact that these acts may produce on executive–legislative relations. Resolutions were not mentioned in the 1958 Constitution to prevent this practice from being abused, as happened in the preceding 'regimes'.[222] It was introduced only 50 years later, through the 2008 constitutional amendment (article 34.1 of the Constitution), to enable the Chambers to express a position that is not binding on the government,[223] insofar as its adoption or rejection does not invoke the responsibility of the executive and the act does not address any order.[224] French resolutions closely relate to the legislative function, because they prevent the adoption of laws devoid of any statutory scope, as in the case of the *lois mémorielles* (memory laws).[225] At the same time, they are instrumental to the oversight function, replacing the ex post oversight with an anticipated scrutiny which is only apparently inoffensive,[226] because the power to stage issues and concerns cannot be underestimated by the executive.[227]

In the countries where preventive parliamentary tools are most developed, including Italy and Spain, motions (or resolutions) are used as a means to foster a general debate, surrounded by extensive publicity, and to 'advise' the government on the conduct of public policies.[228] In many cases, they tend to press the government to adopt certain legislative

---

[218] The question of confidence is not formally regulated in the Constitution, but acts as a constitutional convention, recognised by the Rules of Procedure of the two Houses (art 116 Chamber of Deputies Rules of Procedure; and art 161 Senate Rules of Procedure).

[219] Art 112 of the Constitution; and ss 173 and 174 Spanish Congress Standing Orders, on the 'question of confidence' submitted by the Prime Minister in his/her programme or in a general policy statement.

[220] Pursuant to Art 69 of the German Basic Law, the Federal Chancellor can submit a motion for a vote of confidence.

[221] s 193 of the Spanish Congress Standing Orders.

[222] This 'silence' was given a rigorous interpretation by the Conseil Constitutionnel in two renowned decisions (Décision 24 June 1959, 59-2 DC, and Décision 25 June 1959, 59-3 DC), which considered as legitimate only the resolutions addressing either Chamber (rather than the government) on 'internal' issues. Pursuant to the Conseil Constitutionnel, the only oversight procedures available are those regulated by arts 49 and 50 of the Constitution, consisting of a vote on a motion of censure or a question of confidence. L Favoreu and L Philip, *Les grandes décisions du Conseil constitutionnel*, 14th edn (Paris, Dalloz, 2007) 33 f.

[223] E Balladur, *Une Ve République plus démocratique – Comité de réflexion et de proposition sur la modernisation et le rééquilibrage des institutions de la Ve République* (Paris, La Documentation Française, 2007) 57. The nature of resolutions as non-binding tools is stressed by Boudet (n 207) 271 f.

[224] Art 136 Assembly Rules of Procedure.

[225] M Frangi, 'Les lois mémorielles: de l'expression de la volonté générale au législateur historien' (2005) 1 *Revue du Droit Public* 241.

[226] S Niquège, 'Les résolutions parlementaires de l'article 34-1 de la Constitution' (2010) 84 *Revue française de droit constitutionnel* 865.

[227] The new procedure introduced by art 6 of Organic Law no 2009-403 of 15 April 2009, on the application of the revised art 34.1 of the Constitution, finds its main limit in the plenary regime associated to resolutions.

[228] Sánchez de Dios (n 7) 16, 20 and 26 (on the non-competitive nature of these tools, based on cross-party mode).

solutions; in others, the expected outcome from the executive is a non-legislative one. The experience of the House of Commons provides examples of substantive motions as a mechanism that, on the one hand, allows the opposition to bring into the political debate the salient political issues[229] and, on the other, enables backbenchers to show support for or opposition to selected issues.[230]

In order to favour the transparent representation of party positions, non-legislative motions are usually introduced as collective tools that must clearly indicate the referent party.[231] These acts are generally debated in plenary sittings, open to the intervention not just of the proponent group and of the government, but also to other members. Their discussion may be held in parallel with other motions concerning the same issue and may allow the tabling of amendments.[232]

Finally, the third instance consists of the drafting of resolutions or other 'proposals' as a means for concluding ongoing procedures through a vote in the plenary. Broadly speaking, the difference between the second and third instances lies in the procedural regime: the former are autonomous items, the latter non-autonomous items. Simply put, although different labels are used in the Constitution and Rules of Procedure, whereas motions usually deal with substantial policy issues, resolutions are meant to enable a vote – usually on the initiative of a committee – on a pending procedure. These may include government communications or policy statements,[233] interpellations,[234] resolutions of the European Parliament and EU documents in general,[235] decisions of the Constitutional Court, and so forth.

Different types of act can be included within this category. In the German Bundestag, 'motions for resolutions' are voted on after the end of the debate on the 'major' procedure to which they refer.[236] The Italian Parliament experiences different types of 'resolutions', regulated either directly in the Rules of Procedure or in sectorial legislation as a mechanism to submit to the approval of the plenary a certain document or proposal.[237] There can

---

[229] Motions supported by the opposition may find an opportunity of being tabled based on Rule 14.2 of the House of Commons Standing Orders that sets 20 days or 120 hours in each session for proceedings on opposition business.

[230] Early-Day Motions are the motions submitted for debate in the House of Commons with no specific time allocated to their discussion. Very few motions are debated and yet this tool may gain public interest and media coverage. Ministers, whips and parliamentary private secretaries do not usually sign Early Day Motions, which are rather used by backbenchers. Once tabled, they can be amended. See Rule 22.2 and Rule 83I of the House of Commons Standing Orders.

[231] In the Italian Parliament, motions are strictly regulated as collective tools, that can be tabled in the Lower House by one president of a parliamentary group or 10 members (art 110 Chamber Rules of Procedure) and in the Upper House by eight members (art 157.1 Senate Rules of Procedure – for urgent motions subscribed by at least one fifth of the members, see art 157.3).

[232] s 194 Spanish Congress Standing Orders; arts 112 and 113 Italian Chamber Rules of Procedure; arts 158 and 160 Italian Senate Rules of Procedure.

[233] Parliamentary groups can table draft resolutions to conclude the debate on the government's communication (ss 196 and 197 Spanish Congress Standing Orders).

[234] s 184 Spanish Congress Standing Orders.

[235] See below ch 7, section III.

[236] Rule 88 of the Bundestag Rules of Procedure.

[237] E Griglio, 'I poteri di controllo del Parlamento italiano alla luce del bicameralism paritario' in Vv Aa, *Il Filangieri. Quaderno 2015–2016. Il Parlamento dopo il referendum costituzionale* (Napoli, Jovene, 2017) 217 (resolutions in the Italian Parliament are a multifaceted tool, acting as a means of evaluation, authorisation, political direction).

be resolutions debated in committee[238] or submitted to the plenary to conclude an 'affair' formally assigned to the committee;[239] resolutions approved in the same text by the two Houses on the Economy and Finance Document submitted by the government to present its plans for the future budgetary manoeuvre;[240] resolutions approved by the defence committees to approve new military engagements;[241] and resolutions voted for by the committees for European affairs on EU legislative or non-legislative proposals.[242] In the case of the Danish Folketing, the expression 'proposals to be passed' is used to identify an ancillary act that, during another procedure, may foster a debate and lead to a vote on a proposal.[243] The Riksdag Act entitles standing committees to introduce proposals in the plenary on any subject falling within their remit (committee reports).[244] Also, the Parliamentary Ombudsman may take submissions to the Riksdag on account of an issue that has arisen in its supervisory activity.[245]

On the whole, these procedures may serve different purposes, relating either to the conduct of the general policy or to the tackling of sectorial issues, and they may integrate variably in the parliamentary machinery. Nonetheless, they all produce a common impact on executive–legislative relations, consisting of the adoption of non-binding directions that, without invoking the responsibility of the government, may however set the premises for a reinforced ex post oversight aimed at assessing the correspondence to what has been shared and agreed in the ex ante stage. In this vein, tracking the recommendations made by parliaments and the responses received from government and granting publicity to these statistics would prove a valuable means for supporting the executive's moral obligation to provide a follow-up.[246]

C. Other Ex Ante Oversight Procedures: The Advisory and 'Participatory' Capacity of Parliaments

Parliaments receive a wide range of executive documents and proposals, drafted either by the national government or by EU institutions. Some of them are submitted to Parliament to

---

[238] Art 117.1 Chamber Rules of Procedure enables standing committees to vote on resolutions on 'affairs' included in their scope that normally do not require the approval of the plenary, unless they deal with issues of major relevance or the government does not agree with the merit of the act.

[239] Art 50.2 Senate Rules of Procedure.

[240] Art 118-bis.3 Chamber Rules of Procedure; and 125-bis.3 Senate Rules of Procedure. G Rivosecchi, *L'indirizzo politico finanziario tra Costituzione italiana e vincoli europei* (Padova, Cedam, 2007) 294 ff.

[241] Law no 145 of 21 July 2016, on Italian participation in military missions. Misalignments between the two Houses in the selection and implementation of the procedure are highlighted in E Griglio, 'I seguiti parlamentari della nuova legge quadro sulle missioni internazionali' (2017) 2 *Quaderni costituzionali* 397.

[242] See below section C (nn 259–70).

[243] During the debate on an interpellation and the debate on an account of the Prime Minister, a '*proposal to be passed*' may be introduced, insofar that it is 'naturally linked to the debate going on' (s 24 Folketing Standing Orders); this is not amendable.

[244] Art 16 Riksdag Act.

[245] Supplementary provision 9.17.5 of the Riksdag Act. The submissions from the Auditors General are regulated by supplementary provision 9.17.6, arts 18 and 19 of the Riksdag Act.

[246] IPU and UNDP, *Global Parliamentary Report 2017* (n 27) estimates that 24% of parliaments track recommendations and responses on an ad hoc basis. Ad hoc bodies may be created to fulfil this role, an example being provided by the Parliamentary Evaluation and Research Unit of the Swedish Parliament.

be debated and scrutinised, usually at committee level, and possibly leading to the adoption of an 'opinion' or an 'authorisation' addressed to the government.

Among the most traditional procedures is parliamentary appreciation of government appointments, which is usually carried out at committee level. In parliamentary regimes, no legislature has the power to veto government appointments of senior officials, as in the case of the *advice and consent* of the US Senate.[247] The traditional formula of ministerial responsibility strongly limits Parliament's power to oversee government appointments. Nonetheless, even in the UK, where the government has traditionally been reluctant to submit its appointments to Parliament, since 2004 the House of Commons select committees have been allowed to hold 'confirmation hearings' in respect of certain appointments.[248] This procedure was strengthened in 2008, following the Green Paper on *The Governance of Britain*, which suggested the submission of pre-appointment hearings with the relevant select committee and a list of nominees for key positions.[249] The hearings conclude with the adoption of an opinion which is not considered as binding on a government's right of appointment.

Where Parliament's power to oversee government appointments finds more extensive regulation is probably in Italy and France. In Italy, since 1978[250] it also covers appointments in public bodies at arm's length from ministers: such nominees are subject to Parliament for a preliminary opinion of relevant committees, which is not binding on the government. This procedure was introduced to allow Parliament to gain back the oversight and political direction of some pivotal spheres of policy-making, ensuring transparency and pluralistic control.[251] In literature, it was criticised because it apparently violated the separation of powers, enabling the Parliament to exercise a sort of co-decision and co-management in sensitive areas of public economy.[252] In fact, Parliament has always made moderate use of this prerogative. Moreover, since the 1990s, the nomination of some apical positions of independent authorities has been subject to a pre-appointment parliamentary appraisal productive of binding effects on the executive. As a matter of fact, the government cannot formalise the appointment if it is not supported by the positive opinion of the relevant committees of both Houses, adopted by a two-thirds majority.[253] This is probably the most advanced form of ex ante oversight applicable to government appointments in a parliamentary regime, which in no case could reach the 'consociational' patterns typical to presidential systems.[254]

---

[247] MP Carey, *Presidential Appointment, the Senate's Confirmation Process, and Changes Made in the 112th Congress* (Washington, Congressional Research Service, 2012).

[248] The practice of the confirmation hearings was launched by the House of Commons Liaison Committee, *Shifting the Balance: Unfinished Business. First Report of Session 2000–01* (2000, HC 321) para 13.

[249] Cabinet Office, 'The Governance of Britain' (July 2007).

[250] Law no 14 of 24 January 1978, on parliamentary oversight of appointments in public bodies.

[251] S Cassese, 'Intervento' in Vv Aa, *L'altro potere in economia. La questione delle nomine negli enti pubblici* (Bari, De Donato, 1978) 185.

[252] S Labriola, 'Il controllo parlamentare sulle nomine negli enti pubblici' (1980) 4 *Politica del diritto* 543; and GF Ciaurro, 'Il controllo parlamentare sulle nomine negli enti pubblici' in GF Ciaurro, *Le istituzioni parlamentari* (Milano, Giuffrè, 1982).

[253] The procedure is applied to appointments in the Authority for electric energy and gas (art 2.7 of Law no 481 of 14 November 1995); in the Communications Authority (art 3 of Law no 24 of 31 July 1997, 9); and in the National Institute for Statistics (art 16.1 of Legislative Decree no 322 of 6 September 1989).

[254] D Siclari, 'Il controllo parlamentare sugli atti non normativi del Governo e l'esame di documenti trasmessi al Parlamento dal Governo e da altre Autorità: profili evolutivi' in R Dickmann and S Staiano (eds), *Funzioni parlamentari non legislative* (n 87) 348 f.

A similar procedure was introduced in France by the 2008 constitutional amendment. Some presidential appointments, on account of their importance in the protection of rights and liberties or for the economic and social life of the Nation, can be made only following a public opinion by the relevant standing committees of each Assembly.[255] The President of the Republic cannot formalise the appointment if at least three-fifths of the votes expressed in the committees of the two Houses are against the nominee.[256] The high majority required for vetoing the appointment strongly limits the effectiveness of this tool, and yet the publicity associated with the opinion released by the committee makes it extremely difficult for the President to oppose this position.[257] As a matter of fact, the introduction of this procedure has raised the perception that committee members are de facto co-authors of the appointment.[258]

Beyond these 'national' instances of ex ante oversight, it is in the field of EU affairs where parliaments have recently experienced a significant reinforcement of their scrutiny prerogatives in regard to the early stages of EU decision-making. The Treaty of Lisbon established an ad hoc procedure, the Early Warning System (EWS), aimed at engaging national parliaments in the monitoring of the 'principle of subsidiarity', as indicated by Article 5(3) of the Treaty on European Union, and regulated by Protocol no. 2, on the application of the principles of subsidiarity and proportionality.[259] National parliaments are asked to verify the respect of the subsidiarity principle by scrutinising all draft legislative acts and issuing 'reasoned opinions', addressed to EU institutions.[260] Beyond the formal procedure of the EWS, another procedure, established through a sort of constitutional convention by the Barroso Commission and known as 'political dialogue', has enabled national parliaments to monitor the respect of the principles of subsidiarity and proportionality in all legislative and non-legislative draft EU proposals.

The new scrutiny tools vested in national parliaments reveal at least three distinctive features from the perspective of the executive oversight machinery. First, for the very first time, the legal basis of national parliaments' scrutiny prerogative is not to be found in national constitutions, statutory laws or parliamentary Rules of Procedure, but in an act – the Lisbon Treaty – which is external to the traditional sphere of the national constitutional dimension. Second, the reasoned opinions released by national parliaments find their direct interlocutor in the European Commission, but are indirectly addressed also to the national government. As a matter of fact, these procedures have a two-fold oversight effect, as they enable national parliaments to assess the proposals of the

---

[255] Art 13.5 of the French Constitution.

[256] The list of appointments subject to the new procedure was defined in two steps by Organic Law no 2009-257 of 5 May 2009, on the appointment of the presidents of the societies *France Télévisions* and *Radio France*, and by Organic Law no 2010-838 of 23 July 2010, on the implementation of the fifth paragraph of art 13 of the Constitution. AM Le Pourhiet, 'Le pouvoir de nomination du Chef de l'État contrôlé par le Parlement' in JP Camby, P Fraisseix and J Gicquel (eds), *La révision de 2008: une nouvelle Constitution?* (Paris, LGDJ, 2011) 57 f.

[257] Houillon (n 41) 66.

[258] B Montay, 'Le pouvoir de nomination de l'Executive sous la Ve République' (2013) 11 *Jus Politicum* 1.

[259] P Casalena, N Lupo and C Fasone, 'Commentary on Protocol No 1 annexed to the Treaty of Lisbon (On the role of National Parliaments)' in HJ Blanke and S Mangiameli (eds), *The Treaty on European Union* (Berlin, Springer, 2013).

[260] National parliaments' reasoned opinions produce procedural effects only in the event that a certain number of parliaments raise concerns regarding subsidiarity ('yellow card' and 'orange card').

European Commission, with the purpose of influencing future policies,[261] and at the same time they may also be used as a mechanism for evaluating the conduct of EU affairs by the national government.[262] Third, the new mechanism is shaped as an instance of scrutiny of executive proposals, but its impact is not confined to legislative–executive interaction, as it actually enables national parliaments to become directly involved in the European decision-making processes.[263]

In practice, national parliaments have engaged quite proactively in the EWS and even more proactively in the political dialogue. They have adopted systemic procedures for scrutinising the draft proposals submitted by the European Commission. From a European perspective, the new mechanisms have proved not to be too influential in overall decision-making.[264] However, the impact on national parliamentary regimes has been quite relevant. National parliaments have gained an additional channel to influence executive decisions in the field of EU policy-making,[265] which complements pre-existing prerogatives, consisting of the power to scrutinise the domestic government.

As for the type of oversight mechanism associated with the EWS, the nature of the scrutiny task vested in national parliaments is highly controversial.[266] Following a strict interpretation of the EWS, national parliaments would be called on to monitor the respect of the subsidiarity principle by playing the role of mere legal advisers.[267] In contrast, the implementing practice seems to confirm that in many cases the EWS is interpreted and enforced by parliaments as a political, rather than merely as a legal, instrument:[268] the reasoned opinions approved so far confirm that parliaments tend to interpret in an extensive way the parameters of their own assessment, going beyond mere consideration of the

---

[261] G Martinico, 'Dating Cinderella: On Subsidiarity as a Political Safeguard of Federalism in the European Union' (2011) 4 *European Public Law* 649; and K Boronska-Hryniewiecka, 'Legitimacy through Subsidiarity? The Parliamentary Control of EU Policy-making' (2013) 1 *Polish Political Science Review* 84.

[262] T Raunio, 'The gatekeepers of European integration? The functions of national parliaments in the EU political system' (2011) 33 *Journal of European Integration* 303, 315; and C Fasone, 'Gli effetti del Trattato di Lisbona sulla funzione di controllo parlamentare' (2011) 2 *Rivista italiana di diritto pubblico comunitario* 353.

[263] C Fasone and N Lupo, 'Constitutional Review and The Powers of National Parliaments in EU Affairs. Erosion or Protection?' in D Jančić (ed), *National Parliaments after the Lisbon Treaty and the Euro Crisis. Resilience or Resignation?* (Oxford, Oxford University Press, 2017).

[264] Only in three cases has the minimum threshold for raising a yellow card been reached and only in one of those three did the Commission actually decide to withdraw its proposal.

[265] K Granat, *The Principle of Subsidiarity and its Enforcement in the EU Legal Order. The Role of National Parliaments in the Early Warning System* (Oxford, Hart Publishing, 2018) 227 ff.

[266] M Goldoni and A Jonsson Cornell, 'The Trajectory of the Early Warning System' in A Jonsson Cornell and M Goldoni (eds), *National and Regional Parliaments in the EU-Legislative Procedure Post-Lisbon The Impact of the Early Warning Mechanism* (Oxford, Hart Publishing, 2017); I Cooper, 'Is the Early Warning Mechanism a Legal or a Political Procedure? Three Questions and a Typology' in A Jonsson Cornell and M Goldoni (eds), *National and Regional Parliaments in the EU-Legislative Procedure Post-Lisbon The Impact of the Early Warning Mechanism* (Oxford, Hart Publishing, 2017).

[267] This vision is supported by P Kiiver, *The Early Warning System for the Principle of Subsidiarity: Constitutional Theory and Empirical Reality* (New York, Routledge, 2012); and F Fabbrini and K Granat, '"Yellow card, but no foul": The role of the national parliaments under the Subsidiarity Protocol and the Commission proposal for an EU regulation on the right to strike' (2013) 50 *Common Market Law Review* 115.

[268] M Goldoni, 'The Early Warning System and the Monti II Regulation: The Case for a Political Interpretation' (2014) 10 *European Constitutional Law Review* 90; and N Lupo, 'National Parliaments in the European Integration Process: Re-aligning Politics and Policies' in M Cartabia, N Lupo and A Simoncini (eds), *Democracy and Subsidiarity in the EU. National Parliaments, Regions and Civil Society in the Decision-Making Process* (Bologna, Il Mulino, 2013).

legal basis.[269] In this vein, given the ambiguous nature of the subsidiarity scrutiny, which lies in between law and politics, legal analysis and political assessment,[270] participation in the EWS can be clearly referred to the political oversight of executive action.

The intrusion of a supranational legal source into the scrutiny toolbox of national parliaments has created a precedent, which has since been replicated. Some of the measures adopted by the EU in response to the economic and financial crisis started in 2008, including the Treaty on Stability, Coordination and Governance in the Economic and Monetary Union, the *Six-Pack* and *Two-Pack*, have introduced a direct reference to the powers of national parliaments in the scrutiny of public finance.[271] The issue is highly controversial in literature,[272] but it is worth noting that some of the EU regulations ascribable to European economic governance include some direct (although isolated) references to ex ante 'participatory' powers of national parliaments, of a rather different nature. These are aimed at strengthening parliaments' right to be informed, in a timely way, on intergovernmental decision-making,[273] fostering a dialogue between representative assemblies and executive bodies[274] and, in the most advanced instances of scrutiny, foreseeing national legislatures' direct involvement in the 'European semester' stage of economic governance. The reference is to national parliaments' participation in the adoption of stability and convergence programmes, which is formulated in rather vague and imprecise terms by the EU Regulations, thus paving the way for an extremely differentiated range of national implementing mechanisms.[275]

The European legal framework is complemented by national legislation, which has defined and structured the participation of domestic parliaments in the economic governance, thus giving origin to a multifaceted system of informative, advisory, authorisation procedures.[276] Notwithstanding national variations, the new ex ante procedures can be

---

[269] This vision is supported by the experience of the third yellow card, which was used almost exclusively by Eastern and Central European parliaments to oppose a directive on the posted workers which their governments opposed (D Fromage and V Kreilinger, 'National parliaments' third yellow card and the struggle over the revision of the posted workers directive' (2017) 10 *European Journal of Legal Studies* 125).

[270] The principle of subsidiarity is defined as 'politically complex and legally uncertain' by G de Búrca, 'The principle of subsidiarity and the Court of Justice as an institutional actor' (1998) 36 *Journal of Common Market Studies* 217. On the principle as a 'chamelon', M Evans and A Zimmermans, 'Editors' Conclusions: Future Directions for Subsidiarity' in M Evans and A Zimmermans (eds), *Global Perspectives on Subsidiarity* (Wiesbaden, Springer, 2014).

[271] See below ch 8, section III.

[272] D Jančić (ed), *National Parliaments after the Lisbon Treaty and the Euro Crisis. Resilience or Resignation?* (Oxford, Oxford University Press, 2017). Crum, 'Parliamentary accountability in multilevel governance: what role for parliaments in post-crisis EU economic governance?' (2017) 25 *Journal of European Public Policy* 268.

[273] See the Premise no 1 and arts 3.1, 14.3 Reg no 472/2013/UE; art 11.2 Reg no 473/2013/UE.

[274] Arts 3.8, 3.9, 7.11, 14.5 Reg no 472/2013/UE and art 7.3 Reg no 473/2013/UE on the possibility offered to national parliaments to consult the Commission on the budget Bill.

[275] Arts 3.4 and 7.4 Reg no 1466/1997/CE, as modified by Reg no 1175/2011/UE, provide that stability and convergence programmes 'shall include information on its status in the context of national procedures, in particular whether the programme was presented to the national parliament, and whether the national parliament had the opportunity to discuss the Council's opinion on the previous programme or, if relevant, any recommendation or warning, and whether there has been parliamentary approval of the programme'. D Capuano and E Griglio, 'La nuova *governance* economica europea. I risvolti sulle procedure parlamentari italiane' in A Manzella and N Lupo (eds), *Il sistema parlamentare euro-nazionale. Lezioni* (Torino, Giappichelli, 2014) 247 ff; E Griglio and N Lupo, 'Parliamentary democracy and the Eurozone crisis' (2012) 1 *Law and Economics Yearly Review* II, 313, 345 ff.

[276] See below ch 8, section III.

appreciated as an attempt to enhance anticipated parliamentary scrutiny, granting the respect of budgetary balance, enforcing the monitoring of public finance, and promoting the protection of financial rights of territorial entities. In fact, the oversight potential of these procedures is largely dependent on national parliaments' capacity to frame their budgetary power in the ex ante (and ex post) stage, rather than in the stage of budget approval.[277]

V. Questioning the Government: A Hybrid Oversight Tool

Parliamentary questioning is a constant function of national parliaments worldwide.[278] The 'right' of MPs to question members of the executive came out of the parliamentary practice, dating back to the first question recorded in the House of Lords in 1721. The question was tabled by Earl Cowper asking the government whether there was any truth in the report on the departure from the country and the arrest in Brussels of the Chief Cashier of the South Sea Company, Robert Knight.[279] In Continental Europe, the right to question members of government entered the history of parliamentarism in the second half of the nineteenth century:[280] the *Interpellationsrecht* (right of interpellation) was formally recognised by the internal Rules of Procedure of the Prussian Landtag approved on 28 March 1849.[281] Nowadays, this tool finds regulation in constitutional clauses[282] or, more commonly, in the parliamentary Rules of Procedure. It is considered among the most strategic oversight tools available to Parliament to hold the government to account in a public and transparent manner.[283]

A. Questioning and its Multiple Shapes in Parliamentary Regimes

Questioning, grown out of the Westminster tradition, is peculiar to parliamentary regimes. The US Congress has no significant parliamentary questioning, thus representing a notable exception to the general practice of questions as part of parliamentary procedures.[284] Congressional committees may question witnesses, but there is no questioning procedure taking place on the floor of the Houses, nor can members of Congress table written questions. This peculiarity is explained by the competitive rather than cooperative relation linking the executive and the legislative branches in a presidential-type regime.

---

[277] G Rivosecchi, 'Il Parlamento di fronte alla crisi economico-finanziaria' (2012) 3 *Rivista AIC* 1, 4.

[278] M Franklin and P Norton (eds), *Parliamentary Questions* (Oxford, Clarendon Press, 1993).

[279] House of Commons Information Office, 'Parliamentary Questions' (2010) *Factsheet P1 Procedures Series* 2.

[280] P Galeazzi, 'Le interrogazioni parlamentari al Governo' (1918) 10 *Rivista di diritto pubblico e della pubblica amministrazione in Italia* 72, with regard to Italy.

[281] J Hatschek, *Das Interpellationsrecht im Rahmen der modern Ministerverantwortlichkeit* (Leipzig, GJ Göschen, 1909).

[282] An example is offered by art 48, last paragraph of the French Constitution, amended in 2008, providing that at least one week per month should be reserved as a priority to questions from MPs.

[283] On questioning as a manifestation of the oversight function, see the Spanish Tribunal Constitucional, SSTC 225/1992, para 2; 107/2001, para 4; 33/2010, para 4; 200/2014, para 8; 201/2014, para 4; 23/2015, para 8.

[284] S Martin, 'Parliamentary Questions' (2013) SUNY/CID Comparative Assessment of Parliaments (CAP) Note 2.

In contrast, in parliamentary systems, questioning envisages multiple relational patterns.[285] The basic scheme unfolds through the question tabled by one or more MPs and the answer (that may be written or oral) by one or more members of the government. This entry-level scheme is usually enriched by further patterns, allowing the questioner not only to get an answer from the government, but also to respond, raise supplementary questions, turn the question into a motion or a resolution. Such a variety of relational modules is typical to pure parliamentary systems, encompassing the parliamentary appointment of government, the confidence relationship and the alignment of the executive with a parliamentary majority. In semi-presidential systems, questioning is instead stuck in the entry-level scheme of the question/answer mechanism, with rather limited options of further interaction.

The European style of questioning has been transposed from national parliamentary traditions to the European Parliament. The latter has actually inherited many of the tools implemented at national level[286] and yet questioning in this legislature shows two rather unique features. On the one hand, it has multiple addresses, because the fragmented nature of the EU executive[287] enables the European Parliament to address questions both to the Commission and to the other executive bodies, including the Council, the President of the European Council and even the European Central Bank.[288] On the other hand, in addition to standard purposes, questioning by the European Parliament also serves as a means to signal to the European Commission the upcoming risks of infringement of EU law.[289]

Questioning as a relational mechanism between the legislative–executive branches serves the purpose of parliamentary oversight in many ways. Beyond the original aim of obtaining information, in modern-day parliaments questioning might act both as an ex ante

---

[285] The variety of purposes associated with this mechanism is extensively studied in political science: S Martin, 'Parliamentary Questions, the Behaviour of Legislators, and the Function of Legislatures: An Introduction' (2011) 17 *The Journal of Legislative Studies* 259; and the articles included in the special issue (ivi). Questioning in the benchmark parliaments is addressed in multiple ways: for Denmark, E Damgaard, 'Parliamentary Questions and Control in Denmark' in M Wiberg (ed), *Parliamentary Control in the Nordic Countries* (Jyväskylä, The Finnish Political Science Association, 1994); H Jensen, 'Committees as Actors or Arenas? Putting Questions to the Danish Standing Committees' in M Wiberg (ed), *Parliamentary Control in the Nordic Countries* (Jyväskylä, The Finnish Political Science Association, 1994); for Sweden, I Mattson, 'Parliamentary Questions in the Swedish Riksdag' in M Wiberg (ed), *Parliamentary Control in the Nordic Countries* (Jyväskylä, The Finnish Political Science Association, 1994); for the United Kingdom, K Bird, 'Gendering Parliamentary Questions' (2005) 7 *The British Journal of Politics and International Relations* 353; for the European Parliament, SO Proksch and JB Slapin, 'Position-Taking in European Parliament Speeches' (2010) 40 *British Journal of Political Science* 587; S Lazardeux, '"Une Question Ecrite, Pour Quoi Faire" The Causes of the Production of Written Questions in the French Assemblée Nationale' (2005) 3 *French Politics* 258; for Germany, HM Kepplinger, 'Kleine Anfragen: Funktionale Analyse einer parlamentarischen Praxis' in JW Patzelt, M Sebaldt and U Kranenpohl (eds), *Res publica semper reformanda. Wissenschaft und politische Bildung im Dienste des Gemeinwohls. Estschrift für Heinrich Oberreuter* (Wiesbaden, VS Verlag für Sozialwissenschaften, 2007); for Italy, F Russo, 'The Constituency as a Focus of Representation: Studying the Italian Case through the Analysis of Parliamentary Questions' (2011) *The Journal of Legislative Studies* 290.

[286] R Corbett, F Jacobs and M Shackleton, *The European Parliament*, 8th edn (London, John Harper, 2011) 315 ff.

[287] D Curtin, *Executive Power of the European Union. Law, Practices, and the Living Constitution* (Oxford, Oxford University Press, 2009).

[288] Rule 136 European Parliament Rules of Procedure. On questions for written answers to the ECB, Rule 140 European Parliament Rules of Procedure.

[289] This is an instance of 'fire alarm' that brings the European Parliament closer to the oversight dynamics of presidential systems; McCubbins and T Schwartz, 'Congressional oversight overlooked: police patrol versus fire alarms' (1984) 28 *The American Journal of Political Science* 165.

tool for gathering information and checking (or pressing for) future policy actions;[290] and as an ex post mechanism for asking the government to give an account of the conduct of past policies.[291] Its implementation demonstrates that the oversight potential of this tool is conditional on the party system[292] and the executive–party dimension.[293] On the one hand, parliamentary questioning is deemed to be a typical opposition tool, acting as one of the guarantees available to minorities.[294] On the other hand, majority groups may find in the tabling of questions and interpellations a strategic means of interaction with the government, especially in cases of mismatch in the management of current policy issues.[295] The latter hypothesis is most likely to occur in consensual democracies with large coalition governments or in cases of minority governments.[296]

The party positioning of questions is deeply influenced by the regulation of the power of initiative. Whereas in the history of the Westminster Parliament this was conceived as an individual tool, the German tradition of the *interpellationsrecht* reinterpreted the procedure in a collective perspective, resulting in the two mechanisms of the *Große Anfrage* (major interpellation) and the *Kleine Anfrage* (minor interpellation).[297] Also, some types of oral questions are now regulated as a collective tool, requiring a minimum quorum of subscriptions to be tabled.[298] Individual interests are therefore interacting with party interests in determining the use of questioning in daily parliamentary practice.[299]

In a relational mechanism, questioning unfolds in a rather different way depending on the position that the reference Chamber holds in regard to the executive branch and the confidence relationship. This point represents a distinctive element of Lower and Upper Houses, where questioning pursues rather unique purposes, largely dependent on the nature of the bicameral system involved.[300] Combining all these factors, it is therefore easily

---

[290] Questioning is seen as a means not just to combat information asymmetries but also to give orientations and directions to the executive; see M Sánchez de Dios and M Wiberg, 'Questioning in European Parliaments' (2011) 17 *The Journal of Legislative Studies* 354; G Filippetta, 'L'illusione ispettiva: le interrogazioni e le interpellanze parlamentari tra ricostruzioni dottrinali, rappresentanza politica e funzione di indirizzo' (1991) 36 *Giurisprudenza costituzionale* 4203.

[291] Comparative analysis on the use of questioning shows that representation of constituency interests is a recurring concern for MPs when addressing members of government. Martin, 'Parliamentary Questions' (n 284) 15 f; Garcia Roca, 'Control parlamentario' (n 3); and Russo (n 285).

[292] The use of parliamentary questions in terms of party competition is analysed by S Otjes, '"No politics in the agenda-setting meeting": plenary agenda setting in the Netherlands' (2019) 42 *West European Politics* 728. See also M Wiberg and A Koura, 'The Logic of Parliamentary Questioning' in M Wiberg (ed), *Parliamentary Control in the Nordic Countries* (Helsinki, Finnish Political Science Association, 1994) 23.

[293] A Lijphart, *Patterns of Democracy. Government Forms and Performance in Thirty-Six Countries*, 2nd edn (New Haven, CT, Yale University Press, 2012).

[294] Minorities may be allowed specific time assignments to address their questions to the government. Arts 133.2 and 133.4 of the French Assembly Rules of Procedure reserves to opposition members half of the questions that, each week, must be debated in the plenary pursuant to art 48.6 of the Constitution.

[295] On questioning as a 'potential mechanism for parties in coalition governments to keep tabs on each other's ministers', Martin and Whitaker (n 69) 1469.

[296] O Rozenberg and S Martin, 'Questioning parliamentary questions' (2011) 17 *The Journal of Legislative Studies* 400.

[297] See below (nn 307 and 326–28).

[298] For instance, according to art 136 of the European Parliament Rules of Procedure, parliamentary questions followed by a debate can by tabled by either a committee, a political group or 40 MEPs.

[299] On the use of questions as a means available to individual MPs for pursuing electoral purposes, Damgaard, 'Parliamentary Questions' (n 285); and Mattson (n 285).

[300] On this point, see below ch 5.

demonstrated that questioning is a rather versatile oversight tool, able to adapt to different constitutional and political arrangements and to support a wide range of goals. This adaptability is mirrored by the variety of implementing rules and practices.

Comparing procedures is not always an easy task due to linguistic asymmetries in labelling the main acts used to question the government. To give some examples, the word 'interpellation' usually identifies major questions addressing general and complex topics,[301] whose aim is not to verify whether a specific fact has occurred or whether certain information is available, but rather to check the reasons and motivations behind a government's action in certain policy areas.[302] In fact, the comparative picture shows cases of interpellations that are devoid of these features[303] and cases of questions that respect these conditions, however are not called 'interpellations'. Notwithstanding all these variations, the formal classification of an act as either a 'question' or an 'interpellation' cannot be underestimated, due to the different procedural follow-ups associated with these categories.

On procedural grounds, questioning mechanisms may differ according to a number of variables:[304] the oral or written form of the answer; the timing of questioning (whereas questions are submitted in advance or spontaneous); the possibility to implement the answer with a debate (in the form of a further reply by the questioner, the development of supplementary questions or the integration of other members); and the possibility to vote on a motion or resolution.[305]

B. Questions and Interpellations: Different Procedures with a Common Purpose?

Focusing on the main types of act, it can be argued that written questions are the most recurring tool in parliamentary practice and yet they are considered the least effective questioning mechanism.[306] On the one hand, this is a typical individual oversight tool: it was introduced in Germany by the small parliamentary reform of 1969 to provide an alternative means for questioning ministers to the 'collective' mechanisms of the *Große* and *Kleine Anfrage*.[307] Individual MPs usually resort to written questions to have easy access to information from the government, concerning either a specific policy issue or a constituency concern. To prevent stalemate in parliamentary activity, some parliaments limit the power to submitting questions.[308]

---

[301] According to s 181 of the Spanish Congress Standing Orders, interpellations shall be concerned 'with the reasons for, or intentions underlying, the conduct of the Executive in matters of general policy, whether of the Cabinet itself or of any Ministerial Department'.

[302] G Bruyneel, 'Interpellations, Questions and Analogous Procedures for the Control of Government Actions and Challenging the Responsibility of the Government' (1978) *Constitutional and Parliamentary Information* 66, 84.

[303] Apparently, § 21.1 of the Folketing Standing Orders, which refers interpellations to the wish of a member to submit a public matter for debate and to request a statement from one or several ministers.

[304] Russo and Wiberg (n 12) 218 f.

[305] Substantive criteria for classifying parliamentary questions are discussed in Rozenberg and Martin (n 296) 394.

[306] Martin, 'Parliamentary Questions' (n 284) 9.

[307] S Morscher, *Die parlamentarische Interpellation* (Berlin, Dunckler and Humblot, 1973).

[308] In the German Bundestag, for instance, any MP can table a maximum number of four questions per month (Annex 4 to the Bundestag Rules of Procedure, on 'Guidelines for Question Time and for written questions').

On the other hand, written questions unfold through a lengthy and complex process, since the answers are usually drafted by the administration of the relevant ministry and are delayed. This factor limits the political relevance of the act and tends to bureaucratise the overall mechanism, raising several implementing problems: these include providing partial and incomplete answers, referring to vague and imprecise data and most of all answering late.[309] The Rules of Procedure usually set time limits on the government to provide an answer,[310] but the high number of questions tabled makes it daunting to respect these deadlines. Delays are an ordinary practice and many questions remain unanswered by the end of the legislative term.[311]

A rather different outcome, in terms of legislative–executive relations, is associated with oral questions, which are asked and answered on the floor of the Chamber or in committee. They may be addressed to any minister on issues concerning the activity of his/her department, including ministers that are not members of any Chamber, usually following a rotation.[312] The only limitation followed by Westminster parliaments is that ministers can receive and answer questions only in the Chamber of which they are members.[313]

In oral questioning, three procedural factors exercise a major influence on the effectiveness of the procedure. The first factor affects the option for spontaneous questions, raised directly on the floor of the House or communicated with very limited notice;[314] the alternative option provides the preventive written submission of the question before it is taken and debated in the Chamber.[315] Whereas the former hypothesis has grown out of the original Westminster questioning tradition, the latter hypothesis has been worked on

In the European Parliament, the limit is of 20 written questions every three months (art 138 European Parliament Rules of Procedure). Art 135 of the French National Assembly Rules of Procedure leaves to the Conference of the Presidents the determination of the maximum number of questions that can be submitted by each member during each session.

[309] P Novak, *Parliamentary questions in selected legislative chambers* (Brussels, European Parliament – Directorate General for Internal Policies, 2014) 8 ff; and Yamamoto (n 11) 58 f. The quality and timeliness of answers in the practice of the House of Commons is discussed in the Report of the House of Commons Procedure Committee, *Monitoring of written Parliamentary questions: progress report for Session 2015–2016* (2016, HC 191).

[310] These range from the four days of the Swedish Riksdag to the six weeks for answering ordinary questions in the European Parliament. Intermediate deadlines are foreseen in Denmark (six days), Britain (seven days), Germany (one week), Italy and Spain (20 days), France (one month).

[311] This problem is widespread in Italy. A detailed study of the Italian Senate on the practice of questioning from the beginning of the fifteenth parliament to the seventeenth parliament (28 April 2006–31 December 2016) reported that senators had resorted to it 28.360 times, submitting 1.271 interpellations, 7.780 oral questions and 19.309 questions requiring a written reply. Follow-ups covered an extremely limited part of the overall questions, totalling 6.913 acts (about 24% of the total). Ufficio Valutazione Impatto, 'Gli atti di sindacato ispettivo in Senato' (2016) 6 *Senato della Repubblica – Documento di analisi*.

[312] In Sweden, the incompatibility rule (Chapter 4 – art 13 of the Instrument of Government) prevents ministers from, at the same time, being MPs. Nonetheless, they are answerable to it and participate in questioning sessions.

[313] See below ch 5, section II (n 62).

[314] For instance, Rule 21 of the House of Commons Standing Orders provides that questions shall be taken up to one hour after the House sits. Spontaneous questions are unknown in the Italian, Spanish and German parliaments. They do exist in France and Denmark, where this tool does not however allow other representatives to join the debate. In the United Kingdom and in Sweden, spontaneous questions may be followed by a debate open to the participation of other MPs. Russo and Wiberg (n 12) 222 f.

[315] Oral questions anticipated in a written form are foreseen in all the benchmark parliaments. In all cases, the tabling of a question allows for a debate, but in Italy, Spain and the European Parliament the procedure may result in the vote of a motion. ibid.

in Continental European parliaments as a means of 'protecting' the government during Parliament exposition. In both cases, the tabling of the question may allow for a debate, either limited to the questioner and the relevant minister or also open to other MPs. However, only questions that are anticipated in a written form may be open to the vote of a motion. This is the most powerful questioning procedure and is found in Italy, Spain and the European Parliament.

The second factor relates to the committee-plenary regime. Whereas oral questions originated during a plenary debate, questioning in committee is now a common rule in many parliaments. Having oral questions discussed in committee offers procedural and substantial advantages since it is time saving (more committees can debate questions at the same time, thus contributing to a reduced workload) and it allows the discussion of more focused and sectorial issues. In contrast, questioning in the plenary is always associated with gains in terms of representativeness of the associated debate and publicity.

Finally, the third factor concerns the 'question and answer' timing. Since the number of questions outweighs the time available, an important issue concerns how to allocate oral questions in plenary sessions.[316] Available solutions encompass, on the one hand, time limits for discussion and, on the other, the introduction of dedicated time spots for 'emergency' questions tabled by MPs to address urgent issues. Procedural rules on the selection of emergency questions vary across parliaments:[317] in many cases, the qualification of a question as urgent is left to the proponent and checked by the presiding officer.

The most efficient questioning mechanism in terms of speed and publicity is in any case represented by the 'Question Time'. This formula is labelled[318] and regulated in many ways:[319] introduced in 1961 in the United Kingdom as a procedure specifically addressing the Prime Minister, it has been 'transplanted', with modifications, into many other countries. In Germany, it addresses the whole of government. In Italy, it affects either departmental ministers or the President of the Council of Ministers. In Denmark, it is called 'Question Hour' and addresses the Prime Minister only.[320] In the European Parliament, it may have multiple addressees.[321] What apparently brings together all these instances of Question Time is the chance offered to MPs to have a weekly questioning session, which is usually broadcast, on political salient issues. The broadcast of this tool makes Question Time an

---

[316] Martin, 'Parliamentary Questions' (n 284) 6.

[317] In the Danish Folketing 'urgent interpellations' should be read at the earliest possible date (§ 21.4 Folketing Standing Orders). In the European Parliament, priority written questions should get an answer in three rather than six weeks (art 138.3 European Parliament Rules of Procedure).

[318] In some parliaments, the label 'Question Time' identifies the standard procedure for debating oral questions. This is the case in Denmark (§ 20.2 Folketing Standing Orders) and Sweden (art 8 Riksdag Act).

[319] In France, the possibility to introduce a 'Question Time' has been opposed by the Conseil constitutionnel through *Décision* 63-25 DC, 21 January 1964. A Delcamp, 'Le Conseil constitutionnel et le Parlement' (2004) 57 *Revue française de droit constitutionnel* 37, 43; P Avril and J Gicquel, *Droit parlementaire*, 5th edn (Paris, LGDJ, 2014) 108.

[320] § 20.10 Folketing Standing Orders. The Speaker may limit the possibility of putting questions to certain parliamentary groups, to members who do not belong to parliamentary groups or to party chairmen.

[321] Art 137 of the European Parliament Rules of Procedure sets a 90-minute session on issues decided one month before by the Conference of the Presidents. Questions can be addressed to the Council, the President of the Commission, the Vice President of the Commission/ High Representative for foreign affairs and the President of the Eurogroup.

extremely theatrical procedure, where the opposition tries to challenge the government both in terms of competency and in terms of communication skills.[322]

Finally, interpellations are typically a collective and an opposition tool[323] and they are expected to address major political issues of national relevance.[324] The standard scheme unfolds through the debate in the whole Chamber, open to more than one parliamentarian, that may be followed up either by a motion for a resolution or by a vote of censure.[325] The origins of this form of question date back to the *interpellationsrecht* of the Prussian Landtag, later recovered by the Bundestag distinguishing among two 'collective' procedures: the *Große Anfrage*, which allows each parliamentary group or a number of proponents equal to at least 5 per cent of all MPs to question the government either to provide information or to explain political issues in the plenary. The interpellation is tabled in writing but, on request, the answer is publicly debated.[326] By contrast, the *Kleine Anfrage*, introduced in the Reichstag in 1912, does not allow any debate in the plenary, since the answer is only provided in writing.[327] In parliamentary practice, the number of minor interpellations outweighs major interpellations.[328] Similar mechanisms have been introduced in Italy, where both Houses acknowledge the distinction between ordinary[329] and urgent interpellations,[330] in Spain[331] and in the European Parliament.[332]

---

[322] British Question Time shows a dual scheme, which sets the addressed minister in strong opposition to the questioner, RK Alderman, 'The leader of the opposition and Prime Minister's question time' (1992) 45 *Parliamentary Affairs* 66 ff.

[323] Sánchez de Dios (n 7) 8. A Maccanico, 'Interrogazioni e interpellanze' in *Enciclopedia giuridica*, XVII (Roma, Istituto della Enciclopedia italiana, 1989) 4.

[324] It has already been noted that the label covers a large variety of different procedures. In Denmark, for instance, the 'interpellation' is regulated as an individual tool (§ 21.1 Folketing Standing Orders). The same happens in Sweden, according to Chapter 13, art 5 of the Instrument of Government. In Spain (s 180 Congress Standing Orders), interpellations can be tabled by 'members and parliamentary groups'.

[325] Yamamoto (n 11) 60.

[326] According to Rule 100 of the Bundestag Rules of Procedure, interpellations 'must be brief and succinct and may be accompanied by a short memorandum'. On the conditions for placing the interpellation in the agenda of the Bundestag, see Rule 101.

[327] Rule 104 of the Bundestag Rules of Procedure explicitly prohibits including in the drafting of minor interpellations subjective statements or evaluations.

[328] From the foundation of the Federal Republic until the end of the XVI legislative term in 2009, 15,505 minor interpellations versus 1,323 major interpellations have been tabled (ST Siefken, 'Parlamentarische Frageverfahren – Symbolpolitik oder wirksames Kontrollinstrument?' (2010) 41 *Zeitschrift für Parlamentsfragen* 18). In both cases, the high quorum required to table the act has allowed this tool to display party positions.

[329] Both in the Chamber of Deputies (art 136 Rules of Procedure) and in the Senate (art 154 Rules of Procedure), each member can table an interpellation. Only in the Lower House, however, is the interpellation (art 137 Rules of Procedure) expected to be debated within two weeks.

[330] Urgent interpellations are regulated as collective tools in both Houses. In the Chamber of Deputies, they prove a quite powerful oversight mechanism, associated with a 'fast-track' procedure (the interpellations tabled before Tuesday are debated in the Thursday sitting – art 138 bis Rules of Procedure). In the Senate, urgent interpellations are debated in 15 days from the submission (art 156 bis Rules of Procedure).

[331] Unlike the German precedent, interpellations can also be introduced in the Spanish Congress by individual MPs. Nonetheless, if compared with questions, they enjoy a 'reinforced' procedure, consisting of their being dealt with within plenary sittings, in an open debate that allows the participation of other parliamentary groups, which can give rise to a motion (ss 180–84 Congress Standing Orders).

[332] Rule 139 of the European Parliament Rules of Procedure regulates the major interpellations for written answer, which must be 'of general interest'. They are distributed among political groups, in the limit of one per month, within a maximum of 30 interpellations every year for the Chamber. They are answered in writing, but a group or a minimum quorum of MEPs can require that certain interpellations are debated in the plenary.

To conclude, depending on a number of procedural variables and on the legal and political framework,[333] questioning pursues two main oversight goals: gathering information and promoting a confrontation with the government.[334] The first goal serves the connection between the informative and the oversight function in two senses.[335] On the one hand, it provides MPs with useful information that may be used in other oversight procedures to orient future policies and hold the government accountable for past decisions. On the other hand, the extensive publicity regime allowed to questions[336] makes this tool a valuable means for connecting parliamentary oversight to the wider public. Although the media attraction to questioning may be limited,[337] the procedure – especially in the case of Prime Minister's Question Time – offers citizens the opportunity to have a direct view of how their representatives perform their functions. With regard to the second goal, Parliament is not fully equipped to engage in an open confrontation with the government. The practice confirms that Parliament does not have the power to compel the government to fulfil the questioning duty, providing in due time an answer that is compliant with the question. The respect of these expectations is at the exclusive remit of government and it relies on the political relationship with Parliament.

In fact, it could be argued that answering a question is not just a political, but potentially a constitutional duty, for government. The constitutional basis of this obligation and the legal means for preventing and remedying any violations vary across countries. In Italy, scholars have debated the potential remedies against the recurring violation of the rule calling the President of the Council of Ministers to appear before Question Time at least twice in each calendar,[338] assuming that this violation could be brought before the Constitutional Court as a form of jurisdictional conflict between organs of the state.[339] The event of no-answer or no-show of the government is sometimes explicitly regulated in the Rules of Procedure, with rather different solutions. In the United Kingdom, a minister is not legally compellable to answer any parliamentary question.[340]

---

[333] Rozenberg and Martin (n 296) 400 f (legislatures such as the Italian parliament and the European Parliament that are known for being influential in policy-making are expected to spend less time in questioning).

[334] Russo and Wiberg (n 12) 224 ff. W Ismayr, *Der Deutsche Bundestag im politischen System der Bundesrepublik Deutschland*, 2nd edn (Stuttgart, UTB, 2001) 299 ff defined the *Große Anfrage* as the most important informative and oversight procedure.

[335] On questioning that can be 'as much about sending information as getting information', Rozenberg and Martin (n 296) 402.

[336] Parliamentary questions are generally publicly available and recorded in an electronic database published on the website of the Chamber. See Martin, 'Parliamentary Questions, the Behaviour' (n 285) 264.

[337] Questioning is deemed 'not a very media-friendly scrutiny mechanism because answers often lack the contest and rationale that journalists need to create a story'; H White, *Parliamentary Scrutiny of Government* (London, Institute for Government, 2015) 20. In fact, on the importance of the *Kleine Anfrage* as a means of giving media relevance to parliamentary oversight, Kepplinger (n 285).

[338] Art 135 bis Chamber of Deputies Rules of Procedure.

[339] G Rivosecchi, 'Quali rimedi all'inattuazione del "Premier Question Time?" A proposito di statuto dell'opposizione e giustiziabilità dei regolamenti parlamentari per conflitto di attribuzione' (2004) 4 *Quaderni costituzionali* 811; and F Rosa, 'Interrogazioni e interpellanze fra XIII e XIV legislatura: il confronto mutilato fra Parlamento e Governo' in E Gianfrancescon and N Lupo (eds), *Le regole del diritto parlamentare nella dialettica tra maggioranza e opposizione* (Rome, Luiss University Press, 2007) 410.

[340] C Turpin and A Tomkins, *British Government and the Constitution: Text and Materials*, 7th edn (Cambridge, Cambridge University Press, 2011) 612 f; P Cane, *Controlling Administrative Power: An Historical Comparison* (Cambridge, Cambridge University Press, 2016) 422.

In Denmark, the Folketing Standing Orders allow the prime minister or the ministers to declare that he/she is not in a position to answer the question; in these cases, the matter is considered closed.[341] A similar opportunity is apparently excluded by the Spanish Congress Standing Orders that formally allow the government to only postpone the answer to written and oral questions, not even to 'decline' the reply.[342] Similarly, in Germany, if the federal government refuses to reply to a major interpellation or does not do so within the following three weeks, the Bundestag may place the interpellation on the agenda for debate.

Beyond legal provisions, it is easily demonstrated that the inner logic of parliamentary regimes requires the government to grant maximum cooperation in accomplishing questioning requirements. At the same time, the fulfilment of this expectation depends on Parliament's authority more than on its powers.[343] Framed in these terms, questioning turns out to be a rather effective means for leading the government to give clarifications and explanations of its actions.

VI. Oversight Tools Following Government Action

Different tools support the ex post dimension of the oversight function, whose aim is to monitor and evaluate the past conduct of government affairs. Some of them may also act in the ex ante stage and these include questions and interpellations. The most typical ex post oversight tool is represented by inquiry and select committees in their capacity as parliamentary bodies specifically devoted to oversight tasks and entrusted with reinforced powers of investigation.[344] Parliamentary inquiries are seen as the vanguard, the 'fer de lance'[345] of parliamentary oversight. Being associated with an implied power of representative bodies,[346] they are not deemed to be an autonomous function of Parliament, but rather a mechanism instrumental to the fulfilment of typical functions, including oversight.[347] This fundamental need is satisfied by the two models of the inquiry and select committees that have similar purposes and similar means of action, but distinctive internal structure and composition.

---

[341] § 20.4 on a minister's possibility of declining written questions; § 20.11 on the Prime Minister's power to refuse to reply to questions put during Question Time. § 21.2 on the possibility to postpone an interpellation if the minister finds it contrary to the interests of the country.

[342] ss 188.4 and 190.2 Congress Rules of Procedure.

[343] Meinel (n 29) 330.

[344] The etymological meaning of the noun 'inquiry' and the difference with the term 'investigation' is debated in A Arévalo Gutiérrez, 'Las comisiones de investigación de las Cortes generals y de las Asambleas legislativas de las Comunidades Autonómas' (1995) 43 *Revista Española de Derecho Constitutional* 113.

[345] E Vallet, 'Les commissions d'enquête parlementaires sous la Cinquième République' (2003) 54 *Revue française de droit constitutionnel* 249. E Thiers, 'Le contrôle parlementaire et ses limites juridiques: un pouvoir presque sans entraves' (2010) 134 *Pouvoirs* 71, 78 defines inquiries as the final stage of parliamentary oversight.

[346] P Eugéne, *Traité de Droit politique, electoral et parlementaire*, 5th edn (Paris, Librairies Imprimeries Reunies, 1919) 678. N Pérez-Serrano, *Tratado de Derecho Político*, 2nd edn (Madrid, Ed Civitas, 1984) 814.

[347] The connection is manifest in France where Loi no 91-698 of 20 July 1991, in amending Ordonnance no 58-1100 of 17 November 1958 on the functioning of parliamentary assemblies, introduced the formula of the *commissions d'enquête et de contrôle*.

A. Inquiry Committees

Inquiry committees are established during the course of a legislative term to investigate specific issues.[348] Their object must be clearly defined, but can cover a wide range of salient political items of business, including the conduct of public policies on the part of administration, but potentially also on the part of politicians,[349] and the management of public services or national enterprises.[350] Whereas permanent committees carry out a systematic oversight of government departments, inquiry committees are strictly shaped as temporary bodies: the constitutive act must predetermine the maximum duration of the committee,[351] which can in any case experience an anticipated dissolution, depending on several factors.

This mechanism is rooted in the parliamentary tradition – in many cases it has grown out of nineteenth century practice[352] – and it is acknowledged, in different forms, by contemporary parliaments, with the exception of Denmark and Sweden[353] that do not have inquiry committees. In some countries, including Italy, Spain and Germany, the possibility to establish a committee of inquiry is provided directly in the Constitution. This legal basis is required by the nature and scope of the powers of investigation that bring parliamentary oversight at its extreme legal consequences, bridging it to the prerogatives of judicial power. This is made explicit in the Italian Constitution (article 82) that allows each House to start an inquiry on issues of public interest by setting a committee which is allowed the same powers and limitations of the judiciary.[354] Whereas the Constitution apparently refers to unicameral inquiries,[355] the practice has shown an extensive use of bicameral committees of inquiry, participated in by members of both Houses, and established through the approval of a law. Also, the Spanish Cortes generales, pursuant to Article 76 of the Constitution, admits cases of unicameral or bicameral committees appointed to inquiry 'on any matter of public interest'. In Germany, Article 44 of the Basic Law vests only the Bundestag with the power to establish inquiry committees. In France, Ordonnance no 58-1110 of 17 November 1958 gives a legal basis to the power of each Assembly to start an inquiry, which has been

---

[348] Specific inquiry tasks may be vested on standing committees. For instance, art 22 ter of the French Senate Rules of Procedure, pursuant to art 5 ter of Ordonnance no 58-1100 of 17 November 1958, allows standing or special committees to ask for the allotment of the prerogatives entrusted on inquiry committees; the mission cannot exceed a period of six months.

[349] This is explicitly provided by Art 44 of the German Basic Law as one of the possible items of inquiry.

[350] Art 6 French Ordonnance no 58-1100.

[351] In France, inquiry committees have a very limited duration of six months. The Conseil constitutionnel (Décision 66-28 DC of 8 July 1966) considered as unlawful any attempt to suspend and postpone the six-month term.

[352] Rens (n 52) 321. R Bonghi, 'Dei limiti del potere di inchiesta nelle Assemblee' (1869) 11 *Nuova Antologia* 822; and G Arcoleo, *L'inchiesta nel governo parlamentare* (Napoli, De Ruberto, 1881).

[353] In Sweden, inquiry committees are appointed by the government in connection with the drafting of a new law, as a body charged with the task of evaluating policy alternatives and legislative solutions. They are a fundamental component of the Swedish process of policy- and rule-making. Individual MPs, including members from the opposition parties, may participate in these committees. OECD, *Better Regulation in Europe: Sweden 2010* (Paris, OECD, 2010) 96 f; and Arter, 'From "Parliamentary Control"' (n 62) 125.

[354] A Pace, 'Le inchieste parlamentari nei nuovi regolamenti delle Camere' (1971) 4 *Studi parlamentari e di politica costituzionale* 17; G De Vergottini, 'Limitazioni alla tutela giurisdizionale dei diritti e inchieste parlamentari' in G De Vergottini, *Le inchieste delle assemblee parlamentari* (Rimini, Maggioli, 1985); and C Chimenti, 'Le commissioni di inchiesta come organi bicamerali' in G De Vergottini, *Le inchieste delle assemblee parlamentari* (Rimini, Maggioli, 1985).

[355] C Mortati, *Istituzioni di diritto pubblico*, II, 9th edn (Padova, Cedam, 1976) 693.

part of the French parliamentary tradition since 1832.[356] The unicameral nature of inquiries is seen as a binding principle, but the two Houses may nonetheless establish an inquiry committee on the same issue.[357]

The principle of non-interference between inquiry committees and the judiciary is a major concern for most parliaments. In France, the activity of inquiry committees is conceived of as strictly alternative to judicial investigations: they cannot investigate on affairs that are under judicial proceedings; they are expected to immediately conclude their activity if a judicial proceeding is started during their mandate.[358] These rigorous limits were criticised by some scholars, alleging that they would prevent the right of parliamentary assemblies to hold an inquiry on issues that were perceived as politically relevant by public opinion.[359] Article 76 of the Spanish Constitution clarifies that the conclusions of inquiry committees shall not be binding on the courts, nor shall they affect judicial decisions; nonetheless, the results of investigations may be referred to the Public Prosecutor for the exercise of appropriate action whenever necessary.[360]

Compared with standing committees, inquiry committees enjoy two channels for collecting information and data on the addressed issue.[361] On the one hand, they can resort to the compelling procedures and tools available to the judicial power.[362] These include questioning of witnesses and experts, access to data and documents,[363] including confidential material,[364] the conduct of direct investigations[365] and request for further investigations to be carried out by courts or administrative authorities.[366] Access to these investigative tools is usually regulated in the constitutive act of the inquiry committee. By common practice, appearance before inquiry committees is also set as an obligation for members of government[367] and non-appearance is usually supported by penalties.[368]

---

[356] Art 6 French Ordonnance no 58-1110 provides that inquiry committees are established to collect pieces of information on specific issues concerning the management of public services and public enterprises, with the purpose of submitting conclusions to the referent Chamber.

[357] Vallet (n 345) 259.

[358] Art 6 of Ordonnance no 58-1110 and art 141 of the National Assembly Rules of Procedure. The rigorous application of these limits has de facto prevented the establishment of any inquiry committee on events affecting the violation of individual rights or public liberties. L Hamon and C Emeri, 'Les pouvoirs d'enquête du Parlement' (1962) 2 *Revue de droit public* 270, 280.

[359] G Carcassonne and M Guillaume, *La Constitution*, 14th edn (Paris, Seuil, 2017) 260 ff.

[360] E Recoder de Casso, 'Comentario al artículo 76' in F Garrido Falla (ed), *Comentarios a la Constitución* (Madrid, Ed. Civitas, 1985); A Arévalo Gutiérrez, 'Reflexiones sobre las Comisiones de Investigación o Encuesta parlamentarias en el ordenamiento constitucional español' (1987) 11 *Revista de las Cortes Generales* 159.

[361] R Altenhof, *Die Enquete-Kommissionen des Deutschen Bundestages* (Wiesbaden, Westdeutscher, 2002). G Silvestri, 'Considerazioni sui poteri e limiti delle commissioni parlamentari di inchiesta' (1970) 1 *Il Politico* 538, 559 ff; and A D'Amato, 'Possibilità e limiti delle inchieste parlamentari' (2002) 6 *Dike* 41.

[362] Art 44 German Basic Law (the rules of criminal procedure shall apply *mutatis mutandis* to the taking of evidence in inquiry committees). Art 82 Italian Constitution.

[363] In Spain, committees of inquiry have full access to data and documents of finance administration (Royal Decree 5/1994 of 29 April).

[364] Exceptions can be set for those acts that are under secrecy regimes or that affect national defence, foreign affairs, internal or external security (see art 6 of French Ordonnance no 58-1110).

[365] The possibility to carry out investigations through documents or *in loco* visits is provided by art 6 of French Ordonnance no 58-1110 and art 142 Italian Chamber of Deputies Rules of Procedure.

[366] Art 44 German Basic Law.

[367] In France, the 1977 amendment to Ordonnance no 58-1110 has made the appearance before inquiry committees compulsory for ministers.

[368] See the Spanish Organic Law 5/1984 of 24 May, on the appearance before inquiry committees, and art 6 of French Ordonnance no 58-1110.

On the other hand, the existence of this reinforced channel does not prevent inquiry committees from resorting to the standard tools available to standing committees for collecting evidence and information. The choice between each channel should be carefully pondered by the committee: broadly speaking, the 'judicial-type' procedures should be applied only when it is so required by the nature of the investigation.[369] In contrast, standard procedures give ease of use to inquiry committees to collect information by means of inter-institutional cooperation. Connecting with experts and other institutions is a recurring option to enrich the extra-parliamentary contribution. To this purpose, for instance, Article 44.3 of the German Basic Law provides that courts and administrative authorities shall be required to provide legal and administrative assistance to inquiry committees and the French Court des comptes supports the work of inquiry committees.

The reinforced investigative prerogatives entrusted on these bodies explain why the setting, composition and chair of inquiry committees have always been sensitive issues. The establishment of an inquiry committee is among the typical guarantees offered to minorities. The government could have political interest in starting an inquiry into the activities of the previous government but usually finds little incentive to set up an inquiry into its own action.[370] In fact, rules and practices on the majority-opposition relation in the regulation of inquiry committees are quite inconsistent. On the one hand, German inquiries are solidly framed among opposition rights: pursuant to Article 44 of the German Basic Law, a committee of inquiry shall be created on a motion supported by one quarter of its members. On the other hand, in France the procedure for setting an inquiry committee leaves this tool in the full control of the majority,[371] which explains why in the Fifth Republic the government has been able to orient the use of the mechanism.[372] Moreover, membership should be unbiased by political affiliation: this is a fundamental prerequisite for enabling these bodies to act in an independent way. Therefore, rules providing adequate representation to minorities[373] and allotting the chair of the committee to a member of the opposition are standard guarantees in many parliaments.

In their capacity as temporary bodies, inquiry committees are expected to conclude their activity with the publication of a report,[374] to be submitted to the pertinent Chamber.[375]

---

[369] R Dickmann, 'Profili costituzionali dell'inchiesta parlamentare' (2007) 3 *Diritto e società* 459, 493.

[370] IPU and UNDP, *Global Parliamentary Report 2017* (n 27) 55.

[371] The motion for resolution to establish an inquiry committee is checked in advance by the relevant standing committee. Since standing committees are controlled by the majority, this stage gives the government the opportunity to filter the inquiries (art 6 of Ordonnance no 58-1110). According to Thiers (n 345) 76, the appropriateness evaluation stage raises some problems from the point of view of the rights allotted to minority groups.

[372] An intermediate solution is adopted by the Italian Senate: proposals of inquiries subscribed by at least one tenth of the members must be debated in five days by the relevant committee, but there is no guarantee that they are approved in the end (art 162.2 Rules of Procedure). In the Lower House, the guarantee for minorities is that no question of confidence can be proposed on the approval or rejection of the proposal to set an inquiry committee (art 116.4 Chamber of Deputies Rules of Procedure).

[373] The proportional representation of political groups in Parliament is the standard rule for the composition of inquiry committees both in Italy (art 82 of the Constitution) and in France (art 6 of Ordonnance no 58-1100).

[374] In France, only after the 1977 amendment to Ordonnance no 58-1110 has the publication of the final report become a standard rule for inquiry committees; intermediate reports may be released.

[375] In France, inquiry committees must conclude their work in six months and the Chamber cannot establish a new committee on the same item in the following 12 months (art 6 of Ordonnance no 58-1110). By contrast, in the Bundestag the deadline for submitting the report is the end of the legislative term (art 56 Bundestag Rules of Procedure).

The submission of the report can result in a debate in the plenary.[376] Debating the results of an inquiry is in fact directly instrumental to the mediatisation of the outcomes of this mechanism. As a matter of fact, publicity is a constitutive component of the effectiveness of parliamentary inquiries and it contributes to the 'democratisation' of the overall procedure. Different publicity regimes are accorded to inquiry committees. The standard rule is that committee hearings are open to the public, but the committee itself can decide when a confidential regime must be applied to guarantee the protection of individual rights and to contribute to the effectiveness of investigation.[377] In any case, the 'political' outcomes are there to be shared with the largest public:[378] the publicity associated with the inception of an inquiry is in many cases more important than the results achieved through the investigative activity.

In this vein, inquiries turn out to be multipurpose tools,[379] impacting executive–legislative relations in many ways. There are at least three ways to frame the oversight potential behind this mechanism. First, inquiries are a powerful oversight tool because they give Parliament the opportunity to exercise real 'vigilance' over a certain issue or policy perceived as a priority by public opinion. The possibility to make a direct assessment on selected items of government is particularly relevant for the opposition, as it gives minorities the opportunity to advocate *in concreto* government responsibility.[380] Second, inquiries give Parliament the power to collect strategic information instrumental to other oversight activities. The third potential is associated with the indirect impact exercised on public opinion. In this vein, the real power behind inquiry committees is not in the internal capacity of Parliament to exercise a direct compelling force on the government. Rather, its strength lies in the external impact on public opinion which leads the executive to give public explanations of its conduct.[381] If inquiries are rarely able to offer something more than a public tribune, some exceptions are offered by those landmark cases that demonstrate how the inquiry activity may lead to major legislative reforms.[382]

In this vein, it can be argued that inquiries are unable to pursue government's responsibility in a direct and legally binding manner.[383] Rather, in the parliamentary practice inquiries prove a valuable means for engaging in an enlarged dialogue, which can set the premises

---

[376] Art 56 Bundestag Rules of Procedure. In Italy, the publication of the final report can give rise to a debate in the plenary, but this has occurred in a very few cases.

[377] Art 6 (IV) French Ordonnance no 58-1110.

[378] Arévalo Gutiérrez, 'Las comisiones de investigación' (n 344) 123.

[379] F Santaolalla López, *El Parlamento y sus instrumentos de información (preguntas, interpelaciones y Comisiones de investigación)* (Madrid, Edersa, 1982) 19 ff. E Alvarez Conde, *Curso de Derecho Constitucional*, II (Madrid, Tecnos, 1993) 166.

[380] Vallet (n 345) 251 assumes that inquiry committees have become real bodies of investigation thanks to their technical approach more than to their compelling powers: they have reinforced their capacity to pursue the truth while remaining political bodies.

[381] Arévalo Gutiérrez, 'Reflexiones' (n 360) 166; and Arévalo Gutiérrez, 'Las comisiones de investigación' (n 344) 130.

[382] Examples of these landmark cases are offered by the inquiry committees promoted by the Bundestag in the 1980s to approach the 'Flich and Neue Heimat' affairs, which resulted in the reform of legislation on the funding of political parties. See Le Divellec, 'Des effets du contrôle' (n 46) 136. G Kretschmer, 'Enquete-Kommissionen – ein Mittel politischer Problemlösung? in HH Hartwich (ed), *Gesellschaftliche Probleme als Anstoß und Folge von Politik* (Wiesbaden, VS Verlag für Sozialwissenschaften, 1983).

[383] Dickmann, 'Profili costituzionali' (n 369) 488 f.

for future reforms.[384] Their potential impact is not confined to the executive–legislative relation, but rather tends to cover the overall public machinery, thus assuming the role of a real constitutional guarantee.

B. Select Committees

The second committee model involved in the conducting of inquiries corresponds to the select committees typical to the UK Parliament. House of Commons Select Committees date back to the nineteenth century, when they were established to provide scrutiny of a certain issue and report to Parliament.[385] During the 1960s, new committees – the 'Crossman Committees' – were created on selected policy issues. In 1979, following the review of the Procedure Committee, in response to pressure from backbenchers demanding for greater involvement in the scrutiny of government,[386] the select committee structure was reorganised.[387] This led to the establishment of 12 new committees, responsible for the scrutiny of each department. The setting of departmental select committees in 1979 represented an attempt to expose the government to more systematic and more comprehensive scrutiny.[388]

There are currently 20 departmental select committees in the House of Commons. These consist of 11 members, selected to proportionally represent parties' overall strength in the plenary. The proportional rule grants the majority full control of the committee's activity and decisions. In fact, to limit the dependence from party whips, the 2010 Reform of the House of Commons Committee – also known as the Wright Committee – suggested the introduction of a new mechanism for electing committee members and chairs,[389] which contributed to 'democratising' the composition of these bodies.[390] Their scrutiny commitment includes the fulfilment of a list of core tasks, including the comment on the policy of the department, the examination of the expenditure and of the administration of the department, the assistance to the House in debate and decision.[391]

---

[384] Vallet (n 345) 272.

[385] Norton, 'Nascent Institutionalisation' (n 68) 145.

[386] ibid, 146.

[387] D Naztler and M Hutton, 'Select Committees: Scrutiny à la carte?' in P Giddings (ed), *The Future of Parliament* (London, Palgrave, 2005).

[388] L Maer and M Sandford, *Select Committees Under Scrutiny* (London, The Constitution Unit, 2004) 14.

[389] The Report of the Committee (House of Commons Reform Committee, *Rebuilding the House* (2009, HC 117) para 36 ff) suggested that individual political parties should arrange for the election of their members of select committees in a transparent and democratic way. The chairs of most select committees were to be elected by a secret ballot of all MPs rather than chosen by each committee. These recommendations were adopted by the House of Commons in March 2010 (Rule 122B House of Commons Rules of Procedure). In the practice, there is no formal rule on the allotment of the chair of select committees: being elective, this is in theory under the control of the parliamentary majority, but in fact they are chosen through the 'usual channels'; see M Rush and C Ettinghausen, *Opening Up the Usual Channels* (London, The Hansard Society, 2002).

[390] M Russell, 'Never Allow a Crisis Go To Waste: The Wright Committee Reforms to Strengthen the House of Commons' (2011) 64 *Parliamentary Affairs* 612. See also M Flinders, 'Shifting the Balance? Parliament, the Executive and the British Constitution' (2002) 50 *Political Studies* 23.

[391] The list of core task for select committees was set by the Liaison Committee on 2 March 2002 (House of Commons Liaison Committee, *Annual Report 2002* (2003, HC 558) para 13) and then revised in November 2012 (House of Commons Liaison Committee, *Select Committee Effectiveness, Resources and Powers* (2012, HC 697) para 16).

Moreover, since 2008, the House of Commons select committees have been engaged in the scrutiny of the memoranda drafted by the government as part of post-legislative scrutiny, to assess whether an Act of Parliament has met its objectives within three to five years after Royal Assent.[392] Select committees are expected to engage in additional scrutiny of the government memoranda.[393]

To fulfil all these tasks, select committees use an inquiry process, unfolding through the definition of an issue, the selection of specialist advisers, the collection of written and oral evidence and the publication of a report.[394] They usually start the inquiry by organising a private introductory seminar open to the participation of academics and experts. They consequently issue a call for written evidence, which is publicised through a press release. They then continue with the taking of oral evidence from officials, representative groups and experts.

Like inquiry committees, select committees may also resort to evidence-gathering procedures much strengthened, compared with those available to standing committees. They can 'send for persons, papers and records',[395] but this option can be enforced only through a resolution of the whole House: this procedural requirement limits the power of the initiative of select committees, that need to negotiate with the government the selection of witnesses.[396] Whereas private individuals can be compelled to attend committee hearings, there is no compulsory mechanism applicable to ministers. In fact, following a long-standing convention, ministers do appear[397] and tend to resist appearing before a select committee only when they are convened by a committee that does not scrutinise their department. Select committees have started to take regular evidence from each minister at least once a year. Civil servants' dealings with select committees are instead regulated by the Osmotherly Rules,[398] an executive document offering guidance to civil servants that, in line with the principle of ministerial responsibility, sets several restrictions on their audition. When they appear before a committee, they should act strictly on behalf of their ministers and under their direction; they can provide factual information and evidence, but they are not called to give explanations or justifications. This set of limits has been considered to a large extent anachronistic, because it makes select committees' right of access to civil service policy advice much weaker than the standards provided by the Freedom of Information Act 2000.[399]

Other tools available to select committees comprise the undertaking of domestic and international visits and the staging of online consultations with the public through the Hansard Society. Both activities are cost-intensive, which implies that select committees need to apply to the Liaison Committee to seek funding. Moreover, the fulfilment of these

---

[392] Office of the Leader of the House of Commons, 'Post-Legislative Scrutiny – The Government's Approach' (March 2008).

[393] T Caygill, 'A Tale of Two Houses?' (2019) 2 *European Journal of Law Reform* 87.

[394] House of Commons Liaison Committee, *Select Committee Effectiveness* (n 391) para 47.

[395] Rule 152 House of Commons Standing Orders.

[396] Maer and Sandford (n 388) 10.

[397] Shepard (n 189) 45 argues that the most important government concession to select committee scrutiny has been the Prime Minister's agreement, in April 2002, to be questioned twice a year by the Liaison Committee.

[398] Cabinet Office, 'Giving Evidence to Select Committees. Guidance to Civil Servants', October 2014. See A Blick, *The Codes of the Constitution* (Oxford, Hart Publishing, 2016) 183.

[399] Constitution Committee, *The Accountability of Civil Servants*, Sixth Report (2013, HL 61) para 92.

scrutiny tasks largely depends on the staff capacities allowed for select committees.[400] This capacity was significantly improved in 2002 with the creation of the central resource structure of the Scrutiny Unit,[401] providing specialist support for committees.

The main outcome of select committee inquiries is the publication of a report which includes conclusions and recommendations for government action. On the one hand, the release of the report starts a proactive dialogue with the government, which is obliged to respond within 60 days of the report's publication.[402] Very often, important recommendations made by select committees are accepted and acted upon by the government; others are rejected, but might be adopted at a later stage.

On the other hand, the publication of the report is expected to foster a public debate and to raise public consciousness of the issue.[403] On the request of select committees, reports may be linked to other debates and if the initiator of the main business agrees, the report is open to discussion on the floor of the House of Commons. The introduction of parallel debates in Westminster Hall in 1999[404] has increased the opportunity to debate with the select committee. As a matter of fact, on average 30 reports each year are debated on the floor of the House or in Westminster Hall.[405] Other follow-up tools comprise written correspondence, oral evidence sessions and the undertaking of a follow-up inquiry. The opportunity to foster a public debate on the outcomes of the inquiry, jointly with the publicity regime associated with the activity of select committees,[406] are part of the mediatisation strategy that plays a fundamental role in giving effectiveness to committee work.[407] Press coverage for select committee work offers Parliament the opportunity to promote a wider debate and provides an indirect channel for influencing the government.

On the whole, even if the committee system continues to attract calls for reform,[408] the oversight potential of select committees is unquestionable.[409] Over the years, they have increasingly been seen 'as a central part of strengthening Parliament against the executive'.[410] The structural scrutiny of government departmental action has been used as a

---

[400] The standard staff capacity allotted to each select committee comprises from three to seven officials, of which one or two are clerks of the committee; special advisers can also be appointed.

[401] The Scrutiny Unit was established in November 2002, following the recommendations of the Liaison Committee (House of Commons Liaison Committee, *Shifting the Balance* (n 248) para 76 f).

[402] On the minimum standards that government replies should respect in addressing a committee's recommendations, see Hansard Society, *The Challenge for Parliament: Making Government Accountable*, Report of the Hansard Society Commission on Parliamentary Scrutiny (London, Hansard Society Publications, 2011) para 3.42.

[403] Rule 134 House of Commons Standing Orders.

[404] House of Commons Select Committee on Modernisation of the House of Commons, *Sittings in the House in Westminster Hall. Second Report* (1998–99, HC 194) para 30.

[405] Maer and Sandford (n 388) 39.

[406] According to Rule 125 of the House of Commons Standing Orders, a select committee has the power to admit the public during oral evidence sessions.

[407] On exposure of wrongdoing or poor decision-making in a public arena as an important form of influence available to select committees, Benton and Russell (n 48) 791.

[408] Shepard (n 189) 45 (the lack of prime time in Parliament to consider select committee reports, the lack of power to require the attendance of ministers and civil servants, the lack of power to force them to answer questions represent some 'key hurdles to effective oversight of government department').

[409] Hansard Society, *The Challenge for Parliament* (n 402) 131 ff; and House of Commons Liaison Committee, *Shifting the Balance: Select Committees and the Executive. First Report of Session 1999–2001* (2000, HC 300) para 4 ff.

[410] Maer and Sandford (n 388) 13. Similarly, also Norton, 'Nascent Institutionalisation' (n 68) 151.

means not for assessing responsibilities but for influencing the policy process,[411] thus interacting in a proactive and constructive way with executive decision-making.[412] Two main
features contribute to this end. First, their oversight potential is directly associated with the
committee structure which is not infected by the engagement in highly party-adversarial
activities, such as the passage of legislation and the budget.[413] Select committees tend to act
on a cross-party basis and depend on the choices made by individual MPs more than by
parties.[414] Second, select committee analytical capacities in the detailed scrutiny of executive action favours a structural and constructive dialogue with government departments,
which contributes to make their recommendations heard.[415]

---

[411] Benton and Russell (n 48) 773. Even those reports that 'simply evaluate how policy is being handled rather
than necessarily recommending change' turns out to have an impact on government, 'encouraging better executive
decision-making' (ibid, 791).

[412] It is argued that 'oversight committees strengthen the policy-making process inside and outside government
by exposing decision-making to rigorous tests, and by encouraging more careful consideration of options'
(ibid, 793).

[413] Caygill (n 393) 88.

[414] P Giddings, 'Select Committees and Parliamentary Scrutiny: Plus Ça Change?' (1994) 47 *Parliamentary Affairs*
669. Norton, 'Nascent Institutionalisation' (n 68) 150 (bi-partisanship in select committees is symbolically represented by the horseshoe table where members sit; it usually results in the adoption of unanimous reports).

[415] Caygill (n 393) 88.

5

Parliamentary Oversight in Bicameral Systems: What Role for Upper Houses?

The role of Upper Houses in the oversight of the executive is a highly debated topic in literature.[1] On the one hand, their general exclusion from the confidence relationship, which finds an exception only in the Italian symmetric bicameralism, deprives them of all the instances of 'hard' oversight, thus limiting the formal oversight mechanisms available. In fact, the Spanish Tribunal Constitucional in STC 124/2018 confirmed that the oversight function is exercised by each of the two Houses that compose the bicameral Parliament, which implies that the Senate – although disconnected from the confidence relationship and from the dimension of political responsibility linking the government to the Congress – also participates in this power.[2]

On the other hand, the constitutional position of Upper Houses prevents them from the risk of early dissolution, which is instead a real threat for Lower Houses.[3] Their political composition, permeated by party cleavages usually not corresponding to those of the Lower House and consequently external to the *continuum* between the government and its parliamentary majority, gives them larger margins for manoeuvre.[4] Whereas party discipline in Lower Houses risks inhibiting the effectiveness of executive oversight, their political independence offers the opportunity to approach this function based on a non-party or cross-party approach.[5]

Comparative studies seem to confirm that the combination of these factors creates favourable conditions for the involvement of Upper Houses in oversight of the executive.[6] It may therefore be questioned whether Upper Houses, generally marginalised in the law-making process, find in the oversight function, in its soft conception, an alternative policy-influencing tool.

---

[1] AA Preece, 'Bicameralism at the end of the Second Millennium' (2000) 21 *University of Queensland Law Journal* 67, 81 f; M Russell, 'What are Second Chambers for?' (2001) 54 *Parliamentary Affairs* 442; J Waldron, 'Bicameralism and the separation of powers' (2012) 65 *Current Legal Problems* 31.

[2] STC 124/2018, 7 (see above ch 2, section III).

[3] Such a threat is defined by some scholars through the image of the Parliament and government who 'hold a gun to each other's head'. M Gallagher, M Laver and P Mair, *Representative Government in Western Europe* (London, McGraw Hill, 1992) 22; and Russell, 'What are Second Chambers for?' (n 1) 447.

[4] Waldron (n 1) 43 f (independence from the executive, at least in Westminster-style parliamentary systems, is the main feature of Upper Houses and the main difference with Lower Houses).

[5] R Scully, 'Dealing with big brother: relations with the first chambers' (2011) 17 *The Journal of Legislative Studies* 93 ff (the chance offered to Upper Houses to exercise an effective oversight of the executive entirely depends on the presence of political majorities diverging from those of the Lower House); on this thesis, see also A Vatter, 'Bicameralism and policy performance. The effects of cameral structure in comparative perspective' (2005) 11 *The Journal of legislative Studies* 194.

[6] Preece (n 1) 81.

Three national cases can best represent the alternative patterns of executive oversight available to Upper Houses. Italy, the United Kingdom and Germany are three parliaments associated with different bicameral arrangements. The Italian Senate is the ultimate example of symmetric bicameralism, with the two Houses sharing the same powers both in the confidence relationship and in law-making. From the point of view of the political composition, there are no structural constitutional criteria of differentiation between the two Houses and asymmetries only result from the application of electoral mechanisms. In contrast, the UK House of Lords and the German Bundesrat are two examples of asymmetric bicameralism, with the Upper House excluded from the confidence circuit. The House of Lords falls into the model of unelected representative assemblies endowed with limited powers of reconsideration of legislative Bills approved by the Lower House. The German Bundesrat is a prototype of a federal House acting more as an interpreter and guarantor of territorial entities, rather than as a 'parliamentary' assembly in the traditional meaning. The combination of the three case studies offers the opportunity to assess which type of oversight potential Upper Houses can embody and which are the determinant legal and political factors.

I. Oversight in Symmetric Bicameralism: The Informal Search for Influence by the Italian Senate

Oversight in the Italian bicameralism shows a unique feature, consisting of the perfect duplication of executive–legislative relations in both Houses.[7] In law-making, the position of the Italian Senate is perfectly symmetrical to the Chamber of Deputies.[8] In the field of non-legislative functions, the Senate meets the same prerogatives of the Lower House and substantially the same tools and procedures.[9] From a comparative viewpoint, these factors make the Italian Senate an exceptional Upper House, endowed with a wide set of hard powers on the executive, including the vote of no confidence.

The composition of the Senate relies on political cleavages not too dissimilar from those in the Chamber of Deputies, but differences in the passive and active electoral rights and in the electoral formula may determine some asymmetries in the party structure of the two Houses. As a matter of fact, in the last few legislative terms, the Senate has played a strategic role in the political legislative bargaining due to the small margins for manoeuvre met by the parliamentary majority in the plenary of Palazzo Madama.[10]

---

[7] *Ex multis*, G Negri, 'Bicameralismo' in *Enciclopedia del diritto*, V (Milano, Giuffrè, 1959) 347; L Paladin, 'Tipologia e fondamenti giustificativi del bicameralismo. Il caso italiano' (1984) *Quaderni costituzionali* 219, 220; G Ferrara, 'Articolo 55' in G Branca (ed), *Commentario alla Costituzione. Articoli 55-63: Le Camere. Tomo I* (Bologna, Zanichelli, 1984) 4.

[8] Art 70 Italian Constitution.

[9] Arts 145–56 *bis* Senate Rules of Procedure. G Rivosecchi, 'I poteri ispettivi e il controllo parlamentare dal question time alle Commissioni di inchiesta' in E Gianfrancesco and N Lupo (eds) *Le regole del diritto parlamentare nella dialettica tra maggioranza e opposizione* (Roma, LUP, 2007).

[10] These derive from existing asymmetries in the electoral rules applied to the two Houses; see G Ferri, 'I sistemi elettorali delle Camere dopo le sentenze della Corte costituzionale (n 1/2014 e n 35/2017) e la legge n 165/2017' (2017) 3 *Osservatorio sulle fonti* 1.

From a broad perspective, distinguishing the oversight potential of the Upper and Lower House in the Italian system is therefore rather complicated. In both Houses, oversight powers have generally played quite a marginal role. Parliamentary oversight of the executive does not find formal recognition in the Constitution, although article 82 regulates committees of inquiry[11] and constitutional law no 1/2012 now recognises Parliament's role in the oversight of public finance.[12] The primacy recognised in law-making[13] has undoubtedly prevented both Houses from structuring an effective oversight capacity. This trade-off is clearly represented in the field of budget: the traditional hard legislative powers in the approval of budgetary and financial laws[14] enjoyed by both Houses[15] have inhibited advancements in the oversight of budget execution.

From a procedural viewpoint, the oversight apparatus of the Italian Senate is composed of a wide range of ex ante and ex post tools which show four main features. First, they replicate the oversight toolbox of the Chamber of Deputies, thus creating a perfect 'duplication' which raises some fundamental questions on how to coordinate the oversight actions of the two Houses in a system of symmetric bicameralism. Apart from inquiries, which are frequently implemented on a bicameral basis, it is extremely difficult to compose the oversight initiatives of the two Houses, thus exposing the government to the risk of manifest political asymmetries in the outcomes and directions received from Parliament.

The only possible way to cope with this problem is through informal mechanisms of bicameral coordination. This method has actually become the dominant practice in the case of the resolutions that both Houses adopt in the scrutiny of the Document of Economy and Finance (DEF), the fundamental government plan that sets the general directions for the future macro-economic manoeuvre. The DEF is submitted to both Houses every year, before 10 April, 'for the implied parliamentary deliberations'.[16] The scrutiny procedure relies on the joint development of preliminary investigations by the two referent committees of the Chamber of Deputies and the Senate. This practice finds a legal base in article 118 *bis*.3 of the Chamber Rules of Procedure and article 125 *bis*.3 of the Senate Rules of Procedure, but its practical implementation strongly relies on informal agreements between the two branches of Parliament.[17] Through this bicameral procedure the two Houses, while

---

[11] A Manzella, *I controlli parlamentari* (Milano, Giuffrè, 1970) 68 ff; and C Chimenti, *Il controllo parlamentare nell'ordinamento italiano* (Milano, Giuffrè, 1974) 95 ff.

[12] Art 5.4 of Law no 1/2012. The implications of this 'new' function are debated in E Griglio, 'Il "nuovo" controllo parlamentare sulla finanza pubblica: una sfida per i "nuovi" regolamenti parlamentari' (2013) 1 *Osservatoriosullefonti* 1.

[13] The use of a 'negative' definition for all activities exceeding legislation – as 'non-legislative' functions – confirms the marginal interest vested in this sphere of intervention. N Lupo, 'Funkcja kontrolna parlamentu we Włoszech (La funzione di controllo parlamentare nell'ordinamento italiano)' in Z Witkowski, GC De Martin and KM Witkowska-Chrzczonowicz (eds), *Gwarancje konstytucyjne i srodki kontroli w panstwie demokratycznym z perspektywy dorobku konstytucyjnego Wloch i Polsi* (Torun, Tnoik, 2008).

[14] Since these laws are fully amendable, MPs have tried to exercise their influence mainly by the tabling of amendments. N Lupo, 'Le sessioni di bilancio, ieri e oggi' in G Carboni (ed), *La funzione finanziaria del Parlamento. Un confronto tra Italia e Gran Bretagna* (Torino, Giappichelli, 2009) 36 ff.

[15] On the inverse proportion between the role that parliaments can exercise in budgetary decision-making and budgetary oversight, E Griglio and N Lupo, 'Parliamentary democracy and the Eurozone crisis' (2012) 1 *Law and Economics Yearly Review* II, 313, 345.

[16] Arts 7.2 (a), 9.1 of Law no 196 of 31 December 2009, which includes two fundamental documents of the 'European Semester': the stability programme and the national reform programme.

[17] C Goretti and L Rizzuto, 'Il ruolo del Parlamento italiano nella decisione di bilancio: evoluzione recente e confronto con gli altri paesi' (2011) 1–3 *Rivista di politica economica* 29, 51 f.

remaining formally autonomous in the scrutiny of the document, have come de facto to adopt identical resolutions on the DEF.[18] This textual correspondence has significantly reinforced Parliament's capacity to exercise a unitary influence on government's macro-economic and financial policy.[19]

The joint method developed in the scrutiny of the DEF has not been replicated in other sectors. The implementation of the recent law on international military missions has reproduced the traditional historic asymmetries in the oversight bicameral mechanisms.[20] Pursuant to articles 2.2 and 3 of law no 145 of 21 July 2016, the two Houses are called to intervene ex ante to authorise[21] the launch, continuation or termination of an international military mission through non-legislative acts.[22] Both Houses implemented the new task in a strictly unicameral perspective, grounded on the adoption of resolutions, to be voted in committee and then potentially in the plenary, but following distinct procedures.[23] Apart from the conduct of joint preliminary hearings, the two Houses have not recovered the informal practice of bicameral agreements on the text of the resolution which is typical of the DEF. As a matter of fact, the possibility to transform the ex ante authorisation into an effective oversight mechanism has been seriously compromised.[24]

Second, notwithstanding attempts made in the last 25 years to move the Italian political system towards a majoritarian model, the oversight toolbox has substantially confirmed its original consensual structure.[25] The oversight machinery of the Senate has not undergone significant transformations over time:[26] internal reforms of the Rules of Procedure[27] have followed an incremental strategy, which has not allowed the adaptation of the oversight tools to the logic of a majoritarian democracy.[28] The last organic reform of the Rules of

---

[18] G Rivosecchi, *L'indirizzo politico finanziario tra Costituzione italiana e vincoli europei* (Padova, Cedam, 2007) 294 ff; V Di Ciolo and L Ciaurro, *Il diritto parlamentare nella teoria e nella pratica* (Milano, Giuffrè, 2013) 622.

[19] On the necessity for the two Houses to develop joint preliminary investigations instrumental to parliamentary oversight and strengthen the analysis of technical aspects of public finance and budget, see Art 4.2 of Law no 196/2009, reforming the budgetary procedures; and R Dickmann, 'La riforma della legislazione di finanza pubblica e del sistema del bilancio dello Stato e degli enti pubblici' (2010) 1 *Federalismi.it* 1.

[20] A De Guttry, 'Participating in Peace-Keeping Operations: the Italian Decision-Making Process' in A De Guttry (ed), *Italian and German Participation in Peace-Keeping: From Dual Approaches to Co-operation* (Pisa, ETS, 1996).

[21] On the political nature of Parliament's authorisation of military missions, U Villani, 'Missioni militari all'estero e competenze degli organi costituzionali' in Vv Aa, *Quaderno dell'Associazione per gli studi e le ricerche parlamentari* (Torino, Giappichelli, 1996) 186 ff. *Contra*, V Lippolis, 'Parlamento e potere estero' in S Labriola (ed), *Il Parlamento repubblicano* (Milano, Giuffrè, 1999) 566.

[22] M Benvenuti, 'Luci ed ombre della l n 145/2016 in tema di partecipazione dell'Italia alle missioni internazionali. Una prima lettura' (2017) 1 *Rivista AIC* 1, 29.

[23] Arts 117, 124 and 143 Chamber of Deputies Rules of Procedure. Art 50.2 Senate Rules of Procedure. E Griglio, 'I seguiti parlamentari della nuova legge quadro sulle missioni internazionali' (2017) 2 *Quaderni costituzionali* 397.

[24] On the role of 'authorisation' in administrative law as a form of ex ante oversight, see S Cassese (ed), *Istituzioni di diritto amministrativo*, 5th edn (Milano, Giuffrè, 2015) 410 ff. *Contra*, F Caringella, *Manuale di diritto amministrativo*, III, 10th edn (Roma, Dike Giuridica, 2016) 1374 f.

[25] According to Rivosecchi, 'I poteri ispettivi' (n 9) 201, the rationalisation of the relationship between government and its parliamentary majority should result in a strengthening of non-legislative powers.

[26] R Moretti, 'Le attività informative, di ispezione, di indirizzo e di controllo' in T Martines et al (eds), *Diritto parlamentare* (Milano, Giuffrè, 2011).

[27] On the rather different 'rhythm' followed by the reforms of the Rules of Procedures in the two Houses, N Lupo, 'La persistente ispirazione proporzionalistica dei regolamenti parlamentari dal 1920 ad oggi' (2009) 8 *Ventunesimo Secolo, Il 'secolo breve' della democrazia italiana (1919–2008)* 77, 86.

[28] The relationship between the reform of the Rules of Procedure and the transformation of the form of government is highlighted by S Curreri, 'Riforme dei regolamenti parlamentari e forma di governo' in E Gianfrancesco

Procedure, adopted in 2017, has perpetuated this spirit of substantial 'conservation',[29] but at the same time it has contributed to filling in one of the major gaps in the oversight toolbox of the Italian Senate: the lack of a 'question time'. Whereas questioning of the government is performed in the two Houses through the same tools,[30] only the Chamber of Deputies has experienced the introduction, in 1997, of a question time shaped in a real adversarial style.[31] In 1999, the Senate limited itself to adopting a rather mild and 'bureaucratic' instance of question time, to be debated once a month on issues selected by the conference of the presidents of parliamentary groups.[32] For almost a decade, these procedural limits inhibited the oversight potential of this tool and marginalised its relevance in the executive–legislative relations. The 2017 reform has tried to overcome this situation by replicating the same scheme as the question time in use at the Chamber of Deputies. In practice, so far, the new tool has been proof of an extremely vital part of the political confrontation, carried out in a real adversarial style.

Third, ex post oversight has been poorly implemented as a means of checking and pursuing government responsibility; rather, oversight mechanisms tend to be used as a means of policy influence. Different tools contribute to this outcome. The wide set of written and oral questions are used to pursue a variety of political goals:[33] raising the attention of public opinion on unimplemented government policies; signalling unattended local concerns; and advancing alternative political solutions. Whereas the Chamber of Deputies has recently tried to limit this 'hybrid' use of questions as policy-influencing mechanisms,[34] the practice does not find formal backstops in the legal framework of the Italian Senate. Admissibility rules for all types of questions and interpellations are applied in a flexible manner, thus enabling the questioner to convey a large variety of political messages. This trend, originally fostered by opposition groups, is now also intensively used by majority members as a means of pressing for action when the tabling of amendments is not possible.[35] This approach confirms the conception of non-legislative procedures by parliamentary majority as a 'residual' tool for fulfilling political goals that exceed the direct relationship with the government.[36]

---

and N Lupo (eds), *La riforma dei regolamenti parlamentari al banco di prova della XVI Legislatura* (Roma, LUP, 2009) 231; V Lippolis, 'La riforma del regolamento della Camera dei eputati del 1997 e il Parlamento del bipolarismo' in Vv Aa, *Il Parlamento del bipolarismo: un decennio di riforme dei regolamenti delle Camere. Il Filangieri – Quaderno 2007* (Napoli, Jovene, 2008) 20.

[29] E Gianfrancesco, 'La riforma del regolamento del Senato: alcune osservazioni generali' (2018) 1 *Federalismi.it* 1.

[30] A Manzella, 'Interrogazione e interpellanza' in *Enciclopedia del diritto*, XII (Milano, Giuffrè, 1972) 407 ff.

[31] V Lippolis, 'Maggioranza, opposizione e governo nei regolamenti e nelle prassi parlamentari dell'età repubblicana' in L Violante (ed), *Il Parlamento. Storia d'Italia. Annale n 17* (Torino, Einaudi, 2001) 616 f; and G Rivosecchi, *Regolamenti parlamentari e forma di governo nella XIII legislatura* (Milano, Giuffré, 2002).

[32] Art 151 *bis* Senate Rules of Procedure.

[33] F Russo, 'The Constituency as a Focus of Representation: Studying the Italian Case through the Analysis of Parliamentary Questions' (2011) *The Journal of Legislative Studies* 290.

[34] The Senate Rules of Procedure are more synthetic than the Chamber Rules of Procedure in setting admissibility rules for the questions and interpellations (arts 97 and 146 Senate Rules of Procedure). Furthermore, only the Chamber of Deputies has specified admissibility criteria through the circular letter of 21 February 1996 and the opinion of the Commission on the Rules of Procedure of 1 October 2016. Attempts to limit the admissibility of questions and interpellations in the Senate were made in the current legislative term, without being transposed into a formal decision (see the Communication to the plenary in the sitting of 11 September 2018).

[35] N Lupo, 'Alcuni dati e qualche considerazione sulle procedure (tradizionali e nuove) di controllo parlamentare' in E Rossi (ed), *Maggioranza e opposizioni nelle procedure parlamentari* (Padova, Cedam, 2004).

[36] S Sicardi, 'Il problematico rapporto tra controllo parlamentare e ruolo dell'opposizione nell'esperienza repubblicana' (2002) 44 *Rassegna parlamentare* 961, 988.

Similarly, the establishment of unicameral inquiry committees has offered the Italian Senate another policy-influencing channel,[37] in order to grant transparency on certain issues of public interest and address future policy choices.[38] The latter purpose is pursued through the establishment of 'legislative' inquiry committees addressing controversial, highly mediatic and politically sensitive issues, in view of defining legislative actions to be undertaken.[39]

Furthermore, the Senate has always made intense use of motions, resolutions and orders as policy-influencing tools.[40] These mechanisms act as a means of reaching a political goal which cannot be fulfilled through a legislative decision because this is temporarily precluded or is not possible at all (as in the case of the policies, including defence and foreign affairs, which basically unfold through non-legislative decisions).

Four, from the formal point of view, the Senate (and similarly the Chamber of Deputies) has shown a limited internal capacity to adapt the internal procedures and rules to the external pushes demanding more specialised forms of executive oversight. The oversight of public finance, introduced by article 5.4 of constitutional law no 1/2012 on the balanced budget,[41] has not found appropriate implementation in the internal Rules of Procedure of the Senate.[42] The 'new' function would require a structural reconsideration of ex ante and ex post scrutiny mechanisms,[43] including the establishment of ad hoc committees with reinforced means of investigation and surveillance in the field of public finance.[44]

Moreover, the 2017 reform of the Senate Rules of Procedure has only partially adapted the internal procedures to the new 'European' powers set in favour of the two Houses by law no 234 of 24 December 2012, on Italian participation in the EU. The latter has strengthened parliamentary scrutiny of European affairs by reinforcing government's informative duties on EU policy-making and setting a 'parliamentary reserve',[45] but its novelties have not been fully incorporated in the Senate Rules of Procedure.

---

[37] A Pace, 'Articolo 82' in G Branca (ed), *Commentario alla Costituzione. Articoli 76–82: La formazione delle leggi. Tomo II* (Bologna, Zanichelli, 1979) 322 f, G Recchia, *L'informazione delle Assemblee rappresentative. L'inchiesta* (Napoli, Jovene, 1979) 284; L Ciaurro, 'Recenti sviluppi in materia di inchieste parlamentari' (1990) 4 *Nuovi Studi Politici* 95, 136 ff.

[38] These two tasks roughly correspond to the two main categories of inquiry committees grounded on art 82 of the Constitution, respectively the 'political' and the 'legislative' committees. Moretti (n 26) 347 f.

[39] See for instance the establishment, in the XVII legislative term (2013–18), of the Inquiry committee on Feminicide and Gender-based Violence (Senate Deliberation, 18 January 2017) and of the Inquiry Committee on Intimidations against Local Public Officials (Senate Deliberation, 3 October 2013).

[40] Such tools find their discipline respectively in arts 50.3; 144 *ter*; 157–61 Senate Rules of Procedure.

[41] Griglio, 'Il "nuovo" controllo parlamentare' (n 12).

[42] Similarly, the Senate Rules of Procedure did not incorporate the new powers of surveillance in case of macroeconomic and financial imbalances entrusted on both Houses by Law no 243/2012, which implemented the 2012 constitutional reform. D Capuano and E Griglio, 'La nuova *governance* economica europea. I risvolti sulle procedure parlamentari italiane' in A Manzella and N Lupo (eds), *Il sistema parlamentare euro-nazionale. Lezioni* (Torino, Giappichelli, 2014) 247 ff.

[43] N Lupo, 'A proposito della necessaria politicità del controllo parlamentare' (2002) 6 *Le istituzioni del federalismo* 959, 969.

[44] In support of this solution, R Perna, 'Costituzionalizzazione del pareggio di bilancio ed evoluzione della forma di governo italiana' in Vv Aa, *Costituzione e pareggio di bilancio. Il Filangieri – Quaderno 2011* (Napoli, Jovene, 2012) 42. On the neutrality of the committee structure for providing effectiveness to the oversight of public finance, Griglio, 'Il "nuovo" controllo parlamentare' (n 12).

[45] P Caretti, 'La legge n 234/2012 che disciplina la partecipazione dell'Italia alla formazione e all'attuazione della normativa e delle politiche dell'Unione europea: un traguardo o ancora una tappa intermedia?' (2012)

On the one hand, the reform has overcome the procedural asymmetries in the participation of the two Houses in the Early Warning System.[46] The revised text of article 144 of the Rules of Procedure replicates in the Senate the scrutiny procedure adopted, on an informal basis, by the Chamber of Deputies: participation in political dialogue is entrusted in sectoral committees and the subsidiarity monitoring is deferred to the Committee for EU policies. In fact, the original procedure of the Senate, consisting of the simultaneous legal and political scrutiny in sectoral committees or in the Committee for European Affairs, resulted in stronger substantial control.[47] The Italian Senate has been extremely proactive in the scrutiny of EU proposals,[48] placing itself among the national chambers with the highest number of opinions and contributions submitted under Protocol 2 of the Lisbon Treaty.[49]

On the other hand, the 2017 reform failed to incorporate in the Rules of Procedure other opportunity structures in the field of EU affairs which had already found a legal base in statutory legislation. The reference is to the 'comply or explain' rule set by article 7 of law no 234/2012,[50] to the parliamentary reserve as a means of suspending government decisions at EU level, and to the scrutiny of the communications submitted to the two Houses at the start of an infringement procedure according to articles 258 and 260 of the Treaty on the Functioning of the European Union.[51] Moreover, the reform did not formalise the criteria for selecting EU proposals to be scrutinised and it has not overcome existing asymmetries in the informative duties posed on the government in relation to the meetings of the Council and the European Council.[52]

To conclude, the Italian Senate's participation in the oversight of the executive does not show substantial differences with regard to the Lower House. Existing procedural asymmetries derive from the full 'internal' autonomy constitutionally allowed to each Chamber. From the political perspective, in the last few legislative terms the Senate has unexpectedly been permeated by greater political cleavages compared with the Lower House. This feature has made this House particularly proactive in the use of policy-influencing oversight tools rather than in the sphere of ex post oversight.

5–6 *Le Regioni* 837, 838 ff; G Rivosecchi, 'La partecipazione dell'Italia alla formazione e attuazione della normativa europea. Il ruolo del Parlamento' (2013) 5 *Giornale di diritto amministrativo* 463, 470.

[46] C Fasone, 'Qual è la fonte più idonea a recepire le novità del Trattato di Lisbona sui Parlamenti nazionali' (2010) 3 *Osservatorio sulle fonti* 1.

[47] N Lupo, 'La riforma del 20 dicembre 2017 del (solo) regolamento del Senato, nella faticosa ricerca di un'omogeneità regolamentare tra i due rami del Parlamento' (2017) 50 *Studi parlamentari e di politica costituzionale* 23, 35 ff.

[48] The Lisbon Treaty has opened new 'opportunity structures' for the Italian Senate, see C Neuhold and A Strelkov, 'New opportunity structures for the "unusual suspects"? Implications of the Early Warning System for the role of national parliaments within the EU system of governance' (2012) 4 *OPAL Online Paper Series* 13.

[49] Statistics are available on the IPEX platform.

[50] The rule states that the position adopted by the government at the EU level shall be consistent with the political directions set by the two Houses. A Esposito, 'La legge n 234/2012 sulla partecipazione dell'Italia alla formazione e all'attuazione della normativa e delle politiche dell'Unione europea. Parte I – Prime riflessioni sul ruolo delle camere' (2013) 1 *Federalismi.it* 1, 36 f.

[51] Art 15.2 of Law no 234/2012 provides that the Houses, in compliance with their Rules of Procedure, can adopt any appropriate decision to follow up the communication. The lack of a dedicated procedure clearly inhibits the exercise of this scrutiny prerogative.

[52] F Scuto, 'L'evoluzione del rapporto parlamento-governo nella formazione e nell'attuazione della normativa e delle politiche dell'Unione europea' (2015) 1 *Rivista AIC* 1, 5.

II. When Asymmetric Bicameralism Does Not Hinder the Influence Capacity of the Upper House: Oversight by the House of Lords

Acknowledging the atypical representative nature of the UK House of Lords is prelimi-nary to understanding parliamentary oversight and its dimensions in that legal order and practice.[53] Different from other Upper Houses, the House of Lords is composed of unelected members: this feature determines not just the 'political strength' of the House and its capacity to have legislative influence,[54] but also its relation with the oversight dimension. If oversight is considered as a function embedded in the chain of delegation linking citizens to elected agents, it should be questioned whether the House of Lords could at all oversee the executive.[55]

From a constitutional perspective, the two Houses have distinctive positions both in law-making, where the House of Commons is given primacy, and in the formation of government. Apart from the powers of absolute veto set by the 1911 and 1949 Parliament Acts,[56] for all other public non-money Bills the Lords can only delay the approval of the proposal.[57] In comparative terms, legislative powers entrusted in the House of Lords are not negligible.[58] Nonetheless, the House of Lords is considered a weak legislature, due to its unwillingness to make full use of its powers even in the approval of highly controver-sial Bills.[59]

Because the House of Lords is unelected and excluded from the confidence circuit, governmental accountability is seen as a dimension primarily, if not exclusively, for the Lower House.[60] It is generally acknowledged that the Commons should play a leading role in holding the government to account, while the Lords are only expected to complement and reinforce oversight of the Lower House, without duplications.[61] The main limit faced by the Lords lies in the long-standing convention according to which members of one

---

[53] H Bochel and A Defty, '"A more representative Chamber": Representation and the House of Lords' (2012) 18 *The Journal of Legislative Studies* 82.

[54] M Russell, 'A Stronger Second Chamber? Assessing the impact of the House of Lords Reform in 1999 and the lessons for bicameralism' (2010) 58 *Political Studies* 866.

[55] The issue was highly debated in the 2012 Democratic Audit Report, S Wilks-Heeg, A Blick and S Crone, *How Democratic is the UK? The 2012 Audit* (Liverpool, Democratic Audit, 2012).

[56] The reference is to Bills first introduced into Parliament in the Lords, Bills extending the duration of Parlia-ment beyond the present maximum of five years, and secondary legislation.

[57] Among such conventions, it is worth mentioning the 'Salisbury–Addison doctrine' which, since 1945, requires the Lords not to obstruct Bills passed by the Commons foreshadowed in the majority party's general election manifesto. Joint Committee on Conventions, 'Conventions of the UK Parliament – Report of Session 2005–2006' (31 October 2006).

[58] M Russell, 'The British House of Lords: A Tale of Adaptation and Resilience' in J Luther, P Passaglia and R Tarchi (eds), *A World of Second Chambers. Handbook for Constitutional studies on Bicameralism* (Milano, Giuffrè, 2006) 65.

[59] See the 2012 Democratic Audit Report (n 55) ch 2.4.2.

[60] On parliamentary oversight of the executive in the British tradition as a function rooted in the convention of ministerial responsibility, F Rosa, *Il controllo parlamentare sul governo nel Regno Unito. Un contributo allo studio del parlamentarismo britannico*, XIV (Milano, Giuffrè, 2012) 59 ff.

[61] Cabinet Office, 'A House for the Future: Royal Commission on the Reform of the House of Lords' (20 January 2000) ch 8, 80 f.

Chamber should not speak in the other, which implies that Commons ministers can make statements and be questioned in the Lower House while the Lords can address questions only to ministers drawn from the Upper House.[62] As a matter of fact, from the beginning of the twentieth century the number of ministers selected from the Lords has radically declined and the large majority of members of Cabinet sit in the Commons. Therefore, the ability of the Lords to hold ministerial accountability is extremely weak.[63] Such limitation affects both the questioning of ministers as well as ministerial statements on matters of public importance made for the purposes of information rather than for debate[64] and it is seen as a potential inhibition of the practical influence of such tools.[65]

Notwithstanding these limits, the Lords can pose questions independently of the Commons, thus creating the premise for permanent scrutiny of government activity. Questions may be submitted for oral and written answers. Among oral questions, two questions per week are discussed as 'topical questions', drawn from a ballot 48 hours in advance. Ministers can be asked up to four 'starred questions' a day, which are tabled on a 'first-come, first-served basis': they are considered more effective than similar practices in the Lower House, due to the time available, much longer than in the Commons, and the topicality and random nature of the selection mechanism.[66] Questions not directed to Lords ministers are addressed to 'Her Majesty's Government' as a whole and it is up to the government to decide which department should answer.[67] This practice is different from the Commons, where the questions must relate to the responsibility of the concerned government department. Another difference between the two Houses is Prime Minister's Question Time, which is exclusive to the Commons.

The use of parliamentary questions to influence policy is not typical of the House of Lords. Formally, the Lords Companion to the Standing Orders limits the purpose of parliamentary questions to elicit information from the government of the day and assist members in holding the government to account. Oral questions should be addressed for information only, 'and not with a view to stating an opinion, making a speech or raising a debate'.[68] In contrast, the Factsheet note on parliamentary questions of the House of Commons Information Office explicitly states that 'parliamentary questions are tools that can be used by members of parliament to seek information or to press for action'. The implications of these formal differences should not be overestimated, but – apart from starred questions – scope, cost, length or time limits posed in the Lords on questions[69] confirm a rigorous approach to this tool.

---

[62] Hansard Society Commission on Parliamentary Scrutiny, *The Challenge for Parliament: Making Government Accountable* (London, Hansard Society, 2012) 71.

[63] V Bogdanor, 'Ministerial accountability' (1997) 50 *Parliamentary Affairs* 71.

[64] House of Lords Companion to the Standing Orders, ch 6.02 ff. P Milner, 'Scrutiny by the House of Lords' in C Leston Bandeira and L Thompson (eds), *Exploring Parliament* (Oxford, Oxford University Press, 2018). P Dunleavy, A Park and R Taylor (eds), *The UK's Changing Democracy. The 2018 Democratic Audit* (London, LSE Press, 2018) 182–92.

[65] Cabinet Office, 'A House for the Future' (n 61) 81.

[66] Hansard Society, *The Challenge for Parliament* (n 62) 72.

[67] House of Lords Companion to the Standing Orders, ch 6.24.

[68] ibid, ch 6.26.

[69] ibid, ch 6.17.

Even though excluded from the confidence circuit, the Lords are entitled to debate, make political statements and approve decisions on any items of business, thus fulfilling the 'expressive' function of Parliament.[70] Different types of motion can satisfy these needs. The 'motions to take note' are meant to start a debate on a certain situation or policy action without coming to any decision; they should not include a statement of opinion or demonstrate a point of view (and they are not amendable), but they can advance controversial points of view. Shorter debates may be initiated by any member of the House through a 'question for short debate', lasting one or half an hour, which does not give right to reply to the questioner after the minister has referred on the issue. Resolutions can be tabled when a member wishes the House to adopt a formal opinion or decision on a certain matter.[71]

Thanks to these procedures, the House of Lords continues to act as a distinctive forum for general debate. Compared with the Commons, where political issues tend to be more radicalised, public issues are discussed in the Lords in an easier environment for rational analysis and objectivity. The presence of cross-benchers is crucial for political parties in order to win a vote.[72] What is still lacking is an 'intelligent selection' of items, able to identify the issues which might be of interest to MPs and the public.[73]

In the field of ex post oversight, increasing work is being carried out in the Lords through specialist investigations by select committees. Both the Lords and the Commons have their structures of select committees, without duplications:[74] compared with Commons departmental select committees, the Lords tend to promote more thematic and cross-cutting committees, involving various government departments,[75] and to engage in more strategic, long-term and in-depth evaluation.[76] Legislative and investigative select committees undertake inquiries, gathering information from relevant stakeholders and holding evidence sessions with witnesses.[77] Committee meetings are public, they are webcast and sometimes

---

[70] W Bagehot, *The English Constitution*, 2nd edn (London, HS King, 1872).

[71] House of Lords Companion to the Standing Orders, ch 6.52 ff.

[72] Cabinet Office, 'Modernising Parliament – Reforming the House of Lords' (19 January 1999) ch 7. Cabinet Office, 'A House for the Future' (n 61) 87.

[73] House of Lords, 'Report of the Leader's Group on Working Practices', Session 2010–12 (26 April 2011) 41 ff.

[74] The case of the Select Committee on Science and Technology is of particular interest in this regard: the Lords established this Committee in 1980, after the Commons decided not to reappoint the Select Committee on Science and Technology. Norton, 'Nascent Institutionalisation: Committees in the British Parliament' (1998) 4 *The Journal of Legislative Studies* 143, 157.

[75] Lords select committees may cover large-spectrum issues, including intergenerational fairness, nuclear waste management, the rural economy, inequality, public health and food sustainability. P Leyland, 'The Westminster Parliament and Executive Accountability: The Oversight Function of Departmental Select Committees with Reference to the Millennium Dome and the David Kelly Affair' in E Rossi (ed), *Studi pisani sul Parlamento* (Pisa, Edizioni Plus, 2008) 413 ff.

[76] There are three kinds of select committees: legislative committees engaged in pre- and post-legislative scrutiny; investigative committees focused on a particular topic of public policy; domestic committees addressing members' services, the administration of the House and matters of governance and discipline. See the 2012 Democratic Audit Report (n 55) ch 2.4.3; and M Russell, *The Contemporary House of Lords* (Oxford, Oxford University Press, 2013).

[77] After the selection of the topic, the committee issues a call for evidence inviting any interested people or organisation to submit their views or information in writing; it may also take evidence from government. Lord Sewel, 'The role and work of House of Lords Select Committees' (2014) Open Lecture delivered on 3 December 2014.

shown on *BBC Parliament*. After public hearings, the committee works on the draft report, which is usually considered and agreed by consensus. The government is given eight weeks to reply. Lords inquiry reports are highly regarded and they enable the Lords to develop public opinion on major issues. At the same time, they contribute to spurring the executive into acting to address long-term planning. To give some examples, the Report of the Science and Technology Committee inquiry into nuclear research and development, seeking a long-term, strategic plan for science capital investment, was accepted and implemented by the government.[78] The 2011 Report of the Committee on HIV/AIDS led to the introduction of free testing of migrants for HIV.[79]

Furthermore, since 2012 the Liaison Committee has advocated the appointment of at least one ad hoc committee per session to undertake post-legislative scrutiny on a given issue.[80] Compared with the Commons, where post-legislative scrutiny is carried out by departmental select committees,[81] the arrangement of post-legislative scrutiny in the Lords shows an added value and a limit. On the one hand, Lords ad hoc committees tend to produce more recommendations relating to policy and practice:[82] this is the result of a more technical approach to scrutiny which is favoured by expertise, experience, time and by the dominant consensual approach.[83] On the other hand, the temporary nature of Lords committees engaging in post-legislative scrutiny limits the opportunity for a follow-up: since committees cease to function after the publication of the report, it is up to the Liaison Committee to follow up post-legislative recommendations with the government. This is seen as one of the major weaknesses of the Lords select committee system.[84]

The most significant case study of policy-influencing through select committees is the European Union Committee.[85] The Committee, unique for its size (74 members) and staff resources,[86] is entrusted with the scrutiny of draft EU legislation and the UK government's responses. In the last few decades, it has played a major role in influencing the direction of EU-related political choices. Even before the entry into force of the Treaty of Lisbon,[87] the Committee started a praxis of in-depth scrutiny of EU proposals in which it sifts out documents requiring investigation (on average, 30–40 per year), conducts inquiries and adopts reports addressing recommendations to the government. Such reports are extremely valuable and widely regarded. These scrutiny arrangements

---

[78] On the role played by the House of Lords Select Committee on Science and Technology in undertaking long and wide-ranging inquiries and in adopting influential reports, Norton, 'Nascent Institutionalisation' (n 74) 158.

[79] All these cases are reported in Lord Sewel (n 77).

[80] House of Lords Liaison Committee, *Review of Select Committee Activity and Proposals for New Committee Activity* (2012, HL 279).

[81] In the Lords, the creation of the committee is at the remit of the Liaison Committee, which selects the act to be scrutinised, on the basis also of expertise available. T Caygill, 'A Tale of Two Houses?' (2019) 2 *European Journal of Law Reform* 87.

[82] ibid, 98.

[83] P Norton, *Parliament in British Politics*, 2nd edn (New York, Palgrave, 2013).

[84] Caygill (n 81) 103.

[85] P Milner, 'Scrutiny by the House of Lords' in C Leston Bandeira and L Thompson (eds), *Exploring Parliament* (Oxford, Oxford University Press, 2018) 201 ff.

[86] The Committee and its six sub-committees are supported by 24 members of staff and enjoy considerable financial resources.

[87] Cabinet Office, 'A House for the Future' (n 61) 83 f.

integrate the rapid assessment of all EU proposals by the Commons, thus creating a model of complementary EU affairs scrutiny by the two Houses which is considered to a large extent best practice.[88] Lords scrutiny is now supplemented by the European Scrutiny Reserve, like the Commons. The reserve implies that UK ministers should not engage in any new commitment at European level until parliamentary scrutiny is complemented. The entry into force of the Lisbon Treaty and the establishment of the Early Warning System (EWS) has contributed to keeping the UK House of Lords extremely active in this field. The high number of opinions and contributions adopted by the Lords in the subsidiarity scrutiny is an indicator of the capacity of this Chamber 'to flex its muscles' vis-a-vis the government.[89]

From a general viewpoint, the fortune met by the essential oversight tools in the House of Lords confirms that the non-elected composition of this Chamber does not necessarily diminish its capacity to exercise an influence through oversight, even if many structural and functional changes have been advocated in the ongoing debates on the reform of the House.[90]

III. Oversight as a Means of (Administrative) Territorial Influence in the German Bundesrat

The role of the Bundesrat in the oversight of the executive is deeply embedded in the tradition, nature and evolution of German federalism:[91] whereas the Bundestag stands for federal unity, the Bundesrat is meant to represent *Länder*'s interests.[92] It has three main functions: representing the position of each *Land* vis-a-vis the federation; holding the responsibility of the governance of the federation; and ensuring cooperation between territorial and central administrations. Pursuant to Article 51 of the Basic Law, the Bundesrat is an indirectly elected assembly composed of members of *Länder* governments:[93] power is entrusted on each *Land*, rather than on individual members who even lack basic parliamentary immunities. Moreover, existing cleavages follow territorial, rather than political lines:[94] *Länder*'s interests tend to prevail in party positions due to

---

[88] Hansard Society, *The Challenge for Parliament* (n 62) 75.

[89] Neuhold and Strelkov (n 48).

[90] On more recent proposals for reform, Russell, 'The British House of Lords' (n 58) 91 f; A Kelso, 'Reforming the House of Lords: Navigating Representation, Democracy and Legitimacy at Westminster' (2006) 59 *Parliamentary Affairs* 563; and A Kelso, *Parliamentary Reform at Westminster* (Oxford, Oxford University Press, 2009); C Ballinger, *The House of Lords 1991–2011. A Century of Non-Reform* (London, Hart Publishing, 2012) 159 ff.

[91] The meaning of extra-legislative functions of federal Upper Houses is discussed by E Happacher, 'Extra-legislative Functions of Second Chambers in Federal Systems' (2018) 10 *Perspectives on Federalism* 134.

[92] Art 50 Basic Law.

[93] Territorial representation is unequally distributed among the *Länder*, depending on dimensional criteria, in a sort of compromise between the 'Senate' and the 'Bundesrat' model; N Johnson, 'Territory and Power: Some Historical Determinants of the Constitutional Structure of the Federal Republic of Germany' in C Jeffery (ed), *Recasting German Federalism* (London, Pinter, 1999).

[94] C Jeffery, 'Party politics and territorial representation in the Federal Republic of Germany' (1999) 22 *West European Politics* 130.

long-standing constitutional conventions[95] and to the dominating institutional culture, procedurally reinforced by the territorial unitary vote.[96]

These features make it difficult to identify a real 'parliamentary' nature in the Bundesrat, which is rather considered as a democratic-federative body of the Bund, a forum of coordination of territorial governments not subject to external directions.[97] On procedural grounds, it nonetheless follows the traditional rules and practices of parliamentary assemblies, embodying the ideal 'working parliament'.

In law-making, the role of the Bundesrat changes according to the type of procedure:[98] in some areas, it has the same prerogatives of the Bundestag,[99] in others, it can only slow down the procedure by exercising opposition (*Einspruchsrecht*), which implies a new deliberation by the Bundestag with a reinforced majority.[100] On the whole, it acts more as a policy-influencing Chamber than as a real decision-maker. The relation of the Bundesrat with the federal government is structured in terms of sharp separation. The Bundestag holds an exclusive democratic *liaison* with the national executive, both in terms of accountability and cabinet affiliation.[101] The federal government is not accountable to the Bundesrat, nor is it subject to any vote of no confidence in the Second Chamber. Members of the Bundesrat cannot be appointed to the federal government, in order to prevent any conflict between loyalty at the federal or state level. Conversely, the Bundesrat cannot be dissolved by the federal government.

Based on these premises, oversight by the German Bundesrat is not about holding the government to account, but rather about overseeing 'the efficient management and coordination of many of the wide ranging institutional interdependencies arising from the intergovernmental structure'.[102] This function is grounded not in general politics, but first and foremost in administrative action.

From the procedural viewpoint, the Bundesrat, being excluded from the confidence circuit, does not hold powers of investigation in regard to the executive, but is allowed to gather information on governmental decisions and directions. The relationship with the federal government is regulated by Article 53 of the Basic Law: members of the federal

---

[95] From the constitutional point of view, there is no formal limitation to the role of parties in the Bundesrat. Party politics is actually not at all irrelevant in the Bundesrat's relation with the Bundestag and the federal government. R Sturm, 'Party Competition and the Federal System: The Lehmbruch Hypothesis Revisited' in C Jeffery (ed), *Recasting German Federalism* (London, Pinter, 1999).

[96] Every *Land* is expected to cast its votes in a unitary mode, downsizing individual members to mere spokespersons of the *Land* positions. A Gunlicks, *The Länder and German Federalism* (Manchester, Manchester University Press, 2003) esp 44 ff.

[97] R Herzog, 'Der Bundesrat' in J Isensee and P Kirchhof (eds), *Handbuch des Staatsrechts der Bundesrepublik Deutschland*, III (Heildelberg, Müller, 2008).

[98] M Brunner and M Debus, 'Between Programmatic Interests and Party Politics: The German Bundesrat in the Legislative Process' (2008) 17 *German Politics* 232.

[99] The 'symmetric' bicameral procedure includes constitutional revisions and the policy areas listed in the Constitution (*Zustimmung*), which was significantly reduced by the 2006 constitutional reform (*Föderalismusreform I*), to avoid the proliferation of bicameral laws caused by the theory of the unity of the bicameral legislative act (*Einheitslehre*), see BVerfGE 8, 274 (294) and 55, 274 (319). G Limberger, *Die Kompetenzen des Bundesrates und ihre Inanspruchnahme* (Duncker & Humblot, Berlin, 1982) 41.

[100] Art 77(4) Basic Law.

[101] DG Williamson, *Bismarck and Germany: 1862–1890*, 3rd edn (New York, Routledge, 2011) 45 ff.

[102] U Leonardy, 'The institutional structures of German federalism' (1999) Friedrich-Ebert-Stiftung Working Papers.

government have the right, and if requested the duty, to participate in plenary or committee meetings; they have the right to be heard at any time; and they must keep the Bundesrat informed on the conduct of federal policies.

Questioning is probably the most used oversight tool. Questions can be tabled in the plenary[103] by single members or by *Länder* delegations.[104] Individual questions are developed orally and they can only address issues on the agenda. *Länder* questions are submitted and answered in writing, unless the *Land* insists on an oral answer, and they can also tackle other issues. Due to the prevailing 'collective' nature of the procedure and to potential limitations in the publicity regime, the use of questions in the German Bundesrat has proved a 'weak' tool for political influence.[105] It has nevertheless enabled individual *Länder* to get information on specific territorial matters, engaging in a dialogue with the government. The set of tools and procedures allowing the Bundesrat to address directions to the executive is limited, compared with non-territorial Houses. Recommendations can be submitted by committees to the plenary on any matter referred to them. Motions can be drafted and tabled by each *Land*.[106] Both acts are debated and potentially voted on in the plenary.[107]

On the whole, standard parliamentary tools and procedures for 'political' oversight of the executive are quite narrow in the Bundesrat, compared with ongoing practices in the Bundestag. Only the Lower House can make use of strategic instruments to hold the executive accountable, among which the interpellations put in the *Grosse Anfrangen* (major interpellation) and the *Aktuelle Stunden* (topical questions).

Conversely, the Bundesrat plays a significant role in the 'administrative' oversight, grounded on the cooperative relations between the federation and the *Länder*. Apart from the role played in the oversight of budget, which is at an intermediate stage between the political and the administrative spheres of action,[108] it has several 'administrative' oversight prerogatives that fulfil its role of protector of *Länder* competencies and intergovernmental bodies. It consents to regulations at the federal level, with a power of absolute veto.[109] It must give its consent before the federal government adopts the two decisions of major impact on *Länder* autonomy: the control on the implementation of federal laws by the *Länder* by means of commissioners in case of denial by one or more *Länder* governments (*Bundesaufsicht*); and the exercise of substitutive powers in case of unfulfilment of a certain legal obligation (*Bundeszwang*).[110] In both procedures, the *Land* affected by federal action

---

[103] Art 40.2 of the Bundesrat Rules of Procedure allows members of the federal government to also be questioned in committee meetings.

[104] Art 19 Bundesrat Rules of Procedure.

[105] At the request of the government, questions related to matters falling within the scope of Art 53.3 of the Basic Law may be debated in a non-public meeting. See art 17 Bundesrat Rules of Procedure on the motions to exclude the public.

[106] Art 26 Bundesrat Rules of Procedure.

[107] ibid, art 24.

[108] The two Houses have the same role in the discharge of budget (Art 114.1 Basic Law) and they hold an equal right to receive information from the Court of Auditors. Bundesrat (Arts 106 and 107 Basic Law) is required to participate in the approval of federal laws regulating the mechanisms of the fiscal equalisation between the *Bund* and the *Länder* (vertical equalisation) and between the *Länder* (horizontal equalisation). W Heun, 'Artikel 107' in H Dreier (ed), *Grundgesetz Kommentar. Band III: Artikel 83–146* (Tübingen, Mohr Siebeck, 2008).

[109] Art 80 Basic Law. M Kloepfer, *Verfassungsrecht*, I (München, Beck, 2011) 520.

[110] Art 37.1 Basic Law.

participates in the decision adopted by the Bundesrat,[111] which plays the role of a legitimate court of first instance (decisions can be appealed before the Federal Constitutional Court), evaluating alleged infringements.[112]

Furthermore, the Bundesrat is expected to oversee governmental conduct in case of an internal state of emergency threatening the existence of the liberal and democratic legal order in the federation or in any *Land*.[113] In these circumstances, if the federal government has judged the reaction by one or more *Länder* to be inadequate and has consequently decided to place state administrations or governments under its control, the Bundesrat can ask for the immediate removal of the *Bund* decree. These forms of oversight prove closer to administrative (if not judicial) control.

It is instead in the scrutiny of EU affairs where the German Bundesrat has been able to develop a policy-influencing capacity. This prerogative is grounded in Article 23 of the Basic Law, revised in 1992 following the Maastricht Treaty,[114] in view of strengthening the information and participatory rights of the two Houses in the formation of EU decisions.[115] Some of these scrutiny arrangements affect the Bundestag and the Bundesrat in the same way. Both Houses share the right to be informed, comprehensively and at the earliest possible time, on matters concerning the EU and to take part in the discussion of such issues. Even in this field, the Bundesrat has the distinctive task of promoting the balancing and the integration of federal and state interests in the management of EU affairs. Article 23.4 of the Basic Law sets a sort of 'non-variation' clause enabling the Bundesrat to participate in the EU-related decision-making process of the federation insofar as it is competent at domestic level or insofar as the subject falls within *Länder* domestic competences.[116] Participatory powers of the Bundesrat are graduated according to the impact on *Länder*'s internal competences.[117] These provisions allow the Bundesrat the exercise of a 'reinforced' influence on government decisions in the EU policy-making process, in a spirit of factual cooperation.

The system of mutual support between the *Bund* and the *Länder* called for by Article 23 of the Basic Law, and further implemented by the Agreement of Cooperation between the federation and the *Länder* on matters concerning the EU of 12 March 1993,[118] has worked

---

[111] Art 38 Bundesrat Rules of Procedure. Some criticism on this point has been expressed by H Schäfer, *Der Bundesrat* (Heymann, Köln, 1955) 111 ff.

[112] G Dux, *Bundesrat und Bundesaufsicht* (Duncker & Humblot, Berlin, 1963).

[113] Art 91 Basic Law.

[114] Based on Art 23 of the Basic Law, negotiations of European decisions affecting *Länder* interests may be conducted by the competent minister, assisted by a representative from the Bundesrat.

[115] N Foster and S Sule, *German Legal System and Laws* (Oxford, Oxford University Press, 2010) 63.

[116] 'As the *Bundesrat* is to reflect federalism, rather than parliamentarism', is argued by P Kiiver, *The National Parliaments in the European Union: A Critical View on EU Constitution-building* (The Hague, Kluwer Law, 2006) 58, 'its participatory powers in European affairs depend on the extents to which the *Länder* or the *Bundesrat* are affected by EU measures'.

[117] If *Länder* interests are merely 'affected' by the EU matter at stake, the federal government shall 'take into account' the position of the Bundesrat. When *Länder* legislative powers, the structure of *Länder* authorities, or *Länder* administrative procedures are 'primarily affected', the position of the Bundesrat 'shall be given the greatest possible respect'. Finally, when exclusive legislative powers of the *Länder* are primarily involved, the mandate for conducting negotiations within the Council shall be delegated to a *Länder* representative (usually a minister) designated by the Bundesrat. Arts 23.5 and 6 of the German Basic Law.

[118] See also art 45a Bundesrat Rules of Procedure.

well in practice.[119] This institutional architecture was further enhanced after the entry into force of the Lisbon Treaty and the judgment of 30 June 2009 by the Federal Constitutional Court which declared the partial unconstitutionality of the original accompanying law.[120] A strengthened participatory framework was provided through the incorporation into a formal Act of the 1993 Agreement of Cooperation. In response to these changes, the Bundesrat has proactively participated in the political dialogue and the EWS.[121] The scrutiny is carried out by the Committee on European Union, which rarely triggers a report on its own, mostly relating to EU documents following recommendations from sectoral committees. The latter rely on sifting through procedures and on the functional division of expertise among *Länder* senior civil servants, which enables the Bundesrat to sift through and scrutinise almost half of the available documents, thus representing a very effective response to the overflow of information which affects both Houses. The *Länder* have made use of these tools mostly to defend their competences,[122] granting utmost respect to the position of the federal government. As a matter of fact, the scrutiny outcome remains 'characteristically of an administrative-technical nature'.[123]

Overall, oversight in the Bundesrat is deeply embedded in its nature as a 'cooperative' intergovernmental body rather than a pure 'parliamentary' assembly. The function is primarily shaped as an 'administrative' or 'para-judicial' control as it stands outside the framework of a political relationship between the executive and legislative branches, addressing the cooperative architecture between the *Bund* and the *Länder*. However, as an authentic interlocutor of state interests, the Bundesrat has been able to strengthen its position vis-a-vis the Bundestag and the federal government.

IV. Explaining National Variations in Upper Houses' Parliamentary Oversight

The focus on Upper Houses is an ideal testing ground for assessing the multifaceted nature of the oversight function. Due to their institutional position in the bicameral architecture, their political relationship with the executive and their role in legislative decision-making, Upper Houses offer ideal conditions for evaluating the practice of parliamentary oversight in its two dimensions of governmental accountability and policy-influencing.

---

[119] E Dette-Koch, 'German Länder participation in European policy through the Bundesrat' in AB Gunlicks (ed), *German Public Policy and Federalism* (New York, Berghahn Books, 2003) 184 ff. Y Lejeune, 'Participation of subnational units in the foreign policy of the Federation' in R Blindenbacher and A Koller (eds), *Federalism in a Changing World: Learning from Each Other* (Montreal, McGill-Queen's University Press, 2003) 108 f.

[120] The Federal Constitutional Court declared that the Act Extending and Strengthening the Rights of the Bundestag and the Bundesrat in European Union Matters – so called 'accompanying law' to the ratification of the Lisbon Treaty – infringed Art 38.1 and Art 23.1 of the Basic Law insofar as it did not grant the Bundestag and the Bundesrat sufficient rights of participation in the EU law-making and treaty amending procedure.

[121] O Höing, 'With a little Help from the Constitutional Court. The Bundestag on its way to an Active Policy-shaper' in C Hefftler, C Neuhold, O Rozenberg and J Smith (eds), *The Palgrave Handbook of National Parliaments and the European Union* (London, Palgrave, 2015) 195 ff.

[122] M Romaniello, 'Upper Chambers in EU Affairs. Scrutinising German and Belgian Bicameralism' (2015) *Federalismi.it* 1.

[123] T Saalfeld, 'The German Houses of Parliament and European integration' in P Norton (ed), *National Parliaments and the European Union* (London, Frank Cass, 1996) 26 f.

The involvement of Upper Houses in the oversight of the executive is influenced by three main factors. First, institutional factors, relating to the formal arrangement of oversight tools and procedures, show what type of interaction the Chamber is allowed to start with the government. Second, political factors, pertaining to the internal political composition of the House and its interaction with governmental majority, measure the degree of political independence from the executive, which can both support and endanger the House's oversight potential in terms of policy influence.[124] Third, motivational factors[125] explain why the activism of Upper Houses in the oversight function may often represent a reaction to successes and failures of other parliamentary functions.[126]

The Italian Senate demonstrates that even an Upper House with 'hard' oversight powers may find convenience in engaging in policy-influencing tools rather than using a 'hard stick' approach. In the last few decades, Parliament's loss of direct policy-making powers and its inability to adapt to a majoritarian democracy have revitalised 'non-legislative' tools and procedures. The marginalisation of both Houses in the legislative field[127] has been partially counterbalanced with a strengthening of ex ante oversight, in view of scrutinising government proposals and addressing future choices. What is still lacking is the capacity to compensate for marginalisation in the legislative field with a proportional reinforcement of the ex post oversight capacity.[128]

In the case of the House of Lords, the unelected nature of the Chamber and its exclusion from the confidence circuit apparently create favourable conditions for ex post oversight and unfavourable conditions for ex ante oversight. In fact, the House has been able to play its role as a policy-influencing assembly: it complements the work of the Commons, not just assessing, but often influencing government action. Questions are used primarily to gather information and to a lesser extent to hold the government to account, but in many cases they enable broader issues to be faced and examined in depth compared with that of the Commons. The capacity of the House of Lords to promote a debate on potentially any issue has not been jeopardised over time. The activity of select committees offers a strategic contribution to each of the three primary tasks of the Lords: scrutinising legislation; holding the executive to account; and providing a forum to inform public debate. This outcome is strongly supported by favourable political conditions related to low rates of party adversarial approach, generalised cross-party cooperation, weakened party discipline, and solid reputation grounded on the expertise.

---

[124] On 'informal' powers that Upper Chambers may exercise on respective governments, JN Druckman, LW Martin and MF Thies, 'Influence without Confidence: Upper Chambers and Government Formation' (2005) 30 *Legislative Studies Quarterly* 529.

[125] K Gattermann and C Hefftler, 'Political motivation and institutional capacity: assessing national parliaments' incentives to participate in the early warning mechanism' (2013) 15 *OPAL Online Paper Series*.

[126] 'Weak' second Chambers 'are trying to overcome their relative weakness in the internal legal order by increasingly resorting to the mechanisms provided for by the Lisbon Treaty', Neuhold and Strelkov (n 48) 24; and K Auel, O Rozenberg and A Tacea, 'Fighting Back? And, if so, How? Measuring Parliamentary Strength and Activity in EU Affairs' in C Hefftler, C Neuhold, O Rozenberg and J Smith (eds), *The Palgrave Handbook Handbook of National Parliaments and the European Union* (London, Palgrave, 2015) 86 f.

[127] S Fabbrini, 'Governare l'Italia: il rafforzamento dell'esecutivo tra pressioni e resistenze, Governare le democrazie. Esecutive, leader e sfide' in *Il Filangieri. Quaderno 2010* (Napoli, Jovene, 2011).

[128] L Violante, 'Il Parlamento nell'età della globalizzazione' (2003) *Rassegna parlamentare* 41, 50 ff; and G Rivosecchi, 'Il ruolo delle Assemblee rappresentative di fronte ai processi di globalizzazione: spunti ricostruttivi' (2003) 45 *Giurisprudenza costituzionale* 499.

As for the German Bundesrat, its nature as a 'cooperative' intergovernmental body and its position in the institutional and political framework explain why this Chamber tends to exert very low rates of political influence through oversight. Nevertheless, through available instances of 'administrative' or 'para-judicial' control, the Bundesrat exercises an 'administrative' influence on the federal government which eschews the political relationship linking the executive to the legislature, opening to an enlarged dialogue between territorial entities. Even in the scrutiny of the federal government's EU-related activity, the intervention of the Bundesrat is always mediated by the protection of territorial interests.

Overall, comparative analysis confirms that oversight from Upper Houses is an extremely variegated dimension. Depending on structural, functional and political factors, it may encompass instances of ex ante oversight in the shape of an *indirizzo politico* performed through standard parliamentary mechanisms of policy direction, as in the case of Italy. It may include other forms of influential oversight based on expertise, political independence and political reputation, as in the experience of the House of Lords. It can manifest itself in a sort of administrative control grounded in an enlarged vision of the executive–legislative relation, also encompassing territorial entities, as the Bundesrat clearly shows.

PART II

Instances of Parliamentary Oversight in Sectorial Policy Fields

6

Parliaments in International Affairs: Fostering Democracy Through the Oversight of Government Action

I. Introduction. The Role of Parliaments in International Affairs: Overcoming the Idea of 'Executive Dominance'

International affairs as a policy area comprising issues of security, defence and diplomacy is traditionally regarded as a field of executive dominance, as opposed to domestic policy. Historically, the executives have conducted international relations through bilateral confidential diplomacy,[1] while it was parliaments' role to simply ratify international agreements. Only a few prominent Houses (such as the Senate of the United States) enjoyed a stronger role in foreign affairs.

In the twentieth century, the increase of multilateral cooperation and the establishment of international organisations sparked a flourishing of intergovernmental relations: within international institutions, agreements and treaties were negotiated and adopted by governments without prior consultation of parliaments, which could only intervene in the ratification and implementation stage.

This situation still applies. Nowadays the decision-making powers of parliaments vis-a-vis intergovernmental relations in the international sphere are limited, both formally and substantially.[2] In this framework, part of the relevant literature has assumed that 'a democratic deficit in world politics' is hindering the legitimacy of international organisations according to democratic standards.[3] However, over the years, parliaments have managed to regain room for manoeuvre in the sphere of intergovernmental relations.[4] Rather than insisting on direct decision-making powers, they have developed the capacity to examine, verify, question, debate, support, influence, challenge, criticise, amend and censure

---

[1] The executive prerogative (the so-called 'Crown Prerogative') in foreign affairs is topical in the British legal tradition, see AW Bradley and KD Ewing, *Constitutional and Administrative Law*, 15th edn (London, Longman, 2011) 233 and 309 ff.

[2] SA Riesenfeld and FM Abbott, *Parliamentary Participation in the Making and Operation of Treaties: A Comparative Study* (Dordrecht, Kluwer Academic Publishers, 1994). C Carstairs and R Ware (eds), *Parliament and International Relations* (Bristol, Open University Press, 1991).

[3] A Moravcsik, 'Is there a "Democratic Deficit" in World Politics? A Framework for Analysis' (2004) 39 *Government and Opposition* 336.

[4] A Malamud and S Stavridis, 'Parliaments and Parliamentarians as International Actors' in B Reinalda (ed), *The Ashgate Research Companion to Non-State Actors* (Farnham, Ashgate, 2011).

government proposals, decisions and actions. They have established oversight procedures in different stages of policy-making, which include a large variety of tools.

Parliamentary oversight of international affairs has helped to hold governments to account for their intergovernmental activity, engaging them in a sort of 'two-level game'. This 'two-level' scheme has traditionally described the influence that domestic constraints concerning parliamentary participation in the ratification of treaties exercise on government engagement in international bargaining processes.[5] This scheme confirms that domestic (parliamentary) actors' preferences are definitely relevant for executives involved in intergovernmental cooperation.

The same metaphor of the two-level game could be used, however, to describe parliaments' involvement in the oversight of government foreign policy. In the international sphere, parliaments don't tend to just scrutinise (ex ante) and oversee (ex post) the national government's decisions and actions; since international decision-making affects their sovereignty in the national domain, they also aim to boost their power on the supranational level. Following game theory, holding the executive accountable for the conduct of intergovernmental affairs might expand Parliament's win-set and offer political leverage in the domestic arena.[6] Party strategies and oversight incentives arising from the two-level game have also been hypothesised, drawing on the principal–agent theory.[7]

From a constitutional point of view, the possibility for national parliaments to engage in a two-level game, however, is not always apparent. It requires a permanent multilateral organisation with a structured intergovernmental dimension. These conditions are easier to meet at EU level, due to the existence of a double circuit of legislative–executive relations linking national parliaments to domestic governments and to the supranational bodies of the fragmented EU executive.[8] In other international organisations, by contrast, national parliaments' connection with the intergovernmental sphere is always mediated by national governments. This structural difference explains why scrutiny procedures are different for the EU and for international affairs.[9]

The lack of research on legislative–executive relations in the international domain has therefore led part of the literature to question whether the traditional 'executive dominance' thesis is supported by empirical evidence. In comparative terms, national parliaments' capacity to engage in the oversight of international policy depends on a variety of legal and pre-legal factors. On the one hand, it is determined by the type and intensity of formal constitutional powers that Parliament may enjoy vis-a-vis the government. On the other

---

[5] See RD Putnam, 'Diplomacy and Domestic Politics: The Logic of Two-Level Games' (1988) 42 *International Organization* 427; PB Evans, HK Jacobson and RD Putnam (eds), *Double-edged Diplomacy: International Bargaining and Domestic Politics* (Berkeley, CA, University of California Press, 1993); J Mo, 'The logic of two-level games with endogenous domestic coalitions' (1994) 38 *The Journal of Conflict Resolution* 402.

[6] R Pahre, 'Endogenous domestic institutions in two-level games and parliamentary oversight of the European Union' (1997) 41 *The Journal of Conflict Resolution* 147, 148 (in a parliamentary system, conditions influencing the two-level game are identified in the 'problem of hand tying': 'the same parties make up the legislature, choose a government, and form an opposition').

[7] T Raunio and W Wagner, 'Towards Parliamentarisation of Foreign and Security Policy?' (2017) 40 *West European Politics* 1, 8 f.

[8] See below ch 7, section I.

[9] J Fitzmaurice, 'National parliaments and European policy-making: The case of Denmark' (1976) 76 *Parliamentary Affairs* 281, 282 (a strong tradition of parliamentary involvement in foreign policy is a pre-requisite for a successful system of parliamentary oversight).

hand, it is influenced by the executive–party dimension, the party system, the system of political-party incentives faced by parliamentarians, the accessibility of information, the availability of adequate administrative structures, and the relationship with external independent authorities acting in support of parliamentary investigation. In short, it is strongly affected by the standard oversight capacity that Parliament is able to exercise in respect of the executive.

Both legal and pre-legal factors can only be understood within the relevant form of government, which explains, for example, why foreign powers of the US Congress[10] do not find corresponding counterparts in systems featuring a confidence relationship between the legislative and the executive powers. Of the variety of influencing conditions, three dimensions serve to explain the course of parliamentary oversight of international affairs.[11]

The first dimension is the timing of and access to relevant information related to intergovernmental cooperation and co-decision. It is assumed that parliaments are more likely to exercise effective and intense oversight of international affairs if they intervene before intergovernmental decisions, rather than afterwards. The second dimension consists of the tools and procedures supporting the oversight of international affairs. These are usually derived from the general oversight toolbox available to parliaments. Other informal practices may develop in response to concrete oversight requirements. Finally, the third dimension is associated with the transparency and publicity of intergovernmental oversight processes. Under certain conditions, higher standards of publicity can foster government accountability in international policy-making. In contrast, under other conditions, privacy of meetings and confidentiality of information are necessary preconditions to allow MPs to become acquainted with the status of intergovernmental negotiations and diplomatic relations.

These three dimensions are used as a frame of reference in order to assess the oversight role of parliaments in the international domain. The comparative analysis is expected to provide a good basis for evaluating the respective roles of politics and of the judiciary when setting the executive–legislative balance of powers in international affairs; the *Miller* case is assumed as a form of non-interpretive judicial review of parliamentary scrutiny in the domain of foreign policy.

II. How Parliaments Oversee Government Foreign Policy at the Domestic Level: A Comparative Overview

Parliamentary oversight of foreign policy can take different forms: ex ante oversight to influence government action beforehand; ex post oversight aimed at holding the government to account for its past decisions; and oversight through information providing citizens with increased levels of transparency.

---

[10] HV Milner and D Tingley, *Sailing the Water's Edge: The Domestic Politics of American Foreign Policy* (Princeton, NJ, Princeton University Press, 2015); CC Campbell and DP Auerswald (eds), *Congress and Civil-Military Relations* (Washington DC, Georgetown University Press, 2015).

[11] O Rozenberg and C Hefftler, 'Introduction' in C Hefftler, C Neuhold, O Rozenberg and J Smith (eds), *The Palgrave Handbook of National Parliaments and the European Union* (London, Palgrave, 2015) 11 ff (testing these dimensions on national parliaments' participation in EU policy-making).

The oversight toolbox available to parliaments in foreign policy is not entirely the same as the one applicable to domestic matters.[12] On the one hand, due to the two-level nature of international cooperation, even standard oversight procedures and practices (such as questions, debates, inquiries, hearings) gain a distinctive institutional relevance when applied to foreign affairs. On the other hand, the need to cope with traditional executive dominance in foreign matters has enabled parliaments to acquire means of influence and control over policy-making that are unique to this sector.[13]

A. Ex Ante Oversight of Foreign Policy

In foreign policy, parliaments have a variety of ex ante oversight tools at their disposal to scrutinise government action in foreign policy before any formal decision is adopted. Many tools are derived from the standard oversight toolbox. They include resolutions and motions to give the government political instructions. Parliamentarians also make frequent use of questions to force the government to share information or state its position on specific foreign policy issues. Inquiries might also be triggered to provide parliaments with investigative prerogatives on selected foreign affairs. Moreover, over the years, parliaments have developed other tools unique to this sector. The most influential are those related to the treaty-making process (see below, section II.B).

A large part of the ex ante scrutiny activity is embedded in the daily work of foreign affairs committees.[14] Committees' continuous relationships with government representatives offer them the opportunity for formal and informal interaction on upcoming foreign policy issues. With some exceptions, these relationships are usually developed in private meetings, close to the public. Committees may have access to confidential information concerning ongoing diplomatic relations, treaty negotiations or other forms of government engagement in foreign affairs. This input may be debated in one of the committees to draft reports addressed to the plenary.

This is the scheme as followed by the Committee on Foreign Affairs of the Swedish Riksdag. In a number of matters that do not fall within the competence of other committees,[15] the Committee prepares a report that serves as a basis for debate and decision in the Chamber.[16] In some parliaments, the Foreign Affairs Committee enjoys a special status. This is true for the Danish Folketing's Foreign Policy Committee that is accorded reinforced information prerogatives, stipulated in the Act on the Foreign Policy Committee.[17] As a result, the Danish government is bound to discuss with the Committee, *in camera*, matters of importance to Denmark's foreign policy.

---

[12] *Contra*, Raunio and Wagner (n 7) 12.

[13] See the Inter-Parliamentary Union Parline Database on National Parliaments, 'National reports on oversight of foreign affairs' (www.ipu.org/parline-e/parlinesearch.asp); and Inter-Parliamentary Union, 'Parliamentary Involvement in International Affairs' (2005) Report presented to the Second World Conference of Speakers of Parliaments, New-York, 7–9 September 2005.

[14] C Fasone, *Sistemi di commissioni parlamentari e forme di governo* (Padova, Cedam, 2008).

[15] Supplementary Provision 4.6.6. to the Rules of Procedure (Riksdag Act). M Jerneck, A Sannerstedt and M Sjdlin, 'Internationalization and Parliamentary Decision-making: The Case of Sweden 1970–1985' (1988) 11 *Scandinavian Political Studies* 169.

[16] D Arter, *The Scottish Parliament: A Scandinavian-Style Assembly?* (New York, Routledge, 2004) 137 ff.

[17] Act no 54 of 5 March 1954.

The Foreign Affairs Committee of the German Bundestag also enjoys a wide variety of oversight tools and procedures in foreign policy based on the standard oversight prerogatives, as stipulated among other things by Article 43 of the Basic Law.[18] It is the main, but not the sole, parliamentary body in charge of the scrutiny of government foreign policy which often falls under the scope of sectorial committees. Compared with the other standing committees of the Bundestag, it is a 'necessary' commission enjoying a special constitutional status, directly provided by Article 45a of the Basic Law. As opposed to plenary sittings, its meetings are held *in camera*.[19] The committee is convened on the state of government action in the different areas of German foreign policy; however, over the years, there have been gaps in the government's capacity to fulfil these duties.[20]

In the Spanish Congreso de los Diputados (Chamber of Deputies), by way of contrast, issues of foreign policy are ordinarily shared by the Second Committee on Foreign Affairs with the Nineteenth Committee on International Cooperation for Development. The establishment (in both Houses, according to their Rules of Procedure) of a permanent, non-legislative committee on matters relating to international cooperation and development was foreseen by Article 15.3 of Act no 23/1998 of 7 July 1998, thus highlighting the political relevance of cooperation policy. Uniquely, the Nineteenth Committee and not the Second Committee is the body endowed with reinforced informative prerogatives,[21] in addition to the standard oversight tools provided to standing committees by s 44 of the Congreso Standing Orders.

A peculiar prerogative of the Foreign Relations Committee of the French National Assembly is the right to engage in extensive hearings of the Minister for Foreign Affairs, to be held approximately once every five or six weeks. These hearings, like all the Committee's activity in foreign affairs, are held in open sessions. Moreover, by common practice the National Assembly does not allow the creation of a committee of inquiry on foreign affairs or defence issues.[22] However, since 2000 frequent use has been made of informative missions[23] as a standard oversight tool aimed at gathering evidence on specific matters related to French foreign policy.[24]

In contrast, the Foreign Affairs Committee of the UK House of Commons usually undertakes inquiries in its area of competence, comprising – according to Standing Order 152 – oversight of the policy, administration and expenditure of the Foreign and Commonwealth Office. Inquiry powers in foreign policy allow the Committee to obtain

---

[18] E Majonica, 'Bundestag und Außenpolitik' in HP Schwarz (ed), *Handbuch der Außenpolitik* (München, R Piper, 1975) 122 f.

[19] Annex (Rule 2) Bundestag's Rules of Procedure.

[20] C Tomuschat, 'Parliamentary Control over Foreign Policy in the Federal Republic of Germany' in A Cassese (ed), *Parliamentary Control over Foreign Policy: Legal Essays* (Alphen aan den Rijn, Sijthoff & Noordhoff International Publishers, 1980) 34.

[21] Art 15.3 of Law no 23/1998.

[22] Article 5-*bis* of Ordinance no 58-1100 of 17 November 1958, as modified in 2000. Practice has acknowledged some exceptions over the years, as in the case of the Inquiry Committee on the conditions to set free some Bulgarian nurses and medical professionals in Libya and on the French–Libyan agreements, created on 27 October 2007. E Thiers, 'Le contrôle parlementaire et ses limites juridiques: un pouvoir presque sans entraves' (2010) 134 *Pouvoirs* 71.

[23] Art 145 Rules of Procedure.

[24] P Brana, 'Retour sur la Mission d'information parlementaire française sur les événements de Srebrenica (2001)' (2007) 65 *Culture & Conflicts* 51, 52 ff.

documents and records, hear persons and periodically report to the House of Commons on the state of the inquiries. Scrutiny of foreign policy is also performed by other committees, among which the Liaison Committee, the Joint Committee on Human Rights, composed of members from both Houses, and the Intelligence and Security Committee. Although they face resource constraints, committees still prove an efficient scrutiny tool in the UK tradition of foreign affairs, as they take evidence from the government binding its members to provide timely responses.[25]

In Italy, inquiry powers have been used in foreign affairs through the appointment of temporary inquiry committees, most often bicameral. In contrast, the Foreign Policy Standing Committees in the Chamber and in the Senate make use of the standard oversight toolbox to scrutinise government management of international affairs.[26]

The activity of foreign affairs committees does not cover the entire spectrum of preventative scrutiny tools. First, another relevant practice relates to the participation of parliamentary delegations in intergovernmental meetings. Pursuant to written rules or informal conventions, MPs may be enabled to be part of government delegations in international conferences, multilateral or bilateral meetings. Parliamentary involvement at this stage may offer the opportunity to obtain direct and timely access to privileged and confidential information concerning the state of foreign affairs. Moreover, MPs' direct dialogue with government representatives may result in early reconsideration or reframing of the national position in the intergovernmental sphere.

This practice is followed in Denmark, where MPs can participate in intergovernmental meetings at the request of the government. Also in France, parliamentarians from both Houses regularly attend intergovernmental meetings on the government's initiative. A parliamentary delegation is always present at the UN General Assembly and at the WTO conferences. Moreover, parliamentary delegations usually join most relevant foreign missions involving the President of the Republic, the Prime Minister or the Minister for Foreign Affairs. In the UK, the participation of a parliamentary delegation in an intergovernmental conference depends entirely on the initiative of the government. It is up to the government to appoint members of the delegation, where appropriate allowing the Houses to make proposals through non-binding resolutions.

Second, another instance of preventative scrutiny, mainly implemented in Nordic countries, unfolds through the establishment of sectorial parliamentary advisory bodies competent in foreign affairs. Such bodies may serve as a source of privileged and confidential information, where necessary subject to secrecy requirements, and as a means to address opinions to the government prior to any strategic decision at the international level.

This is true for the Swedish Advisory Council on Foreign Affairs, chaired by the head of state and composed of the Speaker and nine other MPs elected by the Riksdag for the entire electoral period.[27] The government must regularly inform the Council on any foreign policy

---

[25] S Weir (ed), *A World of Difference. Parliamentary Oversight of British Foreign Policy. A Report by the Democratic Audit, the Federal Trust and One World Trust* (London, Democratic Audit, The Federal Trust and One World Trust, 2007) 8.

[26] A Cassese, *Parlamento e politica estera: il ruolo delle Commissioni Affari esteri* (Padova, Cedam, 1982); and F Longo, *Parlamento e politica estera: il ruolo delle commissioni* (Bologna, Il Mulino, 2011).

[27] Supplementary Provision 8.8.1 to the Riksdag Act (on the appointment of the Secretary of the Council by the government) and Chapter 13, art 2 of the Instrument of Government.

issue of specific relevance for the security of the country; moreover, it is required to consult this body before taking any decision of major importance. Highly restrictive confidentiality requirements are in place to ensure respect for foreign policy's secrecy standards.[28]

Similar prerogatives and powers are entrusted by article 19.3 of the Danish Constitution Act to the standing Foreign Affairs Committee of the Folketing, in its function as advisory body in foreign policy. The government is required to consult the Committee before making any decision of major importance in foreign policy.

A temporary solution was instead adopted by the French Parliament in October 2008, when the National Assembly and the Senate established a temporary working group with a sectorial competence concerning the international financial crisis. This body was expected to make proposals on how to face the international financial and economic crisis and thus allow a parliamentary contribution to the definition of the French national position in the G20 intergovernmental meetings.

On the whole, the comparative picture confirms that preventative scrutiny of international affairs is mainly carried out at committee level. Foreign affairs committees may resort to standard oversight tools to fulfil this function and their oversight activity may ordinarily serve as a basis for debate and decision in the plenary. However, in some parliaments (the Danish Folketing, the German Bundestag and the Spanish Cortes Generales), sectorial committees enjoy (more or less formalised) reinforced informative prerogatives allowing them to engage in a preferred dialogue with the government. Other ex ante oversight tools, including participation of parliamentary delegations in intergovernmental meetings and advisory parliamentary bodies competent on foreign affairs, are much less systematic. Nonetheless, where present, they may support a proactive engagement of Parliament in the preventative scrutiny of foreign affairs.

B. Parliaments in Treaty-Making: Ex Ante and Ex Post Oversight

In most Western democracies, treaty-making is a prerogative of governments, but parliaments have their say in scrutinising or overseeing government action. Parliamentary prerogatives, based on the constitution or the law, range from the power to sanction treaties under negotiation and demand that the government issues reservations to the power to approve treaties signed by the government. Even when the approval of the treaty takes the form of a parliamentary law, this is considered as part of the oversight rather than the decision-making powers of Parliament. The latter is in fact not authorised to modify the content of the treaty and can therefore only approve or reject it as a whole. In some countries, Parliament is responsible for the adoption of international law into domestic law.

Tools and procedures offered to national parliaments in treaty-making vary significantly depending on a number of factors. One is the dualist or monist nature of the relationship between international law and the domestic legal system.[29] In monist systems, where international treaties do not need to be implemented through domestic legislation, the executive

---

[28] Art 7 Riksdag Act.
[29] L Fisler Damrosch and SD Murphy, *International Law: Cases and Materials*, 6th edn (St Paul, MN, West Academic Publishing, 2014) 621 ff.

is usually bound to ask for the approval of Parliament prior to making any binding international commitments. This verification prevents the executive from unilaterally altering domestic legislation through its treaty-making power. In contrast, in dualist systems, prior parliamentary authorisation is less common: here, parliaments intervene at a later stage, after the treaty is concluded, but before its ratification.[30] Comparison shows that the monist–dualist dichotomy is far from clear-cut.[31] However, it is useful to highlight that the participation of parliaments in treaty-making could take the form of ex ante or ex post oversight, depending on the timing of parliamentary involvement that could either precede or follow the formal signing of the treaty.

In a number of countries, parliamentary intervention precedes the conclusion of the treaty and can therefore be classified as a form of ex ante oversight. In theory, this practice could be considered typical of monist states, but, in practice, this assumption is less explanatory.[32] Parliament is usually unable to place any conditions on government negotiations. The long-standing tradition of the US Senate's involvement during treaty negotiations through 'consultations', leading to the conditional approval of the treaty by the Senate itself,[33] does not have similar examples in European democracies. Parliaments in Europe are not usually formally involved in shaping the text of the treaty, as they only have the power to approve or reject it as a whole. However, some formal tools (such as reservations) or informal practices (for example, inter-branch bargaining with the government) may offer representative assemblies the opportunity to exercise some influence on the government.

For instance, in Sweden the Riksdag's approval is required before the government concludes an international agreement which is binding upon the Realm in three cases: if the agreement requires changes in statutory legislation; if it otherwise concerns a matter to be decided by the Riksdag; or if the agreement is of major significance, as in the case of treaties involving human rights, defence alliances, amendments of criminal law, environmental and association agreements.[34] In these hypotheses, the government may act without the Riksdag's approval if the interests of the Realm so require, conferring with the Advisory Council on Foreign Affairs before concluding the agreement.[35] This procedure clearly gives the Parliament a strong influence on treaty-making:[36] although it does not have any formal right to amend treaties, in practice it can make its approval subject to specific conditions. For more important treaties, the Riksdag is consulted during negotiations and it can vote

---

[30] PH Verdier and M Versteeg, 'International Law in National Legal Systems: an Empirical Investigation' (2015) 109 *The American Journal of International Law* 514.

[31] J Crawford, *Brownlie's Principles of Public International Law*, 8th edn (Oxford, Oxford University Press, 2012) 50.

[32] J Grimheden, 'The Self-reflective Human Rights Promoter' in J Grimheden and R Ring (eds), *Human Rights Law: From Dissemination to Application. Essays in Honour of Göran Melander* (Leiden, Martinus Nijhoff Publishers, 2006) 120.

[33] KC Kennedy, 'Conditional Approval of Treaties by the US Senate' (1996) 19 *Loyola International & Comparative Law Journal* 89; US Congressional Research Service, *Treaties and Other International Agreements: The Role of the United States Senate* (106th Congress, Committee Print, January 2001).

[34] Chapter 10, arts 3.1 and 3.2 of the Instrument of Government.

[35] Chapter 10, art 3.3 of the Instrument of Government.

[36] S Stromholm (ed), *An Introduction to Swedish Law*, I (New York, Springer, 2013) 67; J Matz, 'Parliamentary decision making and foreign policy: Sweden's participation in international armed missions and the crucial role of the Riksdag' (2013) 33 *Parliaments, Estates and Representation* 186.

to demand that the government either modifies its position or ceases negotiations.[37] These decisions may be binding, depending on the nature of the treaty. In any case, a motion of censure may be used if the government does not comply with the political instructions voted by Parliament.[38]

The Danish Folketing has a similar role in international treaty-making:[39] it must approve beforehand any international obligation which for fulfilment requires the concurrence of Parliament or which is otherwise of major importance.[40] By common practice, the Ministry of Foreign Affairs confers with Parliament while negotiating the treaty: this is not a constitutional duty, as a binding mandate system is limited to negotiations in the European Council or in the Council; however, ministerial statements and questioning in the Committee for Foreign Policy are a common practice. After having examined the treaty, the Committee issues a report with recommendations to the plenary. The Committee's views are not binding on the government, but they may pose political conditions for the ratification of the treaty. As soon as negotiations are concluded, the treaty is presented to Parliament for ratification and implementation.

In Germany, the conclusion of selected categories of international agreement is subject to prior parliamentary approval. This is true for treaties involving 'political relations' of the state or relating to subjects of federal legislation,[41] whose identification is not always easy to define legally. There is no compulsory involvement of the German Parliament when negotiations are ongoing; during this stage, Parliament cannot object to the international treaty, but competent committees may address the plenary with non-binding recommendations.[42] When negotiations are formally closed, Parliament's approval is binding for the adoption of the treaty and for its transposition into the domestic legal system. Pursuant to Article 59.2 of the Basic Law, the Federal President can submit the proposal for approval of the treaty to the other negotiation partners only once it has obtained the consent of the Bundestag and the Bundesrat in the form of a federal law.[43] The procedure follows the ordinary *iter legis*, but the Houses may only adopt or reject the whole proposal, without amending it or selecting parts of it.[44]

Consistent with Spain's monist approach to international law, the Cortes Generales enjoy a wide range of ex ante oversight tools in the field of treaty-making.[45] In a number of cases, stipulated by Article 94 of the Constitution, prior authorisation of Parliament is

---

[37] Chapter 10, arts 6.2, 7.1 and 7.2 of the Instrument of Government.

[38] I Cameron, 'Swedish Parliamentary Participation in the Making and Implementation of Treaties' (2005) 74 *Nordic Journal of International Law* 429.

[39] C Gulmann, 'The Position of International Law within the Danish Legal Order' (1983) 52 *Nordisk Tidsskrift for International Ret* 45 (on Denmark's classification as a dualist system).

[40] Art 19 of the Constitution. S Thorpe, 'Denmark' in R Gaebler and A Shea (eds), *Sources of State Practice in International Law*, 2nd edn (Leiden, Brill Nijhoff, 2014) 179.

[41] Arts 32 and 59 Basic Law.

[42] Deutscher Bundestag, 'Parliament's Role in International Treaties' (2017) WD 2 – 3000 – 038/17 (on the political influence that these recommendations can exert on the government, directing the decision-making process in the plenary).

[43] Arts 24.1 and 24.2 Basic Law.

[44] Art 82.2 Bundestag Rules of Procedure.

[45] A Remiro Brotons, 'De los Tratados Internacionales (Artículos 93–96 de la Constitución)' in O Alzaga Villaamil (ed), *Comentarios a la Constitución española de 1978. Tomo VII* (Madrid, Cortes Generales-Edersa, 1998); R Riquelme Cortado, 'La tramitación de los tratados internacionales y el reglamento del Congreso de los Diputados de 1982' (1982) 34 *Revista española de derecho internacional* 409.

a condition for the state to enter into any commitment through treaty or other international agreement. Authorisation has the formal aspect of a statutory law, as Parliament has no substantial powers regarding the treaty.[46] In these cases, the Cortes Generales cannot amend the treaty, but can make reservations or interpretative declarations.[47] The Houses' Rules of Procedure make reference to the standard law-making procedure, with some adaptations and limitations.[48] In contrast, in cases provided by Article 93 of the Constitution (treaties allowing the transfer of powers derived from the Constitution to an international organisation or institution), the authorisation by the Cortes Generales takes the form of an organic law, to be approved by absolute majority. This reinforced procedure requires solid parliamentary consensus.[49] Treaties not subject to parliamentary authorisation are submitted to both Houses without delay after being concluded by the government.[50]

In other countries, mostly following a dualist approach to international law, Parliament only intervenes after the government has concluded the negotiation process and has signed the treaty: at the stage preceding ratification, the government presents the treaty to Parliament to obtain its explicit or implicit consent, depending on the applicable rules. Due to the different time frame, parliaments following this scheme tend to exercise a form of ex post oversight of government action. This is true for France and Italy, where the ratification of selected treaties requires parliamentary authorisation by means of a law.

In France, the ratification of treaties considered of paramount importance, listed in article 53 of the Constitution, must be authorised by law. The Council of State monitors the respect of these parliamentary prerogatives.[51] Parliament does not vote on the treaty as signed by the executive article by article, nor does it have the right to amend it, but it can only accept or deny the authorisation for ratification.[52] The Houses cannot amend the text or propose reservations; government reservations and interpretative declarations are nonetheless reported in the explicative documents annexed in the ratification Bill.[53] Article 128 of the National Assembly Rules of Procedure prevented deputies from tabling amendments concerning Bills authorising the ratification of an international treaty. The provision was repealed in 2003, but the Conseil constitutionnel (Constitutional Council) specified that this modification cannot be interpreted as an implicit authorisation enabling deputies to submit reservations, interpretative conditions or other modifications.[54] Between signing and ratification, significant delays may occur.[55] To overcome this risk,

---

[46] F Santaolalla López, 'La ley y la autorización de las Cortes a los tratados internacionales' (1981) 11 *Revista de derecho político* 29; and JM Serrano Alberca, 'Artículo 94' in F Garrido Falla et al (eds), *Comentarios a la Constitución*, 3rd edn (Madrid, Civitas, 2001) (framing parliamentary authorisation as a sort of legislative delegation to the government to negotiate and ratify a treaty, following the guidelines approved in Parliament).

[47] Art 21 of Law 25/2014 of 27 November, on Treaty and International Agreements.

[48] Arts 155 and 156 Spanish Congreso Rules of Procedure; art 144 Senado Rules of Procedure. Art 158 Congreso Rules of Procedure; and art 145 Senado Rules of Procedure (on the resolution of disagreements between the two Houses).

[49] Art 93 Spanish Constitution.

[50] ibid, Art 94.2.

[51] Council of State, *Arrêt Nicolo* of 20 October 1989, 108243. Council of State, *SARL du Parc d'activité de Blotzheim* of 18 December 1998, 181249.

[52] Art 128 National Assembly Rules of Procedure.

[53] Organic Law of 15 April 2009.

[54] Decision No 2003-470 DC of 9 April 2003.

[55] On average, the parliamentary stage of the ratification procedure covers three years and two months.

shortened procedures and simplified practices have been introduced. The shortened procedure enables the conference of the presidents of parliamentary groups to avoid preliminary discussions and move directly to the final vote;[56] this procedure is applied in the National Assembly in the large majority of cases.[57] Moreover, a simplified and de facto unicameral procedure for the approval of ratification Bills was agreed by the chairs of the Foreign Affairs Committees of both Houses: according to this practice, any ratification Bill approved by one of the two Houses can only be presented to the Committee in a simplified report. The activation of this fast-tracking process can be reconsidered at any time by the rapporteur.

Likewise in Italy, the approval of Parliament is required to authorise the ratification of a number of treaties listed in article 80 of the Constitution, which comprise, among other things, treaties of a political nature, implying territorial changes, involving financial obligations or legislative amendments.[58] This parliamentary authorisation takes the form of a law, approved by both Houses in the ordinary procedure.[59] Parliamentary authorisation follows the formal conclusion of the treaty by the government, thus preventing Parliament from playing a formal role in the negotiations stage. It is debated whether the law of authorisation is adopted in the exercise of a legally binding oversight function or rather relates to the power to issue instructions to the government.[60] More recently, Parliament's oversight of treaty-making has been defined as a political action consisting of the evaluation of government conduct in view of a sanction (the denial of the authorisation).[61] The parliamentary law of authorisation cannot be amended by Parliament: this principle is not laid down in the Constitution or in the Houses' Rules of Procedure, but it is regarded as a constitutional convention.[62] The text of the treaty itself cannot be modified by Parliament nor be subjected to any interpretative clauses; it can only be entirely approved or rejected by the Houses. However, consistent with the dualistic nature of the Italian system, Parliament can amend the rules of the authorisation law providing for the treaty execution in the internal legal system, as long as they do not impact the treaty itself. In some cases, international controversies have arisen concerning the adoption of statutory provisions instrumental to treaty execution which allegedly contrasted with treaty obligations.[63] Moreover, the law of

---

[56] Art 103 National Assembly Rules of Procedure.

[57] During the XIV legislative term of the National Assembly (20 June 2012–20 June 2017), 156 treaties were examined through the shortened procedure and 23 were debated in the usual procedure. Assemblée Nationale, 'Fiche de syntèse n 42: La ratification des traités' (1 June 2017).

[58] A Cassese, 'Articolo 80' in G Branca (ed), *Commentario alla Costituzione. Articoli 76–82: La formazione delle leggi. Tomo II* (Bologna, Società editrice del Foro italiano, 1979) 150 (on the ambiguity of the 'political nature' criterion that leaves wide margins of discretion to the government).

[59] Art 72 Constitution.

[60] S Romano, 'Saggio di una teoria sulle leggi di approvazione' (1898) *Il Filangieri* 249, 250 f; C Mortati, *Le leggi provvedimento* (Milano, Giuffrè, 1968).

[61] V Lippolis, *La Costituzione italiana e la formazione dei trattati internazionali* (Rimini, Maggioli, 1989) 62 ff.

[62] On the unamendable nature of the law of authorisation, L Lai, 'Il controllo parlamentare sul controllo estero del Governo: l'autorizzazione alla ratifica dei trattati internazionali in prospettiva comparata' in Vv Aa, *Il Parlamento della Repubblica: organi, procedure, apparati* 3 (Roma, Camera dei Deputati, 2013) 1022 f; D Piccione, 'Il falso mito del 'principio di non regressione' nel procedimento di autorizzazione alla ratifica del Trattato costituzionale europeo' (2005) 50 *Giurisprudenza costituzionale* 2225.

[63] See the Agreement between Italy and Switzerland on letters rogatory, concluded on 10 September 1998. Switzerland delayed the ratification of the Treaty until 2003, after Italian case law had settled a restrictive interpretation of the Italian law of authorisation and execution (Law no 367, 5 October 2001), contested by the Swiss authorities.

authorisation can include further provisions, adapting the internal legal system to the new international obligations, which can be amended, as long as there are margins of discretion available to Parliament.[64]

A different form of 'negative' power in the treaty-making process is instead reserved to the UK Parliament. Under the Royal Prerogative, it is for the UK government to negotiate, sign and ratify treaties. Parliament traditionally enjoyed a limited role in this process:[65] according to the informal 'Ponsonby Rule',[66] the government was required to lay before Parliament treaties that, after having been signed, had to be ratified. Parliament had no statutory role in the ratification process and could only exercise political pressure on the government. Formal parliamentary approval was only required for those treaties implying a change in UK legislation, requiring a grant from public funds or altering the territory of the Kingdom.

After a long debate on how to strengthen the parliamentary role in treaty-making, the Constitutional Reform and Governance Act, entering into force on 11 November 2010, gave Parliament the statutory power to block treaty ratification.[67] Pursuant to this reform, any treaty subject to ratification must be laid before Parliament jointly with an Explanatory Memorandum reporting on the treaty's financial implications, on its implementing means and on any UK reservation or declaration to the treaty. This procedure involves both Houses, but only the Commons have the power to block ratification indefinitely by repeatedly passing motions that a treaty should not be ratified. Neither House has resolved against ratification under the new procedure so far. Although the reform has significantly reinforced Parliament's participation in treaty-making, three factors seem to limit its role.[68] In the first place, this is a 'negative resolution' procedure, enabling the Houses only to oppose the treaty, without debate and vote on ratification. Second, some treaties are excluded from the procedure: the Act only covers treaties that are binding under international law (thus excluding Memorandums of Understanding) and in exceptional cases the government can ratify the treaty without laying it before Parliament.[69] Third, the Act does not provide any mechanism for Parliament to scrutinise treaties during negotiations, when the text of the treaty can still be changed: parliamentary debates may take place at this stage, but they only have political significance.[70] In practice, the dominant format followed by the UK Parliament in the oversight of government foreign policy still rests on

---

[64] L Paladin, 'Ciò che rimane del concetto di legge in senso formale' in Vv Aa, *Studi in onore di Manlio Udina*, II (Milano, Giuffrè, 1975).

[65] S Templeman, 'Treaty-Making and the British Parliament' (1991) 67 *Chicago–Kent Law Review* 459.

[66] J Harrington, 'Scrutiny and Approval: the Role of Westminster-style Parliaments in Treaty-Making' (2006) 55 *International and Comparative Law Quarterly* 121, 127 ff.

[67] UK Ministry of Justice, *The Governance of Britain: War Powers and Treaties: Limiting Executive Powers* (Cm 7239, 2007).

[68] A Lang, 'Parliament's role in ratifying treaties' (2017) 5855 House of Commons Library Briefing Paper 1.

[69] Some EU treaties (treaties that amend the main EU treaties) are excluded from the 'negative resolution' procedure (European Union Act 2011, pt 1). In contrast, the Constitutional Reform and Governance Act applies to agreements concluded by the EU with third parties (and, potentially, also to the withdrawal from agreements concluded between the UK and the EU under art 50 TEU – on this point, see below section III.C).

[70] See the debate on the EU–US trade and investment agreement (TTIP), started soon after the inception of formal negotiations in July 2013 by the Commons Backbench Business Committee, followed by the Commons European Scrutiny Committee and the Lords EU Committee.

the adoption of domestic implementing legislation: the UK government tries to ensure that domestic law is adjusted to international obligations before the treaty is formally ratified and it is up to Parliament to adopt any implementing legislation, following the usual legislative procedures.

In conclusion, the variety of practices featuring the role of parliaments in treaty-making does not allow for the question to be answered of whether ex ante or ex post parliamentary involvement is more protective of domestic accountabilitz and sovereignty.[71] The picture is even more complex if one considers that parliaments' engagement cannot simply be explained in terms of formal procedures and binding powers. The relationship between MPs and government representatives is often developed in an informal arena, through non-procedural communications and exchanges of information that are influenced by tactical or strategic evaluations rooted in the two-level game. These political forms of interaction bypassing formal powers and procedures may nonetheless exercise a relevant impact on international law.[72]

C. Oversight of Foreign Affairs Through Information

Intergovernmental negotiations of international agreements normally take place in secret. This makes transparency of decision-making and publicity of information particularly relevant issues when it comes to the oversight of foreign policy. In this sphere, parliaments' involvement may hence reveal their added value in providing public access to information and documents that are free from confidentiality requirements.

Two main stages deserve attention here. The first considers formal publicity of parliamentary proceedings, including plenary debates on international affairs, as a means to hold the government to account for its foreign policy action. In the second stage, the conduct of interparliamentary relations is examined among the tools instrumental to parliamentary oversight of foreign policy.

First, plenary debates on foreign policy are common practice in most parliaments. These occur not just when there are plenary votes on treaty ratification or other statutory laws dealing with foreign policy, but also through hearings, motions, resolutions and questions. Some assemblies have the formal right to be periodically informed on the status of government foreign policy through dedicated procedures. This is true for the Swedish Riksdag where a foreign policy debate is held every February in the plenary room.[73] The debate is opened with a presentation by the Minister of Foreign Affairs of the Statement of Government Policy on Foreign Affairs and it is attended by diplomats from a large number of countries. Recurring debates on foreign policy are placed on the agenda of the Danish Folketing for each parliamentary session.[74] In the German

---

[71] Verdier and Versteeg (n 30) 517.

[72] NL Cope, 'Treaty Law and National Legislative Politics' in W Sandholtz and CA Whytoc (eds), *Research Handbook on the Politics of International Law* (Cheltenham, Edward Elgar Publishing, 2017) 124.

[73] See the Statement of Government Policy, released in the Parliamentary Debate on Foreign Affairs, 15 February 2017.

[74] Art 38 of the Constitution Act.

Bundestag, debates on foreign policy are mainly held at committee level, thus falling short of publicity requirements;[75] however, political parties can urge the government to provide answers in the plenary on government foreign policy guidelines. Based on political input, often relating to contingencies in foreign policy government action, these debates do not respect precise deadlines.[76]

In Spain, a special plenary procedure is foreseen by article 15 of Act No 23/1998 of 7 July 1998. The Congreso is involved at the beginning of each legislative term and then again every year, at the government's initiative, on the definition of the guidelines and the fundamental directions concerning Spanish policy for international cooperation and development. To this purpose, every four years the government is required to submit to the Congreso the Pluriannual Director Plan, serving as the fundamental programmatic document on international cooperation for development.

In other parliaments, there are no sectorial procedures allowing the plenary to debate and oversee the conduct of foreign policy, but this issue is commonly debated in the plenary by means of the standard oversight procedures. This is true for the Italian Parliament, where foreign policy is ordinarily debated on the occasion of government reports to the House and motions.[77] In France, due to the open publicity regime of the Foreign Affairs Committee, oversight of foreign affairs represents a recurring issue for debate not just in the plenary, but also at committee level. The Minister of Foreign Affairs holds a hearing in committee twice a year. As for the plenary, foreign policy is primarily debated through oral questions, held twice a week.

Second, one relevant channel of information instrumental to the oversight of foreign policy is through the practice of parliamentary diplomacy and interparliamentary cooperation.[78] Parliaments engaging in occasional bilateral or multilateral meetings and in the structured forms of cooperation in International Parliamentary Institutions (IPIs) gain access to privileged information and documents on the current state of international affairs. Parliaments conduct these interparliamentary relations through delegations of MPs, governed by rather differentiated rules and practices. The dominant format is that of permanent delegations of MPs, whose duration corresponds to the legislative term, reflecting the numerical strength of each party in Parliament. This format is expected to guarantee continuity and consistency in the activity of the delegation. Selection criteria in the formation of delegations prove a rather relevant issue in the case of international parliamentary institutions, where the Parliament is permanently represented. With the exception of Sweden,[79]

---

[75] This practice proves consistent with the Bundestag's characterisation as an 'Arbeitsparlament', W Steffani, *Parlamentarische und präsidentielle Demokratie. Strukturelle Aspekte westlicher Demokratien* (Opladen, Springer, 1979) 77 f.

[76] See the German Minister for Foreign Affairs statement on 26 January 2017, deploring that 'almost exactly three years have passed since we first discussed the grand coalition's foreign policy guidelines here in the German *Bundestag*'.

[77] Weir (ed) (n 25) 10.

[78] C Decaro and N Lupo (eds), *Il 'dialogo' tra Parlamenti: obiettivi e risultati* (Roma, Luiss University Press, 2009).

[79] Supplementary Provision 7.1.1 to the Rules of Procedure (Riksdag Act), providing for the election of Swedish delegations to the Nordic Council, the Council of Europe and the Parliamentary Assembly of the Organisation for Security and Cooperation in Europe.

most parliamentary cases examined (Denmark,[80] Germany,[81] France,[82] Spain[83] and Italy)[84] have no formal regulations on the issue and rather tend to manage the formation of delegations through parliamentary conventions or agreements between the two Houses, at least in the case of bicameral delegations that are common practice in Italy, France and Spain. In contrast, other asymmetric bicameralisms do not always compose parliamentary delegations as bicameral bodies; for instance, in Germany a very limited number of delegations support a bicameral composition, including representatives from the Bundesrat. An exceptional procedure features the formation of the UK Parliament's delegations to interparliamentary assemblies: it is up to the government and specifically to the Prime Minister to appoint members of the delegation, selecting them from both Houses by means of a written statement in Parliament.[85] The party distribution of seats must reflect the composition of the House of Commons; nonetheless, the derivation from a government appointment risks undermining the independence and autonomy of action of selected members.

Some permanent interparliamentary regional fora seem to gain a specific role in the scrutiny of intergovernmental conduct of foreign relations. This is the case, among others, of the Assemblée parlementaire de la Francophonie for the French Parliament, or the Latin American Parliamentary Forum for the Spanish Cortes Generales, of the Adriatic–Ionian Initiative for the Italian Parliament. In Scandinavian countries, an exceptional forum for regional interparliamentary cooperation is the Nordic Council, complemented by the Nordic Council of Ministers to form an intergovernmental forum.[86] The Council has the power to initiate proposals and to give advice; it may adopt recommendations or issue statements addressing one or more Nordic countries' governments or the Council of Ministers. Moreover, it has the opportunity to state its views on major issues of Nordic cooperation.[87] Also due to the exceptional structure of the Secretariat, which shares its

---

[80] The Danish Folketing appoints delegations to the Inter-Parliamentary Union (IPU), the OSCE Parliamentary Assembly, the NATO Parliamentary Assembly, the Parliamentary Assembly of the Council of Europe, the Parliamentary Assembly of the Union for the Mediterranean, and the Nordic Council.

[81] The German Bundestag includes delegations to the NATO Parliamentary Assembly, the OSCE Parliamentary Assembly, the Parliamentary Assembly of the Union for the Mediterranean, the Black Sea Economic Cooperation and the Baltic Sea Parliamentary Conferences. The formation of delegations is determined on a conventional basis.

[82] The French Parliament has permanent (bicameral) delegations to the IPU, the Assemblée parlementaire de la Francophonie, the parliamentary assemblies of the Council of Europe, OSCE, the Organisation of the Treaty of the Nord Atlantique, the Organization of the Black Sea Economic Cooperation, the Union for the Mediterranean and the Parliamentary Assembly of the Mediterranean.

[83] The organisation of parliamentary delegations representing the Spanish Cortes Generales abroad is agreed at the beginning of each legislative term through bicameral agreements involving the Bureau of the two Houses. Cortes Generales, 'Actividad internacional de las Cortes Generales en la XI Legislatura' (16 February 2016).

[84] In the current legislative term (the seventeenth term, which started in March 2013), five international parliamentary delegations have been established, representing the Italian Parliament before NATO, the Council of Europe, the OECD, the Central Europe Initiative and the Union for the Mediterranean. These delegations enjoy a representative mandate for the electoral term. E Griglio, 'Procedures vis-à-vis the European Parliament and the Other National Parliaments: Inter-parliamentary Cooperation' in N Lupo and G Piccirilli (eds), *The Italian Parliament in the European Union* (Oxford, Hart Publishing, 2017).

[85] The UK Parliament has permanent delegations to the Parliamentary Assembly of the Council of Europe, the North Atlantic Treaty Organisation Parliamentary Assembly, and the OSCE. For the NATO Assembly, the appointment of the parliamentary delegation falls under the responsibility of the Secretary of State for Foreign and Commonwealth Affairs.

[86] Arts 47–48 of the Helsinki Treaty, the Treaty of Co-Operation between Denmark, Finland, Iceland, Norway and Sweden signed on 23 March 1962, entered into force on 1 July 1962.

[87] Arts 44, 45 and 46 of the Helsinki Treaty.

premises with the Secretariat of the Nordic Council of Ministers in Copenhagen, the Nordic Council may constitute a tool of cooperative dialogue between the interparliamentary and the intergovernmental dimension.

A common feature of all these practices of interparliamentary relations is their instrumental role in parliamentary oversight. The creation of some IPIs has been connected with the democratic oversight rationale, defined as the requirement of providing additional democratic legitimation 'in a transparent and deliberative way embedded in and responsive to the affected publics'.[88] This task does not always find concrete follow-up in the experience of IPIs, which do not seem to go beyond the sharing of information and best practices. Participation in these fora by national parliamentary delegations may nonetheless contribute to strengthening the capacity to oversee government foreign policy at domestic level.

III. Political Versus Judicial Interpretation of the Executive–Legislative Balance of Powers in International Affairs

Formal procedures supporting the oversight of foreign affairs alone cannot explain how parliaments interpret this function in the daily management of the confidence relationship with the government. It is at this stage that political interpretations (from Parliament itself or urged by the government) of how to implement parliamentary formal prerogatives in foreign affairs may lead to unexpected results. Such interpretations may completely overturn the original aim and scope of formally provided tools and procedures; or they may lead to different procedural solutions, either created for this purpose or derived from the standard oversight toolbox.

This sphere of political interpretation finds its limits in the judicial interpretation of the executive–legislative balance of power in foreign affairs.[89] Constitutional provisions or conventions establishing the formal role of Parliament vis-a-vis the government are subject to constitutional courts' interpretation. Judicial decisions shed light on the practical implications and on the limits of parliamentary involvement in foreign affairs. However, the question is what restrictions these judicial interpretations may find due to the intrinsically political nature of the role played by Parliament in the oversight of foreign affairs. These remarks refer to those countries envisaging a well-established system of judicial review. As a consequence, Denmark and Sweden are not specifically taken into consideration, although their Supreme Courts have the competence to execute (an essentially limited but growing form of) judicial review.[90] Moreover, in Scandinavian countries, constitutional review is performed by different subjects, including domestic bodies ultimately accountable to

---

[88] A von Bogdandy, 'The European Lesson for International Democracy: The Significance of Articles 9–12 EU Treaty for International Organizations' (2012) 23 *European Journal of International Law* 315, 328.

[89] On the role played by a combination of judicial and political methods in promoting accountability, see N Balmforth, 'Accountability of and to the Legislature' in N Balmforth and P Leyland (eds), *Accountability in the Contemporary Constitution* (Oxford, Oxford University Press, 2013) 259 ff.

[90] PE Lindblom, 'The Role of the Supreme Courts in Scandinavia' (2000) 39 *Scandinavian Studies in Law* 325.

Parliament, such as parliamentary committees or ombudsmen.[91] This argument explains why in these countries the distinction between political and judicial interpretations of the legislative–executive balance of power proves to be a less significant argument.

A. Political Interpretation

The comparative overview provided in previous sections shows that in foreign affairs parliaments may enjoy oversight powers that, under certain conditions, are legally binding to the government. However, contrary to the US Senate, parliaments in Europe are somewhat weaker, if not in the access to, at least in the practical implementation of these tools.

In most European parliamentary democracies, the role of Parliament in international affairs depends on a variety of political and pre-legal factors. Its interaction with the executive can hardly be forced into predefined legal schemes resulting in formal constraints and veto powers and is better explained in terms of political influence.[92] It is without question that procedures do matter; however, when the available formal tools are not enough, European parliaments can still count on the political confidence relationship to exercise some influence on foreign policy. Literature has suggested 'conceiving of legislative–executive relations as a continuous process of (re)calibration of powers and competences in response to developments within the political arena, on the one hand, and in a state's international environment on the other'.[93] This assumption is supported by evidence from parliamentary practice.

On the one hand, certain practices of parliamentary involvement in foreign policy-making have been developed without a clear legal basis, in response to political contingencies or institutional strategies. Even when it lacks a specific title, Parliament may always resort to standard oversight tools embedded in the confidence relationship to hold the government accountable or issue instructions affecting the conduct of foreign policy. These may vary from adopting a motion to making an announcement in the House; and from calling a parliamentary question to be answered to starting an investigation on government action. All these standard methods of parliamentary oversight may, especially in cases of emergency, be used by Parliament to influence government foreign policy.[94] Some examples may clarify these trends.

The 2013 House of Commons vote on military involvement in Syria offers a relevant example of political influence exercised beyond any specific institutional, legal or constitutional authority. The defeat of the government motion submitted by UK Prime Minister David Cameron offered Parliament a decisive influence on UK foreign policy, thus marking a historical decision in British parliamentarism.[95] According to some commentators, explanations of this success for Parliament must be found in a political ground, namely

---

[91] A Follesdal and M Wind, 'Introduction – Nordic Reluctance towards Judicial Review under Siege' (2009) 27 *Nordisk Tidsskrift for Menneskerettigheter* 131, 132.

[92] MA Baum and PBK Potter, *War and Democratic Constraint: How the Public Influences Foreign Policy* (Princeton, NJ, Princeton University Press, 2015).

[93] Raunio and Wagner (n 7) 6.

[94] House of Commons Information Office, 'Treaties' (2010) *Factsheet P14 Procedure Series* 1.

[95] The only precedent was Lord North's defeat in 1782 in the House of Commons on a matter of war and peace.

the assumption that tighter legislative oversight can be triggered by a lack of trust in the government.[96]

In contrast, reverse political conditions may lead to the opposite outcome. On 16 November 2001, the Bundestag approved the vote of confidence tabled by the government on the decision regarding the participation of German troops in the so-called 'War on Terrorism' in Afghanistan. Since the decision was highly controversial and was met with opposition by majority parliamentary groups, the decision to secure a positive outcome with a confidence vote was interpreted as a blow in the exercise of strong, binding, parliamentary control of executive power in Germany. In this precedent, two factors inhibited strong parliamentary oversight. On the one hand, there was the decision of the government to transform one of the most important foreign policy debates in the Bundestag into a more general policy debate constrained by the vote of confidence. On the other hand, there was the decision by a considerable number of members of the Bundestag to vote in favour of the government in spite of their continuing opposition to the provision of German troops in Afghanistan.[97]

In some cases, the informal involvement of Parliament beyond codified procedures is deliberately pursued by the government to prevent potential stalemate on the international stage. For instance, in Germany the government is not formally bound to inform Parliament on ongoing treaty negotiations. However, to prevent the risk that Parliament might reject the treaty at the ratification stage pursuant to Article 59.2 of the Basic Law, the executive tends to inform the Foreign Affairs Committee of the Bundestag in advance of any treaty negotiations and to inform it, jointly with other competent sectorial committees, about the stage of negotiations. The government's will to engage in an early involvement of Parliament depends on tactical evaluations well explained by the two-level games metaphor.

Occasionally, the government may try to foster prior parliamentary involvement by means of extra-parliamentary forms of scrutiny. This occurred during the UK government's public consultation on amending the 1972 Biological and Toxin Weapons Convention; the consultation, carried out between April and September 2002 while negotiations were ongoing, was directed at defining the position to be adopted at the international level. Through the consultation, the executive sought views not just from public opinion, but also from MPs.[98] The practice of engaging in a public consultation prior to treaty ratification was started in 2000, with the consultation on the draft International Criminal Court Bill, leading to the ratification of the 1998 Rome Statute for the International Criminal Court.

On the other hand, parliaments often prefer using informal rather than formal powers when the latter threatens to undermine national commitments assumed or to be assumed at the international and supranational level. To give some examples, the German Bundestag has so far never rejected the ratification of an international treaty negotiated by the government.

---

[96] J Kaarbo and D Kenealy, 'Precedents, Parliaments and Foreign Policy; Historical Analogy in the House of Commons Vote on Syria' (2017) 40 *West European Politics* 62, 63.

[97] AL Paulus, 'Quo vadis Democratic Control? The Afghanistan Decision of the Bundestag and the Decision of the Federal Constitutional Court in the NATO Strategic Concept Case' (2002) 3 *German Law Journal* 1.

[98] See the Consultation Paper presented to Parliament by the Secretary of State for Foreign and Commonwealth Affairs by Command of Her Majesty, *Strengthening the Biological and Toxin Weapons Convention: Countering the Threat from Biological Weapons* (Cm 5484, 2002).

The single case of rejection of an international treaty by the German Bundestag dates from 1962 and concerns the treaty on the cession to France of the Mundatwald, in the Land of South Palatinate.[99] In contrast, MPs (and especially Foreign Affairs Committee members) are willing to play an indirect role in influencing treaty negotiations by means of their political relations with government representatives.[100]

Similarly, the French National Assembly has been reluctant to push its formal prerogatives to the limit. In case of disagreement over a treaty negotiated by the government, rather than vetoing the ratification and exposing the country to major international responsibilities, it has resorted to alternative, less constraining, solutions. These may entail that the Foreign Affairs Committee, after having formally approved its report on the ratification law, takes action calling on the government to prevent or delay the placing of the item on the plenary agenda. In some cases, the government renounced discussing the ratification in the plenary due to informal solicitations by political groups after a formal vote was celebrated on the ratification law at committee level. Some precedents can be mentioned: in the twelfth legislative term, after having approved the authorisation to ratify a fiscal convention between France and Libya, the Foreign Affairs Committee demanded that the Bill was not placed on the plenary's agenda before some hostages held by Libya were released; in the thirteenth legislative term, a similar practice was followed during the examination of the Partnership and Cooperation Agreement with Turkmenistan. In the last legislative term, in January 2017, the government, at the specific request of some political groups represented in the Conference of the Presidents of the National Assembly, withdrew from the agenda of the plenary the Bill authorising the agreement with Mauritius on the co-determination of the île de Tromelin that had already been approved by the French Senate in 2012 and by the Assemblée Nationale in 2013.[101]

Informal arrangements may also be resorted to either by Parliament or by the government to overcome the rigidity of parliamentary prerogatives and procedures by means of soft powers. An interesting case is offered by the French National Assembly. During the past legislative term (the fourteenth), in view of the ratification of the agreement with the United States on the indemnification of Shoah victims deported in France, the Foreign Affairs Committee overcame the prohibition to amend the treaty by means of a diplomatic note, based on Article 79 of the Vienna Convention, aiming to modify the content of article 1 of the agreement. In this case, an extra-parliamentary tool was used by the National Assembly to exercise formal influence on the decision-making process.

There might be cases in which the government itself tries to bypass formal constraints associated with parliamentary involvement in treaty ratification in order to speed up the entry into force of an international treaty or agreement. This occurred in Spain in 1998, when the government adopted a Decree Law on the adhesion of Spain to different agreements of the International Monetary Fund. Some of these agreements clearly fell within the scope of treaties subject to preventative parliamentary approval pursuant to Article 94.1 of the Constitution. Since in Spain a Decree Law has immediate legal effects, which

---

[99] JR Anderson, 'Parliamentary Control and Foreign Policy in Germany. The Bundestag's Use of Formal Instrumentalities in Overseeing the Administrations' Foreign Policy' (2002) 64 *German Politics and Society* 1.

[100] ibid, 10 f.

[101] R Herreros, 'L'accord de cogestion sur l'îlot Tromelin retiré de l'ordre du jour de l'Assemblée nationale' (*Huffington Post politique*, 17 January 2017).

enter into force from the publication in the *Official Journal*, using this mechanism the government managed to bypass the requirement of prior parliamentary approval.[102]

B. Judicial Interpretation

National constitutional traditions include a large variety of jurisprudential cases dealing with the interpretation and implementation of constitutional clauses affecting the conduct of foreign affairs. This interpretative function may offer constitutional courts a strategic role in shaping the institutional design of the executive–legislative relationship.

In some countries, the constitution itself explicitly provides for the intervention of the constitutional court in the event of uncertainties regarding international treaties' compliance with the constitution. This judicial review formally scrutinises the material consistency of the treaty with the constitution; however, it may indirectly serve as a tool for solving conflicts between the legislative and the executive power. In Spain, for instance, according to Article 95 of the Constitution, the conclusion of an international treaty containing stipulations contrary to the Constitution requires prior constitutional amendment. Access to the Constitutional Court to declare whether or not such a contradiction exists is open to the government or to either House, following specific procedures.[103]

The French Constitution offers two methods of direct access to the Conseil constitutionnel for a preventative scrutiny of international treaties' compliance with the Constitution. One is provided by article 54, enabling the President of the Republic, the Prime Minister and the President of either House to refer to the Conseil constitutionnel an international undertaking suspected of infringing the Constitution. The other is regulated by the so-called '*saisine*': the procedure authorising 60 Members of the National Assembly or 60 Senators to challenge a Bill before the Conseil constitutionnel.[104] These two methods of access were realigned by the constitutional law on 25 June 1992 in order to standardise the appeal procedures and enable both categories of subjects to challenge the ratification Bill at any time during the parliamentary proceedings. Before the entry into force of the constitutional law of 25 June 1992, pursuant to art. 61 of the Constitution, ratification Bills could only be challenged by means of the *saisine parlementaire* after having been approved by Parliament.[105] If the Constitutional Council finds that the international undertaking is unconstitutional, authorisation to ratify or approve it may only be given after amending the Constitution.

---

[102] AM Carmona Contreras, 'Decreto-ley y relaciones internacionales: una compatibilidad constitucionalmente problemática' (2000) 110 *Revista de Estudios Políticos* 59.

[103] Art 157 of the Congreso Rules of Procedure; and art 147 of the Senado Rules of Procedure. In May 2017, the Congreso rejected the proposal submitted by the political group Unidos Podemos to raise the issue of the CETA agreement's constitutional compliance before the Constitutional Tribunal.

[104] See for instance the *saisine*, submitted on 22 February 2017 to the Conseil constitutionnel by 60 deputies, on the constitutional compliance of the CETA agreement (Affaire 2017-749 DC: *Accord économique et commercial global (AECG) entre le Canada, d'une part, et l'Union Européenne et ses Etats Membres, d'autre part*).

[105] C Maugüé, 'Le Conseil constitutionnel et le droit supranational' (2003) 105 *Pouvoirs* 53 ff.

A formal role is granted to the German Constitutional Court in the form of a preliminary injunction.[106] Lately, this power has enabled the Court to exercise a major influence on the national government's position assumed at the European level during the negotiation of the EU–Canada Comprehensive and Economic Trade Agreement with Canada (CETA).[107] Reacting to the appeals lodged by some NGOs, the Court issued a preliminary injunction that rejects the request of preliminary legal protection and at the same time binds the signing of the Agreement to a number of conditions. The German federal government set these conditions during negotiations in the EU Council of Ministers and managed to have them fulfilled through declarations annexed to the Council's meeting minutes.[108]

Apart from these reserved competences, constitutional courts may play a pivotal role in interpreting general constitutional clauses on treaty ratification procedures, thus factually contributing to defining the respective position of the government and the Parliament. In many countries, the constitutional court may have large margins of discretion due to the rather generic formula provided by the constitution for filtering treaties subject to parliamentary scrutiny.

In Spain, for instance, in case of a disagreement regarding the treaty classification first determined by the government,[109] the court may intervene, either assessing the treaty's compliance with the Constitution (Article 95 of the Constitution) or judging on the conflict between the government and the Cortes (article 32 of the Law on the the Constitutional Court).[110] Some of the decisions adopted by the Tribunal Constitucional have exercised a major impact on the role of Parliament in foreign affairs. For example, the decision of the Tribunal Constitucional on Law 13/1999 regulating the adhesion of Spain to various International Monetary Fund Agreements[111] highlighted the specificity of the parliamentary procedure for the approval of the authorisation law, which is the only one admissible pursuant to Article 94 of the Constitution.

In Germany, the Federal Constitutional Court has interpreted the expression 'political relationship' provided by the Constitution as allowing the filtering of treaties subject to prior parliamentary approval. Its case law has contributed to restricting the application of this tool only to agreements that affect the German State in the territorial integrity, independence, position or influence in the international community.[112] It has therefore prevented an

---

[106] Art 32 Federal Constitutional Court Act.

[107] See 2 BvR 1368/16, 2 BvR 1444/16, 2 BvR 1823/16, 2 BvR 1482/16, 2 BvE 3/16; see Bundesverfassungsgericht Press Release, 'Application for a Preliminary Injunction in the "CETA" Proceedings Unsuccessful' (31 October 2016) 71.

[108] Council of the European Union, 'Outcome of the council meeting. 3493rd Council Meeting Foreign Affairs on Trade Issues' (8 October 2016) 13310/16 PRESSE 52 PR CO 51.

[109] This is based on the advisory procedure involving the Council of State (Art 17 of Law 25/2014 of 27 November, on Treaty and International Agreements); see for instance the debate urged by parliamentary groups on the occasion of the Spanish adhesion to the North Atlantic Treaty. A Linares, 'La adhesión de España a la Otan: notas para una revisión crítica' (2013) 32 *Historia Actual Online* 23.

[110] Santaolalla López, 'La ley y la autorización' (n 46).

[111] STC 155/2005 of 9 June 2005. M Urrea Corres, 'La autorización parlamentaria en la celebración de Tratados Internacionales: una reserva orgánica y de procedimiento; comentario a la sentencia del Tribunal Constitucional 155/2005, de 9 de junio' (2006) 10 *Revista General de Derecho Europeo* 20; F Santaolalla López, 'Decreto ley, ley y tratado internacional. Comentario a la ley STC 155/2005 de 9 Junio' (2006) 18 UNED. *Teoría y Realidad Constitucional* 399.

[112] BVerfGE 1, 372, in the complaint (2BvE 2/51 of 29 July 1952) on the French–German economic agreement of 10 February 1950, lodged by the socialist political group of the Bundestag.

expansive interpretation of article 59.2 of the Grundgesetz, combining 'an (unnecessarily) broad reading of the executive power in foreign affairs with a narrow construction of parliamentary participation in treaty-making'.[113]

In France, pursuant to article 55 of the Constitution, international engagements supersede statutory laws if they are duly ratified or approved. The Conseil constitutionnel has no formal role in assessing that these procedural conditions are respected; however, it might incidentally engage in this scrutiny during the examination of an appeal under articles 54 and 61 of the Constitution. In some case law, it has provided judicial interpretation of categories of treaties subject to parliamentary authorisation.[114] In fact, it is the Conseil d'Etat – jointly with the Court of Cassation – that has come to play a pivotal role in the defence of parliamentary prerogatives.[115] The Conseil d'Etat has the right to review those treaties that are ratified pursuant to a parliamentary law of authorisation: in such cases, administrative jurisdiction yields to constitutional jurisdiction. In the *Arrêt SARL du parc d'activité de Blotzheim*,[116] the Conseil d'Etat formally established its administrative jurisdiction over the review of the regularity of treaty ratification procedures, up to the assessment of whether or not a treaty belongs to the categories listed in article 53 of the Constitution and is therefore subject to prior parliamentary authorisation. The Conseil d'Etat eventually conceded that in litigation based on the application of an international treaty or agreement any party might argue that the treaty or agreement was not regularly ratified or approved.[117]

All these cases should be assessed in light of the dichotomy between the two prevailing approaches to constitutional adjudication, labelled as 'interpretive' (or 'clause-bound interpretive') and 'non-interpretive' judicial review:[118] the former refers to constitutional decisions based on a value premise that is explicit either in the Constitution's text or in the government structure created by the Constitution; the latter, in contrast, includes all other types of review referring to a value judgement other than one constitutionalised.[119]

---

[113] Paulus (n 97).

[114] eg, Décision no 70-39, 19-6-1970 on the scope of international engagement 'modifiant des dispositions de nature législative'.

[115] The Conseil d'Etat's engagement in this form of judicial review dates back to the *Arrêt Nicolo* of 20 October 1989. G Carcassonne, 'Faut-il maintenir la jurisprudence issue de la décision n. 74-54 DC du 15 janvier 1975?' (1999) 7 *Cahiers du Conseil constitutionnel* 93.

[116] Conseil d'Etat (Assemblée), 18 December 1998, no 181249. See F Raynaud and P Fombeur, 'Conditions d'application en France d'un traité international dont la ratification ou l'approbation est intervenue sans avoir été autorisé par une loi' (1999) *AJDA* 127; JF Lachaume, 'Jurisprudence française relative au droit international' (1999) 45 *Annuaire français de droit international* 843.

[117] Conseil d'Etat (Assemblée), 5 March 2003, *Arrêt Aggoun*, no 242860.

[118] J Perry, *The Constitution, the Courts, and Human Rights* (New Haven, CT, Yale University Press, 1982) 6 ff (detecting in the legitimacy of non-interpretive judicial review 'the central problem of contemporary constitutional theory' – ibid, 6). AA Morris, 'Interpretive and Noninterpretive Constitutional Theory' (1984) 94 *Ethics* 501 (on the difference between interpretive review and textualism). WN Eskridge, 'All About Words: Early Understandings of the "Judicial Power" in Statutory Interpretation, 1776–1806' (2001) 1516 *Columbia Law Review Faculty Scholarship Series* 990 (for an overview of the background understanding of the judiciary's role in the interpretation of legislative texts in the US tradition). LM Eig, 'Statutory Interpretation: General Principles and Recent Trends' (2011) 7-5700 *Congressional Research Service* 1 (on interpretative methods applied in the exercise of judicial review by the US Supreme Court).

[119] JH Ely, *Democracy and Distrust: A Theory of Judicial Review* (Cambridge, MA, Harvard University Press, 1980) 2 f (depicting the dichotomy between interpretive and non-interpretive judicial review as 'false'; to reduce the potential anti-democratic character of judicial review, the author therefore elaborates a theoretical basis for a broadly 'interpretive' judicial review).

This debate might be considered out of date, due to the shift towards a modern judicial review based on the assumption that courts exercise what is fundamentally a legislative power.[120] However, the distinction can still shed light on the differentiated institutional implications of an interpretive or non-interpretive approach to judicial review. With specific reference to the addressed issue of the executive–legislative balance of power in foreign affairs, it is clear that non-interpretive methods of constitutional adjudication are more likely to encroach on the political interpretation of the parliament–government relationship, and therefore more likely to fall short of expected outcomes. This hypothesis is discussed in the following section, focusing on the *Miller* case.

C. The Miller Case as an Instance of Non-Interpretive Judicial Review

The *R (Miller) v Secretary of State for Exiting the European Union* judgment by the UK Supreme Court[121] offers a significant case of non-interpretive judicial interpretation of the relationship between Parliament and the government.

On the question whether Article 50 of the Treaty on the European Union for exiting the EU could be triggered by the executive without the intervention of Parliament, the Supreme Court ruled against the government. It considered the Resolution of the House of Commons of 7 December 2016 calling on ministers to commit to publishing the government's plan for leaving the EU to be a politically relevant act and stated that parliamentary legislation embodied in a statute was required to establish a certain kind of prerogative power in favour of ministers enabling them to give Notice of the EU exit.

The *Miller* case can be critically assessed focusing on the arguments in support of the justiciability of the executive–legislative relationship rather than on the conclusions, which base the need for a parliamentary statutory law on the protection of individual rights.

Majority judges and minority judges have supported similar arguments on the appropriate extent of judicial control on the executive–legislative relationship in foreign affairs. They all agreed that the treaty-making prerogative and foreign relations in general are not justiciable. In support of this premise, majority judges recalled the dualist theory, arguing that the exercise of prerogative power to make or unmake treaties is consistent with the rule that ministers cannot alter UK domestic law.[122] Further arguments relating to the idea that courts should not overlook the constitutional importance of ministerial accountability to parliament are in Lord Reed's dissenting opinion[123] and also in Lord Carnwath's opinion.[124]

---

[120] C Wolfe, *The Rise of Modern Judicial Review* (New York, Basic Books, 1986) 215 ff (reviewing the three contemporary theories – those by Ronald Dworkin, Jesse Choper and John Hart Ely – sharing the acceptance of modern judicial review).

[121] *R (Miller) v Secretary of State for Exiting the European Union* [2017] UKSC 5, (2017) 2 WLR 583. For an overview of the arguments identified by the Divisional Court in the Miller case (*R (Miller) v Secretary of State for Exiting the European Union* (2016) EWHC 2768, (2017) 1 All ER 158, see, among others, D Feldman, 'Brexit, the Royal Prerogative, and Parliamentary Sovereignty' (*UK Constitutional Law Blog*, 8 November 2016).

[122] *R (Miller) v Secretary of State* [2017] (n 121) [55–56].

[123] ibid [240].

[124] ibid [249].

However, the conclusions of majority judges on the role of Parliament in triggering Article 50 of the Treaty on European Union seem to contradict the above-mentioned premises. Soon after having recalled the non-justiciability of the prerogative power in foreign affairs, in response to the suggestion 'that it should not cause surprise if ministers could exercise prerogative powers to withdraw from the EU Treaties, as they would be accountable to Parliament for their actions', majority judges highlighted that:

> There is a substantial difference between (i) ministers having a freely exercisable power to do something that may have to subsequently be explained to parliament and (ii) ministers having no power to do anything unless it is first accorded to them by parliament. The major practical difference between the two categories, in a case such as this where the exercise of power is irrevocable, is that the exercise of power in the first category pre-empts any parliamentary action. When the power relates to an action of such importance to the UK Constitution as withdrawing from the Treaties, it would clearly be appropriate for the power to be in the second category.[125]

It is clear that the 'appropriateness' argument supporting the submission of ministerial action to prior parliamentary approval bypasses the judicial restraint on the exercise of prerogative power in foreign relations.

Against this argument, one first concern involves the dichotomy between political and legal constitutionalism.[126] On the one hand, this affects the question as to what extent parliamentary oversight of the executive should be taken into account when determining the appropriate extent of judicial control.[127] Conversely, it has to do with the question as to whether judicial control finds a legally relevant criterion in the political oversight embedded in the confidence relationship.

From a statutory point of view, under the Constitutional Reform and Governance Act 2010, the withdrawal from agreements concluded between the UK and EU should follow the same procedure as that provided for agreements concluded by the EU with third parties: the government negotiates and concludes the agreement under the prerogative power and when the agreement is concluded, it is formally sent to both Houses to be scrutinised and possibly blocked by the House of Commons. Due to statutory silence, what happens in the stage that precedes the beginning of negotiations is entirely left to the responsibility of the government, which is accountable to Parliament.[128]

Through the 'appropriateness' argument, the Supreme Court introduced into the executive–legislative management of foreign affairs an external, binding constraint (the approval of a parliamentary statutory law) that is not formally required by the UK constitutional system. As far as this constraint does not have a direct legal basis in the UK constitution, it acts as a court-made rule of constitutional construction.[129]

---

[125] ibid [92].

[126] In response to the post by N Barber, T Hickman and J King, 'Pulling the Article 50 "Trigger": Parliament's Indispensable Role' (*UK Constitutional Law Blog*, 27 June 2016) on the legal obligation to obtain parliamentary approval before triggering art 50 TEU, one main argument relates to the idea that 'it is to Parliament itself, not the courts, to ensure that the Government allows it to exercise the influence it should have, and to decide what it is' – S Law, 'Article 50 and the Political Constitution' (*UK Constitutional Law Blog*, 18 July 2016).

[127] M Elliott, 'Analysis/The Supreme Court's Judgment in Miller' (*Public Law for Everyone*, 25 January 2017).

[128] D Howart, 'On Parliamentary Silence' (*UK Constitutional Law Blog*, 13 December 2016) (on the cases behind statutory silence on the issue of whether legislation was needed to trigger art 50 TEU).

[129] M Elliott, 'The Supreme Court's judgment in Miller: in search of constitutional principle' (2017) 76 *Cambridge Law Journal* 257, 284.

A second concern involves the activism of the Supreme Court and the risk that it may fall short of expected outcomes. Arguments in support can be found in US scholars' defence against judicial activism and hence in the idea that

> The judge's authority to compel obedience comes from that external decision (that is, from the decision settled by the Framers of the Constitution or the drafters of a statute), not from the judge's own desires. This is not to say that judges must 'find' rather than 'make' law … The point of this discussion is that the more meaning added by the judge, the less powerful the judge's claim to obedience.[130]

The parliamentary follow-up of the *Miller* decision, resulting in the approval of the European Union (Notification of Withdrawal) Act 2017, seems to offer two elements in support of this argument. One relates to the nature of the Bill, an extremely short measure, comprising only one substantive and formal provision enabling the Prime Minister to notify the European Council of the United Kingdom's intention to withdraw from the EU. The second element derives from the 'semi-fast-tracked' procedure followed in Parliament in the passage of the Bill.[131] Critics of the *Miller* decision did not find in the procedure strong arguments in support of an effective parliamentary scrutiny.[132]

In a broader perspective, it might be questioned whether the recognition stated in the *Miller* decision – that a resolution of the House of Commons does not have any legislative effect, but is nevertheless 'an important political act'[133] – has contributed to confirm the necessity of parliamentary scrutiny during the process of approving the withdrawal agreement and also in the implementation stage. As a matter of fact, between the notification of the withdrawal and the publication of the agreement, Parliament's participation in a number of 'meaningful votes' gave the two Houses (primarily, the Commons) the power to potentially block the whole process and in any case to give their view on the substance of the long-term relationship between the UK and the EU.[134] This trend was first confirmed by the EU Withdrawal Act 2018 which strengthened Parliament's role (with a main focus on the Commons) in the next stages of the Brexit process.[135] It was then reconsidered in the EU Withdrawal Agreement Act 2020, which repealed the specific rules for approval of the agreement in the EU Withdrawal Act 2018 (the 'meaningful vote') and the general rules of approval of international treaties in the Constitutional Reform and Governance Act 2010. These changes allowed the government to ratify the withdrawal agreement without a further vote in Parliament.[136] Parliamentary oversight was also precluded over the

---

[130] FH Easterbrook, 'Legal Interpretation and the Power of the Judiciary' (1984) 7 *Harvard Journal of Law and Public Policy* 97.

[131] On this point, see the conclusions of the report approved by the House of Lords Select Committee on the Constitution, *European Union (Notification of Withdrawal) Bill* 8th Report (HL 2016–17, 119) para 13.

[132] D Chalmers, 'Brexit and the renaissance of parliamentary authority' (2017) 19 *The British Journal of Politics and International Relations* 663 (on the risk that Brexit will weaken representative democracy within the United Kingdom at the stage of the reform of EU-derived law).

[133] *R (Miller) v Secretary of State* [2017] (n 121) [123].

[134] J Simson Card, 'Parliament and the withdrawal agreement: the "meaningful vote"' (*Commons Library Insight*, 9 February 2018). See also the position stressed by the UK government in the White Paper HM Government *The United Kingdom's Exit from and New Partnership with the European Union* (Cm 9417, 2017).

[135] s 13 of the EU Withdrawal Act 2018. G Cowie, 'Withdrawal Agreement Bills: Parliament's role in the future UK–EU relationship' (*Commons Library Insight*, 22 October 2019).

[136] ss 31 and 32 of the EU Withdrawal Agreement Act 2020.

extension of the transition period (since the Act formally removed this hypothesis)[137] and, more significantly, over the negotiations on the future relationship with the EU.[138] A one-off instance of parliamentary oversight remained for the review of EU legislation in the implementation period. When such legislation raises 'a matter of vital national interest to the United Kingdom', the European Scrutiny Select Committee is allowed to set the wording of a motion to be debated and voted on in the Commons within 14 sitting days. The EU Withdrawal Agreement Act 2020, overall, has reaffirmed the idea that the executive's conduct of international relations is not a matter for the Parliament to deal with and regulate.[139] Parliamentary scrutiny over the implementation of the withdrawal agreement and the negotiation of future relations with the EU was therefore severely restrained. The subsequent limitation of accountability may raise regrets[140] as well as doubts with respect to the compliance with the principles held in the *Miller* case.

A remarkably different balance between political and legal constitutionalism is to be found in the *Cherry/Miller (No 2)* decision,[141] adopted by the UK Supreme Court on whether the advice from the Prime Minister that Parliament should be prorogued from a date between 9 and 12 September until 14 October was lawful or not. The Supreme Court ruling found that the power of prorogation is limited by 'the ability of Parliament to carry out its constitutional functions as a legislature and as the body responsible for the supervision of the executive'.[142] The decision brought about two main principles, one substantial, the other methodological. First, relying on the principle of parliamentary sovereignty and accountability, the Court confirmed that not just the act, but the actions of Parliament, including meeting, debating, legislating, are where the heart of power lies in the UK's (uncodified) constitution. Second, the fact that ministers have political accountability to Parliament does not negate legal accountability to the courts.[143]

Both cases deal with the justiciability of political conventions, however with a different impact on the political interaction between the legislative and the executive branches. As opposed to the *Miller (No 1)* case, what the Court offered in the *Cherry/Miller (No 2)* case is the factual condition – ie, the limitation of the prorogation period – required for Parliament to exercise its scrutiny prerogative and hold the government accountable.[144] In this case, the Court did not enter into the oversight mechanisms linking the executive with the legislative branch; rather, it set a limit on the Prime Minister's unilateral power to

---

[137] ibid, s 33.

[138] A previous version of the Bill – European Union (Withdrawal Agreement) Bill (Bill 7 2019)) clause 31, inserting s 13C in the EU Withdrawal Act 2018 – contained a clause providing for parliamentary oversight of negotiations on the future relationship between the UK and the EU.

[139] S Peers, 'The Withdrawal Agreement Act: Implementing the Brexit Withdrawal Agreement in the UK' (*EU Law Analysis*, 17 February 2020).

[140] House of Lords Select Committee on the Constitution, *European Union (Withdrawal) Agreement Bill* (2020, HL 114).

[141] *R (Miller) v The Prime Minister and Cherry v Advocate General for Scotland* [2019] UKSC 41.

[142] ibid [50].

[143] J Grogan, 'The Rule of Law, not the Rule of Politics: Commentary on the Cherry/Miller No 2 Judgment' (*Reconnect*, 8 October 2019).

[144] On this point see P Craig, 'The Supreme Court, Prorogation and Constitutional Principle' (29 October 2019), forthcoming in (2019) 57 Oxford Legal Studies Research Paper 1, 8 (it is legitimate to use constitutional principles to delimit the scope of prerogative power which, as a species of discretionary power, should be subject to control).

determine the length of the prorogation period.[145] The deviation between the two cases can be related to their different interaction with the Bill of Rights of 1688. Article IX of the Bill of Rights states that 'proceedings in Parliament ought not to be impeached or questioned in any Court'. However, in the *Cherry/Miller (No 2)* case, what the Court is policing – ie, the proroguing power – is recognised as a proceeding which takes place within Parliament, but is not 'a proceeding in Parliament': prorogation is not something on which MPs can deliberate, but rather 'it is something which is imposed upon them from outside'.[146] This explains why *Miller (No 1)* and *Cherry/Miller (No 2)*, which similarly result in the judicial protection of Parliaments prerogatives, have a rather differentiated impact on the political dimension which runs the accountability relationship.

From a theoretical point of view, these cases, which address the boundaries of the separation of power and the limitations on executive power, recall functionalist explanations highlighting the overlapping between the 'political' and the 'legal' constitution.[147] The inter-penetration of law and politics in cases involving government policy confirms that the judicial control can reinforce the political oversight embedded in the confidence relationship if its outcomes are duly interpreted and translated in the formal recognition of parliamentary prerogatives vis-a-vis the government. However, it is necessary to acknowledge that judicial review has a limited reach in balancing the role of Parliament in fields of action under executive dominance, such as international affairs. This fundamentally remains a core task of politics, and the follow-up of the *Miller (No 1)* decision seems to confirm it.

IV. The Non-Binding Potential of Parliamentary Oversight in International Affairs

The comparative overview of parliamentary participation in foreign policy confirms that various procedural schemes are applicable: preventative scrutiny suitable to influence government action beforehand; ex post oversight aimed at holding the government to account for its past decisions; and oversight through information supporting publicity and transparency on the conduct of international affairs. The large variety of relational schemes driving legislative–executive interaction explains why one single model cannot fully describe parliamentary oversight of foreign policy. Some common trends may however be identified.

One major feature lies in the prevailing reliance on non-binding oversight mechanisms whose institutional outcome can only be understood within the domain of the confidence relationship.

---

[145] *Contra*, the *Cherry/Miller (No 2)* decision was criticised by J Finnis, *The Unconstitutionality of the Supeme Court's Prorogation Judgment* (London, Policy Exchange, 2019) 5 f as an example of a judgment which does not merely protect the boundaries of the proroguing power, but rather intrudes into its modes of exercise, thus transferring into the domain of justiciable law constitutional conventions which have traditionally been policed politically.

[146] *R (Miller) v The Prime Minister* (n 141) [68]. On this argument, M Loughlin, *The Case of Prorogation, the UK's Constitutional Council Ruling on Appeal from the Judgment of the Supreme Court* (London, Policy Exchange, 2019) 10 f.

[147] JAG Griffith, 'The Common Law and the Political Constitution' (2001) 117 *Law Quarterly Review* 49. See also JAG Griffith, *The Politics of the Judiciary* (Manchester, Manchester University Press, 1977) 127 ff.

Ex ante oversight of foreign policy is mainly conducted at committee level. Committees' oversight potential entirely rests on tools aimed at gathering information, fostering a dialogue with the government, addressing to the executive instructions or opinions on the conduct of foreign relations without any association with veto powers.[148] All these procedures and tools clearly fall within the 'soft' conception of parliamentary oversight. This is specifically true for plenary debates. The interparliamentary and international activity developed by parliaments is another dimension instrumental to the oversight function as a cooperative relationship. In this respect, in some parliaments (especially parliaments of Nordic countries, such as Denmark and Sweden) structural organisational solutions have been developed in the form of advisory councils competent in foreign affairs.

Apart from these 'soft' mechanisms, in the sphere of treaty-making and treaty ratification parliaments can exercise binding, mandatory forms of parliamentary oversight. The time frame, intensity and scope of parliamentary involvement varies substantially. Some parliaments may be asked to give formal consent before the conclusion of treaties and agreements (Sweden, Denmark, Germany and Spain), while others authorise the ratification of the treaty after the government has assumed formal obligations at the international level (Italy and France). A preventative involvement in treaty-making may grant some parliaments (particularly, Sweden, Denmark and Spain) a large variety of scrutiny prerogatives and tools. Parliamentary participation in treaty-making and ratification may be part of a reinforced procedure (Spain) and be solidly anchored in judicial review; or it may be subject to a discretional and purely negative parliamentary intervention (UK). The scope of treaties subject to parliamentary scrutiny or oversight also varies significantly.

However, regardless of these formal and procedural differences, parliaments are often unwilling to use formal veto powers that might seriously compromise government engagements at the international level. Rather, the analysis of political dynamics shows that in many cases parliaments prefer to use their influence through informal and soft, relational mechanisms of interaction with the government.

This priority of political dynamics over formalised procedures raises some major questions on the sustainability of the executive–legislative network of actual relations vis-a-vis expectations of accountability and democratic scrutiny in the domain of international affairs. To limit governments' political discretion in the management of foreign policy, reinforce parliamentary scrutiny and minimise the risk of disagreements between the government and Parliament regarding international engagements, one could advocate the introduction of more formalised and binding scrutiny tools, such as the mandating mechanism that binds the government before an international treaty is formally concluded.

Recently, many national democracies have seen themselves presented with this option as a potential means for strengthening democratic accountability in the management of foreign policy. However, a preliminary question arises here on the desirability of statutory reforms to be adopted at domestic level, aimed at reinforcing the formal position of Parliament vis-a-vis the government in the oversight of foreign policy. Attempts made in the UK to strengthen formal tools available to parliament in treaty-making have not proved

---

[148] As noted by P Norton, *Parliament in the 1980s* (Oxford, Basil Blackwell, 1985) 53, committees' influence relies not only on the expertise and cogency of their reports, but also on 'how far government is willing to initiate, review or change a polity'.

completely satisfactory. The Constitutional Reform and Governance Act 2010 has left the oversight relationship at the discretion of Parliament, thus entirely relying on the political dimension.

Limits faced by statutory reforms of this sort lie in the endogenous nature of changes introduced: as they are negotiated with the government through parliamentary proceedings, these changes are not likely to enable Parliament to go much further in the formal regulation of oversight powers. It is unusual for government to accept any substantial limitation of its foreign policy capacity and allow Parliament to play an increasingly constraining role.

These internal factual limits explain why only an external subject, endowed with definitive power, such as constitutional and supreme courts, may prove capable of introducing substantial innovations in the executive–legislative relationship. Paradoxically, however, this external factor is deemed to face the same limits that it is supposed to overcome. In fact, the political relevance of the executive–legislative relationship in international affairs raises a major question on the feasibility of non-interpretive judicial decisions, as in *Miller*.

Two arguments have been taken into consideration in this respect. The formal argument refers to the constitutional significance of the confidence relationship that risks being challenged and potentially weakened by the intrusion of external legal arguments, such as those dealing with the protection of individual rights, forcing the executive–legislative relationship to respect specific procedures. This risk is emphasised in bicameral procedures involving Upper Houses excluded by the confidence relationship. Moreover, the effectiveness argument highlights that a judicial interpretation may fall short of expected outcomes: judicial attempts to crystallise the executive–legislative interaction may result in the external imposition of a formal parliamentary engagement, discouraging the examination of politically agreed procedural solutions that may favour substantial participation of Parliament in the decision-making process. To overcome this risk, judicial control must be interpreted as a preliminary step that does not preclude but rather encourages the setting of new formal and informal prerogatives in favour of Parliament in the interaction with the government in the field of foreign affairs.

7

Parliamentary Oversight in the EU Constitutional Dimension: The Polycentric Paradigm

I. Parliamentary Oversight of the EU 'Fragmented' Executive

The constitutional traditions of EU Member States appreciate parliamentary oversight as one of the pivotal aspects of the executive–legislative interaction, centred on the confidence relation. This prerogative, rooted in the origins of parliamentarism,[1] has represented a natural point of reference for the construction and development of European institutional architecture. As a matter of fact, the oversight dimension has always been seen as instrumental to the strengthening of EU democratic legitimacy[2] and to the 'parliamentarisation' of its form of government,[3] consisting in the transplant of confidence mechanisms derived from parliamentary systems.

In fact, the legal transplant of parliamentary oversight modules from the national to the European level has shown a clear propensity for rejection.[4] First, the 'model' to be transplanted is not at all homogeneous. The first part of the volume has demonstrated that, depending on the legal tradition, on the internal form of government and on the party structure, parliamentary oversight shows rather different conceptions and procedural implementations at Member State level.

Second, the lack of homogeneity in the model to be transplanted is aggravated by the peculiar arrangement featuring both the legislative and the executive branch at the European level. On the side of the controller, representation is divided and shared between the two channels of the European Parliament and of national parliaments (within their domestic forms of government)[5] and is enriched by the presence of sub-national representative assemblies. On the side of the controlled, due to the fragmented nature of EU government(s),[6] oversight does not address one single body, but more institutions that substantially differ

---

[1] See above ch 2, section I.

[2] C Crombez, 'The Democratic Deficit in the European Union: Much Ado about Nothing?' (2003) 4 *European Union Politics* 101; P Mair and J Thomassen, 'Political representation and government in the European Union' (2010) 17 *Journal of European Public Policy* 20.

[3] B Rittberger, '"No integration' without representation!" European integration, parliamentary democracy, and two forgotten Communities' (2006) 13 *Journal of European Public Policy* 1211. *Contra*, S Fabbrini, 'The European Union and the puzzle of parliamentary government' (2015) 37 *Journal of European Integration* 571.

[4] P Magnette, 'Appointing and censuring the European Commission: the adaptation of parliamentary institutions to the Community context' (2001) 7 *European Law Journal* 292, 307.

[5] Art 10 Treaty on European Union (TEU).

[6] D Curtin, 'Challenging Executive Dominance in European Democracy' (2014) 77 *Modern Law Review* 12.

in their internal composition, democratic legitimacy and relationship with the directly elected bodies. Beyond the European Commission, an intrinsically supranational body, parliamentary oversight comprises intergovernmental institutions (such as the Council and the European Council) or less formalised bodies (for example, the Euro-Group and the Euro-Summit) and independent authorities (the European Central Bank and the agencies). Intergovernmental bodies have acknowledged a significant expansion of their role in response to the financial and economic crisis[7] and yet their accountability represents a factor of vulnerability for the democratic legitimacy of the EU structure.[8]

Third, the network of relations linking the two channels of parliamentary representation and the fragmented EU executive makes it hard to provide a definition of the EU form of government based on traditional national categories. The hybrid nature of the EU institutional architecture combines and matches features derived both from parliamentary and from presidential systems, thus leading to a rather atypical model defined as 'quasi-parliamentary'[9] or 'semi-parliamentary', which resembles the prehistory of the Westminster system.[10] Due to the lack of a traditional separation among governing institutions and to the mixing up of their roles, the EU institutional architecture has been associated with a 'dynamic confusion of powers'. In the horizontal perspective, the rather low horizontal division between the main branches of government[11] mirrors the ambiguities of the EU decision-making structure, relying on the mixing of three accountability regimes:[12] the supranational regime, based on the Community method; the regulatory regime,[13] as referring to laws, rules or principles that are prescribed by EU authorities in one form or another in order to control or govern conduct; and the intergovernmental regime, resembling international negotiations, which confers accountability at the national level.[14] In the vertical perspective, the EU leaves large margins of manoeuvre to Member States, much greater than in any federal system. This arrangement explains the wide range of explicative formulas (*multilevel constitutionalism, multilevel parliamentary field, composite European constitution*, and *euro-national parliamentary system*)[15] defining the structural participation of decentralised levels to the institutional governance of the centre.

---

[7] F Fabbrini, EH Ballin and F Somsen, 'Introduction: A New Look at the Form of Government of the European Union and the Eurozone' in F Fabbrini, EH Ballin and F Somsen (eds), *What Form of Government for the European Union and the Eurozone?* (Oxford, Hart Publishing, 2015).

[8] E Griglio, 'Divided Accountability of the Council and the European Council. The Challenge of Collective Parliamentary Oversight' in D Fromage and A Hérranz-Surallés (eds), *Executive–Legislative (Im)balance in the European Union* (Oxford, Hart Publishing, forthcoming).

[9] S Hix, *The Political System of the European Union* (London, Macmillan, 1999) 47; and S Hix, 'Executive Selection in the European Union; Does the Commission President Investiture Procedure Reduce the Democratic Deficit?' in K Neunreither and A Wiener (eds), *European Integration After Amsterdam: Institutional Dynamics and Prospects for Democracy* (Oxford, Oxford University Press, 2000) 97.

[10] Magnette (n 4) 302.

[11] V Schmidt, 'Federalism and State Governance in the European Union and the United States: An Institutional perspective' in K Nicolaïdis and R Howse (eds), *The Federal Vision: Legitimacy and Levels of Governance in the United States and the European Union* (Oxford, Oxford University Press, 2001) 339.

[12] B Crum and D Curtin, 'The Challenge of Making European Union Executive Power Accountable' in S Piattoni (ed), *The European Union: Democratic Principles and Institutional Architectures in Times of Crisis* (Oxford, Oxford University Press, 2015) 67 ff.

[13] See above, ch 1, section II (nn 70–72).

[14] S Fabbrini, 'The European Union and the puzzle of parliamentary government' (2015) 37 *Journal of European Integration* 571 (on the constant swinging of EU integration between supranational and intergovernmental logic).

[15] See above, ch 1, section II (nn 62–66).

The peculiar conditions met in the EU institutional architecture provide the premises of what can be defined as the polycentric paradigm[16] of parliamentary oversight of the EU fragmented executive. This paradigm is based on a modular concept of the oversight function, declined in a polycentric system of modules of interaction between representative assemblies acting at the European, national and sub-national levels and the EU governments. The following sections analyse the democratic oversight modules respectively vested on the European Parliament, on national parliaments and national form of government (including sub-national parliaments) and on the interparliamentary cooperation.

II. The Oversight Module Centred on the European Parliament

The oversight powers of the European Parliament stem from the combination of majoritarian and regulatory democracy. The failure in the legal transplant of the parliamentary oversight modules grown out of the constitutional traditions of Member States brings the European Parliament closer to the category of legislatures rather than to that of parliaments.[17] Over the decades, the European Parliament has seen its position strengthened in regard to the executive branch,[18] and yet its oversight prerogatives are not fully comparable with those of national parliaments.[19] The legal base for the oversight power of the European Parliament is set by Article 14 TEU which gives this body the task of exercising 'functions of political control and consultation as laid down in the Treaties'.[20] To fulfil this mandate, the European Parliament also resorts to regulatory mechanisms which are less rooted in the tradition of majoritarian parliamentarism.

To understand in what manner the European Parliament exercises its oversight prerogatives, it is necessary to distinguish the constitutional role vested in each of the institutions of the fragmented EU executive, which identifies three distinct oversight modules: the confidence-type, non-confidence type and regulatory oversight modules.

A. The Confidence-Type Oversight Modules: The Relationship with the Commission

The European Parliament oversees the European Commission resorting to oversight mechanisms shaped according to the confidence modules developed in national parliamentary systems (*confidence-type oversight*). In the EU fragmented executive, the Commission

---

[16] The definition of polycentric paradigm is provided by L Besselink, 'National Parliaments in the EU's Composite Constitution: A Plea for a Shift in Paradigm' in P Kiiver (ed), *National and Regional Parliaments in the European Constitutional Order* (Groningen, Europa Law Publishing, 2006). See also E Griglio, 'I circuiti e I "buchi neri" del controllo parlamentare sull'esecutivo frammentato dell'Unione europea' in R Ibrido and N Lupo (eds), *La forma di governo dell'Unione europea* (Bologna, Il Mulino, 2018).

[17] On the distinction between legislatures and parliaments, see above ch 2, section II (n 64).

[18] R Dehousse, 'European institutional architecture after Amsterdam: parliamentary system or regulatory structure?' (1998) 35 *Common Market Law Review* 595.

[19] C Lord, 'The European Parliament, not a very European Parliament?' (2003) 9 *Politique européenne* 30.

[20] M Kohler, 'European Governance and the European Parliament: From Talking Shop to Legislative Powerhouse' (2014) 52 *Journal of Common Market Studies* 600, 602.

is the institution which mostly resembles a real 'government'.[21] Its relations with the European Parliament have been built over the years by imitating and transplanting the confidence mechanisms developed in national constitutional traditions.

The oversight circuit linking the European Parliament to the Commission develops in the three stages of the investiture, censure and horizontal control of the body. The first two stages – the investiture and censure – have acknowledged a process of incremental 'parliamentarisation' aimed at strengthening the participation of the European Parliament in significant moments in the life of the institution.[22] This trend has inflated elements derived from national forms of government into the institutional architecture of the EU, promoting the supranational over the intergovernmental dimension.

The investiture procedure, now regulated by Article 17, paragraphs 7 and 8 TEU, was introduced by the Maastricht Treaty in 1992 in order to align the mandate of the Commission and the European Parliament and give a legal base to the parliamentarisation of this topical institutional moment.[23] The formation of the Commission unfolds in the three stages of the election of the President of the Commission, on proposal of the European Council, the confirmation of commissioners-designate by the appropriate parliamentary committees, and the approval of the college and programme by the European Parliament in plenary sitting. These stages developed in practice, after the 1994 attempt by the European Parliament – on the occasion of the first implementation of the Maastricht Treaty – to maximise its prerogatives.[24] The double parliamentary vote on the President and on the collegial composition of the Commission was then formally recognised by the Amsterdam Treaty. Another step in the direction of the parliamentarisation of the investiture procedure was enabled by the reform of the European Parliament Rules of Procedure that introduced majority rule for the election of the President of the Commission.[25] The power vested in the President of the European Parliament to ask the candidate for the presidency of the Commission to make a statement, followed by debate, or to submit his or her political guidelines to the plenary, completed the parliamentary dimension of the investiture procedure.[26]

A different purpose is instead associated with the confirmation procedure that submits the nominees to the various posts of commissioners to a consultation procedure by the referent parliamentary committee before the collegial vote in the plenary.[27] This mechanism finds its precedent in the confirmation hearing organised by the European Parliament in 1981 during the formation of the Thorn Commission. It is completed by the presentation of the college of commissioners and of their programme at a sitting of Parliament.[28]

---

[21] Hix, *The Political System of the European Union* (n 9) 21.

[22] R Corbett, F Jacobs and D Neville (eds), *The European Parliament*, 9th edn (London, John Harper, 2016) 235 f. D Judge and D Earnshaw, 'The European Parliament and the Commission Crisis: a new assertiveness?' (2002) 15 *Governance: An International Journal of Policy, Administration, and Institutions* 345, 355 f.

[23] J Fitzmaurice, 'The European Commission' in A Duff, J Pinder and R Pryce (eds), *Maastricht and Beyond: Building the European Union* (London, Routledge, 1994).

[24] Lord (n 19) 32.

[25] Rule 32 European Parliament Rules of Procedure 1996, 11th edn, now Rule 124 European Parliament Rules of Procedure 2019.

[26] Rule 124.1 European Parliament Rules of Procedure 2019.

[27] Rule 33 European Parliament Rules of Procedure 1996, now Rule 125.2 European Parliament Rules of Procedure 2019.

[28] Rule 125.5 European Parliament Rules of Procedure 2019.

This mechanism offers an example of legal transplant, derived from presidential systems,[29] whose purpose is related more to the evaluation of the technical competences of the candidates than to consideration of their political programme.

The last step in the direction of the parliamentarisation of the investiture procedure was made with the introduction, in 2014, of the *Spitzenkandidaten* formula,[30] whose main aim was to strengthen the political connection between the preferences expressed by the electors and the selection of the President of the Commission.[31] As a matter of fact, the 'parliamentarisation' of the investiture procedure found one major weakness in the dependence from the candidatures proposed by Member States, which left limited margins of action to the representative institution. In the *Spitzenkandidaten* design, the European parties are called to advance proposals for the position of President of the Commission,[32] with the purpose of binding the European Council to select the candidate of the party which has obtained the relative majority in the European elections.

The first application of this new modus operandi on occasion of the formation of the Juncker Commission in 2014 apparently confirmed the expectations.[33] In contrast, the subsequent application, which took place in 2019 during the formation of the von der Leyen Commission, was interpreted as a backstop in the fortune of the *Spitzenkandidaten* formula. Both interpretations fail to catch the complex nature of the investiture proceedings, whereby the full parliamentarisation of the procedure is hardened by the lack of real majoritarian party dynamics and by the mixing of intergovernmental and supranational logics.

With regard to the 2014 investiture procedure, the success of the *Spitzenkandidaten* formula[34] did not limit the role of the European Council which saw national representatives gain an ever more relevant position in the selection of commissioners-designate expressing national, rather than political, interests.[35] Moreover, the European Council preserved a leading position in the definition of the political programme and of the agenda of the future Commission.

With regard to the 2019 investiture procedure, the failure of the *Spitzenkandidaten* formula was apparently determined by the European Parliament's inability to find a majority in favour of any candidate and by the substantial imposition of the candidate agreed by the European Council. In fact, this situation did not prevent the European Parliament exhibiting its muscles in the hearings with the commissioners-designate, up to the rejection of the French candidate, Sylvie Goulard. The refusal of trust, based on issues of independence

---

[29] Magnette (n 4) 297.

[30] Connecting the formation of the Commission to the electoral results pursuant to the formula of the responsible government was advocated by V Bogdanor, 'Legitimacy, accountability and democracy in the European Union' (2007) *A Federal Trust Report* 1, 5.

[31] S Hobolt, 'A vote for the President? The Role of *Spitzenkandidaten* in the 2014 European Parliament elections' (2014) 21 *Journal of European Public Policy* 1528; and J Priestley, G Schollgen and N Peñalver Garcia, *The Making of a European President* (London, Palgrave, 2015).

[32] The desirability of this transformation is debated by M Kumm, B de Witte and M Maduro, 'The Euro-crisis and the democratic governance of the Euro' (2012) 8 RSCAS Paper 1.

[33] J Müller Gómez and W Wessels, 'The Spitzenkandidaten procedure: reflecting on the future of an electoral experiment' (2016) 8 IAI Working Paper 1.

[34] M Goldoni, 'Politicising EU Lawmaking? The Spitzenkandidaten Experiment as a Cautionary Tale' (2016) 22 *European Law Journal* 279.

[35] S Fabbrini, *Which European Union?* (Oxford, Oxford University Press, 2015) 169.

and integrity, was criticised as a form of abuse of power.[36] Indeed, this muscular manifestation by the European Parliament resembled some presidential experiences of veto power expressed by congressional bodies in regard to the executive appointments. At the same time, many of the questions addressed to the commissioners-designate either related to the political programme or affected issues of accountability towards the European Parliament, which brings the mechanism back to parliamentary standards.

On the whole, recent steps made towards the parliamentarisation of the Commission investiture procedure have significantly empowered the confidence-type oversight tools of the European Parliament. However, results achieved so far are not fully comparable to practices at national level, due also to the position of independence which is a feature of the Commission pursuant to Article 17, paragraph 3 TEU.[37]

The participation of the European Parliament in the investiture of the Commission is mirrored by the power to vote a motion of censure which, if approved by a two-thirds majority, forces all the commissioners to resign. This procedure recalls similar mechanisms of censure at the national level and yet there are both formal and substantial divergences. On the one hand, the double quorum required by Article 234 TEU – the censure must be approved by a two-thirds majority and the majority of members must attend the vote – limits the practicability of this tool, which is deemed to be a 'nuclear weapon'.[38] On the other hand, the strict collegial nature of the Commission has acted as a protective shield limiting the individual responsibility before Parliament.[39] To compensate this gap, the principle of commissioners' individual responsibility before the President of the Commission was introduced on a conventional basis in 1988 before being regulated by the Treaty of Nice; this principle, rooted in the tradition of German constitutionalism, enables the indirect control of the European Parliament on individual commissioners. In practice, the motions of censure examined by the European Parliament, so far, have always been rejected, while the Santer Commission resigned before the censure was voted on in the European Parliament. As a matter of fact, this tool was introduced more as a form of impeachment, to sanction illegal behaviours on behalf of the Commission, and still today shows a hybrid nature,[40] which combines elements of political and judicial control, practices of national parliamentarism and technocratic meritocracy.

In between the investiture and the eventual censure, the European Parliament is engaged in the 'horizontal' control of the Commission, whose purpose is to pursue the collective responsibility of the body ex Article 17, paragraph 8 TEU. This instance has grown out of the spontaneous initiative of the European Parliament, mostly developed in response to the requests submitted by MEPs which were aimed at reproducing at European level the oversight procedures and practices – from questions and interpellations to hearings and inquiry committees – that they knew from the experience of their

---

[36] I Pernice, 'Fairness, Trust and the Rule of Law. Statement on the European Parliament's confirmation procedure concerning Sylvia Goulard' (*Verfassungsblog*, 21 October 2019).

[37] P Oliver and Martenczuk, 'The Commission' in R Schütze and T Tridimas (eds), *Oxford Principles of European Union Law. The European Legal Order*, I (Oxford, Oxford University Press, 2018) 559 ff.

[38] M Westlake, *A Modern Guide to the European Parliament* (London, Pinter, 1994) 115.

[39] Judge and Earnshaw (n 22) 348.

[40] Magnette (n 4) 295 and 305.

national parliaments. In response to these inputs, the right of the European Parliament to obtain information and documents and to scrutinise both ex ante and ex post the actions of the Commission was strengthened. These purposes are now supported by ad hoc tools and procedures, including the debate in a public sitting of the annual general report of the European Commission,[41] the tabling and debate of oral and written questions and interpellations,[42] and the request addressed to the Commission to submit any appropriate proposal on matters on which it considers that a Union act is required for the purpose of implementing the Treaties.[43] On the whole, these tools structure a rather variegated picture of the European Parliament's prerogatives regarding the Commission, ranging from the information rights and reporting duties to the debates and sharing of political directions. Many of these tools are not exclusively referred to the Commission but, in certain cases, can also be addressed to the other bodies of the fragmented executive, thus escaping from the traditional confidence-type patterns.

B. The Non-Confidence Type and Regulatory Oversight Modules

A different instance of non-confidence type oversight connects the European Parliament to the intergovernmental institutions formally provided in the Treaties, including the European Council, the Council[44] and the bodies grown out of the practice of relations between national governments, such as the Euro-Group and the Euro-Summits.

All these bodies are part of the EU fragmented executive and are composed of members of the national executives, but they do not exclusively exercise executive functions.[45] The institutional role of the European Council has been assimilated to a 'collective head of state',[46] while the role of a 'second Chamber', representative of Member States, has been attributed to the Council.[47] Due to their peculiar position and to the recent growth in their decision-making powers,[48] these intergovernmental bodies experience a 'softened' responsibility arrangement before the European Parliament, which explains why the confidence module plays a marginal role.

---

[41] Art 233 of the Treaty on the Functioning of the European Union (TFEU).

[42] Art 230 TFEU.

[43] Art 225 TFEU; and <u>art</u> 45 European Parliament Rules of Procedure.

[44] D Naurin, 'Representation in the Councils of the EU' in S Kroger (ed), *Political Representation in the European Union. Democracy in a Time of Crisis* (London, Routledge, 2014).

[45] D Curtin, *Accumulated Executive Power in Europe. The 'Most Dangerous' Branch of Government in the European Union* (Amsterdam, Knaw Press, 2009) 13 (although the executive power is mainly exercised by the Commission and by the Council, the European Council itself is responsible for executive functions, both political and administrative).

[46] J Lewis, 'Is the Council becoming an Upper House?' in N Jabcko and C Parsons (eds), *The State of the European Union. Vol 7. With US or Against US? European Trends in American Perspective* (Oxford, Oxford University Press, 2005) 146. See also W Wessels, *The European Council* (London, Palgrave, 2016).

[47] S Fabbrini, 'Intergovernmentalism and its Limits: Assessing the European Union's Answer to the Euro Crisis' (2013) 46 *Comparative Political Studies* 1003, 1005 f. *Contra*, D Curtin, *Executive Power of the European Union. Law, Practices, and the Living Constitution* (Oxford, Oxford University Press, 2009). U Puetter, 'Europe's deliberative intergovernmentalism: the new role of the Council and the European Council in EU economic governance' (2012) 19 *Journal of European Public Policy* 161.

[48] YS Rittelmeyer, 'The Institutional Consecration of the European Council: Symbolism Beyond Formal Text' in F Foret and YS Rittelmeyer (eds), *The European Council and European Governance: The Commanding Heights of the EU* (New York, Taylor & Francis, 2014).

In regard to these bodies, the European Parliament is not expected to apply the traditional patterns of parliamentary oversight, but rather tends to engage in a form of 'supervision'. The Parliament is lacking formal prerogatives and sanctions that might bind the intergovernmental bodies or censure ex post their conduct of public affairs. Even for the President of the European Council no mechanism of political removal is provided in the Treaties. Only the European Council, by qualified majority, has the power to end the President's term of office in the event of an impediment or serious misconduct.[49] It can therefore be asserted that the formal de jure accountability arrangement between the European Parliament and the Council or the European Council is very limited.[50] Tools available to the European Parliament do not seem to satisfy the fundamental conditions of a comprehensive accountability regime. These provide that the controlled *be obliged* to explain and justify its conduct, that the controller can pass *judgement* and that the controlled may face *consequences*.[51] Nonetheless, both the Council and the European Council have some informative duties in the regard to the European Parliament.[52] Other prerogatives, provided in the European Parliament Rules of procedure, aim at holding the Council accountable. Many of them affect the legislative procedure,[53] although standard oversight tools can also be used in the non-legislative field.[54] Further informative prerogatives with respect to the Council and the European Council have been set for the European Parliament in the realm of economic governance.[55]

With regard to these informative prerogatives, there are no binding judgements available to the European Parliament. However, the latter can pass a sort of 'soft' judgement resorting to its standard scrutiny tools.[56] To conclude, no binding consequences can be derived from these parliamentary prerogatives, whose aim is to foster transparency and debate, but with little corrective capacity. It has been observed that 'the nature of all these rights is facilitative and informative, rather than obligatory and pressurising'.[57] The European Parliament holds no real formal power regarding the Council and the European Council; however, it is not prevented from exercising a general 'supervision' that occasionally may result in de facto accountability arrangements.[58]

---

[49] Art 15(5) TEU.

[50] M van de Steeg, 'Public Accountability in the European Union: Is the European Parliament able to hold the European Council accountable?' (2009) 13 *European Integration Online Papers* 1 ff.

[51] M Bovens, 'Analysing and Assessing Accountability: A Conceptual Framework' (2007) 13 *European Law Journal* 447.

[52] See art 4 TEU, on the European Council's obligation to inform the European Parliament submitting a report after each summit and a yearly report on the progress achieved by the Union.

[53] See for instance Rules 44 and 45 and the Rules under Title II – Chapter 3 European Parliament Rules of Procedure.

[54] See Rules 136, 137.3, 138 and 139 of the European Parliament Rules of Procedure.

[55] See art 2a.4 of the Council Regulation No 1466/97 of 7 July 1997, as amended by Regulation No 1175/2011, on the appearance of the President of the Council, and, where appropriate, of the European Council, before the relevant European Parliament committee to discuss the broad guidelines of economic policy and any conclusions drawn by the European Council on orientations for economic policies in the context of the European Semester.

[56] For instance, according to Rule 132 of the European Parliament Rules of Procedure, on request of members of the Council or the European Council, a statement with debate may be placed on its agenda. However, no real negative consequences may be attached to this procedure.

[57] Crum and Curtin (n 12) 81.

[58] van de Steeg, 'Public Accountability' (n 50) 17.

The relationship of the European Parliament with the European Central Bank (ECB) is instead far more complex. Oversight of the ECB monetary policy can be related to the European Parliament's non-confidence type module. The ECB is clearly a 'non-majoritarian' institution,[59] which is not directly responsible to the electors and to representative bodies. Nonetheless, it can be argued that it has a 'softened' responsibility before the European Parliament that can address to the ECB some of the surveillance tools and procedures used for the Council and the European Council. To show some examples, the European Parliament can question the ECB.[60] It must be consulted before the European Council appoints the President, Vice President and Executive Committee of the ECB.[61] The President of the ECB can be invited to present to Parliament the Bank's Annual Report.[62] The European Parliament interacts with the ECB through the 'monetary dialogue' which has significantly acted as a reference model for the setting of the 'economic dialogue' with the Council, the European Council and the Euro-Group.[63] Oversight of ECB banking supervision is instead subject to the regulatory module.

Regulatory oversight is the third module featuring the European Parliament and it is mostly exercised in regard to the agencies and of public administration. This module is a genuine European specificity and it is rooted in the regulatory legitimacy of European integration. It comprises forms of ex ante and ex post supervision, including the appointment and dismissal of non-elective officials, budgetary oversight, the assessment of performances, and it may unfold through the implementation of a wide range of parliamentary oversight tools, such as hearings, interrogations and inquiries.

The European Parliament makes use of this machinery in regard to the decentralised agencies, set up on a case-by-case basis in response to clear-cut policy needs. Although the oversight powers may vary *in concreto*, depending on the operating conditions set upon each agency, parliamentary control of EU agencies by the European Parliament usually unfolds through budgetary discharge, participation in the appointment of the executive director, membership of management boards, consultation on work programmes and scrutiny of annual reports.[64] These mechanisms are mainly carried out at committee level, in sectorial committees and in committees on budget and budgetary control.[65] Relying on the European Parliament's capacity as a working parliament, these oversight prerogatives enable MEPs to intrude into the regulatory activity of the agencies, addressing their activity and assessing their performances. As a matter of fact, they prove closer

---

[59] B Rittberger, 'The Creation and Empowerment of the European Parliament' (2003) 41 *Journal of Common Market Studies* 203, 205.

[60] Rules 140 and 141 European Parliament Rules of Procedure.

[61] Art 283 TFEU.

[62] Rule 135 European Parliament Rules of Procedure.

[63] C Fasone, 'European Economic Governance and Parliamentary Representation. What Place for the European Parliament?' (2014) 20 *European Law Journal* 164, 175 f.

[64] R Korver (ed), *EU Agencies, Common Approach and Parliamentary Scrutiny* (Brussels, European Parliamentary Research Service, 2018) 7 f. F Jacobs, 'EU Agencies and the European Parliament' in M Everson, C Monda and E Vos (eds), *European Agencies in between Institutions and Member States* (Alphen aan den Rijn, Kluwer Law International, 2014).

[65] European Parliament Committee on Constitutional Affairs, 'Report on the implementation of the legal provisions and the Joint Statement ensuring parliamentary scrutiny over decentralized agencies' (30 January 2019) 2018/2114(INI).

to instances of congressional oversight of administrative agencies, as grown out in the history of the United States.[66]

The oversight of the new banking supervision powers vested in the ECB at the apex of the financial and economic crisis[67] is also part of the regulatory oversight module. It consists of the oversight on the appointments and on standard activity. Both instances were strengthened by the Interinstitutional Agreement of 30 November 2013, signed by the European Parliament and the ECB, which reinforced the accountability of the ECB in the framework of the Single Resolution Mechanism. Oversight powers vested in the European Parliament in the appointment of apical positions and in the daily monitoring of the ECB's activity are never binding and they are interpreted as a form of interinstitutional cooperation, aimed at fostering transparency and enhanced democratic legitimacy.[68]

Broadly speaking, all these modules confer to the European Parliament oversight or supervision powers that in no case can be assimilated to the prerogatives of national parliaments. Rather, these powers result in the implementation of non-binding tools and procedures, often related to mechanisms of participative democracy,[69] which are aimed at fostering either the interinstitutional dialogue or the transparency of decision-making. In fact, the European Parliament experiences a third sphere of action, cross-cutting all these modules, which exercises a binding force over all the bodies of the fragmented EU executive. The reference is to the budgetary powers vested on the European Parliament for both the ex ante and ex post (see below chapter eight, section IV).

III. Indirect Oversight by National Parliaments and National Forms of Government

The oversight dimension centred on national parliaments contributes to the circuit of democratic oversight in the EU constitutional dimension in several ways. First, it has acted as a reference model for the introduction at the European level of oversight modules inspired by the majoritarian parliamentary tradition.

Second, the national dimension provides a laboratory for testing new 'Europeanised' oversight modules, resulting from the transformation experienced by this function in the EU space due to the melting of the constitutional experiences and to the hybridisation of the procedures. As a matter of fact, in the last few years the oversight of EU affairs by national parliaments has undergone an intensive process of Europeanisation,[70] aimed at adjusting

---

[66] Congressional oversight of administrative agencies fulfils the idea that 'the legislature has a continuous obligation to study and assess the operations of an agency', see Association of the Bar of the City of New York, 'Congressional Oversight of Administrative Agencies. A Report of the Committee on Administrative Law' (1950) 5 *Record of the Association of the Bar of the City of New York* 11, 13 ff.

[67] Council Regulation (EU) No 1024/2013, on the ECB's prudential supervision of credit institutions, and Reg (EU) No 806/2014 on the EU's Single Resolution Mechanism.

[68] R Ibrido, *L'Unione bancaria europea. Profili costituzionali* (Torino, Giappichelli, 2017) 259 ff.

[69] A Simoncini, 'Beyond Representative Democracy: The Challenge of Participatory Democracy and the Boundless Galaxy of Civil Society' in M Cartabia, N Lupo and A Simoncini (eds), *Democracy and Subsidiarity in the EU. National Parliaments, Regions and Civil Society in the Decision-Making Process* (Bologna, Il Mulino, 2013) esp 66 f.

[70] T Bergman, WC Müller and K Strøm, 'Democratic Delegation and Accountability: Cross-national Patterns' in T Bergman, WC Müller and K Strøm (eds), *Delegation and Accountability in Parliamentary Democracies* (Oxford, Oxford University Press, 2003).

the oversight function to the main changes in the European architecture and governance.[71] In many cases, this process has been fostered by national reforms or spontaneous initiatives adopted at Member State level; a typical example is the reinforcement of the prerogatives of the Bundestag and of the Bundesrat fostered by the Bundesverfassungsgericht.[72] In other cases, the Europeanisation has been implemented in an informal manner, acting on the grounds of administrative practices and procedures; the adaptation of the Italian Parliament to the novelties introduced by the Lisbon Treaty is a clear example of this approach.[73] On the whole, the arrangement at national level is deeply asymmetric.

Third, national parliaments are an active component of the democratic oversight exercised in regard to the fragmented EU executive. They contribute to this function in two ways: by overseeing their own national governments in the forms and limits provided by the respective constitutional orders (national segment); and by connecting directly to European institutions through the dynamics of the 'collective' oversight or the mechanisms of privileged 'dialogue' (European segment).[74]

The 'national' segment of parliamentary oversight, mediated by domestic governments, is featured by an intense variety of experiences between Member States. The first differentiating factor affects the formal oversight prerogatives vested in national parliaments. Only a few assemblies have the authority to mandate their government to act in the European intergovernmental institutions according to the instructions voted in Parliament.[75] In other cases, the parliament only has the power to postpone the expression of a formal position at the European level by formulating a 'reserve';[76] or it can interact with the government by requesting information and documents, by expressing an opinion or by addressing political directions, but in no case can these initiatives bind executive action.[77]

Another differentiating factor stems from the impact produced by EU integration on the national model for delegation and accountability, which has been multifaceted and open-ended. Trying to reduce the potential agency loss in the relationship with the national executives, some parliaments have set new control instruments.[78] In response to the euro crisis, many legislatures have tried to increase their influence and control of government

---

[71] E Damgaard, 'Conclusion: The Impact of European Integration on Nordic Parliamentary Democracies' in T Bergman and E Damgaard (eds), *Delegation and Accountability in European Integration: The Nordic Parliamentary Democracies and the European Union* (London, Frank Cass, 2000) 167.

[72] P Kiiver, 'German Participation in EU Decision-Making after the Lisbon Case: A Comparative View on Domestic Parliamentary Clearance Procedures' (2009) 10 *German Law Journal* 1287; and O Höing, 'Differentiation of Parliamentary Powers. The German Constitutional Court and the German Bundestag within the Financial Crisis' in M Cartabia, N Lupo and A Simoncini (eds), *Democracy and Subsidiarity in the EU. National Parliaments, Regions and Civil Society in the Decision-Making Process* (Bologna, Il Mulino, 2013). On the Lissabon Urteil, see above ch 1, section IV (n 118).

[73] E Griglio, 'La funzione di controllo' (e il rapporto con le pubbliche amministrazioni)' (2019) 1 *Rassegna di diritto pubblico europeo* 31.

[74] O Rozenberg, *The Role of National Parliaments in the EU After Lisbon: Potentialities and Challenges* (Brussels, European Parliament – Directorate General for Internal Policies, 2017).

[75] See above ch 4, section II.B (nn 78–83).

[76] K Auel, O Rozenberg and A Thomas, 'Lost in Transaction? Parliamentary Reserves in EU Bargains' (2012) 10 *OPAL Online Paper Series*.

[77] W Wessels and O Rozenberg, *Democratic Control in the Member States of the European Council and the Euro Zone Summits* (Brussels, EU Parliament – Directorate General for internal policies, 2013) 30 ff.

[78] Damgaard (n 71) 167.

positions inside the national arena in issues dealt with by intergovernmental bodies, including the European Council.[79]

Third, different factual constraints relating either to the political continuity of government with parliamentary majority or to the lack of oversight incentives faced by MPs may endanger or limit the implementation of EU-related oversight mechanisms. In some cases, the national Parliament has its hands tied regarding its own executive;[80] in other cases, European policy-making by national legislatures is strongly biased by national interests.[81] Some parliaments are proactive in the participation in EU decision-making, others are not.[82] As a matter of fact, approaches to the scrutiny of EU affairs remain extremely differentiated.[83]

Regardless of these differences, in all European parliamentary systems legislative–executive interaction relies on the confidence relationship.[84] This formal arrangement is what ultimately thickens the accountability scheme in the national segment. It could be objected that this is not true for directly elected heads of state participating in the European Council that are not responsible to Parliament, as in the case of Cyprus, France and Lithuania.[85] Nevertheless, the ultimate weapon is almost always there.[86]

The effectiveness of the accountability arrangement stemming from national parliaments is not yet able to release its effect in the European dimension. On the one hand, national parliaments' oversight can only cover the intergovernmental bodies of the EU (primarily, the Council and the European Council). Its spill-overs onto supranational bodies, including the European Commission, are rather marginal, because national control of the Commission is exhausted by the formulation of the commissioners-designate.[87] On the other hand, the mere aggregation of domestic accountability mechanisms does not support the structuring of a new collective architecture. National lines of accountability become blurred due to the negotiating process in the Council and in the European Council.[88] This risk has become

---

[79] W Wessels, 'The European Council' in R Schütze and T Tridimas (eds), *Oxford Principles of European Union Law* 513.

[80] R Pahre, 'Endogenous domestic institutions in two-level games and parliamentary oversight of the European Union' (1997) 41 *The Journal of Conflict Resolution* 147, 148.

[81] W Wessels, 'National Parliaments and the EP in Multi-tier Governance: In Search for an Optimal Multi-level Parliamentary Architecture. Analysis, Assessment, Advice' in I Pernice et al (eds), *Challenges of Multi-tier Governance in the European Union* (Brussels, European Parliament – Directorate General for Internal Policies, 2013) 104.

[82] K Auel and O Höing, 'Parliaments in the Euro Crisis: can the losers of integration still fight back?' (2014) 52 *Journal of Common Market Studies* 1184, 1192.

[83] *Ex multis*, J Neyer, 'Justified Multi-level Parliamentarism: Situating National Parliaments in the European Polity' (2014) 20 *The Journal of Legislative Studies* 125, 126.

[84] See above ch 1, section II (n 52).

[85] Against this objection, M van de Steeg, 'The European Council's Evolving Political Accountability' in M Bovens, D Curtin and P 't Hart, *The Real World of EU Accountability. What Deficit?* (Oxford, Oxford University Press, 2010) 121. Beyond formal ex post constraints, also informal ex ante constraints should be taken into consideration (S Blavoukos, D Bourantonis and G Pagoulatos, 'A President for the European Union: A New Actor in Town' (2007) 45 *Journal of Common Market Studies* 235) and these are extremely variegated (Wessels and Rozenberg (n 77) 30 ff).

[86] The reference is to the removability of the government by Parliament. See W Steffani, *Parlamentarische und Präsidentielle Demokratie. Strukturelle Aspekte westlicher Demokratien* (Opladen, Springer, 1979) 45; and MS Shugart and JM Carey, *Presidents and Assemblies. Constitutional Design and Electoral Dynamics* (New York, Cambridge University Press, 1992) 18 ff.

[87] Judge and Earnshaw (n 22) 355 f.

[88] F Hayes-Renshaw and H Wallace, 'Executive power in the European Union: The functions and limits of the Council of Ministers' (1995) 2 *Journal of European Public Policy* 559.

manifest once majority voting has been elected as a general rule in the Council:[89] under such conditions, each national Parliament is no more able to influence and control the final outcome. However, a similar risk may occur even when unanimity is applied, due to collective dynamics involving national representatives in a sort of 'two-level game'[90] and informal settings[91] triggering a particular mode of interaction-deliberative intergovernmentalism.[92] The overall lack of transparency over decision-making in intergovernmental institutions still represents a structural limit for national parliaments willing to control the behaviour of their ministers.

With the entry into force of the Lisbon Treaty, the traditional segment of national parliamentary oversight has been complemented by another 'European' segment, which enables national parliaments to exercise direct control over EU institutions without any form of intermediation by domestic governments. Different mechanisms and practices feed the European segment.

On the one hand, instances of collective oversight[93] are fostered by national parliaments through their 'European powers'.[94] The reference is to the subsidiarity control and to the political dialogue in their capacity as mechanisms of ex ante monitoring of the legislative and non-legislative proposals adopted by the European Commission. These mechanisms find in the European Commission the direct referent of national parliaments; they do not produce binding effects, but can result in the stiffening of the decision-making procedures of the Commission.[95] Two distinctive features identify these oversight mechanisms: their being independent from the mediation of national governments; and their being exclusive to national parliaments. Other instances of collective oversight have been established in regard to intergovernmental institutions, including the European Council. However, they rely on the existing mechanisms of interparliamentary cooperation (see below, section IV), thus also including the European Parliament beyond national parliaments in the patterns of interaction with the executive branch.

---

[89] D Naurin and H Wallace, *Unveiling the Council of the European Union* (New York, Palgrave, 2008) esp 23 ff; and M Widgrén, 'The Impact of Council Voting Rules on EU Decision-Making' (2009) 55 *CESifo Economic Studies* 30.

[90] RD Putnam, 'Diplomacy and Domestic Politics: The Logic of Two-Level Games' (1988) 42 *International Organization* 427; PB Evans, HK Jacobson and RD Putnam (eds), *Double-edged Diplomacy: International Bargaining and Domestic Politics* (Berkeley, CA, University of California Press, 1993); J Mo, 'The logic of two-level games with endogeneous domestic coalitions' (1994) 38 *The Journal of Conflict Resolution* 402.

[91] T Christiansen and C Hefftler, 'Informal Politics in the EU' (2013) 51 *Journal of Common Market Studies* 1196, esp 1200.

[92] U Puetter, 'Informal Circles of Ministers: A Way Out of the Eu's Institutional Dilemmas?' (2003) 9 *European Law Journal* 109. E Fouilleux, J Maillard and A Smith, 'Technical or political? The working groups of the EU Council of Ministers' (2005) 12 *Journal of European Public Policy* 609.

[93] I Cooper, 'A 'Virtual Third Chamber' for the European Union? National Parliaments after the Treaty of Lisbon' (2012) 35 *West European Politics* 441, 441 f; and A Cygan, 'Collective Subsidiarity Monitoring by National Parliaments after Lisbon: The Operation of the Early Warning Mechanism' in M Trybus and L Rubini (eds), *The Treaty of Lisbon and the Future of European Law and Policy* (Cheltenham, Edward Elgar, 2012).

[94] N Lupo, 'National Parliaments in the European Integration Process: Re-aligning Politics and Policies' in M Cartabia, N Lupo and A Simoncini (eds), *Democracy and Subsidiarity in the EU* (n. 72) 107 ff.

[95] D Jančić, 'The Game of Cards: National Parliaments in the EU and the Future of the Early Warning Mechanism and the Political Dialogue' (2015) 52 *Common Market Law Review* 939; GA Moens and J Trone, 'The Principle of Subsidiarity in EU Judicial and Legislative Practice: Panacea or Placebo?' (2015) 41 *The Journal of Legislative Studies* 65, 78.

On the other hand, the European segment of parliamentary oversight also comprises the powers of privileged 'dialogue' that national parliaments exercise in regard to the ECB and EU agencies. National parliaments are devoid of formal powers of control in the field of the ECB's monetary policy, but they have privileged information rights in the framework of the 'banking dialogues', based on Article 21 of Regulation (EU) No 2014/2013, that unfold through the standard oversight parliamentary tools (hearings, questions and annual reporting). Banking dialogues rely on the same mechanisms used by national parliaments in the interaction with the domestic government, but the associated finalities and relational dynamics are rather different, because they address a piece of the EU fragmented executive with high levels of independence and autonomy.

The prerogatives of national parliaments in regard to EU agencies are far from being homogeneous: relevant asymmetries can be detected both across Member States and depending on the nature and place of the EU agency. Apparently, the most advanced 'accountability' arrangement (at least from a legal perspective) affects the position of Europol and Eurojust before national representative assemblies. Article 12 TEU gives a legal base to national parliaments' involvement in the 'political monitoring' and 'evaluation' respectively of Europol and Eurojust's activities.[96] Articles 88.2 and 85.1 TFEU further develop this provision by foreseeing 'procedures for scrutiny of Europol's activity by the European Parliament, together with national Parliaments' and 'arrangements for involving the European Parliament and national Parliaments in the evaluation of Eurojust's activities'. The legal framework provided by the Europol and Eurojust regulations[97] sets several oversight prerogatives in favour of national parliaments; these include questioning and access to relevant documents/reports.[98] In fact, in both cases the scrutiny/evaluation machinery is not intended to be used by national parliaments alone, but rather to give origins to instances of joint oversight (see below, section IV). As a matter of fact, national parliaments can be said to exercise a form of democratic control in regard to EU agencies and independent institutions merely from the perspective of increased transparency and general accountability before the citizens.[99]

In Member States with a regional or federal arrangement, the circuit of parliamentary oversight is further enriched by the participation of sub-national legislative assemblies to both segments of parliamentary oversight vested in national parliaments.[100] With regard to the first national segment, the legal base is offered by the constitutional and sub-constitutional rules that regulate the conferral of power between sub-national and national institutions and between the legislative and executive branches. This framework draws a

---

[96] On the scope and impact of the notion of 'evaluation', including the European Parliament and national parliaments' right 'to actively reflect upon Eurojust activities', see P Jeney, *The Future of Eurojust* (Brussels, European Parliament – Directorate for Citizens' Rights and Constitutional Affairs, 2012) 118.

[97] Respectively, Regulation 2016/794/EU and Regulation 2018/1727/EU.

[98] See M Schininà, 'What balance between Europol and Eurojust from a parliamentary angle?' (2020) *New Journal of European Criminal Law* 1, 1 ff.

[99] F Meinel, 'Confidence and Control Control in Parliamentary Government: Parliamentary Questioning, Executive Knowledge, and the Transformation of Democratic Accountability' (2018) 66 *The American Journal of Comparative Law* 317, 318 ff.

[100] C Panara, *The Sub-national Dimension of the EU. A Legal Study of Multilevel Governance* (Springer, Heidelberg, 2015) 11 ff.

rather complex and interwoven network of interactions which sees sub-national parliaments' degree of participation in EU affairs ultimately dependent on their institutional motivations.[101]

With the Lisbon Treaty, this traditional segment of intervention has been complemented by the introduction of a semi-direct form of participation of regional legislative assemblies in the democratic oversight of the EU. Article 6 of Protocol No 2 annexed to the Lisbon Treaty has called national parliaments to consult, when appropriate, with sub-national assemblies entitled with legislative powers.[102] The intermediation of national parliaments has produced rather differentiated outcomes on the grounds of sub-national parliaments' effective capacity to control EU decision-making.[103] Broadly speaking, regional assemblies lack the real power to exercise an influence on the final outcome and in many cases they do not even have the guarantee that their voice might be heard at European level. For these reasons, regional participation in this segment of parliamentary oversight has proved rather marginal.[104]

IV. Filling the Gaps of Parliamentary Oversight Through Interparliamentary Cooperation

The union of the two oversight circuits centred on the European Parliament and on national parliaments does not cover the whole decision-making process. Some areas of activity of the fragmented EU executive are actually escaping any form of parliamentary surveillance.[105] On the one hand, the European Parliament is lacking formal oversight powers that might bind every single body of the EU executive branch, similar to what happens in national parliamentary systems. The European Parliament's oversight prerogatives do not seem to satisfy the prerequisites advocated in literature for the accountability regime.[106] On the other hand, each national Parliament is bound through a confidence relationship only to its domestic government. The summation of all the national confidence circuits does not grant effective oversight on the decisions of EU institutions because, where supranational decision-making prevails over intergovernmentalism, the political directions and mandates adopted by national parliaments are exhausted.

---

[101] R Ladrech, 'Europeanisation and Subnational Parliaments. A Research Perspective' in G Abels and A Eppler (eds), *Subnational Parliaments in the EU Multi-level Parliamentary System: Taking Stock of the Post-Lisbon Era* (Innsbruck, Studienverlag, 2016) 82 ff. E Griglio, 'The Europeanization of Regional Assemblies: A Comparison between Different Ways of Approaching the Representative Challenge in EU Affairs' in D Friedrich and S Kröger (eds), *Representation in the European Union: Coping with Present Challenges to Democracy*? (London, Palgrave, 2012).

[102] P Schmitt, T Ruys and A Marx, *The Subsidiarity Early Warning System of the Lisbon Treaty – The Role of Regional Parliaments with Legislative Powers and Other Subnational Authorities* (Brussels, Committee of the Regions, 2013).

[103] C Fasone, 'Towards New Procedures between State and Regional Legislatures in Italy, Exploiting the Tool of the Early Warning System' (2013) 5 *Perspectives on Federalism* 122; JI Navarro Mendez, *Parlamentos regionales europeos y principio de subsidiariedad* (Aranzadi, Madrid, 2014).

[104] D Fromage, 'Regional Parliaments and the early warning system: an assessment six years after the entry into force of the Lisbon Treaty' (2016) 33 SOG Working Papers 1.

[105] Crum and Curtin (n 12) 67 f.

[106] Bovens (n 51).

The presence of 'black holes' in the democratic oversight dimension is therefore a structural component of EU decision-making.[107] Nonetheless, some remedies might be detected, focusing on the individual position of each executive body. With regard to the European Commission, the strengthening of its accountability condition should be primarily pursued by reinforcing the European Parliament's oversight prerogatives. The confrontation with the experience grown out of national parliamentary traditions confirms that the evolution towards a full confidence regime between the European Parliament and the Commission is a strategic goal.[108]

A different solution should instead be proposed for the intergovernmental bodies, including the Council, the European Council, the Euro-Group and the Euro-Summit. The peculiar position of these bodies in the EU institutional architecture explains why the confidence module cannot be applied to these spheres of decision-making. To fill in existing gaps, there is widespread opinion that formal changes are needed. These may comprise the creation of a new channel of parliamentary representation (a second – or third – Chamber),[109] the transformation of the European Parliament into a variable geometry institution,[110] or the redesign of the relationship between the executive and the legislature.[111]

However, an alternative, less intrusive, and more conservative solution may be available – under existing Treaties – by focusing on the opportunities offered by the interparliamentary dimension. Interparliamentary Cooperation (IPC) in the EU is a rather controversial topic. On the one hand, this practice is contested as inefficient[112] and of minor importance.[113] On the other hand, a further strengthening of IPC is seen as a kind of 'third way' for increased democratic participation and legitimacy in the Union,[114] an 'added value' in order to bring about parliamentary scrutiny of EU affairs.[115]

---

[107] P Lindseth, *Power and Legitimacy Reconciling Europe and the Nation-State* (Oxford, Oxford University Press, 2010) 2 (on the thesis of the democratic *disconnect* between the above-national regulatory power and the sources of democratic and constitutional legitimacy).

[108] On the structural limits that this perspective meets in the EU system of government, see M Goldoni, 'Politicising EU Lawmaking? The Spitzenkandidaten Experiment as a Cautionary Tale' (2016) 22 *European Law Journal* 279.

[109] V Kreilinger and M Larhant, 'Does the Eurozone Need a Parliament?' (2016) 176 Jacques Delors Institute Policy Paper 1 (on the proposal for the establishment of a Euro-zone parliamentary assembly). *Contra*, I Cooper, 'A separate Parliament for the Eurozone? Differentiated Representation, Brexit, and the Quandary of Exclusion' (2017) 70 *Parliamentary Affairs* 655.

[110] E Griglio and N Lupo, 'Towards an asymmetric European Union, without an asymmetric European Parliament' (2014) 20 SOG Working Papers 1 (on the problems raised by this perspective for the European Parliament).

[111] M Shackleton, 'Transforming representative democracy in the EU? The role of the European Parliament' (2017) 39 *Journal of European Integration* 191.

[112] B Rittberger, 'Constructing Parliamentary Democracy in the European Union: How did it Happen?' in B Kohler-Koch and B Rittberger (eds), *Debating the Democratic Legitimacy of the European Union* (Lanham, Rowman & Littlefield Publishers, 2007) 111; J O'Brennan and T Raunio, 'Conclusion: National Parliaments Gradually learning to Play the European Game' in J O'Brennan and T Raunio (eds), *National Parliaments within the Enlarged European Union: From Victims of Integration to Competitive Actors?* (Oxford, Routledge, 2007).

[113] A Cygan, 'Legal implications of economic governance for national parliaments' (2017) 70 *Parliamentary Affairs* 715.

[114] A Manzella, 'Is the EP Legitimate as a Parliamentary Body in EU Multi-tier Governance?' in I Pernice et al (eds), *Challenges of Multi-tier Governance in the European Union* (Brussels, European Parliament – Directorate General for Internal Policies, 2013) 141 ff.

[115] J Wouters and K Raube, 'Europe's Common Security and Defence Policy: The Case for Inter-Parliamentary Scrutiny' (2012) 90 Leuven Centre for Global Governance Studies Working Paper 1.

Notwithstanding these different perceptions, after the entry into force of the Lisbon Treaty, this field has been revitalised. IPC is not a recent phenomenon in the history of European integration:[116] the interparliamentary dialogue was implicit in the original structure of the European Parliament and has continued after the direct elections for the European Parliament with the progressive institutionalisation of the Speakers Conference started in 1975 and the establishment of the Conference of Parliamentary Committees for Foreign Affairs of Parliaments of the European Union in 1989. However, it is in the last decade that the interparliamentary dimension has seen its scope and institutional purposes significantly expanded.[117] New interparliamentary formats focused on sectorial policy areas have specifically led to an extension of the latitude and intensity of interparliamentary relations:[118] the Conferences on Common Foreign Security Policy – Common Security Defence Policy (CFSP–CSDP) and on Stability, Economic Coordination and Governance (SECG), respectively established in 2012 and 2013; the Joint Parliamentary Scrutiny Group (JPSG) on Europol, started in October 2017; the Interparliamentary Committee Meeting on Eurojust, introduced by Article 67 of Regulation (EU) 2018/1727, but still not established;[119] and the Joint Parliamentary Scrutiny Group on the European Border and Coast Guard Agency, foreseen by Regulation (EU) 2019/1896, but still not established.

The institutional aims of these new formats do not merely coincide with those assigned to pre-existing forms of interparliamentary relations, that were threefold: the exchange of information and best practices between parliaments at national and European level; the effective exercise of national parliamentary competences in EU affairs; and the promotion of partnerships between EU parliaments and the parliaments of third countries.[120] In addition to these three objectives, the new interparliamentary formats are also entitled to evaluate the mechanisms implementing EU policies in those policy areas where the influence of the executive branch is overwhelming and oversight by representative assemblies represents a major issue of discussion.[121] Therefore, they are expected to achieve another, more ambitious, aim: that is, to strengthen the capacity of parliaments to fulfil the oversight function and consequently to improve the democratic legitimacy of the EU.[122]

---

[116] E Griglio and S Stavridis, 'Inter-parliamentary cooperation as a means for reinforcing joint scrutiny in the EU: upgrading existing mechanisms and creating new ones' (2018) 10 *Perspectives on Federalism* 1.

[117] N Lupo and C Fasone, *Interparliamentary Cooperation in the Composite European Constitution* (Oxford, Hart Publishing, 2016). See also the Special issue by E Griglio and S Stavridis, 'Joint scrutiny of EU policies: the contribution of interparliamentary cooperation' (2018) 10 *Perspectives on Federalism* 1.

[118] D Fromage, 'Increasing Interparliamentary cooperation in the EU: Current Trends and Challenges' (2016) 22 *European Public Law* 749.

[119] E Griglio, 'I Parlamenti dell'Unione europea alla prova di Europol: verso un esercizio "collettivo" del controllo parlamentare?' (2016) 3 *Quaderni costituzionali* 548. V Kreilinger, 'A Watchdog over Europe's policemen: the new Joint Parliamentary Scrutiny Group for Europol' (2017) 197 Jacques Delors Institute Policy Paper 1.

[120] Conference of Speakers of the European Union Parliaments, 'Guidelines for Inter- parliamentary Co-operation in the European Union' (Lisbon, 19–21 June 2008).

[121] V Kreilinger, 'The new inter-parliamentary conference for economic and financial governance' (2013) 100 Notre Europe – Jacques Delors Institute Policy Paper 1; J Wouters and K Raube, 'The Interparliamentary Conference on Common and Security Policy: A Quest for Democratic Accountability in EU Security Governance' in N Lupo and C Fasone (eds), *Interparliamentary Cooperation in the Composite European Constitution* (Oxford, Hart Publishing, 2016).

[122] I Cooper, 'Parliamentary oversight of the EU after the crisis: on the creation of the 'Article 13' Inter-parliamentary Conference' (2014) 21 SOG Working Paper 1.

The two sectorial Conferences established after Lisbon show a clear connection with this institutional aim, although in rather different ways. In the case of the SECG Conference, article 2.1. of the Rules of Procedure entitles the body both to provide a framework for debate and exchange of information and best practices and to ensure 'democratic accountability in the area of economic governance and budgetary policy in the EU, particularly in the EMU, taking into account the social dimension and without prejudice to the competences of EU Parliaments'.[123] In contrast, in the case of the Conference on CFSP–CSDP, there is no formal provision that includes the oversight rationale within its institutional aims. However, the Conclusions of the first Conference held in Pafos from 9 to 10 September 2012 formally recognised the Conference's role in assessing, reviewing and evaluating the decision-making, thus contributing to promoting democratic values and accountable systems of good governance.[124]

The connection with the oversight rationale is far more explicit and developed for the JPSG. The Group has an explicit mandate to scrutinise, which addresses not a whole policy field but an agency.[125] Grounded on a solid legal base,[126] this mandate is supported by procedural rules – including continuity of membership, access to EU officials and documents, questioning – that favour a stable oversight relationship.

In fact, results achieved so far have not been considered to be fully satisfactory.[127] The EU interparliamentary model has not been able to fully develop its *sui generis* nature and depart from the formats of International Parliamentary Institutions.[128] The lack of effectiveness in the implementation of the joint scrutiny function is a product of multiple causes. These stem from both the procedural and organisational constraints undermining the scrutiny potential of the interparliamentary forums, and the lack of motivation and capacity that prevents parliamentary actors from proactive engagement. The internal disputes between the European Parliament and national parliaments on the conception itself of the new interparliamentary bodies,[129] the non-binding setting of the IPC forums and the difficulty faced by parliaments in bridging from the 'domestic' to the 'collective' dimension have failed to develop transnational schemes of interaction.[130]

---

[123] The presidency conclusions adopted at the end of the meeting held in Vilnius from 16–17 October 2013 (para 5) confirmed that the first purpose of the conference is 'to find the right balance between national parliaments and the European Parliament in organising the exercise of parliamentary control in the area of economic and financial governance'.

[124] See paras 1, 2, 4, 5 and 7 of the Conclusions.

[125] I Cooper, 'A New Form of Democratic Oversight in the EU: The Joint Parliamentary Scrutiny Group for Europol' (2018) 10 *Perspectives on Federalism* 184.

[126] See above section III (nn 96–99).

[127] D Fromage, 'A comparison of existing forums for interparliamentary cooperation in the EU and some lessons for the future' (2018) 10 *Perspectives on Federalism* 1; A Maatsch and I Cooper, 'Governance Without Democracy? Analysing the Role of Parliaments in European Economic Governance after the Crisis: Introduction to the Special Issue' (2017) 70 *Parliamentary Affairs* 645, 650 f.

[128] E Griglio and N Lupo, 'Inter-parliamentary Cooperation in the EU and outside the Union: Distinctive Features and Limits on the European Experience' (2018) 10 *Perspectives on Federalism* 56.

[129] A Hérranz-Surrallés, 'The EU's Multilevel Parliamentary (Battle)Field: Inter-Parliamentary Cooperation and Conflict in Foreign and Security Policy' (2014) *West European Politics* 957. I Cooper, 'The Politicization of Interparliamentary Relations in the EU: Constructing and Contesting the "Article 13 Conference" on Economic Governance' (2016) 14 *Comparative European Politics* 196. D Fromage, 'European Economic Governance and Parliamentary Involvement: Some Shortcomings of the Article 13 Conference and A Solution' (2016) 1 *Les Cahiers européens de Sciences Po* 1.

[130] K Raube and D Fonck, 'Transnational Parliamentarism and the Dynamics of the IPC CFSP/CSDP: Policy-making, Accountability and Cooperation' (2018) 10 *Perspectives on Federalism* 137.

However, from a normative point of view, IPC might play a strategic role in view of filling the gaps in parliamentary oversight in the EU. Interparliamentary bodies lack both the powers and the procedures to exercise, if not a veto or a sanction, at least joint parliamentary 'influence' over the EU executive. However, IPC can offer an instrumental contribution to the oversight relationship linking national parliaments and the European Parliament, in their domestic arenas, to the executive power. Moreover, it may contribute to strengthen the 'European' segment of the oversight circuit by alleviating some of the problems of 'multi-level parliamentarism': asymmetric information; limited oversight of intergovernmental decisions; and differentiated approaches to the scrutiny of EU affairs.[131] In response to these limits, participation in the interparliamentary dimension may enable national parliaments to expand their focus beyond merely holding their own executive to account, simultaneously improving horizontal coordination between them to forge a 'Euro response';[132] in other words, to balance collective and individual engagement in EU decision-making. Moreover, IPC may also support the supervisory powers of the European Parliament, facilitating the access to information, reinvigorating the exercise of 'soft' oversight powers[133] in regard to all the EU executive bodies and providing a complete and exhaustive vision of the political directions defined at national level.

To make this perspective true, some major changes in the conception of the aims, scope and functional organisation of the different IPC formats would be required, either fostering interparliamentary cooperation 'in committee' (for example, in small working groups that might favour specialisation and continuity of action)[134] or promoting a 'document-based' working method, coordinated with the agenda of the main EU institutions, that might bring the interparliamentary bodies to oversee single proposals and documents.[135]

V. The Hybridisation of Parliamentary Oversight in the EU

Parliamentary oversight in the European dimension confirms its atypical nature compared with the experience of national majoritarian parliamentarism. The political oversight machinery is integrated by mechanisms of regulatory oversight, open also to forms of participative democracy. This combination has determined the hybridisation of parliamentary oversight tools with other mechanisms typical to presidential systems. One example is offered by the introduction in the European Parliament Rules of Procedure of the confirmation hearings with individual commissioners-designate before the plenary vote on the college of the Commission. Another case is offered by parliamentary oversight of

---

[131] T Raunio, 'Holding Governments Accountable in European Affairs: Explaining Cross-National Variation' (2005) 11 *The Journal of Legislative Studies* 319.

[132] C Hefftler and W Wessels, 'The Democratic Legitimacy of the EU's Economic Governance and National Parliaments' (2013) 13 IAI Working Papers 1.

[133] A Benz, 'Linking multiple demoi. Inter-parliamentary relations in the EU' (2011) 6 *IEV-Online* 1.

[134] C Hefftler and K Gattermann, 'Interparliamentary Cooperation in the European Union: Patterns, Problems and Potential' in C Hefftler, C Neuhold, O Rozenberg and J Smith (eds), *The Palgrave Handbook of National Parliaments and the European Union* (London, Palgrave, 2015) 98 ff.

[135] N Lupo and E Griglio, 'The Conference on Stability, Economic Coordination and Governance: Filling the Gaps of Parliamentary Oversight in the EU' (2018) 40 *Journal of European Integration* 358, 370 ff.

EU agencies in the European Parliament, whose scope and means resemble congressional oversight of administrative agencies, as developed in the experience of the United States.

This hybridisation determines the coexistence of several oversight modules, with a rather differentiated degree of intrusiveness in the sphere of action of the controlled. Within these modules, the institutional responsibility of the EU executive can be raised both directly and indirectly, resorting to a wide range of tools and procedures:

a. The *confidence* module features the relationship between national parliaments and their domestic executive and it is shaped by the tools typical to majoritarian parliamentarism.

b. The *confidence-type* oversight module connects the European Parliament to the Commission, resulting in the exercise of investiture and censure prerogatives that resemble, in a softened appearance, the confidence tools of majoritarian parliamentarism.

c. The *non-confidence* oversight module supports the interaction of the European Parliament with intergovernmental bodies and with the ECB, limited to the monetary policy: it does not allow the binding or sanctioning of the body controlled, but it aims to foster an interinstitutional 'dialogue' on selected spheres of activity thus resulting in more transparency and participation.

d. The *regulatory* oversight module identifies the relationship of the European Parliament with the agencies and European administration; it enables 'supervision' in different spheres of activity of these structures.

e. The *collective* oversight module is specifically addressing the European Commission; it is associated with the exercise of European powers by national parliaments and with the latest trends in the dimension of interparliamentary cooperation.

The interaction of these modules is not able to cover all the requirements of democratic oversight raised by the fragmented nature of the EU executive branch, which escapes the interaction with one single Parliament. For this reason, connecting existing parliamentary channels also through the interparliamentary dimension turns out to be under the existing Treaties one of the few feasible answers to the complexities of democratic oversight raised by the fragmented EU executive.[136]

---

[136] Griglio and Stavridis, 'Inter-parliamentary cooperation' (n 116) 9 ff.

8

Parliamentary Oversight of Budget: A Trade-Off with Budgetary Decision-Making?

I. How Parliaments Relate to Budgeting

Probably due to the influence exercised by the principle of the 'no taxation without representation', the 'power of the purse' of parliaments has mainly been associated with the appropriation of budgetary resources, unfolding through the determination of spending priorities and level of taxation. The prerogative dates back to the enactment of the Statute *De tallagio non concedendo*, in 1297.[1] In fact, either adopting a synchronic or embracing a diachronic approach, the institutional dynamics reveals much more complexity.

From the diachronic perspective, the type and degree of parliamentary involvement have evolved over time and will continue to evolve in the future. Broadly speaking, parliaments' ownership of budget has followed cyclical changes over the last 70 years,[2] swinging from the limitation of their influence in the setting of a budget to the strengthening of their control over budget execution.[3] From the synchronic point of view, parliaments' involvement in the budgetary process varies considerably across national constitutional systems. Depending on a variety of factors – including the form of government, electoral system, executive-parties dimension and bicameral arrangement – legislatures show different levels of involvement in the subsequent stages of the budgetary process and diversified capacities to influence the preparation, setting and implementation of a budget.[4]

In a broad perspective, the 'power of the purse' should be referred not only to the setting of a budget, but rather to the entire budgetary cycle, which mirrors the evolution of the balance of power between constitutional bodies.[5] The cycle is structured in three main stages. The ex ante oversight dimension covers the period that precedes the submission of

---

[1] The Statute (*De tallagio non concedendo*, 1297, ch 1, 25 Ed I) provides that no tax or aid can be introduced without the consent of the archbishops, bishops, earls, barons, knights, bourgeoisie and of the other free men of the country. W Stubbs, *The Constitutional History of England*, I (Oxford, Clarendon Press, 1880) 401; H Richardson, 'The Origins of Parliament' (1928) 11 *Transactions of the Royal Historical Society* 159.

[2] In the mid-1970s, D Coombes, *The Power of the Purse: The Role of European Parliaments in Budgetary Decisions* (London, Allen and Unwin, 1976) noted that Parliament's power over the purse is everywhere in decline.

[3] W Krafchik and J Wehner, 'The role of Parliament in the budget process' (2005) 66 *South African Journal of Economics* 242, 243.

[4] J Johnson and R Stapenhurst, 'Legislative Budget Offices: International Experience' in R Stapenhurst, R Pelizzo, D Olson and L von Trapp (eds), *Legislative Oversight and Budgeting: A World Perspective* (Washington DC, World Bank, 2008).

[5] R Stapenhurst, *The Legislature and the Budget* (Washington, World Bank, 2004) 1 ff. J Wehner, 'Back from the Sidelines? Redefining the Contribution of Legislatures to the Budget Cycle' (2004) 1 World Bank Institute Working Paper 1.

the yearly budgetary and financial manoeuvre, now roughly corresponding to the European Semester. The involvement in the setting of a budget unfolds through the parliamentary approval of the yearly budget/finance fundamental acts. The ex post oversight stage engages representative assemblies in the surveillance over budget execution.

In each of these three stages, parliaments use different skills. The setting of a budget is part of the decision-making prerogatives of the legislative branch and it is one of the most politically divisive decisions in the relationship between the government, parliamentary majority and opposition.[6] The ex ante and ex post oversight of budget are instead an expression of the dialectic between the legislature and the executive, which covers the setting of political directions and the surveillance in the implementing stage. Both dimensions, expressing the 'supervision' or 'watchfulness' of legislatures over delegated authority,[7] are instrumental to the dimension of accountability. They are carried out in a less adversarial manner, compared with the adoption of budgetary legislation, and most often result in a bipartisan consultative effort to improve the performance and accountability of the executive.

The aggregation of these three stages draws the cycle of Parliament's involvement in budgeting. In all stages, parliamentary action is carried out in close interaction with the government, anticipating, scrutinising and following up the drafting and approval of budget and financial measures. Parliaments have developed alternative answers in response to these requirements, which result from the combination of different factors. One major factor is the formal legal framework, usually (but not necessarily) adopted with legislative acts.[8] Other contextual factors include the access to budgetary information, the technical expertise available and the complexity and flexibility of the internal financial architecture.[9]

Three main models, corresponding to the experience of the British, French and Italian Parliaments, witness the coexistence of different degrees of parliamentary involvement in the three stages of the budgetary cycle. After considering these models, the chapter analyses the influence of the European economic governance on national experiences, drawing insights from the German constitutional jurisprudence. The trade-off between budgetary decision-making and oversight is hence explained, with reference also to the experience of the European Parliament.

II. Parliamentary Oversight of Budget: Alternative Models

Comparative analysis shows alternative models of parliamentary oversight of budget, which are centred on the role of parliamentary committees. The presence of strong committees is a

---

[6] In fact, some authors include the setting of a budget among Parliament's oversight prerogatives. See A Brazier and V Ram, *The Fiscal Maze. Parliament, Government and Public Money* (London, Hansard Society, 2006) 17.

[7] WJ Oleszek, 'Congressional Oversight: An Overview' (2010) *Congressional Research Service Report for Congress* 1, 4.

[8] I Lienert and MK Jung, 'Le cadre juridique des systèmes budgétaires. Une comparaison internationale' (2004) 4 *Revue de l'OCDE sur la gestion budgétaire* 1, 26 f.

[9] R Pelizzo, R Stapenhurst and D Olson, *The Role of Parliaments in the Budget Process* (Washington, World Bank Institute, 2005). J Wehner, 'Assessing the Power of the Purse: An Index of Legislative Budget Institutions' (2006) 54 *Political Studies* 767.

facilitator of effective parliamentary oversight.[10] Committee expertise is determinant above all for those highly technical policy areas, such as the budget, requiring competence and commitment. In the field of budgetary oversight, the presence of proactive and powerful committees becomes strategic for structuring a permanent vigilance over public accounts. Their relationship with the supreme audit institutions is another determinant factor.[11] Whereas committee work favours technical engagement over political posturing, plenary debates rather tend to linger on broad criticism.[12]

Two types of committee expertise are involved in the budget sector. The first type is committed to participate in budgetary law-making: this task is carried out mainly through the examination of the budget or finance Bill to be submitted to the plenary for approval. The second type of expertise is competent in the oversight of budget: acting in close interaction with the supreme auditor, it is involved in the all-year monitoring of public accounts and government budgetary performances. These types of committee expertise do not always come together. On the one hand, Westminster systems allocate expertise on different committees, respectively involved in the scrutiny of the budget and finance Bill and in the ex post oversight of budget execution. The latter is allotted to the Public Accounts Committee, which does not intervene in the setting of budget but is exclusively responsible for overseeing its execution.[13] On the other hand, parliaments in continental Europe experience involvement in the whole budgetary cycle of standing committees tasked, at the same time, with budgetary legislation and oversight. These hybrid committees are the exclusive reference body for all parliamentary procedures which are not neutral on budget. A further variable (typical to the Italian Parliament) sees the presence of two distinct hybrid committees, one for expenditures, the other for revenues.

The following sections will analyse three models of parliamentary involvement in budgeting, based on different committee expertise and associated with varied degrees of involvement in the ex ante and ex post oversight stages.

A. The Westminster Model for the Ex Post Oversight of Budget

The Westminster model shows Parliament engaging in intensive ex post and limited ex ante oversight of budget.[14] This arrangement is deeply rooted in the history of the United Kingdom and has not been substantially altered by the participation in the European economic governance.[15] In the UK, government accountability for public spending is assured mainly through the intervention of two parliamentary bodies: the Public Accounts Committee (PAC) of the House of Commons and the National Audit Office (NAO).

---

[10] I Mattson and K Strøm, 'Parliamentary Committees' in H Döering (ed), *Parliaments and Majority Rule in Western Europe* (New York, St Martin's Press, 1995) 250.

[11] OECD, 'Relations between Supreme Audit Institutions and Parliamentary Committees' (2002) 33 SIGMA Papers 1.

[12] Krafchik and Wehner (n 3).

[13] J Wehner, 'Legislative Arrangements for Financial Scrutiny: Explaining Cross-national Variation' in R Pelizzo, R Stapenhurst and D Olson (eds), *The Role of Parliaments in the Budget Process* (Washington, World Bank Institute, 2005) 13.

[14] House of Commons Procedure Committee, *Should there be a Budget Committee?* (2019, HC 1482).

[15] See below, section III.

This oversight architecture does not exclude the existence of other accountability circuits, such as the one related to ministers' separate accountability before Parliament and the public for their policy outcomes.[16]

One of the non-departmental select committees of the House of Commons, PAC dates back to the Standing Orders of 1862[17] and is purely an oversight body: whereas the Treasury Select Committee participates in the scrutiny of budget and the finance Bill, the PAC exclusively covers the ex post oversight during budget execution. It is composed of 16 MPs, selected among members with high technical expertise, excluding front-benchers, who reflect the overall proportion of parties in Parliament; it is chaired, by convention, by a member of the opposition. It is tasked to examine reports produced by the NAO in its value for money studies of the economy, efficiency and effectiveness of governmental use of public resources. The PAC does not evaluate the formulation or merits of different governmental policies, which is under the scope of departmental select committees, but focuses strictly on value-for-money criteria.[18]

The NAO, the UK's Supreme Audit Institution created by the National Audit Act 1983, is a parliamentary agency endowed with a high degree of independence. The most powerful figure in the internal organisation of the NAO is the Controller and Auditor General, head of the agency, who is appointed by the Queen from the Officers of the House of Commons and moved by an address of the Prime Minister, which guarantees his or her independence from the executive.[19] According to the National Audit Act 1983, the NAO is called on to test the operation of government departments and agencies from the perspective of the 'three Es' (economy, efficiency, effectiveness). Every year, the NAO audits more than 450 government accounts, releasing one report a year, and produces from 50 to 150 (around 60 on average) value-for-money reports on selected issues and policies. Approximately 70 per cent of NAO reports are reviewed by the PAC, which in turn, after a series of hearings, on average produces 17 reports for each 100 days of parliamentary sessions. The oversight process is concluded by the submission of the government's reply to the PAC report, which takes the form of a published Treasury Minute: the Minute faithfully follows up the PAC's findings and discusses recommendations which, on average, are accepted by over 93 per cent.[20]

The twofold oversight process carried out by the NAO and PAC covers both the technical and political requirements of budgetary scrutiny. Their reports are highly attractive to the press and television, mainly due to the influential nature of both parliamentary bodies within public opinion. As a matter of fact, three factors are key conditions for the effectiveness of the PAC's oversight: these include the *capacity building* (mainly related to the availability of adequate resources and expertise); the *independence* (from political or legal constraints); and the *information exchange*.[21]

---

[16] Public Accounts Committee, 'Accountability for public money', 28th Report (5 April 2011) 3.

[17] Now see Rule no 148 House of Commons Standing Orders.

[18] K Strøm, 'Parliamentary committees in European democracies' (1998) 1 *The Journal of Legislative Studies* 21, 31.

[19] R Stapenhurst, V Sahgal, W Woodley and R Pelizzo, 'Scrutinizing Public Expenditures. Assessing the Performance of Public Accounts Committees' (2005) 3613 World Bank Policy Research Working Paper 1, 3.

[20] P Dunleavy, C Gilson, S Bastow and J Tinkler, *The National Audit Office, the Public Accounts Committee and the Risk Landscape in UK Public Policy* (London, LSE, 2009).

[21] D McGee, *The Overseers – Public Accounts Committees and Public Spending* (London, Pluto Press, 2002). According to Stapenhurst, Sahgal, Woodley and Pelizzo (n 19) 24, the institutional factors which most account for

The solid parliamentary architecture supporting the ex post oversight of budget does not find correspondence in the ex ante stage. The UK's ex ante oversight of budget is deemed to be the weakest, compared with other OECD countries.[22] In the last two decades, the UK government has reinforced the Spending Review process as a mechanism to plan national finances in the medium term.[23] However, there is no systematic mechanism for parliamentary scrutiny of the Spending Review, which basically remains a process of negotiation between the Treasury and the departments.[24] Departmental select committees may be involved in the consultation process on the Spending Review and they may interact with departments for collecting information on the targets and related strategies. However, this dialogue occurs on a voluntary basis and is occasional in frequency.

The most significant development in the ex ante stage is the establishment, in 2010, of the Office for Budget Responsibility, an independent agency entitled to provide authoritative analysis of public finances and assess the Treasury's costing of budget measures. The Office, regulated by the Budget Responsibility and National Audit Act 2011, enjoys a strategic relationship with Parliament. It specifically serves as a source of information and analytical studies to parliamentary committees. According to section 16.6, Schedule 1 of the National Audit Act 2011, every report prepared by the Office must be laid before Parliament. The Office is actively involved in parliamentary activity, answering questions and giving evidence to committees. The integration of its authoritative assessment as part of the scrutiny of budget has become an added value to Parliament, leading 'to much higher standards for the forecasting process'.[25]

B. The French Model: In between Ex Ante and Ex Post Oversight of Budget

Within European continental systems, the French Parliament has experienced a meaningful strengthening of budgetary oversight, both in the ex post and in the ex ante stage. In the setting of a budget, significant attempts have been made to rationalise the participation of both Houses in the legislative process leading to the approval of the *loi de finances*, the yearly financial law which traditionally saw an active role by Parliament.[26] This is the outcome of a number of reforms, including: the revision of the national accounting legislation[27] which

---

the success of the Public Accounts Committee are the focus on the government's financial activity rather than on its policies, the power to investigate all past and present government expenses and, to urge a follow up, the relationship with the Auditors General.

[22] Procedure Committee (n 14) para 39.

[23] M Wheatley, B Maddox and TK Bishop, *The 2019 Spending Review. How to run it well* (London, Institute for Government, 2018).

[24] Committee Office Scrutiny Unit, *Financial scrutiny uncovered. How the Government manages its finances and how Parliament scrutinises them* (London, House of Commons, 2007) 13.

[25] House of Commons Treasury Committee, 'Budget 2018. Twenty-Sixth Report of Session 2017–19' (2019, HC 1606) 6.

[26] Parliament is free to amend the budget on the side of the expenditures, but it cannot change overall revenue and expenditure, it cannot create new 'missions' or programmes, and it cannot propose amendments to revenue measures. OECD, 'France – High Council for Public Finances' (2015) 2 *Journal on Budgeting* 117, 120 f.

[27] Loi organique no 2001-692, relative aux lois de finances, of 1 August 2001, revised by Loi organique no 2005-779 of 12 July 2005, which changed the internal structure of the budget.

extended the scope of the control of public expenditure from the verification of regularity to the evaluation of administrative efficiency;[28] the entry into force of the 2008 constitutional amendment on parliamentary oversight;[29] the related 2009 adaptation of the Rules of Procedure of the National Assembly; and organic Law no 2012-1403 of 17 December 2012, on the planning and governance of public finances.[30]

Budgetary surveillance is deeply rooted in the French parliamentary tradition, as indicated by article 14 of the 1789 Declaration of the Rights of Man and of the Citizen. Nevertheless, the fortune of this function revealed some quirks of coincidence with the evolution of the form of government.[31] Because of the mutual influence between parliamentary decision and oversight in the public spending area, the revision of the budgetary process started by the 1958 rationalised parliamentarism did not weaken but instead revived parliamentary control of public finances.[32] Thereafter, parliamentary oversight of budget[33] has complemented the other two pillars of the budgetary control chain, consisting of the 'administrative' control, aimed at detecting possible irregularities, and the jurisdictional control, exercised by the Cour des comptes, assessing compliance with the law in order to sanction hypotheses of malpractice.[34]

The main difference with the Westminster model is not in the nature of the oversight prerogatives conferred on Parliament, but rather in the subjects involved. In France, the Finance Committees of the two Houses take the lead on all budget related matters, including the approval of the annual *loi des finances* (LF). Other oversight prerogatives are vested on the plenary through the adoption of the *loi de règlement*, occurring at the very final stage of the budget execution.

The budgetary prerogatives of the Finance Committees were significantly strengthened in 2001, with the approval of the *Loi organique no 2001-692 du 1er aout 2001 relative aux lois de finances* (LOLF) which repealed part of the *Ordinance organique no 59-2* of 2 January 1959, up to that moment considered the real financial Constitution of the State. Article 57 of the LOLF entitles Finance Committees to control the implementation of the LF and provide a general evaluation of public finances, thus extending their scope from the formal monitoring of public accounts to the assessment of policy performances. Finance committees have a wealth of budgetary oversight tools available, covering both the *contrôle sur place* and the *contrôle sur piece*.[35] Specific oversight missions may be attributed

---

[28] M Lascombe and X Vandendriessche, 'La loi organique relative aux lois de finances (LOLF) et le contrôle des finances publiques' (2006) 117 *Revue française de l'administration publique* 131.

[29] P Türk, *Le contrôle parlementaire en France* (Paris, LGDJ, 2011) 176 ff.

[30] The incorporation of the principles of the Treaty on Stability, Cooperation and Governance (TSCG) through an organic law (instead of a constitutional law) was judged as a legitimate procedure by the Conseil constitutionnel in Décision no 2012-653 DC of 9 August 2012.

[31] I Bouhadana, *Les commission des finances des assemblées parlementaires en France: origines, évolutions et enjeux* (Paris, LDGJ, 2007) 273 ff.

[32] P Carcelle and G Mas, 'Les pouvoirs du Parlement en matière financière' (1959) 68 *La Revue administrative* 129.

[33] On the political nature of the parliamentary oversight of budget, MA Lambert, 'Reinforcer le contrôle du Parlement sur l'exécutif' in OECD – Sénat, *Processus budgétaire. Vers un nouveau rôle du Parlement. Les actes du Réunion international des Présidents et Hauts responsables des commissions budgétaires des pays membres de l'OCDE, 24–25 janvier 2001* (Paris, Imprimerie du Sénat, 2002) 150.

[34] A Barilari, *Les contrôles financiers, comptables, administratifs et juridictionnels des finances publiques* (Paris, LGDJ, 2003); M Bouvier, MC Esclassan and JP Lassale, *Finances Publiques*, 18th edn (Paris, LGDJ, 2019) 529 ff.

[35] Commission des finances – Sénat, 'Guide de bonnes pratiques du contrôle budgétaire' (19 April 2007).

to different rapporteurs speciaux, charged with the scrutiny of ministerial budgets. Each rapporteur carries out the assignment through different instrumental activities, including the dispatch of questionnaires and hearings. Once a year, during the scrutiny of the LF, each rapporteur drafts a report on the management of the ministerial budget controlled. Moreover, the Committee can decide to start a cross-sectional oversight mission, coordinated by the chair of the Committee and/or by the rapporteur general, involving all the relevant rapporteurs speciaux.

In addition to this machinery, the Finance Committee of the National Assembly can rely on the Mission d'évaluation et de controle, the parliamentary body created in February 1999 in order to evaluate political and administrative responsibilities on the management of public finance and conduct advanced investigations on sectorial public policies. This is a perfectly joint organism, composed of 16 members selected from the Finance Committee following an equal division between majority and opposition, and it is co-chaired by a deputy of the majority and by a deputy of the opposition. The Mission d'évaluation et de controle has access to a wide range of government reports and documents, listed in articles 34 and 37 LOLF. It can use a variety of parliamentary tools, regulated by articles 57, 59 and 60 LOLF, including the dispatch of questionnaires to government officials, in loco controls and hearings, inquiries on sectorial public policies. This activity is reported to the Finance Committee which, in turn, may publish informative reports:[36] if the report includes observations notified to the government, the latter is asked to give a formal written reply within two months.[37]

The Cour des comptes is another strategic actor providing assistance to the Finance Committee in the oversight of budget execution.[38] Pursuant to article 47 of the Constitution and article 58.2 of LOLF, the Finance Committees of the two Houses have the power to assign to the Cour des comptes the task of carrying out special inquiries on specific issues, to be completed within eight months.

Beyond these oversight instances during budget execution, another relevant oversight tool is the approval of the *loi de règlement* by the plenary, which formally concludes the budgetary cycle. The *loi de règlement*, submitted to Parliament every year before 1 June, presents the overall amount of revenues and expenditures and their variations during the financial year. This procedure enables Parliament to oversee the implementation of the LF of the previous year, assessing government spending and revenues. To support an effective parliamentary scrutiny, the LOLF strengthened the information to be made available to parliament. This framework has contributed to transform the *loi de règlement* into an instrument for assessing budgetary and financial performances, beyond the traditional formal verification of accounts.

On the side of the ex ante oversight of budget, the role of Parliament was significantly reinforced by the 2008 constitutional amendment, which temporarily coincided with the inception of a new European economic governance. The revised article 34 of the Constitution enables Parliament, through the approval of the *Loi de programmation de finances publiques*, to set long-term directions on public finance. This multiyear perspective

---

[36] Art 146 National Assembly Rules of Procedure.
[37] Art 60 LOLF.
[38] The principle of cooperation between the Cour des comptes and Parliament is advocated and analysed in the Decision of the Conseil Constitutionnel no 2001-448 DC of 25 July 2001.

started a more structural and continuous parliamentary control on budgetary provisions.[39] Moreover, Organic Law no 2012-1403 established the Haut Conseil des finances publiques, the French Fiscal Council created at the premises of the Cour des comptes, whose advisory activity is expected to support Parliament's capacity to evaluate the macro-economic and financial framework.

Parliament's involvement in the ex ante oversight of budget starts in April, when the Minister of Finance submits a report to the two Assemblies on the main documents of the European Semester (the National Reform Programme and the Stability Programme);[40] the report is debated in committee, after the Minister's hearing. Before 10 July, the special rapporteurs of the Finance Committee submit a questionnaire to the referent ministers in view of drafting their report on the following financial manoeuvre. The government is required to provide an answer before 10 October.[41] This activity precedes Parliament's involvement in the drafting of the finance Bill, framed in a general debate on the state of public finance, which is supported by the hearing of the First President of the Cour de comptes and by the presentation of the government report on the following year's finance legislation. This calendar of activities confirms that, whereas the government has primacy in budgetary decision-making due also to constrained amending powers of the two Houses, Parliament is involved in the pre-budget stage through long and active debates which are aimed at evaluating and orienting executive budgeting from the onset.[42]

C. The Italian Model: Strong Ex Ante and Weak Ex Post Oversight of Budget

The Italian experience signifies a model of strong ex ante and weak ex post parliamentary oversight of budget. The procedure for the approval of the traditional *legge finanziaria* – now reframed in the *legge di bilancio* (budget law)[43] – has attributed to Parliament a highly influential power over the setting of a budget.[44] Conversely, the two Houses have always been extremely weak in overseeing government performances during the execution of a budget.[45] Recent attempts to enhance the role of Parliament in the control of public finances have not brought about substantial changes.[46]

---

[39] E Oliva, *Les principes budgétaires et comptables à valeur constitutionelle. Considérations autour de la 'vrai' Constitution financière de la France* (Paris, Dalloz, 2014) 453.

[40] D Moretti and D Kraan, 'Budgeting in France' (2018) 2 *OECD Journal on Budgeting* 53 (on Parliament's debate as a strong political endorsement of government strategy).

[41] Art 49 LOLF.

[42] Moretti and Kraan (n 40) 61 (on the persistent weaknesses of finance committees in the pre-budget and budget execution stages).

[43] Law no 196 of 31 December 2006, as amended by Law no 163 of 4 August 2016.

[44] E De Giorgi and L Verzichelli, 'Still a Difficult Budgetary Process? The Government, the Legislature and the Finance Bill' (2008) 13 *South European Society & Politics* 87.

[45] G Rivosecchi, 'I poteri ispettivi e il controllo parlamentare a dieci anni dalla riforma del regolamento della Camera dei deputati' in Vv Aa, *Il Parlamento del bicameralismo. Un decennio di riforme dei regolamenti delle Camere. Il Filangieri* (Napoli, Jovene, 2008). M Degni, *La decisione di bilancio nel sistema maggioritario* (Roma, Ediesse, 2004) 244 ff. G Arconzo, 'Le scelte di finanza pubblica in una "democrazia decidente": alla ricerca di un nuovo ruolo per Governo e Parlamento' (2008) 4 *Quaderni costituzionali* 813, 829 f.

[46] See art 5.4 of Law no 243 of 24 December 2012.

The lack of a real culture of ex post oversight of budget is mirrored by the absence of ad hoc parliamentary tools addressing this function. The Budget and Finance Standing Committees of the two Houses take the lead both in the setting of a budget and in the oversight stage. To perform this role, they exclusively resort to the standard oversight tools and procedures, including questioning, hearings, fact-finding missions and potentially also inquiries. However, these mechanisms are not able to support the collection of complete and independent information, documents and analytical reports which are a prerequisite for an effective oversight of budget. The lack of ad hoc budgetary oversight tools is hence one main gap in the expertise of Italian budget and finance committees.

The only 'typical' tool is represented (in line with the French experience) by the *rendiconto*, the final balance referred to the previous financial year, which must be submitted to Parliament before 30 June.[47] Through the approval of the *rendiconto*, the legislative branch is expected to verify the correspondence between expenses authorised and resources effectively spent. However, in its concrete application, this mechanism never involved Parliament in an effective and detailed scrutiny of public accounts.[48] Time spent in the consideration of the *rendiconto* has always been limited both in committee and in the plenary. The two Houses have basically restricted their participation to a mere confirmation of the judgment of the Corte dei conti, the Supreme Audit Institution. The *rendiconto* has little appeal in Parliament due also to its unamendable nature, which only enables a single vote, either favourable or contrary.[49]

Somehow more attractive for the two Houses is the *assestamento*, the Bill submitted every year, by 30 June, in order to adjust (on the basis also of the *rendiconto*) revenues and expenses expectations contained in the budget. Formally related to the law-making, rather than to the oversight function, the scrutiny of the *assestamento* actually gives Parliament the opportunity to evaluate the government's budgetary decisions on the basis of the effective trend of public accounts.

Weakness in the budgetary oversight capacity of Parliament also relates to its dependence on the executive branch for accessing information: the legislature often lacks fully coherent and reliable data,[50] sometimes due to information gaps at the executive level, sometimes due to malpractices in interinstitutional cooperation. Law no 196/2009 tried to improve this situation by committing the government and public administrations to cover the informative requirements of parliamentary committees (articles 4 and 6). In fact, these provisions did not substantially innovate what was already included in the prerogatives of the two Houses. To reinforce the channel of independent information, the two Houses have enhanced the role of parliamentary administration through the creation,

---

[47] Arts 21 and 24 of Law no 468 of 5 August 1978 (now replaced by Law no 196 of 30 December 2009).

[48] C Chiappinelli, 'La evoluzione del sistema dei controlli e la relazione sul rendiconto generale dello Stato' (2009) 2 *Rivista della Corte dei conti* 256.

[49] A precedent occurred in 2011, due to the increased political weakness of the parliamentary majority leading to the rejection by the Chamber of Deputies of art 1 of the rendiconto. To solve the stalemate, the government was forced to present a new Bill, exactly reproducing the content of the rejected proposal, which was soon approved by both Houses. See Camera dei Deputati – Giunta per il regolamento, Session of 12 October 2011.

[50] C Goretti and L Rizzuto, 'Il ruolo del Parlamento italiano nella decisione di bilancio: evoluzione recente e confronto con gli altri paesi' (2011) 1–3 *Rivista di politica economica* 29, 49 ff.

in 2001, of dedicated oversight units entitled to scrutinise the huge amount of incoming reports.[51] Another source of parliamentary information is the Corte dei conti, which regularly submits its reports to Parliament. In fact, cooperation with the Supreme Audit Institution has not yet been fully exploited, especially at the stage of budget execution.[52] The availability of complete and exhaustive data still represents a major gap for Parliament's engagement in the oversight of budget.

A different framework features the ex ante oversight of budget. In this field, Parliament has experienced a revitalisation of its power to set the fundamental political directions, urged by major trends in European economic governance. Since the entry into force of the National Accounting Act, Law no 468/1978, the Italian Parliament has been involved in the adoption of the budgetary and financial plans drafted by the government by means of the approval of unicameral resolutions.[53] These procedures, incorporated in the Rules of Procedure of both Houses,[54] were updated as to adjust to the proceedings of the 'European Semester'.[55] The content of the budgetary and financial plan submitted by the government in spring, the 'Document of Economy and Finance', was revised so as to absorb the National Reform Programme.[56] Also, the Note of Adjournment to the Document of Economy and Finance, submitted in the autumn, is often incorporating the authorisation to the correction mechanisms in the event of significant observed deviations from the medium-term objective, to be approved by an absolute majority.[57]

Other ex ante oversight procedures were introduced by Law no 234/2012, on participation in the EU. The government is required to periodically inform and consult both Houses on the coordination of economic and budgetary policies and on the functioning of the financial stability mechanisms (article 4.4). The rule of the 'comply or explain' (article 5), inspired by the rulings of the German Constitutional Court,[58] binds the government to inform the two Houses of any negotiation of agreement between EU Member States that set or reinforce financial or monetary rules or produce relevant consequences in the sphere of public finance. During the negotiations, the Houses can address directions to the government, which in case of non-compliance is required to give explanations.[59]

These trends confirm a strong involvement of the Italian Parliament in the early stages of the budgetary cycle which precede the setting of a budget.[60] However, this trend was not compensated by a corresponding reinforcement of the ex post oversight of public finance, which still represents the main vulnerability of the Italian model.

---

[51] F Rosa, 'Le relazioni governative al Parlamento sullo stato di attuazione delle leggi' in M Carli (ed), *Il ruolo delle Assemblee elettive. Vol I. La nuova forma di governo delle regioni* (Torino, Giappichelli, 2001) 442.

[52] V Lippolis, 'Il rapporto tra Corte dei conti e Parlamento e le prospettive della "valutazione delle politiche pubbliche"' (2009) 12 *Federalismi.it* 4.

[53] Art 3.1 of Law no 468/1978, now replaced by art 7.2(a) of Law no 196/2009. On the promotion of bicameral synergies in the scrutiny of these acts, see art 4.2. of Law no 196/2006.

[54] Art 118-*bis*.1 Chamber of Deputies Rules of Procedure; art 125 *bis* 1 Senate Rules of Procedure.

[55] Law no 39 of 7 April 2011.

[56] Art 10.5 of Law no 196/2006.

[57] Art 6.3 of Law no 243/2012.

[58] See below, section IV.

[59] Art 46 Senate Rules of Procedure; and art 143 Chamber of Deputies Rules of Procedure.

[60] P De Ioanna, 'La nuova cornice costituzionale: economia, istituzioni e dinamica delle forze politiche' in Vv Aa, *Il Filangieri. Quaderno 2011* (Napoli, Jovene, 2012) 45.

III. The Impact of European Economic Governance

In European Member States, common pushes towards the revitalisation of budgetary oversight in Parliament can be detected. These trends find their origins in European economic governance, defining the complex and multilevel set of rules and measures adopted within and outside the EU legal order to coordinate economic and financial policies and prevent major imbalances.[61] In the last decade, in view of promoting a strengthened cooperation between Member States and EU institutions, European economic governance[62] has experienced a deep transformation.[63] This change raised a number of accountability concerns, affecting national legal orders and requiring an adaptation also on the side of parliamentary oversight of budget and public finance.[64]

In response to these pressures, domestic models have not experienced a radical change, but a rationalisation of the pre-existing budgetary oversight architecture. Four major trends can be detected. First, for the very first time the European legal order has imposed into national democracies some parameters and binding rules which are conditioning the 'realm' of the relationship between the domestic legislative and executive branches. To give some examples, the Treaty on Stability, Coordination and Governance (TSCG) required the introduction of the principle of balanced budgets, as specified in article 3, paragraph 2, 'preferably' in national Constitutions; or, at least, in another provision 'of binding force and permanent character ... guaranteed to be fully respected and adhered to throughout the national budgetary process'. This sets a clear parameter that parliaments are required to use to oversee the compliance of governmental measures with the expected budgetary outcomes.[65] On the side of the procedures, some of the rules of European economic governance introduced forms of parliamentary 'participation' and 'involvement' in the budgetary process, thus leading the European legal system to its furthest border.[66]

Second, one of the Six-pack EU Regulations (No 1175/2011) established the European Semester, the architecture legally based on Article 121 of the Treaty on the Functioning of the European Union (TFEU) and designed to develop a new working method spurring the ex ante coordination of EU Members' economic policies. Its aim is to ensure

---

[61] Some rules have been adopted through intergovernmental agreements between Members States: this is the case for the European Financial Stability Facility, the Treaty to establish the European Stability Mechanism, and the TSCG. Other rules are set in EU secondary norms, including the Six-pack, made up of five regulations and one directive which entered into force on 13 December 2011; and the Two-pack, consisting of two regulations.

[62] A Hatje, 'The Economic Constitution within the Internal Market' in A von Bogdandy and J Bast (eds), *Principles of European Constitutional Law* (Oxford, Hart Publishing, 2010) (highlighting the difference with the notion of European economic constitution).

[63] F Naert, 'The new European Union economic governance: what about accountability?' (2016) 82 *International Review of Administrative Sciences* 638.

[64] L Besselink, 'Parameters of Constitutional Development: The Fiscal Compact in between EU and Member States Constitutions' in LS Rossi and F Casolari (eds), *The EU after Lisbon: Amending or Coping with the Existing Treaties?* (Heidelberg, Springer, 2014).

[65] See art 3.2 TSCG also, which provides that the correction mechanisms 'shall fully respect the prerogatives of national Parliaments'.

[66] See above, ch 4, section IV.C (nn 271–75).

that the collective discussion on key priorities about public policies takes place at the EU level before, and not after, national decisions are made.[67] This innovation contributed to formal and informal adaptations at the national level leading to the reinforcement of the legislature's ability to interact with the planning of public finances before the setting of a budget.

Third, the radical changes in European economic governance urged a reconsideration of parliaments' role in the budgetary and financial processes at the level also of constitutional jurisdictions. The reference is to the role exercised by the Bundesverfassungsgericht (BVG) in protecting the prerogatives of the German Parliament both in a normative perspective and, more concretely, in the setting of the big options of the European economic and monetary policy. With the Lissabon Urteil adopted on 30 June 2009,[68] the Constitutional Court judged as unconstitutional the 2008 'accompanying law' to the ratification of the Lisbon Treaty, insofar as it did not grant the Bundestag and Bundesrat sufficient rights of participation in the EU's law-making and treaty amendment procedures. Four other decisions followed, from September 2011 to September 2012. The first ruling[69] affected the euro rescue package for Greece and other highly indebted euro zone countries: rejecting three lawsuits against euro bail-out measures, the BVG stated that the Bundestag should have a greater say and participation in future bail outs. The second ruling, adopted on 28 February 2012,[70] judged as largely unconstitutional the new committee of law-makers set up by *StabMechG* (the Act on the Assumption of Guarantees in Connection with a European Stabilisation Mechanism) since it violated the Bundestag's budgetary prerogatives, which should be exercised by the whole body and not through selected Members. The third ruling, of 19 June 2012[71] and referring to the structuring of the European Stability Mechanism (ESM), confirmed the government's duty to provide comprehensive information to the Bundestag in EU matters. Finally, the decision of 12 September 2012 on the ESM and on the TSCG[72] recognised the mandatory overall budgetary responsibility of the Bundestag regarding German electors, which implies the independence of the German Federal Assembly from directives coming from the EU institutions. More recently, in July 2019, the Second Senate of the Federal Constitutional Court, while dismissing constitutional complaints against the foundational acts of the EU Banking Union and the related federal Acts, confirmed that the Bundestag's overall budgetary responsibility is an inalienable fundamental democratic principle.[73]

Reasons alleged by the Court are based on the exclusive role assigned to the Bundestag in the scrutiny of the decisions that shape the state budgetary and financial responsibility in European economic governance.[74] This jurisdictional defence of parliamentary democracy

---

[67] M Marzinotto, B Wolff and GB Hallerberg, *An Assessment of the European Semester* (Brussels, European Parliament – Directorate-General for Internal Policies, Study, 2012) esp 68 ff.

[68] Judgment of the Federal Constitutional Court of 30 June 2009–2 BvE 2/08.

[69] Judgment of the Federal Constitutional Court of 7 September 2011–2 BvR 987/10, 2 BvR 1485/10, 2 BvR 1099/10.

[70] Judgment of the Federal Constitutional Court of 28 January 2012–2 BvE 8/11.

[71] Judgment of the Second Senate of 19 June 2012–2 BvE 4/11.

[72] Judgment of the Federal Constitutional Court of 12 September 2012 – 2 BVR 1390/12. JHR and WTE, 'Watching Karlsruhe/Karlsruhe Watchers' (2012) 8 *European Constitutional Law Review* 367, 368 ff.

[73] Judgment of the Second Senate of 30 July 2019–2 BvR 1685/14, 2 BvR 2631/14, para 123.

[74] 2 BvE 8/11, para 113.

in Europe[75] confirms that the apparent loss of autonomy and weight of national parliaments can be compensated by reinforcing their informative, participative and oversight prerogatives.

Fourth, the EU provided for the establishment, at the national level, of fiscal agencies, better known as 'fiscal councils', independent institutions composed mainly of economic experts and academics, whose pivotal task is to enhance the transparency of decision-making on budgetary and financial matters.[76] The set of EU regulatory norms fixed a wide range of structural and functional requirements for these institutions, to be completed at national level.[77]

In fact, some Member States had previously experienced the creation of fiscal agencies: Denmark (1962), Germany (1963), Austria (1970), Belgium (1989) and Sweden (2007). The United Kingdom, which did not sign the TSCG, autonomously provided for the creation, in 2010, of the Office for Budget Responsibility. After the entry into force of the TSCG, the presence of a fiscal council has become mandatory for signatory Member States. As a matter of fact, in Italy, based on Constitutional Law no 1/2012, Law no 243 of 20 December 2012 established the Parliamentary Budget Office as a sort of 'parliamentary' agency, whose Council members are appointed through bicameral agreements by the presidents of the two Houses. In France, article 11 of the *loi organique* of 17 December 2012 created the High Council of Public Finances, an independent body alongside the Cour des comptes, but enjoying a special relationship with Parliament. In Spain, the Independent Authority for Spanish Fiscal Responsibility was set up in 2013 at the premises of the government,[78] as an authority serving the executive branch and sub-national entities.

Notwithstanding the large variety of fiscal authorities acting at the national level, the EU design seems to advocate their stable relationship with the legislative branch. While protecting the independence of these authorities, EU legislation also requests Member States to introduce the most suitable tools for making them accountable to parliaments.[79] This innovation is adding another pivotal element to strengthen parliamentary oversight. The diffusion of fiscal councils fostered by the TSCG is sometimes described as the second wave of delegation to technocratic non-majoritarian institutions.[80] In fact, their

---

[75] L Besselink and JH Reestman, 'The Fiscal Compact and the European Constitutions: "Europe Speaking German"' (2012) 8 *European Constitutional Law Review* 1.

[76] L Calmfors, 'The Role of Fiscal Rules, Fiscal Councils, and Fiscal Union in the EU Integration' in H Badinger and V Nitsch (eds), *Routledge Handbook of the Economics of European Integration* (Abingdon, Routledge, 2015).

[77] See Art 6 of Directive 2011/85/UE, art 3.2. TSCG, art 2.1(a) Reg (EU) no 473/2013 and the Communication from the Commission defining the Common principles on national fiscal correction mechanisms (COM 2012) 342.

[78] Organic Law no 6/2013 of 14 November 2013.

[79] C Fasone and E Griglio, 'Can Fiscal Councils Enhance the Role of National Parliaments in the European Union? A Comparative analysis' in B De Witte, A Héritier and AH Trechsei (eds), *The Euro Crisis and the State of European Democracy* (Florence, EUI, 2013). M Horvath, 'EU Independent Fiscal Institutions: An Assessment of Potential Effectiveness' (2018) 56 *Journal of Common Market Studies* 504.

[80] T Tesche, '"The troika is dead, long live to the domestic troikas?" Varieties of technocracy and the diffusion of national fiscal councils in the European Union: Agents, trustees or orchestrators of fiscal discipline?' (2018) 3 TARN Working Paper 1.

institutional mission does not result in a 'depoliticisation' of economic issues,[81] but rather serves the existing channels of democratic representation by providing highly specialised expertise and advice. Fiscal institutions are specifically reinforcing Parliament's independent sources of information and analytical capacity regarding fiscal and economic data.[82] Their presence does not substitute, but rather supports, parliamentary oversight, bridging it to pursue substantial outcomes.[83]

IV. The Trade-Off between Budgetary Decision-Making and Oversight: Unchallenged by the European Parliament

The traditional conception of Parliament's ownership of budget as centred on legislative decision-making is no longer able to explain the actual involvement of representative assemblies in economic and financial governance. The interweaving of the national and the European dimensions has emphasised the all-year cyclical structure of budget, which sees parliaments participating in three stages of the ex ante oversight, setting of budget and ex post oversight. These dimensions are not equally relevant and effective across legislative assemblies.

The comparative analysis witnesses a sort of trade-off between budgetary decision-making and oversight: where Parliament is intensively involved in the setting of the yearly budget/finance law, its role in the oversight of budget execution may be undermined; in contrast, oversight of budget execution naturally tends to counterbalance the parliamentary degree of involvement in budgetary decision-making. Different motivations may contribute to explain the trade-off effect. On the one side, it is the paradox of the controlled–ontroller, which reaches its apex when the setting of budget is not fully placed under the responsibility of the government, but comes from the compromise reached in Parliament between the legislative and executive branches. On the other side, it is the lack of oversight incentives for MPs when 'electoral' outcomes can be maximised through the amending of budget.

The trade-off effect combines with alternative balancing of the decision-oversight dimensions. The UK shows a strong executive dominance over the budgetary decision, a low level of Parliament's ex ante engagement in the pre-budget stage and an effective system of ex post oversight of budget execution. The opposite happens in Italy, where the legislature confirms itself as highly influential in budgetary legislation, but keeps an extremely weak structure of ex post oversight, only partially balanced by the relaunching of Parliament's engagement in the ex ante stage. France turns out to be in an intermediate position, having experienced a limitation of Parliament's amending of budgetary and financial legislation and, at the same time, a strengthening of ex ante and ex post oversight.

---

[81] I Sánchez-Cuenca, 'From a Deficit of Democracy to a Technocratic Order: The Postcrisis Debate on Europe' (2017) 20 *Annual Review of Political Science* 351.

[82] D Fromage, 'Creation and Reform of Independent Fiscal Institutions in EU Member States: Incomplete and Insufficient Work in Progress?' in T Beukers, B De Witte and C Kilpatrick (eds), *Constitutional Change through Euro-Crisis Law* (Oxford, Oxford University Press, 2017) 109.

[83] B Anderson, 'The Value of a Nonpartisan, Independent, Objective Analytic Unit to the Legislative Role in Budget Preparation' in R Stapenhurst, R Pelizzo, D Olson and L von Trapp (eds), *Legislative Oversight and Budgeting: A World Perspective* (Washington DC, World Bank, 2008).

Figure 1 Alternative arrangements for parliamentary involvement in the main stages of the budgetary cycle

	United Kingdom (Westminster Model)	France (Continental Europe)	Italy (Continental Europe)
Type of Committee	Select Committees: • Commons Treasury Select Committee (Budget & Finance Bill) • Public Account Committees (ex post oversight)	In both Houses, Finance Committees acting as hybrid committees	In both Houses, involvement of two hybrid committees: the Budget Committee and the Finance Committees (respectively, for expenditures and for revenues)
Ex ante oversight of budget	• Absorbed in the debate on the budget • Weak role of Parliament	• Dedicated ex ante oversight tools • Impact of the European Semester procedure on the promotion of ex ante oversight mechanisms	• Dedicated ex ante oversight tools • Impact of the European Semester procedure on the promotion of ex ante oversight mechanisms
Setting of a budget	• Strong governmental control of the merit of the budgetary decision/main financial measures • Parliament merely 'authorises' the budgetary decision	Limited capacity of Parliament to influence the merit of budgetary/financial legislation	Advanced capacity of Parliament to influence the merit of the budgetary/financial legislation
Ex post oversight of budget	Parliament's strong involvement in the examination of public expenditure and formulation of recommendations to the government	• Advanced capacity of Parliament to oversee the execution of a budget • Approval of the *loi de règlement* including reports on the evaluation of the performance	• Extremely weak capacity of Parliament to oversee the execution of budget • Approval of the *rendiconto* as a formal prerogative, non-associated with effective oversight

The trade-off effect, in its different variations, is only apparently contradicted by the experience of the European Parliament which in the budgetary field finds one of its core competences, linked to the exercise of formal prerogatives, with a binding outcome on the other institutions.[84] On the one hand, the European Parliament participates, jointly with

---

[84] C Fasone and N Lupo, 'The Union Budget and the Budgetary Procedure' in R Schütze and T Tridimas (eds), *Oxford Principles of European Union Law. The European Legal Order*, I (Oxford, Oxford University Press, 2018).

the Council, in approval of the yearly budget of the Union, and formulates its last will.[85] On the other hand, through the discharge procedure, it oversees the execution of budget, assessing the management of public accounts by the Commission and the other institutions.[86]

Simplifying, the European Parliament may be considered an example of strong involvement in budgetary decision-making and an equivalent level of participation in the oversight of budget. In fact, the lack of a real trade-off in the experience of the European Parliament can be attributed to the hybrid nature of the European form of government more than to any other reason. From a diachronic perspective, the reinforcement of European Parliament budgetary prerogatives[87] has represented an attempt to compensate for the ongoing marginalisation experienced by national representative assemblies, which have lost control of a number of competences.[88] Nonetheless, solutions adopted to fulfil this institutional need have brought the European Parliament closer to a legislature than to a parliament sharing the features of European national constitutional traditions.[89] In the comparison between presidential systems and Westminster models, the separateness of the legislature shows a linear relationship with its budgetary authority.[90] Therefore, it can be argued that the European Parliament budgetary authority resembles the experience of the United States more than that of the United Kingdom. It specifically recalls the US 'conflict and resolution' between the President and Congress,[91] whereby the legislature, acting as a powerful counterweight to the executive, combines an unfettered amending power with an effective ex post oversight of budget.

Since these features are traceable to the atypical EU relationship between the branches of government, the trade-off effect does not seem to be contradicted by the experience of the European Parliament. Rather, the European dimension, in respect of its impact on national constitutional systems, validates even more the idea that Parliament's strong role in the budgetary decision is largely anti-historical. The EU budgetary and financial architecture, permeated by the mixing of European and national rules and by the intruding of technical parameters into political priorities, has deeply affected the role of representative assemblies in the field of budget and public finance. Parliaments have undoubtedly lost much of their

---

[85] Art 314 TFEU. G Benedetto, 'The EU budget after Lisbon: Rigidity and reduced spending? (2013) 33 *Journal of Public Policy* 345; S Neheider, 'Reframing the EU Budget Decision-Making Process' (2011) 49 *Journal of Common Market Studies* 631.

[86] Art 319 Treaty on the Functioning of the European Union (TFEU).

[87] MW Bauer and S Becker, 'Assessing the European Parliament's Power of the Purse: Rights, Capabilities and Strategies' in S Backer, MW Bauer and A De Feo (eds), *The New Politics of the European Union Budget* (Baden-Baden, Nomos, 2017).

[88] A De Feo, *A history of budgetary powers and politics in the EU: the Role of the European Parliament. Part II: the non-elected Parliament 1957–1978* (Luxembourg, Publications Office of the European Union, 2016) 9. R Crowe, 'The European Budgetary Galaxy' (2017) 13 *European Constitutional Law Review* 428, esp. 431.

[89] C Fasone, 'What is a legislature in the twenty-first century? Classification and evolution of a contested notion' (2019) 15 *Federalismi.it* 1, 4 ff.

[90] I Lienert, 'Who Controls the Budget: The Legislature or the Executive?' (2005) 5/115 IMF Working Paper 1, 8 ff.

[91] A Schick, *The Federal Budget Politics, Policy, Process* (Washington, Brookings Institution, 2002) 1 ff.

ability to define the detail of budgetary legislation, which is shifting from increased technicism to ever expanding executive dominance. However, the need to compensate these trends with hits of democratic legitimacy has urged the definition of new patterns of parliamentary 'participation' in the fundamental stages of economic and financial governance. In this vein, the medium fiscal outlook is gaining increased relevance and it is at this stage that parliaments can contribute to overseeing the budget framework that guides the executive in setting the annual budget and fiscal strategy.

9

Conclusions. From Law-Making to Oversight? A Concrete Perspective for European Parliamentarism

Parliamentarism has traditionally seen in the effectiveness of oversight procedures a meas-ure of the overall 'strength' of parliaments.[1] Different instances of public virtue make this function a particularly topical dimension: improving the quality of the decisions of those who exercise a direct power on the public sphere; and enabling elected representatives to mediate between government action and citizens' preferences.[2] Parliamentary over-sight serves the fundamental values of representative democracies, including government responsibility and legitimacy[3] and is therefore the sole democratic counterweight to trends of executive dominance and opaqueness in public decision-making. Especially in policy areas where the role of the executive is overwhelming, parliamentary oversight brings about higher standards of information and participation,[4] thus contributing to improving input and throughput legitimacy.[5] An effective oversight dynamic is therefore an added value not just for parliaments but also for responsive governments willing to be held accountable before elected assemblies in the spirit of good governance.

To date, an overarching formula apt to guaranteeing effective parliamentary oversight has not been devised. A catch-all system is inconceivable. Every legislature has adapted its own machinery in response to the demands and challenges raised by the interplay between the executive-parties dimension and the form of government. And rightly so. Different combinations of legislative and oversight prerogatives, often interacting in a sort of trade-off, can be found across parliaments.[6] This makes it hard to assess what oversight arrangements and procedures are most effective. As a matter of fact, oversight outcomes largely depend on the types of procedures available, on their degree of intrusiveness and capacity to bind the executive. Nonetheless, parliaments are increasingly called to confront themselves with oversight mechanisms whose outcomes – in terms of transparency, informal cooperation and sharing of political directions between the branches of government – either depend on party interactions or rely on pre-legal factors.

---

[1] M Ameller, *Les questions, instrument du contrôle parlementaire* (Paris, LGDJ, 1964) 9.

[2] P Houillon, 'Le contrôle extraordinaire du parlement' (2010) 134 *Pouvoirs* 64, 66.

[3] A Le Divellec, 'Des effets du contrôle parlementaire' (2010) 134 *Pouvoirs* 123.

[4] R Dahl, *On Democracy* (New Haven, CT, Yale University Press, 1998) 126.

[5] V Schmidt, 'Democracy and Legitimacy in the European Union Revisited: Input, Output and "Throughput"' (2013) 61 *Political Studies* 2.

[6] Both functions are undergoing change and facing new challenges. For the UK Parliament, see A Horne and A Le Sueur (eds), *Parliament. Legislation and Accountability* (Oxford, Hart Publishing, 2016).

The solutions adopted at the national level, in connection with the oversight enforcing mechanisms, vary along two main areas of differentiation. First, parliaments show different combinations of the two fundamental conceptions of parliamentary oversight observed on comparative grounds. The hard conception stands for oversight serving a hierarchical means to hold the government accountable vis-a-vis Parliament. In the soft conception, parliamentary oversight is interpreted as a horizontal dimension serving Parliament's attempt to exercise influence over the executive. Switching between these two conceptions, parliamentary oversight may either trigger legally binding sanctions to address governmental responsibility or act as a non-binding power that nonetheless may result in strong political commitments. Whereas the possibility to overthrow the government is the ultimate weapon in the Parliament's armoury, soft oversight powers are at the very heart of legislative–executive daily interaction. The Spanish Tribunal Constitucional explicitly recognised that not all oversight tools find their purpose in the breaking of the confidence relationship, because in principle they can also be exercised when such a relationship is lacking.[7] Ongoing trends of parliamentary oversight in European national systems seem to confirm that the hard conception, brought to its extreme implications (ie, the censure of the government), may be unfit or excessive for the purpose of bringing about more democratic legitimacy. Rather, over the course of the confidence relationship, parliaments react to the oversight challenge following two main strategies.

On the one hand, they may harden the oversight machinery by revising the tools and procedures available so as to reinforce government accountability, but without challenging the continuity of the confidence relationship. Hardened oversight procedures are setting binding requirements on the government, forcing it to provide information, explanation and follow-up, or are introducing reinforced proceedings and majorities. Through reforms of the constitution, of the parliamentary rules of procedure, of statutory legislation, parliaments resort to this strategy mostly to compensate the challenges raised by the transformation of executive–legislative interaction.[8] Examples can be found in the ongoing adaptation of the tools and procedures related to the scrutiny of European affairs or to the oversight of budget and public finance, which have involved the large majority of EU Member States. The 2008 amendment of the French Constitution is another major case for the hardening of the oversight relationship. In most cases, however, the hardened effect is not able to fully constrain the executive.

On the other hand, parliaments increasingly resort to soft and informal oversight tools, including relationships with the media. Their capacity to perform this role does not exclusively depend on the formal powers that they share; rather, it is strongly influenced by other pre-legal factors, such as the willingness and ability to engage in oversight throughout the decision-making process, the political independence from the executive, the access to independent sources of information, technical expertise and analytical capacity. The technical factor is becoming an increasingly relevant asset for parliamentary oversight. The modern

---

[7] STC 124/2018, para 7.

[8] Bundesverfassungsgericht Press Release, 'If interpreted strictly, the framework for the European Banking Union does not exceed the competences of the European Union' (30 July 2019) 52 depicts transparency requirements or reporting and accountability obligations vis-a-vis the national parliaments as a form of 'compensation' for the losses in the level of democratic legitimation related to the functioning of the European Banking Union.

state is so vast and complex that it is 'no longer possible for Parliament alone to ensure accountability across the wide range of activities of central departments, let alone the myriad of other public sector bodies'.[9] Representative assemblies should therefore be placed at the apex of the pyramid of accountability, drawing on the investigations of outside regulators and commissions[10] and on the evaluation of public policies[11] to more effectively perform their functions.

Transparency and publicity are other potentially powerful 'soft' oversight mechanisms, which may be used to make governments directly accountable to citizens. To fulfil this target, representative assemblies can rely on the traditional means of parliamentary publicity or they can connect to the media. Whereas these instances may prove a rather powerful means of interinstitutional dialogue, in many cases the difficulty in tracing their effects raises increasing dissatisfaction on the grounds of their effectiveness.[12]

The second of the main areas of differentiation across parliaments relates to the combination of the oversight dimensions alongside the subsequent stages of decision-making. Oversight potentially permeates all spheres of parliamentary activity. Its versatility emerges in the objectives, scope, tools and interaction with other parliamentary powers. Forms of 'oversight' are detected both in the 'follow-up' procedures through which parliaments hold governments to account for past action and in the mechanisms aimed at exercising an ex ante 'influence' on the sphere of action of the executive. Oversight is not just a form of a *contre-rôle*, a reaction to the action of another subject.[13] Rather, it is a cyclical function encompassing the whole life of the executive–legislative relation and the entire decision-making process.[14] This implies that the oversight dynamics may draw on governmental action not as a premise, but also as an expected output,[15] according to the 'policy-influencing' relational scheme.[16]

As a matter of fact, parliaments have different preferences towards ex ante and ex post mechanisms, which may change from one policy area to another. For instance, the British Parliament has a well-rooted ex post oversight machinery and, in the Brexit case, has recently seen the judicial endorsement of its ex ante prerogatives. The French Parliament has identified in the strengthening of parliamentary ex post oversight, extended to the evaluation of public policies, one of the core aspects of the constitutional rebalancing of executive–legislative interaction. The Danish Folketing, followed by the Swedish Riksdag, has one of

---

[9] Hansard Society, *The Challenge for Parliament: Making Government Accountable*, Report of the Hansard Society Commission on Parliamentary Scrutiny (London, Hansard Society Publications, 2011) 1.

[10] A Tomkins, 'What is Parliament for?' in N Bamforth and P Leyland (eds), *Public Law in a Multi-Layered Constitution* (Oxford, Hart Publishing, 2003) 70.

[11] J Chevallier, 'L'évaluation législative: un enjeu politique' in A Delcamp, JL Bergel and A Dupas, *Contrôle parlementaire et évaluation* (Paris, La Documentation française, 1995) 27.

[12] F Meinel, 'Confidence and Control in Parliamentary Government: Parliamentary Questioning, Executive Knowledge, and the Transformation of Democratic Accountability' (2018) 66 *The American Journal of Comparative Law* 317, 367 ff.

[13] Le Divellec, 'Des effets du contrôle' (n 3) 125.

[14] Council of Europe Commissioner for Human Rights, *Democratic and Effective Oversight of National Security Services* (Paris, Council of Europe, 2015) 61 argues that, in relation to national security services, the oversight system should be 'ex ante (where appropriate), contemporaneous and ex post'.

[15] M Mezey, *Comparative Legislatures* (Durham, NC, Duke University Press, 1979) 48 (effective oversight 'can create new demands for which new policies must be formulated, deliberated and decided upon').

[16] P Norton, 'Parliaments: A Framework for Analysis' (1990) 13 *West European Politics* 1, 5.

the strongest ex ante oversight tools available to parliaments, the mandate system on EU affairs, and extensive experience of interaction with the public on their complaints about the conduct of public action through the ombudsmen. The Italian Parliament has a rather weak ex post oversight toolbox and a preference for ex ante oversight, which has enabled the codetermination of the *indirizzo politico* between the legislative and the executive branches, remarkably in the field of the scrutiny of EU affairs. The German Bundestag has lately witnessed the judicial endorsement of its oversight prerogatives, including the information and participatory mechanisms of the ex ante stage, as an unalienable fundamental democratic principle vis-a-vis participation in European integration. The Spanish Parliament has recently sought support from the Constitutional Tribunal to assert the imperativeness of its oversight prerogatives, even in cases of a transitional government acting without the confidence of Parliament.

From a comparative perspective, the ex ante oversight dimension is gaining increasing relevance across parliaments, thus confirming that governmental accountability can be challenged at the very beginning of the decision-making process, even before executives take a formal decision or start an action. The challenge is therefore moving from a 'negative' to a 'positive' approach to parliamentary oversight. Representative assemblies are called on not just to react to government action in order to set a sanction in the case of misuse of power. Rather, the real challenge is how to influence the general conduct of government affairs and public administration in a supportive mode which does not weaken the executive.[17] This vision is also true for the dimension of ex post oversight which, on procedural grounds, remains the weakest at comparative level. Ex post oversight can be a means to evaluate what has been done also in view of advancing new policy solutions. It is at this stage that parliaments are called on to invest new energies and resources to face the challenges of post-legislative scrutiny and evaluation of public policies.

In this vein, parliaments have revived their interest in the wide range of oversight mechanisms supporting the confidence relationship between the legislative and executive branches.[18] This machinery dates back to the very origins of parliamentarism and yet it seems to experience a new life in the current institutional framework. To face contemporary accountability challenges, parliaments are called on to seriously tackle the original paradox of the political identity between the controller and the controlled, resorting to solutions suitable to compensate if not to relieve the paradox.[19] In response to these pushes, traditional patterns of executive oversight in parliamentary regimes based on party modes are complemented by non-party modes involving the legislature as a whole vis-a-vis the executive. Oversight is therefore experiencing a shift from cooperative to more adversarial modes, where competitiveness not only works on a party basis, but also on the institutional

---

[17] A Le Divellec, 'La problématique du contrôle parlementaire de l'administration' in B Seiller (ed), *Le contrôle parlementaire de l'administration* (Paris, Dalloz, 2010) 16 f.

[18] An example of the revived interest towards parliamentary oversight is confirmed by the proposals for reform included in the final report of the French Working Group on the Future of Institutions, released in November 2016, C Bartolone and M Winock, 'Refaire la démocratie' (2016) 3100 *Assemblée Nationale – Rapport* 110 ff.

[19] As argued by D Woodhouse, *Ministers and Parliament: Accountability in Theory and Practice* (Oxford, Oxford University Press, 1994) 298: 'The corruption of ministerial accountability to Parliament, mainly through the operation of party solidarity, challenges Parliament to continue to play its constitutional role in accountable government, or to accept a diminished constitutional position and concede the accountability function to others'.

dynamics between the legislature and the executive. This shift brings parliamentary regimes closer to the antagonistic style of presidential systems in interpreting and implementing the oversight function.[20] EU integration has been a major determinant of this change, because an increased number of decisions are addressed not to a national party-based government, but rather to a fragmented executive with limited connections to traditional party lines. The whole area of the scrutiny of EU affairs increasingly relies on hybridised patterns of parliamentary oversight. Similar trends are affecting other 'technical' oversight tasks, including the scrutiny of government appointments[21] and the evaluation of public policies. The role of Upper Houses disconnected from the confidence circuit in holding the government to account is gaining increased interest.[22] These trends do not prevent the configuration of party power from exercising a decisive influence on the oversight relation between Parliament and the executive.[23]

In a broad perspective, several trends call for a strengthening of the oversight function: the crisis of legislatures' involvement in law-making;[24] the overarching role of the executives, paired with the increased technical complexity of decision-making; the collapse of the traditional architecture of the separation of powers;[25] the euro crisis, which aggravated the democratic accountability concerns of the Union;[26] the transformation of European governance, with its expanding penetration into national constitutional systems;[27] and the rise of a 'new intergovernmentalism'.[28] All these factors are profoundly challenging the established constitutional methods of control and accountability in the EU. Representative assemblies have suffered from a form of marginalisation, at least in their traditional role as legislators and hence decision-makers.[29]

The need to cope with these trends and regain spheres of democratic control brings us back to the idea that oversight of the executives is a measure of parliaments' ability to respond to contemporaneity. This acknowledgement dates back to the decision of *Matthews v The United Kingdom* of the European Court of Human Rights, which 20 years ago clearly opened the path to a 'comprehensive' vision of the role of Parliament. On the one hand, the decision confirmed that the most fundamental attribute of a legislature is 'the power

---

[20] In fact, presidential systems have also experienced the hybridisation of political competition, that is increasingly channelled not through the branches of government, but through political parties, see DJ Levinson and RH Pildes, 'Separation of Parties, Not Powers' (2006) 119 *Harvard Law Review* 2311.

[21] F Matthews and M Flinders, 'The watchdogs of 'Washminster' – parliamentary scrutiny of executive patronage in the UK' (2015) 53 *Commonwealth and Comparative Politics* 153.

[22] On the advantages related to the splitting of parliamentary oversight between two assemblies, E Spagna Musso, 'Bicameralismo e riforma del Parlamento' in Vv Aa, *Parlamento, istituzioni, democrazia: seminario di studio, Roma, 11–13 dicembre 1979* (Milano, Giuffrè, 1980) 127.

[23] D Beetham, *Parliament and Democracy in the twenty-first century: A guide to good practice* (Geneva, Inter-Parliamentary Union, 2006).

[24] See above (n 12).

[25] T Ginsburg and AZ Huq, *How to Save a Constitutional Democracy* (Chicago, IL, University of Chicago Press, 2018) 10 ff.

[26] G Majone, 'From Regulatory State to a Democratic Default' (2014) 52 *Journal of Common Market Studies* 1216.

[27] S Dullien and JI Torreblanca, 'What is the Political Union?' (2012) 70 *European Council on Foreign Relations* 2.

[28] J Bickerton, D Hodson and U Puetter (eds), *The New Intergovernmentalism. States and Supranational Actors in the Post-Maastricht Era* (Oxford, Oxford University Press, 2015).

[29] M Loughlin, 'The Contemporary Crisis of Constitutional Democracy' (2019) 39 *Oxford Journal of Legal Studies* 442.

to initiate legislation and the power to adopt it'.[30] On the other hand, based on article 3 of Protocol no 1 of the European Convention on Human Rights, it granted the European Parliament the nature of a *corp législatif* recognising that, beyond participation in the legislative process, it is 'sufficiently involved in the general democratic supervision of the activities of the European Community',[31] thus representing the principal form of political accountability in that system.[32] This approach has recently been reflected in initiatives on a global level that detect parliaments' added value in securing democratic oversight of strategic policy fields, including counter-terrorism,[33] internal security services[34] and the protection of human rights.[35] In an ever more integrated constitutional dimension, the benefits of an effective system of parliamentary oversight are a safeguard not just within the boundaries of domestic executive–legislative interaction, but also in view of the fulfilment of the substantial values related to global democracy and justice. It is thus demonstrated that a fully-fledged contemporary parliament is a *contrôleur* more than a *corp législatif*, the accountability dimension turning out as the real cornerstone of parliamentary democracy.

---

[30] European Court of Human Rights, *Case of Matthews v the United Kingdom* (18 February 1999) App no 24833/94, para 45.

[31] ibid, para 54.

[32] N Lupo, 'The Transformation of Parliamentary Functions: Are Parliaments Still Legislative Bodies?' in P Falconer, C Smith and CWR Webster (eds), *Managing Parliaments in the 21st Century* (Amsterdam, Ios Press, 2001).

[33] International Institute for Justice and the Rule of Law, *The Role of Parliamentarians in Developing an Effective Response to Terrorism. Valletta recommendations Relating to Contributions by Parliamentarians in Developing an Effective Response to Terrorism* (Valletta, IIJ, 2016).

[34] European Commission for Democracy through Law (Venice Commission), 'Report on the Democratic Oversight of the Security Services' (2015) *Studies no 388/2006 and no 719/2013*, adopted on 15 December 2015.

[35] Council of Europe Parliamentary Assembly, 'The role of parliaments in implementing ECHR standards: overview of existing structures and mechanisms' (2016) 19 PPSD.

BIBLIOGRAPHY

Abazi, V, *Official Secrets and Oversight in the EU: Law and Practices of Classified Information* (Oxford, Oxford University Press, 2019).

Abels, G and Eppler, A (eds), *Subnational Parliaments in the EU Multi-level Parliamentary System: Taking Stock of the Post-Lisbon Era* (Innsbruck, Studienverlag, 2016).

Aberbach, JD, *Keeping a Watchful Eye: The Politics of Congressional Oversight* (Washington DC, Brookings Institution, 1990).

Achterberg, N, 'Parlamentarische Kontrollrechte' (1977) 30 *Die öffentliche verwaltung* 548.

—— *Parlamentsrecht* (Tübingen, Mohr, 1984).

Aguiar de Luque, L, 'La estructura del proceso de formación de gobierno: el caso español en el marco del Derecho comparado' (1980) 6 *Revista de derecho político* 61.

Alderman, RK, 'The leader of the opposition and Prime Minister's question time' (1992) 45 *Parliamentary Affairs* 66.

Allemand, F and Martucci, F, 'La légitimité démocratique de la gouvernance économique européenne: la mutation de la fonction parlementaire' (2014) 134 *Revue de l'OFCE* 115.

Altenhof, R, *Die Enquete-Kommissionen des Deutschen Bundestages* (Wiesbaden, Westdeutscher, 2002).

Alvarez Conde, E, *Curso de Derecho Constitucional*, II (Madrid, Tecnos, 1993).

Alventosa, JR, 'La Cour des comptes: une place constitutionnelle confortée (L'article 47-2 de la Constitution)' (2008) 254 *Les Petites affiches* 82.

Amato, G, *L'ispezione parlamentare* (Milano, Giuffrè, 1968).

Ameller, M, *Les questions, instrument du contrôle parlementaire* (Paris, LGDJ, 1964).

Amselek, P, 'Le budget de l'État et le parlement sous la V République' (1998) 5–6 *Revue du droit public* 1444.

Anderson, B, 'The Value of a Nonpartisan, Independent, Objective Analytic Unit to the Legislative Role in Budget Preparation' in R Stapenhurst, R Pelizzo, D Olson and L von Trapp (eds), *Legislative Oversight and Budgeting: A World Perspective* (Washington DC, World Bank, 2008) 131–40.

Anderson, JR, 'Parliamentary Control and Foreign Policy in Germany. The Bundestag's Use of Formal Instrumentalities in Overseeing the Administrations' Foreign Policy' (2002) 64 *German Politics and Society* 1.

Andeweg, RB, 'Role Specialisation or Role Switching? Dutch MPs between Electorate and Executive' (1997) 3 *The Journal of Legislative Studies* 110.

Andeweg, RB and Nijzink, L, 'Beyond the Two-Body Image: Relations between Ministers and MPs' in H Döering (ed), *Parliaments and Majority Rule in Western Europe* (New York, St Martin's Press, 1995) 152–78.

Angiolini, V, 'La difficile convivenza tra responsabilità politica e responsabilità giuridica' in N Zanon and F Biondi (eds), *Percorsi e vicende attuali della rappresentanza e della responsabilità politica: atti del convegno* (Milano, Giuffrè, 2001) 3–19.

Anglmayer, I, *Evaluation and Ex-post Impact Assessment at EU Level* (Brussels, European Parliamentary Research Service, 2016).

—— *Better Regulation practices in national parliaments* (Brussels, European Parliamentary Research Service Study, 2020).

Anglmayer, I and Scherrer, A, 'Ex-post evaluation in the European Parliament: an increasing influence on the policy cycle' (2020) *Journal of legislative studies*.

Anschütz, G, *Die Verfassung des Deutschen Reiches vom 11. 8. 1919*, 14th edn (Berlin, Georg Stilke, 1933).

Aragón Reyes, M, 'El control parlamentario como control político' (1986) 23 *Revista de Derecho Político* 9.

—— 'El control como elemento inseparable del concepto del Constitución' (1987) 19 *Revista Española de Derecho Constitucional* 15.

Arangio-Ruiz, G, *Delle guarentigie costituzionali* (Napoli, Pierro, 1886).

Arcoleo, G, *Il gabinetto nei governi parlamentari* (Napoli, Jovene, 1881).

—— *L'inchiesta nel governo parlamentare* (Napoli, De Ruberto, 1881).

Arconzo, G, 'Le scelte di finanza pubblica in una "democrazia decidente": alla ricerca di un nuovo ruolo per Governo e Parlamento' (2008) 4 *Quaderni costituzionali* 813.

Arévalo Gutiérrez, A, 'Reflexiones sobre las Comisiones de Investigación o Encuesta parlamentarias en el ordenamiento constitucional español' (1987) 11 *Revista de las Cortes Generales* 159.

——— 'Las comisiones de investigación de las Cortes generales y de las Asambleas legislativas de las Comunidades Autónomas' (1995) 43 *Revista Española de Derecho Constitucional* 113.

Arter, D, 'Parliamentary Democracy in Scandinavia' (2004) 57 *Parliamentary Affairs* 581.

——— *The Scottish Parliament: A Scandinavian-Style Assembly?* (New York, Routledge, 2004).

——— 'Conclusion. Questioning the "Mezey Question": an interrogatory framework for the comparative study of legislatures' (2006) 12 *Journal of Legislative Studies* 462.

——— 'Introduction: comparing the legislative performance of legislatures' (2006) 12 *The Journal of Legislative Studies* 245.

——— 'From "Parliamentary Control" to "Accountable Government"? The role of public committee hearings in the Swedish Riksdag' (2008) 61 *Parliamentary Affairs* 122.

Association of the Bar of the City of New York, 'Congressional Oversight of Administrative Agencies. A Report of the Committee on Administrative Law' (1950) 5 *Record of the Association of the Bar of the City of New York* 11.

Aström, C, 'Evaluation et qualité de la législation: Quel rôle pour les parlements?' (2013) 1 *Sénat, Actes de colloque*.

Auel, K, 'Democratic Accountability and National Parliaments: Redefining the Impact of Parliamentary Scrutiny in EU Affairs' (2007) 13 *European Law Journal* 487.

Auel, K and Höing, O, 'Parliaments in the Euro Crisis: can the losers of integration still fight back?' (2014) 52 *Journal of Common Market Studies* 1184.

——— 'National Parliaments and the Eurozone Crisis: Taking Ownership in Difficult Times?' (2015) 38 *West European Politics* 375.

Auel, K, Rozenberg, O and Tacea, A, 'Fighting Back? And, if so, How? Measuring Parliamentary Strength and Activity in EU Affairs' in C Hefftler, C Neuhold, O Rozenberg and J Smith (eds), *The Palgrave Handbook of National Parliaments and the European Union* (London, Palgrave, 2015) 60–93.

——— 'To Scrutinise or Not to Scrutinise? Explaining Variation in EU-Related Activities in National Parliaments' (2015) 38 *West European Politics* 282.

Auel, K, Rozenberg, O and Thomas, A, 'Lost in Transaction? Parliamentary Reserves in EU Bargains' (2012) 10 *OPAL Online Paper Series*.

Avril, P, 'Responsabilité et *accountability*' in O Beaud and JM Blanquer (eds), *La responsabilité des gouvernants* (Paris, Descartes & Cie, 1999) 85–93.

——— 'La nature de la Ve République' (2001) 300 *Cahiers français* 3.

——— 'Quel équilibre entre exécutif et législatif?' (2002) 1–2 *Revue du droit public* 268.

——— 'Le contrôle. Exemple du Comité d'évaluation et de contrôle des politiques publiques' (2008) 6 *Jus Politicum* 1.

——— 'Le statut de l'opposition: un feuilleton inachevé? (Les articles 4 et 51-1 de la Constitution) (2008) 254 *Petites affiches* 1.

——— 'L'introuvable contrôle parlementaire' (2009) 140 *Petites affiches* 7.

——— 'L'introuvable contrôle parlementaire (après la révision constitutionelle française de 2008' (2009) 3 *Jus Politicum* 1.

Avril, P and Gicquel, J, *Droit parlementaire*, 5th edn (Paris, LGDJ, 2014).

Badura, P, 'Die Parlamentarische Verantwortlichkeit Der Minister' (1980) 11 *Zeitschrift Für Parlamentsfragen* 573.

Bagehot, W, *The English Constitution*, 2nd edn (London, HS King, 1872).

——— 'The Non-Legislative Functions of Parliament' (1860) in N St John-Stevas (ed), *The Collected Works of Walter Bagehot*, VI (London, The Economist, 1986) 41–45.

——— 'The Unseen Work of Parliament' (1861) in N St John-Stevas (ed), *The Collected Works of Walter Bagehot*, VI (London, The Economist, 1986) 45–48.

Baghestani, L, 'A propos de la loi tendant à renforcer les moyens du Parlement en matière de contrôle de l'action du Gouvernement et d'évaluation des politiques publiques' (2011) 78 *Les Petites affiches*.

Bailer, S, 'People's Voice or Information Pool? The Role and Reasons for Parliamentary Questions in the Swiss Parliament' (2011) 17 *The Journal of Legislative Studies* 302.

Baldassarre, A, 'I poteri di indirizzo-controllo del parlamento' in Vv Aa, *Il parlamento: analisi e proposte di riforma* (Roma, Editori Riuniti, 1978) 181–220.

——— 'Il Parlamento come soggetto di indirizzo e di controllo politico' in Vv Aa, *Attualità e attuazione della Costituzione* (Roma, Bari, 1979) 16–41.

Balladur, E, *Une Ve République plus démocratique – Comité de réflexion et de proposition sur la modernisation et le rééquilibrage des institutions de la Ve République* (Paris, La Documentation Française, 2007).

Ballinger, C, *The House of Lords 1991–2011. A Century of Non-Reform* (London, Hart Publishing, 2012).

Balmforth, N, and Leyland, P, 'Introduction: Accountability in the Contemporary Constitution' in N Balmforth and P Leyland (eds), *Accountability in the Contemporary Constitution* (Oxford, Oxford University Press, 2013) 1–26.

Balmforth, N, 'Accountability of and to the Legislature' in N Balmforth and P Leyland (eds), *Accountability in the Contemporary Constitution* (Oxford, Oxford University Press, 2013) 259–288.

Bar Cendón, A, 'Accountability and Public Administration: Concepts, Dimensions, Developments' in M Kelly (ed), *Openness and Trasparency in Governance: Challenges and Opportunities* (Bratislava, NISPAcee Press, 2000) 22–61.

Baranger, D, *Parlamentarisme des origines. Essai sur les conditions de formation d'un exécutif responsable en Angleterre* (Paris, PUF, 1999).

Barber, N, Hickman, T and King, J, 'Pulling the Article 50 "Trigger": Parliament's Indispensable Role' (*UK Constitutional Law Blog*, 27 June 2016).

Barilari, A, *Les contrôles financiers, comptables, administratifs et juridictionnels des finances publiques* (Paris, LGDJ, 2003).

Barthélemy, J, *L'introduction du régime parlementaire en France sous Louis XVIII et Charles X* (Paris, Giard & Brière, 1904).

—— Le rôle du pouvoir exécutif dans le Républiques modernes (Paris, Giard et Brière, 1906).

—— *Essai sur le travail parlementaire et le système des commissions* (Paris, Librairie Delagrave, 1934).

Bartolone, C and Winock, M, 'Refaire la démocratie' (2016) 3100 *Assemblée Nationale – Rapport* 1.

Bastien, F, 'II. Un parlementarisme "rationalisé"' in F Bastien (ed), *Le régime politique de la Ve République* (Paris, La Découverte, 2011) 29–62.

Baudu, A, *Contribution à l'étude des pouvoirs budgétaires du Parlement en France: éclairage historique et perspectives d'évolution* (Paris, Dalloz, 2010).

Bauer, MW and Becker, S, 'Assessing the European Parliament's Power of the Purse: Rights, Capabilities and Strategies' in S Backer, MW Bauer and A De Feo (eds), *The New Politics of the European Union Budget* (Baden-Baden, Nomos, 2017) 173–94.

Baum, MA and Potter, PBK, *War and Democratic Constraint: How the Public Influences Foreign Policy* (Princeton, NJ, Princeton University Press, 2015).

Bäumlin, R, *Die Kontrolle des Parlaments über Regierung und Verwaltung* (Basel, Helbing & Lichtenhahn, 1966).

Beaud, O, 'Le transfert de la responsabilité politique du ministre verse ses proches subordonnés' in O Beaud and JM Blanquer (eds), *La responsabilité des gouvernants* (Paris, Descartes & Cie, 1999) 203–34.

Beaud, O and Blanquer, JM, 'Comment réintroduire une responsabilité des gouvernants sous la Vᵛ République' in O Beaud and JM Blanquer (eds), *La responsabilité des gouvernants* (Paris, Descartes & Cie, 1999) 7–14.

Beetham, D, *Parliament and democracy in the twenty-first century: A guide to good practice* (Geneva, Inter-Parliamentary Union, 2006).

Belorgey, JM, *Le Parlement à refaire* (Paris, Gallimard, 1991).

Benedetto, G, 'The EU budget after Lisbon: Rigidity and reduced spending? (2013) 33 *Journal of Public Policy* 345.

Benton, M and Russell, M, 'Assessing the Impact of Parliamentary Oversight Committees: The Select Committees in the British House of Commons' (2013) 66 *Parliamentary Affairs* 772.

Benvenuti, M, 'Luci ed ombre della l n 145/2016 in tema di partecipazione dell'Italia alle missioni internazionali. Una prima lettura' (2017) 1 *Rivista AIC* 1.

Benz, A, 'Linking multiple demoi. Inter-parliamentary relations in the EU' (2011) 6 *IEV-Online* 1.

Benz, A and Broschek, J, *Nationale Parlamente in der europäischen Politik: Funktionen, Probleme und Lösungen* (Berlin, Friedrich-Ebert-Stiftung: Internationale Politikanalyse, 2010).

Bergman, T, 'Formation rules and minority governments' (1993) 23 *European Journal of Political Research* 55.

—— 'Constitution rules and party goals in coalition formation: an analysis of winning minority governments in Sweden' (Umeå, Umeå universitet, 1995).

—— 'When Minority Cabinets are the Rule and Majority Coalitions the Exception' in W Müller and K Strøm (eds), *Coalition Governments in Western Europe* (Oxford, Oxford University Press, 2000) 193–225.

Bergman, T and Damgaard, E (eds), *Delegation and Accountability in European Integration: The Nordic Parliamentary Democracies and the European Union* (London, Frank Cass, 2000).

Bergman, T, Müller, WC and Strøm, K, 'Democratic Delegation and Accountability: Cross-national Patterns' in T Bergman, WC Müller and K Strøm (eds), *Delegation and Accountability in Parliamentary Democracies* (Oxford, Oxford University Press, 2003) 109–220.

Besselink, L, 'National Parliaments in the EU's Composite Constitution: A Plea for a Shift in Paradigm' in P Kiiver (ed), *National and Regional Parliaments in the European Constitutional Order* (Groningen, Europa Law Publishing, 2006) 117–31.

—— *A Composite European Constitution* (Groningen, Europa Law Publishing, 2007).

—— 'Parameters of Constitutional Development: The Fiscal Compact in between EU and Member States Constitutions' in LS Rossi and F Casolari (eds), *The EU after Lisbon: Amending or Coping with the Existing Treaties?* (Heidelberg, Springer, 2014) 21–37.

Besselink, L and Reestman, JH, 'The Fiscal Compact and the European Constitutions: "Europe Speaking German"' (2012) 8 *European Constitutional Law Review* 1.

Beuve-Méry, H, 'De la dictature temporaire au régime semi-présidentiel' *Le Monde* (8 January 1959), now in D Colas and C Émeri (eds), *Droit, institutions et systèmes politiques: mélanges en hommage à Maurice Duverger* (Paris, PUF, 1988) 533–40.

Beyme, K von, 'Does the Constitution Need Remorming?' in O Petersson et al (eds), *Democracy the Swedish Way* (Stockholm, SNS Forlag, 1999) 17–46.

—— *Parliamentary Democracy* (Basingstoke, Macmillan, 2000).

Bickerton, J, Hodson, D and Puetter, U (eds), *The New Intergovernmentalism. States and Supranational Actors in the Post-Maastricht Era* (Oxford, Oxford University Press, 2015).

Birch, AH, *Representative and Responsible Government. An Essay on the British Constitution* (Toronto, University of Toronto Press, 1969).

Bird, K, 'Gendering Parliamentary Questions' (2005) 7 *The British Journal of Politics and International Relations* 353.

Birnbaun, P, Hamon, F and Troper, M, *Reinventer le parlement* (Paris, Flammarion, 1978).

Blachèr, P, *Le Parlement en France* (Paris, LGDJ, 2012).

Blackburn, R and Kennon, A et al, *Griffith and Ryle on Parliament: Functions, Practice and Procedures* (London, Sweet & Maxwell, 2003).

Blavoukos, S, Bourantonis, D and Pagoulatos, G, 'A President for the European Union: A New Actor in Town' (2007) 45 *Journal of Common Market Studies* 231.

Blick, A, *The Codes of the Constitution* (Oxford, Hart Publishing, 2016).

Blischke, W, 'Parliamentary Staff in the German Bundestag' (1981) 6 *Legislative Studies Quarterly* 533.

Blondel, J, *Comparative Legislatures* (Englewood Cliffs, NJ, Prentice-Hall, 1973).

Bluntschi, M, *Théorie générale de l'Etat*, fr trad (Paris, Librairie Guillaumin, 1877).

Bochel, H and Defty, A, '"A More Representative Chamber": Representation and the House of Lords' (2012) 18 *The Journal of Legislative Studies* 82.

—— 'Parliamentary Oversight of Intelligence Agencies: Lessons from Westminster' in AW Neal (ed), *Security in a Small Nation: Scotland, Democracy, Politics* (Cambridge, Open Book Publishers, 2017) 103–24.

Bodenheim, DG, *Kollision parlamentarischer Kontrollrechte. Zum verfassungsrechtlichen Verhältnis von parlamentarischem Frage – und Untersuchungsrecht* (Hamburg, Joachim Heitmann, 1979).

Bogdandy, A von, 'The European Lesson for International Democracy: The Significance of Articles 9–12 EU Treaty for International Organizations' (2012) 23 *European Journal of International Law* 315.

Bogdandy, A von, Cruz Villalón, P and Huber, PM (eds), *Handbuch Ius Publicum Europaeum*, I (Heidelberg, Müller, 2007).

Bogdanor, V, 'The Government Formation Process in the Constitutional Monarchies of North-West Europe' in D Kavanagh and G Peele (eds), *Comparative Government and Politics: Essays in Honour of SE Finer* (London, Heinemann, 1984) 49–72.

—— 'Ministerial accountability' (1997) 50 *Parliamentary Affairs* 71.

—— 'Legitimacy, accountability and democracy in the European Union' (2008) *A Federal Trust Report* 1.

Bonghi, R, 'Dei limiti del potere di inchiesta nelle Assemblee' (1869) 11 *Nuova Antologia* 822.

Born, H, Fluri, PH and Lunn, S (eds), *Oversight and guidance: the relevance of parliamentary oversight for the security sector and its reform. A collection of articles on foundational aspects of parliamentary oversight of the security sector* (Brussels, DCAF and NATO Parliamentary Assembly, 2003).

Born, H and Leigh, I, *Making Intelligence Accountable: Legal Standards and Best Practice for Oversight of Intelligence Agencies* (Oslo, Parliament of Norway, 2005).

Boronska-Hryniewiecka, K, 'Legitimacy through Subsidiarity? The Parliamentary Control of EU Policy-making' (2013) 1 *Polish Political Science Review* 84.

Borring Olesen, T, 'Denmark in Europe 1973–2015: Processes of Europeanization and "Denmarkization"' (2015) 11 *Journal of Contemporary European Research* 321.

Boudet, F, 'La force juridique des résolutions parlementaires' (1958) 2 *Revue de droit publique* 271.

Bouhadana, I, *Les commission des finances des assemblées parlementaires en France: origines, évolutions et enjeux* (Paris, LDGH, 2007).

Boulet, L, 'La notion de fonction administrative' (1966) 113 *La Revue administrative* 474.

Bouvier, M, Esclassan, MC and Lassale, JP, *Finances Publiques*, 18th edn (Paris, LGDJ, 2019).

Bovens, M, *The Quest for Responsibility: Accountability and Citizenship in Complex Organisations* (Cambridge, Cambridge University Press, 1998).

—— 'Analysing and Assessing Accountability: A Conceptual Framework' (2007) 13 *European Law Journal* 447.

Bovens, M, Curtin, D and 't Hart, P, *The Real World of EU Accountability. What Deficit?* (Oxford, Oxford University Press, 2010).

Bradley, AW and Ewing, KD, *Constitutional and Administrative Law*, 15th edn (London, Longman, 2011).

Bradley, AW and Pinelli, C, 'Parliamentarism' in M Rosenfeld and A Sajó (eds), *The Oxford Handbook of Comparative Constitutional Law* (Oxford, Oxford University Press, 2012) 650–70.

Bragaglia, A, *Il sindacato parlamentare, principi, norme, forme: studio giuridico e politico* (Torino, Casa Editrice Nazionale, 1903).

Brana, P, 'Retour sur la Mission d'information parlementaire française sur les événements de Srebrenica (2001)' (2007) 65 *Culture & Conflicts* 51.

Brazier, A, 'Post-Legislative Scrutiny' (2017) 8 *Global Partners Governance, Guide to Parliaments* 1.

Brazier, A and Ram, V, *The Fiscal Maze. Parliament, Government and Public Money* (London, Hansard Society, 2006).

Broglie, A de, *Vues sur le Gouvernement de la France* (Paris, Michel Levy Frères, 1870).

Brunclik, A, 'Patterns of Government Formation in Europe: the Role of the Head of State' (2015) 1 *Czech Journal of Political Science* 26.

Brunner, M and Debus, M, 'Between Programmatic Interests and Party Politics: The German Bundesrat in the Legislative Process' (2008) 17 *German Politics* 232.

Bruyneel, G, 'Interpellations, Questions and Analogous Procedures for the Control of Government Actions and Challenging the Responsibility of the Government' (1978) *Constitutional and Parliamentary Information* 66.

Budge, I, 'Great Britain and Ireland: Variations on Dominant Party Govenment' in JM Colomer (ed), *Political Institutions in Europe*, 3rd edn (London, Routledge, 2008) 17–57.

Budge, I and Keman, H, *Parties and Democracy. Coalition Formation and Government Functioning in Twenty States* (Oxford, Oxford University Press, 1990).

Bulmer, E, *Government Formation and Removal Mechanisms* (Stockholm, International IDEA, 2017).

Búrca, G de, 'The principle of subsidiarity and the Court of Justice as an institutional actor' (1998) 36 *Journal of Common Market Studies* 217.

Burdüau, G, *Traité de Science Politique* (Paris, Librairie Genérale de Droit et de Jurisprudence, 1976).

Burgess, M and Tarr, GA, 'Introduction: Sub-national Constitutionalism and Constitutional Development' in M Burgess and GA Tarr (eds), *Constitutional Dynamics in Federal Systems: Sub-national Perspectives* (Montreal, McGill-Queen's University Press, 2012).

Busch, E, *Parlamentarische Kontrolle. Ausgestaltung und Wirkung* (Heidelberg, Decker und Müller, 1983).

Bustos Gisbert, R, *La responsabilidad política del Gobierno: Realidad o ficción?* (Madrid, Colex, 2001).

Busuioc, M, *European Agencies. Law and Practices of Accountability* (Oxford, Oxford University Press, 2013).

Butler, D, *Governing without a Majority. Dilemmas for Hung Parliaments in Britain* (Basingstoke, Macmillan, 1987).

—— 'Hung Parliaments: Context and Background' in A Brazier and S Kalitowski (eds), *No Overall Control: The Impact of a 'Hung Parliament' on British Politics* (London, Hansard Society, 2008) 7–13.

Caiden, GE, 'The Problem of Ensuring the Public Accountability of Public Officials' in JG Jabbra and OP Dwivedi (eds), *Public Service Accountability: A Comparative Perspective* (West Hartford, CT, Kumarian, 1989) 17–38.

Calabresi, SG and Yoom, CS, *The Unitary Executive. Presidential Power from Washington to Bush* (New Haven, CT, Yale University Press 2008).

Califano Placci, L, *Le commissioni parlamentari bicamerali nella crisi del bicameralismo italiano* (Milano, Giuffrè, 1993).

Calmette, JF, 'L'évaluation des politiques publiques: un moyen de control de l'action du gouvernement' in X Magnon et al (eds), *Pouvoir exécutif et Parlement: de nouveaux équilibres?* (Aix-en-Provence, PUAM, 2012) 91–121.

Calmfors, L, 'The role of fiscal rules, fiscal councils, and fiscal union in the EU integration' in H Badinger and V Nitsch (eds), *Routledge Handbook of the Economics of European Integration* (Abingdon, Routledge, 2015) 157–70.

Cameron, I, 'Swedish Parliamentary Participation in the Making and Implementation of Treaties' (2005) 74 *Nordic Journal of International Law* 429.

Campbell, CC and Auerswald, DP (eds), *Congress and Civil-Military Relations* (Washington DC, Georgetown University Press, 2015).

Campbell, S and Laporte, J, 'The Staff of the Parliamentary Assemblies in France' (1981) 6 *Legislative Studies Quarterly* 521.

Cane, P, *Controlling Administrative Power: An Historical Comparison* (Cambridge, Cambridge University Press, 2016).

Capitant, R, 'L'aménagement du pouvoir exécutif et la question du chef de l'État' in *Encyclopédie française. Tome X: L'État* (Paris, Société nouvelle de l'Encyclopédie française, 1964) 142–63.

Capuano, D and Griglio, E, 'La nuova *governance* economica europea. I risvolti sulle procedure parlamentari italiane' in A Manzella and N Lupo (eds), *Il sistema parlamentare euro-nazionale. Lezioni* (Torino, Giappichelli, 2014) 225–63.

Carcassonne, G, 'La primauté de l'élection présidentielle: rapports entre les consultations populaires. La leçon des résultats' in N Wahl and JL Quermonne (eds), *La France présidentielle: l'influence du suffrage universel sur la vie politique* (Paris, Presses de Sciences Po, 1995) 31–45.

—— 'Faut-il maintenir la jurisprudence issue de la décision n 74-54 DC du 15 janvier 1975?' (1999) 7 *Cahiers du Conseil constitutionnel* 93.

Carcassonne, G and Guillaume, M, *La Constitution*, 14th edn (Paris, Seuil, 2017).

Carcelle, P and Mas, G, 'Les pouvoirs du Parlement en matière financière' (1959) 68 *La Revue administrative* 122.

Carducci, M, 'Controllo parlamentare e "autonomia" politica del governo' (1993) 41 *Studi Parmensi* 53.

—— *Controllo parlamentare e teorie costituzionali* (Padova, Cedam, 1996).

Caretti, P, 'La legge n 234/2012 che disciplina la partecipazione dell'Italia alla formazione e all'attuazione della normativa e delle politiche dell'Unione europea: un traguardo o ancora una tappa intermedia?' (2012) 5–6 *Le Regioni* 837.

Carey, MP, *Presidential Appointment, the Senate's Confirmation Process, and Changes Made in the 112th Congress* (Washington DC, Congressional Research Service, 2012).

Caringella, F, *Manuale di diritto amministrativo*, III, 11th edn (Roma, Dike Giuridica, 2016).

Carmona Contreras, AM, 'Decreto-ley y relaciones internacionales: una compatibilidad constitucionalmente problemática' (2000) 110 *Revista de Estudios Políticos* 59.

Carré de Malberg, R, *Contribution à la Théorie Générale de l'Etat*, II (Paris, Recueil Sirey, 1929).

Carstairs, C and Ware, R (eds), *Parliament and International Relations* (Bristol, Open University Press, 1991).

Casalena, P, Lupo, N and Fasone, C, 'Commentary on Protocol No 1 annexed to the Treaty of Lisbon (On the role of National Parliaments)' in HJ Blanke and S Mangiameli (eds), *The Treaty on European Union* (Berlin, Springer, 2013) 1529–634.

Casamassima, V, *L'opposizione parlamentare: le esperienze britannica ed italiana a confronto* (Pisa, Il Campano, 2008).

Cascajo, JL, 'El Congreso de los Diputados y la forma de gobierno en Espana' in A Martinez (ed), *El Congreso de los Diputados* (Madrid, Tecnos, 2000) 21–36.

Cassese, A, 'Articolo 80' in G Branca (ed), *Commentario alla Costituzione. Articoli 76–82: La formazione delle leggi. Tomo II* (Bologna, Società editrice del Foro italiano, 1979) 150–96.

—— *Parlamento e politica estera: il ruolo delle Commissioni Affari esteri* (Padova, Cedam, 1982).

Cassese, S, 'Intervento' in Vv Aa, *L'altro potere in economia. La questione delle nomine negli enti pubblici* (Bari, De Donato, 1978) 185–89.

Cassese, S (ed), *Istituzioni di diritto amministrativo*, 5th edn (Milano, Giuffrè, 2015).

Cassese, S and Perez, R, *Istituzioni di Diritto Pubblico* (Roma, La Nuova Italia Scientifica, 1989).

Caygill, T, 'A Tale of Two Houses?' (2019) 2 *European Journal of Law Reform* 87.

Chalmers, D, 'Brexit and the renaissance of parliamentary authority' (2017) 19 *The British Journal of Politics and International Relations* 663.

Chamon, M, *EU Agencies: Legal and Political Limits to the Transformation of the EU Administration* (Oxford, Oxford University Press, 2016).

Chandernagor, A, *Un parlement pour quoi faire?* (Paris, Gallimard, 1967).

Chantebout, B (ed), *Le contrôle parlementaire* (Paris, La Documentation Française, 1998).

Chapus, R, *Droit administratif général*, I, 13th edn (Paris, Montchrestien, 1999).

Cheli, E, *Atto politico e funzione di indirizzo politico* (Milano, Giuffrè, 1968).

—— 'Articolo 89' in G Branca (ed), *Commentario alla Costituzione. Articoli 88–91: Il Presidente della Repubblica. Tomo II* (Bologna, Zanichelli, 1983) 96–148.

Chevallier, J, 'L'évaluation législative: un enjeu politique' in A Delcamp, JL Bergel and A Dupas, *Contrôle parlementaire et évaluation* (Paris, La Documentation française, 1995) 13–30.

Chiappinelli, C, 'La evoluzione del sistema dei controlli e la relazione sul rendiconto generale dello Stato' (2009) 2 *Rivista della Corte dei conti* 256.

Chimenti, C, *Il controllo parlamentare nell'ordinamento italiano* (Milano, Giuffrè, 1974).

—— 'Centralità e funzionalità del Parlamento' (1978) 4 *Democrazia e diritto* 627.

—— 'Le commissioni di inchiesta come organi bicamerali' in G De Vergottini, *Le inchieste delle assemblee parlamentari* (Rimini, Maggioli, 1985) 103–14.

Christiansen, T and Hefftler, C, 'Informal Politics in the EU' (2013) 51 *Journal of Common Market Studies* 1196.

Ciaurro, GF, 'Il controllo parlamentare sulle nomine negli enti pubblici' in GF Ciaurro, *Le istituzioni parlamentari* (Milano, Giuffrè, 1982) 130–63.

Ciaurro, L, 'Recenti sviluppi in materia di inchieste parlamentari' (1990) 4 *Nuovi Studi Politici* 95.

—— 'Maggioranza e opposizioni nelle procedure di controllo parlamentare: l'esperienza del Senato' in E Rossi (ed), *Maggioranza e opposizioni nelle procedure parlamentari* (Padova, Cedam, 2004).

Cobreros Mendazona, E, 'El status parlamentario como derecho fundamental' in Vv Aa, *Estudios sobre la Constitución española. Homenaje al profesor E Garcia de Enterrìa*, III (Madrid, Ed Civitas, 1991) 2125–84.

Coglianese, C, 'Administrative Law: The U.S. and Beyond' (2016) 1656 *Faculty Scholarship Paper* 1.

Constant, B, *De la responsabilité des ministres* (Paris, H Nicolle, 1815).

Colliard, JC, *Les régimes parlementaires contemporains* (Paris, Presses de la Fondation nationale des sciences politiques, 1978).

Colombo, P, 'La question du pouvoir exécutif dans l'évolution institutionelle et le débat politique révolutionnaire' (2000) 319 *Annales historiques de la Révolution française* 1.

Colomer, JM, 'Spain and Portugal: Rule by Party Leadership' in JM Colomer (ed), *Political Institutions in Europe*, 3rd edn (London, Routledge, 2008) 174–207.

Coombes, D, *The Power of the Purse: The Role of European Parliaments in Budgetary Decisions* (London, Allen and Unwin, 1976).

Cooper, I, 'A 'Virtual Third Chamber' for the European Union? National Parliaments after the Treaty of Lisbon' (2012) 35 *West European Politics* 441.

—— 'Parliamentary oversight of the EU after the crisis: on the creation of the "Article 13" Inter-parliamentary Conference' (2014) 21 SOG Working Paper Series 1.

—— 'The politicization of interparliamentary relations in the EU: Constructing and contesting the "Article 13 Conference" on economic governance' (2016) 14 *Comparative European Politics* 196.

—— 'A separate Parliament for the Eurozone? Differentiated Representation, Brexit, and the Quandary of Exclusion' (2017) 70 *Parliamentary Affairs* 655.

—— 'Is the Early Warning Mechanism a Legal or a Political Procedure? Three Questions and a Typology' in A Jonsson Cornell and M Goldoni (eds), *National and Regional Parliaments in the EU-Legislative Procedure Post-Lisbon* (Oxford, Hart Publishing, 2017) 18–49.

—— 'A New Form of Democratic Oversight in the EU: The Joint Parliamentary Scrutiny Group for Europol' (2018) 10 *Perspectives on Federalism* 184.

Cope, NL, 'Treaty law and national legislative politics' in W Sandholtz and CA Whytoc (eds), *Research Handbook on the Politics of International Law* (Cheltenham, Edward Elgar Publishing, 2017) 116–48.

Copeland, GW and Patterson, SC (eds), *Parliaments in the Modern World* (Ann Arbor, MI, Michigan University Press, 1997).

Coppola, G and Toniato, FS, 'La valutazione delle politiche pubbliche' in F Bassanini and A Manzella (eds), *Due Camere, un Parlamento: per far funzionare il bicameralismo* (Bagno a Ripoli, Passigli, 2017) 151–77.

Corbett, R, Jacobs, F and Shackleton, M, 'The European Parliament at Fifty: A View from the Inside' (2003) 41 *Journal of Common Market Studies* 353.

Corbett, R, Jacobs, F and Neville, D (eds), *The European Parliament*, 9th edn (London, John Harper, 2016).

Corbett, R, Jacobs, F and Shackleton, M (eds), *The European Parliament*, 8th edn (London, John Harper, 2011).

Cornu, G (ed), *Vocabulaire juridique*, 12th edn (Paris, PUF, 2018).

Costa, M, *The Accountability Gap in EU Law: Mind the Gap* (New York, Routledge, 2016).

Costa, O, *Le Parlement européen, assemblée deliberante* (Bruxelles, Editions de l'Université de Bruxelles, 2001).

Costa, O, Jabko, N, Lequesne, C and Magnette, P, 'La diffusion des mécanismes de contrôle dans l'Union européenne: vers une nouvelle forme de démocratie?' (2001) 51 *Revue française de science politique* 859.

Costa, O, Kerrouche, E and Magnette, P, 'Introduction. Le temps du parlementarisme désenchanté? Les parlements face aux nouveaux modes de gouvernance' in O Costa, E Kerrouche and P Magnette (eds), *Vers un renouveau du parlementarisme en Europe?* (Brussels, Ed de l'Université de Bruxelles, 2004) 9–32.

Cotta, M, 'Il sotto-sistema governo-parlamento' (1987) 2 *Rivista italiana di Scienza Politica* 241.

Cowie, G, 'Withdrawal Agreement Bills: Parliament's role in the future UK-EU relationship' (*Commons Library Insight*, 22 October 2019).

Crabbe, VCRAC, 'The ethics of legislative drafting' (2010) 36 *Commonwealth Law Bulletin* 11.

Craig, P, 'The Supreme Court, Prorogation and Constitutional Principle' (29 October 2019), forthcoming in (2019) 57 *Oxford Legal Studies Research Paper* 1.

Crawford, J, *Brownlie's Principles of Public International Law*, 8th edn (Oxford, Oxford University Press, 2012).

Creswell, JW, *Research Design: Qualitative, Quantitative, and Mixed Methods Approaches* (Thousand Oaks, CA, SAGE, 2014).

Crick, B, *The Reform of Parliament* (London, Weidenfeld and Nicolson, 1964).

Crisafulli, V, 'Per una teoria giuridica dell'indirizzo politico' (1939) 1–4 *Studi urbinati* 53, now in Crisafulli, V, *Prima e dopo la Costituzione* (Napoli, Editoriale Scientifica, 2015).

—— 'Aspetti problematici del sistema parlamentare vigente in Italia' (1958) 2 *Jus* 151.

Crombez, C, 'The Democratic Deficit in the European Union: Much Ado about Nothing?' (2003) 4 *European Union Politics* 101.

Crowe, R, 'The European Budgetary Galaxy' (2017) 13 *European Constitutional Law Review* 428.

Crum, B, 'Parliamentary accountability in multilevel governance: what role for parliaments in post-crisis EU economic governance?' (2017) 25 *Journal of European Public Policy* 268.

Crum, B and Curtin, D, 'The Challenge of Making European Union Executive Power Accountable' in S Piattoni (ed), *The European Union: Democratic Principles and Institutional Architectures in Times of Crisis* (Oxford, Oxford University Press, 2015) 63–87.

Crum, B and Fossum, JE, 'The Multilevel Parliamentary Field: a framework for theorizing representative democracy in the EU' (2009) 1 *European Political Science Review* 249.

Curreri, S, 'Riforme dei regolamenti parlamentari e forma di governo' in E Gianfrancesco and N Lupo (eds), *La riforma dei regolamenti parlamentari al banco di prova della XVI Legislatura* (Roma, LUP, 2009) 230–33.

Curtin, D, 'Betwixt and Between: Democracy and Transparency in the Governance of the European Union' in J Winter, D Curtin, A Kellerman and B de Witte (eds), *Reforming the Treaty on the European Union – The Legal Debate* (Maastricht, Kluwer Law International, 1996) 95–121.

—— 'Democracy, Transparency and Political Participation: Some Progress Post-Amsterdam' in V Deckmyn and I Thomson (eds), *Openness and Transparency in the European Union* (Maastricht, European Institute of Public Administration, 1998) 107–20.

—— 'Transparency and political participation in EU governance: A role for civil society?' (1999) 3 *Cultural Values* 445.

—— *Accumulated Executive Power in Europe. The 'Most Dangerous' Branch of Government in the European Union* (Amsterdam, Knaw Press, 2009).

—— *Executive Power of the European Union. Law, Practices, and the Living Constitution* (Oxford, Oxford University Press, 2009).

—— 'Challenging Executive Dominance in European Democracy' (2014) 77 *Modern Law Review* 12.

Curtin, D, Mair, P and Papadopoulos, I (eds), *Accountability and European Governance* (London, Routledge, 2012).

Curtin, D and Mendes, J, 'Transparence et Participation: des Principes Démocratiques Pour l'Administration de L'Union Européenne' (2011) 137–38 *Revue Française d'Administration Publique* 101.

Curtin, D and Wille, A (eds), *Meaning and Practice of Accountability in the EU Multi-Level Context* (Mannheim, Connex Report Series No 07, 2008).

Cygan, A, 'Collective Subsidiarity Monitoring by National Parliaments after Lisbon: The Operation of the Early Warning Mechanism' in M Trybus and L Rubini (eds), *The Treaty of Lisbon and the Future of European Law and Policy* (Cheltenham, Edward Elgar, 2012) 55–73.

—— *Accountability, Parliamentarism and Transparency in the EU* (Cheltenham, Edward Elgar, 2013).

—— 'Legal implications of economic governance for national parliaments' (2017) 70 *Parliamentary Affairs* 710.

Dahl, R, *Modern Political Analysis*, 5th edn (Englewood Cliffs, NJ, Prentice-Hall, 1991).

—— *On Democracy* (New Haven, CT, Yale University Press, 1998).

D'Amato, A, 'Possibilità e limiti delle inchieste parlamentari' (2002) 6 *Dike* 41.

Damgaard, E (ed), *Parliamentary Change in the Nordic Countries* (Oslo, Scandinavian University Press, 1992).

—— 'Parliamentary Questions and Control in Denmark' in M Wiberg (ed), *Parliamentary Control in the Nordic Countries* (Helsinki, Finnish Political Science Association, 1994) 44–76.

—— 'How Parties Control Committee Members' in H Döering (ed), *Parliaments and Majority Rule in Western Europe* (New York, St Martin's Press, 1995) 308–25.

—— 'Conclusion: The Impact of European Integration on Nordic Parliamentary Democracies' in T Bergman and E Damgaard (eds), *Delegation and Accountability in European Integration. The Nordic Parliamentary Democracies and the European Union* (London, Frank Cass, 2000) 151–69.

Damgaard, E and Jensen, H, 'Europeanisation of Executive–Legislative Relations: Nordic Perspectives' (2005) 11 *The Journal of Legislative Studies* 394.

Damgaard, E and Svensson, P, 'Who Governs? Parties and Policies in Denmark' (1989) 17 *European Journal of Political Research* 731.

Daugeron, B, 'La cohabitation et ses faux-semblants: réflexions sur le présidentialisme minoritaire' (2004) 1 *Revue du droit public* 67.

De Benedetto, M, Martelli, M and Rangone, N, *La qualità delle regole* (Bologna, Il Mulino, 2011).

Decaro, C and Lupo, N (eds), *Il 'dialogo' tra Parlamenti: obiettivi e risultati* (Roma, Luiss University Press, 2009).

De Feo, A, *A history of budgetary powers and politics in the EU: the Role of the European Parliament. Part II: the non-elected Parliament 1957–1978* (Luxembourg, Publications Office of the European Union, 2016).

De Giorgi, E and Verzichelli, L, 'Still a Difficult Budgetary Process? The Government, the Legislature and the Finance Bill' (2008) 13 *South European Society & Politics* 87.

Degni, M, *La decisione di bilancio nel sistema maggioritario* (Roma, Ediesse, 2004).

De Guttry, A, 'Participating in Peace-Keeping Operations: the Italian Decision-Making Process' in A De Guttry, *Italian and German Partecipation in Peace-Keeping: From Dual Approaches to Co-operation* (Pisa, ETS, 1996) 3–40.

Dehousse, R, 'European institutional architecture after Amsterdam: parliamentary system or regulatory structure?' (1998) 35 *Common Market Law Review* 595.

De Ioanna, P, 'La nuova cornice costituzionale: economia, istituzioni e dinamica delle forze politiche' in Vv Aa, *Il Filangieri. Quaderno 2011* (Napoli, Jovene, 2012) 45–79.

Delcamp, A, 'Le Conseil constitutionnel et le Parlement' (2004) 57 *Revue française de droit constitutionnel* 37.

—— 'La perception du contrôle parlementaire. Comment le rendre plus attractif?' (2010) 134 *Pouvoirs* 109.

Delcamp, A, Bergel, JL and Dupas, A, *Contrôle parlementaire et évaluation* (Paris, La Documentation française, 1995).

Dette-Koch, E, 'German Länder participation in European policy through the Bundesrat' in AB Gunlicks (ed), *German Public Policy and Federalism* (New York, Berghahn Books, 2003) 182–96.

De Vergottini, G, *Lo 'Shadow Cabinet'. Saggio comparativo sul rilievo costituzionale dell'opposizione nel regime parlamentare britannico* (Milano, Giuffrè, 1973).

De Vergottini, G, *Diritto costituzionale comparato* (Padova, Cedam, 1981).

De Vergottini, G, 'Limitazioni alla tutela giurisdizionale dei diritti e inchieste parlamentari' in G De Vergottini, *Le inchieste delle assemblee parlamentari* (Rimini, Maggioli, 1985) 191–222.

De Vrieze, F, *Principles of Post-Legislative Scrutiny by Parliaments* (London, Westminster Foundation for Democracy, 2018).

—— 'Introduction to Post-Legislative Study' (2019) 21 *European Journal of Law Reform* 84.

—— *Post-Legislative Scrutiny in Europe. How the oversight on the implementation of legislation by Parliaments in Europe is getting stronger* (London, Westminster Foundation for Democracy, 2019) 1–28.

De Winter, L, 'The Role of Parliament in Government Formation and Resignation' in H Döering (ed), *Parliaments and Majority Rule in Western Europe* (New York, St Martin's Press, 1995) 115–51.

Di Ciolo, V and Ciaurro, L, *Il diritto parlamentare nella teoria e nella pratica* (Milano, Giuffrè, 2013).

Dickmann, R, 'Profili costituzionali dell'inchiesta parlamentare' (2007) 3 *Diritto e società* 459.

—— 'Atti e attività parlamentari con funzione conoscitiva' in R Dickmann and S Staiano (eds), *Funzioni parlamentari non legislative e forma di governo. L'esperienza dell'Italia* (Milano, Giuffrè, 2008) 495–528.

—— 'La riforma della legislazione di finanza pubblica e del sistema del bilancio dello Stato e degli enti pubblici' (2010) 1 *Federalismi.it* 1.

Dickmann, R and Staiano, S (eds), *Funzioni parlamentari non legislative e forma di governo. L'esperienza dell'Italia* (Milano, Giuffrè, 2008).

—— *Le funzioni parlamentari non legislative. Studi di diritto comparato* (Milano, Giuffrè, 2009).

Diermeier, D and van Roozendaal, P, 'The duration of cabinet formation processes in western multi-party democracies' (1998) 28 *British Journal of Political Science* 609.

Díez-Picazo Giménez, ML, 'Actos de los procedimientos de control, impulso e información' in F Sáinz Moreno (ed), *Los actos del Parlamento (Instituciones de Derecho Parlamentario II)* (Vitoria, Parlamento Vasco, 1999) 135–56.

Dobbels, M and Neuhold, C, 'The Roles bureaucrats play: The input of European Parliament (EP) administrators into the ordinary legislative procedure: A case study approach' (2012) 35 *Journal of European Integration* 375.

Dodd, LC and Schott, RL, *Congress and the Administrative State* (New York, Wiley & Sons, 1979).

Döering, H (ed), *Parliaments and Majority Rule in Western Europe* (New York, St Martin's Press, 1995).

Döering, H, 'Time as a Scarce Resource: Government Control of the Agenda' in H Doering (ed), *Parliaments and Majority Rule in Western Europe* (New York, St Martin's Press, 1995) 223–46.

Dogliani, M, *Indirizzo politico. Riflessioni su regole e regolarità nel diritto costituzionale* (Napoli, Jovene, 1985).

—— 'Indirizzo politico' in *Digesto delle discipline pubblicistiche*, VIII (Torino, Utet, 1993) 244–59.

Dolzer, R et al, *Das parlamentarische Regierungssystem und der Bundesrat – Entwicklungsstand und Reformbedarf. Rechtliche Optimierungsgebote oder Rahmensetzungen für das Verwaltungshandeln?* (Berlin, Walter de Gruyter, 1999).

Donati, F, *La responsabilità politica dei ministri nella forma di governo italiana* (Torino, Giappichelli, 1997).

D'Onofrio, F, Le *indagini conoscitive delle commissioni parlamentari. Problemi e prospettive* (San Giorgio al Cremano, Istituto Grafico Italiano, 1971).

Dorey, P and Purvis, M, 'Representation in the Lords' in C Leston Bandeira and L Thompson (eds), *Exploring Parliament* (Oxford, Oxford University Press, 2018) 244–54.

Dosière, R, 'Le contrôle ordinaire' (2010) 134 *Pouvoirs* 37.

Draper, H, 'Marx on Democratic Forms of Government' (1974) *Social Register* 101.

Druckman, JN, Martin, LW and Thies, MF, 'Influence without Confidence: Upper Chambers and Government Formation' (2005) 30 *Legislative Studies Quarterly* 529.

Duguit, L, *Traité de droit constitutionnel*, II, 3rd edn (Paris, E de Boccard, 1928).

Dullien, S and Torreblanca, JI, 'What is the Political Union?' (2012) 70 *European Council on Foreign Relations* 1.

Dunleavy, P, Gilson, C, Bastow, S and Tinkler, J, *The National Audit Office, the Public Accounts Committee and the Risk Landscape in UK Public Policy* (London, LSE, 2009).

Dunleavy, P, Park, A and Taylor, R (eds), *The UK's Changing Democracy. The 2018 Democratic Audit* (London, LSE Press, 2018).

Duprat, JP, 'Le parlement évaluateur' (1998) 2 *Revue Internationale de Droit Comparé* 551.

—— 'Le Parlement entre modernisation et attentisme (L'article 24 de la Constitution)' (2008) 254 *Les Petites affiches* 35.

Duverger, M, *Institutions politiques et droit constitutionnel*, 11th edn (Paris, Presses Universitaires de France, 1970).

—— *La monarchie républicaine* (Paris, Robert Laffont, 1974).

—— 'A new political system model: semi-presidential government' (1980) 8 *European Journal of Political Research* 165.

Dux, G, *Bundesrat und Bundesaufsicht* (Duncker & Humblot, Berlin, 1963).

Easterbrook, FH, 'Legal Interpretation and the Power of the Judiciary' (1984) 7 *Harvard Journal of Law and Public Policy* 87.

Egeberg, M, Gornitzka, A, Trondal, J and Johannessen, M, 'Parliament staff: Unpacking the behaviour of officials in the European Parliament' (2012) 20 *Journal of European Public Policy* 495.

Egeberg, M and Trondal, J, 'Researching European Union Agencies: What Have We Learnt (and Where Do We Go from Here)? (2017) 55 *Journal of Common Market Studies* 657.

Eichenberger, K, 'Die Problematik der parlamentarischen Kontrolle im Verwaltungsstaat' (1965) 18 *Schweizerische Juristen-Zeitung* 269.

Eig, LM, 'Statutory Interpretation: General Principles and Recent Trends' (2011) 7-5700 *Congressional Research Service* 1.

Elia, L, 'Governo (forme di)' in *Enciclopedia del diritto*, XIX (Milano, Giuffrè, 1970).

Elliott, M, 'Analysis/The Supreme Court's Judgment in Miller' (*Public Law for Everyone*, 25 January 2017).

—— 'The Supreme Court's judgment in Miller: in search of constitutional principle' (2017) 76 *Cambridge Law Journal* 257.

Ely, JH, *Democracy and Distrust: A Theory of Judicial Review* (Cambridge, MA, Harvard University Press, 1980).

Embid Irujo, A, 'El control parlamentario del gobierno en la jurisprudencia del Tribunal constitucional' (1991) 31 *Revista Vasca de Administración Pública* 179.

—— 'El control parlamentario y el principio de la mayoria parlamentaria' (1992) 25 *Revista de las Cortes Generales* 7.

Emmerling, S, *Kontrolle im parlamentarischen Regierungssystem der Bundesrepublik Deutschland* (Kiel, Grin, 2004).

Epstein, LD, 'Parliamentary Government' in *International Encyclopedia of the Social Sciences*, II (New York, Macmillan, 1968) 419–26.

Erkkilä, T, *Government Transparency. Impacts and Unintended Consequences* (New York, Palgrave, 2012).

Eskens, S, Daalen, O van and Eijk, N van, *Ten standards for oversight and transparency of national intelligence services* (Amsterdam, Institute for Information Law, 2015).

Eskridge, WN, 'All About Words: Early Understandings of the "Judicial Power" in Statutory Interpretation, 1776–1806' (2001) 1516 *Columbia Law Review Faculty Scholarship Series* 990.

Esmein, A, *Eléments de droit constitutionnel*, 1st edn (Paris, Larose et Forcel, 1896).

—— *Éléments de Droit Français et comparé*, I (Paris, Recueil Sirey, 1927).

Esposito, A, 'La legge n 234/2012 sulla partecipazione dell'Italia alla formazione e all'attuazione della normativa e delle politiche dell'Unione europea. Parte I – Prime riflessioni sul ruolo delle camere' (2013) 1 *Federalismi.it* 1.

Eugéne, P, *Traité de Droit politique, electoral et parlementaire*, 5th edn (Partis, Librairies Imprimeries Reunies, 1919).

Evans, PB, Jacobson, HK and Putnam, RD (eds), *Double-edged Diplomacy: International Bargaining and Domestic Politics* (Berkeley, CA, University of California Press, 1993).

Evans, M and Zimmermans, A, 'Editors' Conclusions: Future Directions for Subsidiarity' in M Evans and A Zimmermans (eds), *Global Perspectives on Subsidiarity* (Wiesbaden, Springer, 2014) 221–23.

Fabbrini, S, 'Governare l'Italia: il rafforzamento dell'esecutivo tra pressioni e resistenze, Governare le democrazie. Esecutive, leader e sfide' in *Il Filangieri. Quaderno 2010* (Napoli, Jovene, 2011) 33–54.

—— 'Intergovernmentalism and its Limits: Assessing the European Union's Answer to the Euro Crisis' (2013) 46 *Comparative Political Studies* 1003.

—— 'The European Union and the puzzle of parliamentary government' (2015) 37 *Journal of European Integration* 571.

—— *Which European Union?* (Oxford, Oxford University Press, 2015).

Fabbrini, F, Ballin, EH and Somsen, F, 'Introduction: A New Look at the Form of Government of the European Union and the Eurozone' in F Fabbrini, EH Ballin and F Somsen (eds), *What Form of Government for the European Union and the Eurozone?* (Oxford, Hart Publishing, 2015) 1–16.

Fabbrini, F and Granat, K, '"Yellow card, but no foul": The role of the national parliaments under the Subsidiarity Protocol and the Commission proposal for an EU regulation on the right to strike' (2013) 50 *Common Market Law* Review 115.

Fasone, C, *Sistemi di commissioni parlamentari e forme di governo* (Padova, Cedam, 2008).

—— 'Qual è la fonte più idonea a recepire le novità del Trattato di Lisbona sui Parlamenti nazionali' (2010) 3 *Osservatorio sulle fonti* 1.

—— 'Gli effetti del Trattato di Lisbona sulla funzione di controllo parlamentare' (2011) 2 *Rivista italiana di diritto pubblico comunitario* 353.

—— 'Le commissioni parlamentari come "categoria a sè stante" di comitati' in Vv Aa, *Le autonomie in cammino. Scritti dedicati a Gian Candido De Martin* (Padova, CEDAM, 2012) 329–48.

—— 'Towards New Procedures between State and Regional Legislatures in Italy, Exploiting the Tool of the Early Warning System' (2013) 5 *Perspectives on Federalism* 122.

—— 'European Economic Governance and Parliamentary Representation. What Place for the European Parliament?' (2014) 20 *European Law Journal* 164.

—— 'What is a legislature in the twenty-first century? Classification and evolution of a contested notion' (2019) 15 *Federalismi.it* 1.

Fasone, C and Griglio, E, 'Can Fiscal Councils Enhance the Role of National Parliaments in the European Union? A Comparative Analysis' in B de Witte, A Héritier and AH Trechsei (eds), *The Euro Crisis and the State of European Democracy* (Florence, EUI, 2013) 264–305.

Fasone, C and Lupo, N, 'Constitutional Review and The Powers of National Parliaments in EU Affairs. Erosion or Protection?' in D J Jančić (ed), *National Parliaments after the Lisbon Treaty and the Euro Crisis. Resilience or Resignation?* (Oxford, Oxford University Press, 2017) 59–75.

—— 'The Union Budget and the Budgetary Procedure' in R Schütze and T Tridimas (eds), *Oxford Principles of European Union Law. The European Legal Order*, I (Oxford, Oxford University Press, 2018) 809–46.

Fasone, C and Piccirilli, G, 'Le procedure euro-nazionali' in F Bassanini and A Manzella (eds), *Due Camere, un Parlamento. Per fare funzionare il bicameralismo* (Firenze, Passigli, 2017) 87–95.

Favoreu, L and Philip, L, *Les grandes décisions du Conseil constitutionnel*, 14th edn (Paris, Dalloz, 2007).

Fearon, JD, 'Electoral accountability and the control of politicians: Selecting Food Types Versus Sanctioning Poor Performance' in A Przeworski, SC Stokes and B Manin (eds), *Democracy, Accountability, and Representation* (Cambridge, Cambridge University Press, 1999) 55–97.

Feldman, D, 'Brexit, the Royal Prerogative, and Parliamentary Sovereignty' (*UK Constitutional Law Blog*, 8 November 2016).

Ferejohn, J, 'Accountability and Authority: Toward a Theory of Political Accountability' in A Przeworski, SC Stokes and B Manin (eds), *Democracy, Accountability, and Representation* (Cambridge, Cambridge University Press, 1999) 131–53.

Férnandez-Fontecha Torres, M, 'Un Gobierno en funciones: su responsabilidad. Comentario a la Sentencia del Tribunal Constitucional 124/2018 de 14 de noviembre, en el conflicto entre órganos constitucionales 3102-2016 (B.O.E. núm.301, de 14 de diciembre 2018)' (2019) 106 *Revista de las Cortes Generales* 595.

Fernández Sarasola, I, 'El control parlamentario y su regulación en el ordenamiento español' (2000) 60 *Revista Española de Derecho Constitucional* 89.

—— 'Dirección política y función del gobierno en la Historia constitucional' (2003) 4 *Revista Electrónica de Historia Constitucional*.

Ferrara, G, 'Bicameralismo e riforme del Parlamento' (1981) 21 *Democrazia e diritto* 11.

—— 'Articolo 55' in G Branca (ed), *Commentario alla Costituzione. Articoli 55–63: Le Camere. Tomo I* (Bologna, Zanichelli, 1984) 1–42.

Ferri, G, 'I sistemi elettorali delle Camere dopo le sentenze della Corte costituzionale (n 1/2014 e n 35/2017) e la legge n 165/2017' (2017) 3 *Osservatorio sulle fonti* 1.

Filippetta, G, 'L'illusione ispettiva: le interrogazioni e le interpellanze parlamentari tra ricostruzioni dottrinali, rappresentanza politica e funzione di indirizzo' (1991) 36 *Giurisprudenza costituzionale* 4203.

—— 'Il controllo parlamentare e le trasformazioni della rappresentanza politica' (2014) *Rivista AIC* 1.

Finer, H, 'The Individual Responsibility of Ministers' (1956) *Public Administration* 377.

Finke, D and Herbel, A, 'Coalition Politics and Parliamentary Oversight in the European Union' (2018) 53 *Government and Opposition* 388.

Finke, D and Melzer, M, *Parliamentary Scrutiny of EU Law Proposals in Denmark: Why do Governments request a Negotiation Mandate?* (Vienna, Institute for Advanced Studies, 2012).

Finnis, J, *The Unconstitutionality of the Supeme Court's Prorogation Judgment* (London, Policy Exchange, 2019).

Fisler Damrosch, L and Murphy, SD, *International Law: Cases and Materials*, 6th edn (St Paul, MN, West Academic Publishing, 2014).

Fitsilis, F and Koutsogiannis, A, 'Strengthening the Capacity of Parliaments through Development of Parliamentary Research Services' (2017) Paper presented at the 13th Workshop of Parliamentary Scholars and Parliamentarians, Wroxton.

Fitzmaurice, J, 'National parliaments and European policy-making: The case of Denmark' (1976) 76 *Parliamentary Affairs* 281.

—— 'The European Commission' in A Duff, J Pinder and R Pryce (eds), *Maastricht and beyond: building the European Union* (London, Routledge, 1994) 183–90.

Flinders, M, *The Politics of Accountability in the Modern State* (Aldershot, Ashgate Publishing, 2001).

—— 'Shifting the Balance? Parliament, the Executive and the British Constitution' (2002) 50 *Political Studies* 23.

Follesdal, A and Wind, M, 'Introduction – Nordic Reluctance towards Judicial Review under Siege' (2009) 27 *Nordisk Tidsskrift for Menneskerettigheter* 131.

Font, N, 'Designing Accountability Regimes at the European Union Level' in AC Bianculli, X Fernández-i-Marín and J Jordana (eds), *Accountability and Regulatory Governance. Audiences, Controls and Responsibilities in the Politics of Regulation* (London, Palgrave, 2015) 123–42.

Forsberg, A, 'Contribution to the General Debate on "The work of parliamentary committees"' (2008) Paper presented at the Meeting of the Association of Secretary Generals of Parliament, Cape Town, April 2008.

Foster, N and Sule, S, *German Legal System and Laws* (Oxford, Oxford University Press, 2010).

Fouilleux, E, Maillard, J de and Smith, A, 'Technical or political? The working groups of the EU Council of Ministers' (2005) 12 *Journal of European Public Policy* 609.

Fox, R and Korris, M, *Making Better Law. Reform of the Legislative process from Policy to Act* (London, Hansard Society, 2010).

Frangi, M, 'Les lois mémorielles: de l'expression de la volonté générale au législateur historien' (2005) 1 *Revue du droit public* 241.

Franklin, M and Norton, P (eds), *Parliamentary Questions* (Oxford, Clarendon Press, 1993).

Friedel, A, *Blackbox Parlamentarisches Kontrollgremium des Bundestages. Defizite und Optimierungsstrategien bei der Kontrolle der Nachrichtendienste* (Berlin, Springer, 2019).

Friedrich, CJ, *Constitutional Government and Democracy: Theory and Practice in Europe and America*, 4th edn (Waltham, MA, Blaisdell, 1968).

Friesenhahn, E, 'Die politischen Grundlagen des Bonner Grundgesetzesin' in H Wandersleb (ed), *Recht, Staat, Wirtschaft*, II (Dusseldorf, Schwann, 1950) 164–82.

Friesenhahn, E et al (eds), *Parlement und Regierung in modernen Staat. Die Organisationsgewalt* (Berlin, Walter de Gruyter, 1966).

Fromage, D, *Les Parlements dans l'Union Européenne après le Traité de Lisbonne – La Participation des Parlements allemands, britanniques, espagnols, français et italiens* (Paris, Harmattan, 2015).

—— 'European Economic Governance and Parliamentary Involvement: Some Shortcomings of the Article 13 Conference and A Solution' (2016) 1 *Les Cahiers européens de Sciences Po* 1.

—— 'Increasing Interparliamentary cooperation in the EU: Current Trends and Challenges' (2016) 22 *European Public Law* 749.

—— 'Regional Parliaments and the early warning system: an assessment six years after the entry into force of the Lisbon Treaty' (2016) 33 SOG Working Papers 1.

—— 'Creation and Reform of Independent Fiscal Institutions in EU Member States: Incomplete and Insufficient Work in Progress?' in T Beukers, B de Witte and C Kilpatrick (eds), *Constitutional Change through Euro-Crisis Law* (Oxford, Oxford University Press, 2017) 108–42.

—— 'A comparison of existing forums for interparliamentary cooperation in the EU and some lessons for the future' (2018) 10 *Perspectives on Federalism* 1.

Fromage, D and Hérranz-Surallés, A (eds), *Executive–Legislative (Im)balance in the European Union* (Oxford, Hart Publishing, forthcoming).

Fromage, D and Ibrido, R, 'Democratic Accountability and Parliamentary Oversight over the ECB. The Banking Union Experience' (2016) 40 SOG Working Papers 1.

Fromage, D and Kreilinger, V, 'National parliaments' third yellow card and the struggle over the revision of the posted workers directive' (2017) 10 *European Journal of Legal Studies* 125.

Furlong, P, 'Institutional fragmentation in parliamentary control: the Italian case' (2004) 10 *Journal of Legislative Studies* 174.

Fuzier-Herman, E, *La séparation des pouvoirs d'après l'histoire et le droit constitutionnel* (Paris, Librairie de A Marescq Ainé, 1880).

Gailmard, S and Patty, JW, 'Slackers and Zealots: Civil Service, Policy Discretion, and Bureaucratic Expertise' (2007) 51 *The American Journal of Political Sciencè* 873.

Galeazzi, P, 'Le interrogazioni parlamentari al Governo' (1918) 10 *Rivista di diritto pubblico e della pubblica amministrazione in Italia* 72.

Galeotti, S, 'Controlli costituzionali' in *Enciclopedia del Diritto*, X (Milano, Giuffrè, 1962) 319–48.

—— *Introduzione alla teoria dei controlli costituzionali* (Milano, Giuffrè, 1963).

Galizia, M, *Studi sui rapporti fra Parlamento e Governo*, I (Milano, Giuffrè, 1972).

Gallagher, M, Laver, M and Mair, P, *Representative Government in Western Europe* (London, Mc-Graw Hill, 1992).

Ganghof, S and Stecker, C, 'Investiture Rules in Germany: Stacking the Deck against Minority Government' in BE Rasch, S Martin and JA Cheibub (eds), *Parliaments and Government Formation: Unpacking Investiture Rules* (Oxford, Oxford University Press, 2015) 67–85.

García Fernández, J, 'El control parlamentario desde la perspectiva del Gobierno' (1997) 2 *Cuadernos de Derecho Público* 195.

García Morillo, J, 'Control parlamentario' in JJ González Encinar (ed), *Diccionario del sistema político español* (Madrid, Akal, 1984) 145–56.

—— *El control parlamentario del Gobierno en el ordenamiento español* (Madrid, Congreso de los Diputados, 1985).

——— 'Aproximación a un concepto del control parlamentario' (1986) 10 *Revista de la Facultad de Derecho de la Universidad Complutense* 31.

García Morillo, J and Montero, JR, *El control parlamentario* (Madrid, Tecnos, 1984).

García Roca, FJ, 'El control del Gobierno desde la perspectiva individual del parlamentario (y a la luz del art 23.2 de la Constitución)' (1995) 42 *Revista Vasca de Administración Publica* 161.

——— 'Del principio de la división de poderes' (2000) 108 *Revista de Estudios Politicos* 41.

——— 'Control parlamentario y convergencia entre presidencialismo y parlamentarismo' (2016) 38 *Teoría y Realidad Constitucional* 61.

——— 'Puede rechazar el control parlamentario un Gobierno en funciones?' in E Aranda Álvarez (ed), *Lecciones constitucionales de 314 días con el Gobierno en funciones* (Barcelona, Tirant lo Blanch, 2017) 131–50.

García Roca, FJ and Ibrido, R, 'El control parlamentario en Italia. Un estudio comparado sobre el concepto y algunas de sus mejores prácticas: el Comité para la legislación y la Comisión de presupuestos' in F Pau i Vall (ed), *El control del Gobierno en democracia* (Madrid, Tecnos, 2013) 105–36.

Garner, JF, 'The British Ombudsman' (1968) 18 *University of Toronto Law Journal* 158.

Garrett, J, *Westminster: Does Parliament Work?* (London, Gollancz, 1992).

Garritzmann, JL, 'How much power do opposition have? Comparing the opportunity structures of parliamentary oppositions in 21 democracies' (2017) 23 *The Journal of Legislative Studies* 1.

Gattermann, K and Hefftler, C, 'Political motivation and institutional capacity: assessing national parliaments' incentives to participate in the early warning mechanism' (2013) 15 *OPAL Online Paper Series* 1.

Gaudin, JP, *La démocratie participative* (Paris, Armand Collin, 2007).

Gehrig, N, *Parlament – Regierung – Opposition. Dualismus als Voraussetzung für eine parlamentarische Kontrolle der Regierung* (München, Beck, 1969).

Gertler, PJ, Martinez, S, Premand, P, Rawlings, LB and Vermeersch, CJ, *Impact evaluation in Practice*, 2nd edn (Washington, World Bank Institute, 2016).

Geslot, C, Monjal PY and Rossetto, J (eds), *La responsabilité politique des exécutifs des États membres du fait de leur action européenne* (Brussels, Bruylant, 2016).

Ghevontian, R, 'La révision de la Constitution et le Président de la République: l'hyperprésidentialisation n'a pas eu lieu' (2009) 70 *Revue française de droit constitutionnel* 119.

Gianfrancesco, E, 'La riforma del regolamento del Senato: alcune osservazioni generali' (2018) 1 *Federalismi.it* 1.

Giannini, MS, 'Controllo: nozioni e problemi' (1974) 4 *Rivista trimestrale di diritto pubblico* 1263.

Gianniti, L, 'The 2016 Attempted Reform of the Italian Senate in a European Perspective' in N Lupo and G Piccirilli (eds), *The Italian Parliament in the European Union* (Oxford, Hart Publishing, 2017) 305–16.

Giddings, P, 'Select Committees and Parliamentary Scrutiny: Plus Ça Change?' (1994) 47 *Parliamentary Affairs* 669.

Gil-Robles y Gil-Delgado, JM and Marín Riaño, F, 'Naturaleza jurídica del control sobre el Gobierno y la Administración' in Vv Aa, *Gobierno y Administración en la Constitución*, I (Madrid, Instituto de Estudios Fiscales, 1988) 729–46.

Gill, P, 'Evaluating intelligence oversight committees: The UK intelligence and security committee and the "war on the terror"' (2007) 22 *Intelligence and National Security* 14.

Giménez Sánchez, IM, 'Indirizzo politico, dirección política, impulso político: el papel del Parlamento' (2008) 18 *Revista Jurídica de la Universidad de Madrid* 83.

Ginsburg, T and Huq, AZ, *How to Save a Constitutional Democracy* (Chicago, IL, University of Chicago Press, 2018).

Giulj, S, *Le Statut de l'Opposition en Europe* (Paris, La Documentation française, 1980).

——— 'Confrontation or Conciliation: the Status of the Opposition in Europe (1981) 16 *Government and Opposition* 476.

Gneist, R, *L'amministrazione e il diritto amministrativo inglese*, III (Torino, Unione Tipografico-editrice, 1896).

Golder, M, Golder, S and Siegel, DA, 'Modeling the Institutional Foundations of Parliamentary Government Formation' (2012) 74 *Journal of Politics* 427.

Goldoni, M, 'The Early Warning System and the Monti II Regulation: The Case for a Political Interpretation' (2014) 10 *European Constitutional Law Review* 90.

——— 'Politicising EU Lawmaking? The Spitzenkandidaten Experiment as a Cautionary Tale' (2016) 22 *European Law Journal* 279.

Goldoni, M and Jonsson Cornell, A, 'The Trajectory of the Early Warning System' in A Jonsson Cornell and M Goldoni (eds), *National and Regional Parliaments in the EU-Legislative Procedure Post-Lisbon* (Oxford, Hart Publishing, 2017) 335–55.

Gordon, S, *Controlling the State: Constitutionalism from Ancient Athens to Today* (Cambridge, MA, Harvard University Press, 1999).

Goretti, C and Rizzuto, L, 'Il ruolo del Parlamento italiano nella decisione di bilancio: evoluzione recente e confronto con gli altri paesi' (2011) 1–3 *Rivista di politica economica* 29.

Götz, F, 'Das Informationsungleichgewicht zwischen Regierung, Verwaltung und Parlament' (1988) 33 *Publizistik. Vierteljahresschrift für Kommunikationsforschung* 633.

Gouet, Y, 'Qu'est-ce que le Régime Parlamentaire' (1932) *Revue de Droit Public* 179.

Granat, K, *The Principle of Subsidiarity and its Enforcement in the EU Legal Order. The Role of National Parliaments in the Early Warning System* (Oxford, Hart Publishing, 2018).

Grandguillaume, N, *Théorie générale du contrôle* (Paris, Economica, 1994).

—— 'Le demande de contrôle' (2000) 318 *La Revue Administrative* 641.

Griffith, JAG, *The Politics of the Judiciary* (Manchester, Manchester University Press, 1977).

—— 'The Common Law and the Political Constitution' (2001) 117 *Law Quarterly Review* 42.

Griglio, E, 'The Europeanization of Regional Assemblies: A Comparison between Different Ways of Approaching the Representative Challenge in EU Affairs' in D Friedrich and S Kröger (eds), *Representation in the European Union: Coping with present challenges to democracy?* (London, Palgrave, 2012) 192–209.

—— 'Il "nuovo" controllo parlamentare sulla finanza pubblica: una sfida per i "nuovi" regolamenti parlamentari' (2013) 1 *Osservatoriosullefonti* 1.

—— 'I Parlamenti dell'Unione europea alla prova di Europol: verso un esercizio "collettivo" del controllo parlamentare?' (2016) 3 *Quaderni costituzionali* 548.

—— 'Better Law-Making and the Integration of Impact Assessment in the Decision-Making Process: The Role of National Parliaments' in A De Feo and B Laffan (eds), *Scrutiny of EU Policies* (Fiesole, European University Institute, 2017) 63–94.

—— 'I poteri di controllo del Parlamento italiano alla luce del bicameralismo paritario' in Vv Aa, *Il Filangieri. Quaderno 2015–2016. Il Parlamento dopo il referendum costituzionale* (Napoli, Jovene, 2017) 199–238.

—— 'I seguiti parlamentari della nuova legge quadro sulle missioni internazionali' (2017) 2 *Quaderni costituzionali* 397.

—— 'Procedures vis-à-vis the European Parliament and the Other National Parliaments: Inter-parliamentary Cooperation' in N Lupo and G Piccirilli (eds), *The Italian Parliament in the European Union* (Oxford, Hart Publishing, 2017) 195–214.

—— 'I circuiti e i "buchi neri" del controllo parlamentare sull'esecutivo frammentato dell'Unione europea' in R Ibrido and N Lupo (eds), *La forma di governo dell'Unione europea* (Bologna, Il Mulino, 2018) 207–33.

—— 'La funzione di controllo' (e il rapporto con le pubbliche amministrazioni)' (2019) 1 *Rassegna di diritto pubblico europeo* 31.

—— 'Post-Legislative Scrutiny as a Form of Executive Oversight. Tools and Practices in Europe' (2019) 2 *European Journal of Law Reform* 118.

—— 'Divided Accountability of the Council and the European Council. The Challenge of Collective Parliamentary Oversight' in D Fromage and A Hérranz-Surallés (eds), *Executive–Legislative (Im)balance in the European Union* (Oxford, Hart Publishing, forthcoming).

Griglio, E and Lupo, N, 'Parliamentary democracy and the Eurozone crisis' (2012) 1 *Law and Economics Yearly Review* II, 313.

—— 'Towards an asymmetric European Union, without an asymmetric European Parliament' (2014) 20 SOG Working Papers 1.

—— 'Inter-parliamentary Cooperation in the EU and outside the Union: Distinctive Features and Limits on the European Experience' (2018) 10 *Perspectives on Federalism* 56.

Griglio, E and Stavridis, S, 'Inter-parliamentary cooperation as a means for reinforcing joint scrutiny in the EU: upgrading existing mechanisms and creating new ones' (2018) 10 *Perspectives on Federalism* 1.

—— 'Joint scrutiny of EU policies: the contribution of interparliamentary cooperation' (2018) 10 *Perspectives on Federalism* 1.

Grimheden, J, 'The Self-reflective Human Rights Promoter' in J Grimheden and R Ring (eds), *Human Rights Law: From Dissemination to Application. Essays in Honour of Göran Melander* (Leiden, Martinus Nijhoff Publishers, 2006) 119–28.

Grogan, J, 'The Rule of Law, not the Rule of Politics: Commentary on the Cherry/Miller No 2 Judgment' (*Reconnect*, 8 October 2019).

Gröhe, H and Naundorf, S, 'Bürokratieabbau und bessere Rechtsetzung, Eckpunkte, Erfahrungen und Perspektiven' (2009) 24 *Zeitschrift für Gesetzgebung* 367.

Guerin, B, McCrae, J, and Shepheard, M, 'Accountability in modern government: what are the issues? A discussion paper' (London, Institute for Government, 2018).

Guidi, M, 'Modelling the Relationship Between Independence and Accountability of Regulatory Agencies' in AC Bianculli, X Fernández-i-Marín and J Jordana (eds), *Accountability and Regulatory Governance. Audiences, Controls and Responsibilities in the Politics of Regulation* (London, Palgrave, 2015) 105–22.

Gulmann, C, 'The Position of International Law within the Danish Legal Order' (1983) 52 *Nordisk Tidsskrift for International Ret* 45.

Gunlicks, A, *The Länder and German Federalism* (Manchester, Manchester University Press, 2003).

Gustavsson, S, Karlsson, C and Persson, T (eds), *The Illusion of Accountability in the European Union* (New York, Routledge, 2009).

Gusy, C, 'Privatisierung und parlamentarische Kontrolle' (1998) 31 *Zeitschrift für Rechtspolitik* 265.

Hayek, F von, Law, *Legislation and Liberty. A New Statement of the Liberal Principles of Justice and Political Economy*, III (London, Routledge, 1979).

Hayes-Renshaw, F and Wallace, H, 'Executive power in the European Union: The functions and limits of the Council of Ministers' (1995) 2 *Journal of European Public Policy* 559.

Hamon, L, '[Note sous decision n° 64-27 DC]' (1966) *Recueil Dalloz* 17.

Hamon, F and Troper, M, *Droit constitutionnel*, 26th edn (Paris, LGDJ, 1999).

Hamon, L and Emeri, C, 'Les pouvoirs d'enquête du Parlement' (1962) 2 *Revue de droit public* 270.

Happacher, E, 'Extra-legislative Functions of Second Chambers in Federal Systems' (2018) 10 *Perspectives on Federalism* 134.

Harlow, C, 'Freedom of Information and Transparency as Administrative and Constitutional Rights' (1999) 2 *Cambridge Yearbook of European Legal Studies* 285.

—— *Accountability in the European Union* (Oxford, Oxford University Press, 2002).

Harlow, C and Rawlings, R, 'Promoting Accountability in Multi-Level Governance: A Network Approach' (2007) 13 *European Law Journal* 542.

Harrington, J, 'Scrutiny and Approval: the Role of Westminster-style Parliaments in Treaty-Making' (2006) 55 *International and Comparative Law Quarterly* 121.

Harris, JP, *Congressional Control of Administration* (Washington DC, Brookings Institution, 1964).

Hauriou, M, *Précis de droit administratif: contenant le droit public et le droit administratif* (Paris, Larose, 1892).

—— *Précis de Droit Constitutionnel*, 2nd edn (Paris, Recueil Sirey, 1929).

Hatje, A, 'The Economic Constitution within the Internal Market' in A von Bogdandy and J Bast (eds), *Principles of European Constitutional Law* (Oxford, Hart Publishing, 2010) 589–625.

Hatschek, J, *Das Interpellationsrecht im Rahmen der modern Ministerverantwortlichkeit* (Leipzig, GJ Göschen, 1909).

Hazell, R and Young, B, *The Politics of Coalition: How the Conservative–Liberal Democrat Government Works* (London, Bloomsbury Publishing, 2012).

Hefftler, C and Gattermann, K, 'Interparliamentary Cooperation in the European Union: Patterns, Problems and Potential' in C Hefftler, C Neuhold, O Rozenberg and J Smith (eds), *The Palgrave Handbook of National Parliaments and the European Union* (London, Palgrave, 2015) 94–115.

Hefftler, C and Wessels, W, 'The Democratic Legitimacy of the EU's Economic Governance and National Parliaments' (2013) 13 IAI Working Papers 1.

Hegeland, H and Neuhold, C 'Parliamentary participation in EU affairs in Austria, Finland and Sweden: Newcomers with different approaches' (2002) 6 *European Integration Online Papers* 6.

Hegemann, H, 'Towards "normal" politics? Security, parliaments and the politicization of intelligence oversight in the German Bundestag' (2018) 20 *The British Journal of Politics and International Relations* 175.

Héritier, A, 'Elements of democratic legitimation in Europe: an alternative perspective' (1999) 6 *Journal of European Public Policy* 269.

Hermán, V and Mendel, F (eds), *Parliaments of the World* (London, Macmillan, 1976).

Hérranz-Surrallés, A, 'The EU's Multilevel Parliamentary (Battle)Field: Inter-Parliamentary Cooperation and Conflict in Foreign and Security Policy' (2014) *West European Politics* 957.

Herrero, M, 'El Estado de partidos y la vida parlamentaria' in M Ramirez (ed), *El Parlamento a debate* (Madrid, Trotta, 1997) 45–58.

Herreros, R, 'L'accord de cogestion sur l'îlot Tromelin retiré de l'ordre du jour de l'Assemblée nationale' (*Huffington Post politique*, 17 January 2017).

Herreros López, JM, 'El control parlamentario del Gobierno en funciones. Comentario de la STC 124/2018, de 14 de noviembre' (2019) 6 *Actualidad administrativa* 1.

Herzog, R, 'Der Bundesrat' in J Isensee and P Kirchhof (eds), *Handbuch des Staatsrechts der Bundesrepublik Deutschland*, III (Heildelberg, Müller, 2008) 943–90.

Heun, W, 'Artikel 107' in H Dreier (ed), *Grundgesetz Kommentar. Band III: Artikel 83–146* (Tübingen, Mohr Siebeck, 2008) 803.

Hintze, O, 'Preussens Entwicklung zum Rechtstaat' (1920) in O Hintze, *Geist und Epochen der preussichen Geschichte*, III (Leipzig, Koehler & Amelang, 1943).

Hix, S, *The Political System of the European Union* (London, Macmillan, 1999).

—— 'Executive Selection in the European Union; Does the Commission President Investiture Procedure Reduce the Democratic Deficit?' in K Neunreither and A Wiener (eds), *European Integration After Amsterdam: Institutional Dynamics and Prospects for Democracy* (Oxford, Oxford University Press, 2000).

Hobolt, S, 'A vote for the President? The Role of *Spitzenkandidaten* in the 2014 European Parliament elections' (2014) 21 *Journal of European Public Policy* 1528.

Hochedez, D, 'La mission d'évaluation et de côntrole (MEC). Une volonté de retour aux sources du Parlement: la défense du citoyen-contribuable' (1999) 68 *Revue française de finances publiques* 261.

Högenauer, AL, Neuhold, C and Christiansen, T (eds), *Parliamentary Administrations in the European Union* (Basingstoke, Palgrave, 2016).

Hogwood, BW, 'Autonomía burocrática y responsabilidad' (1999) 15 *Gestion y Análisis de Políticas Públicas* 19.

Höing, O, 'Differentiation of Parliamentary Powers. The German Constitutional Court and the German Bundestag within the Financial Crisis' (2009) 9 *OPAL Online Paper Series* 1.

—— 'Differentiation of Parliamentary Powers. The German Constitutional Court and the German Bundestag within the Financial Crisis' M Cartabia, N Lupo and A Simoncini (eds), *Democracy and Subsidiarity in the EU. National Parliaments, Regions and Civil Society in the Decision-Making Process* (Bologna, Il Mulino, 2013) 259–83.

—— 'With a little Help from the Constitutional Court. The Bundestag on its way to an Active Policy-shaper' in C Hefftler, C Neuhold, O Rozenberg and J Smith (eds), *The Palgrave Handbook of National Parliaments and the European Union* (Basingstoke, Palgrave, 2015) 191–208.

Hönle, R, 'Bundesrat und Europapolitik – kein kontrollfreier Raum. Eine Replik auf Erich Röper' (2009) 40 *Zeitschrift für Parlamentsfragen* 683.

Horne, A and Le Sueur, A (eds), *Parliament. Legislation and Accountability* (Oxford, Hart Publishing, 2016).

Horvath, M, 'EU Independent Fiscal Institutions: An Assessment of Potential Effectiveness' (2018) 56 *Journal of Common Market Studies* 504.

Houillon, P, 'Le contrôle extraordinaire du parlement' (2010) 134 *Pouvoirs* 59.

Howart, D, 'On Parliamentary Silence' (*UK Constitutional Law Blog*, 13 December 2016).

Huntington, SP, 'Congressional Responses to the Twentieth Century' in DB Truman (ed), *The Congress and America's Future* (Englewood Cliffs, NJ, Prentice Hall, 1965).

Ibrido, R, *L'Unione bancaria europea. Profili costituzionali* (Torino, Giappichelli, 2017).

Ihalainen, P, Ilie, C and Palonen, K, 'Parliament as a Conceptual Nexus' in P Ihalainen, C Ilie and K Palonen (eds), *Parliament and Parliamentarism: A Comparative History of a European Concept* (New York, Berghahan, 2016).

Ismayr, W, 'Jahre Parlamentarismus in der Bundesrepublik Deutschland' (1999) 20 *Aus Politik und Zeitgeschichte* 14.

—— *Der Deutsche Bundestag im politischen System der Bundesrepublik Deutschland*, 2nd edn (Stuttgard, UTB, 2001).

Jacobs, F, 'EU Agencies and the European Parliament' in M Everson, C Monda and E Vos (eds), *European Agencies in between Institutions and Member States* (Alphen aan den Rijn, Kluwer Law International, 2014) 201–28.

Jančić, D, 'The Game of Cards: National Parliaments in the EU and the Future of the Early Warning Mechanism and the Political Dialogue' (2015) 52 *Common Market Law Review* 939.

—— (ed), *National Parliaments after the Lisbon Treaty and the Euro Crisis: Resilience or Resignation?* (Oxford, Oxford University Press, 2017).

Janssen, A, *Über die Grenzen des legislativen Zugriffsrechts* (Tübingen, Mohr, 1990).

Jeffery, C, 'Party politics and territorial representation in the Federal Republic of Germany' (1999) 22 *West European Politics* 130.

Jeney, P, *The Future of Eurojust* (Brussels, European Parliament – Directorate for Citizens' Rights and Constitutional Affairs, 2012).

Jennings, I, *Cabinet Government*, 2nd edn (Cambridge, Cambridge University Press, 1951).

Jensen, H, 'Committees as Actors or Arenas? Putting Questions to the Danish Standing Committees' in M Wiberg (ed), *Parliamentary Control in the Nordic Countries* (Jyväskylä, The Finnish Political Science Association, 1994) 77–102.

Jensen, TK, 'Party Cohesion' in P Esaiasson and K Heidar (eds), *Beyond Westminster and Congress. The Nordic Experience* (Columbus, OH, Ohio State University Press, 2000) 210–36.

Jerneck, M, A Sannerstedt and M Sjdlin, 'Internationalization and Parliamentary Decision-making: The Case of Sweden 1970–1985' (1988) 11 *Scandinavian Political Studies* 169.

JHR and WTE, 'Watching Karlsruhe/Karlsruhe Watchers' (2012) 8 *European Constitutional Law Review* 367.

Jiménez Campo, J, 'Sobre el control parlamentario en Comisión' in Vv Aa, *Política y sociedad. Homenaje al profesor Murillo Ferrol* (Madrid, CIS-CEC, 1987) 477–92.

Johnson, JK, 'The Role of Parliament in Government' (2005) WBI Working Papers 1.

Johnson, J and Stapenhurst, R, 'Legislative Budget Offices: International Experience' in R Stapenhurst, R Pelizzo, D Olson and L von Trapp (eds), *Legislative Oversight and Budgeting: A World Perspective* (Washington DC, World Bank, 2008) 141–57.

Johnson, N, 'Committees in the West German Bundestag' in JD Lees and M Shaw (eds), *Committees in Legislatures: A Comparative Analysis* (Oxford, Martin Robertson, 1979) 102–47.

—— 'Territory and Power: Some Historical Determinants of the Constitutional Structure of the Federal Republic of Germany' in C Jeffery (ed), *Recasting German Federalism* (London, Pinter, 1999) 23–40.

—— *State & Government in the Federal Republic of Germany: Executive at Work*, 2nd edn (Oxford, Pergamon Press, 2016).

Juberías, CF, 'Spain: Delegation and Accountability in a Newly Established Democracy' in K Strøm, W Müller and T Bergman (eds), *Delegation and Accountability in Parliamentary Democracies* (Oxford, Oxford University Press, 2003) 573–93.

Judge, D and Earnshaw, D, 'The European Parliament and the Commission Crisis: A new assertiveness?' (2002) 15 *Governance: An International Journal of Policy, Admninistration, and Institutions* 345.

Kaarbo, J and Kenealy, D, 'Precedents, Parliaments and Foreign Policy; Historical Analogy in the House of Commons Vote on Syria' (2017) 40 *West European Politics* 62.

Kaiser, FM, 'Congressional Oversight of the Presidency' (1988) 499 *The Annals of the American Academy of Political and Social Science* 75.

Kaiser, FM, Oleszek, WJ and Tatelman, TB, *Congressional Oversight Manual* (Washington DC, Congressional Oversight Service, 2011).

Kam, CJ, *Party Discipline and Parliamentary Politics* (Cambridge, Cambridge University Press, 2009).

Kanis, AM (ed), *Parliamentary Control of Budget Implementation* (Brussels, European Parliament, 2012).

Karlas, J, 'National Parliamentary Control of EU Affairs: Institutional Design after Enlargement' (2012) 35 *West European Politics* 1095.

Karpen, U, 'Comparative Law: Perspectives of Legislation' (2003) 17 *Anuario Iberoamericano de Justicia Constitucional* 141.

—— 'On the State of Legislation Studies in Europe' (2005) 7 *European Journal of Law Reform* 59.

—— 'Good Governance through Transparent Application of the Rule of Law' (2009) 11 *European Journal of Law Reform* 213.

—— 'Regulatory Impact Assessment: Current Situation and Prospects in the German Parliament' (2015) 101 *Amicus Curiae* 14.

—— 'Introduction' in U Karpen and H Xanthaki (eds), *Legislation in Europe. A Comprehensive Guide for Scholars and Practitioners* (Oxford, Hart Publishing, 2017) 1–16.

Katsaitis, A and Eriksen, A, 'Accountability through Mutual Attunement: Parliamentary Hearings & Agency Oversight in the European Union (2019) Paper prepared for EUSA, Denver, 9–11 May 2019.

Katz, R, 'Party Government: A Rationalistic Conception' in F Castles and R Wildenmann (eds), *The Future of Party Government. Vol I: Visions and Realities of Party Government* (Berlin, De Gruyter, 1987) 31–71.

Kelly, R and Everett, M, 'Post-Legislative Scrutiny' (2013) SN/PC/05232 *UK House of Commons Library Standard Note* 1–16.

Kelsen, H, *General Theory of Law and State* (Cambridge, MA, Harvard University Press, 1945).

Kelso, A, 'Reforming the House of Lords: Navigating Representation, Democracy and Legitimacy at Westminster' (2006) 59 *Parliamentary affairs* 563.

—— *Parliamentary Reform at Westminster* (Oxford, Oxford University Press, 2009).

Kennedy, KC, 'Conditional Approval of Treaties by the US Senate' (1996) 19 *Loyola International & Comparative Law Journal* 89.

Kenny, C, Rose, D, Hobbs, A, Tyler, C and Blackstock, J, *The Role of Research in the UK Parliament*, I (London, Houses of Parliament, 2017).

Kepplinger, HM, 'Kleine Anfragen: Funktionale Analyse einer parlamentarischen Praxis' in JW Patzelt, M Sebaldt and U Kranenpohl (eds), *Res publica semper reformanda. Wissenschaft und politische Bildung im Dienste des Gemeinwohls. estschrift für Heinrich Oberreuter* (Wiesbaden, VS Verlag für Sozialwissenschaften, 2007) 304–19.

Khandker, SR, Koolwal GB and Hussain, AS, *Handbook on Impact Evaluation: Quantitative Methods and Practices* (Washington, World Bank, 2010).

Kiewiet, DR and McCubbins, MD, *The Logic of Delegation* (Chicago, IL, University of Chicago Press, 1991).

Kiiver, P, *The National Parliaments in the European Union: A Critical View on EU Constitution-building* (The Hague, Kluwer Law, 2006).

—— 'German Participation in EU Decision-Making after the Lisbon Case: A Comparative View on Domestic Parliamentary Clearance Procedures' (2009) 10 *German Law Journal* 1287.

—— *The Early Warning System for the Principle of Subsidiarity: Constitutional Theory and Empirical Reality* (New York, Routledge, 2012).

Kimmel, A, *L'Assemblée nationale sous la Cinquième République* (Paris, Presses de Sciences Po, 1991).

King, A, 'Modes of Executive–Legislative Relations: Great Britain, France, and West Germany' (1976) 1 *Legislative Studies Quarterly* 11.

Kloepfer, M, *Verfassungsrecht*, I (München, Beck, 2011).

Kohler, M, 'European Governance and the European Parliament: From Talking Shop to Legislative Powerhouse' (2014) 52 *Journal of Common Market Studies* 600.

Korver, R (ed), *EU Agencies, Common Approach and Parliamentary Scrutiny* (Brussels, European Parliamentary Research Service, 2018).

Kouroutakis, A, *The Constitutional Value of Sunset Clauses: An Historical and Normative Analysis* (New York, Routledge, 2017).

Krafchik, W and Wehner, J, 'The role of Parliament in the budget process' (2005) 66 *South African Journal of Economics* 242.

Krause, J, 'Der Bedeutungswandel parlamentarischer Kontrolle: Deutscher Bundestag und US-Kongreß im Vergleich' (1999) 30 *Zeitschrift für Parlamentsfragen* 534.

Krebs, W, *Kontrolle in staatlichen Entscheidungsprozessen. Ein Beitrag zur rechtlichen Analyse von gerichtlichen, parlamentarischen und Rechnungshof-Kontrollen* (Heildelberg, Muller, 1984).

Kreilinger, V, 'The new inter-parliamentary conference for economic and financial governance' (2013) 100 Notre Europe – Jacques Delors Institute Policy Paper 1.

—— *National Parliaments, Surveillance Mechanisms and Ownership in the EuroArea* (Berlin, Jacques Delors Institute Studies and Report, 2016).

—— 'A Watchdog over Europe's policemen: the new Joint Parliamentary Scrutiny Group for Europol' (2017) 197 Jacques Delors Institute Policy Paper 1.

Kreilinger, V and Larhant, M, 'Does the Eurozone Need a Parliament?' (2016) 176 Jacques Delors Institute Policy Paper 1.

Kreppel, A, 'Moving beyond procedure. An empirical analysis of European Parliament legislative influence' (2002) 35 *Comparative Political Studies* 784.

—— 'Understanding the European Parliament from a Federalist Perspective: The Legislatures of the United States and the European Union Compared' in A Menon and MA Schain (eds), *Comparative Federalism. The European Union and the United States in Comparative Perspective* (Oxford, Oxford University Press, 2006) 245–74.

Kretschmer, G, 'Enquete-Kommissionen – ein Mittel politischer Problemlösung? in HH Hartwich (ed), *Gesellschaftliche Probleme als Anstoß und Folge von Politik* (Wiesbaden, VS Verlag für Sozialwissenschaften, 1983) 261–74.

Kriner, D and Schwartz, L, 'Divided Government and Congressional Investigations' (2008) 33 *Legislative Studies Quarterly* 295.

Kubicek, P, *European Politics*, 2nd edn (New York, Routledge, 2017).

Kumm, M, Witte, B de and Maduro, M, 'The Euro-crisis and the democratic governance of the Euro' (2012) 8 RSCAS Paper 1.

Laband, P, *Das Budgetrech nach den Bestimmungen der Preussichen Verfassungsurkunde* (Berlin, Guttentag, 1871).

—— *Des Staatsrecht des Deutschen Reiches*, I (Tubingen, Laupp, 1876).

Labriola, S, 'Il controllo parlamentare sulle nomine negli enti pubblici' (1980) 4 *Politica del diritto* 543.

Lachaume, JF, 'Jurisprudence française relative au droit international' (1999) 45 *Annuaire français de droit international* 842.

Ladrech, R, 'Europeanisation and Subnational Parliaments. A Research Perspective' in G Abels and A Eppler (eds), *Subnational Parliaments in the EU Multi-level Parliamentary System: Taking Stock of the Post-Lisbon Era* (Innsbruck, Studienverlag, 2016) 77–90.

Laferrière, E, *Traité de la jurisdiction administrative et des recours contentieux* (Paris, Berge-Levrault, 1896).

Lai, L, 'Il controllo parlamentare sul controllo estero del Governo: l'autorizzazione alla ratifica dei trattai internazionali in prospettiva comparata' in Vv Aa, *Il Parlamento della Repubblica: organi, procedure, apparati* 3 (Roma, Camera dei deputati, 2013) 999–1088.

Lambert, MA, 'Reinforcer le contrôle du Parlement sur l'exécutif' in OECD – Sénat, *Processus budgétaire. Vers un nouveau rôle du Parlement. Les actes du Réunion international des Présidents et Hauts responsables des commissions budgétaires des pays membres de l'OCDE, 24–25 janvier 2001* (Paris, Imprimerie du Sénat, 2002) 149–52.

Lang, A, 'Parliament's role in ratifying treaties' (2017) 5855 House of Commons Library Briefing Paper 1.

Larsson, T, Sweden: the New Constitution' in J Blondel and F Müller-Rommel (eds), *Cabinets in Western Europe* (London, Macmillan, 1988) 197–212.

—— 'How Open Can a Government Be? The Swedish Experience' in V Deckmyn and I Thomson (eds), *Openness and Transparency in the European Union* (Maastricht, European Institute of Public Administration, 1998) 39–52.

Lascombe, M and Vandendriessche, X, 'La loi organique relative aux lois de finances (LOLF) et le contrôle des finances publiques' (2006) 117 *Revue française de l'administration publique* 131.

Lasswell, HD and Kaplan, A, *Power and Society. A Framework for Political Inquiry* (New Haven, CT, Routledge, 1950).

Lathrop, D and Ruma, L, *Open Government: Collaboration, Transparency and Participation in Practice* (Beijing, O'Reilly, 2010).

Laursen, F, 'The role of national parliamentary committees in European scrutiny: Reflections based on the Danish case' (2005) 11 *The Journal of Legislative Studies* 412.

Lauvaux, P, *Destins du présidentialisme* (Paris, PUF, 2002).

—— 'Le contrôle, source du régime parlementaire, priorité du régime présidentiel' (2010) 134 *Pouvoirs* 23.

Laver, M, 'Overview: Legislatures and Parliaments in Comparative Context' in B Weingast and D Wittman (eds), *Oxford Handbook of Political Economy* (Oxford, Oxford University Press, 2008) 195–211.

Laver, M, Marchi, S de and Mutlu, H, 'Negotiation in Legislatures over Government Formation' (2011) 147 *Public Choice* 285.

Laver, M and Schofield, N, *Multiparty Government. The Politics of Coalitions in Europe* (Oxford, Oxford University Press, 1990).

Laver, M and Shepsle, KA (eds), *Cabinet Ministers and Parliamentary Government* (Cambridge, Cambridge University Press, 1994).

Laver, M and Shepsle, KA, *Making and Breaking Governments: Cabinets and Legislatures in Parliamentary Democracies* (Cambridge, Cambridge University Press, 1996).

Law, S, 'Article 50 and the Political Constitution' (*UK Constitutional Law Blog*, 18 July 2016).

Lazardeux, S, '"Une Question Ecrite, Pour Quoi Faire" The Causes of the Production of Written Questions in the French Assemblée Nationale' (2005) 3 *French Politics* 258.

Le Divellec, A, *Le gouvernement parlementaire en Allemagne. Contribution à une théorie générale* (Paris, LGDJ, 2004).

—— 'Le Gouvernement, portion dirigeante du Parlement. Quelques aspects de la réception juridique hésitante du modèle de Westminster dans les Etats européens' (2009) 1 *Jus Politicum* 185.

—— 'Des effets du contrôle parlementaire' (2010) 134 *Pouvoirs* 123.

—— 'La problématique du contrôle parlementaire de l'administration' in B Seiller (ed), *Le Contrôle parlementaire de l'administration* (Paris, Dalloz, 2010) 5–19.

Lees, JD, 'Legislatures and Oversight: A Review Article on a Neglected Area of Research' (1977) 2 *Legislative Studies Quarterly* 193.

Lees, JD and Shaw, M (eds), *Committees in Legislatures: A Comparative Analysis* (Oxford, Martin Robertson, 1979).

Leibholz, G, 'Die Kontrollfunktion des Parlaments' in *Macht und Ohnmacht der Parlamente* (Stuttgart, Friedrich-Naumann-Stiftung, 1965) 57–74.

Lejeune, Y, 'Participation of Sub-national Units in the Foreign Policy of the Federation' in R Blindenbacher and A Koller (eds), *Federalism in a Changing World: Learning from Each Other* (Montereal, McGill-Queen's University Press, 2003) 169–99.

Leonardy, U, 'The institutional structures of German federalism' (1999) Friedrich-Ebert-Stiftung Working Papers.

Le Pourhiet, AM, 'Le pouvoir de nomination du Chef de l'État contrôlé par le Parlement' in JP Camby, P Fraisseix and J Gicquel (eds), *La révision de 2008: une nouvelle Constitution?* (Paris, LGDJ, 2011) 57–69.

Leston Bandeira, C and Thompson, L (eds), *Exploring Parliament* (Oxford, Oxford University Press, 2018).

Levinson, DJ and Pildes, RH, 'Separation of Parties, Not Powers' (2006) 119 *Harvard Law Review* 2311.

Lewin, L, 'Majoritarian and Consensus Democracy: the Swedish Experience' (1998) 21 *Scandinavian Political Studies* 195.

Lewis, J, 'Is the Council becoming an Upper House?' in N Jabcko and C Parsons (eds), *The State of the European Union. Vol. 7. With US or Against US? European Trends in American Perspective* (Oxford, Oxford University Press, 2005) 145–57.

Leyland, P, 'The Westminster Parliament and Executive Accountability: The Oversight Function of Departmental Select Committees with Reference to the Millennium Dome and the David Kelly Affair' in E Rossi (ed), *Studi pisani sul Parlamento* (Pisa, Edizioni Plus, 2008) 409–24.

Liebert, U, 'The Centrality of Parliament in the Consolidation of Democracy: A Theoretical Exploration' (1989) 7 Political Science Institute Heidelberg – Working Paper 12.

Lienert, I, 'Who Controls the Budget: The Legislature or the Executive?' (2005) 5/115 IMF Working Paper 1.

Lienert, I and Jung, MK, 'Le cadre juridique des systèmes budgétaires. Une comparaison internationale' (2004) 4 *Revue de l'OCDE sur la gestion budgétaire* 1.

Lijphart, A, *Democracies. Patterns of Majoritarian and Consensus Government in Twenty-One Countries* (New Haven, CT, Yale University Press, 1984).

—— *Patterns of Democracy. Government Forms and Performance in Thirty-Six Countries*, 2nd edn (New Haven, CT, Yale University Press, 2012).

Limberger, G, *Die Kompetenzen des Bundesrates und ihre Inanspruchnahme* (Duncker & Humblot, Berlin, 1982).

Lin, NCN, 'Informative Committees and Legislative Performance in the American States' (2015) 40 *Legislative Studies Quarterly* 391.

Linares, A, 'La adhesión de España a la Otan: notas para una revisión crítica' (2013) 32 *Historia Actual Online* 23.

Lindblom, PE, 'The Role of the Supreme Courts in Scandinavia' (2000) 39 *Scandinavian Studies in Law* 325.

Lindseth, P, '"Weak" Constitutionalism? Reflections on Comitology and Transnational Governance in the European Union' (2001) 21 *Oxford Journal of Legal Studies* 145.

—— 'The Paradox of Parliamentary Supremacy: Delegation, Democracy and Dictatorship in Germany and France, 1920s–1950s' (2004) 49 *University of Connecticut School of Law Articles and Working Papers* 1341.

—— *Power and Legitimacy. Reconciling Europe and the Nation-State* (Oxford, Oxford University Press, 2010).

Lindseth, P, Aman, AC and Raul, AC, *Oversight* (Chicago, American Bar Association, 2008).

Lippolis, V, 'Indagini conoscitive' in *Enciclopedia giuridica*, XVI (Roma, Treccani, 1989) 1–6.

—— *La Costituzione italiana e la formazione dei trattati internazionali* (Rimini, Maggioli, 1989).

—— 'Parlamento e potere estero' in S Labriola (ed), *Il Parlamento repubblicano* (Milano, Giuffrè, 1999) 525–73.

—— 'Maggioranza, opposizione e governo nei regolamenti e nelle prassi parlamentari dell'età repubblicana' in L Violante (ed), *Il Parlamento. Storia d'Italia. Annale n 17* (Torino, Einaudi, 2001) 613–58.

—— 'La riforma del regolamento della Camera dei deputati del 1997 e il Parlamento del bipolarismo' in Vv Aa, *Il Parlamento del bipolarismo: un decennio di riforme dei regolamenti delle Camere. Il Filangieri – Quaderno 2007* (Napoli, Jovene, 2008) 5–26.

—— 'Il rapporto tra Corte dei conti e Parlamento e le prospettive della "valutazione delle politiche pubbliche"' (2009) 12 *Federalismi.it* 1.

Littré, E, *Dictionnaire de la langue française*, 1st edn (Paris, Hachette, 1973).

Loewenberg, G and Patterson, SC, *Comparing Legislatures* (Boston, Little, Brown and Company, 1979).

Loewenstein, K, *Political Power and the Governmental Process* (Chicago, IL, The University of Chicago Press, 1957).

Longhi, V, *Elementi di diritto e procedura parlamentare* (Milano, Giuffrè, 1982).

Longo, F, *Parlamento e politica estera: il ruolo delle commissioni* (Bologna, Il Mulino, 2011).

López Guerra, L, 'El control parlamentario como instrumento de las minorias' (1996) 8 *Anuario de derecho constitucional y parlamentario* 81.

Lord, C, 'The European Parliament, not a very European Parliament?' (2003) 9 *Politique européenne* 30.

Loughlin, M, 'The Contemporary Crisis of Constitutional Democracy' (2019) 39 *Oxford Journal of Legal Studies* 435.

—— *The Case of Prorogation, the UK's Constitutional Council Ruling on Appeal from the Judgment of the Supreme Court* (London, Policy Exchange, 2019).

Lowi, T and Ginsberg, B, *American Government: Freedom and Power* (London, WW Norton, 1996).

Luciani, M, 'Democrazia rappresentativa e democrazia partecipativa' in Vv Aa, *La sovranità popolare nel penisero di Esposito, Crisafulli, Paladin* (Padova, Cedam, 2004).

—— 'Funzione di controllo e riforma del Senato' (2016) 1 *Rivista AIC* 1.

—— 'Un giroscopio costituzionale. Il Presidente della Repubblica dal mito alla realtà (passando per il testo della costituzione)' (2017) 2 *Rivista AIC* 1.

Luhmann, N, *Legitimation durch Verfahren*, 6th edn (Frankfurt am Main, Suhrkamp, 2006).

Lupia, A, 'Delegation and its Perils' in K Strøm, W Müller and T Bergman (eds), *Delegation and Accountability in Parliamentary Democracies* (Oxford, Oxford University Press, 2003) 33–54.

Lupo, N, 'The Transformation of Parliamentary Functions: Are Parliaments Still Legislative Bodies?' in P Falconer, C Smith and CWR. Webster (eds), *Managing Parliaments in the 21st Century* (Amsterdam, Ios Press, 2001) 29–39.

—— 'A proposito della necessaria politicità del controllo parlamentare' (2002) 6 *Le istituzioni del federalismo* 959.

—— 'Alcuni dati e qualche considerazione sulle procedure (tradizionali e nuove) di controllo parlamentare' in E Rossi (ed), *Maggioranza e opposizioni nelle procedure parlamentari* (Padova, Cedam, 2004) 109–38.

—— 'Funkcja kontrolna parlamentu we Włoszech (La funzione di controllo parlamentare nell'ordinamento italiano)' in Z Witkowski, GC De Martin and KM Witkowska-Chrzczonowicz (eds), *Gwarancje konstytucyjne i srodki kontroli w panstwie demokratycznym z perspektywy dorobku konstytucyjnego Wloch i Polsi* (Torun, Tnoik, 2008) 105–48.

—— 'La persistente ispirazione proporzionalistica dei regolamenti parlamentari dal 1920 ad oggi' (2009) 8 *Ventunesimo Secolo, Il 'secolo breve' della democrazia italiana (1919–2008)* 77.

—— 'Le sessioni di bilancio, ieri e oggi' in G Carboni (ed), *La funzione finanziaria del Parlamento. Un confronto tra Italia e Gran Bretagna* (Torino, Giappichelli, 2009) 16–42.

—— 'National Parliaments in the European Integration Process: Re-aligning Politics and Policies' in M Cartabia, N Lupo and A Simoncini (eds), *Democracy and Subsidiarity in the EU. National Parliaments, Regions and Civil Society in the Decision-Making Process* (Bologna, Il Mulino, 2013) 108–31.

—— 'Parlamento europeo e Parlamenti nazionali nella Costituzione "composita" dell'Unione europea: le diverse letture possibili' in A Ciancio (ed), *Nuove strategie per lo sviluppo democratico e l'integrazione politica in Europa* (Roma, Aracne, 2014) 365–96.

—— 'La riforma del 20 dicembre 2017 del (solo) regolamento del Senato, nella faticosa ricerca di un'omogeneità regolamentare tra i due rami del Parlamento' (2017) 50 *Studi parlamentari e di politica costituzionale* 23.

—— 'The Scrutiny of the Principle of Subsidiarity in the Procedures and Reasoned Opinions of the Italian Chamber and Senate' in AJ Cornell Jonsson and M Goldoni (eds), *National and Regional Parliaments in the EU-Legislative Procedure Post-Lisbon. The Impact of the Early Warning Mechanism* (Oxford, Hart Publishing, 2017) 225–52.

Lupo, N and Fasone, C, *Interparliamentary Cooperation in the Composite European Constitution* (Oxford, Hart Publishing, 2016).

Lupo, N and Griglio, E, 'The Conference on Stability, Economic Coordination and Governance: Filling the Gaps of Parliamentary Oversight in the EU' (2018) 40 *Journal of European Integration* 358.

Lupo, N and Piccirilli, G (eds), *The Italian Parliament in the European Union* (Oxford, Hart Publishing, 2017).

Maatsch, A and Cooper, I, 'Governance Without Democracy? Analysing the Role of Parliaments in European Economic Governance after the Crisis: Introduction to the Special Issue' (2017) 70 *Parliamentary Affairs* 645.

Maccanico, A, 'Interrogazioni e interpellanze' in *Enciclopedia giuridica*, XVII (Roma, Istituto della Enciclopedia italiana, 1989) 1–7.

Mackenzie, K, *The English Parliament* (Middlesex, Penguin, 1959).

Mader, L, 'Evaluating the Effects: A Contribution to the Quality of Legislation' (2001) 22 *Statute Law Review* 119.

Maer, L and Sandford, M, *Select Committees Under Scrutiny* (London, The Constitution Unit, 2004).

Maffio, R, '*Qui custodiet ipsos custodes?* Il controllo parlamentare dell'attività di governo in prospettiva comparata' (2002) 9 *Quaderni di scienza politica* 333.

Magnette, P, 'Appointing and censuring the European Commission: the adaptation of parliamentary institutions to the Community context' (2001) 7 *European Law Journal* 292.

Magnon, X et al (eds), *Pouvoir exécutif et Parlement: de nouveaux équilibres?* (Aix-en-Provence, PUAM, 2012).

Mair, P and Thomassen, J, 'Political representation and government in the European Union' (2010) 17 *Journal of European Public Policy* 20.

Majone, G, 'The European Community: An "Independent Fourth Branch of Government?"' in G Brüggemeier (ed), *Verfassungen für ein ziviles Europa* (Baden-Baden, Nomos, 1994) 23–44.

—— 'Regulatory Legitimacy' in G Majone (ed), *Regulating Europe* (New York, Routledge, 1996) 283–301.

—— 'Europe's "Democratic Deficit": The Question of Standards' (1998) 4 *European Law Journal* 5.

—— 'Two logics of delegation: agency and fiduciary relations in EU governance' (2001) 2 *European Union Politics* 103.

—— 'From Regulatory State to a Democratic Default' (2014) 52 *Journal of Common Market Studies* 1216.

Magone, J, *Contemporary European Politics: A Comparative Introduction* (New York, Routledge, 2010).

Majonica, E, 'Bundestag und Außenpolitik' in HP Schwarz (ed), *Handbuch der Außenpolitik* (München, R Piper, 1975) 112–23.

Malamud, A and Stavridis, S, 'Parliaments and Parliamentarians as International Actors' in B Reinalda (ed), *The Ashgate Research Companion to Non-State Actors* (Farnham, Ashgate, 2011) 101–15.

Manin, B, *Los principios del Gobierno representativo* (Madrid, Alianza Editorial, 1998).

Mannino, A, *Indirizzo politico e fiducia nei rapporti fra governo e parlamento* (Milano, Giuffrè, 1973).

—— *Rapporti tra maggioranza e opposizioni. Note introduttive* (Milano, Giuffrè, 1999).

Manzella, A, *Per un riesame dei controlli parlamentari nell'esperienza repubblicana* (Firenze, Vallecchi, 1968).

—— *I controlli parlamentari* (Milano, Giuffrè, 1970).

—— 'Interrogazione e interpellanza' in *Enciclopedia del diritto*, XII (Milano, Giuffrè, 1972) 406–27.

—— 'Le funzioni del Parlamento in Italia' (1974) 24 *Rivista Trimestrale di Diritto Pubblico* 375.

—— *Il Parlamento* (Bologna, Il Mulino, 1977).

—— 'Controllo parlamentare e forme di governo' (1995) 15 *Quaderni costituzionali* 311.

—— 'La funzione di controllo' in Vv Aa, *Associazione italiana dei costituzionalisti, Annuario 2000. Il Parlamento* (Padova, Cedam, 2001).

—— *Il Parlamento* (Bologna, Il Mulino, 2003).

—— 'Le origini dei regolamenti parlamentari a quarant'anni dal 1971' in A Manzella (ed), *I regolamenti parlamentari a quarant'anni dal 1971* (Bologna, Il Mulino, 2012) 11–19.

—— 'Is the EP legitimate as a Parliamentary Body in EU Multi-tier Governance?' in I Pernice et al (eds), *Challenges of Multi-tier Governance in the European Union* (Brussels, European Parliament – Directorate General for Internal Policies, 2013) 138–51.

—— 'Il Parlamento come organo costituzionale di controllo' (2017) 1 *Nomos* 1.

Manzella, A and Lupo, N (eds), *Il sistema parlamentare euro-nazionale. Lezioni* (Torino, Giappichelli, 2014).

Marcou, G, 'Les inspections générales et le contrôle de l'administration' in G Marcou (ed), *Le contrôle de l'administration par elle-même* (Paris, Editions du CNRS, 1983) 9–193.

—— 'Le Contrôle de l'Administration Aujourd'hui' (2011) 45 *Zbornik Radova* 797.

Marshall, G, *Constitutional Conventions: The Rules and Forms of Political Accountability* (Oxford, Oxford University Press, 1987).

—— (ed), *Ministerial Responsibility* (Oxford, Oxford University Press, 1989).

Martin, LW and Stevenson, RT, 'Government Formation in Parliamentary Democracies' (2001) 45 *Journal of Political Science* 33.

Martin, LW and Vanberg, G, *Parliaments and Coalitions: The Role of Legislative Institutions in Multiparty Governance* (Oxford, Oxford University Press, 2011).

Martin, S, 'Parliamentary Questions, the Behaviour of Legislators, and the Function of Legislatures: An Introduction' (2011) 17 *The Journal of Legislative Studies* 259.

Martin, S, 'Parliamentary Questions' (2013) *SUNY/CID Comparative Assessment of Parliaments (CAP)* Note 1.

Martin, S and Whitaker, R, 'Beyond Committees: parliamentary oversight of coalition government in Britain (2019) 42 *West European Politics* 1464.

Martines, T, 'Indirizzo politico' in *Enciclopedia del diritto*, XXI (Milano, Giuffrè, 1971) 134–71.

Martinico, G, 'Dating Cinderella: On Subsidiarity as a Political Safeguard of Federalism in the European Union' (2011) 4 *European Public Law* 649.

Marzinotto, M, Wolff, B, Hallerberg, GB, *An Assessment of the European Semester* (Brussels, European Parliament – Directorate-General for Internal Policies, Study, 2012).

Massot, J, La cohabitation, quelles conséquences pour les institutions?' (2001) 300 *Cahiers français* 28.

Mattei, P, 'Party system change and parliamentary scrutiny of the executive in Italy' (2005) 11 *Journal of Legislative Studies* 16.

Matthews, F and Flinders, M, 'The watchdogs of "Washminster" – parliamentary scrutiny of executive patronage in the UK' (2015) 53 *Commonwealth and Comparative Politics* 153.

Mattson, I, 'Parliamentary Questions in the Swedish Riksdag' in M Wiberg (ed), *Parliamentary Control in the Nordic Countries* (Helsinki, Finnish Political Science Association, 1994) 276–356.

Mattson, I and Strøm, K, 'Parliamentary Committees' in H Döering (ed), *Parliaments and Majority Rule in Western Europe* (New York, St Martin's Press, 1995) 249–307.

Matz, J, 'Parliamentary decision making and foreign policy: Sweden's participation in international armed missions and the crucial role of the Riksdag' (2013) 33 *Parliaments, Estates and Representation* 186.

Maugüé, C, 'Le Conseil constitutionnel et le droit supranational' (2003) 105 *Pouvoirs* 53.

Maurer, A, 'The legislative powers and impact of the European Parliament' (2003) 41 *Journal of Common Market Studies* 227.

Maus, D, *Le parlement et les cohabitations* (1999) 91 *Pouvoirs* 71.

Mayer, O, *Deutsches Verwaltungsrecht*, 1st edn (Leipzig, Duncker & Humblot, 1895).

Mazzoni Honorati, ML, *Lezioni di diritto parlamentare*, 3rd edn (Torino, Giappichelli, 1999).

McCanse Wright, A, 'Constitutional Conflict and Congressional Oversight' (2014) 98 *Marquette Law Review* 881.

McCubbins, MD and Schwartz, T, 'Congressional oversight overlooked: police patrol versus fire alarms' (1984) 28 *The American Journal of Political Science* 165.

McCune Lindsay, S, 'Constitutional Limitations on Government Powers' (1915) 5 *Proceedings of the Academy of Political Science in the City of New York* 93.

McGee, D, *The Overseers – Public Accounts Committees and Public Spending* (London, Pluto Press, 2002).

McIlwain, CH, *Constitutionalism Ancient and Modern* (Ithaca, NY, Cornell University Press, 1940).

McKay, W and Johnson, CW, *Parliament and Congress: Representation and Scrutiny in the Twenty-first Century* (Oxford, Oxford University Press, 2010).

Meijer, AJ, 'Transparent Government: Parliamentary and legal accountability in an information age' (2003) 8 *Information Polity* 69.

Meijer, AJ and Bovens, M, 'Public accountability in the information age' in M Palmirani, T van Engers and MA Wimmer (eds), *Workshop in conjunction with JURIX 2003* (Laxenburg, International Federation for Information Processing, 2003).

Meijer, AJ, Curtin, D and Hillebrandt, M 'Open Government: connecting vision and voice' (2012) 78 *International Review of Administrative Science* 15.

Meinel, F, 'Confidence and Control in Parliamentary Government: Parliamentary Questioning, Executive Knowledge, and the Transformation of Democratic Accountability' (2018) 66 *The American Journal of Comparative Law* 317.

Mello, P and Peters, D, 'Parliaments in security policy. Involvement, politicization, and influence' (2018) 20 *The British Journal of Politics and International Relations* 3.

Mendel, T, *Parliament and Access to Information: Working for Transparent Governance*, WBI Working Paper Series (Washington, World Bank Institute, 2005) 1.

Mény, Y, 'France: The Institutionalization of Leadership' in JM Colomer (ed), *Political Institutions in Europe*, 3rd edn (London, Routledge, 2008) 94–134.

Merkl, A, *Allgemeines Vewaltungsrech* (Berlin, Springer, 1927).

Metcalf, MF, *The Riksdag: A History of the Swedish Parliament* (Stockholm, Bank of Sweden Tercentenary Foundation, 1987).

Meuwese, A and Popelier, P, 'The Legal Implications of Better Regulation: An Introduction' (2011) 17 *European Public Law* 455.

Meuwese, CM, *Impact Assessment in EU Lawmaking* (The Netherlands, Kluwer Law International, 2008).

Meyer, K, 'Legislative influence: toward theory development through casual analysis' (1980) 5 *Legislative Studies Quarterly* 563.

Meyn, KU, *Kontrolle als Verfassungsprinzip* (Baden-Baden, Nomos, 1982).

Mezey, M, *Comparative Legislatures* (Durham, NC, Duke University Press, 1979).

Michon, L, *Le Gouvernement perlementaire sous la Restauration* (Paris, Librairie générale de droit et de jurisprudence, 1905).

Mill, JS, 'Considerations on Representative Government' (1861) in JS Mill, *The Collected Works of John Stuart Mill, XIX – Essays on Politics and Society*, 3rd edn (London, Longman-Green, 1865).

Millard, E, 'La signification juridique de la responsabilité politique' in P Ségur (ed), *Gouvernants, quelle responsabilité?*, 1st edn (Paris, PUF, 1998) 81–100.

Miller, GJ, 'The Political Evolution of Principal-Agent Models' (2005) 8 *Annual Review of Political Science* 203.

Miller, R, Pelizzo, R and Stapenhurst, R, *Parliamentary Libraries, Institutes and Offices: The Sources of Parliamentary Information* (Washington, World Bank, 2004).

Milloz, P, *Les inspections générales ministérielles dans l'administration française* (Paris, Economica, 1983).

Milner, HV and Tingley, D, *Sailing the Water's Edge: The Domestic Politics of American Foreign Policy* (Princeton, NJ, Princeton University Press, 2015).

Milner, P, 'Scrutiny by the House of Lords' in C Leston Bandeira and L Thompson (eds), *Exploring Parliament* (Oxford, Oxford University Press, 2018) 196–205.

Mirkine-Guetzévitch, B, *Les nouvelles tendances du droit constitutionnel* (Paris, Marcel Giard, 1931).

—— 'Le régime parlementaire dans les récentes Constitutions européennes' (1950) 2–4 *Revue internationale de droit comparé* 605.

Mitnick, BM, 'Agency Theory' in RE Freeman and OH Werhane (eds), *The Blackwell Encyclopedic Dictionary of Business Ethics* (Malden, Blackwell, 1998) 12–5.

Mo, J, 'The logic of two-level games with endogenous domestic coalitions' (1994) 38 *The Journal of Conflict Resolution* 402.

Moens, GA and Trone, J, 'The Principle of Subsidiarity in EU Judicial and Legislative Practice: Panacea or Placebo?' (2015) 41 *The Journal of Legislative Studies* 65.

Molas, I and Pitarch, I, *Las Cortes Generales en el sistema parlamentario de Gobierno* (Madrid, Tecnos, 1987).

Möllers, C, *The Three Branches: A Comparative Model of Separation of Powers* (Oxford, Oxford University Press, 2013).

Montay, B, 'Le pouvoir de nomination de l'Executive sous la Ve République' (2013) 11 *Jus Politicum* 1.

Montero Gibert, JR, *El control parlamentario* (Madrid, Tecnos, 1984).

Montesquieu, C de Secondat de, *De l'esprit des lois*, XI, ch VI (Paris, Nourse, 1772).

Mora-Donatto, C, 'Instrumentos constitucionales para el control parlamentario' (2001) *Cuestiones constitucionales* 85.

Moravcsik, A, 'Is there a "Democratic Deficit" in World Politics? A Framework for Analysis' (2004) 39 *Government and Opposition* 336.

Moretti, D and Kraan, D, 'Budgeting in France' (2018) 2 *OECD Journal on Budgeting* 1.

Moretti, R, 'Le attività informative, di ispezione, di indirizzo e di controllo' in T Martines et al (eds), *Diritto parlamentare* (Milano, Giuffrè, 2011) 335–79.

Morichetti Franchi, M, 'Efficacia e limiti del sindacato ispettivo parlamentare' (1989) 19 *Nuovi studi politici* 105.

Morris, AA, 'Interpretive and Noninterpretive Constitutional Theory' (1984) 94 *Ethics* 501.

Morscher, S, *Die parlamentarische Interpellation* (Berlin, Dunckler and Humblot, 1973).

Mortati, C, *L'ordinamento del governo nel nuovo diritto pubblico italiano* (Roma, Anonima Romana Editoriale, 1931).

—— *Le leggi provvedimento* (Milano, Giuffrè, 1968).

—— *Istituzioni di diritto pubblico*, II, 9th edn (Padova, Cedam, 1976).

Moser, C, How open is 'open as possible'? Three different approaches to transparency and openness in regulating access to EU documents (Vienna, Institute for Advanced Studies, 2001).

Mujica, A and Sanchez-Cuenca, I, 'Consensus and Parliamentary Opposition: the Case of Spain' (2006) 41 *Government and Opposition* 86.

Mulgan, R, 'Accountability: An Ever-Expanding Concept?' (2000) 78 *Public Administration* 555.

Müller, W and Strøm, K, 'Conclusion: Coalition Governance in Western Europe' in W Müller and K Strøm (eds), *Coalition Governments in Western Europe* (Oxford, Oxford University Press, 2000) 559–92.

Müller Gómez, J and Wessels, W, 'The Spitzenkandidaten procedure: reflecting on the future of an electoral experiment' (2016) 8 IAI Working Paper 1.

Müller-Graff, PC, 'Das Karlsruher Lissabon-Urteil: Bedingungen, Grenzen, Orakel und integrative Optionen' (2009) 32 *Integration* 331.

Nabli, B, 'L'opposition parlementaire: un contre-pouvoir politique saisi par le droit' (2010) 133 *Pouvoirs* 125.

Naert, F, 'The new European Union economic governance: what about accountability?' (2016) 82 *International Review of Administrative Sciences* 638.

Nardone, C, 'Il controllo parlamentare sui servizi di informazione e sicurezza e sul segreto di Stato' in R Dickmann and S Staiano (eds), *Funzioni parlamentari non legislative e forma di governo. L'esperienza dell'Italia* (Milano, Giuffrè, 2008) 375–415.

National Democratic Institute for International Affairs, 'Strengthening Legislative Capacity in Legislative-Executive Relations' (2000) 6 *NDI Legislative Research Series* 4.

Naundorf, S and Radaelli, C, 'Regulatory Evaluation *Ex Ante* and *Ex Post*: Best Practice, Guidance and Methods' in U Karpen and H Xanthaki (eds), *Legislation in Europe: A Comprehensive Guide for Scholars and Practitioners* (Oxford, Hart Publishing, 2017) 187–215.

Naurin, D, 'Representation in the Councils of the EU' in S Kroger (ed), *Political Representation in the European Union. Democracy in a Time of Crisis* (London, Routledge, 2014) 69–87.

Naurin, D and Wallace, H, *Unveiling the Council of the European Union* (New York, Palgrave, 2008).

Navarro Mendez, JI, *Parlamentos regionales europeos y principio de subsidiariedad* (Aranzadi, Madrid, 2014).

Naztler, D and Hutton, M, 'Select Committees: Scrutiny à la carte?' in P Giddings (ed), *The Future of Parliament* (London, Palgrave, 2005) 88–97.

Negri, G, 'Bicameralismo' in *Enciclopedia del diritto*, V (Milano, Giuffrè, 1959) 345–54.

Neheider, S, 'Reframing the EU Budget Decision-Making Process' (2011) 49 *Journal of Common Market Studies* 631.

Neuhold, C and Ruiter, R de, 'Out of reach? Parliamentary control of EU affairs in the Netherlands and the UK' (2010) 16 *The Journal of Legislative Studies* 57.

Neuhold, C and Smith, J, 'Conclusion' in C Hefftler, C Neuhold, O Rozenberg and J Smith (eds), *The Palgrave Handbook of National Parliaments and the European Union* (London, Palgrave, 2015) 668–86.

Neuhold, C and Strelkov, A, 'New opportunity structures for the "unusual suspects"? Implications of the Early Warning System for the role of national parliaments within the EU system of governance' (2012) 4 *OPAL online Paper Series* 1.

Neuhold, C and Vahoonacker, S, 'Introduction' in C Neuhold et al (eds), *Civil Servants and Politics* (Basingstoke, Palgrave, 2013) 3–11.

Neunreither, K, 'Elected legislators and their unelected assistants in the European Parliament' (2006) 8 *The Journal of Legislative Studies* 40.

Neyer, J, 'Justified Multi-level Parliamentarism: Situating National Parliaments in the European Polity' (2014) 20 *The Journal of Legislative Studies* 125.

Nipperdey, T, *Deutsche Geschichte 1866–1918*, II (München, Beck, 1992).

Niquège, S, 'Les résolutions parlementaires de l'article 34-1 de la Constitution' (2010) 84 *Revue française de droit constitutionnel* 865.

Noll, P, *Gesetzgebungslehre* (Hamburg, Reinbeck, 1973).

Norton, M, 'Origins and Functions of the UK Parliamentary Office of Science and Technology' in J Norman and H Paschen (eds), *Parliaments and Technology: The Development of Technology Assessment in Europe* (New York, State University of New York Press, 2000) 65–91.

Norton, P, *Parliament in the 1980s* (Oxford, Basil Blackwell, 1985).

—— 'Parliaments: A Framework for Analysis' (1990) 13 *West European Politics* 1.

—— (ed), *Parliaments in Western Europe* (London, Frank Cass, 1990).

—— *Does Parliament Matter?* (Hemel Hempstead, Harvester Wheatsheaf, 1993).

—— 'Nascent Institutionalisation: Committees in the British Parliament' (1998) 4 *The Journal of Legislative Studies* 143.

—— 'Making Sense of Opposition' (2008) 14 *The Journal of Legislative Studies* 236.

—— 'La nature du contrôle parlementaire' (2010) 134 *Le Seuil* 5.

—— *Parliament in British Politics*, 2nd edn (New York, Palgrave, 2013).

Novak, P, *Parliamentary questions in selected legislative chambers* (Brussels, European Parliament – Directorate General for Internal Policies, 2014).

Ntaba, Z, 'Pre-legislative Scrutiny' in C Stefanou and H Xanthaki (eds), *Drafting Legislation: A Modern Approach* (London, Routledge, 2008) 118–30.

O'Brennan, J and Raunio, T, 'Conclusion: National Parliaments Gradually Learning to Play the European Game' in J O'Brennan and T Raunio (eds), *National Parliaments within the Enlarged European Union: From Victims of Integration to Competitive Actors?* (Oxford, Routledge, 2007) 272–86.

O'Brien, M, Stapenhurst, R and Trapp, L von, *Benchmarking and Self-Assessment for Parliaments* (Washington, World Bank Group, 2016).

Ogul, MS, Congress *Oversees the Bureaucracy: Studies in Legislative Supervision* (Pittsburgh, PN, University of Pittsburgh Press, 1976).

—— 'Congressional oversight: structure and incentives' in L Dodd and B Oppenheimer (eds), *Congress Reconsidered* (New York, Praeger, 1977) 207–21.

Oleszek, WJ, 'Towards a Stronger Legislative Branch' (1975) 3 *The Bureaucrat* 456.

—— 'Integration and Fragmentation: Key Themes of Congressional Change' (1983) 466 *The Annals of the American Academy of Political and Social Science* 193.

—— 'Congressional Oversight: An Overview' (2010) *Congressional Research Service Report for Congress* 1–17.

Oleszek, WJ et al, *Congressional Procedures and the Policy Process*, 11th edn (Washington, CQ Press, 2019).

Oliva, E, *Les principes budgétaires et comptables à valeur constitutionelle. Considérations autour de la 'vrai' Constitution financière de la France* (Paris, Dalloz, 2014).

Oliver, D, 'Executive Accountability: A Key Concept' in L Verhey, P Kiiver and S Loeffen, *Political Accountability and European Integration* (Groningen, Europa Law Publishing, 2009) 9–32.

Oliver, P and Martenczuk, B, 'The Commission' in R Schütze and T Tridimas (eds), *Oxford Principles of European Union Law. The European Legal Order*, I (Oxford, Oxford University Press, 2018) 549–80.

Olson, D, *The Legislative Process: A Comparative Approach* (New York, Harper and Row, 1980).

—— 'Legislatures and Administration in Oversight and Budgets: Constraints, Means, and Executives' in R Stapenhurst, R Pelizzo, D Olson and L von Trapp (eds), *Legislative Oversight and Budgeting: A World Perspective* (Washington DC, World Bank, 2008) 161–72.

Olson, D and Norton, P, 'Legislatures in Democratic Transition' (1996) 2 *The Journal of Legislative Studies* 1.

Oppenheim, FE, 'An Analysis of Political Control: Actual and Potencial' (1958) 3 *Journal of Politics* 515.

Oppenheimer, FE, *System der soziologie*, I (Jena, Fischer, 1992).

Oppermann, T et al, *Das parlamentarische Regierungssystem des Grundgesetzes. Organisierte Einwirkungen auf die Verwaltung* (Berlin, Walter de Gruyter, 1975).

Orlando, VE, 'La decadenza del sistema parlamentare' (1884) 2 *Rassegna di scienze sociali e politiche* 589.

—— (ed), *Primo trattato completo di diritto amministrativo italiano* (Milano, Società Editrice Libraria, 1900).

Osborne, D and Gaebler, T, *Reiventing Government: How the Entrepreneurial Spirit is Transforming the Public Sector* (Reading, Addison-Wesley, 1992).

Otjes, S, '"No politics in the agenda-setting meeting": plenary agenda setting in the Netherlands (2019) 42 *West European Politics* 728.

Ottman, H and Barisic, P (eds), *Deliberative Demokratie* (Baden-Baden, Nomos, 2015).

Pace, A, 'Le inchieste parlamentari nei nuovi regolamenti delle Camere' (1971) 4 *Studi parlamentari e di politica costituzionale* 17.

—— 'Articolo 82' in G Branca (ed), *Commentario alla Costituzione. Articoli 76–82: La formazione delle leggi. Tomo II* (Bologna, Zanichelli, 1979) 303–92.

Pacelli, M, 'Le amministrazioni delle Camere tra politica e burocrazia' in L Violante (ed), *Il Parlamento* (Torino, Einaudi, 2001) 743–69.

Packenham, RA, 'Legislatures and Political Development' in A Kornberg and LD Musolf (eds), *Legislatures in Developmental Perspective* (Durham, NC, Duke University Press, 1970) 521–82.

Pahre, R, 'Endogenous domestic institutions in two-level games and parliamentary oversight of the European Union' (1997) 41 *The Journal of Conflict Resolution* 147.

Paladin, L, 'Ciò che rimane del concetto di legge in senso formale' in Vv Aa, *Studi in onore di Manlio Udina*, II (Milano, Giuffrè, 1975) 1735–53.

—— 'Tipologia e fondamenti giustificativi del bicameralismo. Il caso italiano' (1984) *Quaderni costituzionali* 219.

—— 'Presidente della Repubblica' in *Enciclopedia del diritto*, XXXV (Milano, Giuffrè, 1986).

—— 'Bicameralismo' in *Enciclopedia giuridica*, V (Roma, Treccani, 1988) 1–8.

Palma, L, *Corso di diritto costituzionale*, II (Firenze, Pellas, 1884).

Panara, C, *The Sub-national Dimension of the EU. A Legal Study of Multilevel Governance* (Springer, Heidelberg, 2015).

Pariente, A, 'Evaluation parlementaire et responsabilité politique du Gouvernement' (2000) 14 *Les Petites affiches* 9.

Panebianco, A, 'Parlamento-arena e partiti' (1987) 17 *Rivista italiana di scienza politica* 203.

Pappalardo, A, 'Dal pluralismo polarizzato al pluralismo moderato. Il modello di Sartori e la transizione italiana' (1996) 26 *Rivista Italiana di Scienza Politica* 103.

Parkhurst, J, *The Politics of Evidence: From evidence-based Policy to the Good Governance of Evidence* (London, Routledge, 2016).

Pasquino, G, 'Executive–legislative relations in Southern Europe' in R Gunther, P Nikiforos Diamandourous and HJ Puhle (eds), *The Politics of Democratic Consolidation. Southern Europe in Comparative Perspective* (Baltimore, John Hopkins University Press, 1995) 261–83.

—— 'Tricks and Threats: The 2005 Italian Electoral Law and Its Consequences' (2007) 12 *South European Society & Politics* 79.

—— 'Italy: The Never-ending Transition of a Democratic Regime' in JM Colomer (ed), *Political Institutions in Europe*, 3rd edn (London, Routledge, 2008) 135–73.

—— 'Governments in European Politics' in JM Magone (ed), *Routledge Handbook of European Politics* (London, Routledge, 2015) 295–310.

Pasquino, G and Pelizzo, R, *Parlamenti democratici* (Bologna, Il Mulino, 2006).

Pasquino, P, 'Sieyès, Constant e il "governo dei moderni". Contributo alla storia del concetto di rappresentanza politica' (1987) 1 *Filosofia politica* 77.

Patzelt, WJ, 'Ein latenter Verfassungskonflikt? Die Deutschen und ihr parlamentarisches Regierungssystem' (1998) 39 *Politische Vierteljahresschrift* 725.

Paulus, AL, 'Quo vadis Democratic Control? The Afghanistan Decision of the Bundestag and the Decision of the Federal Constitutional Court in the NATO Strategic Concept Case' (2002) 3 *German Law Journal* 1.

Pedersen, AM and Jørgensen, RF, *National intelligence authorities and surveillance in the EU: Fundamental rights safeguards and remedies. Denmark* (Copenhagen, Danish Institute for Human Rights, 2014).

Peers, S, 'The Withdrawal Agreement Act: Implementing the Brexit Withdrawal Agreement in the UK' (*EU Law Analysis*, 17 February 2020).

Peled, R and Rabin, Y, 'The constitutional right to information' (2011) 42 *Columbia Human Rights Law Review* 357.

Pelizzo, R and Stapenhurst, F, *Parliamentary Oversight Tools. A Comparative Analysis* (New York, Routledge, 2011).

—— *Government Accountability and Legislative Oversight* (New York, Routledge, 2014).

Pelizzo, R and Stapenhurst, R, 'Legislature and Oversight: a note' (2004) 9 *Quaderni di scienza politica* 175.

Pelizzo, R, Stapenhurst, R and Olson, D, *The Role of Parliaments in the Budget Process* (Washington, World Bank Institute, 2005).

Pennings, P, 'Beyond dichotomous explanations: Explaining constitutional control of the executive with fuzzy sets' (2003) 42 *European Journal of Political Research* 541.

Perassi, T, *Le attuali istituzioni e la bancarotta del parlamentarismo* (Pavia, Officina d'arti grafiche, 1907).

Pérez-Serrano, N, *Tratado de Derecho Político*, 2nd edn (Madrid, Ed. Civitas, 1984).

Perna, R, 'Costituzionalizzazione del pareggio di bilancio ed evoluzione della forma di governo italiana' in Vv Aa, *Costituzione e pareggio di bilancio. Il Filangieri – Quaderno 2011* (Napoli, Jovene, 2012) 19–43.

Pernice, I, 'Multilevel Constitutionalism in the European Union' (2002) 5 *European Law Review* 511.

—— 'Fairness, Trust and the Rule of Law. Statement on the European Parliament's confirmation procedure concerning Sylvia Goulard' (*Verfassungsblog*, 21 October 2019).

Pernice, I et al (eds), *Challenges of Multi-tier Governance in the European Union* (Brussels, European Parliament – Directorate General for Internal Policies, 2013).

Pernice, I and Mayer, FC, 'De la Constitution composée de l'Europe' (2000) 36 *Revue trimestrielle de droit européen* 623.

Perry, J, *The Constitution, the Courts, and Human Rights* (New Haven, CT, Yale University Press, 1982).

Petersson, O, 'The Swedish Constitution of 1809' in E Özdalga and S Persson (eds), *Contested Sovereignties: Government and Democracy in Middle Eastern and European Perspectives* (Istanbul, Swedish Research Institute in Instanbul, 2009) 53–66.

—— 'Constitutional History' in J Pierre (ed), *The Oxford Handbook of Swedish Politics* (Oxford, Oxford University Press, 2016) 89–102.

Piccione, D, 'Il falso mito del 'principio di non regressione' nel procedimento di autorizzazione alla ratifica del Trattato costituzionale europeo' (2005) 50 *Giurisprudenza costituzionale* 2225.

Piccirilli, G, 'Il ricorso alla legge per l'esercizio dei poteri "europei" da parte del Parlamento italiano. Spunti per una lettura costituzionalmente orientata' (2013) 2 *Osservatorio sulle fonti* 1.

Piccirilli, G and Zuddas, P, 'Assisting Italian MPs in Pre-Legislative Scrutiny: The Role Played by Chambers' Counsellors and Legislative Advisors in Enhancing the Knowledge and Skills Development of Italian MPs: The Assistance Offered to an Autonomous Collection of Information' (2012) 65 *Parliamentary Affairs* 672.

Pissaloux, JL, 'Les inspections générales au sein de l'administration française: structures, fonctions et évolution' (2015) 155 *Revue française de l'administration publique* 601.

Pitruzzella, G, 'Responsabilità politica' in Digesto delle discipline *pubblicistiche*, XIII (Torino, Utet, 1997) 289–304.

Plagemann, H, 'Mehr parlamentarische Kontrolle durch Untersuchungsausschüsse. Zu den Empfehlungen der Enquete-Kommission Verfassungsreform' (1977) 8 *Zeitschrift für Parlamentsfragen* 242.

Polsby, NW, 'Legislatures' in FI Greenstein and NW Polsby (eds), *Handbook of Political Science*, V (Reading, Addison-Wesley, 1975) 257–319.

Popelier, P, 'Governance and Better Regulation: Dealing with the Legitimacy Paradox' (2011) 17 *European Public Law* 555.

—— 'Management of Legislation' in U Karpen and H Xanthaki (eds), *Legislation in Europe. A Comprehensive Guide for Scholars and Practitioners* (Oxford, Hart Publishing, 2017) 53–72.

—— 'A legal perspective on Regulatory Impact Assessment' (2017) Paper for the International Symposium on Regulatory Impact Analysis, Luxembourg – 23, 24 November 2017.

Poptcheva, EM, 'Policy and legislative evaluation in the EU' (European Parliament, Library of the European Parliament Briefing, 3 April 2013).

Praino, D, 'The Structure of the EU System of Government' (2015) 5 ARENA Working Papers 1.

Predieri, A, 'Mediazione e indirizzo nel parlamento italiano' (1975) 5 *Rivista italiana di scienze politiche* 407.

Preece, AA, 'Bicameralism at the end of the Second Millennium' (2000) 21 *University of Queensland Law* Journal 67.

Preuvot, P, 'Réflexion sur les remèdes aux difficultés d'application des lois' (2011) VIII Congrès Français de Droit constitutionnel, Nancy, 18 June 2011.

Price, DK, 'The Parliamentary and Presidential Systems' (1943) 3 *Public Administration Review* 317.

Priestley, J, Schollgen, G and Peñalver Garcia, N, *The Making of a European President* (London, Palgrave, 2015).

Proksch, SO and Slapin, JB, 'Institutions and Coalition Formation: The German Election of 2005' (2006) 29 *West European Politics* 540.

—— 'Position-Taking in European Parliament Speeches' (2010) 40 *British Journal of Political Science* 587.

Puetter, U, 'Informal Circles of Ministers: A Way Out of the Eu's Institutional Dilemmas?' (2003) 9 *European Law Journal* 109.

—— 'Europe's deliberative intergovernmentalism: the new role of the Council and the European Council in EU economic governance' (2012) 19 *Journal of European Public Policy* 161.

Putnam, RD, 'Diplomacy and Domestic Politics: The Logic of Two-Level Games' (1988) 42 *International Organization* 427.

Quintero González, F, 'Debates del estado de la nación: control parlamentario o puesta en escena para medio de comunicación? (2014) 19 *Historia y Comunicación Social* 793.

Racioppi, F and Brunelli, I, *Commento allo Statuto*, III (Torino, Unione tipografico editrice, 1909).

Radaelli, CM and De Francesco, F, 'Regulatory impact assessment' in R Baldwin, M Cave and M Lodge (eds), *The Oxford Handbook of Regulation* (Oxford, Oxford University Press, 2010) 279–301.

Rani Sharma, M et al, *Expert report on the implementation of ex-post evaluations. Good practice and experience in other countries* (Berlin, NKR, 2013).

Rasch, BE, Martin S and Cheibub, JA (eds), *Parliaments and Government Formation: Unpacking Investiture Rules* (Oxford, Oxford University Press, 2015).

Rasch, BE, Martin, S and Cheibub, JA, 'Investiture Rules Unpacked' in BE Rasch, S Martin and JA Cheibub (eds), *Parliaments and Government Formation: Unpacking Investiture Rules* (Oxford, Oxford University Press, 2015) 331–56.

Raube, K and Fonck, D, 'Transnational Parliamentarism and the Dynamics of the IPC CFSP/CSDP: Policy-making, Accountability and Cooperation' (2018) 10 *Perspectives on Federalism* 137.

Raunio, T, 'Holding Governments Accountable in European Affairs: Explaining Cross-National Variation' (2005) 11 *The Journal of Legislative Studies* 319.

—— 'The gatekeepers of European integration? The functions of national parliaments in the EU political system' (2011) 33 *Journal of European Integration* 303.

Raunio, T and Wagner, W, 'Towards Parliamentarisation of Foreign and Security Policy?' (2017) 40 *West European Politics* 1.

Raynaud, F and Fombeur, P, 'Conditions d'application en France d'un traité international dont la ratification ou l'approbation est intervenue sans avoir été autorisé par une loi' (1999) *AJDA* 127.

Recchia, G, *L'informazione delle Assemblee rappresentative. L'inchiesta* (Napoli, Jovene, 1979).

Recoder de Casso, E, 'Comentario al artículo 76' in F Garrido Falla (ed), *Comentarios a la Constitución* (Madrid, Ed. Civitas, 1985) 1169–81.

Regonini, G, 'Parlamenti analitici' (2012) 1 *Rivista Italiana di Politiche Pubbliche* 33.

Remiro Brotons, A, 'De los Tratados Internacionales (Artículos 93–96 de la Constitución)' in O Alzaga Villaamil (ed), *Comentarios a la Constitución española de 1978. Tomo VII* (Madrid, Cortes Generales-Edersa, 1998) 491–651.

Renda, A, *Impact Assessment in the EU. The State of the Art and the Art of the State* (Brussels, Centre for European Policy Studies, 2006).

—— 'European Union and Better Law-Making: Best Practices and Gaps' in The Best Practices in Legislative and Regulatory Processes in a Constitutional Perspective (workshop), Study for the AFCO Committee (Brussels, European Parliament, 2015).

Rens, I, 'Les commissions parlementaires en droit comparé' (1961) 13 *Revue internationale de droit comparé* 309.

Rescigno, GU, *La responsabilità politica* (Milano, Giuffrè, 1967).

—— 'Responsabilità (diritto costituzionale)' in *Enciclopedia del diritto*, XXXIX (Milano, Giuffrè, 1988) 1341–69.

—— 'Responsabilità politica e responsabilità giuridica' (2012) 3 *Rivista italiana per le scienze giuridiche* 333.

Revenga Sánchez, M, *La formación del gobierno en la Constitución española de 1978* (Madrid, Centro de Estudios Constitucionales, 1988).

Richardson, H, 'The Origins of Parliament' (1928) 11 *Transactions of the Royal Historical Society* 137.

Riddell, P, 'Impact of Transparency on Accountability' in N Bowles, JT Hamilton and DA Levy (eds), *Transparency in Politics and the Media. Accountability and Open Government* (New York, Palgrave, 2014) 19–30.

Riesenfeld, SA and Abbott, FM, *Parliamentary Participation in the Making and Operation of Treaties: A Comparative Study* (Dordrecht, Kluwer Academic Publishers, 1994).

Rinella, A, 'L'opposizione parlamentare. Profili di diritto costituzionale' in G Dalla Torre (ed), *Studi in onore di Giovanni Giacobbe*, II (Milano, Giuffrè, 2010) 186–217.

Riquelme Cortado, R, 'La tramitación de los tratados internacionales y el reglamento del Congreso de los Diputados de 1982' (1982) 34 *Revista española de derecho internacional* 409.

Rittberger, B, 'The Creation and Empowerment of the European Parliament' (2003) 41 *Journal of Common Market Studies* 203.

—— '"No integration without representation!" European integration, parliamentary democracy, and two forgotten Communities' (2006) 13 *Journal of European Public Policy* 1211.

—— 'Constructing Parliamentary Democracy in the European Union: How did it Happen?' in B Kohler-Koch and B Rittberger (eds), *Debating the Democratic Legitimacy of the European Union* (Lanham, Rowman & Littlefield Publishers, 2007) 111–37.

—— 'Institutionalizing Representative Democracy in the European Union: The Case of the European Parliament' (2012) 50 *Journal of Common Market Studies* 18.

Rittberger, B and Winzen, T, 'The EU's Multilevel Parliamentary System' in J Richardson and S Mazey (eds), *European Union: Power and Policy-Making*, 4th edn (London, Routledge, 2015) 107–34.

Rittelmeyer, YS, 'The Institutional Consecration of the European Council: Symbolism Beyond Formal Text' in F Foret and YS Rittelmeyer (eds), *The European Council and European Governance: The Commanding Heights of the EU* (New York, Taylor & Francis, 2014) 25–43.

Rivosecchi, G, *Regolamenti parlamentari e forma di governo nella XIII legislatura* (Milano, Giuffrè, 2002).

—— 'Il ruolo delle Assemblee rappresentative di fronte ai processi di globalizzazione: spunti ricostruttivi' (2003) 45 *Giurisprudenza costituzionale* 499.

—— 'La funzione di controllo parlamentare tra Parlamento europeo e Parlamenti nazionali' in A Lucarelli and A Patroni Griffi (eds), *Studi sulla Costituzione europea: percorsi e ipotesi* (Napoli, ESI, 2003) 289–304.

—— 'Quali rimedi all'inattuazione del "Premier Question Time?" A proposito di statuto dell'opposizione e giustiziabilità dei regolamenti parlamentari per conflitto di attribuzione' (2004) 4 *Quaderni costituzionali* 811.

—— 'I poteri ispettivi e il controllo parlamentare dal question time alle Commissioni di inchiesta' in E Gianfrancesco and N Lupo (eds) *Le regole del diritto parlamentare nella dialettica tra maggioranza e opposizione* (Roma, LUP, 2007) 155–202.

—— *L'indirizzo politico finanziario tra Costituzione italiana e vincoli europei* (Padova, Cedam, 2007).

—— 'I poteri ispettivi e il controllo parlamentare a dieci anni dalla riforma del regolamento della Camera dei deputati' in Vv Aa, *Il Parlamento del bicameralismo. Un decennio di riforme dei regolamenti delle Camere. Il Filangieri* (Napoli, Jovene, 2008) 201–42.

—— 'Il Parlamento di fronte alla crisi economico-finanziaria' (2012) 3 *Rivista AIC* 1.

—— 'La partecipazione dell'Italia alla formazione e attuazione della normativa europea. Il ruolo del Parlamento' (2013) 5 *Giornale di diritto amministrativo* 463.

Rizzoni, G, *Opposizione parlamentare e democrazia deliberativa. Ordinamenti europei a confronto* (Bologna, Il Mulino, 2012).

Rockman, BA, 'Legislative-executive relations and legislative oversight' (1984) 9 *Legislative Studies Quarterly* 387.

Romaniello, M, 'Upper Chambers in EU Affairs. Scrutinising German and Belgian Bicameralism' (2015) *Federalismi.it* 1.

Romano, S, 'Saggio di una teoria sulle leggi di approvazione' (1898) *Il Filangieri* 161–69; 249–71; 330–45.

Romzek, BS and Dubnick, MJ, 'Accountability in the public sector: lessons from the challenger tragedy' (1987) 47 *Public Administration Review* 227.

Romzek, BS and Utter, A, 'Congressional legislative staffs: political professional or clerks' (1997) 41 *American Journal of Political Science* 1251.

Röper, E, 'Europapolitische Bundesratsbeschlüsse ohne demokratisch-parlamentarische Kontrolle' (2009) 40 *Zeitschrift für Parlamentsfragen* 3.

Rosa, F, 'Le relazioni governative al Parlamento sullo stato di attuazione delle leggi' in M Carli (ed), *Il ruolo delle Assemblee elettive. Vol I. La nuova forma di governo delle regioni* (Torino, Giappichelli, 2001) 442–63.

—— 'Interrogazioni e interpellanze fra XIII e XIV legislatura: il confronto mutilato fra Parlamento e Governo' in E Gianfrancesco and N Lupo (eds), *Le regole del diritto parlamentare nella dialettica tra maggioranza e opposizione* (Rome, Luiss University Press, 2007) 395–411.

—— *Il controllo parlamentare sul Governo nel Regno Unito. Un contributo allo studio del parlamentarismo britannico* (Milano, Giuffrè, 2012).

Rose-Ackerman, S, Egidy, S and Fowkes, J, *Due Process of Lawmaking. The United States, South Africa, Germany and the European Union* (New York, Cambridge University Press, 2015).

Rosegger, HL, *Das parlamentarische Interpellationsrecht. Rechts-vergl eichende und politische Studie* (Leipzig, von Duncker & Humblot, 1907).

Rosen, B, *Holding Government Bureaucracies Accountable* (New York, Praeger, 1982).

Rousseau, JJ, *Du contrat social* (Paris, Bordas, 1762).

—— 'Considerations sur le gouvernement de la Pologne et sur sa réformation projetée (1771–1772)' in *Collection complète des oeuvres de JJ Rousseau*, I (Genève, Société typographique de Genève, 1780–89).

Rozenberg, O, *The Role of National Parliaments in the EU After Lisbon: Potentialities and Challenges* (Brussels, European Parliament – Directorate General for Internal Policies, 2017).

—— 'Comparer les parlements' in JM de Waele and Y Déloye (eds), *Politique comparé* (Bruxelles, Bruylant, 2018) 303–64.

Rozenberg, O and Hefftler, C, 'Introduction' in C Hefftler, C Neuhold, O Rozenberg and J Smith (eds) *The Palgrave Handbook of National Parliaments and the European Union* (London, Palgrave, 2015) 1–39.

Rozenberg, O and Martin, S, 'Questioning parliamentary questions' (2011) 17 *The Journal of Legislative Studies* 394.

Rubio Llorente, F, 'El control parlamentario' (1985) 1 *Revista Parlamentaria de Habla Hispana* 83.

—— *La forma del poder (Estudios sobre la Constitución)* (Madrid, CEC, 1993).

Rush, M and Ettinghausen, C, *Opening Up the Usual Channels* (London, The Hansard Society, 2002).

Russo, F, 'The Constituency as a Focus of Representation: Studying the Italian Case through the Analysis of Parliamentary Questions' (2011) *The Journal of Legislative Studies* 290.

Russo, F and Wiberg, M, 'Parliamentary Questioning in 17 European Parliaments: Some Steps towards Comparison' (2010) 16 *The Journal of Legislative Studies* 215.

Russell, M, 'The Territorial Role of Second Chambers' in N Baldwin and D Shell (eds), *Second Chambers* (London, Frank Cass, 2001).

—— 'What are Second Chambers for?' (2001) 54 *Parliamentary Affairs* 442.

—— 'The British House of Lords: A Tale of Adaptation and Resilience' in J Luther, P Passaglia and R Tarchi (eds), *A World of Second Chambers. Handbook for Constitutional studies on Bicameralism* (Milano, Giuffrè, 2006) 65–95.

—— 'Assessing the policy impact of Parliament: methodological challenges and possible future approaches' (2009) Paper for PSA Legislative Studies Specialist Group Conference, 24 June 2009.

—— 'A Stronger Second Chamber? Assessing the impact of the House of Lords Reform in 1999 and the lessons for bicameralism' (2010) 58 *Political Studies* 866.

—— 'Never Allow a Crisis Go To Waste: The Wright Committee Reforms to Strengthen the House of Commons' (2011) 64 *Parliamentary Affairs* 612.

Russell, M, *The Contemporary House of Lords* (Oxford, Oxford University Press, 2013).

Russell, M and Benton, M, 'Assessing the policy impact of Parliament: methodological challenges and possible future approaches' (2009) Paper for PSA Legislative Studies Specialist Group Conference.

Russell, M and Cowley, P, 'The Policy Power of the Westminster Parliament: The Parliamentary State and the Empirical Evidence' (2017) 29 *Governance* 121.

Saalfeld, T, 'The German Houses of Parliament and European integration' in P Norton (ed), *National Parliaments and the European Union* (London, Frank Cass, 1996) 12–34.

—— 'Members of parliament and governments in Western Europe: agency relations and problems of oversight' (2000) 37 *European Journal of Political Research* 353.

—— 'Institutions, Chance and Choices. The Dynamics of Cabinet Survival in the Parliamentary Democracies of Western Europe' in K Strøm, WC Müller and T Bergman (eds), *Cabinets and Coalition Bargaining: The Democratic Life Cycle in Western Europe* (Oxford, Oxford University Press, 2008) 327–68.

—— 'Parliamentary Questions as Instruments of Substantive Representation: Visible Minorities in the UK House of Commons, 2005–10' (2011) 17 *The Journal of Legislative Studies* 271.

Sáenz Royo, E, 'El papel del parlamento español en la democracia de partidos' (2007) 73 *Revista de Derecho Político* 149.

Saiegh, SM, 'Lawmaking' in S Martin, T Saalfeld and KW Strøm (eds), *The Oxford Handbook of Legislative Studies* (Oxford, Oxford University Press, 2014) 482–523.

Sáiz Arnáiz, A, 'El Gobierno y la dirección de la política' (1992) 34 *Revista Vasca de Administración Pública* 189.

Sajó, A, *Limiting Government: An Introduction to Constitutionalism* (Budapest, Central European Press, 1999).

Samuels, DJ and Shugart, MS, *Presidents, Parties, and Prime Ministers. How the Separation of Powers Affects Party Organization and Behavior* (New York, Cambridge University Press, 2010).

Sánchez Agesta, L, 'Gobierno y responsabilidad' (1960) 113–14 *Revista de estudios políticos* 35.

Sánchez-Cuenca, I, 'From a Deficit of Democracy to a Technocratic Order: The Postcrisis Debate on Europe' (2017) 20 *Annual Review of Political Science* 351.

Sánchez de Dios, M, *La moción de censura* (Madrid, Congreso de los Diputados, 1992).

—— 'Parliamentary Accountability in Europe: How do parliaments of France, Italy and Spain fight information asymmetries? (2008) Paper prepared for the Workshop 'Comparing legislatures worldwide: roles, functions and performance in old and new democracies – ECPR Joint Sessions, Rennes, 11–16 April 2008.

Sánchez de Dios, M and Wiberg, M, 'Questioning in European Parliaments' (2011) 17 *The Journal of Legislative Studies* 354.

Sánchez Navarro, AJ, *La oposición parlamentaria* (Madrid, Congreso de los Diputados, 1997).

Sannerstedt, A and Sjölin, M, 'Sweden: Changing Party Relations in a More Active Parliament' in E Damgaard (ed), *Parliamentary Change in the Nordic Countries* (Oslo, Scandinavian University Press, 1992) 100–49.

Santangelo Spoto, I, *La giustizia nell'amministrazione: la burocrazia ed il Governo parlamentare* (Torino, Unione tipografico-editrice, 1902).

Santaolalla López, F, 'La ley y la autorización de las Cortes a los tratados internacionales' (1981) 11 *Revista de derecho político* 29.

—— *El Parlamento y sus instrumentos de información (preguntas, interpelaciones y Comisiones de investigación)* (Madrid, Edersa, 1982).

—— 'Decreto ley, ley y tratado internacional. Comentario a la ley STC 155/2005 de 9 Junio' (2006) 18 UNED. *Teoría y Realidad Constitucional* 399.

Sanz Pérez, AL, 'El artículo 77 de la Constitución. Las comisiones de peticiones de las Cortes Generales y las de los Parlamentos autonómicos' (2018) 31 *Corts: Anuario de derecho parlamentario* 279.

Sartori, G, *Elementi di scienza politica* (Bologna, Il Mulino, 1987).

—— *Comparative Constitutional Engineering. An Inquiry into Structures, Incentives and Outcomes*, 2nd edn (New York, NYU Press, 1997).

Schäfer, D, Roethe, G and Wagner, A (eds), *Preussen. Deutschlands Vergangenheit und Deutschland Zukunft* (Berlin, von Reimar Hobbing, 1913).

Schäfer, H, *Der Bundesrat* (Heymann, Köln, 1955).

Schedler, A, Diamond, L and Plattner, M, *The Self-Restraining State: Power and Accountability in New Democracies* (Boulder, Lynne Rienner Publishers, 1999).

Scher, S, 'Conditions for Legislative Control' (1963) 25 *Journal of Politics* 526.

Schick, A, 'Congress and the "details" of administration' (1976) 36 *Public Administration Review* 516.

—— *The Federal Budget Politics, Policy, Process* (Washington DC, Brookings Institution, 2002).

Schiller, T, 'Direct Democracy and Theories of Participatory Democracy: Some Observations' in ZT Pállinger, B Kaufmann, W Marxer and T Schiller (eds), *Direct Democracy in Europe. Developments and Prospects* (Wiesbaden, Springer, 2007) 52–63.

Schininà, M, 'What balance between Europol and Eurojust from a parliamentary angle?' (2020) *New Journal of European Criminal Law* 1–12.

Schleiter, P, Belu, V and Hazell, R, 'Hung Parliaments and the Need for Clearer Rules of Government Formation' (2017) 88 *The Political Quarterly* 404.

Schmidt, J, *Die demokratische Legitimationsfunktion der parlamentarischen Kontrolle* (Berlin, Duncker & Humblot, 2007).

Schmidt, MG, 'Germany: The Grand Coalition State' in JM Colomer (ed), *Political Institutions in Europe*, 3rd edn (London, Routledge, 2008) 58–93.

Schmidt, V, 'European "Federalism" and its Encroachments on National Institutions' (1999) 29 *Publius: The Journal of Federalism* 19.

—— 'Federalism and State Governance in the European Union and the United States: An Institutional perspective' in K Nicolaïdis and R Howse (eds), *The Federal Vision: Legitimacy and Levels of Governance in the United States and the European Union* (Oxford, Oxford University Press, 2001) 335–54.

—— 'Democracy and Legitimacy in the European Union Revisited: Input, Output and "Throughput"' (2013) 61 *Political Studies* 2.

Schmitt, P, Ruys, T and Marx, A, *The Subsidiarity Early Warning System of the Lisbon Treaty – The Role of Regional Parliaments with Legislative Powers and Other Subnational Authorities* (Brussels, Committee of the Regions, 2013).

Schneider, HP, *Entscheidungsdefizite der Parlamente: über die Notwendigkeit einer Wiederbelebung der Parlamentsreform* (Tübingen, Mohr Siebeck, 1980).

Schorkopf, F 'The European Union as an Association of Sovereign States: Karlsruhe's Ruling on the Treaty of Lisbon' (2009) 10 *German Law Journal* 1219.

Schuett-Wetschky, E, 'Gouvernementale Parlamentskontrolle? Politische Führung, Regierungsmehrheiten und das Verhältnis von Parlament und Regierung' in W Patzelt and E Holtmann (eds), *Parlamentarische Regierungskontrolle – Gouvernementale Parlamentskontrolle. Theorie und Fallbeispiele* (Lesk, Opladen, 2004) 17–42.

Schütze, R, *From Dual to Cooperative Federalism. The Changing Structure of EU Law* (Oxford, Oxford University Press, 2009).

Schwarzmeier, M, *Parlamentarische Mitsteuerung* (Wiesbaden, Westdeutscher, 2001).

Scully, R, 'Dealing with big brother: relations with the first chambers' (2011) 17 *The Journal of Legislative Studies* 93.

Scuto, F, 'L'evoluzione del rapporto parlamento-governo nella formazione e nell'attuazione della normativa e delle politiche dell'Unione europea' (2015) 1 *Rivista AIC* 1.

Ségur, P, *La responsabilité politique* (Paris, PUF, 1998).

Seiller, B (ed), *Le contrôle parlementaire de l'administration* (Paris, Dalloz, 2010).

Serrano Alberca, JM, 'Artículo 94' in F Garrido Falla et al (eds), *Comentarios a la Constitución*, 3rd edn (Madrid, Civitas, 2001) 1475–88.

Sewel, Lord, 'The role and work of House of Lords Select Committees' (2014) Open Lecture delivered on 3 December 2014.

Seyd, B, *Coalition Government in Britain: Lessons from Overseas* (London, The Constitution Unit, 2002).

Shackleton, M, 'Transforming representative democracy in the EU? The role of the European Parliament' (2017) 39 *Journal of European Integration* 191.

Shaw, M, 'Parliamentary Committees: A Global Perspective' (1998) 4 *The Journal of Legislative Studies* 225.

Shepard, M, 'Administrative Review and Oversight: The Experience of Westminster' in R Pelizzo, R Stapenhurst and D Olson (eds), *Trends in Parliamentary Oversight* (Washington DC, World Bank Institute, 2004) 40–46.

Shugart, MS and Carey, JM, *Presidents and Assemblies. Constitutional Design and Electoral Dynamics* (New York, Cambridge University Press, 1992).

Sicardi, S, 'Controllo e indirizzo parlamentare' in *Digesto delle discipline pubblicistiche*, IV (Torino, Utet, 1989) 94–139.

—— 'Il problematico rapporto tra controllo parlamentare e ruolo dell'opposizione nell'esperienza repubblicana' (2002) 44 *Rassegna parlamentare* 961.

Siclari, D, 'Il controllo parlamentare sugli atti non normativi del Governo e l'esame di documenti trasmessi al Parlamento dal Governo e da altre Autorità: profili evolutivi' in R Dickmann and S Staiano (eds), *Funzioni parlamentari non legislative e forma di governo. L'esperienza dell'Italia* (Milano, Giuffrè, 2008) 337–73.

Sieberer, U, 'The institutional power of Western European Parliaments: a multidimensional analysis' (2011) 34 *West European Politics* 731.

Siefken, ST, 'Parlamentarische Frageverfahren – Symbolpolitik oder wirksames Kontrollinstrument?' (2010) 41 *Zeitschrift für Parlamentsfragen* 18.

—— *Parlamentarische Kontrolle Im Wandel: Theorie Und Praxis Des Deutschen Bundestages* (Baden-Baden, Nomos, 2018).

Silva Ochoa, J da (ed), *Las Comisiones Parlamentarias* (Vitoria, Parlamento Vasco, 1994).

Silvestri, G, 'Considerazioni sui poteri e limiti delle commissioni parlamentari di inchiesta' (1970) 1 *Il Politico* 538.

Simoncini, A, 'Beyond Representative Democracy: The Challenge of Participatory Democracy and the Boundless Galaxy of Civil Society' in M Cartabia, N Lupo and A Simoncini (eds), *Democracy and Subsidiarity in the EU. National Parliaments, Regions and Civil Society in the Decision-Making Process* (Bologna, Il Mulino, 2013) 45–73.

—— *Administrative Regulation Beyond the Non-Delegation Doctrine. A Study on EU Agencies* (Oxford, Hart Publishing, 2018).

Simson Card, J, 'Parliament and the withdrawal agreement: the "meaningful vote"' (*Commons Library Insight*, 9 February 2018).

Singer, J, *Praxiskommentar Zum Gesetz Über Die Parlamentarische Kontrolle Nachrichtendienstichler Tätigkeit Des Bundes* (Berlin, Springer, 2016).

Smend, R, *Die politische Gewalt im Verfassungsstaat und das Problem der Staatsform* (Tübingen, Mohr, 1923).

Smookler, J, 'Making a difference? The effectiveness of pre-legislative scrutiny' (2006) 59 *Parliamentary Affairs* 522.

Smurra, G, Caputo, M and Goracci, A, 'Gli atti di indirizzo e di sindacato ispettivo' in R Dickmann and S Staiano (eds), *Funzioni parlamentari non legislative e forma di governo: l'esperienza dell'Italia* (Milano, Giuffrè, 2008) 261–312.

Somek, A 'Administration Without Sovereignty' in P Dobner and M Loughlin (eds), *The Twilight of Constitutionalism* (Oxford, Oxford University Press, 2010).

Sonnino, S, *Del governo rappresentativo in Italia* (Roma, Botta, 1872).

Spagna Musso, E, 'Bicameralismo e riforma del Parlamento' in Vv Aa, *Parlamento, istituzioni, democrazia: seminario di studio*, Roma, 11–13 dicembre 1979 (Milano, Giuffrè, 1980) 119.

Spenkuch, H, 'Prussian Governance' in M Jefferies (ed), *The Ashgate Research Companion to Imperial Germany* (London, Routledge, 2015) 33–54.

Sprungk, C, 'Ever more or ever better scrutiny? Analysing the conditions of effective national parliamentary involvement in EU affairs' (2010) 14 *European Integration Online Papers* 1.

—— 'A New Type of Representative Democracy? Reconsidering the Role of National Parliaments in the European Union' (2013) 35 *Journal of European Integration* 547.

Stadler, P, *Die parlamentarische Kontrolle der Bundesregierung* (Berlin, Springer, 1984).

Stammati, S, 'Qualche riflessione ulteriore su democrazia, rappresentanza e responsabilità: dalla rappresentanza democratica alla rappresentanza "sbagliata"' in Vv Aa, *Scritti in onore di Lorenza Carlassare: il diritto costituzionale come regola e limite al potere*, V (Napoli, Jovene, 2009) 2043–103.

Stapenhurst, R, *The Legislature and the Budget* (Washington, World Bank, 2004).

Stapenhurst, R, Pelizzo, R, Olson, D and Trapp, L von (eds), *Legislative Oversight and Government Accountability: A World Perspective* (Washington DC, World Bank Publications, 2008).

Stapenhurst, R, Sahgal, V, Woodley, W and Pelizzo, R, 'Scrutinizing Public Expenditures. Assessing the Performance of Public Accounts Committees' (2005) 3613 World Bank Policy Research Working Paper 1.

Steeg, M van de, 'Public Accountability in the European Union: Is the European Parliament able to hold the European Council accountable?' (2009) 13 *European Integration Online Papers* 1.

—— 'The European Council's Evolving Political Accountability' in M Bovens, D Curtin and P 't Hart (eds), *The Real World of EU Accountability. What Deficit?* (Oxford, Oxford University Press, 2010) 117–49.

Steffani, W, *Parlamentarische und präsidentielle Demokratie. Strukturelle Aspekte westlicher Demokratien* (Opladen, Springer, 1979).

—— 'Formen, Verfahren und Wirkungen der parlamentarischen Kontrolle' in HP Schneider and W Zeh (eds), *Parlamentsrecht und Parlamentpraxis* (Berlin, De Gruyter, 1989) 1325–67.

Stepan, A and Skach, C, 'Constitutional frameworks and democratic consolidation: Parliamentarism and presidentialism' (1993) 46 *World Politics* 1.

Stern, K, *Staatsrecht*, I (Munich, Beck, 1977).

Sternberger, D, 'Gewaltenteilung und parlamentarische Regierung in der Bundesrepublik Deutschland' in T Stammen (ed), *Strukturwandel der modernen Regierung* (Darmstadt, Wissenschaftliche Buchgesellschaft, 1967) 186–209.

Sterzel, F, *Riksdagen Kontrollmakt* (Stockholm, PA Norstedt, 1969).

Stone, B, 'Administrative accountability in "Westminster" democracies: towards a new conceptual framework' (1995) 8 *Governance* 505.

Strøm, K, *Minority Government and Majority Rule* (New York, Cambridge University Press, 1990).

—— 'Parliamentary Government and Legislative Organisation' in H Döering (ed), *Parliaments and Majority Rule in Western Europe* (New York, St Martin's Press, 1995) 51–83.

—— 'Parliamentary committees in European democracies' (1998) 1 *The Journal of Legislative Studies* 21.

—— 'Delegation and accountability in parliamentary democracies' (2000) 37 *European Journal of Political Research* 261.

—— 'Parliamentary Democracy and Delegation' in K Strøm, W Müller and T Bergman (eds), *Delegation and Accountability in Parliamentary Democracies* (Oxford, Oxford University Press, 2003) 55–108.

Stromholm, S (ed), *An Introduction to Swedish Law*, I (New York, Springer, 2013).

Stubbs, W, *The Constitutional History of England*, I (Oxford, Clarendon Press, 1880).

Sturm, R, 'Party Competition and the Federal System: The Lehmbruch Hypothesis Revisited' in C Jeffery (ed), *Recasting German Federalism* (London, Pinter, 1999) 197–216.

Swenden, W, *Federalism and Second Chambers. Regional Representation in Parliamentary Federations: The Australian Senate and German Bundesrat Compared* (Brussels, Peter Lang, 2004).

Templeman, S, 'Treaty-Making and the British Parliament' (1991) 67 *Chicago–Kent Law Review* 459.

Tesauro, A, 'Le funzioni fondamentali dello Stato' (1957) 12 *Rassegna di diritto pubblico* 533.

Tesche, T, '"The troika is dead, long live to the domestic troikas?" Varieties of technocracy and the diffusion of national fiscal councils in the European Union: Agents, trustees or orchestrators of fiscal discipline?' (2018) 3 TARN Working Paper 1.

Thaysen, U, 'Zur Praxis eines grundlegenden parlamentarischen Kontrollrechts: die herbeirufung von regierungsmitgliedern durch das Parlament' (1974) 5 *Zeitschrift für Parlamentsfragen* 459.

Thiers, E, 'Le contrôle parlementaire et ses limites juridiques: un pouvoir presque sans entraves' (2010) 134 *Pouvoirs* 71.

Thorarensen, B, 'Mechanisms for Parliamentary Control of the Executive' in H Krunke and B Thorarensen (eds), *The Nordic Constitutions: A Comparative and Contextual Study* (Oxford, Hart Publishing, 2018) 67–106.

Thornton, GC, *Legislative Drafting*, 4th edn (London, Butterworths, 1996).

Thorpe, S, 'Denmark' in R Gaebler and A Shea (eds), *Sources of State Practice in International Law*, 2nd edn (Leiden, Brill Nijhoff, 2014) 177–86.

Tiilikainen, T 'The concepts of parliamentarism in the EU's political system. Approaching the choice between two models' (2019) 108 FIIA Working Papers 7.

Todd, A, *On Parliamentary Government in England. Its Origin, Development and Practical Operation*, II, 2nd edn (London, Longmans, Green and Co, 1889).

Togeby, L et al, *Power and Democracy in Sweden. Conclusions* (Aarhus, Magtudredningen, 2004).

Tomkins, A, 'What is Parliament for?' in N Bamforth and P Leyland (eds), *Public Law in a Multi-Layered Constitution* (London, Hart Publishing, 2003) 55–78.

Tomuschat, C, 'Parliamentary Control over Foreign Policy in the Federal Republic of Germany' in A Cassese (ed), *Parliamentary Control over Foreign Policy: Legal Essays* (Alphen aan den Rijn, Sijthoff & Noordhoff International Publishers, 1980) 25–49.

Trivelli, L, *Le Bicamérisme. Institutions Comaparées. Étude historique, statistique et critique des rapports entre le conseil national et le conseil des états* (Lausanne, Diffusion Payot, 1975).

Trubek, DM, Cottrell, P and Nance, M, '"Soft Law", "Hard Law", and EU Integration' in G de Búrca and J Scott (eds), *New Governance, Law and Constitutionalism* (Oxford, Hart Publishing, 2006) 65–96.

Tsebelis, G and Money, J, *Bicameralism* (Cambridge, Cambridge University Press, 1997).

Tuori, K, *European Constitutionalism* (Cambridge, Cambridge University Press, 2015).

Turpin, C, 'Responsibility in Government' (1996) 11 *Public Policy and Administration* 35.

Turpin, C and Tomkins, A, *British Government and the Constitution: Text and Materials*, 7th edn (Cambridge, Cambridge University Press, 2011).

Türk, P, *Le contrôle parlementaire en France* (Paris, LGDJ, 2011).

—— *Les institutions de la Ve République*, 12th edn (Paris, LGDJ, 2019/2020).

Uhr, J, 'Bicameralism' in RAW Rhodes, SA Binder and B Rockman (eds), The Oxford Handbook of Political Institutions (Oxford, Oxford University Press, 2006) 474–94.

Urrea Corres, M, 'La autorización parlamentaria en la celebración de Tratados Internacionales: una reserva orgánica y de procedimiento; comentario a la sentencia del Tribunal Constitucional 155/2005, de 9 de junio' (2006) 10 *Revista General de Derecho Europeo* 20.

Urvoas, JJ, 'La lente mais irrépressible renaissance des commissions parlementaires' (2013) 146 *Pouvoirs* 21.

Urvoas, JJ and Vadillo, F, *Réformer les services de renseignement français: efficacité et impératifs démocratiques* (Paris, Fondation Jean Laurès, 2011).

Valbruzzi, M, 'When populists meet technocrats. The Italian innovation in government formation' (2018) 23 *Journal of Modern Italian Studies* 460.

Vallet, E, 'Les commissions d'enquête parlementaires sous la Cinquième République' (2003) 54 *Revue française de droit constitutionnel* 249.

Varela Suárez, J, 'El control parlamentario del gobierno en la Historia constitucional española' in Vv Aa, *El Parlamento a debate* (Madrid, Trotta, 1997) 59–71.

Vatter, A, 'Bicameralism and policy performance. The effects of cameral structure in comparative perspective' (2005) 11 *The Journal of Legislative Studies* 194.

Vedel, G, *Manuel élémentaire de droit constitutionnel* (Paris, Recueil Sirey, 1949).

Verdier, PH and Versteeg, M, 'International Law in National Legal Systems: an Empirical Investigation' (2015) 109 *The American Journal of International Law* 514.

Verhey, L, Kiiver, P and Loeffen, S (eds), *Political Accountability and European Integration* (Groningen, Europa Law Publishing, 2009).

Verhoest, K, Molenveld, A and Willems, T, 'Explaining Self-Perceived Accountability of Regulatory Agencies in Comparative Perspective: How Do Formal Independence and De Facto Managerial Autonomy Interact' in AC Bianculli, X Fernández-i-Marín and J Jordana (eds), *Accountability and Regulatory Governance. Audiences, Controls and Responsibilities in the Politics of Regulation* (London, Palgrave, 2015) 51–77.

Verhoeven, A, 'The Right to Information: a Fundamental Right? in Vv Aa, *An Efficient, Transparent Government and the Right of Citizens to Information, Conference Proceedings* (Maastricht, EIPA, 2000) 1–17.

Verney, D, 'Parliamentary Government and Presidential Government' in A Lijphart (ed), *Parliamentary Versus Presidential Government* (Oxford, Oxford University Press, 1992) 41–47.

Videlin, JC, 'La Mission d'information parlementaire' (1999) 40 *Revue française de droit constitutionnel* 699.

Vila Ramos, B, *Los sistemas de comisiones parlamentarias* (Madrid, Cepc, 2004).

Villani, U, 'Missioni militari all'estero e competenze degli organi costituzionali' in Vv Aa, *Quaderno dell'Associazione per gli studi e le ricerche parlamentari* (Torino, Giappichelli, 1996) 175–92.

Vile, MJC, *Constitutionalism and the Separation of Powers* (Oxford, Oxford University Press, 1967).

Vintzel, C, 'Renforcer le Parlement français: Les leçons du droit comparé' (2017) 17 *Jus Politicum.*

Violante, L, 'Il Parlamento nell'età della globalizzazione' (2003) *Rassegna parlamentare* 41.

Virga, P, 'Dibattito sulle inchieste parlamentari' (1959) 4 *Giurisprudenza costituzionale* 596.

Volpi, M, 'La responsabilité politique en Italie' in Vv Aa, *La responsabilité en droit public: aspects contemporains: colloque de Beyrouth, 3–4 novembre 2004* (Bruxelles, Bruylant, 2005) 117–25.

Vv Aa, 'Le contrôle parlementaire' (2010) 134 *Pouvoirs* 5.

Waldron, J, 'Bicameralism and the separation of powers' (2012) 65 *Current Legal Problems* 31.

Walker, AL et al, 'Supporting evidence-informed policy and scrutiny: A consultation of UK research professionals' (2019) 14 *PloS one* 1.

Waterman, RW and Meier, KJ, 'Principal-agent models: an expansion?' (1998) 8 *Journal of Public Administration Research and Theory* 173.

Weatherhill, S, *Better Regulation* (Oxford, Hart Publishing, 2007).

Weber, M, 'Parliament and Government in a Reconstructed Germany' (1918) in M Weber, *Economy and Society. An Outline of Interpretive Sociology* (New York, Bedminster, 1968).

—— 'Parliament and Government in Germany under a New Political Order' (1917) in P Lassman and R Speirs (eds), *Weber: Political Writings* (Cambridge, Cambridge University Press, 1994) 130–271.

Wehner, J, 'Back from the Sidelines? Redefining the Contribution of Legislatures to the Budget Cycle' (2004) 1 World Bank Institute Working Paper 1.

—— 'Legislative Arrangements for Financial Scrutiny: Explaining Cross-national Variation' in R Pelizzo, R Stapenhurst and D Olson (eds), *The Role of Parliaments in the Budget Process* (Washington DC, World Bank Institute, 2005) 2–17.

—— 'Assessing the Power of the Purse: An Index of Legislative Budget Institutions' (2006) 54 *Political Studies* 767.

Weir, S (ed), *A World of Difference. Parliamentary Oversight of British Foreign Policy. A Report by the Democratic Audit, the Federal Trust and One World Trust* (London, Democratic Audit, The Federal Trust and One World Trust, 2007).

Wessels, B, 'Roles and Orientations of Members of Parliament in the EU Context: Congruence or Difference? Europeanisation or not? (2005) 11 *The Journal of Legislative Studies* 446.

Wessels, W, 'National Parliaments and the EP in Multi-tier Governance: In Search for an Optimal Multi-level Parliamentary Architecture. Analysis, Assessment, Advice' in I Pernice et al (eds), *Challenges of Multi-tier Governance in the European Union* (Brussels, European Parliament – Directorate General for Internal Policies, 2013).

—— *The European Council* (London, Palgrave, 2016).

—— 'The European Council' in R Schütze and T Tridimas (eds), *Oxford Principles of European Union Law. The European Legal Order*, I (Oxford, Oxford University Press, 2018) 490–517.

Wessels, W and Rozenberg, O (eds), *Democratic Control in the Member States of the European Council and the Euro Zone Summits* (Brussels, EU Parliament – Directorate General for Internal Policies, 2013).

Westlake, M, 'Maastricht, Edinburgh, Amsterdam: the "End of the Beginning"' in V Deckmyn and I Thomson (eds), *Openness and Transparency in the European Union* (Maastricht, European Institute of Public Administration, 1998) 120–32.

—— M, *A Modern Guide to the European Parliament* (London, Pinter, 1994).

Wheare, KC, *Government by Committee* (Oxford, Claredon Press, 1955).

Wheatley, M, Maddox, B, Bishop, TK, *The 2019 Spending Review. How to run it well* (London, Institute for Government, 2018).

White, H, *Parliamentary Scrutiny of Government* (London, Institute for Government, 2015).

Wiberg, M and Koura, A, 'The Logic of Parliamentary Questioning' in M Wiberg (ed), *Parliamentary Control in the Nordic Countries* (Helsinki, Finnish Political Science Association, 1994) 19–44.

Widgrén, M, 'The Impact of Council Voting Rules on EU Decision-Making' (2009) 55 *CESifo Economic Studies* 30.

Wieslander, B, *The Parliamentary Ombudsman in Sweden* (Stockholm, Bank of Sweden Tercentenary Foundation, 1994).

Wilks-Heeg, S, Blick, A and Crone, S, *How Democratic is the UK? The 2012 Audit* (Liverpool, Democratic Audit, 2012).

Williamson, DG, *Bismark and Germany: 1862–1890*, 3rd edn (New York, Routledge, 2011).

Willoughby, WW, 'The Prussian Theory of Government' (1918) 12 *The American Journal of International Law* 266.

Wills, A and Vermeulen, M (eds), *Parliamentary oversight of security and intelligence agencies in the European Union* (EU Parliament – Directorate General for Internal Policies, 2011).

Wilson, W, *Congressional Government. A Study in American Politics* (Boston, MA, Houghton Mifflin Company, 1885).

—— *The State: Elements of Historical and Practical Politics* (Boston, MA, DC Heath & Co, 1911).

Winzen, T, 'Technical or political? An exploration of the work of officials in the committees of the European Parliament' (2011) 17 *The Journal of Legislative Studies* 27.

—— 'National Parliamentary Control of European Union Affairs: A Cross-national and Longitudinal Comparison' (2012) 35 *West European Politics* 657.

Witte, B de et al, 'Legislating after Lisbon. New Opportunities for the European Parliament' (2010) 1 *EUDO Report* 1.

Wolfe, C, *The Rise of Modern Judicial Review* (New York, Basic Books, 1986).

Woodhouse, D, *Ministers and Parliament: Accountability in Theory and Practice* (Oxford, Oxford University Press, 1994).

Wouters, J and Raube, K, 'Europe's Common Security and Defence Policy: the Case for Inter-Parliamentary Scrutiny' (2012) 90 Leuven Centre for Global Governance Studies Working Paper 1.

—— 'The Interparliamentary Conference on Common and Security Policy: A Quest for Democratic Accountability in EU Security Governance' in N Lupo and C Fasone, *Interparliamentary Cooperation in the Composite European Constitution* (Oxford, Hart Publishing, 2016) 227–45.

Yamamoto, H, *Tools for Parliamentary Oversight: A Comparative Study of 88 National Parliaments* (Geneva, Inter-parliamentary Union, 2007).

Official Publications

Assemblée Nationale, 'Les enquêtes demandées à la Cour des comptes (art 58-2° de la LOLF)' (2011).

—— 'Le rôle des commissions permanentes en matière de contrôle du Gouvernement' (2016) *Fiche de synthèse n 48*.

—— 'Fiche de synthèse n 52: Le contrôle de l'application des lois et l'évaluation de la législation et des politiques publiques' (6 Juin 2017).

Bundesverfassungsgericht Press Release, 'Application for a Preliminary Injunction in the "CETA" Proceedings Unsuccessful' (31 October 2016) 71.

—— 'If interpreted strictly, the framework for the European Banking Union does not exceed the competences of the European Union' (30 July 2019) 52.

Cabinet Office, 'Modernising Parliament – Reforming the House of Lords' (19 January 1999).

—— 'White Paper: Modernising government' (March 1999).

—— 'A House for the Future: Royal Commission on the Reform of the House of Lords' (20 January 2000).

—— 'The Governance of Britain' (July 2007).

—— 'Giving Evidence to Select Committees. Guidance to Civil Servants' (October 2014).

Commission des finances – Sénat, 'Guide de bonnes pratiques du contrôle budgétaire' (19 April 2007).

Committee Office Scrutiny Unit, *Financial scrutiny uncovered. How the Government manages its finances and how Parliament scrutinises them* (London, House of Commons, 2007).

Conference of Speakers of the European Union Parliaments, 'Guidelines for Inter-parliamentary Co-operation in the European Union' (Lisbon, 19–21 June 2008).

Cortes Generales, 'Actividad internacional de las Cortes Generales en la XI Legislatura' (16 February 2016).

Council of Europe Commissioner for Human Rights, *Democratic and Effective Oversight of National Security Services* (Paris, Council of Europe, 2015).

Council of Europe Parliamentary Assembly, 'The role of parliaments in implementing ECHR standards: overview of existing structures and mechanisms' (2016) 19 PPSD.

Council of the European Union, 'Outcome of the council meeting. 3493rd Council Meeting Foreign Affairs on Trade Issues' (8 October 2016) 13310/16 PRESSE 52 PR CO 51.

Deutscher Bundestag, 'Parliament's Role in International Treaties' (2017) WD 2 – 3000 – 038/17.

European Commission for Democracy through Law (Venice Commission), 'Report on the Democratic Oversight of the Security Services' (2015) *Studies no 388/2006 and no 719/2013*.

European Parliament Committee on Constitutional Affairs, 'Report on the implementation of the legal provisions and the Joint Statement ensuring parliamentary scrutiny over decentralized agencies' (30 January 2019) 2018/2114(INI).

Hansard Society, *The Challenge for Parliament: Making Government Accountable*, Report of the Hansard Society Commission on Parliamentary Scrutiny (London, Hansard Society Publications, 2011).

Hansard Society Commission on the Legislative Process, *Making the Law* (London, Hansard Society, 1992).

Hansard Society Commission on Parliamentary Scrutiny, *The Challenge for Parliament: Making Government Accountable* (London, Hansard Society, 2012).

House of Commons, *Return to an Address of the Honourable House of Commons dated 15th February 1996 for the Report the Inquiry into the Export of Defence Equipment and Dual-use Goods to Iraq and related prosecutions* (1995–96, HC 115).

House of Commons Constitution Committee, *The Accountability of Civil Servants Sixth Report* (2013, HL 61).

House of Commons Information Office, 'Parliamentary Questions' (2010) *Factsheet P1 Procedures Series 2*.

—— 'Treaties' (2010) *Factsheet P14 Procedure Series 1*.

House of Commons Liaison Committee, *Shifting the Balance: Unfinished Business. First Report of Session 2000–01* (2000, HC 321).

—— *Annual Report 2002* (2003, HC 558).

—— *Review of Select Committee Activity and Proposals for New Committee Activity* (2012, HL 279).

—— *Select Committee Effectiveness, Resources and Powers* (2012, HC 697).

House of Commons Procedure Committee, *Monitoring of Written Parliamentary Questions: Progress Report for Session 2015–2016* (2016, HC 191).

—— *Should there be a Budget Committee?* (2019, HC 1482).

House of Commons Reform Committee, *Rebuilding the House* (2009, HC 117).

House of Commons Select Committee on Modernisation of the House of Commons, *Sittings in the House in Westminster Hall. Second Report* (1998–99, HC 194).

House of Commons Political and Constitutional Reform Committee, *Government Formation Post-Election* (2015, HC 1023).

House of Commons Treasury Committee, *Budget 2018. Twenty-Sixth Report of Session 2017–19* (2019, HC 1606).

House of Lords, 'Report of the Leader's Group on Working Practices', Session 2010–12 (26 April 2011).

House of Lords Select Committee on the Constitution, *European Union (Notification of Withdrawal) Bill* 8th Report (HL 2016–17, 119).

—— Constitution, *European Union (Withdrawal) Agreement Bill* (HL 2020, 114).

HM Government *The United Kingdom's Exit from and New Partnership with the European Union* (Cm 9417, 2017).

Interinstitutional Agreement on Better Law-Making [16 December 2003] OJ C 321.

Interinstitutional Agreement on Better Law-Making [13 April 2016] OJ L 123.

International Institute for Justice and the Rule of Law, *The Role of Parliamentarians in Developing an Effective Response to Terrorism. Valletta recommendations Relating to Contributions by Parliamentarians in Developing an Effective Response to Terrorism* (Valletta, IIJ, 2016).

Inter-Parliamentary Union, 'Parliamentary Involvement in International Affairs' (2005) Report presented to the Second World Conference of Speakers of Parliaments, New-York, 7–9 September 2005.

Inter-Parliamentary Union (IPU) and United Nations Development Programme (UNDP), *Global Parliamentary Report 2017. Parliament's power to hold government to account: Realities and perspectives on oversight* (France, Courand et Associés, 2017).

IPU and IFLA, 'Guidelines for Parliamentary Research Services' (2015).

Joint Committee on Conventions, 'Conventions of the UK Parliament – Report of Session 2005–2006' (31 October 2006).

OECD, Better Regulation in Europe: Germany 2010 (Geneva, OECD, 2010).

—— *Better Regulation in Europe: Sweden 2010* (Paris, OECD, 2010).

—— 'France – High Council for Public Finances' (2015) 2 *Journal on Budgeting* 117.

—— 'Recommendation of the Council on Regulatory Policy and Governance' (22 March 2012).

—— 'Relations between Supreme Audit Institutions and Parliamentary Committees' (2002) 33 SIGMA Papers 1.

—— 'The Role of Ombudsman Institutions in Open Government' (2018) OECD Working Paper on Public Governance 29 (Paris, OECD, 2018).

Office of the Leader of the House of Commons, 'Post-Legislative Scrutiny – The Government's Approach' (March 2008).

Public Accounts Committee, 'Accountability for public money' 28th Report (5 April 2011).

Regulatory Fitness and Performance Programme (REFIT), COM (2012) 746 fin.

Sénat, 'Rapport d'information fai tau nom de la délégation du Sénat pour la planification sur l'évaluation des politiques publiques en France' (2004) 391 *Annexe au procés verbale de la Séance du 30 Juin 2004*.

Ufficio Valutazione Impatto, 'Gli atti di sindacato ispettivo in Senato' (2016) 6 *Senato della Repubblica – Documento di analisi*.

UK Ministry of Justice, *The Governance of Britain: War Powers and Treaties: Limiting Executive Powers* (Cm 7239, 2007).

US Congressional Research Service, *Treaties and Other International Agreements: The Role of the United States Senate* (106th Congress, Committee Print, January 2001).

INDEX

Lightning Source UK Ltd.
Milton Keynes UK
UKHW032224290920
370714UK00007B/335